T0234959

Lecture Notes in Computer Science 13055

Yanio Hernández Heredia ·
Vladimir Milián Núñez ·
José Ruiz Shulcloper (Eds.)

Progress in Artificial Intelligence and Pattern Recognition

7th International Workshop
on Artificial Intelligence and Pattern Recognition, IWAIPR 2021
Havana, Cuba, October 5–7, 2021
Proceedings

 Springer

Editors
Yanio Hernández Heredia ⓘ
Universidad de las Ciencias Informáticas
La Habana, Cuba

Vladimir Milián Núñez ⓘ
Universidad de las Ciencias Informáticas
La Habana, Cuba

José Ruiz Shulcloper
Universidad de las Ciencias Informáticas
La Habana, Cuba

ISSN 0302-9743   ISSN 1611-3349 (electronic)
Lecture Notes in Computer Science
ISBN 978-3-030-89690-4   ISBN 978-3-030-89691-1 (eBook)
https://doi.org/10.1007/978-3-030-89691-1

LNCS Sublibrary: SL6 – Image Processing, Computer Vision, Pattern Recognition, and Graphics

This Springer imprint is published by the registered company Springer Nature Switzerland AG
The registered company address is: Gewerbestrasse 11, 6330 Cham, Switzerland

Preface

The 7th International Workshop on Artificial Intelligence and Pattern Recognition (IWAIPR 2021) was the latest edition in a series of biennial conferences aimed at serving the scientific community active in these fields in Cuba and other countries. Due to the COVID-19 pandemic it was necessary to postpone the conference for a year and in this edition, for the same reason, the Organizing Committee decided on a virtual modality.

As has been the case for previous editions of the conference, IWAIPR 2021 hosted worldwide participants with the aim of promoting and disseminating ongoing research on mathematical methods and computing techniques for Artificial Intelligence and Pattern Recognition, and in particular for bioinformatics, cognitive and humanoid vision, computer vision, image analysis and intelligent data analysis, as well as their application in a number of diverse areas such as industry, health, robotics, data mining, opinion mining and sentiment analysis, telecommunications, document analysis, and natural language processing and recognition. Moreover, IWAIPR 2021 was a forum for the scientific community to exchange research experience, to share new knowledge, and to increase the cooperation among research groups working in artificial intelligence, pattern recognition and related areas.

IWAIPR 2021 received 73 contributions from authors in (15) countries. After a rigorous double-blind reviewing process, where three highly qualified reviewers reviewed each submission, 42 papers authored by 147 authors from (11) countries were accepted. The scientific quality of the accepted papers was above the overall mean rating.

Like the most recent editions of the conference, IWAIPR 2021 was a single-track conference in which all papers where presented in oral sessions. IWAIPR 2021 presentations were grouped into four sessions: Artificial Intelligence, Data Mining and Applications; Pattern Recognition and Applications; Biometrics, Image, and Video Analysis; and Signals Analysis and Processing.

We would like to point out that the reputation of the IWAIPR conferences is growing and therefore the proceedings are published, as in the case of IWAIPR 2018, in the series Lecture Notes in Computer Science by Springer.

Besides the 42 accepted submissions, the scientific program of IWAIPR 2021 also included the conference "End-to-end Document Analysis: From Unreadable Data to Operable Information" of an outstanding invited speaker, Professor Apostolos Antonacopoulos (University of Salford, UK), who is the Past President of the International Association for Pattern Recognition.

IWAIPR 2021 was endorsed by the International Association for Pattern Recognition (IAPR) and therefore the conference conferred the IAPR-IWAIPR Best Paper Award. The aim of this award is to acknowledge and encourage excellence, originality, and innovation in new models, methods, and techniques with an outstanding theoretical contribution and practical application to the field of artificial intelligence, pattern recognition, and/or data mining.

The selection of the winners is based on the wish of the author to be considered for the prize, the evaluation and recommendations from members of the Program Committee, and the evaluation of the Award Committee. This committee, carefully chosen to avoid conflicts of interest, evaluate each nominated paper for the Best Paper.

We want to express our gratitude to the prestigious experts Heydi Mendez-Vazquez, Research Director from the CENATAV, DATYS, Cuba; Walter Kropatsch from the Vienna University of Technology, Austria, and Gregory Randall, from the Institute of Electrical Engineering, University of the Republic of Uruguay.

IWAIPR 2021 was organized by Universidad de las Ciencias Informáticas, Cuba (UCI) and the Cuban Association for Pattern Recognition (ACRP) with the sponsorship of the Cuban Society for Mathematics and Computer Sciences (SCMC). We acknowledge and appreciate their valuable contribution to the success of IWAIPR 2021.

We gratefully acknowledge the help of all members of the Organizing Committee and of the Program Committee for their support and for the rigorous work in the reviewing process.

We also wish to thank the members of the local committee for their unflagging work in the organization of IWAIPR 2021 that helped create an excellent conference and proceedings.

We are especially grateful to Alfred Hofmann (Vice President Publishing, Computer Science, Springer), Anna Kramer (Assistant Editor, Computer Science, Springer), and Volha Shaparava (Springer Nature OCS Support) for their support and advice during the preparation of this LNCS volume.

Special thanks are due to all authors who submitted their work to IWAIPR 2021, including those of papers that could not be accepted.

Finally, we invite the artificial intelligence and pattern recognition communities to attend IWAIPR 2023 in Havana, Cuba.

October 2021

Yanio Hernández Heredia
Vladimir Milián Núñez
Jose Ruiz Shulcloper

Organization

Program Chairs

Yanio Hernández Heredia	Universidad de las Ciencias Informáticas, Cuba
Vladimir Milián Núñez	Universidad de las Ciencias Informáticas, Cuba
Jose Ruiz Shulcloper	Universidad de las Ciencias Informáticas, Cuba

Local Organizing Committee

Nadiela Milan Cristo	Universidad de las Ciencias Informáticas, Cuba
Beatriz Aragón Fernández	Universidad de las Ciencias Informáticas, Cuba
José Eladio Medina Pagola	Universidad de las Ciencias Informáticas, Cuba
Héctor Raúl González Diez	Universidad de las Ciencias Informáticas, Cuba

IAPR-IWAIPR Best Paper Award Committee

Heydi Mendez-Vazquez	CENATAV, Cuba
Walter Kropatsch	Vienna University of Technology, Austria
Gregory Randall	University of the Republic, Uruguay

Program Committee

Sergey Ablameyko	Belarusian State University, Belarus
Yudivián Almeida	Universidad de La Habana, Cuba
Rene Alquezar	UPC, Spain
Leopoldo Altamirano	INAOE, Mexico
Mauricio Araya	UTFSM, Chile
G. Arroyo-Figueroa	Instituto Nacional de Electricidad y Energias Limpias, Mexico
Rafael Berlanga	Universitat Jaume I, Spain
Ana Bernardos	Universidad Politécnica de Madrid, Spain
Ramon Brena	Tecnologico de Monterrey, Mexico
Maria Elena Buemi	Universidad de Buenos Aires, Argentina
Lázaro Bustio-Martínez	Universidad Iberoamericana, Mexico
Hiram Calvo	Instituto Politécnico Nacional, Mexico
José Ramón Calvo de Lara	CENATAV, Cuba
Sergio Daniel Cano-Ortiz	Universidad de Oriente, Cuba
Jesús Ariel Carrasco-Ochoa	INAOE, Mexico
César Castellanos	Universidad Nacional de Colombia, Colombia
Eduardo R. Concepcion-Morales	Universidad de Cienfuegos, Cuba
Raúl Cruz-Barbosa	Universidad Tecnológica de la Mixteca, Mexico

Alexandra Moutinho	Instituto Superior Tecnico, Portugal
Alfredo Muñoz-Briseño	CENATAV, Cuba
João Neves	IT - Instituto de Telecomunicações, Portugal
Lawrence O'Gorman	Bell Labs, USA
Martha R. Ortiz-Posadas	Universidad Autónoma Metropolitana Iztapalapa, Mexico
Kalman Palagyi	University of Szeged, Hungary
Joao Papa	São Paulo State University, Brazil
Glauco Vitor Pedrosa	University of Brasilia, Brazil
Billy Peralta	Universidad Andres Bello, Chile
Marieta Peña Abreu	Universidad de las Ciencias Informáticas, Cuba
Ignacio Ponzoni	Universidad Nacional del Sur, Argentina
Osvaldo Andrés Pérez García	CITMATEL, Cuba
Adrián Pérez-Suay	Universitat de València, Spain
Gregory Randall	Universidad de la República, Uruguay
Pedro Real	Univesity of Seville, Spain
Yunia Reyes González	Universidad de las Ciencias Informáticas, Cuba
Carlos A. Reyes-Garcia	INAOE, Mexico
Dayana Ribas	University of Zaragoza, Spain
Edgar Roman-Rangel	ITAM, Mexico
Alejandro Rosete	CUJAE, Cuba
Jose Ruiz Shulcloper	Universidad de las Ciencias Informáticas, Cuba
Cesar San Martin	Universidad de La Frontera, Chile
Guillermo Sanchez-Diaz	Universidad Autónoma de San Luis Potosí, Mexico
Carlo Sansone	University of Naples Federico II, Italy
Alfredo Simón-Cuevas	Universidad Tecnológica de La Habana José Antonio Echeverría, Cuba
Juan Humberto Sossa Azuela	Instituto Politécnico Nacional, Mexico
Antonio-José Sánchez-Salmerón	Universitat Politècnica de València, Spain
Alberto Taboada-Crispi	UCLV, Cuba
Sergio A. Velastin	Queen Mary University of London, UK
Vera Yashina	Federal Research Center "Computer Science and Control" of the Russian Academy of Sciences, Russia

Additional Reviewers

Pablo Layana Castro	Universitat Politecnica de Valencia, Spain
Yanir Díaz	INAOE, Mexico
Antonio García Garví	UPV, Spain
Leonardo Barboni	Universidad de la República, Uruguay

Contents

Pattern Recognition and Applications

Artificial Intelligence, Data Mining and Applications

Layer-Wise Relevance Propagation in Multi-label Neural Networks to Identify COVID-19 Associated Coinfections

Marilyn Bello[1,2]([✉]), Yaumara Aguilera[4], Gonzalo Nápoles[3], María M. García[1], Rafael Bello[1], and Koen Vanhoof[2]

[1] Computer Science Department, Universidad Central de Las Villas,
Santa Clara, Cuba
mbgarcia@uclv.cu
[2] Faculty of Business Economics, Hasselt University, Hasselt, Belgium
[3] Department of Cognitive Science and Artificial Intelligence, Tilburg University,
Tilburg, The Netherlands
[4] Hospital "Comandante Manuel Fajardo Rivero" of Santa Clara city,
Santa Clara, Cuba

Abstract. COVID-19 has been affected worldwide since the end of 2019. Clinical studies have shown that a factor that increases its lethality is the existence of secondary infections. Coinfections associated with the infection SARS-CoV-2 are classified into bacterial infections and fungal infections. A patient may develop one, both, or neither. From a machine learning point of view, this is considered a multi-label classification problem. In this work, we propose a multi-label neural network able to detect such infections in a patient with SARS-CoV-2 and thus provide the medical community with a diagnosis to guide therapy in these patients. However, neural networks are often considered a "black box" model, as their strength in modeling complex interactions, also make their operation almost impossible to explain. Therefore, we propose three adaptations of the Layer-wise Relevance Propagation algorithm to explain multi-label neural networks. The inclusion of this *post-hoc interpretability* stage made it possible to identify significant input variables in a classifier output.

Keywords: COVID-19 · Coinfections · Multi-label scenario · Neural networks · Layer-wise Relevance Propagation

1 Introduction

COVID-19 is a disease that, after its outbreak in November 2019 in Wuhan, has continued to spread to all continents. It is reporting to date 190 affected countries and more than 106 million positive diagnoses of the disease. The knowledge we have is relatively low because of its novelty, although research proliferates in many countries. Artificial Intelligence (AI) has contributed to several dimensions of this problem in tune with all the world's science efforts to confront this pandemic [4,13,15,16].

© Springer Nature Switzerland AG 2021
Y. Hernández Heredia et al. (Eds.): IWAIPR 2021, LNCS 13055, pp. 3–12, 2021.
https://doi.org/10.1007/978-3-030-89691-1_1

An important risk factor in the evolution of COVID-19 is secondary infections. Such infections can lead to a worse prognosis for SARS-CoV-2 infected patients, increasing the disease's lethality [1]. In the first stage of the ongoing research at the "Comandante Manuel Fajardo Rivero" Hospital in Santa Clara, it is evidenced that 60% of the patients with secondary infections coexisting with the SARS-CoV-2 virus died. Hence, there is a need to establish a diagnostic protocol for detecting these coinfections. Thus, it is very convenient to have an AI model to support decision-making in the preventive, diagnostic, and therapeutic order and complement the clinical method.

Clinical studies have grouped these coinfections into bacterial or fungal, i.e., patients may develop one, both, or neither of them. From a machine learning point of view, this is considered a multi-label classification problem [8]. One of the most effective multi-label classification methods is neural networks, which have also been successfully applied in the diagnosis of COVID-19 [5,7,18]. However, one aspect to be taken into account in the construction of neural models, especially in medical applications [6], is their interpretability, which is an essential aspect of the current trends Explainable AI [2]. Therefore, it is necessary to build a model to infer the possible coinfection in a patient with SARS-CoV-2 and to have the ability to explain the inferred output.

In this research, a multi-label neural network is used to predict the possible coinfections present in a patient with SARS-CoV-2. The proposed model is complemented with a *post-hoc interpretability* stage. For this purpose, we propose three adaptations of the Layer-wise Relevance Propagation (LRP) method [3] to operate on multi-label neural networks. This is the most important and novel contribution of this work since it allowed the acceptance of the medical community's neural model, determining the input variables that most influenced the inferred decision.

The paper is organized as follows. Section 2 introduces the LRP algorithm and three adaptations of this algorithm in a multi-label scenario. Section 3 describes the problem under consideration and presents a solution based on a multi-label neural network and some of the results obtained when applying the extended LRP on the proposed neural network. Finally, some concluding remarks are given in Sect. 4.

2   LRP to Explain Multi-label Neural Networks

This section provides an introduction to LRP and three adaptations of it to handle multi-label scenarios.

2.1   LRP

LRP [3] is a technique that provides neural networks the ability to explain themselves. This technique explains the classifier's decisions by decomposition [14]. Mathematically, it redistributes the prediction $f(x)$ backward using local redistribution rules until it assigns a relevance score R_i to each input variable (problem features). Equation (1) summarizes the fundamental property of this redistribution process, which is called conservation of relevance,

$$\sum_i R_i = \cdots = \sum_j R_j = \sum_k R_k = \cdots = f(x). \qquad (1)$$

This property says that at every step of the redistribution process (e.g., at every layer of a neural network), the total amount of relevance is conserved. No relevance is artificially added or removed during redistribution. The relevance scores R_i of each input variable determines how much this variable has contributed to the prediction. Thus, in contrast to sensitivity analysis, LRP truly decomposes the function value $f(x)$.

In the following, we describe the LRP redistribution process for feed-forward neural networks [11]. Let the neurons of the neural network be described by the Eq. (2),

$$a_i = \sigma(\sum_j a_j w_{ji} + b_i) \qquad (2)$$

where a_i is the activation degree of neuron i, a_j the activation degree of neuron j from the previous layer, w_{ji} the weight connecting the neuron j to i, and b_i the neuron's bias parameters. The function σ is a positive and monotonically increasing activation function.

Then, one propagation rule that fulfills local conservation properties is the $\alpha\beta$-rule given by Eq. (3),

$$R_i = \sum_j (\alpha \frac{a_i w_{ij}^+}{\sum_i a_i w_{ij}^+} - \beta \frac{a_i w_{ij}^-}{\sum_i a_i w_{ij}^-}) R_j \qquad (3)$$

where $()^+$ and $()^-$ are the positive and negative weights connecting i to j, respectively, and where the parameters α and β are chosen subject to the constraint $\alpha = \beta + 1$. The relevance of neuron i will depend on its relevance in neuron j, i.e., those neurons where there is a connection from the ith neuron of layer n to the jth neuron of layer $n + 1$. Algorithm 1 describes the LRP step-by-step for a given object.

Algorithm 1. LRP with $\alpha\beta$-rule

1: Compute the degree of activation of the output neuron using the trained neural model, and infer the resulting class.
2: Compute each neuron's relevance for inferring the resulting class:
    a) the output neuron's relevance values correspond to its activation value
    b) the relevance values of the remaining ith neurons are calculated using Equation (3).
3: Rank the features in decreasing order according to the relevance values of the input neurons. In this way, the first three features in the ranking will be the most relevant features to infer the resulting class.

2.2   LRP in Multi-label Scenarios

In multi-label scenarios, each of the data's objects has associated a vector of outputs instead of being associated with a single value [8].

Definition 1. *Let us suppose that $\mathcal{U}$ is a N-dimensional object space called the universe, and $\mathcal{L} = \{l_1, l_2, \ldots, l_K\}$ denotes the label space with K possible class labels. The task of multi-label learning is to learn a function $\Theta : \mathcal{U} \longrightarrow 2^{\mathcal{L}}$ from the multi-label training set $\{(u_i, \mathcal{L}_i) \mid 1 \leq i \leq N\}$, where $u_i \in \mathcal{U}$ is a M-dimensional feature vector $(x_1(i), x_2(i), \ldots, x_M(i))$ and $\mathcal{L}_i \subseteq \mathcal{L}$ is the set of labels associated with u_i.*

Then, each possible class or label is another node in the neural network's output layer. Algorithm 2 describes step-by-step three possible adaptations to the LRP for multi-label neural networks.

Algorithm 2. LRPml with $\alpha\beta$-rule

1: Compute the degree of activation of the output neurons using the trained neural model, and infer the labels $\{L_1, L_2, \ldots L_K\}$.
2: Compute each neuron's relevance for inferring the predicted labels:
   a) the relevance values of the output neurons correspond to the activation values of the output neurons. Three alternatives for doing this in a multi-label scenario are described below.
      Alternative 1: Propagate forward the activation values (obtained in Step **1**) of all output neurons.
      Alternative 2: Propagate forward the activation values of those output neurons whose activation value is greater than a threshold.
      Alternative 3: Propagate forward the activation value of each output neuron independently. This is equivalent to applying Algorithm 2 for each label in the application domain.
   b) the relevance values of the remaining ith neurons are calculated using Equation (3).
3: Rank the features in decreasing order according to the relevance values of the input neurons. In this way, the first three features in the ranking will be the most relevant features to infer the model's predicted labels.

---

3   Identifying COVID-19 Associated Coinfections

Coinfections associated with SARS-CoV-2 are classified into bacterial infections and fungal infections, i.e., patients may develop one, both, or neither of them. This problem is considered a multi-label classification problem. For its solution, we use a multi-label neural network.

3.1 Dataset Under Consideration

We considered as a learning set the clinical histories of 42 patients. Although the number of cases is low since this problem is relatively new, specialists in this medical field consider this information sufficient. Each patient in a dataset has three possible labels associated with it: the patient has no coinfection (l_1), has bacterial coinfection (l_2), has fungal coinfection (l_3). The variables that characterize it are divided into five large groups: *epidemiological* (G1), *clinical* (G2), *radiological* (G3), *clinical laboratory* (G4), and *microbiological* (G5). The latter group including antimicrobial susceptibility and all information related to coinfection. More details about these variable groups are given next.

G1: age ($A0$), sex ($A1$), stay in hospital ($A2$), status at admission ($A3$), hospitalization room ($A4$), personal pathological history ($A18 - A29$).

G2: clinical diagnosis ($A5 - A17$), clinical condition ($A30 - A42$), heart rate ($A43$), respiratory rate ($A44$), evacuation status ($A48 - A50$), medications used ($A51 - A58$), invasive procedures ($A59 - A61$).

G3: x-ray report ($A45 - A47$).

G4: global leukocyte count ($A62$), neutrophil nuclear polymorphs ($A63$), lymphocytes ($A64$), platelets ($A65$), hemoglobin ($A66$), hematocrit ($A67$), creatinine ($A68$), tgp ($A69$), tgo ($A70$), d-dimer ($A71$), ggt ($A72$), ldh ($A73$), fa ($A74$), lactate ($A75$), urea ($A76$), cholesterol ($A77$), triglycerides ($A78$), uric acid ($A79$), glycemia ($A80$).

G5: number of laboratory cultures ($A81$), isolated microorganism ((escherichia coli ($A82$), candida.spp ($A83$), psuedomona aeruginosa ($A84$), coagulase negative staphylococcus ($A85$), staphylococcus aureus ($A86$), acinetobacter baumannnii calcoaceticus complex ($A87$), klebsiella pneumoniae ($A88$), moraxella.spp ($A89$), enterobacter aerogenes ($A90$)), antimicrobial resistance ($A91$), multidrug resistance ($A92$), type of laboratory culture ((stool culture ($A93$), urine culture ($A94$), endotracheal tube culture ($A95$), central venous catheter culture ($A96$), blood culture ($A97$), tracheostomy culture ($A98$)).

3.2 Solution Based on Multi-label Neural Networks

The proposed architecture involves a fully-connected neural network with four layers: an *input layer*, two *hidden layers*, and an *output layer*. The number of hidden neurons is equal to $2 * M$ and $2 * K$, where $M = 99$ and $K = 3$ are the numbers of features and labels of the problem, respectively. This model operates with scaled exponential linear units [10]. These neural units use the transfer function depicted in Eq. (4),

$$f(x) = \begin{cases} \beta x & x > 0 \\ \beta \alpha (e^x - 1) & x \leq 0 \end{cases} \tag{4}$$

where α and β are parameters derived from the inputs. The advantage of this transfer function is that it performs an internal normalization operation such that the current layer preserves the mean and variance of the previous one. When classifying an object, the function's output in the last layer is transformed with the sign function to determine the labels attached to that object.

We have adopted a *squared hinge loss function* [12] to increase the margins between positive and negative labels in terms of the learning algorithm. The theoretical advantage of having well-separated labels is that the model becomes less sensitive to the threshold determining the labels attached to each object. This eventually translates into having fewer misclassifications. Equation (5) displays the regularized squared hinge loss function to be minimized by the model, which is aimed at maximizing the margins between labels,

$$\mathcal{E} = \frac{1}{2}\Big(\sum_{i=1}^{K} \max\{0, l_i(k)a_i^{(T)}(k)\}^2 + \frac{\lambda^{(t)}}{2} \sum_{t=1}^{T} \mathcal{R}^{(t)} \Big) \tag{5}$$

such that

$$\mathcal{R}^{(t)} = \sum_{j=1}^{M^{(t-1)}} \sum_{i=1}^{M^{(t)}} \left(w_{ji}^{(t)} \right)^2 \tag{6}$$

where K is the number of labels, T denote the total number of layers, $M^{(t)}$ stands for the number of neurons in the t-th layer, $l_i(k)$ takes -1 when the i-th label is not associated with the k-th object, otherwise, it takes 1. Also, $a_i^{(T)}(k)$ is the activation value of the i-th neuron in the output layer whereas $\lambda \geq 0$ is a constant to control the ℓ_2 regularization component.

The weights associated with the multi-layer networks are adjusted using an extension to stochastic gradient descent, known as the Adam optimization algorithm [9]. Also, the number of epochs is set to 200.

To measure the classifier's performance, we have adopted the *Hamming Loss* (HL) measure. HL is probably the most commonly used performance metric in multi-label scenarios quantifying the fraction of incorrectly predicted labels [8].

The average HL value associated with the classifier is 0.1545 after performing a leave-one-out cross-validation process [17]. It is a particular case of cross-validation where the number of folds equals the number of objects in the dataset. Thus, the learning algorithm is applied once for each object, using all other objects as a training set and using the selected object as a single-item test set.

3.3 Applying the LRPml Algorithm to the Proposed Neural Network

Figures 1 and 2 show the LRPml algorithm's output using Alternatives 1 and 2, respectively, for a patient X with SARS-CoV-2, who presents bacterial (L_2) and fungal (L_3) coinfection at the same time. Likewise, Figs. 3 and 4 show this result using Alternative 3 as the activation values of labels L_2 and L_3 are propagated forward, respectively. The three alternatives report that attributes $A91$ with a value of 1, $A84$ with a value of 1, and $A92$ with a value of 1 are the most relevant to the patient who has both coinfections. In contrast, $A79$ with a value of 0.4732 has a negative relevance, and several attributes have a near-zero relevance in the presence of any of these coinfections. The differences between these three variants lie in that Alternatives 1 and 2 show higher relevance values than Alternative 3, but this is expected since this case's relevance is distributed individually for each label. LRPml explains the classifier's result for a specific case (in this case, patient X). This means that these attributes need not influence the decision about other patients with different characteristics. This result is evaluated using expert criteria. The experts assessed explanations obtained from cases already known to them. They estimated that the most relevant attributes when a patient presents both coinfections coincide with those obtained by the proposed methods.

A91 1.2347	A84 0.8954	A92 0.8676	A83 0.8464	A4 0.4267	A87 0.3869	A56 0.3683	A53 0.3576	A50 0.3163
A61 0.3111	A95 0.3008	A6 0.1663	A31 0.0068	A1 0.0	A3 0.0	A5 0.0	A7 0.0	A8 0.0
A9 0.0	A10 0.0	A11 0.0	A13 0.0	A14 0.0	A15 0.0	A17 0.0	A18 0.0	A19 0.0
A20 0.0	A21 0.0	A22 0.0	A23 0.0	A25 0.0	A26 0.0	A27 0.0	A28 0.0	A29 0.0
A30 0.0	A32 0.0	A33 0.0	A34 0.0	A35 0.0	A36 0.0	A37 0.0	A38 0.0	A39 0.0
A40 0.0	A41 0.0	A42 0.0	A46 0.0	A47 0.0	A48 0.0	A49 0.0	A51 0.0	A54 0.0
A57 0.0	A58 0.0	A59 0.0	A60 0.0	A82 0.0	A85 0.0	A86 0.0	A88 0.0	A89 0.0
A90 0.0	A96 0.0	A97 0.0	A98 0.0	A64 -0.0006	A67 -0.0007	A63 -0.0177	A94 -0.0241	A77 -0.034
A78 -0.0343	A55 -0.0485	A70 -0.0783	A93 -0.0834	A80 -0.1152	A16 -0.1257	A69 -0.1283	A76 -0.1308	A62 -0.1361
A68 -0.1447	A73 -0.1684	A71 -0.1885	A72 -0.1920	A24 -0.2258	A75 -0.2296	A0 -0.2339	A52 -0.2499	A66 -0.2572
A81 -0.2641	A45 -0.2942	A12 -0.3109	A74 -0.3187	A65 -0.333	A43 -0.4285	A44 -0.4509	A2 -0.4646	A79 -0.7714

Colorbar scale: 1.00, 0.75, 0.50, 0.25, 0.00, -0.25, -0.50, -0.75

Fig. 1. Output of LRPml by using Alternative 1.

A first desirable property of an explanation technique is that it produces a continuous explanation function [11]. It means that: *If two data points are nearly equivalent, then the explanations of their predictions should also be nearly equivalent.* The continuity of the explanation (or lack of it) can be quantified according to Eq. (7),

$$\max_{x \neq x'} \frac{\|R(x) - R(x')\|}{\|x - x'\|} \tag{7}$$

where $R(x)$ and $R(x')$ are the relevance of the objects x and x', respectively, and $\|.\|$ is the L2 norm (i.e., Euclidean norm). A value close to zero means that the quality of the explanation is superior.

The quality of explanation of Alternative 1 is 0.7, of Alternative 2 is 0.37, and of Alternative 3 propagating L_2 and L_3 forward, it is 0.24 and 0.28, respectively. It should be noted that the quality is calculated globally (i.e., a set of

A91 0.6954	A84 0.4899	A92 0.4874	A83 0.3543	A56 0.2957	A4 0.2599	A53 0.2271	A50 0.2064	A61 0.1834
A95 0.1138	A87 0.1113	A55 0.0783	A6 0.062	A67 0.0385	A52 0.0119	A31 0.0039	A1 0.0	A3 0.0
A5 0.0	A7 0.0	A8 0.0	A9 0.0	A10 0.0	A11 0.0	A13 0.0	A14 0.0	A15 0.0
A17 0.0	A18 0.0	A19 0.0	A20 0.0	A21 0.0	A22 0.0	A23 0.0	A25 0.0	A26 0.0
A27 0.0	A28 0.0	A29 0.0	A30 0.0	A32 0.0	A33 0.0	A34 0.0	A35 0.0	A36 0.0
A37 0.0	A38 0.0	A39 0.0	A40 0.0	A41 0.0	A42 0.0	A46 0.0	A47 0.0	A48 0.0
A49 0.0	A51 0.0	A54 0.0	A57 0.0	A58 0.0	A59 0.0	A60 0.0	A82 0.0	A85 0.0
A86 0.0	A88 0.0	A89 0.0	A90 0.0	A96 0.0	A97 0.0	A98 0.0	A64 -0.0002	A63 -0.0092
A78 -0.0159	A77 -0.0277	A94 -0.0404	A70 -0.0455	A0 -0.0543	A80 -0.0649	A62 -0.067	A93 -0.0739	A73 -0.0803
A76 -0.082	A71 -0.0916	A69 -0.0966	A24 -0.1004	A72 -0.1068	A16 -0.1209	A68 -0.1257	A75 -0.1282	A74 -0.129
A81 -0.1396	A66 -0.1708	A65 -0.1774	A43 -0.2209	A45 -0.2493	A12 -0.2555	A2 -0.2705	A44 -0.2736	A79 -0.401

Fig. 2. Output of LRPml by using Alternative 2.

A91 0.2422	A84 0.157	A92 0.1516	A83 0.1475	A4 0.0788	A53 0.0773	A61 0.0734	A56 0.0719	A95 0.0491
A6 0.0463	A87 0.0356	A93 0.0218	A55 0.0203	A1 0.0	A3 0.0	A5 0.0	A7 0.0	A8 0.0
A9 0.0	A10 0.0	A11 0.0	A13 0.0	A14 0.0	A15 0.0	A17 0.0	A18 0.0	A19 0.0
A20 0.0	A21 0.0	A22 0.0	A23 0.0	A25 0.0	A26 0.0	A27 0.0	A28 0.0	A29 0.0
A30 0.0	A32 0.0	A33 0.0	A34 0.0	A35 0.0	A36 0.0	A37 0.0	A38 0.0	A39 0.0
A40 0.0	A41 0.0	A42 0.0	A46 0.0	A47 0.0	A48 0.0	A49 0.0	A51 0.0	A54 0.0
A57 0.0	A58 0.0	A59 0.0	A60 0.0	A82 0.0	A85 0.0	A86 0.0	A88 0.0	A89 0.0
A90 0.0	A96 0.0	A97 0.0	A98 0.0	A64 -0.0001	A78 -0.0033	A63 -0.0037	A67 -0.0041	A94 -0.0045
A16 -0.0141	A31 -0.0141	A77 -0.0147	A70 -0.0162	A24 -0.0163	A50 -0.0174	A69 -0.0194	A80 -0.0233	A52 -0.0243
A76 -0.0243	A68 -0.0334	A45 -0.0334	A62 -0.0342	A12 -0.0352	A71 -0.0378	A73 -0.0385	A72 -0.0395	A0 -0.0463
A75 -0.0493	A65 -0.0503	A81 -0.0509	A74 -0.0569	A66 -0.0661	A43 -0.0797	A2 -0.0885	A44 -0.0918	A79 -0.1416

Fig. 3. Result of LRPml using Alternative 3 while the L_2 label activation value is propagated.

patients) and not locally (i.e., for a given patient). Thus, it can be concluded that Alternatives 2 and 3 can explain the neural network output more accurately for this set of patients.

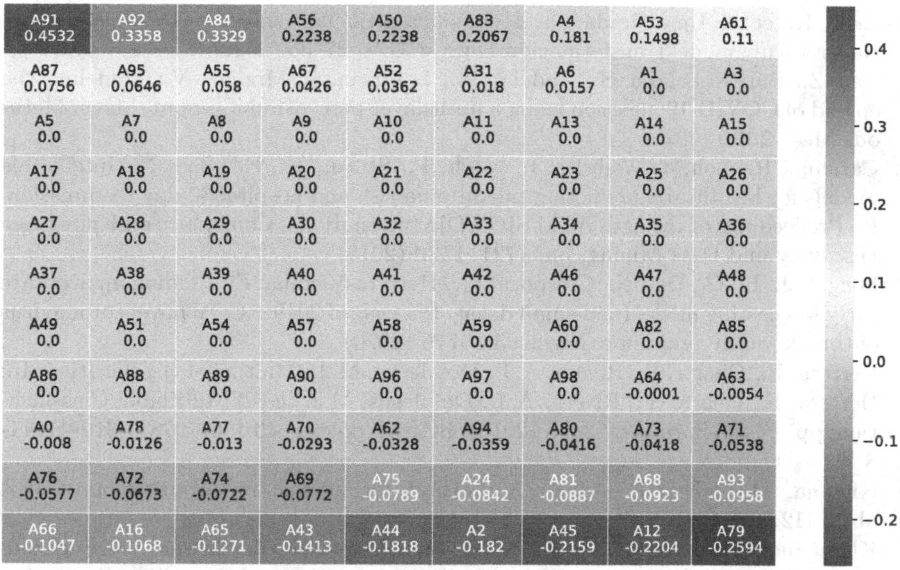

A91 0.4532	A92 0.3358	A84 0.3329	A56 0.2238	A50 0.2238	A83 0.2067	A4 0.181	A53 0.1498	A61 0.11
A87 0.0756	A95 0.0646	A55 0.058	A67 0.0426	A52 0.0362	A31 0.018	A6 0.0157	A1 0.0	A3 0.0
A5 0.0	A7 0.0	A8 0.0	A9 0.0	A10 0.0	A11 0.0	A13 0.0	A14 0.0	A15 0.0
A17 0.0	A18 0.0	A19 0.0	A20 0.0	A21 0.0	A22 0.0	A23 0.0	A25 0.0	A26 0.0
A27 0.0	A28 0.0	A29 0.0	A30 0.0	A32 0.0	A33 0.0	A34 0.0	A35 0.0	A36 0.0
A37 0.0	A38 0.0	A39 0.0	A40 0.0	A41 0.0	A42 0.0	A46 0.0	A47 0.0	A48 0.0
A49 0.0	A51 0.0	A54 0.0	A57 0.0	A58 0.0	A59 0.0	A60 0.0	A82 0.0	A85 0.0
A86 0.0	A88 0.0	A89 0.0	A90 0.0	A96 0.0	A97 0.0	A98 0.0	A64 -0.0001	A63 -0.0054
A0 -0.008	A78 -0.0126	A77 -0.013	A70 -0.0293	A62 -0.0328	A94 -0.0359	A80 -0.0416	A73 -0.0418	A71 -0.0538
A76 -0.0577	A72 -0.0673	A74 -0.0722	A69 -0.0772	A75 -0.0789	A24 -0.0842	A81 -0.0887	A68 -0.0923	A93 -0.0958
A66 -0.1047	A16 -0.1068	A65 -0.1271	A43 -0.1413	A44 -0.1818	A2 -0.182	A45 -0.2159	A12 -0.2204	A79 -0.2594

Fig. 4. Result of LRPml using Alternative 3 while the L_3 label activation value is propagated.

4   Concluding Remarks

This paper proposes a multi-label neural model to predict bacterial and fungal coinfections in patients with SARS-CoV-2. Moreover, considering that in medical domains, it is essential that the results are interpretable, the proposed solution includes a *post-hoc* stage. This research shows that combining a multi-label neural network with the LRPml method allows the construction of an effective (in terms of HL) and interpretable learning method for the problem at hand. The inclusion of a *post-hoc interpretability* stage allowed the acceptance of the medical community's neural model, identifying influential input variables in the classifier output.

References

1. Aguilera Calzadilla, Y., Díaz Morales, Y., Ortiz Díaz, L.A., Gonzalez Martínez, O.L., Lovelle Enríquez, O.A., Sánchez Álvarez, M.d.L.: Infecciones bacterianas asociadas a la covid-19 en pacientes de una unidad de cuidados intensivos. Revista Cubana de Medicina Militar **49**(3) (2020)
2. Arrieta, A.B., et al.: Explainable artificial intelligence (XAI): concepts, taxonomies, opportunities and challenges toward responsible AI. Inf. Fusion **58**, 82–115 (2020)
3. Bach, S., Binder, A., Montavon, G., Klauschen, F., Müller, K.R., Samek, W.: On pixel-wise explanations for non-linear classifier decisions by layer-wise relevance propagation. PloS ONE **10**(7), e0130140 (2015)

4. Bello, R., et al.: Una mirada a la inteligencia artificial frente a la covid-19 en cuba. Revista Cubana de Transformación Digital **1**(3), 27–36 (2020)
5. Car, Z., Baressi Šegota, S., Anđelić, N., Lorencin, I., Mrzljak, V.: Modeling the spread of COVID-19 infection using a multilayer perceptron. Comput. Math. Methods Med. **2020** (2020)
6. Caruana, R., Lou, Y., Gehrke, J., Koch, P., Sturm, M., Elhadad, N.: Intelligible models for healthcare: predicting pneumonia risk and hospital 30-day readmission. In: Proceedings of the 21th ACM SIGKDD International Conference on Knowledge Discovery and Data Mining, pp. 1721–1730 (2015)
7. Fong, S.J., Li, G., Dey, N., Crespo, R.G., Herrera-Viedma, E.: Finding an accurate early forecasting model from small dataset: a case of 2019-NCOV novel coronavirus outbreak. arXiv preprint arXiv:2003.10776 (2020)
8. Herrera, F., Charte, F., Rivera, A.J., Del Jesus, M.J.: Multilabel classification. In: Herrera, F., Charte, F., Rivera, A.J., Del Jesus, M.J. (eds.) Multilabel Classification, pp. 17–31. Springer, Cham (2016). https://doi.org/10.1007/978-3-319-41111-8_2
9. Kingma, D.P., Ba, J.: Adam: a method for stochastic optimization. CoRR abs/1412.6980 (2015)
10. Klambauer, G., Unterthiner, T., Mayr, A., Hochreiter, S.: Self-normalizing neural networks. In: 31st International Conference on Neural Information Processing Systems. NIPS 2017, pp. 972–981. Curran Associates Inc. (2017)
11. Montavon, G., Samek, W., Müller, K.R.: Methods for interpreting and understanding deep neural networks. Digit. Sig. Process. **73**, 1–15 (2018)
12. Nápoles, G., Bello, M., Salgueiro, Y.: Long-term cognitive network-based architecture for multi-label classification. Neural Netw. (2021)
13. Ramón-Hernández, A., Bello Garcia, B., Bello, M., García Lorenzo, M., Bello Pérez, R.: Análisis de escenario utilizando técnicas de inteligencia artificial. Anales de la Academia de Ciencias de Cuba **10**(2) (2020)
14. Samek, W., Wiegand, T., Müller, K.R.: Explainable artificial intelligence: understanding, visualizing and interpreting deep learning models. arXiv preprint arXiv:1708.08296 (2017)
15. Sipior, J.C.: Considerations for development and use of AI in response to COVID-19. Int. J. Inf. Manag. **55**, 102170 (2020)
16. Suárez, A.R., Lorenzo, M.M.G., Caballero, Y., Bello, R.: Un bosquejo de la inteligencia artificial frente a la covid-19 en el mundo. Revista Cubana de Transformación Digit. **1**(3), 05–26 (2020)
17. Wong, T.T.: Performance evaluation of classification algorithms by k-fold and leave-one-out cross validation. Pattern Recogn. **48**(9), 2839–2846 (2015)
18. Yan, T., Wong, P.K., Ren, H., Wang, H., Wang, J., Li, Y.: Automatic distinction between COVID-19 and common pneumonia using multi-scale convolutional neural network on chest CT scans. Chaos, Solitons Fractals **140**, 110153 (2020)

A Machine Learning Based Approach for Estimation of the Lung Affectation Degree in CXR Images of COVID-19 Patients

Eduardo Garea-Llano$^{(\boxtimes)}$, Hector A. Castellanos-Loaces, Eduardo Martinez-Montes, and Evelio Gonzalez-Dalmau

Cuban Neuroscience Center, 190 No. 1520, Playa, 11600 Havana, Cuba
{eduardo.garea,hector.castellanos,eduardo,
evelio.gonzalez}@cneuro.edu.cu

Abstract. The effectiveness of the treatments applied to patients with COVID-19 in serious and critical condition admitted to intensive care units is a necessary element to draw up the strategies and protocols to follow in each particular case. An automatic index that allows to quantify the degree of affectation produced by the disease in the lungs from X-ray images of the thorax has not been investigated so far.

The work presents a method for estimation of a lung affectation index in chest X-ray images in patients diagnosed with COVID-19 in an advanced stage of the disease. The index is obtained from a method that combines image quality evaluation, digital image processing and deep learning for lung region segmentation. This method is capable of facing the problem of very diffuse borders due to the notable effects that COVID-19 patients in serious or critical condition have. The subsequent step of our proposal consist in the classification of the previously segmented image into two classes (healthy region, affected region) establishing the relationship between the number of pixels of each class. The results achieved in the experiments on images of healthy and affected by COVID-19 patients showed high values of sensitivity and specificity.

Keywords: Machine learning · CXR images · COVID-19 · Index of affectation · Deep learning · Image classification

1 Introduction

After more than a year in the fight with the COVID-19 pandemic, the protocols and forms of action in the treatment of patients in serious or critical condition have been in constant renewal in order to achieve in the first instance to save their life. One method of evaluating the degree of effectiveness of the protocols applied in these cases has been the Chest X-ray (CXR) examination by radiologists and intensivists to look for visual indicators associated with the evolution of the SARS-CoV-2 viral infection.

Several recently published studies have shown that abnormalities in chest CXR images that are characteristic of COVID-19 patients [1, 2] may decrease or increase

© Springer Nature Switzerland AG 2021
Y. Hernández Heredia et al. (Eds.): IWAIPR 2021, LNCS 13055, pp. 13–23, 2021.
https://doi.org/10.1007/978-3-030-89691-1_2

depending on the disease severity and the effectiveness of the applied protocols [3–5]. The large number of patients that has caused the collapse of many intensive therapies makes it almost impossible for each of them to have a radiology service with a full-time radiologist, for this reason it is necessary to have an indicator that automatically allows to the intensivists to evaluate the evolution of patients in critical condition based on the degree of affectation of their lungs. However, in the bibliographic review carried out, no research was found that proposes the automatic calculation of an indicator, measure or index to evaluate the degree of lung affectation caused by COVID-19 in patients in advanced stage of the disease in CRX images.

In this work, we propose a method that obtains as a result an affectation index of the lungs in COVID-19 patients in advanced stage of the disease. The method first performs the quality evaluation of the CXR image considering its degree of sharpness and entropy, based on this result applies techniques for its improvement, then the segmentation of the lung region is performed and finally the supervised classification into two classes (healthy region, affected region) is performed on the resulting image. Derived from this result, the affectation index (Iaf) is proposed by calculating the relationship between the number of pixels of each class. In Sect. 2 we discuss the most relevant related works that contribute to our proposal. In Sect. 3 the proposed method is presented. Section 4 presents the experimental results and their discussion. Finally, the conclusions and future works are presented.

2   Related Works

The quality of a medical image is determined by the method of image capture, the characteristics of the equipment, and the image variables selected by the operator. Image quality is not a single factor, but a combination of at least five factors: contrast, blur, noise, artifacts, and distortion [6]. When the image is out of focus as a consequence of this, unwanted effects such as noise and artifacts arise, so solving the problem of blurring could largely imply solving the problems of noise and artifacts present in the image [7].

In [8] an objective evaluation method is proposed in order to adjust the voltages to achieve closed-loop control of the X-ray imaging system. Compared with the traditional image quality evaluation method, the results of the experiments showed that the proposed method based on weighted entropy can evaluate the X-ray image quality effectively. However, the objective of this method is to serve as a guide to correct the problems of the X-ray sensors in order to obtain quality images directly from the equipment and the possibility of an improvement process of the images already acquired is not considered.

In [9] an analysis of the use of the Kang and Park filter was carried out using images of eyes taken in the near infrared spectrum. The filter was used to eliminate high frequencies and is composed of a convolutional kernel represented by a 5×5 matrix. This is formed by the sum of three functions represented by a matrix of 5×5 and amplitude -1, another of 3×3 and amplitude $+5$ and one that is represented by four values of 1×1 and amplitude -5 in the corresponding positions. The kernel is capable of filtering the high frequencies within the texture better than other operators of the state of the art, in addition it has a low computational cost due to its reduced size. On the other hand, the entropy of an image has proven to be a good indicator of the volume of information contained in it [8, 10]. The entropy only depends on the volume of gray levels and the frequency of each level.

The fundamental objective of the lung segmentation process in the CXR image is to be able to concentrate the classification process only in the lung regions, avoiding interference in the process that can be caused by the rest of the image regions. Automatic segmentation of CXRs has been extensively studied since the 1970s, at least with regard to segmentation of the lungs, rib cage, heart, and clavicles [11] Conventional methods are based on previous knowledge [12] to delineate anatomical objects from X-ray images. Modern approaches use deep convolutional networks and have shown superior performance [13]. Despite the great advances in the automatic segmentation of these organs, limitations still persist, such as the need to use small-size CXRs or the irregularity and imprecision of the edges resulting from segmentation that reduce its applicability in clinical settings. Additionally, CXR images of COVID-19 patients in an advanced stage of the disease make the segmentation process a challenging task because the characteristic conditions of this disease cause a whitening of the pulmonary region, which confuses the most of the algorithms trained for this task [14].

In much of the more recent consulted literature on the use of artificial intelligence in the fight against COVID-19, the image classification is understood as the process of assigning a label to the image to assign it a category related to the presence or not of the disease. In [15] a study of the state of the art of the most recent methods used in the identification of COVID-19 from CXR images is carried out. It is clear that the trend is to apply techniques through deep neural networks. Most of the results obtained are encouraging, as they report very good results that even surpass the radiologists themselves, although they do not convince them [16]. The authors of [15] delve into the peculiarities of this task and the characteristics of the databases taken for the training of networks, as well as what are the factors that may be causing biases in them fundamentally referred to the amount of data, samples training, metadata, and sensor characteristics. According to these authors, the problem with deep learning-based methods is that they generate their own descriptors in the network training process, which can produce an overfitting of the classification models. They put forward the idea that the use of traditional methods of computer vision and machine learning could lead to models with greater generalizability.

3   Method for Automatic Estimation of Lung Affectation Degree by COVID-19 in CXR Images

Figure 1 presents the general scheme of the proposed method which consists of 4 main steps: 1) image quality evaluation; 2) image enhancement if necessary; 3) segmentation of lung regions 4) Image classification and Index calculation. The following sections explain each of these steps in detail.

Application Context and Data Characteristics: To achieve the best possible approximation to the context of practical application of the proposed method, we built a database of CXR images of 3 hospitals working in the fight against the COVID-19 pandemic in Havana, Cuba. The images were taken in the period from March to December 2020. The database consists of 333 images, 179 images of patients diagnosed with COVID-19 and

154 images of healthy people. The original images were obtained from the digital scan in jpg format of the plates printed in acetate and from the files in Dicom format directly obtained from the digital x-ray equipment. For the experimental work, all the images were converted to jpg format. Some examples are shown in Fig. 2.

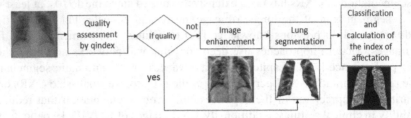

Fig. 1. General scheme of the proposed algorithm.

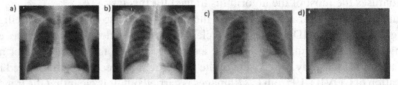

Fig. 2. Examples of the images from our database, a) and b) healthy, c) and d) COVID-19 patients.

This is not a public database and has only been used for research purposes with the consent of hospital institutions. For this, a process was carried out that includes anonymizing the data by the hospital institutions, so the researchers did not have access to the biographical data of the patients.

Image Quality Assessment: In this work we propose a method for evaluating the quality of the chest X-ray image based on the calculation of a quality index (*qindex*). The *qindex* is obtained by the estimation of the image sharpness and the level of diversity of the texture present in it, using a combination of the Kang and Park filter [9] and a measure of the image entropy. The proposed *qindex* measure is obtained by Eq. 1.

$$qindex = \frac{kpk * ent}{tkpk * tent} \tag{1}$$

Where *kpk* is the average value of the image pixels obtained as a result of the convolution of the input x-ray image with the Kang and Park kernel. *tkpk* is the estimated threshold of *kpk* to obtain a quality image, in [9] the authors, based on their experimental results, recommend a threshold = 15. *ent* is the entropy value of the image. *tent* is the estimated threshold of *ent* with which it is possible to obtain a quality image.

The entropy or average information of an image can be roughly determined from the image histogram. The histogram shows the different gray level probabilities in the image. Entropy is useful, for example, for image autofocus: as the focus state of an image varies, so does its entropy. The entropy of an image [10], considers the probability of occurrence of a given gray level value within the image region. For the calculation of the entropy measure, levels of 256 tones are used in the histogram count, so that the pixel values are discrete and correspond directly to a bin value.

To define the entropy threshold (tent) we carried out an experiment that allowed us to empirically establish that good quality CXR images have an entropy greater than 4.

For the experiment, we created a set of 300 CXR images randomly selected from our dataset, it was divided into two subset (images of good and bad quality) by a specialist in radiology. To determine the minimum entropy value for a quality image, the evaluation of each of them was carried out through their response to the Kang and Park filter. The entropy frequency distribution showed that good quality CXR images have an entropy greater than 4, (in a range from 4.3 to 5.6, with X- = 4.9 and S = 0.65), so we propose to assume this value as the value of *tent*. These results show that the higher the entropy there is a more uniform distribution of the image tones, while blurred or poorly sharp images give rise to close values of tones that are repeated a lot in the image, which is expressed in a decrease in the entropy. The combination of low entropy values with high kernel response values means that higher quality images have a more uniform distribution with high and low values that give a high average, since low averages are more related to blurred parts of the image.

The *qindex* measure can reach values that depend on the thresholds selected for *kpk* and *ent*. In this way considering the values of the thresholds *tkpk* = 15 experimentally obtained in [9] and *tent* = 4 experimentally obtained by us, the minimum value of *qindex* to obtain a quality CXR image will be 1, higher values will denote higher image quality and values less than 1 denote lower image quality.

Image Enhancement: After evaluating the quality of the input image, the proposed algorithm establishes a conditional step that allows improving the quality of the input image if it presents a *qindex* < *1*. For this, the contrast-limited adaptive histogram equalization (CLAHE) method [17] was chosen, which has given good results in improving x-ray images [18]. This method allows to improve the image even in regions that are darker or lighter than most of the image.

Lung Segmentation: To perform the segmentation of the lung region, we propose the application of the convolutional neural network (CNN). For this purpose pre-trained CCNs are adapted via transfer learning. Transfer learning is the process of learning from a new tasks through the transfer of knowledge from a related task that has already been learned. This process can be classified into inductive learning or reinforcement learning. In this work, inductive learning over UNet-CNN [19] for segmenting lung regions is performed. UNet is based on a CNN architecture for fast and accurate image segmentation, this network has demonstrated high precision in various tasks dedicated to the segmentation of structures in electron microscopy and was recently successfully used to segment lungs in CXR with the use of manually prepared masks [20].

For the training of the network, 700 images were taken from the Montgomery County Chest X-ray Database (National Library of Medicine, National Institutes of Health, Bethesda, MD, USA) [21, 22] which has their corresponding segmentation masks ("ground truth"). Also we used a set of 50 images corresponding to COVID-19 patients from our database. Their segmentation masks were obtained manually following the methodology established in [21] and [22], under the supervision from a radiologist. These 50 images were chosen under the criteria of having strong effects caused by COVID-19 and correspond to patients who were admitted to Intensive Care Units due to the degree of severity of the disease. The intention in this case was to provide the training with the conditions of the images of patients severely affected by COVID-19 to obtain a robust classifier that would allow the effective segmentation of this type of images.

3.1 Supervised Classification of the Lung Image and Calculation of the Index of Affectation

In our proposal, for the classification of image pixels we chose a classic automatic learning algorithm, the Random Forest. This algorithm creates multiple decision trees and combines them to obtain a prediction. In this algorithm additional randomness is added to the model, as the trees grow, instead of looking for the most important characteristic when dividing a node, it looks for the best characteristic among a random subset of characteristics, this results in a wide diversity that generally results in a better model [23].

The CXR are images in gray levels, where in healthy patients the anatomical elements that make up this region are differentiated, which are the lung mass, the bones of the ribs and clavicles. On the other hand, radiological studies [14] of the affectations caused by COVID-19 have determined that ground glass opacities and consolidation with or without vascular enlargement, interlobular septal thickening and air bronchogram sign are the most common affectations seen on CXR images. These elements are manifested in the change of tones of the lung region from dark tones for the healthy regions of the lung and lighter tones for the affected regions. Taking these elements into account, in this work we propose to use as a feature for the classification of the image the tones of the regions to be classified, which we will divide into two classes: healthy lung + bones and affectations.

For the classifier training, our database was randomly divided into two parts, a first part of 180 images was taken as a training set. The images comprise 90 images of healthy lungs and 90 images of lungs affected by COVID-19. From this set, 4500 samples (pixels) were randomly taken, 1500 samples of each class. All (100%) of the samples corresponding to the affectations caused by COVID-19 were taken from the images of patients with the disease, while 90% of the samples of the two remaining classes (healthy lung and bones) correspond to images of healthy people and 10% to patients with COVID-19. The rest of the images that comprise the subset were designated as the test set. Once the classifier has been obtained, it can be applied to new images to achieve its classification and the subsequent calculation of the index of affectation.

Calculation of the Affectation Index: Taking into account that the image classification is developed pixel by pixel, then as a result of its application it is possible to quantify the number of pixels belonging to the healthy lung class and affectations. For this we propose the calculation of lung affectation index (Iaf) by the following expression (2):

$$Iaf = \frac{P1}{P0 + P2} \tag{2}$$

Where: P1 is the sum of the pixels classified as affected region. P0 is the sum of the pixels classified as healthy region. P2, is the sum of the pixels classified as bone region.

4   Experimental Results and Discussion

The proposed method was integrated into 4 basic functions (quality evaluation, improvement, segmentation and classification) that make up the Beta version pipeline implemented in c++ language, also using the set of functionalities for image processing and computer vision from the OpenCv library (https://opencv.org/).

Evaluation of the Proposed Quality Measure: For the evaluation of the proposed quality measure (*qindex*), the 333 images of our database were taken, and their quality was calculated using the *qindex*. The results obtained show that in the case of images of healthy people, 43 (37%) present poor quality, however, in the images of COVID-19 patients, 143 (80%) images were of poor quality. This may be due to the effect caused by conditions such as ground glass opacities in images with COVID-19 or the origin of a part of these images that were obtained from scanning the plates.

The application of the image enhancement method to the images with *qindex* < 1, showed an increase in the quality of the images and with an increase in the *qindex* for the images of healthy people ($\overline{X} = 0.38$, S = 0.071) and images of COVID- 19 patients ($\overline{X} = 0.30$, S = 0.27) respectively. In the case of the images of healthy people, only 5 images were left with a *qindex* < 1 but very close to this value; while the images of COVID-19 patients also increased their quality even in the 43 images that were left with *qindex* < 1. These results show the usefulness of the enhancement step because with its application it is guaranteed that the images that will go to the process of classification have better quality than the original images, which may lead to better classification results (see an example in Fig. 3).

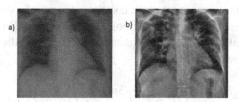

Fig. 3. Results of the application of the enhancement method, a) original b) improved

Evaluation of the Proposed Segmentation Method: For the evaluation of the proposed segmentation method, a subset of images from our database was randomly formed. The selected images were not used in the network training set. Each image was segmented manually by two medical specialists to obtain the ground truth of their segmentation masks. Due to the complexity of the manual segmentation process and the limited time available to specialists, the subset consisted of 20 images (10 normal and 10 COVID-19). As a second step, the 20 images were segmented by the proposed method and the result of the segmentation of each image was compared with its corresponding ground truth, using the calculation of the E1 error rate proposed in the protocol. NICEI (http://nice1. di.ubi.pt/). This metric estimates the proportion of mismatched pixels between segmentation and ground truth, the closer the value of E1 to 0, the better the segmentation result.

In the results, the images corresponding to healthy people reach an average value of E1 smaller ($\overline{X}= 0.17$, $S = 0.031$) than in the images corresponding to patients with COVID-19 ($\overline{X} = 0.25$, $S = 0.051$), this is given by the nature of the affectations caused by the disease that imply the presence of opacities that can be confused by the segmentation method and classified as non-pulmonary areas. Figure 4 show an example of a segmented image.

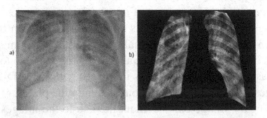

Fig. 4. Results of the segmentation method, a) original b) segmented

Evaluation of the Image Classification Process: For the evaluation of the proposed classification method, a test set formed by the 153 images that were not used in the training set of the classifier was taken. This test set consisted of 77 images of COVID-19 patients and 76 of healthy people. Previously, a process of segmentation and manual labeling of the regions affected by COVID-19 was carried out by two experts. The rest of the pixels were assigned the label corresponding to healthy lung and bones. For the evaluation metrics of the classification efficacy we used Sensitivity and Specificity (3). This was done taking into account for each class the correctly classified pixels (TP), those classified as of that class but that really belong to another class (FP), those classified as of another class but that belong to the evaluated class (FN) and those classified as other classes and that they really are (TN).

$$Sens = \frac{TP}{(TP + FN)} \quad Spec = \frac{TN}{(TN + FP)} \tag{3}$$

A 4 fold cross-validation process was performed for the experiment. The test dataset was divided into four subsets and the cross training and testing process was performed. Table 1 shows the confusion matrix, the average of sensitivity and specificity values and standard deviation (S) obtained. As can be seen in all the results, the sensitivity and specificity values remain high, which indicates a good performance of the obtained classifier. On the other hand, the presence of pixels falsely classified as affectations is due in large part to the similarity of the tones of the bones with the tones that the true affectations present within the lung area (see Fig. 5). This is a problem that we will explore in future research.

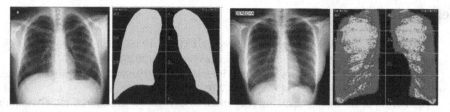

Fig. 5. Examples of segmented and classified images from healthy person (left) COVID-19 patient (right), (in red: class affectations, in green: healthy class) (Color figure online)

Table 1. Confusion matrix (in number of pixels per class) and obtained results

Actual	Number of pixels	No	Yes	Sens.	S	Spec.	S
Class healthy = healthy lung + bones							
No	13683810	13215522	468288	0.964	0.012	0.966	0.018
Yes	10712730	382610	10330120				
Class COVID-19 affectations							
No	53612730	51200269	2412461	0.984	0.01	0.955	0.004
Yes	13788810	220639	13568171				

5 Conclusions and Future Work

In this work, a method for estimation of lung affectation degree in CXR image from COVID-19 patients was proposed. Our proposal focuses on the stages of image quality evaluation and enhancement, lung segmentation and classification and is based on the combination of the evaluation of CXR image quality, the CNN-Unet network for segmentation, and classification of regions affected by COVID-19. The obtained lung segmentation method allows estimating the degree of affectation caused by the disease only in the pulmonary region, which avoids the interference of other anatomical regions that do not intervene in the analysis. The inclusion of the proposed quality evaluation as a stage prior to the lung segmentation process limits the passage of low-quality images to the system, which leads to a more accurate classification of COVID-19 affectations. The application of supervised classification based on Random Forest showed high values of sensitivity and specificity. Future works will be focused on the development of bone suppression methods and on the interaction with medical specialists to fine tune the proposed method.

Acknowledgment. We appreciate the collaboration of the Cuban Society of Imaging and the Hospitals "Luis Díaz Soto" (Naval), Institute of Tropical Medicine "Pedro Kouri" and "Salvador Allende" for providing us with the images that allowed us to develop this research.

References

1. Ng, M.-Y., Lee, Y.P., et al.: Imaging profile of the COVID-19 infection: radiologic findings and literature review. Radiol. Cardiothogracic Imaging **2**(1) (2020)
2. Huang, C., et al.: Clinical features of patients infected with 2019 novel coronavirus in Wuhan, China. The Lancet **395**(10223), 497–506 (2020)
3. Borghesi, A., et al.: Radiographic severity index in COVID-19 pneumonia: relationship to age and sex in 783 Italian patients. Radiol. Med. (Torino) **125**(5), 461–464 (2020). https://doi.org/10.1007/s11547-020-01202-1
4. Monaco, C.G., et al.: Chest x-ray severity score in COVID-19 patients on emergency department admission: a two-centre study. Eur. Radiol. Exp. **4**(1), 1–7 (2020). https://doi.org/10.1186/s41747-020-00195-w
5. Schalekamp, S., Huisman, M., van Dijk R.A., et al.: Model-based prediction of critical illness in hospitalized patients with COVID-19 [published online ahead of print, 2020 Aug 13]. Radiology 202723 (2020)
6. Sprawls, P.: image characteristics and quality. In: Physical Principles of Medical Imaging Online, Resources for Learning and Teaching. http://www.sprawls.org/resources
7. Samajdar, T., Quraishi, M.I.: Analysis and evaluation of image quality metrics. In: Mandal, J.K., Satapathy, S.C., Sanyal, M.K., Sarkar, P.P., Mukhopadhyay, A. (eds.) Information Systems Design and Intelligent Applications. AISC, vol. 340, pp. 369–378. Springer, New Delhi (2015). https://doi.org/10.1007/978-81-322-2247-7_38
8. Chen, F., Pan, J., Han, Y.: An effective image quality evaluation method of x-ray imaging system. J. Comput. Inf. Syst. **7**(4), 1278–1285 (2011)
9. Garea-Llano, E., García-Vázquez, M., Colores-Vargas, J.M., Zamudio-Fuentes, L.M., Ramírez-Acosta, A.A.: Optimized robust multi-sensor scheme for simultaneous video and image iris recognition. Pattern Recogn. Lett. **101**, 44–45 (2018)
10. Gonzalez, R.C., Woods, R.E.: Image compression and watermarking. In: Digital Image Processing, 4th edn, vol. 8 (2018)
11. Toriwaki, J.-I., Suenaga, Y., Negoro, T., Fukumura, T.: Pattern recognition of chest x-ray images. Comput. Vis. Graph **2**(3), 252–271 (1973)
12. Zhu, Y., Prummer, S., Wang, P., Chen, T., Comaniciu, D., Ostermeier, M.: Dynamic layer separation for coronary DSA and enhancement in fluoroscopic sequences. In: Yang, G.-Z., Hawkes, D., Rueckert, D., Noble, A., Taylor, C. (eds.) MICCAI 2009. LNCS, vol. 5762, pp. 877–884. Springer, Heidelberg (2009). https://doi.org/10.1007/978-3-642-04271-3_106
13. Gómez, O., Mesejo, P., Ibáñez, O., Valsecchi, A., Cordón, O.: Deep architectures for high-resolution multi-organ chest x-ray image segmentation. Neural Comput. Appl. **32**(20), 15949–15963 (2019). https://doi.org/10.1007/s00521-019-04532-y
14. Kanne, J.P., Little, B.P., Chung, J.H., Elicker, B.M., Ketai, L.H.: Essentials for radiologists on COVID-19: an update-radiology scientific expert panel. Radiology **296**(2), E113–E114 (2020)
15. López-Cabrera, J.D., Portal Díaz, J.A., Orozco Morales, R., Pérez Díaz, M.: Revisión crítica sobre la identificación de COVID-19 a partir de imágenes de rayos x de tórax usando técnicas de inteligencia artificial. Rev. Cub. Transf. Digit. **1**(3), 67–99 (2020)
16. Laghi, A.: Cautions about radiologic diagnosis of COVID-19 infection driven by artificial intelligence. The Lancet Digit. Health **2**(5), e225 (2020)
17. Zuiderveld, K.: Contrast limited adaptive histogram equalization. In: Graphics Gems IV, pp. 474–485. Academic Press Professional, Inc., San Diego (1994)
18. Koonsanit, K., Thongvigitmanee, S., Pongnapang, N., Thajchayapong, P.: Image enhancement on digital x-ray images using N-CLAHE. In: 2017 10th (BMEiCON), Hokkaido, Japan, pp. 1–4 (2017)

19. Ronneberger, O., Fischer, P., Brox, T.: U-net: convolutional networks for biomedical image segmentation. In: Navab, N., Hornegger, J., Wells, W.M., Frangi, A.F. (eds.) MICCAI 2015. LNCS, vol. 9351, pp. 234–241. Springer, Cham (2015). https://doi.org/10.1007/978-3-319-24574-4_28

20. Candemir, S., Jaeger, S., Musco, J., Xue, Z., et al.: Lung segmentation in chest radiographs using anatomical atlases with nonrigid registration. IEEE Trans. Med, Imaging **33**(2), 577 (2014)

21. Jaeger, S., et al.: Automatic tuberculosis screening using chest radiographs. IEEE Trans. Med. Imaging **33**(2), 233–245 (2014). https://doi.org/10.1109/TMI.2013.2284099. PMID: 24108713

22. Gordienko, Y., et al.: Deep learning with lung segmentation and bone shadow exclusion techniques for chest x-ray analysis of lung cancer. In: Hu, Z., Petoukhov, S., Dychka, I., He, M. (eds.) ICCSEEA 2018. AISC, vol. 754, pp. 638–647. Springer, Cham (2019). https://doi.org/10.1007/978-3-319-91008-6_63

23. Gelbowitz, A.: Decision trees and random forests guide: an overview of decision trees and random forests: machine learning design patterns. Independently Published (2021)

Deep Neural Network to Detect Gender Violence on Mexican Tweets

Grisel Miranda[1], Roberto Alejo[2(✉)], Carlos Castorena[2], Eréndira Rendón[2], Javier Illescas[2], and Vicente García[3]

[1] National Technological Institute of Mexico, TESJo,
Mexico City, Mexico State, Mexico
[2] National Technological Institute of Mexico, IT Toluca,
Metepec, Mexico
{ralejoe,ccastorenal,erendonl,fillescasm}@toluca.tecnm.mx
[3] Autonomous University of Ciudad Juárez, UACJ,
Ciudad Juárez, Mexico
vicente.jimenez@uacj.mx

Abstract. During COVID-19 quarantine, in online sites such as social networks, Gender-Based Violence has alarmingly increased. Online platforms have taken various measures to regulate and prevent broadcasting of violence messages. Multiple proposals based on machine learning and deep learning approaches have been used to address this problem. This work presents an improvement in implementation of a deep learning neural network for detection of Gender-Based Violence in Twitter messages. A total of 32,500 tweets were downloaded from Mexican Twitter accounts and human volunteers manually tagged the tweets as violent and non-violent to be used as training and testing data sets. Experimental results show the effectiveness of the deep neural network (about 90% of the Area Under the Receiver Operating Characteristic) to detect gender violence in Twitter messages using a simple Natural Language Processing approach.

Keywords: Gender-Based Violence · Mexico · Twitter · Deep neural networks · Class imbalance

1 Introduction

Gender-Based Violence (GBV) has been recognized as a public health problem and a violation of human rights that results in the inequality of gender. This inequality can be described as discrimination in the opportunities, responsibilities, and access and control of sources, which has its roots in the notion of males attributed socioculturally as superior to females [1].

The violence exerted on women has become a problem of pandemics dimensions, affecting the whole world and millions of people; among those, who stand out more are women and children [2]. The declaration on the elimination of violence against women defines the GBV as any act that results in physical, sexual

Y. Hernández Heredia et al. (Eds.): IWAIPR 2021, LNCS 13055, pp. 24–32, 2021.
https://doi.org/10.1007/978-3-030-89691-1_3

or psychological harm or any suffering to the woman, including threats and the arbitrary deprivation of her freedom, whether in public or private life [3].

In Mexico, the GBV has existed since ancient times; however, in recent years, a significant increase in the number of victims of gender violence has become visible due to the social, political and economic context in which they live, manifesting gender and race inequality [4]. This problem has been addressed through social movements founded to neutralize their effects; a clear example is #niunamás, whose objective is to combat femicide and raise awareness about violence against women in Mexico [5].

Computer science researchers have implemented algorithms and methodologies based on machine learning and deep learning to address the GBV problem. For instance, [6] presents a prototype based on Support Vector Machines to detect verbal aggressions and then classify the aggressiveness of the messages posted on the social platform Twitter. While [7] propose a model that helped to detect violence against women on social media in the Spanish language using different techniques such as Opinion Mining, Document Term Matrix (DTM), Bag of Words (BoW), and algorithms based on Machine Learning.

On the other hand, [8] presents an application capable of detecting, classifying, analyzing and predicting texts that include signs of violence through data mining and NLP (Natural Language Processing). This work was focused on content related to xenophobia and GBV of Twitter in Ecuador.

Twitter is one of the most public social networks with a great impact, where millions of users post messages daily. These messages can be violent with a symbolic or explicit character that directly undermines women's dignity and highlights gender inequality [9]. Many women experience different types of abuse, and almost a half have experienced online attacks as a part of their daily lives [10]. In [11], authors exposed Twitter as a mean where women suffer violence and abuse considered continuous, normalized, frequent, hostile and sustained. Some of the most relevant characteristics of this abuse are sexual harassment, humiliation and threats of sexual violence that are experienced as degrading violations and can also be used as violent pornographic representations [12]. Although social media platforms and the Internet have recently taken measures to ensure user experience, adding some changes to their privacy and policies, the effectiveness of these efforts and measures still needs constant regulation [13].

This paper proposes an improvement of the results obtained from [14] and some of the changes applied to that work are: 1) the creation of a new corpus including two different classes (violent and non-violent), and 2) the addition of hidden layers and hidden neurons to the deep neural network. The performance of the new approach was evaluated with the Area Under the Receptor Operational Characteristics (AUC), thus showing better results in the classification task related to GBV in Twitter messages.

2   Related Work

In recent years, technologies have significantly advanced and with them the social computing [15]; a clear example of social computing is sentiment analysis, whose objective is to understand the feelings and emotions of citizens. It has been used in areas of interest such as marketing, customer service and violence detection in social networks. Until a few years ago, researchers used to employ traditional algorithms based on machine learning (ML) to deal with the challenge of sentiment analysis; however, today, researchers are already implementing techniques based on deep learning (DL) [16].

Some of the works that implement algorithms based on machine learning employ common architectures like Random Forest (RF) and Support Vector Machines (SVM) to identify violence in Twitter messages. Such is the case of [17], where the use of ML classifiers such as RF and SVM variants are presented. These classifiers were used to detect misogyny in Spanish tweets using Bag of Words (BoW) and word embedding, achieving a precision of 85%.

In the same context, [18] presents an approach based on expanded dictionaries of insults with a supervised classifier (such as SVM). This approach was adapted to the English and Mexican Spanish languages, where the authors determined for both languages that the global expansion of the dictionaries was the best option to have good precision, with 95% and 57% (positive and negative respectively) for the English language and 100% and 46% (positive and negative respectively) for Mexican Spanish. Besides, [19] introduces a study of algorithms such as RF and OneR for the detection of cyber-aggression in social networks for the Mexican Spanish language. In this case, the classification was made up of 3 types of cyber-aggression (racism, violence based on sexual orientation and violence against women) and it achieved good results with the OneR model.

On the other hand, within DL architectures used for the same task, we can find the Convolutional Networks (CNN), Long Short Term Memory networks (LSTM), and the Multilayer Perceptron (MLP). Emphasizing these architectures, [17] exposed the development of 13 DL models based on architectures such as CNN and LSTM for detecting hate speech from Twitter and Facebook messages, concluding that LSTM and one of its variants together with the word embedding technique showed promising results for all data sets. In the same way, [20–22] showed the implementation of an architecture based on CNN together with an n-gram model for the detection of aggressiveness on Mexican tweets; By comparing the results of these studies, the last one obtained the best results for this task. Ramadhami et al. [23] evidenced poor results in the precision of text analysis using a DL model (MLP) and the data mining technique for tweet messages in English and Korean languages.

Based on the work related to detecting GBV in social networks, it is important to note that many of these complex preprocessing methods are necessary. Researchers who have presented their works in English [24] and other languages [25,26] agree that one of the characteristics to achieve good results is to consider the regional language context for the classification of messages. Therefore, this paper focuses on the Mexican Spanish language with a straightforward preprocessing method that includes removing some characters (such as hashtags, symbols, conjunctions, emojis, numbers) and an only tokenize approach (CountVectorizer) for the automatic detection of GBV from tweets generated in Mexico.

3 Theoretical Framework

A Deep Learning Multilayer Perceptron (DL-MLP) model comprises two or more layers hidden between inputs and outputs. It is characterized because there are no connections between neurons of the same layer and no backward connections. Each layer has the function of feeding all the neurons of the next layer, repeating the propagation process up to the output layer [27]. Implementing multiple layers generates a more complex optimization problem; however, a reduction in the number of nodes used per layer within the architecture is obtained with more layers. Likewise, the use of multiple layers increases the abstraction capability of an MLP to complex problems [28].

The learning of a deep neural network can be formulated as a non-convex optimization problem [29]; therefore, the predominant methodology in deep learning training relies on Stochastic Gradient Descent methods [30]: the most common way to optimize neural networks. One of the most common algorithms in descending gradient optimization is Adam [31,32], which is based on the adaptive estimation of first and second order-moments, that is, the Adam algorithm reduces the error of $f(w)$ and $\hat{f}(x, w)$.

Text feature extraction is a process used to extract a list of words from text data and then transform it into a set of unique features that can be used by a classifier [33]. A standard technique based on the Bag of Words (BoW) model is CountVectorizer [34], which considers the frequency of a word that appears in a document a and is then transformed into numerical vector $a = \{t_1, t_2, t_3, ..., t_N\}$, using the t_N value as the weight of each feature in the document a and building a vocabulary of words. Also, this method counts the words found in the document, so it returns an integer vector.

A major challenge for using the sampling method is setting parameters, such as sampling rates, that significantly impact minority class performance. That is why the sampling methods are a very good option for dealing with class imbalance [35]. A straightforward method to deal with the class imbalance problem is the Random Over Sampling (ROS) [36], which duplicates examples of the minority class randomly until it has as many examples as the majority class, that is until it is achieved a balance between the number of samples for the different classes. An alternative to ROS is the Synthetic Minority Over-sampling Technique (SMOTE) [37], whose function is based on generating synthetic samples of the minority class through the interpolation of existing and nearby instances between them.

4 Methodology

Currently, the amount of data generated in social networks shows exponential and massive growth. This simplifies the obtainment of useful information for its analysis. This section shows the methodological aspects of this work, from data collection, preprocessing, classifier parameters to model training.

Data collection. In the first stage, 2,500 tweets containing expressions that promote gender violence were manually extracted and 30,000 more non-violent. Tweets were downloaded with a program made in Python language by using the Twitter streaming API to access public tweets in real-time, only those published within the Mexican territory.

Labeling data. The next stage consists on manually tagging a set of tweets and only for this case we use two different polarity tags (be they violent or non-violent). It is important to note that for this data set, there is a class imbalance. That is, there is a majority class and a minority class, which could mean that this could affect the performance of the classifier model.

Text preprocessing. At this stage, to have only information that provides a better understanding and to eliminate little information relevant to the classification process, three different filters were applied.

In the first filter, identifiers such as hashtags, at and URLs were removed from each tweet. The stop words were removed in the second filter since we think these words do not show importance in the document (such as articles, conjunctions, prepositions). Finally, in the third filter, symbols and other words were removed (such as punctuation marks, emojis).

After applying these filters to the original database, it was divided into training and test sets manually to observe if there is any change by dividing it manually or using a function already predefined in ML libraries.

Text feature extraction. Text tokenization is applied, that is, the qualitative data (tweets) is transformed into quantitative data. This was performed using text vectorization, thus facilitating the text transformation to a number since the neural network only accepts numerical data. This process was carried out using the CountVectorizer method since this technique has shown better results in [14].

Classifier set-up. ML and DL libraries such as Tensorflow, Keras, and Scikit-Learn were used for the network model. In this work, a multilayer perceptron was used with 7 hidden layers of 20, 30, 30, 40, 40, 30, and 30 neurons, respectively. Where both, the number of layers and the number of neurons were determined by the trial-error method. For the output layer, only two neurons and the softmax function were employed. The model was trained using Adam, the learning rate $\eta = 0.0006$, and the stopping criterion was 50 epochs.

Classifier evaluation. Once the architecture and parameters of the classifier were established, the model was run 10 times with 2 different sampling methods to compare the effectiveness of the employed sampling methods. This process was carried out to know the model's effectiveness in classifying both classes using sample methods. Error rates and accuracy are commonly used to assess the performance of learning models. However, for class imbalance problems, both measures are biased for the majority class, so alternative performance metrics should be used. Following this premise, a viable option is the area under the curve ROC (AUC), that is defined as $AUC = (Sensitivity + Specificity)/2$, where the $Sensitivity = tp/(tp + fn)$ corresponds to the percentage of correctly classified positives and the $Specificity = tn/(tn + fp)$ represents the percentage of correctly classified negatives (see Table 1).

Table 1. Confusion matrix for binary classification

		Predicted class	
True class	Positive	True positive (tp)	False negative (fn)
	Negative	False positive (fp)	True negative (tn)

5 Experimental Results and Discussion

This work aimed to improve the classification of gender violence in Twitter messages generated in Mexico. Results were computed in terms of characteristics obtained by the extraction method and three performance measures. Table 2 summarizes the best results previously obtained in [14] and the results presented in this article by using CountVectorizer as extraction method (in [14], this method gave the best results compared to TfidVectorizer and HashingVectorizer) and two sampling methods (ROS and SMOTE).

As shown in Table 2, the number of features obtained is visibly different in contrast to [14], where the best results occur when the dataset presents a greater number of features. In addition, it is possible to note that when using sampling methods, the MLP shows effectiveness in identifying gender violence in tweets. Nevertheless, it is also possible to observe that the classifier's performance continues being affected by class imbalance, since the classification rate in the minority class increases, but in the majority class decreases.

Another relevant aspect to consider as an improvement in the results is that although SMOTE yields higher scores in the different executions for the violent class, its performance for the non-violent class has a somewhat notable decrease. This behavior was also observed with ROS; however, the change is not as noticeable as with SMOTE.

On the other hand, it was also observed that adding more hidden layers and neurons increases the performance of the classifier (the number of neurons and hidden layers for this work was done by trial and error). In this sense, the number of hidden neurons and layers is much higher than the used in [14], where 6 hidden layers were employed with 6, 6, 5, 5, 4, 3 hidden neurons, respectively.

Finally, results in this work surpass the best results in [14]; this can be attributed by the fact that the increase in samples in the violent class means an increase in the number of characteristics, thus adding more elements to the architecture (such as layers and hidden neurons).

Table 2. Comparison of results obtained in [14] and results of this work, using the MLP, the CountVectorizer and ROS and SMOTE as sampling methods. High scores are highlighted in bold, while best scores in [14] are highlighted in bold and italic.

Sampling method	Features	Specificity	Sensitivity	AUC	References
SMOTE	1016 [14]	*0.8659*	*0.7562*	*0.8111*	Best results in [14]
	27885	0.9288	0.8106	0.8697	
		0.9289	0.8188	0.8738	
		0.9306	0.8365	**0.8835**	
		0.8886	**0.8488**	0.8687	
		0.9242	0.8188	0.8715	
		0.8905	0.8229	0.8567	
		0.8915	0.8474	0.8694	
		0.9290	0.8174	0.8732	
		0.9283	0.8297	0.8790	
		0.9234	0.8093	0.8663	
ROS	1018 [14]	*0.8926*	*0.7241*	*0.8083*	Best results in [14]
	27832	**0.9801**	0.7779	0.8790	
		0.9645	0.8174	0.8910	
		0.9591	**0.8395**	**0.8993**	
		0.9731	0.7970	0.8851	
		0.9788	0.7738	0.8763	
		0.9604	0.8311	0.8958	
		0.9740	0.7834	0.8787	
		0.9724	0.8093	0.8909	
		0.9751	0.7916	0.8834	
		0.9664	0.8134	0.8899	

6   Conclusions and Future Work

In this work, an improvement of results from [14] is presented to detect gender violence in Mexican Twitter messages. An MLP was used as a classifier, while the CountVectorizer algorithm was used for feature extraction method, and sampling methods were applied to address the class imbalance. When obtained results were compared to the best results in [14], it was observed that although both works use sampling methods to address the class imbalance problem, this continues affecting the correct classification of the violent messages (for example, when there are more samples for the non-violent class than the violent class).

Because of the new changes performed to the previous work, favorable results could be seen. The best results for this case are given by the ROS sampling method, so it can be seen that some other improvements can still be made in the near future; for example: a study in the increment of the aggressiveness and discriminatory comments for the female gender since they are less frequent concerning non-violent tweets. Also, it is considered as an improvement the experimentation with a more sophisticated feature extraction methods such as word embedding and transformers to compare their influence with text and a DL-based computational model such as the MLP proposed in this paper.

Finally, another future work is using a continuous learning system; that is: it will continue to learn with new entries and at the same time classify the tweets.

References

1. Krantz, G., Garcia-Moreno, C.: Violence against women. J. Epidemiol. Commun. Health **59** (10), 818–821 (2005)
2. Reyes, V.E.H., Gutierrez, Y.A., Castro, V.H.H.: Las consecuencias de la violencia de género para la salud y formación superior de los adolescentes. Revista Médica Electrónica **38**, 697–710 (2016)
3. ONU: Declaration on the elimination of violence against women (1993). https://research.un.org/en/docs/ga/quick/regular/48
4. Bermúdez, G.M., Bonino, A.: Ni una más, ni una menos, manifestaciones de mujeres como fuente del derecho. Inventio: La génesis de la cultura universitaria en Morelos **13**(29) (2017)
5. Castillo, R.: Racialized geographies and the "war on drugs": gender violence, militarization, and criminalization of indigenous peoples. J. Latin Am. Caribbean Anthropol. **24** (2019)
6. Contreras, M.E.R., Alvarez, J.V.: Reconocimiento de agresión verbal en Twitter con el uso de patrones lingüísticos. Ph.D. thesis, Pontificia Universidad Católica de Valparaíso (2017)
7. Cruz, G.A.P., Vasquez, E.E.M.: Modelo de Detección de Violencia Contra la Mujer en Redes Sociales en español, utilizando Opinion Mining. Ph.D. thesis, Universidad Tecnológica de Perú (2020)
8. Arroba, R., Bravo, J.L.V., Enrique, A.: Aplicativo para detectar conductas violentas en Twitter, a través de análisis de sentimientos. Ph.D. thesis, Universidad Central de Ecuador (2020)
9. Montilla, A.M., et al.: Una modalidad actual de violencia de género en parejas jóvenes: Las redes sociales. Educación XX1 (2016)
10. Montaño, P.: #Violencias de género en twitter: análisis desde el trabajo social. Ph.D. thesis, Universidad Complutense de Madrid (2017)
11. Lewis, R., Rowe, M., Wiper, C.: Online abuse of feminists as an emerging form of violence against women and girls. Brit. J. Criminol. **57** (2016)
12. Whittle, H., Hamilton-Giachritsis, C., Collings, B.: A review of online grooming: characteristics and concerns. Aggression Violent Behav. **18**, 62–70 (2013)
13. Abaido, G.M.: Cyberbullying on social media platforms among university students in the united Arab Emirates. Int. J. Adolesc. Youth **25**(1), 407–420 (2020)
14. Castorena, C.M., et al.: Deep neural network for gender-based violence detection on Twitter messages. Mathematics **9**(8) (2021)
15. Schuler, D.: Social computing. Commun. ACM **37**(1), 28–29 (1994)
16. Prashant, K., Asif, E., Dipankar, D.: Investigating deep learning approaches for hate speech detection in social media (2020)

17. García-Díaz, J.A., et al.: Detecting misogyny in Spanish tweets. An approach based on linguistics features and word embeddings. Future Gener. Comput. Syst. **114**, 506–518 (2021)
18. García-Falcón, E.: Detección de lenguaje ofensivo en Twitter basada en expansión automática de lexicones. Master's thesis, Instituto Nacional de Astrofísica, Óptica y Electrónica (2018)
19. Gutiérrez-Esparza, G.O., Vallejo-Allende, M., Hernández-Torruco, J.: Classification of cyber-aggression cases applying machine learning. Appl. Sci. **9**(9) (2019)
20. Frenda, S., Banerjee, S.: Deep analysis in aggressive Mexican tweets, July 2018
21. Frenda, S., Banerjee, S., Rosso, P., Patti, V.: Do linguistic features help deep learning? the case of aggressiveness in Mexican tweets. Computación y Sistemas **24** (2020)
22. Aragon, M., López-Monroy, A.: Author profiling and aggressiveness detection in Spanish tweets: Mex-a3t 2018, August 2018
23. Ramadhani, A.M., Goo, H.S.: Twitter sentiment analysis using deep learning methods. In: 2017 7th International Annual Engineering Seminar (InAES), pp. 1–4 (2017)
24. Watanabe, H., Bouazizi, M., Ohtsuki, T.: Hate speech on Twitter: a pragmatic approach to collect hateful and offensive expressions and perform hate speech detection. IEEE Access **6**, 13825–13835 (2018)
25. Plaza-Del-Arco, F.-M., Molina-González, M.D., López, L.A.U., Martín-Valdivia, M.T.: Detecting misogyny and xenophobia in Spanish tweets using language technologies, **20**(2) (2020)
26. Mubarak, H., Rashed, A., Darwish, K., Samih, Y., Abdelali, A.: Arabic offensive language on Twitter: analysis and experiments (2021)
27. Haykin, S.: Neural Networks: A Comprehensive Foundation, 2nd edn. Prentice Hall, Upper Saddle River (1999)
28. Bengio, Y., Goodfellow, I., Courville, A.: Deep Learning. MIT Press, Cambridge (2016)
29. Zhang, J., Cui, L., Gouza, F.B.: GADAM: genetic-evolutionary ADAM for deep neural network optimization. CoRR, abs/1805.07500 (2018)
30. Le, Q.V., Ngiam, J., Coates, A., Lahiri, A., Prochnow, B., Ng, A.Y.: On optimization methods for deep learning. In: Proceedings of the 28th International Conference on International Conference on Machine Learning, pp. 265–272. Omnipress, Madison (2011)
31. Ruder, S.: An overview of gradient descent optimization algorithms. CoRR, abs/1609.04747 (2016)
32. Kingma, D., Ba, J.: Adam: a method for stochastic optimization. In: International Conference on Learning Representations, vol. 12 (2014)
33. Waykole, R.N., Thakare, A.D.: A review of feature extraction methods for text classification. Int. J. Adv. Eng. Res. Dev. **5** (2018)
34. Sarlis, S., Maglogiannis, I.: On the reusability of sentiment analysis datasets in applications with dissimilar contexts. In: Maglogiannis, I., Iliadis, L., Pimenidis, E. (eds.) AIAI 2020. IAICT, vol. 583, pp. 409–418. Springer, Cham (2020). https://doi.org/10.1007/978-3-030-49161-1_34
35. Abdi, L., Hashemi, S.: To combat multi-class imbalanced problems by means of over-sampling techniques. IEEE Trans. Knowl. Data Eng. **28**(1), 238–251 (2016)
36. Arellano, H.S.: Minería de datos aplicada a clases minoritarias. Master's thesis, Universidad Autónoma Metropolitana (2006)
37. Chawla, N., Bowyer, K., Hall, L., Kegelmeyer, W.: Smote: synthetic minority over-sampling technique. J. Artif. Intell. Res. **16**, 321–357 (2002)

Consumer Price Index Forecasting Based on Univariate Time Series and a Deep Neural Network

Reynaldo Rosado⬭, Aldis Joan Abreu⬭, José C. Arencibia⬭,
Hector Gonzalez$^{(\boxtimes)}$⬭, and Yanio Hernandez⬭

Universidad de las Ciencias Informaticas (UCI), La Habana, Cuba
{rrosado,ajabreu,jcarencibia,hglez,yhernandezh}@uci.cu

Abstract. The global Consumer Price Index (CPI) is a monthly record, which allows measuring the variation of the final consumer prices of a given set of goods and services of households living in a given geographic region, city or country. The present work addresses the problem of CPI forecasting using different Long Short-Term Memory (LSTM) neural network architectures according to state of the art in time series forecasting. Univariate time series data are mapped by a multivariate spatiotemporal representation using a set of Box-Jenkins functions and a time window. Next, a Convolutional Neural Network (CNN) with a specific droop out function combines the feature set to make a more discriminative representation space of the multivariate data. Finally, a LSTM exploits the temporality relationship among the data. The pipeline results, by combining a CNN with a LSTM, showed an improvement in forecasting CPI time series over Ecuador available dataset with respect to other LSTM-based architectures and models.

Keywords: Consumer Price Index · Time series forecasting · Long Short-Term Memory

1 Introduction

The Consumer Price Index (CPI) reflects the variation in the prices of household products and services in a given period of time. It constitutes one of the most important economic indicators for any country. Through it, the inflationary processes of economies can be measured. The CPI is systematically way taken as a reference for decision-making regarding monetary policies by governments and financial entities. It is also used for various aspects of social finance, such as retirement, unemployment and government financing [18].

Both the prices of the products and services that give origin to the CPI estimate, as well as the CPI itself, are calculated systematically, so they are time

This work has been partially funded by FONCI through project: Plataforma para el análisis de grandes volúmenes de datos y su aplicación a sectores estratégicos.

© Springer Nature Switzerland AG 2021
Y. Hernández Heredia et al. (Eds.): IWAIPR 2021, LNCS 13055, pp. 33–42, 2021.
https://doi.org/10.1007/978-3-030-89691-1_4

series data type. As CPI forecast helps to estimate future trends, it is key for decision making. Moreover, it allows the application of price stabilization policies to reduce the economic impact on the prices of products and services demanded by consumers. In those economies that present instability, CPI data fluctuate over time, which translates into a non-linear and non-stationary behavior [13].

Traditionally, time series forecasting is performed using well-established statistical tools such as the Box-Jenkins Auto-Regressive models or the Holt-Winters approach to exponential smoothing [4,8]. Since the computational point of view, the problem of measuring, estimating or forecasting CPI, not the CPI problem inself, has been approached as a univariate time series for the study of the global metric, or as a multivariate problem when the study is extended to the set of products or services that are included in the basic family basket. The most popular statistical method used for CPI forecasting, as a univariate time series problem, has been the autoregressive family of algorithms known as ARIMA [1,2]. Recently, there are several approaches that introduce modern techniques with better accuracy results, however, it is still a tendency to compare the results with ARIMA [12]. The use of machine learning techniques for CPI forecasting has emerged in recent references. Artificial Neural Networks (ANN) [6] and Support Vector Machines (SVM) [15] stand out as learning techniques in the CPI forecast.

The introduction of Deep Neural Networks in the time series forecasting has been widely studied in recent years with results that establish the state of the art in several problems. Particularly the use of ANN architectures with the presence of recurrent mechanisms such as RNN or LSTM shows the best results [9,10,16]. These neural network models have the capability of capturing the temporal dependence in the data, and, at the same time, they are flexible to the forecast of more than one output variable, which corresponds to the multivariate problem. According to the study consulted, this models are more widely used to study the CPI forecast as a univariate problem, as compared to deep networks and recurrent models. Two examples to use a simple LSTM model, are the comparative empirical study of Ecuador with temporal data between 2005–2020 CPI [14] and Indonesia CPI where several optimization approach with LSTM are compared [18].

In the empirical CPI studies of Indonesia and Ecuador mentioned above, the models used are based on classical regression approaches in which the parameters are not tuned, so that possible improvements in accuracy should be expected. Likewise, there are limitations in the representation of the set of attributes, so that the possible temporal non-linearity inherent in the data is not handled, or the attributes are not transformed into spaces with greater discriminative power. Finally, the regularization approach is not clear in either paper. Especially in the LSTM approach, the authors do not combine several interesting architectures such as stacked LSTMs, a CNN combined with LSTMs or, bidirectional LSTMs among other approaches.

The aim of this paper is to develop an empirical evaluation of different models and architectures of LSTM-based deep neural networks, that allow solving the CPI forecasting problem with higher accuracy on the available data set from

Ecuador. In our proposal, the set of attributes must be represented with an adequate treatment of the non-linearity in the time series relationship. On the other hand, the model should consider a droop out schemes that ensure generalization in the learning process and select the most relevant features.

2 General Notation and State of the Art

A univariate time series is defined as a collection of values of a given variable, ordered chronologically and sampled at constant time intervals. Whenever a variable is spatially related and individually shows a temporal relationship, we say that the problem is a multivariate time series. Classical statistical or machine learning models need to consider the univariate or multivariate problem differently, however deep learning models can handle both indistinctly with high accuracy. Time series are usually characterized by three components: trend, seasonality and residuals [16]. In real-world time series and, in particular the CPI problem, seasonality can be affected by external agents such as the economic and financial crisis, prices of the main products in the world market, and emerging situations such as the COVID-19 pandemic.

Let $X = \{x_1, \ldots, x_T\} \in \mathbb{R}$, be a chronological ordered value. For a temporal window of size h, which considers a low seasonality of the problem, each training instance is written as $(\boldsymbol{x}_j, \boldsymbol{y}_j) \in \mathbb{R}^p \times \mathbb{R}^q$, where the input variables are $\boldsymbol{x}_j = \{x_{j-1}, x_{j-2}, \ldots, x_{j-h}, g(x_{j-1}, \ldots, x_{j-h})\}$, with $\boldsymbol{g} = \{g_1, \ldots, g_r\}$ a family of the Box-Jenkins non-linear functions [1], and the outputs variables $\boldsymbol{y}_j = \{x_j, x_{j+1}, \ldots, x_{j+q}\}$. Finally, the corresponding time series forecasting problem consists of the estimating a predictor $F : \mathbb{R}^p \to \mathbb{R}^q$ in such a way that the expected deviation between true and predicted outputs is minimized for all possible inputs.

2.1 LSTM in Time Series Forecasting

In a recent review article [10], long-term time series forecasting based on LSTM models is discussed in more detail. The main contribution of this model to recurrent architectures such as RNNs [11,17] is in the solution of the optimization problem, where classical activation functions tend to gradient vanishing in interactive propagation to capture long-term dependence. The Gated Recurrent Unit (GRU) [3] is the newest generation of RNNs and is quite similar to an LSTM. The main difference between a GRU and an LSTM is that a GRU has gate, an update, and reset gate; while an LSTM has three gates: an input, a forget, and an output gate, which allow for changes in the state vector of a cell while capturing the long-term temporal relationship. When the time series is small, GRU is suggested; on the other hand, if the series is large, it must be LSTM. GRU checks in each iteration and can be updated with short-term information, however LSTM limits the change gradient in each iteration and in this way does not allow the past information to be completely discarded, this is why LSTM is mostly used for the long-term dependency modeling. In [10] he states that there are no significant advantages with respect to the computation time of GRU over

LSTM, although it has a smaller number of parameters in the cells. An additional advantage of the use of LSTM cells is in the incorporation of filters in the input that allows removing unnecessary information. For this reason, the present work proposes the use of cellular architectures based on LSTM.

2.2 Conventional LSTM Architectures

The most simple LSTM model is Vanilla, that has a single hidden layer of units of this type and an output layer used to make a prediction. One of its advantages is its application in time series, given by the fact that its sequence prediction is a function of the previous steps. The use of a simple architecture with an input layer, a hidden cell, and an output layer is effective for prediction problems with short sequences.

Bidirectional LSTM

There are problems in the field of Natural Language Processing (NLP) where, in order to predict a value of a sequence of data at a given time instant, information is needed from the sequence both before and after that instant. Bidirectional Recurrent Neural Networks (BRNN) address this point to solve this type of problem. Their main limitation with BRNNs is that the entire data set is needed beforehand to make the prediction, unlike standard networks that compute the activation values of the hidden units using a one-way feedforward procedure. In a BRNN, information from the past, present and future is used as input for prediction by means of a forward and backward process. Figure 1a show an example of this architecture.

Stacked LSTM

This extension has LSTM layers where each layer contains multiple memory cells. Stack-type architecture is composed of several hidden layers of LSTM memory blocks, and, in some cases MLP layers. For this type of deep architecture good results are recognized for solving problems of high level of complexity. In this type of network, each layer gradually solves a part of the prediction and then passes it to the next layer, until the output information is obtained. A simple example of this architecture is shown in Fig. 1b.

CNN LSTM

Convolutional Neural Networks (CNNs) are one of the most common architectures used in image processing and computer vision. At the same time, convolutional LSTM networks are also suitable for modeling multiple quantities, e.g., spatially and temporally distributed relationships, due to their characteristic properties.

CNNs have three types of layers: convolutional, clustering, and fully connected. The core work of the convolution layers is the learning of features from the input data. For this purpose, filters of a predefined size are applied to the data using the convolution maneuver between matrices. Convolution is the addition of all the products of the features.

Pooling reduces the size of the input, which speeds up the computation and avoids overfitting. The most popular pooling methods are average pooling and maximum pooling, which summarize the values using the average or maximum value, respectively. Once the features have been extracted by the convolutional layers, the prediction is carried out using fully connected layers. The input data for the latter fully connected layers are the attenuated features resulting from the convolutional layers and the dense layers. See example in Fig. 1c.

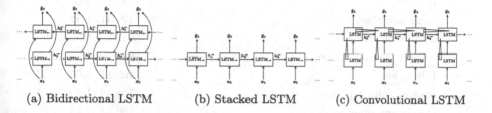

(a) Bidirectional LSTM   (b) Stacked LSTM   (c) Convolutional LSTM

Fig. 1. Architectures of the LSTMs consider in our proposal.

3 Results and Discussion

Results of time series forecasting of the Ecuador CPI and main goods and services are compared in terms of graphs and different classification metrics. Forecasted general CPI and the most ten relevant products are graphically compared in the next sections. Comparison is driven with respect to Stacked, Bi-directional and two Convolutional LSTMs. Additionally, the experimental setup is described, and the main results of the LSTMs models discussed. In the first place, we present technical details related to the datasets, parameter setup and implementations. Finally, a detailed comparison between the LSTMs approach and the machine learning algorithms proposal [14]. Also, the empirical evaluation of the forecasted LSTMs models over the ten critical goods and services gives a fine multivariate solution to CPI problem.

Datasets

The dataset used for the experiments are taken from the Ecuador CPI in the official governmental website https://www.ecuadorencifras.gob.ec. Our study is limited to using LSTMs architectures in univariate ahead forecasting considering only single seasonality, to be able to straightforwardly compare against automatic standard benchmark methods over mentioned datasets as an update[14]. In Table 1, the basic statistics information of general CPI and the ten goods and services considered in the experimentation are shown. The time interval considered for the general CPI is from January 2005 to March 2021, and for goods and services from January 2015 to March 2021. A more detailed characterization of the dataset related to trend, seasonality, and residuals measures [14].

Table 1. Basic information of datasets

Datasets	Mean	Std
General	91,59	13,42
Food and non-alcoholic drinks	105,95	1,51
Alcoholic drinks, tobacco and drugs	125,65	8,33
Clothing and shoes	88,89	5,64
Accommodation, water, electricity, gas and other fuels	113,20	3,21
Furniture and household items	102,64	1,71
Health	108,84	3,98
Transportation	106,31	1,52
Communications	94,95	0,95
Recreation and culture	98,48	1,77
Education	109,11	4,65
Restaurants and hotels	108,18	1,40
Goods and other services	106,34	1,44

Implementation Details

For the experiment, we design two strategies to split the data consequently with the range of dataset employed [14]. In the first one, the predictive model was trained with all CPI data except for the last 12 months, selecting data in the range since January 2005 to June 2019 for model training, and data from July 2019 to June 2020 as the test dataset. The goal of this approach was to compare our results to the machine learning algorithms used in the previous work. Secondly, all data was employed to compare the performance of the LSTMs approaches. The experiment was implemented and run in Python using available libraries to work with deep neural network.

The optimization of the models will determine their quality, and it must be performed based on the adjustment of its hyper-parameters, obtaining the best fit of the model that provides the most accurate results. In deep learning, there are two types of hyper-parameters: model parameters and optimization parameters. Model parameters must be adjusted in the model definition to obtain optimal performance. Optimization parameters are adjusted during the training phase of the model by using the dataset. The number of hyper-parameters used in a predictive model depends on the architecture and layers used in the implementation of each algorithm. One of the most common hyper-parameters used on LSTM algorithms is the number of nodes or neurons that LSTM layer has, therefore we choose this parameter for searching its best fit in order to obtain the best model optimization. For searching the best hyper-parameter optimization, we used a two-level heuristic search. In the first level of search, values between 100 and 1000 nodes were used, with an increase of 100 nodes per iteration, obtaining the range of nodes with the lowest RMSE as the first level search results. For the second search level, values in the best range obtained in the previous level were chosen, with an increment of 10 per iteration, finally obtaining the number of nodes with the lowest RMSE and best precision as the result of the complete search.

Performance Measures

As in other similar works, we use two common metrics, the Root Mean Squared Error (RMSE) and Mean absolute Percentage Error(MAPE). Given a test set, D_{test}, and a predictor, h, this measures are given as

$$RMSE(h; D_{test}) = \sqrt{\frac{\sum_{(x,y) \in D_{test}} (h(x) - y)^2}{N}} \tag{1}$$

$$MAPE(h; D_{test}) = \frac{1}{N} \sum_{(x,y) \in D_{test}} \frac{|(h(x) - y)|}{|y|} \tag{2}$$

In the second experiment, we use the Friedman test procedure with the corresponding post-hoc to compare algorithms over multiple datasets as recommended by Demsar's method [5] and its extensions [7].

Benchmarks

In Table 2, we indicate the results of comparing the predictions in the July 2019 to June 2020 range to previous experimentation. The best performance with the MAPE metric is found in the Bidirectional LSTM (marked in boldface), and the poorest LSTMs results is better than the best of the previous research. These results suggest that the use of an LSTM approach to the general CPI problem in Ecuador is an accurate one and improves the results obtained in previous research.

Table 2. Mean MAPE results and last year estimation for each LSTMs and benchmark models.

Month	Test	SVR Poly	SVR RBF	LSTM	SARIMA (MAPE)	Exp. Smt	Prophet	LSTM Vanilla	LSTM Stacked	LSTM Bid	LSTM CNN	LSTM Conv
2019-07	105,54	105,35	105,26	105,51	105,92	105,37	105,98	105,52	105,54	105,48	105,51	105,63
2019-08	105,43	105,36	105,20	105,57	105,98	105,40	105,89	105,52	105,54	105,48	105,51	105,63
2019-09	105,42	105,36	105,13	105,61	106,00	105,59	105,99	105,51	105,54	105,48	105,51	105,63
2019-10	105,97	105,36	105,06	105,61	106,09	105,55	105,91	105,63	105,66	105,60	105,63	105,74
2019-11	105,22	105,36	104,99	105,61	106,24	105,47	105,89	105,63	105,66	105,60	105,63	105,75
2019-12	105,21	105,35	104,91	105,64	106,39	105,61	105,89	105,34	105,37	105,31	105,33	105,49
2020-01	105,45	105,34	104,82	105,67	106,47	105,87	106,14	105,27	105,30	105,24	105,26	105,41
2020-02	105,29	105,34	104,73	105,64	106,51	105,89	106,30	105,41	105,43	105,37	105,40	105,52
2020-03	105,50	105,32	104,64	105,64	106,58	106,01	106,48	105,55	105,58	105,52	105,55	105,65
2020-04	106,56	105,31	104,55	105,67	106,71	106,28	106,71	106,00	106,04	105,99	106,01	106,06
2020-05	106,28	105,29	104,45	105,68	106,86	106,21	106,57	106,42	106,46	106,41	106,43	106,47
2020-06	105,62	105,27	104,35	105,69	106,95	106,01	106,41	106,14	106,16	106,10	106,13	106,25
MAPE		3,2E−03	7,4E−03	3,0E−03	7,3E−03	2,9E−03	5,4E−03	2,1E−03	2,2E−03	**2,0E−03**	2,1E−03	2,6E−03

In the LSTMs comparative models, we consider a Gaussian filter in the input layer for all models in order to capture the non linearity of the data. As shown in Table 3, the Gaussian filter in the input layer increase, the performance of the LSTMs models for the General CPI Ecuador dataset, and particularly for each good and service. Figure 2 shows the forecasting of General CPI and other three datasets over test set.

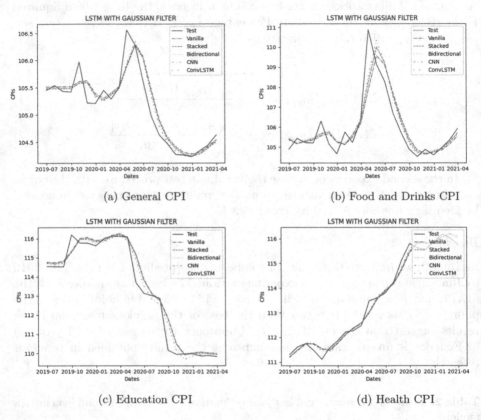

(a) General CPI

(b) Food and Drinks CPI

(c) Education CPI

(d) Health CPI

Fig. 2. Examples of the CPI forecasting of general dataset and three goods and services.

Besides, we compare the results of different algorithms, and, in general, the combination of CNN with LSTM takes advantage of the filter. We use the Friedman test to compare the relative performance of the different LSTMs architectures against each other across all the datasets in terms of RMSE error metric. The relative goodness of each of the five variants considered can be graphically observed in Fig. 3 that corresponds to the result of the Friedman test with Shaffer post-hoc. Even though we have significance differences in the combination of CNN-LSTM neural network respect to rest of LSTMs variants. These results can be seen as very encouraging specially taking into account that we consider in input layer a non-linear transformation with Gaussian filter.

Table 3. Mean RMSE results with Gaussian filters (right columns) and without Gaussian filters (left columns) in the LSTMs models.

Goods and Services	LSTM Vanilla	LSTM Stacked	LSTM Bid	LSTM CNN	LSTM Conv	LSTM Vanilla	LSTM Stacked	LSTM Bid	LSTM CNN	LSTM Conv
General	0,399	0,391	0,397	0,410	0,400	0,250	0,244	0,243	**0,223**	0,257
Food and non-alcoholic drinks	1,305	1,306	1,325	1,376	1,302	0,779	0,726	0,756	**0,708**	0,809
Alcoholic drinks, tobacco and drugs	0,524	0,561	0,568	0,524	0,544	0,415	0,360	0,393	**0,274**	0,481
Clothing and shoes	0,511	0,491	0,515	0,551	0,517	0,223	0,222	0,222	**0,221**	0,224
Accommodation, water, electricity, gas and other fuels	0,159	0,158	0,152	0,156	0,156	0,124	**0,076**	0,099	0,083	0,140
Furniture and household items	0,303	0,297	0,305	0,311	0,304	0,162	0,156	0,159	**0,155**	0,168
Health	0,360	0,357	0,362	0,366	0,363	0,220	0,216	0,216	**0,202**	0,228
Transportation	1,165	1,159	1,185	1,264	1,171	0,592	0,593	0,593	**0,566**	0,605
Communications	0,575	0,574	0,580	0,638	0,577	0,334	0,362	0,330	**0,297**	0,343
Recreation and culture	0,925	0,915	0,934	0,961	0,923	0,553	0,560	0,548	**0,521**	0,552
Education	0,928	0,912	0,909	0,931	0,928	0,561	0,567	0,553	**0,488**	0,573
Restaurants and hotels	1,093	1,091	1,104	1,227	1,080	0,601	0,592	0,592	**0,559**	0,601
Goods and other services	0,406	0,395	0,400	0,404	0,420	0,259	0,256	0,262	**0,236**	0,291

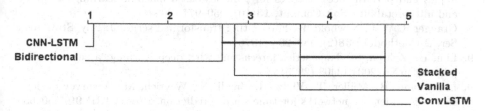

Fig. 3. Results of the Friedman test with Shaffer correction: $p = 1.33e - 7 < 0.05$

4 Concluding Remarks and Further Work

An attempt is made to improve CPI forecasting based on different LSTM architectures of Neural Networks. The application of a Gaussian filter in the input of these architectures has led to competitive results in the preliminary experimentation performed. The proposal was compared using a General CPI Database and specific goods and services of Ecuador, available in previous works. The results of the five LSTM architectures used improve the previous machine learning models, with respect to MAPE and RMSE metrics. The proposal was enriched with the application of a Gaussian filter in the input of all the implemented LSTM variants. The most efficient result is the combination of LSTM with CNN, with an RMSE of 0.243. Future work is being planned in several directions. On the one hand, work is being done to compare this experiment with CPI forecasts from other countries. On the other hand, different optimization schemes can be adopted to improve efficiency and performance. In addition, it is possible to build a multivariate model for CPI forecasting that has as input the prices of different products and services, and to do a simultaneous estimation of those prices.

References

1. Box, G.E.P., Jenkins, G.M.: Time Series Analysis: Forecasting and Control. Holden-Day, San Francisco (1976)
2. Brockwell, P.J., Davis, R.A.: Time Series: Theory and Methods (1987)
3. Chung, J., Gulcehre, C., Cho, K., Bengio, Y.: Empirical evaluation of gated recurrent neural networks on sequence modeling. In: NIPS 2014 Workshop on Deep Learning, December 2014 (2014)
4. Collins, S.: Prediction techniques for box-cox regression models. J. Bus. Econ. Stat. **9**(3), 267–277 (1991)
5. Demšar, J.: Statistical comparisons of classifiers over multiple data sets. J. Mach. Learn. Res. **7**, 1–30 (2006)
6. Fauzan, M., et al.: Epoch analysis and accuracy 3 ANN algorithm using consumer price index data in Indonesia. In: 3rd International Conference of Computer, Environment, Agriculture, Social Science, Health Science, Engineering and Technology, pp. 1–7 (2018)
7. García, S., Fernández, A., Luengo, J., Herrera, F.: A study of statistical techniques and performance measures for genetics-based machine learning: accuracy and interpretability. Soft Comput. **13**(10), 959–977 (2009)
8. Granger, C.W.J., Newbold, P.: Forecasting transformed series. J. Roy. Stat. Soc.: Ser. B (Methodol.) **38**(2), 189–203 (1976)
9. Lim, B., Zohren, S.: Time series forecasting with deep learning: a survey. arXiv preprint arXiv:2004.13408 (2020)
10. Lindemann, B., Müller, T., Vietz, H., Jazdi, N., Weyrich, M.: A survey on long short-term memory networks for time series prediction. Proc. CIRP **99**, 650–655 (2021)
11. Mikolov, T., Karafiát, M., Burget, L., Černockỳ, J., Khudanpur, S.: Recurrent neural network based language model. In: Eleventh Annual Conference of the International Speech Communication Association (2010)
12. Mohamed, J.: Time series modeling and forecasting of Somaliland consumer price index: a comparison of ARIMA and regression with ARIMA errors. Am. J. Theoret. Appl. Stat. **9**(4), 143–153 (2020)
13. Qin, X., Sun, M., Dong, X., Zhang, Y.: Forecasting of China consumer price index based on EEMD and SVR method. In: 2018 2nd International Conference on Data Science and Business Analytics (ICDSBA), pp. 329–333. IEEE (2018)
14. Riofrıo-Valarezo, J., Peluffo-Ordóñez, D.H., Chang, O.: Forecasting consumer price index (CPI) of Ecuador: a comparative study of predictive models. Int. J. Adv. Sci. Eng. Inf. Technol. **10**(3), 1078–1084 (2020)
15. Rohmah, M.F., Putra, I.K.G.D., Hartati, R.S., Ardiantoro, L.: Predicting consumer price index cities and districts in East Java with the Gaussian-radial basis function kernel. J. Phys.: Conf. Ser. **1456**, 012026 (2020)
16. Torres, J.F., Hadjout, D., Sebaa, A., Martinez-Alvarez, F., Troncoso, A.: Deep learning for time series forecasting: a survey. Big Data **9**(1), 3–21 (2021)
17. Williams, R.J., Zipser, D.: A learning algorithm for continually running fully recurrent neural networks. Neural Comput. **1**(2), 270–280 (1989)
18. Zahara, S., Ilmiddaviq, M.B., et al.: Consumer price index prediction using long short term memory (LSTM) based cloud computing. J. Phys.: Conf. Ser. **1456**, 012022 (2020)

Application of a Generalized Regression Neural Network to the Estimation of Average Gait Speed

Elías O. García Alvaredo[1](✉), Gianna Arencibia Castellanos[2],
Fidel E. Hernández Montero[1], and Tania Y. Aznielle Rodríguez[2]

[1] Technological University of Havana, Havana, Cuba
fhernandez@tele.cujae.edu.cu
[2] Cuban Center for Neuroscience, Havana, Cuba
{gianna.arencibia,tania}@cneuro.edu.cu

Abstract. This work addresses the estimation of the average gait speed through a Generalized Regression Neural Network. According to this goal, acceleration and angular velocity signals were gathered from an Inertial Measurement Unit placed in the lumbar region. In order to lead to a more adequate composition of the training and validation subsets, a novel approach, based on route optimization, in particular, the nearest neighbor algorithm, was implemented. Although only five features were extracted from IMU's signals, the results were very promising, since the achieved error and RMSE indexes were in the order of those obtained by the most accurate works.

Keywords: Gait speed · GRNN · IMU · Route optimization

1 Introduction

Human activity monitoring has been applied on medical and sport areas for the assessment of human functional condition, motor ability, frailty and cognitive disorders. In particular, the average gait speed, together with other gait parameters, can bring out important information on human activity condition [1].

In order to estimate spatial-temporal gait parameters, different measuring devices have been applied. For example, in [2], the use of an Inertial Measurement Unit (IMU) and Global Positioning System (GPS) were proposed for outdoor applications. Other technologies, such as Wi-Fi [3], RFID [4] and video-cameras [5], are more suitable to be applied on indoors environments.

Other works have been implemented in order to provide solutions using only IMUs. For example, in [6, 7] and [8], the inverted pendulum model was effectively applied with the aim of using few sensors and proving its performance in different environments. However, such proposals are based on theoretical assumptions that are not close to real living conditions. The Kalman filter [9], which leads to obtain a dynamic gait model, has been used in order to fuse the signals provided by inertial sensors. Nevertheless, in this work, the use of both biometric data that cannot be accurately obtained and the results of the integration of accelerometer signal that is affected by the gravity vector, are

Y. Hernández Heredia et al. (Eds.): IWAIPR 2021, LNCS 13055, pp. 43–51, 2021.
https://doi.org/10.1007/978-3-030-89691-1_5

disadvantages that must be taken into account whether this algorithm is applied. These algorithms must face difficulties inherent to the work with more than one IMU.

Several techniques have been implemented for addressing the use of only one single IMU. In [10], the Zero Velocity Update (ZUPT) algorithm was proposed in order to estimate the velocity drift and the fusion of accelerometer, gyroscope and magnetometer signals for orientation assessment. The combination of both estimations provides walking speed estimation. Since in this work, the direct relationship between IMU's acceleration and angular velocity signals is not ensured, and the adequate effectiveness of the fusion process cannot be guaranteed.

Other works address the application of machine learning techniques on walking speed estimation through one single IMU. In [1], the Markov chain was proposed for processing signals from an IMU attached at the foot. Although successful, this work required to work with a large number of features, very difficult to obtain in some cases. In [11], an algorithm based on Linear Regression was applied. In this case, demographic, biometric and spatial-temporal parameters were used in order to estimate walking speed through the use of an IMU placed at the lumbar region. In this paper, the implementation of acceleration integration discarding the gravity vector effect, as well as the application of acceleration and angular velocity signals fusion when the linear relationship between such signals cannot be assured, do not guarantee to achieve an effective result. In both [1] and [11], biometric parameters are required which leads to errors in the estimated variables.

In this work, the use of the IMU's original signals (to avoid both the negative effects of the integration procedure and the need of gravity vector estimation) and the application of a neural network structure (to deal with the difficult nature of the IMU's original signals) are proposed in order to estimate the average gait speed through one single IMU attached at the lumbar region. The artificial neural network applied in this work was the Generalized Regression Neural Network (GRNN). The use of GRNN is especially advantageous due to its ability to predict results with only a few available training samples, and the amount of additional knowledge needed to get the fit in a satisfying way is relatively small. The choice of this model avoids iterative training and provides a more natural sample collection process, which is suitable for this research. Five features closely linked to the gait speed and extracted from acceleration and angular velocity signals are used.

Since a random selection procedure is not capable to guarantee that the training/validation data is sufficiently diverse (then overfitting is avoided), in this work, an algorithm based on route optimization, the nearest neighbor algorithm, is proposed to be applied.

1.1 Inertial Measurement Unit (IMU)

The IMU is an electronic device composed mainly of accelerometers, gyroscopes and magnetometers. These sensors carry on different drawbacks that must be taken into account by the algorithms implementing signal processing techniques.

The gyroscope measurements are affected by four types of noise: the constant bias, the scale factor, white noise and the bias instability [12]; on the other hand, accelerometers provide a measure of the difference between the linear acceleration of the accelerometer block and the earth's gravitational field vector. Therefore, it is necessary to remove the gravitational component in the subsequent processing steps [13]. Magnetometer sensors measure the magnetic field components through the estimation of orientation with respect to the earth-magnetic field. Such sensors are very useful whenever they do not be exposed to external magnetic field or be close to metallic objects that change the earth-magnetic field [14].

2 Generalized Regression Neural Networks (GRNN)

Artificial Neural Networks (ANN) are inspired in the biologic neural networks. Several classification, clustering and pattern recognition problems can be solved by means of ANN. An example of ANN model is the Generalized Regression Neural Network (GRNN) model, proposed in [15], does not require any iterative training. The learning efficiency and algorithm convergence increase with the number of samples and the training is performed in one pass [15]. These characteristics represent the main advantages of this model.

The operation of the GRNN is based on the theory of nonlinear regression. The prediction of the output of GRNN can be expressed by:

$$\hat{Y}(X) = \frac{\sum_{i=1}^{n} Y_i \exp(-\frac{D_i^2}{2/\sigma^2})}{\sum_{i=1}^{n} \exp(-\frac{D_i^2}{2/\sigma^2})} \tag{1}$$

where $D_i^2 - (X - X_i)^T (X - X_i)$ is the Euclidian Distance between Xi and X, X is the input sample, Xi is the training sample, Yi is the output associated to Xi, $\exp(-\frac{D_i^2}{2/\sigma^2})$ is the activation function, σ is the smoothing factor of the gaussian function, and $\hat{Y}$ is the estimated output of the input X.

The GRNN topology consists of four layers. The first one represent the input vector (input layer). The second layer (pattern layer) has the radial basis function as transfer function [16]. The weights of the pattern layer take the values of the training data Xi. For a given X, the exponent based on the distance between X and each training input data Xi is computed and the product of the exponent value and the corresponding training output data Yi is also calculated. The third layer (summation layer) has two nodes: A and B. The node B computes the summation of each exponential value weighted by the known output Yi, while the A node simply computes the summation of the exponents of the distances. The output layer divides B by A to produce the predicted output. The output layer is a weighted average of the training values close to the input values.

The only adjustable parameter in a GRNN is the smoothing factor, σ, of the gaussian function. The value of σ determines the amplitude of the radial basis function (activation function), and therefore, the area with significant outputs around the input vector. The neural network tends to response with the target vector associated with the closest design input vector [17].

Several techniques can be implemented in order to prevent overfitting in the ANN training process. One of them is the k-folds cross-validation procedure, which is a data resampling method applied for assessing the generalization ability of the models.

2.1 Route Optimization Algorithm

The route optimization algorithms are focused to find an optimal route as a solution to the Traveling Salesman Problem (TSP) [18]. Given a set of nodes and the distances between them, they are intended to find the shortest path that passes through all nodes and returns to the initial node.

Among the heuristic algorithms [19], the nearest neighbor algorithm is classified as a route construction algorithm: initially, the route is not comprised by any node and the nodes are added in one at a time until a complete path is achieved. This is one of the simplest and most straightforward TSP heuristics, which usually leads to the optimal route while the execution time depends on the number of nodes to visit (the time complexity is $O(n^2)$, where n is the number of the nodes). The nearest neighbor algorithm starts at a previously selected starting node, from which the distances are calculated with respect to the other nodes. As result, the nearest node is selected and the previous node is checked as visited for the next iteration. Then, taking the last node selected as the "nearest neighbor" as a reference, the process is repeated with the remaining nodes until all nodes have been visited.

3   Materials and Methods

In order to estimate the average gait speed, in this work only one single IMU was placed in the lumbar region at L3 level. In particular, an IMU BitalinoRIoT [20] was used. This device is based on a 9 DoF LSM9DSO (STMicroelectronics) motion sensor, which includes a triaxial accelerometer (range $\pm$ 8 g, sensibility 0.244 mg/LSB), a triaxial gyroscope (range $\pm$ 2 gauss, sensibility 0.08 mgauss/LSB) and a magnetometer (range $\pm$ 2 gauss, sensibility 0.08 mgauss/LSB). The signals were sampled at 200 Hz. The IMU was fixed at the lumbar region by a velcro tape for achieving a more suitable fixation.

In addition, the BITalino (r)evolution Plugged platform [21] was also used in order to implement markers for the initial and final walking times. This allows for computing the true gait speed through the time calculated by means of the markers and the known distance to walk.

A database was built up order to test and validate the technique proposed in this paper. The database was comprised by the accelerometer and the gyroscope signals registered by the IMU. The measurements involved 23 subjects, including 12 men and 11 women, with age ranging from 20 to 50 years. None of them had any diagnosed disease.

Each subject was asked to walk along a 10 m straight line. Three types of walking were performed: fast, normal, and slow, then, 69 walks were available. Each subject interacted with a button in the Bitalino (r)evolution Plugged for indicating the initial and final walking times.

Five features were proposed to be extracted from the signals provided by the IMU: the vertical acceleration variance, the average of times between maximum peaks of vertical acceleration and the three axes angular velocity variances. The higher the gait speed, the shorter the time interval between maximum peaks of vertical acceleration; that is why the latter was one of the features proposed. Since this time interval is also related with the length of the subject legs, the vertical acceleration variance, other feature related with the physical activity involved in the gait process, was also proposed: the shorter the leg size, the lower the vertical acceleration variance. However, the projection of the gravity vector on this axis must be taken into account. Since the trunk could rotate during the gait, a further variation in vertical acceleration may occur that does not correspond to a movement related to the type of gait being executed. That is why, the three axes angular velocity variances are also proposed to work with; these features will represent the variations due to trunk rotations. The average of times between maximum peaks of vertical acceleration was also a chosen feature because it could provide additional information about the gait dynamics.

In order to estimate the average walking speed, a GRNN was used. The 69 realizations, each corresponding to the 5 computed features, were the inputs of the GRNN model.

The process of selecting the optimal configuration for the GRNN consisted of two parts. First, the value of σ, which leads the neural network to achieve a better generalization, was determined by applying the cross-validation approach (the database was divided into 3 subsets of 23 samples each) and evaluating 100 values of σ ranging from 0.0001 to 1. For each segmentation and each value of σ, the values of the metrics obtained were averaged. Once the value of σ was selected, the work addressed the selection of the best neural network configuration. To do that, two different approaches were carried out.

On one hand, the training and validation subsets, including 52 and 17 walking realizations, respectively, were randomly selected.

Nevertheless, this random selection procedure is not capable to guarantee that the training/validation data is sufficiently diverse, that is, that the composition of both subsets is satisfactorily balanced ("similar" data are uniformly distributed between the training and the validation subsets). In this study, a route optimization algorithm was implemented in order to work with more balanced training and validation subsets. By means of this algorithm, the full set of data is arranged in such a way that the "distance" between consecutives realizations of features is among the shortest possible, that is, they are the most similar as possible. Then, on the basis of the resulting data order, the data is orderly distributed between the training and the validation subset through a given distribution form, for example, 1/1 (one data is included in the training subset, one data is included in the validation subset, and so on), 2/1 (two data are included in the training subset, one data is included in the validation subset, and so on), 3/2 (three data are included in the training subset, two data are included in the validation subset, and so on), etc. In particular, the method implemented in order to reach a suitable rearrange of the full dataset was based on the nearest neighbor algorithm. The input nodes of the algorithm were the feature realizations (5-dimension vectors given by the 69 realizations). The distance between nodes was the Euclidean distance in a 5-dimensional space. Since this algorithm will deliver as many routes as the number of nodes, 69 routes will be generated. Thus, it will be necessary to determine which route leads the neural network to achieve a better performance. In order to train and validate the neural network, a training/validation set was constructed for each route by following the route order and applying a 4/1 distribution form.

In both approaches, the metrics that were used in order to evaluate the performance of the neural network were:

$$\text{Absolute error}: \quad \Delta x = |x_i - x| \tag{2}$$

$$\text{Relative error}: \quad \delta_x = \frac{\Delta x}{x} \tag{3}$$

$$\text{RMSE}: \quad rmse = \sqrt[2]{\frac{1}{n} \sum_{i=1}^{n} \Delta x} \tag{4}$$

where x_i is the estimated velocity, x is the actual velocity, and n is the size of the validation subset.

4   Results and Discussion

The first procedure implemented was the identification of the value of σ that leads to a better neural network performance. As aforementioned, this task was performed through a cross-validation process, which determined that the best neural network performance is obtained for $\sigma = 0.0101$. Figure 1 shows the behavior of the achieved metrics as σ varies. This figure reveals that a minimum of these three curves is reached for $\sigma = 0.0101$. At that point, the values of the metrics are: RMSE = 0.1217, AbsoluteError = 0.0934 and RelativeError = 8.28%.

Then, the neural network training/validation process through two different approaches of selection of the training and the validation subsets was implemented. In case of the application of the route optimization algorithm, specifically, the nearest neighbor method, the route was selected according to the metrics values. Figure 2 shows the different average gait speed estimations computed from the validation subset

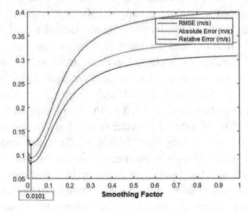

Fig. 1. Behavior of the scale factor (σ) with respect to the metrics.

of features. Figure 2a and 2b show the results obtained when the training/validation set was randomly selected and when this set was selected through the route optimization algorithm.

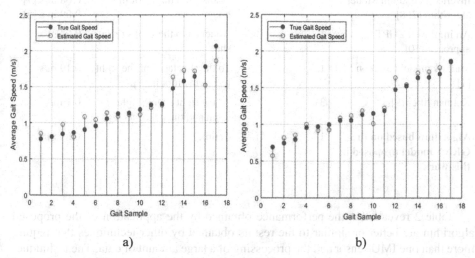

a)   b)

Fig. 2. Average gait speed estimation for a) the GRNN trained through a random selection of the training/validation set, and b) the GRNN trained through a route optimization algorithm for the training/validation set selection. (Color figure online)

In Fig. 2, the blue lines represent the true average gait speed, and the red lines, the average gait speed estimated by the neural network. This figure reveals that in general the values estimated by the model that applies route optimization for the training/validation set selection are closer to the true values than the values estimated by the neural network that applies a random training/validation set selection. Table 1 presents a comparison of the quantitative results obtained from the application of the two approaches of training/validation set selection.

The best results obtained from the application of the GRNN model were compared with results achieved by other research works, such as [1, 7–10]. Table 2 presents this comparison.

Table 1. Comparison of the performance achieved by the neural network according to the two approaches applied for the training/validation set selection.

Set selection algorithm	Absolute error (m/s)	Relative error (%)	RMSE (m/s)
Random selection	0.0963	7.82	0.1192
Route optimization	0.0675	6.23	0.0781

Table 2. Effectiveness of algorithms used to estimate walking speed.

Techniques	Number of IMU	Sensor placement	RMSE
Inverted Pendulum Model algorithm [7, 8]	2	Shanks and thighs of the body	0.08 m/s [7] 0.09 m/s [8]
An improved ZUPT approach [10]	1	Attached to the subject's shoe	0.04 m/s
Markov model based on SDI [1],	1	To the shoelaces of the right feet at the foot instep	0.19 m/s
Kalman filter [9]	3	At the right shank, right thigh and the pelvis	0.1 m/s
Algorithm based on the GRNN model proposed in this work	**1**	**Trunk**	**0.08 m/s**

Table 2 reveals that the performance obtained by the application of the proposed algorithm are better or similar to the results obtained by other techniques that require more than one IMU sensor and the processing of a large amount of data. The technique-proposed in this paper was worse than just one technique. But it should be noticed that, in contrast to the proposed algorithm, the latter requires to implement the complicated and unaccurate gravity vector estimation process.

5 Conclusions

In this work, the application of a GRNN model was proposed in order to estimate the average walking speed. The data acquisition and processing were performed by using a single IMU, placed in the lumbar region at the L3 level.

The GRNN model input was comprised by 5 features closely linked to gait speed: the vertical acceleration variance, the average of times between maximum peaks of vertical acceleration and the three axes angular velocity variances. The proposed approach is significantly effective compared to those found in previous studies, taking into account that neither the estimation of the gravity vector nor the use of patient biometric data was required, and such factors could lead to significant measurement inaccuracies.

In this work, a route optimization algorithm was implemented in order to deal with more balanced training and validation subsets. This procedure led to a better general-ization capability of the neural network and, therefore, to a better performance of the neural network.

Acknowledgments. This research was supported by OGFPI, reference PN305LH13-050.

References

1. Mannini, A., María Sabatini, A.: Walking speed estimation using foot-mounted inertial sensors: comparing machine learning and strap-down integration method. Med. Eng. Phys. **36**, 1312–1321 (2014)
2. Terrier, P., Schutz, Y.: How useful is satellite positioning system (GPS) to track gait parameters? A review. J. NeuroEng. Rehabil. 11 (2005)
3. Liu, A.X., Wang, W., Shahzad, M.: Gait Recognition Using WiFi Signals, vol. 16, Heidelberg, Germany (2016)
4. Hsu, C.-C., Chen, J.-H.: A novel sensor-assisted RFID-based indoor tracking system for the elderly living alone. Sensors **11**, 10094–10113 (2011)
5. Stankovic, V., Yanh, C., Stankovic, L., Kerr, A.: Gait analysis using a single depth camera (2015)
6. Allseits, E., Agrawai, V., Lucarevic, J., Gailey, R., Gaunaurd, I., Bennett, C.: A practical step length algorithm using lower limb angular velocities. J. Biomech. **17**, 137–144 (2017)
7. Chen, S., Cunningham, C.L., Lach, J., Bennett, B.C.: Extracting spatio-temporal information from inertial body sensor networks for gait speed estimation. In: 2011 International Conference on Body Sensor Networks (2011)
8. Li, Q., Young, M., Naing, V., Donelan, J.: Walking speed estimation using a shank-mounted inertial measurement unit. J. Biomech. **43**, 1640–1643 (2010)
9. Qilong, Y., Chen, I.-M.: Localization and velocity tracking of human via 3 IMU sensors. Sens. Actuators A **212**, 25–33 (2014)
10. Byun, S., Lee, H., Han, J., Kim, J., Choi, E., Kim, K.: Walking-speed estimation using a single inertial measurement unit for the older adult. PLoS ONE **14**, 16 (2019)
11. Brzostowski, K.: Novel approach to human walking speed enhancement based on drift estimation. Biomed. Sig. Process. Control **42**, 18–29 (2018)
12. Pasciuto, I., Bergamini, E., Vannozzi, G., Maria Sabatini, A., Cappozzo, A.: How angular velocity features and different gyroscope noise types interact and determine orientation estimation accuracy. Sensors **15**, 23983–24001 (2015)
13. Pedley, M.: Tilt sensing using a three-axis accelerometer. Freescale Semiconductor, vol. AN3461 (2013)
14. Edelstein, S., Lenz, J.: Magnetic sensors and their applications. IEEE Sens. J. **6**, 631–649 (2006)
15. Specht, D.F.: A general regression neural network. IEEE Trans. Neural Netw. **2**, 568–576 (1991)
16. Rojas, I., et al.: Analysis of the functional block involved in the design of radial basis function networks. Neural Process. Lett. **12**, 1–17 (2000)
17. MATLAB: Generalized Regression Neural Networks. Documentation (2017)
18. Rego, C., Gamboa, D., Glover, F., Osterman, C.: Traveling salesman problem heuristics: leading methods, implementations and latest advances. Eur. J. Oper. Res. **3**, 427–441 (2013)
19. Karkory, F.A., Abudalmola, A.A.: Implementation of heuristics for solving travelling salesman problem using nearest neighbour and minimum spanning tree algorithms. Int. J. Comput. Inf. Eng. **7**(10) (2013)
20. Flety, E.: A comprehensive guide to using, programming & flashing the BITtalino R-IoT WiFi sensor module. In: Prototypes & Engineering Team (PIP) - IRCAM, vol. 1.0 (2017)
21. da Silva, H.P., Guerreiro, J., Lourenco, A., Fred, A., Martins, R.: BITalino: a novel hardware framework for physiological computing. In: PhyCS 2014 - Proceedings of the International Conference on Physiological Computing Systems (2014)

Gait Speed Estimation Based on Artificial Neural Network: Comparison with the Application of the Inverted Pendulum Model

Gianna Arencibia Castellanos[1]([⊠]), Fidel E. Hernández Montero[2],
and Tania Y. Aznielle Rodríguez[1]

[1] Cuban Center for Neuroscience, Havana, Cuba
{gianna.arencibia,tania}@cneuro.edu.cu
[2] Technological University of Havana, Havana, Cuba
fhernandez@tele.cujae.edu.cu

Abstract. One of the most analyzed physical activities is the human gait. Among the different gait parameters, the gait speed is widely used in order to quantify improvements and specific functional impairments. Inertial Measurement Unit (IMU) sensors have been used for estimating the gait speed by means of different approaches ranging from physical gait models to machine learning/deep learning algorithms. In this paper, an algorithm based on artificial neural network (ANN) is proposed to be applied on the estimation of the gait speed. The features used by the network were extracted from acceleration and angular velocity signals supplied by a single IMU placed at the lumbar region. The results achieved by this application of a machine learning technique were compared with those obtained by the application of the inverted pendulum model. It proved that the proposed algorithm achieved better results. In order to train the ANN and to measure the performance achieved by both methods, a database, comprised by IMU signals recorded during the walking performed by young and elderly subjects, was built up. The ANN model proved the feasibility of its application on elderly subjects. Hence, it can be applied for monitoring frailty and screening cognitive diseases in older adults.

Keywords: Inertial measurement unit · Inverted pendulum model · Artificial neural network · Gait speed estimation

1 Introduction

Human activity monitoring is applied on different medical areas for the assessment of cognitive disorders [1], motor ability [2], human functional condition [3] and frailty [4]. One of the most analyzed physical activities is the human gait, which has been monitored by means of the application of different technical solutions, such as: the use of GPS (Global Positioning System) for outdoor applications [5], and video-cameras [6], WiFi [7] and RFID [8] for indoors environments.

© Springer Nature Switzerland AG 2021
Y. Hernández Heredia et al. (Eds.): IWAIPR 2021, LNCS 13055, pp. 52–59, 2021.
https://doi.org/10.1007/978-3-030-89691-1_6

Among the different gait parameters that can be processed, the walking speed or gait speed can be associated with specific functional impairments and it is widely used in order to quantify improvements that occur after therapeutic and rehabilitative treatment [9]. Moreover, the walking speed provides personal activity and localization information for health care and pervasive computing applications [10]. Several works have addressed the gait speed estimation through less expensive procedures. It leads to the use of fewer sensors and the ability to be used in different environments. In this context, Inertial Measurement Unit (IMU) sensors have been used for estimating spatiotemporal parameters, such as gait speed [11–13]. The data coming from IMU sensors have been analyzed by means of different approaches ranging from physical gait models to machine learning/deep learning algorithms in order to infer the relationship between the measurements and the gait speed.

2 Related Work

Among the proposals that are based on physical gait model are [11, 14, 15]; these techniques propose different locations for the sensor to be placed at the body: in [11] and [14], the sensor is attached at the lumbar region; in [15], the sensor is attached at the shank. In such works, the applied algorithms deal with different limitations, such as the use of a multiplicative factor that is distinctive to every subject, the need of integration of the vertical acceleration signal for estimating the vertical displacement, and the incapability of ensuring the fulfilment of the initial conditions needed for sensor fusion implementation. In [16], a comparison between algorithms that use physical gait models is presented. This research reveals that the variant of inverted pendulum model (IPM) proposed by Weinberg [11] is more effective than that proposed by Zijlstra et al. [14]. In [12], the application of the IPM through two sensors, each attached at each ankle, is proposed. The estimation of the gait speed was accomplished by a segmentation algorithm similar to zero-velocity update (ZUPT), which was an improvement of the gait parameter estimation when it is compared with previous algorithms. However, in this method the drift inherent to the gyroscope signals is still distorting the parameter estimation.

Currently, there is a predominant use of machine learning techniques for gait speed estimation through IMU-based prediction systems. In such applications, the sensors are attached at the wrist [17], the foot [13], into the pant pockets [18] or the lumbar region [19]. In [17], in order to improve the accuracy of the walking speed estimation for a wide range of speed values, a Support Vector Machine (SVM) based walking speed classifier is combined with a walking speed estimation model based on Gaussian process regression. In this application, the initial conditions required for data fusion are not guaranteed and the gyroscope drift is not removed either. In [13], the use of non-linear and sparse models for solving the drift estimation problem proved to be effective. In [18], the estimation of the gait speed is performed by means of the application of deep learning algorithms. Although this application reported results more satisfactory than those achieved in previous works, its implementation requires a high computational cost. An approach that addressed the use of demographic and anthropometric variables in regression models, combined with IMU measurements, was proposed in [19].

Although the implementation of these two groups of algorithms (model-based and machine learning techniques) exhibited effectiveness, their implementations deal with different limitations, for example, the need of many sensors, the use of demographic and anthropometric variables, the need of parameters that must be set empirically and may change from one subject to another. Besides, such implementations need the integration of some acceleration signal for displacement estimation, the reduction of the gyroscope drift, the fulfilment of the initial conditions required for sensor fusion implementation, and the high computational cost incurred by the implementations. Such limitations jeopardize the accurate and feasible estimation of the gait speed. On the other hand, it's not possible to find a comparison of the performance obtained by the application of two techniques belonging to different groups of algorithms, using data taken from the same dataset. This does not allow for the accurate determination of which technique could achieve a better performance.

In this work, an algorithm based on artificial neural network (ANN) is proposed to be applied on the estimation of the gait speed. The features used by the network were extracted from acceleration and angular velocity signals supplied by a single IMU placed at the lumbar region, that position is more comfortable than other locations; the upper body variables indicate gait disorder and impaired balance in older adults and patient with cognitive disease [20]. The results achieved by this application of a machine learning technique were compared with those obtained by the application of the inverted pendulum model proposed in [11], that is the most effective of those model-based techniques with the sensor attached at the lumbar region. In order to train the ANN and to measure the performance achieved by both methods, a database, comprised by IMU signals recorded during the walking performed by young and elderly subjects, was built up.

3 Methods and Materials

In order to estimate the average gait speed, in this work a single IMU was placed in the lumbar region, at L3 level. In particular, an IMU Bitalino RIoT [21] was used. The signals were sampled at 200 Hz. The IMU was fixed at the lumbar region by means of a velcro tape for achieving a more suitable fixation.

In addition, the BITalino (r)evolution Plugged platform [22] was also used in order to implement markers for the initial and final walking times. This allows to compute the true gait speed using the time calculated from the markers and the walking distance fixed for the experiments.

A database was built up in order to test and validate the technique proposed in this work. The database was comprised by accelerometer and gyroscope signals registered by means of the IMU. Measurements involving 23 healthy subjects, including women and men, with age ranging from 20 years to 50 years, were carried out. Each subject walked along a 10 m straight line. Three types of walking were performed: fast, normal, and slow, then, 69 walks were available.

Five features were proposed to be extracted from the signals provided by the IMU: the vertical acceleration variance, the average of times between maximum peaks of vertical acceleration and the three axes angular velocity variances. The vertical acceleration variance was proposed because it was assumed that the amplitude of the acceleration component in this axis and the physical activity involved in the gait process (the gait speed is just a characteristic) are related to some extent. However, the projection of the gravity vector on this axis must be taken into account. Since the trunk could rotate during the gait, a further variation in vertical acceleration may occur that does not correspond to a movement related to the type of gait being executed. That is why, the three axes angular velocity variances are also proposed to work with; these features will represent the variations due to trunk rotations. The average of times between maximum peaks of vertical acceleration was also a chosen feature because it could provide additional information about the gait dynamics.

A feed-forward multilayer neural network with backpropagation training algorithm was the ANN used in this work for the gait speed estimation. The five features detailed above were used in the ANN training and validation stages. The feature values were normalized within the range $[-1, 1]$ prior to be given at the ANN input. The activation functions were the hyperbolic tangent sigmoid function (hidden layers) and the linear function (output layer). The ANN has one output that corresponds with the average gait speed.

Eleven ANN architectures were used in the experiment. Such networks were used with either one or two hidden layers and with a number of hidden layer neurons that ranged from 5 to 35. A cross-validation ($q = 3$) procedure was implemented in order to select the most effective architecture. The following error metrics, were used for assessing the effectiveness of the gait speed estimation performed by each architecture:

- Absolute error (Δx):

$$\Delta x = |x_i - x|$$

- Relative error (δ_x):

$$\delta_x = \frac{\Delta x}{x}$$

- RMSE ($rmse$):

$$rmse = \sqrt[2]{\frac{1}{n}\sum_{i=1}^{n}\Delta x}$$

where x_i is the estimated gait speed, x is the true gait speed and n is the size of test set.

Then, the weights of the architecture more effective were initialized again and such a model was trained by using the 75% of data; the remaining data was used in the test stage.

To prove the generalization capability of the ANN, new data consisting of signals recorded during 114 tries of the walking of persons with ages varying from 19 to 88, was gathered. The distribution of subject's ages is 20.8% between 19 and 29 years old, 20.8% between 59 and 69 years old, 35.4% between 70 and 79 years old, 18.75% between 80 and 88 years old. Then, for the new data the performance achieved by the application of the ANN was determined and compared with that obtained by the application of the IPM proposed in [11]. The factor K involved in the implementation of the IPM was determined as the average the values of K that yielded the best performance per subject. The value of K was set to 0.4.

4 Results

As result of the 3-folds cross-validation procedure, an ANN architecture with 5 nodes and 1 node at the hidden and the output layers, respectively, was the structure that yielded the best results. Such architecture was trained and tested with 52 and 17 groups of features, respectively. The result of the test stage is shown in Fig. 1. This figure shows the true and estimated gait speeds and reveals the performance achieved. The effectiveness parameters: the RMSE, the relative error and the absolute error, were computed and yielded 0.08 m/s, 5.1% and 0.06 m/s, respectively.

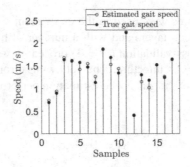

Fig. 1. Result of the test stage of the trained ANN.

The generalization capability achieved by the ANN was assessed through the use of a dataset (comprised by data gathered from 114 tries of the walking of persons) that

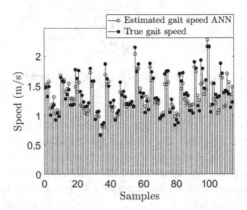

Fig. 2. Results achieved by the ANN through the use of a dataset not used for training or testing.

was not involved in any of the previous stages. The results are shown in Fig. 2. This figure shows the true and the estimated gait speeds. The computation of the effectiveness parameters: the RMSE, the relative error and the absolute error, resulted in 0.1 m/s, 8.4% and 0.11 m/s, respectively. These errors are similar to those achieved by the previous test stage. Hence, it can be said that the ANN reached a high generalization capability as result of the training process. The results showed that the ANN held a good performance for subjects of a wide range of ages, therefore it can be said that the model is balanced and that overfitting does not occur.

The last dataset was also used for the application of the IPM on the estimation of the gait speed. Table 1 presents the values taken by the effectiveness parameters. It reveals that the performance achieved by the ANN was better than that obtained by the IPM.

Table 1. Effectiveness parameters obtained by the application of the IPM and the ANN.

Errors	IPM (state of the art)	ANN (our algorithm)
RMSE (m/s)	0.2	0.1
Relative Error (%)	14.5	8.4
Absolute Error (m/s)	0.17	0.11

Figure 3 shows a box diagram created with the absolute errors achieved by both the IPM and the ANN. On each box, the central mark indicates the median, and the bottom and top edges of the box indicate the 25th and 75th percentiles, respectively. The whiskers extend to the most extreme data points not considered outliers, and the outliers are plotted individually using the '+' symbol. Figure 3 reveals that, unlike the mean of the errors obtained by the IPM, the mean of the errors obtained by the ANN is close to 0 m/s. Besides, the errors achieved by the ANN exhibit less variance that those obtained by the IPM.

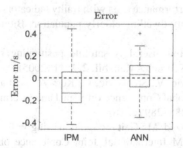

Fig. 3. Absolute errors achieved by the IPM and the ANN

The absolute errors of the IPM and ANN were compared with the Wilcoxon Signed rank test which revealed that difference between both methods is statistically significant with a p-value of 10^{-7}.

5 Conclusions

In this work, an algorithm based on the application of an ANN was proposed for the estimation of the gait speed. An effective ANN model, which does not require to work with biometric, demographic or anthropometric features, nor to estimate the gravity component, nor to guarantee initial conditions, was obtained. Indeed, a good performance was achieved through a relatively simple and low cost solution.

This algorithm was validated through signals recorded by a single IMU attached at the lumbar region in young and elderly subjects during the walking. Moreover, a comparison between the results of the ANN and an algorithm belonging to a different approach, the IPM, was achieved. In fact, it was proved that the proposed algorithm achieved better results. The comparison was performed over the same dataset, which makes the results more reliable.

The technique proved the feasibility of its application on elderly subjects. Hence, it can be applied for monitoring frailty and screening cognitive diseases in older adults.

Acknowledgements. This research was supported by OGFPI, reference PN305LH13-050.

References

1. Schlachetzki, J.C.M., Barth, J., Marxreiter, F., Gossler, J., Kohl, Z., Reinfelder, S., et al.: Wearable sensors objectively measure gait parameters in Parkinson's disease. PLoS ONE 12(10), 1–18 (2017)
2. Agustín, D.G., Morejón, C.D.D.S., Pérez, Z.R.: Physical performance tests in the prognosis of adverse outcomes in the elderly. MEDISAN 22(6), 466–470 (2018)
3. García-Agustin, D., Morgade-Fonte, R.M., Bobes, M.A., Galán-García, L., Rodríguez-Rodríguez, V.: Association between gait speed decline and EEG abnormalities in a cohort of active older adults living in the community. medRxiv, 1 January 2020; 2020.05.03.20089540. http://medrxiv.org/content/early/2020/05/08/2020.05.03.20089540.abstract
4. Munguia, L., Solis, V., Meaney, E., Ramirez-Sanchez, I., Villarreal, F., Perez-Duran, J., et al.: Association of physical performance tests with frailty indicators and oxidative stress markers in a sample of a community-dwelling elderly population. Biomed Res. 29(17), 3344–3350 (2018)
5. Terrier, P., Schutz, Y.: How useful is satellite positioning system (GPS) to track gait parameters? A review. J. Neuroeng. Rehabil. 2, 1–11 (2005)
6. Ye, M., Yang, C., Stankovic, V., Stankovic, L., Kerr, A.: Gait analysis using a single depth camera. In: 2015 IEEE Global Conference on Signal and Information Processing, GlobalSIP 2015, no. December, pp. 285–289 (2016)
7. Wang, W., Liu, A.X., Shahzad, M.: Gait recognition using WiFi signals. In: UbiComp 2016 – Proceedings of 2016 ACM International Joint Conference on Pervasive and Ubiquitous Computing, pp. 363–373 (2016)
8. Hsu, C.C., Chen, J.H.: A novel sensor-assisted RFID-based indoor tracking system for the elderly living alone. Sensors 11(11), 10094–10113 (2011)
9. Soler, B., Ramari, C., Valet, M., Dalgas, U., Feys, P.: Clinical assessment, management, and rehabilitation of walking impairment in MS: an expert review. Expert Rev. Neurother. 20(8), 875–886 (2020). https://doi.org/10.1080/14737175.2020.1801425

10. Bae, J., Tomizuka, M.: A tele-monitoring system for gait rehabilitation with an inertial measurement unit and a shoe-type ground reaction force sensor. Mechatronics **23**(6), 646–651 (2013). http://dx.doi.org/10.1016/j.mechatronics.2013.06.007

11. WeinBerg, H.: AN-602: using the ADXL202 in pedometer and personal navigation applications, pp. 1–8 (2002). http://www.analog.com/static/imported-files/application_notes/513 772624AN602.pdf

12. Mao, Y., Ogata, T., Ora, H., Tanaka, N., Miyake, Y.: Estimation of stride-by-stride spatial gait parameters using inertial measurement unit attached to the shank with inverted pendulum model. Sci. Rep. **11**(1), 1–11 (2021). https://doi.org/10.1038/s41598-021-81009-w

13. Brzostowski, K.: Toward the unaided estimation of human walking speed based on sparse modeling. IEEE Trans. Instrum. Meas. **67**(6), 1389–1398 (2018)

14. Zijlstra, W., Hof, A.L.: Assessment of spatio-temporal gait parameters from trunk accelerations during human walking. Gait Posture **18**(2), 1–10 (2003)

15. Chen, S., Cunningham, C.L., Lach, J., Bennett, B.C.: Extracting spatio-temporal information from inertial body sensor networks for gait speed estimation. In: Proceedings - 2011 International Conference on Body Sensor Networks, BSN 2011, pp. 71–76 (2011)

16. Alvarez, D., González, R.C., López, A., Alvarez, J.C.: Comparison of step length estimators from weareable accelerometer devices. In: Annual International Conference on IEEE Engineering in Medicine and Biology – Proceedings, pp. 5964–5967 (2006)

17. Zihajehzadeh, S., Aziz, O., Tae, C.G., Park, E.J.: Combined regression and classification models for accurate estimation of walking speed using a wrist-worn IMU. In: Proceedings of Annual International Conference on IEEE Engineering in Medicine and Biology Society, EMBS 2018, pp. 3272–3275, July 2018

18. Feigl, T., Kram, S., Woller, P., Siddiqui, R.H., Philippsen, M., Mutschler, C.: A bidirectional LSTM for estimating dynamic human velocities from a single IMU. In: 2019 International Conference on Indoor Positioning and Indoor Navigation, IPIN 2019, pp. 1–8 (2019)

19. Byun, S., Lee, H.J., Han, J.W., Kim, J.S., Choi, E., Kim, K.W.: Walking-speed estimation using a single inertial measurement unit for the older adults. PLoS ONE **14**(12), 1–16 (2019)

20. Buckley, C., Galna, B., Rochester, L., Mazzà, C.: Upper body accelerations as a biomarker of gait impairment in the early stages of Parkinson's disease. Gait Posture **71**, 289–295 (2019). https://doi.org/10.1016/j.gaitpost.2018.06.166

21. Flety, E., Team, E., Edition, I.: A comprehensive guide to using, programming & flashing the BITtalino R-IoT WiFi sensor module, vol. 1, no. March (2017)

22. Da Silva, H.P., Guerreiro, J., Lourenço, A., Fred, A., Martins, R.: BITalino: a novel hardware framework for physiological computing. In: PhyCS 2014 – Proceedings of International Conference on Physiological Computing Systems, no. January, pp. 246–253 (2014)

Scalable Generalized Multitarget Linear Regression With Output Dependence Estimation

Julio Camejo Corona[1(✉)], Hector Gonzalez[2], and Carlos Morell[3]

[1] Universidad de Cienfuegos Carlos Rafael Rodríguez (UCF), Carretera a Rodas, Km. 4, Cienfuegos, Cuba
`jcamejo@ucf.edu.cu`
[2] Universidad de las Ciencias Informaticas (UCI), Havana, La Habana, Cuba
`hglez@uci.cu`
[3] Universidad Central Marta Abreu (UCLV), Villa Clara, Santa Clara, Cuba
`cmorellp@uclv.edu.cu`

Abstract. Nowadays the phenomenon of Big Data is overwhelming our capacity to extract relevant knowledge through classical machine learning techniques. Multitarget regression has arisen in several interesting industrial and environmental application domains, such as ecological modeling and energy forecasting. However, standard multi-target regressors are not designed to perform well with such amounts of data. This paper proposes a scalable implementation for a multi-target linear regression algorithm with output dependence estimation for Big Data analytics in Apache Spark. Our experiments on large-scale datasets show an accurate analysis compared to standard implementation and order of training time reduction as the available number of working nodes in the processing cluster increases.

Keywords: Big data · Apache Spark · Multi-target regression

1 Introduction

Distributed programming is a fundamental tool in the solution of problems involving large volumes of data since it allows an outstanding amount of data to be stored and processed on everyday computers, without the need to invest in high-cost specialized equipment. In addition, they are scalable, which means that more units can be added to the network as the volume of data increases.

There are several algorithms that solve the multivariate linear regression problem, in distributed environment. Also, structured prediction problems [1] in which outputs may exhibit structure along with strong interdependences are particularly discussed in recent works for small data [2,16,17]. Additionally, the Apache Spark MLlib library contains distributed implementations of the Linear Regression, Decision Tree, Random Forest, and Gradient-boosted Trees algorithms. The shortcoming appears when an algorithm is needed to predict simultaneously several output variables with dependency estimation on very large

© Springer Nature Switzerland AG 2021
Y. Hernández Heredia et al. (Eds.): IWAIPR 2021, LNCS 13055, pp. 60–68, 2021.
https://doi.org/10.1007/978-3-030-89691-1_7

datasets, i.e. in the context of Big Data. Taking into account these implementations in [4], variants of MTS and ERC [14] are proposed capable of using any of these as a base regressor, being the only work found that solves the previous problem.

A recent state-of-the-art work that solves the linear regression problem with several output variables efficiently, introducing a space of latent variables, is the method proposed in [6]. This algorithm, called Generalized Multitarget Linear Regression with Output Dependence Estimation (GMLR), introduce a general, flexible and adaptable scheme to different scenarios and regularization schemes. After a detailed review of this algorithm, we propose a distributed extension, which guarantees scalability as the number of examples in the dataset increases. The main contribution of this paper are the new multitarget regression algorithm based on latent variables representation and scalable to very large datasets.

Next, some concepts about Big Data are briefly explained, the MTR problem and the GMLR algorithm are presented, and then our main contribution is introduced. An empirical evaluation is also considered using publicly available data and involving different dimensions of the data set is also considered. Finally, the main conclusions along with lines of future research are outlined.

2   Big Data: Concepts and Frameworks

Humongous amounts of information are stored in data centers now, ready to be processed. The efficient extraction of valuable knowledge from these datasets raises a considerable challenge for data scientists. Gartner [11] introduced the popular concept of Big Data in 2001. In its report, Gartner defines this concept as the conjunction of the 3Vs: high volume, velocity, and variety of the information that require new large-scale processing. This list was extended with 2 extra terms: veracity and value [13].

One of the first frameworks in Big Data analytics is the MapReduce framework [5]. This framework, devised by Google in 2003, allows us to automatically process huge data by distributing the complexity burden among a cluster of machines. Final users only have to design their tasks specifying the Map and Reduce functions. Partitioning and distributing of data, job scheduling or fault-tolerance are responsibilities of the platform.

The MapReduce model offers two primitives -Map and Reduce-, which correspond with two execution stages in the whole process. Firstly, the master node retrieves the dataset (split into several chunks) from the distributed file system so that each node reads those data chunks allocated in its local disk. Each node then starts one or more Map threads to process the raw chunks. The result is a set of key-value pairs (intermediate pairs), which are also stored in disk. After all Map tasks have ended, the master node starts the Reduce phase by distributing those pairs with coincident keys to the same node. Each Reduce task combines those matching pairs to yield the final output. Figure 1 depicts a simplified scheme of MapReduce and its two main functions.

Recently Apache Spark has emerged as a widely used open-source engine. Spark is a fault-tolerant and general-purpose cluster computing system providing APIs in Java, Scala, Python, and R, along with an optimized engine that

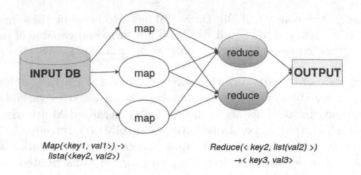

Fig. 1. Scheme of the MapReduce paradigm.

supports general execution graphs. It has several matrix representations and a machine learning library that includes optimization methods, regularization functions, evaluation metrics for regression models, and a well-defined package structure, making it easy to add new regression algorithms.

3   Multitarget Regression

Let $\vec{x}$, $\vec{y}$ be input and output vectors, respectively, and let $\{(\vec{x}^j, \vec{y}^j)\} \in \mathbb{R}^p \times \mathbb{R}^q$, for $i = 1, \ldots, N$, be a given training set. The MTR problem consists of obtaining a predictor $h : \mathbb{R}^p \to \mathbb{R}^q$ in such a way that the expected deviation between true and predicted outputs is minimized for all possible input/output pairs.

Global methods are interesting because they focus on explicitly capturing all interdependencies and internal relationships among targets.

A straightforward adaptation method for MTR is Multivariate Linear Regression with q output variables [2,3]. In this approach it is possible to estimate the coefficient matrix through unconstrained optimization by combining an appropriate loss function, $\mathcal{L}(W)$, and a regularizer, $\mathcal{R}(W)$, as:

$$\hat{W} = \underset{W}{\mathrm{argmin}}\, \mathcal{L}(W) + \lambda\mathcal{R}(W) \tag{1}$$

Like severals previous works on MTR, the loss function used here is the Mean Squared Error (MSE) between real outputs and predictions, $\frac{1}{2N}\|XW - Y\|_F^2$, where $\|\cdot\|_F$ designates the Frobenius norm, and $X \in \mathbb{R}^{N \times p}$ and $Y \in \mathbb{R}^{N \times q}$.

In GMLR, it's defined a set of latent variables $\vec{z} \in \mathbb{R}^r$ between the input and output variables. The latent variables are estimated from the matrix $W_{p \times r}$ which establishes the relationships between the input and output set. In case of $r = q$ it is said that W is a full range structure. Then, to relate the set of output variables through the latent variables, the matrix structure $S_{r \times q}$ is included in the model, which linearly combines the set of individual predictions in the linear regression model.

The main algorithms in MTR consider that the training set has a reasonable size (N and p) to solve the optimization problem and perform various algebraic operations such as the product of matrices. Now, the question is how to solve the MTR problem when the number of instances is very large ($N \rightarrow \infty$), by following a latent variable representation like GMLR approach. In this direction, we introduce in the next section the "Scalable MTR with Output Dependence Estimation" that employs a distributed scenario to improve the performance of this problem.

4 Scalable MTR with Output Dependence Estimation

In general, to estimate the structures that relate the set of input and output variables and between output variables, an optimization problem is defined to minimize the functional loss $\ell(\vec{x}^i, \vec{y}^i, W, S)$ and a regularization function $\mathcal{R}(W, S)$ which controls the generalization of the model and at the same time establishes the structures of each matrix. In very large data sets, we divide the data from the

$$
X = \begin{bmatrix} \mathbf{X}_{11}\mathbf{X}_{12}\cdots\mathbf{X}_{1K} \\ \mathbf{X}_{21}\mathbf{X}_{22}\cdots\mathbf{X}_{2K} \\ \vdots\vdots\ddots\vdots \\ \mathbf{X}_{K1}\mathbf{X}_{K2}\cdots\mathbf{X}_{KK} \end{bmatrix} \text{ and } Y = \begin{bmatrix} \mathbf{Y}_{11}\mathbf{Y}_{12}\cdots\mathbf{Y}_{1K} \\ \mathbf{Y}_{21}\mathbf{Y}_{22}\cdots\mathbf{Y}_{2K} \\ \vdots\vdots\ddots\vdots \\ \mathbf{Y}_{K1}\mathbf{Y}_{K2}\cdots\mathbf{Y}_{KK} \end{bmatrix}
$$

matrices into blocks [7] distributed over K available processing nodes in the cluster. Each processing node computes a local matrix operation with a subset of data and later a global sum operator of the aggregation is computed in the master node. We transform the classical GMLR [6] problem, introducing the following global variables $A = X^T X \in \mathbb{R}^{p \times p}$, $B = X^T Y \in \mathbb{R}^{p \times q}$ and $C = Y^T Y \in \mathbb{R}^{q \times q}$. The block matrix multiplications schema is similar to the Fig. 2. Considering that we only intend to address problems with large numbers of instances, we can assume that p and q are not very large, so we reduce the problem to matrices A, B, and C in the master node. So the general optimization problem can be transformed for our proposal as a follow:

$$
\{W^*, S^*\} = \arg\min_{W,S} \frac{1}{2N} \operatorname{Tr}(S^T W^T A W S - 2B^T W S + C) + \lambda_1 g_1(W) + \lambda_2 g_2(S)
$$

$$(2)$$

where g_1 y g_2 represent the term associated with the regularizer for the matrix W y S respectively. It is worth noting that in this context g_1 y g_2 can be generic, allow various types of rules to be used, and are scalable to different regularization schemes.

To solve this problem, one of the matrices is fixed and the other is updated, alternately (biconvex problem) for each node independently.

$$
W_{t+1} = \arg\min_{W} \frac{1}{2N} \operatorname{Tr}(S_t^T W^T A W S_t - 2B^T W S_t) + \lambda_1 g_1(W) \quad \text{Keeping } S_t \qquad (3)
$$

$$
S_{t+1} = \arg\min_{S} \frac{1}{2N} \operatorname{Tr}(S^T W_{t+1}^T A W_{t+1} S - 2B^T W_{t+1} S) + \lambda_2 g_2(S) \text{ Keeping } W_{t+1} \quad (4)
$$

using the proximal operators:

$$W_{t+1} := \underset{\lambda_1 s_t g_1}{\mathbf{prox}}(W_t - s_t \nabla_W \ell(W_t, S_t)) \tag{5}$$

$$S_{t+1} := \underset{\lambda_2 s_t g_2}{\mathbf{prox}}(S_t - s_t \nabla_S \ell(W_{t+1}, S_t)) \tag{6}$$

where

$$\nabla_W \ell = A(W_t(W_t(SS_t^T))) - BS^T \tag{7}$$

$$\nabla_S \ell = W_{t+1}^T(AW_{t+1})S_t - B^T W_{t+1} \tag{8}$$

In our proposal called *Scalable Generalized Multitarget Linear Regression with Output Dependence Estimation* (SGMLR), is perfectly applicable to different GMLR regularization frameworks proposed in [6] and inherits all its advantages.

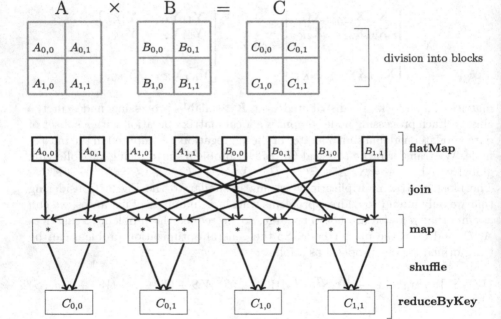

Fig. 2. Graphical representation of the process of multiplication of matrices distributed by blocks.

5   Experiments and Results

This section describes the experimental framework carried out and analyses the results derived from these experiments. These experiments aim to prove the benefit derived from using our distributed solution.

5.1   Convergence Experiments

In this experiment is compared the goodness of fit metric (MSE) of the GMLR algorithm and proposed SGMLR, both in their two variants (1 and 2) for tree datasets. Note that errors' differences between GMLR and SGMLR were apparently the same since differences were in the order of 10^{-5}.

In all cases the training were fixed to 20 iterations. For EDM [10] dataset λ_1 and λ_2 were 0.138 and 0.001 respectively, and for ANDRO [8] 1.914 and 0.001. The results are presented in Figs. 3, 4, 5, and 6.

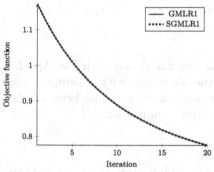

Fig. 3. $SGMLR_1$ vs $GMLR_1$ training error for EDM dataset

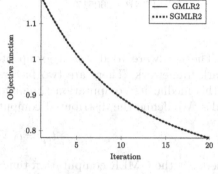

Fig. 4. $SGMLR_2$ vs $GMLR_2$ training error for EDM dataset

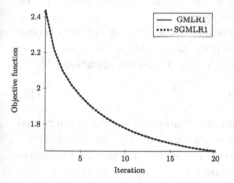

Fig. 5. $SGMLR_1$ vs $GMLR_1$ training error for ANDRO dataset

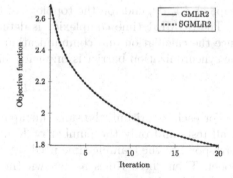

Fig. 6. $SGMLR_2$ vs $GMLR_2$ training error for ANDRO dataset

Although it is not visible to the naked eye in these graphs, there is a slight difference in the order of 10^{-5} between the values of the objective function of GMLR and SGMLR. This is because both implementations are in different programming languages, which results in a difference in the number of decimal places that the real variables store.

5.2   Scalability Experiments

Scalability tests were performed on the UJIIL, HPC, and NPMSMP data sets that have the following properties (Table 1):

Table 1.   Characteristics of the data sets.

Dataset	Number of instance N	Inputs p	Outputs q	Source
HPC	2075259	6	3	[9]
UJIIL	21048	525	4	[15]
NPMSMP	260517	134	10	[12]

The hardware used was a group of homogeneous nodes with the Apache Spark framework. There are two factors of the algorithm with a primary role in this media: its computation time and the communication time between the nodes. We define the distributed computation time complexity as:

$$t_{cp} = c(N, p, q)/K \tag{9}$$

where c is the GMLR computation time complexity function, which depends on the input sizes N, p, and q. The communication time complexity is

$$t_{cm} = f_{cm}(N, p, q, K) \tag{10}$$

where the value of f_{cm} increases with N, p, q and the number of nodes K; the shape of f_{cm} depends on the topology of the media.

The SGMLR time complexity is determined as the sum of the two terms, since the calculation and communication step do not overlap. We assume that the synchronization barrier is implicitly included in the communication.

$$t = t_{cp} + t_{cm} \tag{11}$$

For each algorithm, the same metaparameter configuration was maintained in all tests and only the number of K nodes was varied. The measured times correspond to the training time needed by each algorithm to learn its respective model. Then these times are shown (in seconds) for one, four, eight sixteen processing nodes.

In all cases, a reduction in the necessary training time was obtained from one to four processing nodes, extending to sixteen with the UJIIL data set. The most notable reductions were those obtained in the passage from one to four nodes. Notable are the results with the data set NPMSMP decreases in time 62% and 61% respectively.

The most encouraging results were obtained with the HPC data set because it has very few variables and many instances, a situation for which this proposal is designed.

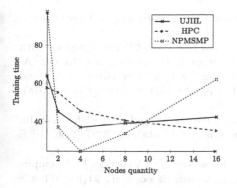 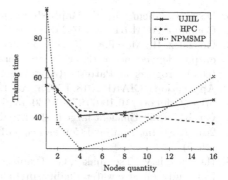

Fig. 7. Training times for data sets and nodes amounts of $SGMLR_1$

Fig. 8. Training times for data sets and nodes amounts of $SGMLR_2$

The complexity of the computation time decreases as the number of nodes grows. At the same time, the communication time increases the final temporal complexity. Consequently, the training time does not decrease indefinitely and begins to increase around 4 nodes. This is the point where the total execution time reaches its minimum for this setting.

6 Conclusions and Further Work

The empirical evaluation showed that the SGMLR algorithm is equivalent in terms of convergence to the GMLR algorithm. This ensures that it inherits the efficiency and adaptability of its predecessor while allowing data sets with virtually unlimited numbers of instances to be processed.

The scalability experiments showed that SGMLR is scalable, although this characteristic is highly determined by the cardinalities of the data set. Distributed computation in SGMLR is used only to limit the cardinality of the matrices involved in the optimization problem to p, q and r, so further research is directed to distribute the computations of these structures so that the algorithm is scalable not only in the number of training examples but also in the number of variables.

References

1. Baklr, G., Hofmann, T., Smola, A.J., Schölkopf, B., Taskar, B.: Predicting Structured Data. MIT Press, Cambridge (2007)
2. Borchani, H., Varando, G., Bielza, C., Larranaga, P.: A survey on multi-output regression. Wiley Interdisc. Rev.: Data Min. Knowl. Discovery **5**(5), 216–233 (2015)
3. Corona, J.C., Gonzalez, H., Morell, C.: Los principales algoritmos para regresión con salidas múltiples. una revisión para big data. Revista Cubana de Ciencias Informáticas **13**(4), 118–150 (2019)
4. Corona, J.C., Gonzalez, H., Morell, C.: Solución distribuida de los algoritmos de predicción con salidas múltiples MTS y ERC. In: XVIII Convención y Feria Internacional Informática 2020 (2020)

5. Dean, J., Ghemawat, S.: MapReduce: simplified data processing on large clusters. Commun. ACM **51**(1), 107–113 (2008)
6. Gonzalez, H., Morell, C., Ferri, F.J.: Generalized multitarget linear regression with output dependence estimation. In: Vera-Rodriguez, R., Fierrez, J., Morales, A. (eds.) Progress in Pattern Recognition, Image Analysis, Computer Vision, and Applications. CIARP 2018. LNCS, vol. 11401, pp. 296–304. Springer, Cham (2018). https://doi.org/10.1007/978-3-030-13469-3_35
7. Gu, R., et al.: Efficient large scale distributed matrix computation with spark. In: 2015 IEEE International Conference on Big Data (Big Data), pp. 2327–2336. IEEE (2015)
8. Hatzikos, E.V., Tsoumakas, G., Tzanis, G., Bassiliades, N., Vlahavas, I.: An empirical study on sea water quality prediction. Knowl.-Based Syst. **21**(6), 471–478 (2008)
9. Hebrail, G., Baillard, A.: UCI machine learning repository: Individual household electric power consumption dataset. Technical report. University of California, Irvine, School of Information and Computer Sciences 2 (2012)
10. Karalič, A., Bratko, I.: First order regression. Mach. Learn. **26**(2), 147–176 (1997)
11. Laney, D., et al.: 3D data management: controlling data volume, velocity and variety. META Gr. Res. Note **6**(70), 1 (2001)
12. Moniz, N., Torgo, L.: Multi-source social feedback of online news feeds (2018)
13. Ramírez-Gallego, S., García, S., Benítez, J.M., Herrera, F.: A distributed evolutionary multivariate discretizer for big data processing on apache spark. Swarm Evol. Comput. **38**, 240–250 (2018)
14. Spyromitros-Xioufis, E., Tsoumakas, G., Groves, W., Vlahavas, I.: Multi-target regression via input space expansion: treating targets as inputs. Mach. Learn. **104**(1), 55–98 (2016)
15. Torres-Sospedra, J., et al.: UJIIndoorLoc: a new multi-building and multi-floor database for WLAN fingerprint-based indoor localization problems. In: 2014 International Conference on Indoor Positioning and Indoor Navigation (IPIN), pp. 261–270. IEEE (2014)
16. Zhen, X., Yu, M., He, X., Li, S.: Multi-target regression via robust low-rank learning. IEEE Trans. Pattern Anal. Mach. Intell. **40**(2), 497–504 (2017)
17. Zhen, X., et al.: Multitarget sparse latent regression. IEEE Trans. Neural Netw. Learn. Syst. **29**(5), 1575–1586 (2017)

Covariance Matrix Adaptation Evolution Strategy for Convolutional Neural Network in Text Classification

Orlando Grabiel Toledano-López[1]([⊠]) [iD], Julio Madera[2] [iD], Héctor González[1] [iD], and Alfredo Simón Cuevas[3] [iD]

[1] Universidad de las Ciencias Informáticas (UCI), La Habana, Cuba
{ogtoledano,hglez}@uci.cu
[2] Universidad de Camagüey, Camagüey, Cuba
julio.madera@reduc.edu.cu
[3] Universidad Tecnológica de La Habana "José Antonio Echeverría",
La Habana, Cuba
asimon@ceis.cujae.edu.cu

Abstract. Text classification has become relevant in recent years because of its usefulness in supporting different text mining solutions. Neural networks for this purpose have benefited from the creation of word embedding for learning semantics among words in a corpus. However, artificial neural network training by conventional methods present several theoretical and computational limitations. In this work, we develop a hybrid training method that combines gradient-based methods and Covariance Matrix Adaptation Evolution Strategy to train Convolutional Neural Network for the text classification task. For this, the training process is divided into two stages taking advantage of the speed of the gradient-based methods for learning the parameters of the convolutional filters and the application of the Covariance Matrix Adaptation Evolution Strategy for learning the weights of the fully connected layer. Our proposal was evaluated using a Spanish dataset for text classification, taken off the EcuRed Cuban Encyclopedia, divided into five classes. The proposed method increases the accuracy significantly of the convolutional network applied to the text classification.

Keywords: Convolutional neural network · Covariance matrix adaptation evolution strategy · Text classification · Word embedding

1 Introduction

Text classification has benefited many areas of knowledge and spheres of society, finding applications in marketing [2], product management [14], E-government [21], education [18] and many other fields. This consists of labeling texts written in natural language (e.g., tweets, news articles, blog posts, and documents library), based on relevant categories as of pre-defined tags from unstructured data [23]. For this purpose, deep learning approaches allow the

Y. Hernández Heredia et al. (Eds.): IWAIPR 2021, LNCS 13055, pp. 69–78, 2021.
https://doi.org/10.1007/978-3-030-89691-1_8

extraction of important elements in the text that improve the performance of the final prediction, such as attentional mechanisms, semantic relationships, and dimensionality reduction of the input text [13].

Convolutional Neural Networks (CNN), as deep learning architecture commonly used, have taken relevance in different NLP tasks due to their use for dimensionality reduction in signal, image, or text processing problems [6]. This has been useful for the considerable reduction of parameters to be learned in the neural network, and it avoids redundant features and overfitting problem [3]. With a CNN, we can extracts more abstract features from the input according to the number of convolutional filters in the sequence, which makes the final classification information of the model more reliable [23]. This kind of artificial neural network takes advantage of the use of distributed text rendering through word embedding. With this, it is possible to create a representation of the words coming from a larger dimensional space to a smaller dimensional space while maintaining the contextual semantic information [12].

Recent research has focused on the use of methods for the reduction of dimensionality from input features as we can observe in [17], where the size of pre-trained word embedding is reduced while achieving similar or better performance than original embeddings. In [9], the use of attentional mechanisms with CNN-based operations to automatically extract and weight multiple granularities and fine-grained representations. The empirical observations made with five databases show that this method has better results in terms of accuracy with less execution time compared to other architectures that only use CNN. Other works combine the use of CNN with Recurrent Neural Network (RNN) [22] and Long Short Term Memory (LSTM) [10] to improve the final classification performance by capturing relevant features from the input text. However, basic approaches for Artificial Neural Network (ANN) training are the methods based on partial derivatives of the objective function, such as Stochastic Gradient Descent (SGD) [4] and Adam [5]. These methods have theoretical-practical limitations that are evident in their probability of convergence to local minimums [19,20], which results in a significant effect on the accuracy of the final model.

Estimation of Distribution Algorithms (EDA) is an extension of the area of evolutionary computing where the model of a candidate population solution is probabilistic. This type of algorithm has been applied as a method of solving the continuous variable optimization problems without restrictions [7]. Based on this, we aim to introduce a hybrid method that combines gradient-based methods with Covariance Matrix Adaptation-Evolution Strategy (CMA-ES) [1] for training a CNN. It should be considered that neural network training for text classification is a problem of high dimensionality that requires a large number of parameters to be optimized. As consequence, this leads to a high computational cost of the training process, so some population meta-heuristics are limited to obtain good results with reasonable population size. CMA-ES is a type of EDA that takes advantage of the eigenvalue decomposition property of the covariance matrix as a search operator for the optimization of continuous variables on non-convex problems.

In the next, we present the design of CNN for text classification tasks and introduce a hybrid method to train CNN that combines gradient-based methods and CMA-ES. We also introduce a new dataset in Spanish for text classification problems created from keywords by groups of contents published in the EcuRed Cuban encyclopedia. Moreover, we discuss the accuracy and statistical results in comparison with gradient-based methods. Finally, some conclusions and recommendations are given.

2 Computational Methodology

In the literature, the use of population meta-heuristics for ANN training has been addressed in [8,11,15,19]. A fundamental criterion for the success of these algorithms has been the balance between exploration of the search space and exploitation of local information. The use of search operators to explore the fitness function has characteristics that hinder the optimization process, such as local minima and non-convexity of the problem.

In [19] a homotopy transformation is performed to modify the fitness function for training an ANN in regression tasks, which allows the application of continuation methods together with other meta-heuristics such as Particle Swarm Optimization (PSO), Firefly Algorithm (FA), and Cuckoo Search (CS). However, the EDAs instead of transforming the fitness function, transform the search operator that is estimated during the training process. It allows the algorithm to build a probabilistic model capable of learning the relationships between the variables of the optimization problem [7,11]. Compared to PSO and other similar meta-heuristics, EDAs constitute a middle ground between the use of problem-specific operators and general-purpose operators. This aspect has motivated the application of CMA-ES for training a CNN in text classification. The decomposition property of the covariance matrix allows the generation of new points and regulates the step-size of the variables, avoiding premature convergence [1].

2.1 Design of Convolutional Neural Network for the Text Categorization

To text classification, we define a CNN architecture, shown in Fig. 1 that receives by input word embedding document representation. In this, we use three sequential convolutional filters, each one of them uses in the output max-pooling and Rectified Linear Unit (ReLU) as activation function. For the features extraction, we use a pre-trained GloVe [16][1] in embedding layer with 300 dimension vectors, 1.4B tokens, and 855,380 words of vocabulary. The last CNN filter is connected with one fully connected layer and log softmax function as the output of the neural network on the last layer.

2.2 Formalization of the Problem and Optimization by Proposed Method

Text classification works in a instance of space X where each instance is a document d and a fixed set classes/categories $C = \{c_0, c_1, c_2, ..., c_{L-1}\}$. Hence, let

---

[1] Available at http://dcc.uchile.cl/~jperez/word-embeddings/glove-sbwc.i25.vec.gz.

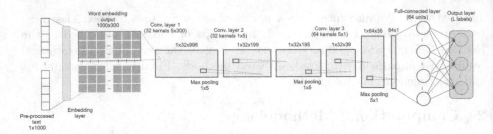

Fig. 1. Design of CNN for text classification

$X = \{d_1, d_2, d_3, ..., d_N\}$ be the set of documents for the training, and let V be the words of vocabulary in the set X. Each document $d_i = \{t_1, t_2, t_3, ..., t_P\}$, represents a sequence of words with $t_p \in V$, $Y = \{y_1, y_2, y_3, ..., y_N\}$ the set of categories in which each document d_i is classified, each $y_i \in C$. The goal of document classification is learn a classifier A that maps instances to classes: $A : X \to C$.

A fitness function allows evaluating the quality of a certain solution. Considering meta-heuristic approaches, this function determines which is the best solution given a population. For an ANN, used for a classification problem, a fitness function is determined by the set of training patterns, the set of parameters, and the set of labels for the classification. In practice, the fitness function in the CNN is a sort of loss function such as the cross-entropy loss. Hence, the model will train for the set of parameters $w \in \mathbb{R}^q$ minimizing the cross-entropy loss in the Eq. 1a:

$$w = \underset{w \in \mathbb{R}^q}{argmin}\, F(w, X) \tag{1a}$$

$$F(w, X) = - \sum_{c=0}^{L-1} \Upsilon_{d_i} \log(P_{d_i,c}(w)) \tag{1b}$$

$$\Upsilon_{d_i} = \begin{cases} 1 \ if \ y_i = \hat{y}_i \\ 0 \ otherwise \end{cases} \tag{1c}$$

Where $\hat{y}_i$ is the prediction for document d_i, and $P_{d_i,c}(w)$ is the predicted probability of d_i in the class c.

We apply gradient-based methods for learning convolutional filters in CNN, and we train fully connected layer via CMA-ES optimization. In this, an individual $w_{fc} = w/\{w_{cnn}\}$ represents parameters of fully connected layer, being w_{cnn} parameters of CNN filters and fitness function is evaluated for w that represent all trainable parameters in the CNN. Algorithm 1.1 describes how to use an hybrid EDA for CNN training. The algorithm receives as input the set of training documents X and the set of categories Y of each document. The fitness function is computed for all trainable parameters in the CNN as we show in Eq. 1a. An $w_{fc} = (u_1, u_2, u_3, ..., u_\gamma)$ is a configuration that corresponds to a distribution $p(w_{fc}) = [P_0 = u_1, P_1 = u_2, P_3 = u_3, ..., P_\gamma = u_\gamma]$. Optimization problem consists to find a minimum configuration w_{fc} where $F(.) : \mathbb{R}^q \to \mathbb{R}$.

Algorithm 1.1: General approach for CNN training via EDA

1: **Require:** Set of training pattern $X = (d_1, d_2, d_3, ..., d_N)$.
2: **Require:** Fitness function $F(w, X)$.
    $\backslash$* *STAGE 1: Learning convolutional layers by gradient-based method.* *$\backslash$
3: **while** Criterion not fulfilled **do**
4:     **for** *batch in X* **do**
5:         Forward pass in *batch* to get output $\hat{y}$.
6:         Backforward propagation to compute gradients.
7:         Update parameters w with computed gradients.
8:     **end for**
9: **end while**
    $\backslash$* *STAGE 2: Learning fully connected layer by EDA optimization.* *$\backslash$
10: Initialize $g \leftarrow 1$.
11: Keep parameters for CNN filters w_{cnn}.
12: Generate initial population $w_{fc,1}, w_{fc,2}, w_{fc,3}, ..., w_{fc,\Lambda}$.
13: **while** Criterion not fulfilled **do**
14:     Evaluate population in $F(w, X)$.
15:     Select an intermediate set CS from M individuals.
16:     Estimate distribution from CS through $p^{CS} = p(w_{fc}, g)$.
17:     Generate new individuals from $p(w_{fc}, g + 1) \approx p^{CS}(w_{fc}, g)$.
18:     $g = g + 1$.
19: **end while**
20: **return** Best individual w_{fc}^* in the population.

In fully connected layer optimization, the most important step is the estimation of the distribution p^{CS} for generating new individuals. In our proposal, covariance matrix $Cov \in \mathbb{R}^\gamma$ is initialized in identity matrix $Cov = I$, this matrix is symmetric and positive. We fix the initial centroid $\Omega \in \mathbb{R}^\gamma$ and the initial step-size $\sigma \in \mathbb{R}$ that corresponds to initial variance. For estimating distribution we sort the individuals by increasing fitness function $F_1 < F_2 < F_3 < ...F_\Lambda$ and select M best individuals in CS. For each generation we obtain new individuals following Eq. 2:

$$w_{fc,\lambda}^{(g+1)} = \Omega^{(g)} + \sigma^{(g)}\mathcal{N}(0, Cov^{(g)}) \tag{2}$$

The matrix Cov has an orthonormal basis of eigenvectors defined as B as results of eigenvalue decomposition of $Cov = BD^2B^T$, being B an orthogonal matrix, where $B^TB = BB^T = I$. $D^2 = diag(d_1^2, ..., d_\gamma^2)$ is a diagonal matrix with eigenvalues of Cov as diagonal elements. Hence, $D = diag(d_1, ..., d_\gamma)$ is a diagonal matrix with square roots of eigenvalues of D as diagonal elements [1].

Using previous eigenvalue decomposition of Cov, $\mathcal{N}(0, Cov^{(g)})$ can be computed as following Eq. 3:

$$\mathcal{N}(0, Cov^{(g)}) = BD\mathcal{N}(0, I) \tag{3}$$

Where $\mathcal{N}(0, I)$ represents a standard normally distributed vector which are realizations from a multivariate normal distribution with zero mean and identity covariance matrix. Selection and recombination is an important step in the evolution strategy to adjust of initial centroid Ω, taking into account initial weights for each point of distribution. Moreover, σ is considered an step-size and we perform its control using property of matrix decomposition Cov and initial evolution path $p \in I\!R^\gamma$. Finally, we perform the covariance matrix adaptation step as described in [1].

2.3   Dataset

We created a dataset composed of public pages in Spanish from EcuRed[2] encyclopedia. EcuRed is a collaborative Cuban encyclopedia, created in 2010, with articles in Spanish. It includes articles on different topics ranging from science, history, culture, sports, education, art, health, among others, reaching more than 200,000 pages of content. Page data were collected using the Sketch Engine[3] tool, which uses the Bing search engine. The dataset[4] is composed of five categories, such as sports, science, history, health, and culture. The dataset also consists of 53,208 unique tokens in a total of 980 documents in HTML format. Table 1 summarizes main statistics for the dataset per labels.

Table 1. Summary statistic of the dataset

Label	Documents	Tokens count	Stop-words
Sports	214	292,127	96,856
Science	221	342,490	130,739
History	100	248,945	93,803
Health	214	285,547	107,686
Culture	231	389,745	143,204

3   Results and Discussion

This section describes the experimental setup and results of the proposed method for CNN optimization. For the SGD and Adam algorithms, we consider hyperparameter tuning through a Grid Search cross-validation with 5-folds, in the portion that represents the training set. We compare the results with SGD and Adam regarding the combination of algorithms as hybrid proposals: SGD-CMAES (Variant 1), Adam-CMAES (Variant 2). Combinations are represented by dash separating the gradient-based algorithm used in the first stage, and the EDA used in the second stage. We specify network-related hyper-parameters taking into account the training algorithm. However, we do not deal with model selection.

Our model is implemented with Pytorch[5], and for performing the EDA algorithm we use the Deap library as an evolutionary computation framework that

---

[2] https://www.ecured.cu/EcuRed:Enciclopedia_cubana.
[3] https://www.sketchengine.eu/.
[4] Dataset available at: https://github.com/ogtoledano/ecured_five_tags.
[5] Source code at: https://github.com/ogtoledano/Text_Cat_Based_EDA.

includes implementations of meta-heuristic algorithms. We run the experiments in a workstation with Intel(R) Xeon(R) E5-2620 v3 2.40 GHz CPU, NVIDIA GeForce GTX 980 GPU with 2 GB of DRAM, and 32 GB of RAM.

To perform the experimental analysis, we split the dataset into 70% for training and 30% for testing. In the pre-processing phase, we parse the HTML file of each document and extract raw text that represents the content. After we removed Spanish stop-words, tokenize the text, and the text size is set to 1000 tokens using zero as the padding value. The amount of parameters for the convolutional filter is 63,488 and the fully-connected layer has 4,485 parameters. In the following, we will use the term ecured-five-tags to refer to the proposed dataset.

Figure 2 shows the influence of different hyper-parameters values considering SGD and Adam. SGD has two hyper-parameters learning rate (α) and momentum (β), different values for each hyper-parameter were tested by performing 100 training epochs and averaging the means of each fold. The color graph on the left shows contour lines ranging from cool to warm colors indicating the fluctuations of the accuracy values for different combinations of hyper-parameters. In the case of Adam, α was considered as a hyper-parameter by searching for the optimal using the same procedure. The final configuration of the hyper-parameters was left for SGD with $\alpha = 0.0085$ and $\beta = 0.97$, and for Adam with $\alpha = 0.01$, such hyper-parameters can be used to reproduce experimental results.

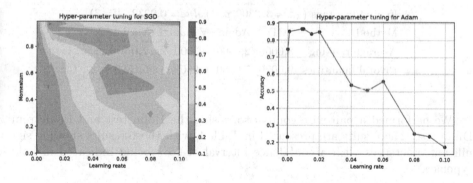

Fig. 2. Effects of hyper-parameter tuning considering SGD and Adam

For training CNN with SGD and Adam, we train with 400 epochs as maximum and 128 documents as batch size. After, we apply the CMA-ES for learning parameters on the fully connected layer making the second stage of the proposed method and comparing the results. To perform the second stage by EDA optimization, we use 200 individuals, 500 generations, initial step-size $\sigma = 0.095$, and mean of initial distribution in Ω vector is set to 0.02 for each parameter. Table 2 summarizes the different accuracy values obtained from a total of 30 measurements for each training algorithm. The results are compared considering the mean of the measurements and the best result is marked in bold typeface.

Table 2. Comparative measurement of accuracy considering the SGD, Adam and proposed methods

	Min	Max	Mean	Std-dev
SGD	0,8265	0,8844	0,8558	0,0132
Adam	0,7789	0,8980	0,8546	0,0265
Variant 1	0,8367	0,8912	0,8612	0,0120
Variant 2	0,7925	0,9014	**0,8627**	0,0243

To find significant statistical differences between the gradient-based methods and our proposals, normality tests were performed on the results using the Shapiro-Wilk test, detecting that some samples did not have a normal distribution. Therefore, we performed nonparametric tests using the Friedman ranking test with the accuracy obtained with the measurements on unseen data. Table 3 shows the results of chi-square statistic (χ^2), p-value, and degree of freedom (df). It can be seen from the average ranking that the results applying CMA-ES to adjust the weights of the fully connected layer achieve better results than using only SGD or Adam to train the entire CNN.

Table 3. Friedman test results for each methods

Ecured-five-tags ($\chi^2 = 3,3300, p-value= 0,0232$, df$= 3$)				
Method	SGD	Adam	Variant 1	Variant 2
Average ranking	3,0000	2,6500	2,3000	**2,0500**
Pivotal quantities	9,0000	7,9500	6,9000	6,1500

We performed a pair-wise comparison using the Holm test and Bonferroni Dunn test. The results are presented in Table 4, with those results showing significant differences with a confidence interval of 95% being indicated in bold typeface.

Table 4. Post-hoc test results considering best method

Holm		Bonferroni Dunn	
SGD	0,0131	SGD	**0,0131**
Adam	0,1437	Adam	0,2156
Variant 1	0,4533	Variant 1	1,0000

From the statistical test results, the proposed algorithm shows a significant improvement in accuracy over SGD. Experimental results indicate that the algorithm can obtain better results even if the previous results achieved in the first phase are worse. With this, the algorithm takes advantage of using the speed of the gradient-based methods to adjust the parameters of the convolutional filters and the ability of the EDA to achieve fine-tuning effects on the fully connected layer.

4   Conclusions and Further Work

In this paper, we present a hybrid gradient-based method and CMA-ES together for training CNN in problems of text classification. The use of SGD and Adam as an optimizer in the first phase takes advantage of the speed of these methods to train the filters of the convolutional layers in the CNN, something that would not be appropriate to apply through population meta-heuristics due to the high parameterization of this type of ANN and the dimensionality of the nature of the problem. The application of EDA in the training of a part of the CNN, with fewer parameters, increases the accuracy of the results, starting from the filters learned by the gradient-based methods and learning the distribution of each variable of the optimization problem. Future analyses could make use of other population meta-heuristics as alternatives to EDA in the way of exploring the search space and transforming the objective function. In addition, to the use of Bayesian optimization methods for hyper-parameters tuning.

References

1. Hansen, N., Ostermeier, A.: Completely derandomized self-adaptation in evolution strategies. Evol. Comput. **9**(2), 159–195 (2001)
2. Hartmann, J., Huppertz, J., Schamp, C., Heitmann, M.: Comparing automated text classification methods. Int. J. Res. Mark. **36**(1), 20–38 (2019)
3. Indolia, S., Kumar, A., Mishra, S.P., Asopa, P.: Conceptual understanding of convolutional neural network- a deep learning approach. Proc. Comput. Sci. **132**, 679–688 (2018)
4. Kiefer, J., Wolfowitz, J.: Stochastic estimation of the maximum of a regression function. Ann. Math. Stat. **23**(3), 462–466 (1952)
5. Kingma, D.P., Ba, J.L.: Adam: a method for stochastic optimization. In 3rd International Conference on Learning Representations, ICLR 2015 - Conference Track Proceedings, pp. 1–15 (2015)
6. Kowsari, K., Meimandi, K.J., Heidarysafa, M., Mendu, S., Barnes, L., Brown, D.: Text classification algorithms: a survey (2019)
7. Larrañaga, P., Lozano, J.A.: Estimation of Distribution Algorithms: A New Tool for Evolutionary Computation, vol. 2. Springer, Heidelberg (2002). https://doi. org/10.1007/978-1-4615-1539-5
8. Le, L.T., Nguyen, H., Dou, J., Zhou, J.: A comparative study of PSO-ANN, GA-ANN, ICA-ANN, and ABC-ANN in estimating the heating load of buildings' energy efficiency for smart city planning. Appl. Sci. (Switzerland) **9**(13), 2630 (2019)
9. Liang, Y., et al.: Fusion of heterogeneous attention mechanisms in multi-view convolutional neural network for text classification. Inf. Sci. **548**, 295–312 (2021)

10. Luan, Y., Lin, S.: Research on text classification based on CNN and LSTM. In: Proceedings of 2019 IEEE International Conference on Artificial Intelligence and Computer Applications, ICAICA 2019, pp. 352–355 (2019)

11. Madera, J., Dorronsoro, B.: Estimation of distribution algorithms. In: Alba, E., Martí, R. (eds.) Metaheuristic Procedures for Training Neural Networks, 1 edn., pp. 87–108. Springer, Boston (2006). https://doi.org/10.1007/0-387-33416-5_5. ISBN: 978-0-387-33415-8

12. Mikolov, T., Sutskever, I., Chen, K., Corrado, G., Dean, J.: Distributed representations of words and phrases and their compositionality. In: Advances in Neural Information Processing Systems, pp. 1–9 (2013)

13. Minaee, S., Kalchbrenner, N., Cambria, E., Nikzad, N., Chenaghlu, M., Gao, J.: Deep learning based text classification: a comprehensive review (2020)

14. Nair, V., Mohapatra, S.K., Malhotra, R.: A machine learning algorithm for product classification based on unstructured text description. Int. J. Eng. Res. Technol. **7**(06), 404–407 (2018)

15. Ojha, V.K., Abraham, A., Snásel, V.: Metaheuristic design of feedforward neural networks?: a review of two decades of research. Eng. Appl. Artif. Intell. **60**, 97–116 (2017)

16. Pennington, J., Socher, R., Manning, C.D.: GloVe: global vectors for word representation. In: Proceedings of the 2014 Conference on Empirical Methods in Natural Language Processing (EMNLP), pp. 1532–1543. Association for Computational Linguistics (2014)

17. Raunak, V., Metze, F.: Effective dimensionality reduction for word embeddings. In: Proceedings of the 4th Workshop on Representation Learning for NLP (RepL4NLP-2019), , Florence, pp. 235–243. Association for Computational Linguistics (2019)

18. Reddy, T., Williams, R., Breazeal, C.: Text classification for AI education. In: Proceedings of the 52nd ACM Technical Symposium on Computer Science Education, SIGCSE 2021, pp. 1381. Association for Computing Machinery, New York (2021)

19. Rojas-Delgado, J., Trujillo-Rasúa, R., Bello, R.: A continuation approach for training Artificial Neural Networks with meta-heuristics. Pattern Recogn. Lett. **125**, 373–380 (2019)

20. Shen, H.: Towards a mathematical understanding of the difficulty in learning with feedforward neural networks. In: Proceedings of the IEEE Conference on Computer Vision and Pattern Recognition (CVPR), pp. 811–820 (2018)

21. Suyan, W., Entong, S., Binyang, L., Jiangrui, W.: TextCNN-based text classification for E-government. In: International Conference on Information Science and Control Engineering, ICISCE 2019, pp. 929–934 (2019)

22. Wang, R., Li, Z., Cao, J., Chen, T., Wang, L.: Convolutional recurrent neural networks for text classification. In: Proceedings of the International Joint Conference on Neural Networks, vol. 2019-July, no. 2018, pp. 1–6 (2019)

23. Wu, H., Liu, Y., Wang, J.: Review of text classification methods on deep learning. Comput. Mater. Continua **63**(3), 1309–1321 (2020)

A Novel Approach for Detection and Location of Cyber-Attacks in Water Distribution Networks

Claudia Rodríguez Martínez[1] [iD], Marcos Quiñones-Grueiro[1] [iD],
Cristina Verde[2] [iD], and Orestes Llanes-Santiago[1]([✉]) [iD]

[1] Universidad Tecnológica de La Habana José Antonio Echeverría, CUJAE,
19390 La Habana, Cuba
orestes@tesla.cujae.edu.cu
[2] Instituto de Ingeniería, UNAM, Mexico City, Mexico
cverde@unam.mx

Abstract. Most scientific contributions addressing cyber-security issues
in water distribution networks present proposals of detection systems and
very few propose location systems. A novel methodology for detection
and location of cyber-attacks in water distribution networks (WDNs) is
proposed in this paper. Structural analysis and autoencoder neural networks are effectively combined with a the control chart Adaptive Exponentially Weighted Moving Average (AEWMA). In the training phase,
the proposed detection and location framework only requires data from
normal operating conditions and knowledge about the behavioral model
of the system which represents an advantage over previous works that
demand for additional data of cyber-attacks. Among other advantages
of the proposed methodology are the high performance in the effective,
robust and early detection and the effectiveness of the location strategy.
The proposal was evaluated with the known case study BATADAL.

Keywords: Ciber-attacks · Water distribution networks · Pattern
recognition · Autoencoders · Structural analysis

1 Introduction

The advances in the information technologies and the industrial computing
have transformed the traditional water distribution networks (WDN) in cyber-
physical systems. The combination of physical processes with cyber-physical systems improves the service of the urban WDN but expose them to the potential
threats of cybernetic attacks [1,12]. In the last years, several water distribution and supply systems have received cyber-attacks [4]. This has motivated the
creation of cyber-security agencies for protecting and defending WDN.

Project No. 27 of National Program of Research and Innovation ARIA of CITMA,
Cuba.

In a bibliographic review about the cyber-security in WDN can be appreciated that the most algorithms address cyber-attack detection but few works are concerned with the location of the attacks being this a current open research problem [4,10,13]. At present, cyber-attack detection is based in the identification of abnormal patterns in the behaviour of the variables. Advanced methods use signal spectral analysis or the comparison between the ideal behaviour of the WDN (by using a model) with its current state [6,13].

The main objective of this paper is to propose a novel methodology for detection and location of cyber-attacks in WDN combining tools of computational intelligence and structural analysis which constitutes its main contribution. The methodology only requires the normal operating data, and it does not require a parameterized physical model of the network constituting both aspects other contributions of the paper. For the validation of the proposal, data from the BATADAL test problem were used [13].

The organization of the paper is as follows: in Sect. 2, the principal characteristics of computational tools and the structural analysis used in the paper are presented. In Sect. 3, the proposed methodology is described. In Sect. 4, this methodology is applied to the C-Town case study. An analysis and discussion of the obtained results is developed in Sect. 5. Finally, the conclusions and recommendations for future works are presented.

2   Materials and Methods

2.1   Adaptive Exponential Weighted Moving Average Chart

Exponentially weighted moving average (EWMA) is a univariate control chart used for detecting deviations in the mean of a signal [11]. The EWMA of a signal $x(t) \in \Re^p$ is defined as:

$$z(t) = \gamma \bar{x}(t) + (1 - \gamma)z(t - 1) \quad z(1) = \mu \tag{1}$$

The Adaptive EWMA (AEWMA) can detect either small or large shifts or both simultaneously. In this paper, the following score function is used [2]:

$$\phi(e) = \begin{cases} e + (1 - \gamma)k & if \ e < -k \\ \gamma e & if \ |e| \leq k \\ e - (1 - \gamma)k & if \ e > k \end{cases} \quad 0 \leq \gamma \leq 1 \text{ and } k \geq 0 \text{ are constants}$$

An abnormal pattern is detected when $z(t)$ exceeds the control limits $\mu \pm h\sigma$, where μ and σ are the mean and the standard deviation parameters of a reference signal and h is chosen with the aim to achieve a desired performance. To avoid false alarms, the Average of the Run Length (ARL) of the control chart is used as performance measure of the AEWMA control chart [2]. Several methods can be used to determine the design parameters γ and k. In this paper, those parameters are calculated as in [2].

$$\lambda = \ln(1.2219 - 0.04697 * \ln(ARL) + 0.45985 * \sqrt{\delta_{min}} - 0.02701 * \sqrt{\delta_{max}}) \quad (2)$$

$$k = \sqrt{4.846 + 1.5852 * \ln(ARL) - 2.8679 * \sqrt{\delta_{min}} - 1.7198 * \sqrt{\delta_{max}}} \quad (3)$$

2.2   Autoencoders

Autoencoders are deep neural networks with the aim to transform input patterns into outputs with a minimum distortion. They encode the input pattern in compressed form to the feature space and after decode this information with the objective to obtain a pattern as similar as possible to the original one [3].

Autoencoders are formally defined in [3] by the following elements: 1) $\mathfrak{X} = \{x_1, ..., x_m\}$ such as $x_i \in \Re^n$ a set of m vectors representing an input pattern, 2) $A : \Re^n \rightarrow \Re^p$ such as $n > p$ a function that represents the encoder, 3) $B : \Re^p \rightarrow \Re^n$ a function that represents the decoder, and 4) Δ is a distortion function (e.g. **L2** norm) defined in $\Re^n$ which measures the distance between the output pattern and the input pattern.

The autoencoder transforms a vector $x_i \in \Re^n$ into an output vector $A \circ B(x_i) \in \Re^n$. The autoencoder problem is to find the functions A and B such that the distortion function is minimized.

The cost function used in the training process is formulated as [8]:

$$J = \frac{1}{n}\sum_{j=1}^{n}\sum_{i=1}^{k}(x_{ij} - \hat{x}_{ij})^2 + \lambda * \Omega_{weights} + \beta * \Omega_{sparsity}$$

where

$$\Omega_{weights} = \frac{1}{2}\sum_{l=1}^{L}\sum_{j=1}^{n}\sum_{i=1}^{k}(\omega_{ji}^{(l)})^2$$

$$\Omega_{sparsity} = \sum_{i=1}^{D^{(2)}} KL(p\|\hat{p}_i) = \sum_{i=1}^{D^{(2)}} p * \log\left(\frac{p}{\hat{p}_i}\right) + (1 - p) * \log\left(\frac{1-p}{1-\hat{p}_i}\right)$$

$\Omega_{sparsity}$ is used to improve the learning in the training, $\Omega_{weights}$ is used to avoid overfitting, n represents the number of observations used in the training set, k represents the number of variables in the data training, L represents the number of hidden layers in the sparse autoencoder, ω_{ji} are the weights, $D^{(2)}$ is the number of neurons in the hidden layer, KL is the Kullback-Leibler divergence, $\hat{p}_i$ is the average activation of a single neuron obtained as $\hat{p}_i = \frac{1}{n}\sum_{j=1}^{n} z_i^{(2)}(x_j))$, $z_i^{(2)}(x)$ is the activation of a single neuron belonging to the hidden layer, p is a restriction imposed for $\hat{p}_i$, the weight decay parameter λ controls the relative importance of the first two terms in the cost function and the parameter β controls the weight of the sparsity penalty term.

2.3   Structural Analysis

Structural analysis is a model-based methodology that has been used for fault diagnosis in industrial processes [5]. In a similar way, it can be used to detect and locate cyber-attacks. The structural model of a system represents an abstraction of its behavioral model that permits to establish analytical redundancy relationships (ARRs) with the goal to detect and locate cyber-attacks in the system. The number of ARRs that can be defined depend on the known variables, and the structure of the system. ARRs represent a set of constraints/rules evaluated during system operation by using the variables calculated from the model and the measurements obtained from the system. If a cyber-attack occurs, one or several ARRs won't be consistent. The advantage of this methodology is the possibility to analyze the detectability and isolability of different cyber-attacks without requiring its analytical model. The behaviour model of a system can be defined by a pair $(\mathcal{C}, \mathcal{V})$ where $\mathcal{V} = v_1, v_2, ..., v_n$ represents a set of variables, and $\mathcal{C} = c_1, c_2, ..., c_m$ represents a set of constrains. The set of variables $\mathcal{V} = \mathcal{K} \cup \mathcal{X}$ where $\mathcal{K}$ represents the subset of known variables and $\mathcal{X}$ represents the subset of unknown variables.

Definition 1. *Structural model* [5]

   The structural model of the system $(\mathcal{C}, \mathcal{V})$ *is a bi-partite graph* $(\mathcal{C}, \mathcal{V}, \mathcal{E})$ *where* $\mathcal{E} \subset \mathcal{C} \times \mathcal{V}$ *is a set of edges defined by:*

$$e_{ij} \in \mathcal{E} = \begin{cases} (c_i, v_j) & \textit{if the variable } v_j \textit{ appears in the constraint } c_i \\ 0 & \textit{in other cases} \end{cases}$$

   A bi-partite graph has associated an incidence matrix [5]. In Structural Analysis, the possibility to establish ARRs implies that the graph has more constraints that unknown variables. Applying the canonical Dulmage-Mendelsohn decomposition [7] to the graph $(\mathcal{G})$, it can be divided in tree parts: the structurally over-constrained part $\mathcal{G}^+$ which has more constrains than unknown variables, the just-determined part $\mathcal{G}^0$ with the same number of constraints and unknown variables, and the structurally under-constrained part $\mathcal{G}^-$ with less constraints than unknown variables. The cyber-attacks that affect the constrains belonging $\mathcal{G}^0$ and $\mathcal{G}^-$ are not detectable.

3   Methodology for Detection and Location of Cyber-Attacks

The methodology proposed for the detection and location of cyber-attacks in this paper is shown in Fig. 1.

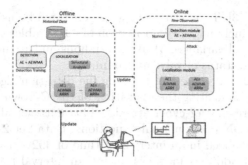

Fig. 1. Methodology proposed for detection and location of cyber-attacks

3.1   Offline and Online Stages

In the offline stage, an autoencoder is trained with data of normal operation for the detection process. In the training, a set of measurements obtained by the supervisory and data acquisition system (SCADA) are used. Together with the autoencoder, the parameters of the AEWMA control chart are tuned for detecting deviations. Also at this stage, experts will use structural analysis of the WDN to determine the ARRs that characterize each DMA into which the network is divided. For each ARR, an autoencoder is then trained with measured variables of the WDN in normal operation present in the respective ARR. Also, an AEWMA chart associated with each autoencoder is tuned to detect a deviation in the normal operation. The detection of an attack in a DMA can be characterized for the activation of one or several AEs simultaneously.

In the online stage, each new observation is analyzed by the detection module. If the observation is considered within the condition of normal operation, it can be used to update the training database in the offline stage. If the observation is not considered within the normal operation of the WDN, then it is analyzed with the combination of Autoencoder plus AEWMA established for each ARR in the location module. This observation should cause that the ARRs involved with the DMA under attack become inconsistent. This allows the location of the DMA where the cyber-attack is taking place.

4   Application of the Proposed Methodology to the C-Town Case Study

4.1   Case Study: C-Town WDN and BATADAL Datasets

C-Town is a medium-sized network based on real-world. The network consists of a single reservoir, 7 storage tanks, 429 pipes, 11 pumps distributed across 5 pumping stations (S1-S5), 388 junctions and 5 valves. Pumps, valves, and level sensors of the tanks are connected to 9 programmable logic controllers (PLCs) which form a cyber-network together with a central computer where a SCADA system coordinates the operations through the PLCs [9]. BATADAL data sets were introduced in [13]. Three data sets were generated by using the simulation package EPANET2 including the information of 43 variables sampled with fixed hourly intervals. Of all variables, 31 are continuous and 12 are binary variables corresponding to the status of valve and pumps.

Data Set 1 and 2 can be used for training the detection algorithms. Data Set 1 was generated by simulating the operation of the C-Town WDN during 365 days without the presence of cyber-attacks. This data set allows to study the operations of the WDN under normal conditions. Data Set 2 contains information of 7 attacks produced in an interval of time of 492 h. Data Set 3 contains the information of 7 additional attacks during an interval time of 407 h, and it should be used to test the performance of the detection algorithm after training. A complete characterization about Data Sets 2 and 3 can be seen in [13].

4.2   Detection Module in the Offline Stage

In the detection module the autoencoder is trained by using 8753 observations from normal operating data, and with a maximum number of epochs of 3000. Root Mean Square Error (RMSE) function is used as performance measure. After a grid search experiment, the parameters that allow to obtain the best performance are $p = 0.99$, $\lambda = 0.0001$, $\beta = 1$. After several experiments for different dimensions of latent space and for different combinations of the activation functions sigmoid and linear, the selected latent space dimension was 24 variables and the sigmoid and linear activation functions were chosen for encoder and decoder, respectively. In the case of the AEWMA chart, the values of the parameters were chosen as $ARL = 400$, $\delta_{min} = 0.5$, $\delta_{max} = 5$ and $h = 0.669338$, considering the results presented in [2]. Furthermore, by evaluating in (2) $\gamma = 0.102013$ and $k = 2.984267$ are obtained.

4.3   Location Module in the Offline Stage

The first step in this module is to establish the possible attack areas (AAs). For C-Town WDN, there are 5 DMAs and the first idea was to identify each DMA with an AA. However, DMA1 contains two sub-areas very important: the first is the Pumping Station 1 and the second is, the valve 2 which controls the distribution of water to DMA2 and DMA3. For that reason, two AAs were established for DMA1.

In the second step, structural analysis is developed by experts to determine if each AA can be characterized by one or several ARRs which allow to locate an attack. The following variables are available: the level (h) of each tank (t), the flow rate (q), the inlet and outlet pressure (p), and the status of each pump (p), as well as the flow and status of valve (v) 2. In the development of the structural analysis three subset of variables were defined: Attacks $(fdma\#, \# : 1, 2, .., 6)$, observable variables (always begin with $y...$), and system variables. The set of equations that describe the behavior of the system is shown in Table 1.

Table 1. Equations defined for the structural analysis

$e_1 : \{qp1, qp2, q1, qt1, h1, fdma1\}$	$e_{15} : \{yqp1, qp1\}$	$e_{29} : \{yp1a, p1a\}$
$e_2 : \{q1, p1a, p1d\}$	$e_{16} : \{yqp2, qp2\}$	$e_{30} : \{yp1d, p1d\}$
$e_3 : \{q1, qt1, q2, q5\}$	$e_{17} : \{yq2, q2\}$	$e_{31} : \{ypva, pva\}$
$e_4 : \{q5, q6, q7\}$	$e_{18} : \{yq3, q3\}$	$e_{32} : \{ypvd, pvd\}$
$e_5 : \{q2, pva, pvd, qt2, h2, fdma6\}$	$e_{19} : \{yq4, q4\}$	$e_{33} : \{yp2a, p2a\}$
$e_6 : \{q2, qt2, q3, q4\}$	$e_{20} : \{yq6, q6\}$	$e_{34} : \{yp2d, p2d\}$
$e_7 : \{q3, p2a, p2d, qt4, h4, fdma2\}$	$e_{21} : \{yq7, q7\}$	$e_{35} : \{yp3a, p3a\}$
$e_8 : \{q3, qt4\}$	$e_{22} : \{yh1, h1\}$	$e_{36} : \{yp3d, p3d\}$
$e_9 : \{q4, p3a, p3d, qt3, h3, fdma3\}$	$e_{23} : \{yh2, h2\}$	$e_{37} : \{yp4a, p4a\}$
$e_{10} : \{q4, qt3\}$	$e_{24} : \{yh3, h3\}$	$e_{38} : \{yp4d, p4d\}$
$e_{11} : \{q6, p4a, p4d, qt5, h5, fdma4\}$	$e_{25} : \{yh4, h4\}$	$e_{39} : \{yp5a, p5a\}$
$e_{12} : \{q6, qt5\}$	$e_{26} : \{yh5, h5\}$	$e_{40} : \{yp5d, p5d\}$
$e_{13} : \{q7, p5a, p5d, h6, h7, fdma5\}$	$e_{27} : \{yh6, h6\}$	
$e_{14} : \{q7, qt6, qt7\}$	$e_{28} : \{yh7, h7\}$	

An analysis of the structural isolability properties shown the possibility to isolate all defined attacks in a unique way. Figure 2a) shows the corresponding Dulmage-Mendelsohn decomposition where it is appreciated the isolability properties because attacks appear in different classes. For designing the residual generators, the structurally over-constrained minimal equation sets (SOMs) are determined. With them, and based on the Fault Sensitivity Matrix, the set of constrains that satisfy the specifications of isolability are determined. In this case, 28 SOMs were obtained and seven analytical redundant residuals (ARRs) were established which are shown in Fig. 2b).

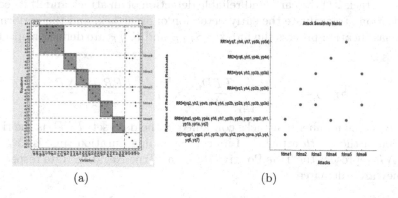

(a)   (b)

Fig. 2. (a) Dulmage-Mendelsohn decomposition (b) Attack sensitivity matrix

For each ARR an autoencoder was trained. In the training process, 8753 samples of normal operation of the WDN were used but only with the variables present in each ARR. Furthermore, the parameters of the AEWMA control charts associated with each autoencoder were established and they are shown in Table 2a) where DLS represents the dimension of the latent space. The same activation functions were used for the seven autoenconders: linear for the encoders and sigmoid for the decoders. After several experiments and considering the results presented in [2] the parameters for the seven AEWMA control charts of the location module in the offline stage were chosen. They are shown in Table 2b). A set of 289 observations of the data set 3 of the C-Town case study were used in the analysis of the performance of the AEWMA control charts because it contains data of attacks made to all AAs except to the AA4.

Table 2. a) Parameters of autoencoders and b) Parameters of AEWMA control charts in the location module

	Parameters of autoencoders				Parameters of AEWMA control charts					
ARRs	λ	p	β	DLS	ARL	δ_{min}	δ_{max}	h	γ	k
ARR1	0.0001	0.1	1	6	100	1.5	4	1.416963	0.416893	2.205357
ARR2	0.01	0.1	1	5	600	0.25	4	0.664883	0.095301	3.178406
ARR3	0.00001	0.1	1	3	300	0.5	5	0.956107	0.192733	2.817520
ARR4	0.00001	0.1	1	3	500	0.25	6	0.660161	0.095073	3.035565
ARR5	0.0001	0.1	1	9	400	0.25	6	0.666165	0.100697	2.969459
ARR6	0.001	0.1	1	12	500	0.25	6	0.660161	0.095073	3.035565
ARR7	0.01	0.1	1	12	600	0.25	6	0.660161	0.095073	3.035565

4.4   Performance Assessment

There are two important characteristics to be satisfied by a system for detection of cyber-attacks: 1) the early and reliable detection of an attack and 2) its correct classification. To evaluate the early detection of an attack, and the performance in the classification process the indexes S_{TTD} and S_{CLF} are defined respectively as:

$$S_{TTD} = 1 - \frac{1}{n_a} \sum_{i=1}^{n_a} \frac{TTD_i}{\Delta t_i}, \quad S_{CLF} = \frac{TPR + TNR}{2} \tag{4}$$

where n_a is the number of attacks contained in the data set, TTD_i is the time to detection of the $i - th$ attack and its corresponding duration time is Δt_i. TPR and TNR represent the True Positive Rate and True Negative Rate respectively, and they are calculated as:

$$TPR = \frac{TP}{TP + FN}, \quad TNR = \frac{TN}{TN + FP} \tag{5}$$

where TP is the true positive alarms, FN is false negative alarms, TN is true negative alarms and FP is false positive alarms.

Both index are integrated in an index of global performance

$$S_{GP} = \varsigma * S_{TTD} + (1 - \varsigma) * S_{CLF} \tag{6}$$

where ς determines the relative importance of the indexes S_{TTD} and S_{CLF} in the general index S_{GP}. In this paper $\varsigma = 0.5$ to give the same weight to early detection and correct classification. The False Alarm Rate (FAR) index is calculated as:

$$FAR = 1 - TNR \tag{7}$$

5   Results and Discussion

The performance of the detection system was evaluated by using 2089 observations from the data set 3 of the C-Town case study which contains the information about 7 cyber-attacks. The results of the detection system, the time to detection (TTD), the duration time (DT) of each cyber-attack expressed in number of observations, and the elements and attack area affected in each attack are shown in Fig. 3. In this figure, the blue line indicates the behaviour of the $z(t)$ variable corresponding to the AEWMA control chart of the detection system. The red horizontal line represents the limit of the AEWMA control chart for the normal operation of the WDN. With vertical lines, the start and the end time of each cyber-attack has been indicated. As can be observed, the seven attacks are detected.

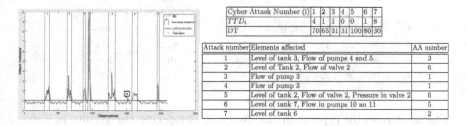

Cyber Attack Number (i)	1	2	3	4	5	6	7
TTD_i		4	1	1	0	0	1	8
DT		70	65	31	31	100	80	30

Attack number	Elements affected	AA number
1	Level of tank 3, Flow of pumps 4 and 5	3
2	Level of Tank 2, Flow of valve 2	6
3	Flow of pump 3	1
4	Flow of pump 3	1
5	Level of tank 2, Flow of valve 2, Pressure in valve 2	6
6	Level of tank 7, Flow in pumps 10 an 11	5
7	Level of tank 6	2

Fig. 3. Detection, time to detection, duration time, and elements and attack area affected in each cyber-attack for the data set 3,

Using the expression (4) the index $S_{TTD} = 0.9451$ was calculated. The observations of the data set were classified as: TP: 350, TN: 1612, FP: 70 and FN: 17. With these values and by using the expressions (5) and (7), the indicators $TNR = 0.9584$, $FAR = 0.0416$ and $TPR = 0.9582$ as well as the indexes $S_{CLF} = 0.9583$ and $S_{GP} = 0.9517$ were obtained. These results indicate the effectiveness of the detection system proposed.

To locate an attack satisfactorily, the observations during the attack should make non-consistent the ARRs that characterize the attacked area. However, four different alternatives can occur when an observation detected as attack is analyzed: A.1) Only the actual AA is activated, A.2) Several AAs are activated and the actual AA is included in them, A.3) One or several AAs are activated and the actual AA is not included and A.4) No AA es activated.

The first result to be pointed out is that the 70 observations classified as FP did not make non-consistent any ARR. Table 3 shows the other results obtained by the cyber-attack location system. The first column (**A**) indicates the attack number. The second column (**B**) indicates the number of observations during the presence of each attack. The third column (**C**) indicates the number of observations that active at least one AA. The next four columns (**D, E, F, G**) indicate the number of observations that satisfy the alternatives A.1, A.2, A.3 and A.4 respectively. The column **H** indicates the location rate (LR, percent of observations that activate at least one AA with respect the total number of observations during the presence of the attack $\frac{C}{B} * 100$). The column **I** shows the exact location rate (ExLR, percent of observations that activate only the actual AA with respect the number of observations that activate at least one AA during an attack $\frac{D}{C} * 100$) The last column (**J**) indicates the effective location rate (EfLR, percent of observations that activate the real AA with respect to the number of observations that activate at least one AA $\frac{D+E}{C} * 100$)

Table 3. Results of the cyber-attack location process

A	B	C	D	E	F	G	$H = \frac{C}{B} * 100$	$I = \frac{D}{C} * 100$	$J = \frac{D+E}{C}$
1	70	44	41	3	0	26	62.85	93.18	100
2	65	48	41	7	0	17	73.84	85.41	100
3	31	29	29	0	0	2	93.54	100	100
4	31	31	29	2	0	0	100	93.54	100
5	100	74	51	23	0	26	74	68.91	100
6	80	23	19	4	0	57	28.75	82.60	100
7	30	16	16	0	0	14	53.33	100	100
Total	407	265	226	39	0	142	65.11	85.28	100

The most relevant aspects of the analysis considering the results in Table 3 are the following:

- The LR index was 65.11%. Note that the cyber-attack 6 is the most affected.
- The ExLR index was 85.25% which represents a satisfactory result. In this case, the most negative incidence is in the attack 5 where 23 observations activate several AAs simultaneously.
- The EfLR index was 100% which is relevant because this indicates that the real AA is always activated for all observations that activate at least one AA. This result is very important for the operators because if the location process indicates several AAs, they can be sure that one of them is the real AA. If operators simultaneously analyze which AA has been activated for the greatest number of observations during the period of time under attack, they can identify the real AA.

6 Conclusions

In this paper, a methodology for detection and location of cyber-attacks in a water distribution network is presented. The proposal is based on the combined use of structural analysis with two computational intelligence tools: autoencoders and AEWMA control chart. The proposal permits to locate an attack which represents an advantage with respect to the most proposals present in the literature. Another advantage of the proposed methodology is that it only needs data corresponding to the normal operation of the WDN for training. To evaluate the detection process the indexes of early detection S_{TTD}, performance in classification S_{CLF} and global performance S_{GP} were defined. The obtained results demonstrates the robustness and attack detection capability of the first part of the proposed methodology. With respect to the location process, very satisfactory results were obtained in the indexes exact location rate, and the effective location rate which ensure the possibility of always determining the real attack area.

References

1. Adepu, S., Palleti, V.R., Mishra, G., Mathur, A., et al.: Investigation of cyber attacks on a water distribution system. In: Zhou, J. (ed.) ACNS 2020. LNCS, vol. 12418, pp. 274–291. Springer, Cham (2020). https://doi.org/10.1007/978-3-030-61638-0_16

2. Aly, A., Hamed, R., Mahmoud, M.: Optimal design of the adaptive exponentially weighted moving average control chart over a range of mean shifts. Commun. Stat.-Simul. Comput. 46(2), 890–902 (2015). https://doi.org/10.1080/03610918.2014.983650

3. Baldi, P.: Autoencoders, unsupervised learning, and deep architectures. In: Guyon, I., Dror, G., Lemaire, V., Taylor, G., Silver, D. (eds.) Proceedings of ICML Workshop on Unsupervised and Transfer Learning. Proceedings of Machine Learning Research, vol. 27, pp. 37–49. JMLR Workshop and Conference Proceedings, Bellevue, 02 July 2012

4. Berglund, E., Pesantez, J., Rasekh, A., Shafiee, M., Sela, L., Haxton, T.: Review of modeling methodologies for managing water distribution security. J. Water Resour. Plan. Manag. 146(8), 1–23 (2020). https://doi.org/10.1061/(ASCE)WR.1943-5452.0001265

5. Blanke, M., Kinnaert, M., Lunze, J., Staroswiecki, M.: Diagnosis and Fault-Tolerant Control. Springer, Heidelberg (2006). https://doi.org/10.1007/978-3-540-35653-0

6. Quiñones Grueiro, M., Llanes-Santiago, O., Prieto Moreno, A., Verde, C.: Decision support system for cyber attack diagnosis in smart water networks. IFAC-PapersOnLine 51(34), 329–334 (2019). https://doi.org/10.1016/j.ifacol.2019.01.024

7. Krysander, M., Frisk, E.: Sensor placement for fault diagnosis. IEEE Trans. Syst. Man Cybern. - Part A: Syst. Hum. 38(6), 1398–1410 (2008)

8. Ng, A.: Sparse autoencoder. Technical report, University of Stanford (2010). https://web.stanford.edu/class/cs294a/sparseAutoencoder.pdf

9. Ostfeld, A., et al.: Battle of the water calibration networks. J. Water Resour. Plann. Manag. **138**(5), 523–532 (2012). https://doi.org/10.1061/(ASCE)WR.1943-5452.0000191
10. Ramotsoela, D.T., Hancke, G.P., Abu-Mahfouz, A.M.: Attack detection in water distribution systems using machine learning. HCIS **9**(1), 1–22 (2019). https://doi.org/10.1186/s13673-019-0175-8
11. Roberts, S.: Control chart tests based on geometric moving averages. Technometrics **1**, 239–250 (1959)
12. Taormina, R., Galelii, S., Tippenhauer, N., Salomons, E., Ostfeld, A.: Characterizing cyber-physical attacks on water distribution systems. J. Water Resour. Plann. Manag. **143**(5), 04017009 (2017). https://doi.org/10.1061/(ASCE)WR.1943-5452.0000749
13. Taormina, R., et al.: The battle of the attack detection algorithms disclosing cyber attacks on water distribution networks. J. Water Resour. Plann. Manag. **144**(8), 04018048 (2018). https://doi.org/10.1061/(ASCE)WR.1943-5452.0000749

Identification of Non-linear Chemical Systems with Neural Networks

Reynold Alejandro Oramas Rodríguez$^{(\boxtimes)}$ ⓘ, Ana Isabel González Santos ⓘ, and Laura García González ⓘ

Technological University of Havana, 114 # 11901/Ciclovía and Rotonda, 19390 Marianao, Havana, Cuba

Abstract. This study proposes the use of neural networks, specifically NARX networks, in the modeling of non-linear chemical systems with the use of the control field systems identification methodology. The chemical reactor of the Tennessee Eastman, responsible for the greater non-linearities of the plant, is studied. First, a simple decentralized control scheme is proposed for the stabilization of the plant, an identification experiment is designed, and two sub-models are trained for the level and pressure of the reactor, obtaining satisfactory results.

Keywords: Tennesse Eastman · Neural networks · NARX · Systems identification · Non-linear systems

1 Introduction

In recent years, great attention has been paid to the modeling and identification of non-linear systems, because all real processes present non-linearities to some degree. The classical approach to this problem for years was to obtain linear models that were quite representative of the systems to be modeled, but there are cases in which non-linearities can cause significant errors in the identification problem. For this reason, several machine learning techniques and especially neural networks have been an important tool in recent years for the modeling of non-linear systems. In this work, the case of study is the Tennessee Eastman (TE) plant. This plant has been the object of study for 27 years and numerous investigations of various kinds have been developed on it. In [3] linear ARX, impulse response and state space models such as N4SID and CVA were identified, the latter being the best results. In [4] models of the plant reactor based on different structures of artificial neural networks trained by regression and the Levenberg-Marquardt (LM) algorithm were identified to compare their effectiveness when used in Model-based Predictive Controllers (MPC). In [5] state space models such as MOESP, N4SID and ORT were identified and compared. In [6] Genetic Programming was used to obtain a model of the plant reactor. In [7] a gray model of ET was obtained by modeling some variables by basic principles and others by identifying HAMMERSTEIN-WIENER models. In [8] a model based on a multilayer perceptron-type neural network was identified using the Swarm of Birds algorithm. In [9] a model based on neural networks trained with bio-inspired algorithms such as the Bat Algorithm, Firefly Algorithm, and Bee Colony

Y. Hernández Heredia et al. (Eds.): IWAIPR 2021, LNCS 13055, pp. 91–102, 2021.
https://doi.org/10.1007/978-3-030-89691-1_10

Algorithm was identified. In [10] a Digital Twin of the complete plant is obtained for monitoring and control. In [2, 11] and [12] decentralized control strategies are developed to stabilize and control the entire plant. In [13] a model of the reactor-separator of the plant is developed in the object-oriented modeling language Modelica.

Although in [4, 8] and [9] good models based on neural networks are obtained for the reactor of the TE plant, there is a lack of clarity in the obtaining process. For example, there is no explanation about the selection of input and output variables, and some that contribute to the dynamics of the system are ignored, such as reactant flows. According to [1] the TE plant is open-loop unstable, which is why an experiment cannot be carried out without its prior stabilization. This topic will be better explained in the next section, but it represents an important step in the identification process. In [4, 8] and [9] the authors are able to obtain a large data set, without giving an explanation of the topic, which leads to a lack of clarity in the assumptions, such as the operating conditions of the plant, this analysis is very important, because they are the conditions in which the obtained models will be valid for use. In addition, questions about the design of the experiment such as the type of signals used or their parameters are not specified, it is not taken into account whether the data sufficiently reflect the transient and stable dynamics of the plant. No explanation is offered on the selected neural network structure and regarding the validation of the obtained models, according to [15], it is necessary to perform a residual analysis, in addition to the fit indices such as the MSE and others. In the field of modeling and systems identification, the quantitative validity given by the adjustment of the obtained models is as important as the qualitative validity reflected in the preparation and rigor of the obtaining method. For these reasons, the objective of this work is to obtain models based on neural networks in a case study process, the TE plant, using the systems identification methodology to detail the process and guarantee the validity of the models.

2 TE Process

The Tennessee Eastman plant, was published in [1] as a simulation process for academic research. The TE process is a highly non-linear chemical process, created by a real system, with slight changes made to protect the identity of reactants and products, and features up to 6 modes of operation. This system is a reference problem for the process control community, providing a realistic simulation of a chemical industrial process of interest for analysis, control, monitoring and identification of systems. The process shown in Fig. 1 consists mainly of five operating units: a two-phase reactor, a condenser, a recycle compressor, a vapor-liquid separator, and a distillation column. The process has eight components, including four gaseous reactants (A, C, D, and E), two liquid products (G and H), an inert component (B), and a byproduct (F). As explained in [1] all reactions are irreversible and exothermic. Reaction rates are a function of temperature through the Arrhenius expression. Furthermore, the reactions are approximately first order with respect to reagent concentrations. The gaseous reactants feed into the reactor, where they react to form the two products. Gas phase reactions are catalyzed by a non-volatile catalyst dissolved in the liquid phase. The reactor has an internal cooling system to remove the heat of the reaction. The products leave the reactor as vapor along with the reactants that did not react while the catalyst remains in the reactor. The product stream from the reactor passes through a condenser and from there to a vapor-liquid separator. The non-condensed components are recycled through a centrifugal compressor to the reactor feed. The condensed components are moved towards a distillation column to remove the reagent residues, distilling them together with the reagent C feed. Products G and H exit the column towards a refining section that is not part of the process. Byproduct F is primarily purged from the system as steam in the separator. The complete plant has 12 manipulated variables, and 41 measured, continuous and discrete variables. All measurements have noise added to simulate the behavior of real sensors.

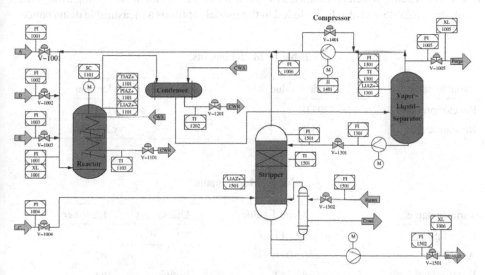

Fig. 1. Flow diagram of the Tennessee Eastman plant.

For this work, only a model of the plant's two-phase reactor will be identified, which is the sub-process responsible for the highest non-linearities of the process. In order to generate an input-output data set to identify a process model, it is first necessary to stabilize the plant, since it is open-loop unstable and has restrictions that when violated, the process stops immediately. The control strategy must prevent these restrictions from being violated while the plant is disturbed by excitation at the inputs. This model can then be used as the basis for a Model-based Predictive Controller, which would act at the supervisory level. However, to preserve as much process dynamics as possible, the number of controllers added to the plant should be kept to a minimum and the controllers are used solely to prevent the plant from violating its limitations. The control strategy is the one proposed in [5], which is a simplification of "Stage 1" and "Stage 2" proposed in [11] and [12]. As a result of the stabilization process, not all the manipulated variables mentioned in [1] are accessible. On the other hand, the controller references constitute additional manipulated variables of the stable process.

The measured variables that represent the outputs of the model are shown in Table 1, it should be clarified that the reactor temperature was not considered as a model output because with the implemented control strategy it becomes the variable manipulated by the pressure controller, in addition, as long as the pressure restriction is met, the temperature restriction is also met. The manipulated variables that will be considered as the inputs of the system for identification and their stable values for Mode 1 of operation of the plant are represented in Table 2. The flow of reactant E is not taken into account because it is the variable manipulated by the level controller. In addition to the manipulated variables, there is a measured variable that influences the behavior of the model outputs, the feed flow to the reactor, which is composed of the flow of A, D, E and the recycling flow of the plant, this variable will also be included in the model inputs as a measurable disturbance.

Table 1. Model outputs.

Variable name	Mode 1 value	Units	Identifier
Reactor pressure	2705.0	kPa	y1
Reactor level	75.0	%	y2

Table 2. Model inputs.

Variable name	Mode 1 value	Units	Identifier
D feed flow	24.644	%	u1
A feed flow	63.053	%	u2
Reactor feed flow	42.239	kscmh	u3
Setpoint reactor pressure	2705.0	kPa	u4
Setpoint reactor level	75.0	%	u5

3   Methodology

Obtaining the model will be based on the systems identification methodology shown in Fig. 2.

3.1   Experiment Design

In order to carry out the experiment for identification, it is necessary to know the excitation limits of the inputs, as well as the time constants of the system. To do this, a simple experiment is carried out, in which one input is varied at a time with a positive and a negative step, each with a duration of 5 h. In order not to violate the plant's restrictions, the inputs will be varied to ±10% of their value in Mode 1, except for the pressure

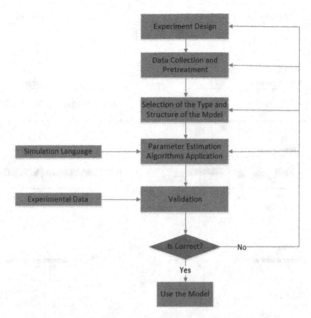

Fig. 2. System identification methodology.

reference in the reactor, which is the most critical, this will be varied by ±100 kPa. Figure 3 shows the response of the system outputs to a stimulus in the D and A flows, and in the pressure and level references. The experiment illustrates the variety in terms of time constants of the system. It is concluded that a pulse width of 5 h is sufficient to capture the transient and stable dynamics of the system and that, for the chosen varia- tions in the inputs, the outputs are far from violating any restriction. There is a risk that by stimulating all the inputs at the same time the variations in the outputs will be much larger, for this reason values relatively close to the operating point were chosen. It is very difficult to incorporate knowledge into a neural network, therefore, the quality of the network is dependent on the data used to train it. The training data must cover the entire range of inputs for which the network will be used, because neural networks, like other nonlinear black box models, do not extrapolate well. To comply with the above, the data for identification were generated by stimulating the manipulated variables with 'skyline' functions, with the maximum variations mentioned above and pulse width of 5 h.

3.2 Data Collection and Pretreatment

The main objective of data pre-treatment is to facilitate network training. The TE process has incorporated in its programming a random noise additive to all measurable variables, therefore, it is necessary to filter the signals to eliminate this noise. In this work, the data were filtered by a second-order Butterworth low-pass filter with a cut-off frequency of 10 rad/s to eliminate noise from high frequencies. A standard practice in data pretreat- ment to train neural networks is data normalization. As the inputs of the process differ

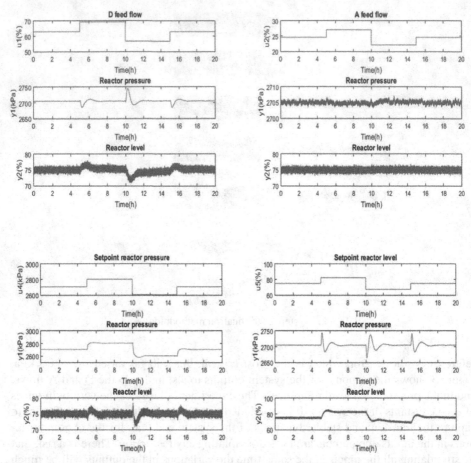

Fig. 3. Output response for a stimulus of + -10% in the flow of D and A and level reference, + -100 kPa in the pressure reference.

in magnitude, there is an undesired effect on the weights of the network, which try to compensate for the magnitude of the input so as not to saturate activation functions. A 500-h experiment was performed. The data obtained were filtered and normalized, remaining as shown in Fig. 4 and Fig. 5.

3.3 Selection of the Type and Structure of the Model

There is a great variety of neural network structures, each with the objective of solving a specific problem, as explain in chapter 6 of [14]. It is a great task to study in depth the characteristics, advantages and disadvantages of each structure in each situation. According to Chapter 14 of [15] neural networks can be classified into static and dynamic. Static are networks in which the output is calculated directly from the inputs through direct connections. In dynamic networks, the output depends not only on the current input of the network, but also on the previous inputs, outputs or states of the network. Dynamic

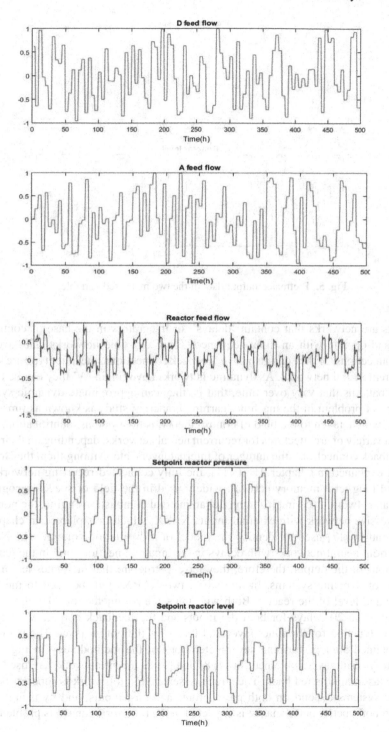

Fig. 4. Pretreated input data for the four manipulated variables and the measurable disturbance.

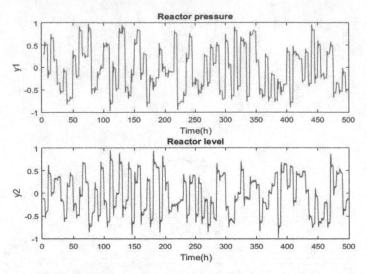

Fig. 5. Pretreated output data of the two measured variables.

networks are networks that contain 'delays', or integrators in the case of continuous inputs, and operate with an input sequence. These dynamic networks can have only direct connections, or they can also have feedback connections, the latter type are known as recurrent neural networks. As dynamic networks have 'memory' they can be trained to learn patterns that vary over time, that is, they can approximate dynamic systems. This type of problem in the machine learning branch of study is known as time series analysis, which, taken to the field of control theory, is the systems identification. There is a great variety of architectures for recurrent neural networks, depending on their direct and feedback connections, the number of internal layers, etc. Among them the Hopfield network explained in Chapter 21 of [15], the fully connected recurring networks, the short and long-term memory network widely used in the field of speech recognition, the Elman network, used in [16] to model an internal combustion engine, the nonlinear autoregressive network with external inputs NARX, which is explained in chapter 27 of [15] and in [17] used to identify the model of a distillation column. The NARXs are recurrent neural networks with delays in the input connections and in the feedback connections of the output, therefore, they have a structure that facilitates learning the behavior of dynamic systems. In this work, two NARXs will be used to model the pressure and level of the reactor. Both with the same parameters of 10 neurons in the input layer and 20 delays for both the inputs and the feedback output, with sigmoid activation function for the inner layer and linear for the output layer. The parameters were obtained after performing several iterations of the methodology in Fig. 2 until satisfactory results were obtained. In [4, 8] and [9] recurrent networks are used where only the last output is fed back. The structure selected in this work is superior because dynamic systems depend on both past outputs and past inputs, and by using several delays in both, better performance is expected in the time series analysis problem.

3.4 Estimation of Parameters, Application of Algorithms

The networks were trained with the Levenberg-Marquardt algorithm using the Neural Networks ToolBox of the MATLAB version R2015a software. To train each network, a 200-h fragment of the data set obtained and pretreated was chosen. Each network was trained a total of 5 times to avoid the local optimum problem and training was stopped when the performance of the network calculated by the least squared error stopped improving significantly.

3.5 Validation

For model identification or prediction problems, it is convenient to perform an analysis of prediction residuals or errors. The residues cannot be related to each other, nor to the sequence of the entries. For this, the autocorrelation function and the cross-correlation function are used. Figure 6 shows the autocorrelation graphs of the residuals for the two networks and in Fig. 7 the cross-correlation of the residuals with the inputs. For the residuals to be unrelated, the autocorrelation function must give an impulse at the instant $T = 0$ and the rest of the values be within the confidence interval denoted by the dashed lines, in Fig. 6 it is observed that this is not fulfilled at all, although it is an acceptable result for this type of problem. For the cross correlation, the residuals must be within the confidence interval at all times. Figure 7 shows that this is true for the two networks. In order to validate whether a black box model is representative of the system that was identified, it is vital to perform a cross-validation, that is, to analyze the behavior of the model in the face of a different data set than the one used for training. Figure 8 and Fig. 9 show the behavior of the two networks for 100 h of data, different from those used during training. Table 3 shows the calculation of the percentage of fit (FIT) and the mean square error (MSE) of the models and their analogues with the best results in [8] and [9], the BSA and the ANN-BA respectively. As can be seen, the models obtained in this work have competitive results, despite the global optimization techniques used for training the networks in [8] and [9]. This is mainly due to the work carried out throughout the identification process, from the selection of the input variables, the design of the experiment and the selection of a better neural network structure.

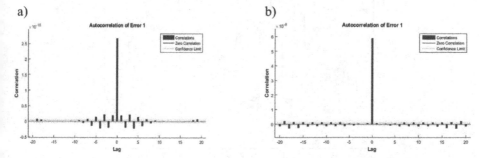

Fig. 6. Autocorrelation of the residuals. a) Reactor pressure, b) Reactor level.

a)   b)

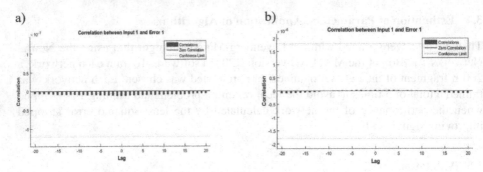

Fig. 7. Cross correlation of the residuals and the inputs. a) Reactor pressure, b) Reactor level.

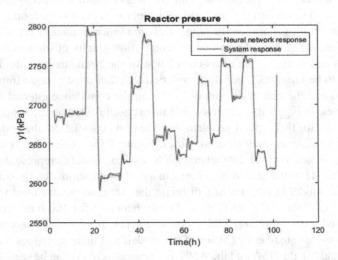

Fig. 8. Response of the reactor pressure network for the validation data.

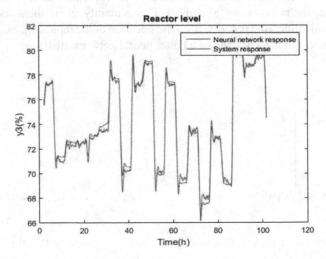

Fig. 9. Response of the reactor level network for the validation data.

Table 3. Validation indices calculated for the models.

Variable name	Reactor pressure	Reactor level	Reactor pressure [8]	Reactor level [8]	Reactor pressure [9]	Reactor level [9]
FIT	96.77%	91.32%	–	–	84.668%	90.167%
MSE	$2.3005*10^{-4}$	$1.1*10^{-3}$	0.0411	0.4321	$9.37*10^{-2}$	$1.29*10^{-2}$

4 Conclusions and Future Work

In the present investigation, a model based on NARX-type neural networks was obtained for the chemical reactor of the Tennessee Eastman plant using the systems identification methodology, the main objective of the work. Specifically, a decentralized control was implemented to stabilize the plant, an identification experiment was carried out to obtain the data with which two recurrent neural networks of the NARX type were trained to model the level and pressure in the reactor. The models obtained present good results. This work shows that rigor and preparation in the system identification process not only gives qualitative validity to the resulting models, but also directly influences their performance. This paper will serve as the basis, for the authors, in future studies on the main problems when using neural networks as models of dynamic systems: the lack of generalization, local minimums in the training process and the lack of tools to incorporate the physical knowledge of the system in the models.

References

1. Downs, J.J., Vogel, E.: A plant-wide industrial process control problem. Comput. Chem. Eng. **17**(3), 245–255 (1993)
2. Ricker, N.L.: Decentralized control of the tennessee eastman challenge process. J. Proc. Cont. **6**(4), 205–221 (1996)
3. Juricek, B.C., Seborg, D.E., Larimore, W.E.: Identification of the Tennessee Eastman challenge process with subspace methods. Control Eng. Pract. **9**, 1337–1351 (2001)
4. Sheta, A., Braik, M., Al-Hiary, H.: Identification and model predictive controller design of the tennessee eastman chemical process using ANN. In: Proceedings of the 2009 International Conference on Artificial Intelligence, ICAI 2009, 13–16 July 2009, Las Vegas Nevada, USA, 2 Volumes (2009)
5. Bathelt, A., Jelali, M.: Comparative study of subspace identification methods on the tennessee eastman process under disturbance effects. In: 5th International Symposium on Advanced Control of Industrial Processes 28–30 May 2014, Hiroshima, Japan (2014)
6. Sheta, A., Faris, H.: Identification of the Tennessee Eastman chemical process reactor using genetic programming. Int. J. Adv. Sci. Technol. **50**, 121–140 (2013)
7. González, L.G., González Santos, A.I.: Desarrollo de un modelo de caja gris para el caso base de la planta Tennessee Eastman. RIELAC **41**, 18–33 (2020)
8. Aljarah, I., Faris, H., Mirjalili, S., Al-Madi, N., Sheta, A., Mafarja, M.: Evolving neural networks using bird swarm algorithm for data classification and regression applications. Clust. Comput. **22**(4), 1317–1345 (2019). https://doi.org/10.1007/s10586-019-02913-5

9. Sheta, A., Braik, M., Al-Hiary, H.: Modeling the Tennessee Eastman chemical process reactor using bio-inspired feedforward neural network (BI-FF-NN). Int. J. Adv. Manuf. Technol. **103**, 1359–1380 (2019)
10. He, R., Chen, G., Dong, C., Sun, S., Shen, X.: Data-driven digital twin technology for optimized control in process systems. ISA Trans. **95**, 221–234 (2019)
11. McVoy, T.J., Ye, N.: Base control for the Tennessee Eastman problem. Comput. Chem Eng. **18**(5), 383–413 (1994)
12. McVoy, T.J., Ye, N., Gang, C.: An improved base control for the Tennessee Eastman problem. In: Proceedings of the American Control Conference, Seatle, Washington, June 1995
13. Martin-Villaba, C., Urquia, A., Shao, G.: Implementations of the Tennessee Eastman process in Modelica. IFAC PapersOnLine. **51**(2), 619–624 (2018)
14. Brunton, S.L., Kutz, J.N.: Data Driven Science & Engineering Machine Learning, Dynamical Systems, and Control. Cambridge University Press, Cambridge (2019)
15. Hagan, M.T., Demuth, H.B., Beale, M.H., De Jesús, O.: Neural Network Design. 2nd edn. PSW Publising (1996). ISBN: 0-971732 1-0-8
16. Contreras, W., Arichávala, M., Jérez, C.: Determinación de la presión máxima de compresión de un motor de encendido provocado basado en una red neuronal artificial recurrente. INGENIUS **19**, 9–18 (2019)
17. Hieu, D.X., Anh, D.T.L., Phuoc, N.D., Thanh, D.V., Cuong, D.D.: Temperature prediction and model predictive control (MPC) of a distillation column using an artificial neural network based model. In: 2017 International Conference on System Science and Engineering (ICSSE), Ho Chi Minh City, pp. 113–118 (2017). https://doi.org/10.1109/ICSSE.2017.8030848

Convolutional Neural Networks as Support Tools for Spinocerebellar Ataxia Detection from Magnetic Resonances

Robin Cabeza-Ruiz[1]([envelope]) [iD], Luis Velázquez-Pérez[2,3] [iD],
and Roberto Pérez-Rodríguez[1] [iD]

[1] CAD/CAM Study Centre, University of Holguin, XX Anniversary, Holguin, Cuba
[2] Cuban Academy of Sciences, Havana, Cuba
[3] Centre for the Research and Rehabilitation of Hereditary Ataxias,
Libertad Street, Holguin, Cuba

Abstract. Spinocerebellar ataxias (SCAs) are a group of neurodegenerative diseases, characterized by loss of balance and motor coordination due to dysfunction of the cerebellum and its afferent and efferent pathways. For a better characterization, usually volumetric analysis is performed using magnetic resonance imaging. This task, which involves cerebellum segmentation, is generally performed by hand, and can be exhausting due to the amount of time and level of expertise needed. For this reason, an automatic tool for performing cerebellum segmentation from magnetic resonances is needed. Convolutional neural networks (CNNs or convnets) are a state-of-the-art deep learning technique, based on the human brain functioning, and have been successfully applied in medical image processing field. In this paper we present and compare two CNN architectures for human cerebellum and brainstem segmentation. Results confirm that convnets are very useful tools for this task, and can be applied on automatic SCAs characterization from magnetic resonances.

Keywords: Spinocerebellar ataxias · Artificial intelligence · Convolutional neural networks · Cerebellum · Segmentation

1 Introduction

1.1 Spinocerebellar Ataxias

Spinocerebellar ataxias (SCAs) are a group of neurodegenerative disorders, phenotypic and genotypically heterogeneous, characterized by loss of balance and motor coordination, due to malfunctioning of the cerebellum and its afferent pathways [1, 2].

These diseases are mainly characterized by gait ataxia, dysarthria, dysmetria, postural instability, which may be accompanied by extracerebellar signs like movement disorders (including dystonia, parkinsonism, and chorea), dementia, epilepsy, visual disorders, neuropathy, etc. [2, 3]. Three patterns of macroscopic atrophy reflecting damage

© Springer Nature Switzerland AG 2021
Y. Hernández Heredia et al. (Eds.): IWAIPR 2021, LNCS 13055, pp. 103–114, 2021.
https://doi.org/10.1007/978-3-030-89691-1_11

of different neuronal system are recognized in spinocerebellar ataxias, named spinal atrophy (SA), olivopontocerebellar atrophy (OPCA) and cortico-cerebellar atrophy (CCA) [4].

Neuroimaging has been widely used to diagnose SCAs, since 1995, when Kumas [5] described their principal characteristics, obtained from computed tomographies, in children with olivopontocerebellar atrophy. In particular, magnetic resonance images (MRIs) are a good option for organs segmentation and volumetric characterizations [6], and have a predominant diagnostic role with respect to other techniques like single-photon emission computed tomographies (SPECTs) and positron emission tomographies (PETs) [7], based on the visual detection of SA, OPCA and CCA. According to Klaes et al. [8], magnetic resonance imaging is the best – studied biomarker candidate for spinocerebellar ataxias.

Medical image segmentation is typically used to locate objects of interest and their boundaries to make the representation of a volumetric image stack more meaningful and easier for analysis [9]. For instance, neurological MRI volumetric studies have been conducted to compare different stages of the disease and their correlation with symptoms severity [10]. Generally, this process is made by hand, slice by slice, and can be very time-consuming. Automatic detection of these features, might improve the speed of the diagnosis process.

1.2 Convolutional Neural Networks

Convolutional neural networks (CNNs or convnets) [11, 12] have demonstrated outstanding performances at tasks such as hand-written digit classification, face and contour detection [13], automatic video processing [14], neurological behavior analysis and prediction [15, 16], and others. A single convnet is composed of a series of layers, each of them including various filters which conduce to the image's processing result.

CNNs have been used in variety of studies for brain MRI processing. Kamnitsas et al. [17] used a standard 3D structure joint with Conditional Random Fields for segmenting brain lesions, while Erden et al. [18] explored the U–Net architecture [19] for the same purpose, taking advantage of combinations of features produced in each layer of the structure.

Moeskops et al. [20] proposed using two U-Net models, joint through adversarial training, achieving good results on anatomic brain structure segmentation. Some approaches [21–24], in the aim of reducing computational cost on training stage, use 2D CNNs, obtaining a faster processing for the same task. Mehta et al. [25] created a convnet which mixes 2D and 3D feature patches, giving the possibility to the system for more combination of features. A similar approach was used by Chen et al. [26], using 2D and 3D Resnet [27] architectures. Recently, Carass et al. [28] performed cerebellum parcellation using three distinct CNN architectures, overpassing scores obtained with other techniques. Han et al. [29, 30] improved this approach, using two convnets for the task: the first one obtains the coordinates of the most – likely cerebellum position on the MRI, and then the second, based on U-Net, makes a fully parcellation, performing a 28-channel binary segmentation, one channel for each cerebellar region. Talo et al. [31], created an architecture for lesion classification over 2D images, obtaining a system which could be integrated in some retrieval system for SCA-like diseases.

Based on the results obtained by previous researches, is our goal to evaluate convolutional neural networks as a tool for helping clinicians to diagnose and characterize spinocerebellar ataxias from brain magnetic resonances. In this paper, we compare two CNN-based methods for automatic cerebellum and brainstem segmentation from MRIs. One of these uses the inception technique [24], configured in small circuits. The best of the models is evaluated for cerebellar volume calculation, comparing against the ground truth segmentations.

2 Materials and Methods

Proposed methods are both based on 3D U-Net. Used layers were max pooling (Max-Pool) for dimensionality reduction, concatenation (Concat), convolution (Conv) and transposed convolution (TranspConv), and all activation layers are Rectified Linear Unit (ReLU) [32]. The models are significantly small (about 500 000 parameters each one), giving the possibility of execution in computers without great resources.

Our first model (M1) is composed of three down sampling and three up sampling sections. The two first sequences in the encoder are composed Conv-Conv-MaxPool (two convolutional layers followed by one max pooling operation), and the third one has three convolutional layers instead of two. For each one of these sequences, the used stride for max pooling operation was two, reducing dimensions by half each step. In decoding section, three Conv-Conv-TranspConv (two convolutional layers followed by a transposed convolution) sequences were used. The outcomes of transposed convolutions are concatenated with partial results from the encoding phase, giving the network more features to analyze. Finally, a single-filter convolutional layer returns the output of the system. The network has a total of 372 521 parameters. We used a small number of parameters with the purpose of reducing computational complexity of the system. Figure 1 shows the model.

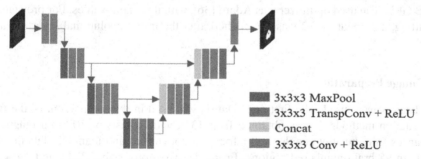

■ 3x3x3 MaxPool
■ 3x3x3 TranspConv + ReLU
▨ Concat
■ 3x3x3 Conv + ReLU

Fig. 1. First U-Net model without inception modules (M1)

Second proposed architecture (M2) results more complex. The system counts with four down samplings, and four up samplings. Besides, all Convolutional layers in the original U-Net [19] were substituted by inception modules: thus, all encoding section consists on Inception-MaxPool sequences, and decoding section is composed of Inception-TranspConv. Also, TranspConv outcomes are concatenated with partial results

from encoding section. The same as in M1 model, the last layer is a single-filter convolution, returning the final segmentation. Inception modules used in this investigation
are composed of 3D convolutions with sizes ($1 \times 1 \times 1$) and ($3 \times 3 \times 3$), one Max-
Pool operation, and one single concatenation as the final layer. This second model was
inspired in [33], but with a much more simple architecture: the used inception modules
are significantly smaller, and the number of filters on each stage is smaller too. The
architecture is slightly bigger than M1, with a total of 550 097 learnable parameters.
Figure 2 shows the architecture. The objective of the inception was to take advantage of
big number of image features, without increasing the network depth. The selected inception architecture (Fig. 2b), with less connections than usual, helps on taking advantage
of a big number of features, while reduces the number of learnable parameters.

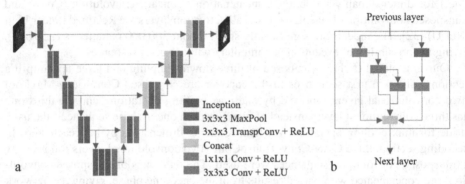

Previous layer

Inception
3x3x3 MaxPool
3x3x3 TranspConv + ReLU
Concat
1x1x1 Conv + ReLU
3x3x3 Conv + ReLU

Next layer

a   b

Fig. 2. Second U–Net model (M2). In (a) the general network structure, and (b) shows the
proposed inception circuit.

Implementation was made with Keras [34] and TensorFlow backend [35], using
Python 3.7 programming language, and the training was done on Tesla P100-SXM2
16 GB GPU. The used optimizer was Adam [36], with its default values. For preventing
overfitting, a dropout of 0.2 was established after the last convolutional layer of each
model.

2.1   Image Preparation

Two datasets were used. The first one (Data1) was used in the comparison of the two
segmentation methods. It was obtained from [37], and consists of 30 brain magnetic
resonances from healthy people, in T1 format, anonymized and manually labelled by
experts in 95 brain numbered regions. From all 95 regions, only 17, 18 and 19 were
used, which correspond to right and left cerebellum, and brainstem, respectively.

The second dataset (Data2) was obtained by joining Data1 with 14 magnetic resonance images retrieved from the Cuban Neurosciences Center. The new acquired MRIs
consisted on five healthy controls, five presymptomatic carriers of SCA2, and four SCA2
patients. The preprocessing stage for this second dataset was the same as Data1, but this
time no skull stripping was made. Also, for this dataset, only the cerebellum segmentation
was available, obtained with help of ACAPULCO [29, 30]. ACAPULCO (Automatic

Cerebellum Anatomical Parcellation using U-net with Locally Constrained Optimization) is a system for performing cerebellum parcellation. For our purposes, the whole cerebellum mask was conformed as the union of all the lobules obtained with ACA-PULCO. Calculated masks were then manually corrected using the software ITK-Snap [38].

On preprocessing stage, all images were passed through a bias field correction (BFC) stage using N4 method [39]. After BFC, a registration was made to MNI 152 space [40], using exhaustive technique. Skull striping was made, removing non-brain tissue (eyes, fat, skull). Finally, intensities were rescaled to range [0; 255], and histogram equalization was applied to all MRIs.

As an extra step with the aim of reducing computational complexity on models, after MNI registration, images were cropped to smaller volume with dimensions ($128 \times 128 \times 96$). The selected volume consists on the localization of cerebellum and brainstem in all MRIs, expanded by a number of slides on each axis. The whole preprocessing stage can be observed in Fig. 3.

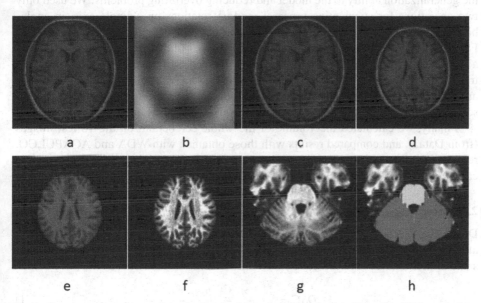

Fig. 3. Preprocessing phases example. Original imaging (a), calculated bias (b), BFC result (c), registration result (d), skull stripping (e), histogram equalization (f), cropping (g) and masks of the interesting organs; red shows the cerebellum, and green represents the brainstem. (Color figure online)

2.2 Analysis Description

The first dataset (Data1), consisting of 30 MRIs of healthy subjects, was used to discern between the most suitable architecture for the segmentation task. In this stage we used 18 images for training, six for validation, and six for testing purposes. Each model was trained over 200 epochs.

After this stage, we took the model we thought was more convenient for anatomic structure segmentation from the MRIs, and retrained it on the second dataset (Data2) with the aim of performing deeper analysis. For that, we used 25 images for training, nine for validation, and 10 for testing purposes. Table 1 shows the created partitions.

Table 1. Partitions created from Data2

Partition	Healthy subjects	Presymptomatic carriers	SCA2 patients
Train	21	3	1
Validation	7	1	1
Evaluation	7	1	2

Data augmentation was used for the training over Data2, with the goal of increasing the generalization ability to the model and reducing overfitting problems. We used only two operations for augmenting process: random rotations on a single axis, in angles between $-45°$ and $45°$, and random shifts in the range $[-20; 20]$ pixels on each axis. For each image on the train and validation sets, 10 new artificial ones were created, giving a total of 384 MRIs. For an evaluation on the incidence of the data augmentation, we trained the model with and without data augmentation (WDA and NDA, respectively), and then compared the results. No data augmentation was performed over the evaluation set, and no postprocessing operations were made for any of the analysis here described.

Finally, we calculated the volume of the whole cerebellum on the 10 test images (from Data2), and compared results with those obtained with WDA and ACAPULCO, respectively. The objective of this step was to verify the possibility of automatically capturing the loss of volume caused by SCA2 on patients, from brain MRIs.

2.3 Metrics

Dice score, Jaccard index, sensitivity and specificity were used as the metrics for evaluating the segmentations. Dice score (DSC) allows comparison between two volumes of same dimensions through the Eq. 1:

$$DSC = \frac{2 \times \sum_i^N p_i g_i}{\sum_i^N p_i^2 + \sum_i^N g_i^2} \tag{1}$$

where N represents the total number of voxels in one image, p belongs to the prediction volume, and g belongs to the ground truth volume [41]. Jaccard index (JI) can be calculated with the Eq. 2 [42]:

$$JI = \frac{\sum_i^N p_i g_i}{\sum_i^N p_i + \sum_i^N g_i - \sum_i^N p_i g_i} \tag{2}$$

Sensitivity (SN) allows to evaluate the voxels which have been correctly classified as positive through the Eq. 3 [43]:

$$SN = \frac{TP}{TP + FN} \tag{3}$$

on the other side, specificity (SP), refers to the proportion of those voxels which do not belong to the ground truth mask, and can be obtained with the Eq. 4 [43]:

$$SP = \frac{TN}{FP + TN} \tag{4}$$

where TP and TN are the number of voxels which have been correctly recognized as part of the mask and as part of the background, respectively, and FP, FN correspond to those voxels incorrectly identified as part of the mask and the background, respectively.

3 Results and Discussion

Figure 4 shows the comparison between evaluation results for the two proposed methods on dataset Data1.

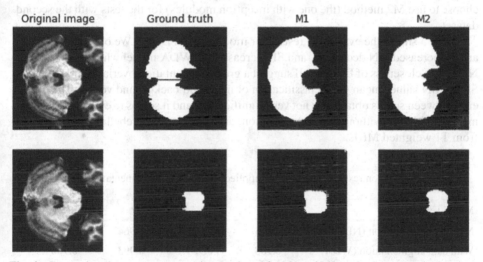

Fig. 4. Comparison between segmentation produced for M1 and M2 methods on Data1. First row shows cerebellum masks, and second row displays brainstem masks

The figure shows that both architectures segmented brainstem and cerebellum with good precision. There are some irregularities on the edges, which can be removed in future investigations. It can be observed than M2 was capable of finding the cerebellum and brainstem boundaries with a better correctness than M1. This gives us an idea of the convenience of using inception modules for segmentation task, increasing the chance of finding the correct feature set. Table 2 shows the scores achieved in evaluation over Data1.

Results are promising for both methods. Nevertheless, all images in Data1 have a very good quality; perhaps this could have some influence in results. The evaluation, performed on six unseen MRIs, shows a good behavior for the anatomic structure segmentation from T1 – weighted images. M2 method (using inception modules) achieved a

Table 2. Evaluation results for comparing M1 and M2 on dataset Data1

Method	Brainstem				Cerebellum			
	DSC	JI	SP	SN	DSC	JI	SP	SN
M1 (no inception)	**0.926**	**0.861**	0.988	0.982	0.946	0.897	0.966	0.993
M2 (inception)	0.923	0.859	0.994	0.966	**0.954**	**0.915**	0.975	0.992

better DSC and JI than M1 (without inception, and less profound) on cerebellum segmentation. M2 method obtained slightly lower scores than M1 for brainstem segmentation, but the difference on DSC and JI (0.003 and 0.002, respectively) is not considered as meaningful for discerning in which is better for segmenting this brain structure. Sensitivity and specificity scores suggest that both methods had a better behavior recognizing background voxels for the cerebellum, and the opposite for the brainstem. However, we choose to use M2 method (the one with inception modules) for the tests with the second dataset.

Table 3 shows the evaluation results for model M2 on Data2. We observe how DSC and JI increased. SN decreased, and SP increased for WDA model while decreased for NDA. The closeness of DSC and JI suggest a good segmentation overlap, while the high SP and SN values mean good classification of mask and background voxels. The difference between scores obtained is not very significative, and it seems to evidence that both models, with and without data augmentation, are suitable for cerebellum segmentation from T1 weighted MRIs.

Table 3. Evaluation results for model M2 applied to cerebellum segmentation from Data2

Model version	DSC	JI	SP	SN
No data augmentation (NDA)	0.963	0.932	0.964	0.941
With data augmentation (WDA)	**0.968**	**0.939**	**0.993**	**0.966**

Interestingly, the absence of skull stripping seems not to have significance in segmentation results. This conclusion, and the opinion of some authors that skull stripping can sometimes remove parts of the cerebellum [30], encourages us to eliminate it from the preprocessing stage on future investigations. Figure 5 shows a comparison between segmentation results for one of the test images, belonging to a SCA2 patient. Both methods seem to be capable of successfully segmenting the cerebellum. Segmentation results are both very close to ground truth. Yet, the results from NDA model contains some greater errors, which can be appreciated marked in red squares in Fig. 5b. This could be related with the difference on training samples, as NDA model used only 25 images. Figure 6 shows a comparison between segmentations produced for a new artificial image, created through data augmentation.

As the figure shows, this time the model without data augmentation (NDA) was not capable of correctly finding the contours of the cerebellum. The error (marked with a red

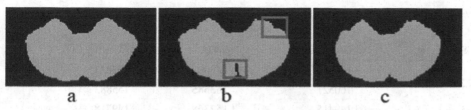

Fig. 5. Segmentation comparison for one of the test MRIs. Ground truth mask (a), followed by mask obtained with NAD model (b) and WAD model (c). The major errors were obtained with NAD model, resulting in a considerably smaller volume estimation.

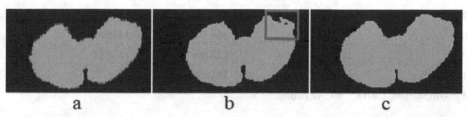

Fig. 6. Segmentation comparison for one test MRI, which has been displaced and rotated. Ground truth segmentation (a), followed by segmentation with NAD model (b), and with WAD model (c). Once again, the major errors were produced with NAD model (marked in red), resulting in the loss of information. (Color figure online)

rectangle), leads to big information loss, as parts of the cerebellum would be ignored. This result clearly indicates that it does not possess sufficient generalization, and is not able to process displaced or rotated MRIs. Based on Fig. 5 and Table 3, however, NDA should be able to perform a good segmentation if the registering process does not fail.

The whole cerebellar volumes were calculated for the masks generated with WAD model. The calculations were made only for the 10 images of the evaluation subset, and the results were compared with ACAPULCO pretrained model outcomes. Comparison can be done in Table 4.

Each architecture performed better on five of the 10 images. The results indicate that WDA model should be more reliable for finding cerebellar volume loss, as it identified the correct volume of the two SCA2 patients with a high grade of precision. ACA-PULCO prediction was closer for the presymptomatic carrier and four of the healthy patients. In most of samples, ACAPULCO predictions were smaller than the ground truth segmentations. We suspect this phenomenon takes place, due to de difference on training datasets, because ACAPULCO was used with a pretrained model provided by the authors. In contrast, WDA model mainly segments greater volumes. We think that adding a postprocessing stage could improve results, as well as bigger number of training epochs. Further analysis should be made in order to discern in which algorithm results better for cerebellar volume estimation, using bigger architectures and new datasets to compare.

Performed tests allow us to confirm that convnets are capable of precisely segment human cerebellum and brainstem from MRIs. The small size of the datasets, as well as the unbalanced imaging types (Data2 consists of 35 healthy subjects, and only five

Table 4. Calculated volumes using each method, compared with the ground truth (in mm^3)

Subject no.	Ground truth	WDA	ACAPULCO
1	138921	143001	**135033**
2	160527	**163685**	155883
3	149415	152368	**149718**
4	150687	**152068**	146179
5	144754	151905	**141942**
6	144416	154712	**152927**
7	173560	**177178**	143293
8 *	140691	144078	**140596**
9 **	126190	**128265**	112160
10 **	161586	**161554**	148233

*Presymptomatic carrier **SCA2 patient

presymptomatic carriers and four SCA2 patients) do not permit us to affirm that our model will correctly obtain the loss of volume on patients. Further investigations must be made on this way, using larger and more balanced datasets. Despite that, based on the accurate segmentation results, our analysis presents convnets as promising tools for being incorporated on SCAs diagnosis and characterization. Results could help specialists to perform various studies on the damaged structures, approximating the stage of the disease, and comparison can be made in different stages for the same patient, evaluating the progression of the disease.

4 Conclusions

Two CNN – based methods have been presented for human cerebellum and brainstem segmentation on MRIs. Produced segmentations could be used for comparing different stages of the SCA patients, showing changes on atrophy of affected brain structures. Convnets are capable of segmenting such structures with a good precision, and can be a powerful tool, helping specialists in decision – making process. The correct use of the inception modules enhances the behavior of CNNs for segmenting anatomic brain structures. In future investigations, we propose the use of convnets for localizing the most relevant atrophic changes in brainstem and cerebellum of SCA patients.

References

1. Dueñas, A.M., Goold, R., Giunti, P.: Molecular pathogenesis of spinocerebellar ataxias. Brain **129**, 1357–1370 (2006). https://doi.org/10.1093/brain/awl081
2. Stevanin, G., Brice, A.: Spinocerebellar ataxia 17 (SCA17) and Huntington's disease-like 4 (HDL4). Cerebellum **7** (2008). https://doi.org/10.1007/s12311-008-0016-1

3. Teive, H.A.G.: Spinocerebellar ataxias. Arq. Neuropsiquiatr. **67**, 1133–1142 (2009). https://doi.org/10.1590/S0004-282X2009000600035

4. Mascalchi, M.: Spinocerebellar ataxias. Neurol Sci. **29**, 311–313 (2008). https://doi.org/10.1007/s10072-008-1005-3

5. Kumar, S.D., Chand, R.P., Gururaj, A.K., Jeans, W.D.: CT features of olivopontocerebellar atrophy in children. Acta Radiol. **36**, 593–596 (1995). https://doi.org/10.1177/028418519503600458

6. Meira, A.T., et al.: Neuroradiological findings in the spinocerebellar ataxias. Tremor Other Hyperkinetic Mov. 1–8 (2019). https://doi.org/10.7916/tohm.v0.682

7. Mascalchi, M., Vella, A.: Neuroimaging applications in chronic ataxias. Int. Rev. Neurobiol. **143**, 109–162 (2018). https://doi.org/10.1016/bs.irn.2018.09.011

8. Klaes, X.A., et al.: MR imaging in spinocerebellar ataxias : a systematic review. Am. J. Neuroradiol. **37**, 1405–1412 (2016)

9. Shao, F., Xie, X.: An overview on interactive medical image segmentation. In: Annals of the BMWA, pp. 1–22 (2013)

10. Reetz, K., et al.: Brain atrophy measures in preclinical and manifest spinocerebellar ataxia type 2. Ann. Clin. Transl. Neurol. **5**, 128–137 (2018). https://doi.org/10.1002/acn3.504

11. LeCun, Y., et al.: Backpropagation applied to digit recognition. Neural Comput. **1**, 541–551 (1989)

12. Zeiler, M.D., Fergus, R.: Visualizing and understanding convolutional networks. Anal. Chem. Res. **12**, 818–833 (2014). https://doi.org/10.1016/j.ancr.2017.02.001

13. Hariharan, B., Arbeláez, P., Bourdev, L., Maji, S., Malik, J.: Semantic contours from inverse detectors. In: International Conference on Computer Vision, pp. 991–998 (2011)

14. Jaroensri, R., et al.: A video-based method for automatically rating ataxia. In: Proceedings of Machine Learning, pp. 1–13 (2017)

15. Kawahara, C., et al.: BrainNetCNN: convolutional neural networks for brain networks; towards predicting neurodevelopment. Neuroimage **146**, 1038–1049 (2017)

16. Stoean, C., et al.: Automated detection of presymptomatic conditions in spinocerebellar ataxia type 2 using Monte Carlo dropout and deep neural network techniques with electrooculogram signals. Sensors **20**, 3032 (2020). https://doi.org/10.3390/s20113032

17. Kamnitsas, K., et al.: Efficient multi-scale 3D CNN with fully connected CRF for accurate brain lesion segmentation. Med. Image Anal. **36**, 61–78 (2016). https://doi.org/10.1016/j.media.2016.10.004

18. Erden, B., Gamboa, N., Wood, S.: 3D convolutional neural network for brain tumor segmentation. Stanford (2017)

19. Ronneberger, O., Fischer, P., Brox, T.: U-Net: convolutional networks for biomedical image segmentation. In: Navab, N., Hornegger, J., Wells, W., Frangi, A. (eds.) Medical Image Computing and Computer-Assisted Intervention – MICCAI 2015. MICCAI 2015. LNCS, vol. 9351, pp. 234–241. Springer, Cham (2015). https://doi.org/10.1007/978-3-319-24574-4_28

20. Moeskops, P., Veta, M., Lafarge, M.W., Eppenhof, K.A.J., Pluim, J.P.W.: Adversarial training and dilated convolutions for brain MRI segmentation. In: Cardoso, M. et al. (eds.) Deep Learning in Medical Image Analysis and Multimodal Learning for Clinical Decision Support, pp. 56–64. Springer, Cham (2017). https://doi.org/10.1007/978-3-319-67558-9_7

21. Mehta, R., Sivaswamy, J.: M-NET : a convolutional neural network for deep brain structure segmentation. In: 2017 IEEE International Symposium on Biomedical Imaging, pp. 437–440 (2017)

22. Havaei, M., et al.: Brain tumor segmentation with deep neural networks. Med. Image Anal. **35**, 18–31 (2017)

23. Chen, L., Bentley, P., Mori, K., Misawa, K., Fujiwara, M., Rueckert, D.: DRINet for medical image segmentation. IEEE Trans. Med. Imaging **37**, 1–11 (2018)

24. Cahall, D.E., Rasool, G., Bouaynaya, N.C., Fathallah-Shaykh, H.M.: Inception modules enhance brain tumor segmentation. Front. Comput. Neurosci. **13**, 1–8 (2019). https://doi.org/10.3389/fncom.2019.00044

25. Mehta, R., Majumdar, A., Sivaswamy, J.: BrainSegNet : a convolutional neural network architecture for automated segmentation of human brain structures. J. Med. Imaging **4** (2017). https://doi.org/10.1117/1.JMI.4.2.024003

26. Mehta, R., Majumdar, A., Sivaswamy, J.: BrainSegNet : a convolutional neural network architecture for automated segmentation of human brain structures. J. Med. Imaging **4** (2017). https://doi.org/10.1016/j.neuroimage.2017.04.041

27. He, K., Zhang, X., Ren, S., Sun, J.: Deep residual learning for image recognition. In: Proceedings of the IEEE Conference on Computer Vision and Pattern Recognition, pp. 1–9 (2016)

28. Carass, A., et al.: Comparing fully automated state-of-the-art cerebellum parcellation from magnetic resonance images. Neuroimage **183**, 150–172 (2018). https://doi.org/10.1016/j.neuroimage.2018.08.003.Comparing

29. Han, S., He, Y., Carass, A., Ying, S.H., Prince, J.L.: Cerebellum parcellation with convolutional neural networks. Proc. SPIE Int, Soc, Opt. Eng. **10949** (2019). https://doi.org/10.1117/12.2512119.Cerebellum

30. Han, S., Carass, A., He, Y., Prince, J.L.: Automatic cerebellum anatomical parcellation using U-Net with locally constrained optimization. IEEE Trans. Med. Imaging **116819** (2020). https://doi.org/10.1016/j.neuroimage.2020.116819

31. Talo, M., Baloglu, U.B., Yildrim, Ö., Acharya, U.R.: Application of deep transfer learning for automated brain abnormality classification using MR images. Cogn. Syst. Res. **54**, 176–188 (2019)

32. Nair, V., Hinton, G.E.: Rectified linear units improve restricted Boltzmann machines. In: International Conference on Machine Learning (2010)

33. Qamar, S., Ahmad, P., Shen, L.: HI-Net: hyperdense inception 3D UNet for brain tumor segmentation. arXivPreprint. arXiv2012.06760, pp. 1–9 (2020)

34. Chollet, F.: Keras: The Python deep learning library. Astrophysics Source Code Library, Record ascl:1806.022 (2018)

35. Agarwal, A., et al.: TensorFlow: large-scale machine learning on heterogeneous distributed systems. arXiv Prepr. arXiv1603.04467 (2016)

36. Kingma, D.P., Ba, J.L.: Adam: a method for stochastic optimization. In: 3rd International Conference for Learning Representations (ICLR) (2015)

37. Brain Development Webpage. https://brain-development.org/brain-atlases/

38. Yushkevich, P.A., Gao, Y., Gerig, G.: ITK-SNAP : an interactive tool for semi-automatic segmentation of multi-modality biomedical images. In: 2016 38th Annual International Conference of the IEEE Engineering in Medicine and Biology Society (EMBC), pp. 3342–3345. IEEE (2016)

39. Tustison, N.J., et al.: N4ITK : improved N3 bias correction. IEEE Trans. Med. Imaging **29**, 1310–1320 (2010)

40. BrainMap Webpage. https://www.brainmap.org/

41. Milletari, F., Navab, N., Ahmadi, S.A.: V-Net: fully convolutional neural networks for volumetric medical image segmentation. In: Proceedings - 2016 4th International Conference 3D Vision, 3DV 2016, pp. 565–571 (2016). https://doi.org/10.1109/3DV.2016.79

42. Miao, S., Liao, R.: Deep Learning and Convolutional Neural Networks for Medical Imaging and Clinical Informatics. Springer, Switzerland AG (2019)

43. Fawcett, T.: An introduction to ROC analysis **27**, 861–874 (2006). https://doi.org/10.1016/j.patrec.2005.10.010

A Hybrid Brain-Computer Interface using Extreme Learning Machines for Motor Intention Detection

Ramón Osmany Ramírez Tasé[1]([⊠]), Denis Delisle Rodríguez[2],
Oluwarotimi Williams Samuel[3], and Alberto López Delis[4]

[1] University of Granma, Bayamo, Granma, Cuba
[2] Postgraduate Program in Electrical Engineering, Federal University of Espirito
Santo, Vitória, Brazil
[3] Shenzhen Institute of Advanced Technology, Chinese Academy of Sciences, Beijing, China
[4] Center of Medical Biophysics, University of Oriente, Santiago de Cuba, Cuba

Abstract. This work proposes a hybrid brain-computer interface (HBCI) using Bayesian method to fuse information from electroencephalography (EEG) and electromyography signals (EMG) for decoding movement intention. For EEG signal feature extraction, Riemannian covariance matrices are computed, whereas other three features into the time and frequency domain are extracted from each EMG channel, such as autoregressive models, signal slope changes, and zero crossing. In this approach, the Bayesian fusion method is used to combine predictions from Extreme Learning Machines (ELMs) classifiers. Our proposed HBCI obtained average accuracy of 96.26%, recall of 93.97, kappa of 0.78, and false positive rate of 3.31%, outperforming solution only based on EEG or EMG, suggesting its potential for neuro-rehabilitation applications.

Keywords: Bayesian fusion · Extreme Learning Machines · Hybrid
Brain-Computer Interface · Motor intention · Riemannian geometry

1 Introduction

Nowadays, there are millions of people with physical disabilities, caused by war, traffic accidents, neural diseases or disorders, and work-related injuries, affecting upper and lower limbs. The hand disability is one of the most frequent impairments worldwide. Besides, the loss of hand movements can be caused by either amputation or a motor function issue, which has motivated the development of technologies for hand rehabilitation, although this research field is a challenging task [1].

Brain-computer interface (BCI) or brain-machine interface (BMI) is a system that provides a communication pathway between both user and end-application (robotic devices, serious games, software, etc.) to facilitate the interaction [2]. This emerging technology has shown great potential to assist movements of patients in the neuro-rehabilitation therapies, in order to recover their lost motor functions [3, 4] by controlling robotic exoskeletons [5, 6], inducing plasticity [7]. Despite their wide use in non-clinical

© Springer Nature Switzerland AG 2021
Y. Hernández Heredia et al. (Eds.): IWAIPR 2021, LNCS 13055, pp. 115–123, 2021.
https://doi.org/10.1007/978-3-030-89691-1_12

applications, these BCI systems using brain signals alone are still limited for clinical neuro-rehabilitation therapy [8].

Many control techniques have been investigated through different types of bio-signals, such as surface electromyography (sEMG) to provide a more natural interaction between both human and robotic devices. sEMG signal, also named myoelectric signal, has been widely used in control applications, as these signals directly reflect the motor intention of muscles [9]. The sEMG -based systems have some limitations because of muscular fatigue, which affects the amplitude and frequency spectrum of myoelectric signals and the muscle contractions [10]. Rocon et al. [11] reported that, involuntary tremor can deteriorate the performance of methods based on this signal. Other research had demonstrated that sEMG signals in individuals with paraplegia or hemiplegia are not sufficient to control a robotic exoskeleton, and enhance the performance of daily living activities [10]. Consequently, the development of rehabilitation technologies for these individuals is still necessary to repair their neural and motor impairments, allowing their autonomy and mobility.

On the other hand, EEG signals are widely used in BCIs due to their low-cost and high temporal resolution [12]. However, factors such as low information transfer rate (ITR) limit the effectiveness, usability, and reliability of these EEG signal systems in real-world operation based on user's movement intention. Additionally, the low ITR may increase the mental load as reported by Padfield et al. [13], which is an undesirable effect. Then, combining both EEG and sEMG signals in a hybrid BCI, we expected to enhance the classification of movement intention of people with amputation or neurological damage [8], as well as their interaction with end-devices.

To reinforce the EEG-based BCI, some studies explored the combination of EEG signals with other signals of less variability across subjects, such as sEMG signals [14]. Hybrid BCIs (HBCIs) can combine or fuse the information of two or more sub-systems, aiming to optimize the overall performance. For instance, various studies have been conducted by fusing both EMG and EEG signals, achieving encouraging results [8, 10 14–21]. These approaches reduce the disadvantages of using these signals indepen-dently, but still new hybrid schemes to improve the effectiveness of these hybrid BCIs in biomedical applications should be investigated [8].

In this work, a hybrid method was developed, based on fusion of sEMG and EEG signals as a parallel input to classify five wrist and hand motions. The proposed method uses the covariance matrices in EEG epochs to obtain a projection matrix onto the Riemannian space, while three features into the time–frequency domain are used in sEMG signals. These features are extracted, and then concatenated to construct the feature vectors. Also, in this approach, for the first time is used ELM algorithm for motion classification in hybrid method, in order to enhance the classification performance. For the outputs fusion Bayesian method is used to combine the decisions of two ELM classifiers.

2 Materials and Methods

2.1 Dataset

An EEG and sEMG dataset of five motion classes, such as hand open, hand close, wrist pronation, wrist supination, and no movement was used, which was acquired in previous studies from four male amputees (average age of 41.50 ± 7.05 years) [8, 9]. To avoid muscle and mental fatigue, the subjects executed each task for a period of 5 s, including between two consecutive tasks a period of 5 s for resting. Each motor task was repeated for a total of 10 trials, completing 50 s of raw EEG and sEMG per task. The sampling rate was fixed at 1024 Hz, and 1000 Hz for EMG and EEG signals, respectively. The high-density sEMG system (REFA 128, TMS International, the Netherlands) of 32 monopolar electrodes was used to simultaneously record both signals, being the sEMG signals acquired around the biceps brachii and triceps brachii muscles on the residual arm of each subject. A cap of 64 EEG electrodes (EasyCap, Herrsching, Germany) placed according to standard 10–20 system, was used to acquire brain signals with the Neuroscan system (Version 4.3).

2.2 Proposed HBCI

The proposed HBCI based on the fusion of both EEG and EMG signals is shown in Fig. 1. This approach is composed of four-stages after signal acquisition: pre-processing, feature extraction, classification, and fusion of classification outputs. Details about each stage are given next.

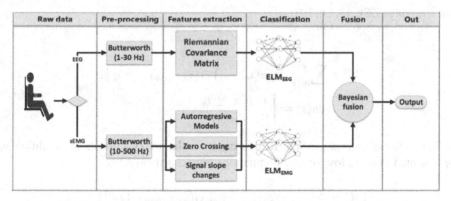

Fig. 1. Proposed HBCI block diagram for motor intent classification

Pre-processing. This phase uses two bandpass filters (Butterworth of 2nd order), one with frequency range from 8 to 30 Hz for pre-processing EEG signals, and other from 10 to 500 Hz for filtering sEMG signals. Furthermore, a 50 Hz notch filter is applied to reject the power-line interference. After, a Common Average Reference for filtering EEG channels is also applied on EEG segments of 5120 sample points to reject common interference. For each motion class these segments are extracted from -0.12 to 5 s (being 0 s the movements onset) over each trial. In sequence, an overlapped segmentation strategy is deployed, getting 250 ms window lengths each 100 ms for processing both EEG and sEMG signals.

Feature Extraction. EEG epochs of 250 ms corresponding to the training set are first used to calculate covariance matrices, which are after analyzed to obtain a projection matrix onto the Riemannian space [22]. Then, the covariance matrices computed on EEG epochs from the training and testing sets, can be also projected onto their tangential space by using this projection matrix. Here, we used the functions covariances, mean-covariances, and Tangent-space [23, 24], available at https://github.com/alexandrebar achant.

For sEMG epochs, the features of each channel are extracted, and then concatenated to construct the feature vectors. Three features into the time and frequency domain are used:

Autoregressive Models (AR). It describes each sample of the sEMG signal as a linear combination of the previous samples x_{t-i} plus a white noise error term ε_t:

$$x_t = \sum_{i=1}^{p} a_i x_{t-i} + \varepsilon_t, \tag{1}$$

where x_t is the EMG signal, a_i are the autoregressive coefficients, p denotes the order of the model, and ε_t an error term [25]. In this case, error trial tests were carried out, and the best result was determined for an order $p = 4$.

Zero Crossing (ZC). [8, 26, 27].

$$ZC = \sum_{n=1}^{N-1} \left[sgn(x_n x_{n+1}) \cap |x_n - x_{n+1}| \geq t_h \right],$$
$$sgn(x) = \begin{cases} 1, & \text{if } x \geq t_h \\ 0, & \text{otherwise} \end{cases} \tag{2}$$

Signal Slope Changes (SSC). In this case, similar to ZC, threshold condition is implemented to avoid low voltage fluctuations or background noises,

$$SSC = \sum_{n}^{N-1} \left[sgn[(x_n - x_{n-1})(x_n - x_{n+1})] = 1 \right],$$
$$sgn(x) = \begin{cases} 1, & \text{if } x \geq t_h \\ 0, & \text{otherwise} \end{cases} \tag{3}$$

In both cases, ZC and SSC, x_i is the sample, N is the total number of samples and *th* is a selected threshold (equal to 5% of the value of the mean amplitude of the signal [27]).

Classification. The classifier based on Extreme Learning Machine (ELM) proposed by Huang et al. [28] is applied in this approach. In Biomedical Engineering applications, several studies have successfully employed ELMs to solve classification problems, such as for motor intention recognition [29]. ELM is a single hidden-layer feedforward neural network (SLFN) network that contains only one hidden layer, where the weights and biases are configured randomly between the input and the hidden layer, whereas the weights between the hidden layer and the output of the network are determined analytically through the solution of a linear system. The classifier is formed through a non-iterative method that does not require the optimization process, and uses a Moore–Penrose pseudo-inverse that allows the achievement of an optimal model, considering an error tolerance [30].

For the N distinct samples $(x_i, t_i) \in R^{(n \times m)}$, where, $x_i = [x_{i_1}, x_{i_2}, \ldots, x_{i_n}]^T \in R^n$, $t_i = [t_{i_1}, t_{i_2}, \ldots, t_{i_n}]^T \in R^m$ and $i = 1, 2, \ldots, N$, standard SLFNs with N hidden nodes and activation Bayesian method is used for function $f(x)$ are mathematically modeled.

Fusion. Bayesian method is used for fusion [31]. It is considered as the conditional model $P(C|O_1, O_2)$ to combine the decisions of two data sources (in this case EEG and sEMG signals), where C denotes the classes (open hand, close hand, wrist pronation, wrist supination or rest), and O_1 and O_2 are the decisions of the two ELMs classifiers corresponding to EEG and sEMG signals, respectively.

$$C_{out} = argmax_c[P(O_1|C = c), P(O_2|C = c)] \tag{4}$$

Unlike traditional fusion by this method [31], in this current work the value of P starting from confusion matrix of each ELM classifier. Equation (4) shows the Bayesian fusion used.

2.3 Evaluation

In order to evaluate the classification performance, a leave-one-out cross validation (LOOCV) method [32, 33] was adopted to partitioning the matrix of extracted features into training, testing, and validation sets before using them for classification. LOOCV provides an approximation of the test error with lower bias, which is more suitable for small sample size datasets such as here. Since our evaluation followed a within-participant design, we performed the LOOCV by participant to avoid introducing possible twinning bias. The first two sets for training and testing were used here to obtain the ELM model, which was later tested with the third set. The accuracy (ACC), recall or sensitivity, Cohen's kappa coefficient (κ), and false positive rate (FPR) [33] were used as metrics for evaluation. 5 folds on each subject were carried out, selecting the mean value. A comparison using independently EEG or sEMG signals was conducted.

3 Results and Discussion

In this work, the systems based on a single source of signals (sEMG or EEG), and fusing both signals were tested and compared. Tables 1 and 2 show the performance of the

ELM classifier for each subject using only EEG and sEMG signals, respectively. We observed using EEG signals alone, average ACC = 81.11%, Recall = 80.02, κ = 0.54 and FPR = 16.73%. For sEMG signals alone, ACC = 86.43%, Recall = 84.47, κ = 0.66 and FPR = 10.39% were achieved, improving slightly the performance employing EEG alone. The best performance was obtained for Subjects S3 and S2, using EEG and sEMG, respectively.

Table 1. Performance comparison-EEG classifier.

Subjects	ACC(%)	Recall	κ	FPR(%)
S1	75.86	81.60	0.46	21.12
S2	80.43	79.57	0.68	16.45
S3	85.48	80.26	0.61	12.29
S4	82.67	78.63	0.39	17.07
Mean	**81.11**	**80.02**	**0.54**	**16.73**
SD	**4.06**	**1.25**	**0.13**	**3.61**

SD: Standard deviation

Table 2. Performance comparison-EMG classifier.

Subjects	ACC(%)	Recall	κ	FPR(%)
S1	83.16	86.19	0.58	10.36
S2	91.09	84.31	0.73	8.02
S3	87.12	83.87	0.69	10.84
S4	84.33	83.49	0.62	12.35
Mean	**86.43**	**84.47**	**0.66**	**10.39**
SD	**3.53**	**1.20**	**0.07**	**1.79**

SD: Standard deviation

Table 3 shows the results achieved using our proposed HBCI based on Bayesian fusion scheme. An average accuracy of 96.26% was obtained, increasing the overall performance, being 15.15% and 9.83% higher in relation of using independently EEG or sEMG signals, respectively. The achieved FPR declined 13.42% and 7.08% with respect of using only EEG and sEMG, respectively, demonstrating the potential of fusing both signals for motor rehabilitation purposes, which agrees with previous studies [8, 12, 16, 18, 20, 21].

The performance stability of the hybrid systems across subjects was better. For instance, the intra-subject variability was higher using EEG-based BCI [19], as shown in Tables 1 and 2. The results showed in Table 3 are comparable with respect to similar hybrid systems that also fuse EEG and EMG. In [8] the authors demonstrated the feasibility of fusing both signals for movement classification of above-elbow amputees,

Table 3. Performance comparison-HBCI classifier.

Subjects	ACC(%)	Recall	κ	FPR(%)
S1	95.73	94.12	0.77	5.02
S2	97.89	93.71	0.86	0
S3	97.28	94.64	0.8	3.87
S4	94.12	93.41	0.67	4.36
Mean	**96.26**	**93.97**	**0.78**	**3.31**
SD	**1.69**	**0.53**	**0.08**	2.26

SD: Standard deviation

obtaining average ACC of 87.0%. Similar to our research, in [20] the classification of five classes of wrist and hands movements was studied, where the authors reported mean accuracy of 91.4% using LDA classifier. Besides, in [34] mean ACC of 96.58% was achieved by classifying three and five classes of movements.

4 Conclusions

In this study, a hybrid classification method based in the combination of EEG and sEMG signals was proposed to recognize hand and wrist motions. The experimental results show that the proposed hybrid BCI performed better compared to traditional systems based only on sEMG or EEG. Our approach can be used in future works to develop EEG and sEMG-based systems for motor neurorehabilitation therapy.

References

1. Anam, K., Al-Jumaily, A.: Evaluation of extreme learning machine for classification of individual and combined finger movements using electromyography on amputees and non-amputees. Neural Netw. **85**, 51–68 (2017). https://doi.org/10.1016/j.neunet.2016.09.004
2. Yadav, D., Yadav, S., Veer, K.: A comprehensive assessment of brain computer interfaces: recent trends and challenges. J. Neurosci. Methods **346**, 20 (2020). https://doi.org/10.1016/j.jneumeth.2020.108918
3. Birbaumer, N., Gallegos, G., Wildgruber, M., Silvoni, S., Soekadar, S.R.: Direct brain control and communication in paralysis. Brain Topogr. **27**, 4–11 (2014)
4. Bouton, C.E.: Restoring cortical control of functional movement in a human with quadriplegia. Nature **533**, 247–250 (2016)
5. Gui, K., Liu, H., Zhang, D.: A practical and adaptive method to achieve EMG-based torque estimation for a robotic exoskeleton. IEEE ASME Trans. Mechatron. **24**, 483–494 (2019)
6. Yun, Y., et al.: Maestro: an EMG-driven assistive hand exoskeleton for spinal cord injury patients, pp. 2904–2910 (2017)
7. Rupp, R., Rohm, M., Schneiders, M., Kreilinger, A., Müeller, G.: Functional rehabilitation of the paralyzed upper extremity after spinal cord injury by noninvasive hybrid neuroprostheses, vol. 103, no. 6, pp. 954–968. IEE (2015)

8. Li, X., Samuel, O.W., Zhang, X., Wang, H., Fang, P., Li, G.: A motion-classification strategy based on sEMG-EEG signal combination for upper-limb amputees. J. NeuroEng. Rehabil. **14**, 1–13 (2017). https://doi.org/10.1186/s12984-016-0212-z

9. Samuel, O.W.: Intelligent EMG pattern recognition control method for upper-limb multi-functional prostheses: advances, current challenges, and future prospects. IEEE Access **7**, 10150–10165 (2019)

10. Chowdhury, A., Raza, H., Dutta, A., Prasad, G.: EEG-EMG based hybrid brain computer interface for triggering hand exoskeleton for neuro-rehabilitation. In: Proceedings of the Advances in Robotics on - AIR'17, New Delhi, India, 2017, pp. 1–6 (2017). https://doi.org/10.1145/3132446.3134909.

11. Rocon, E., Miranda, J., Pons, J.L.: TechFilter: filtering undesired tremorous movements from PC mouse cursor. Technol. Disabil. **18**, 3–8 (2006)

12. Ruhunage, I., Mallikarachchi, S., Chinthaka, D., Sandaruwan, J., Lalitharatne, T.D.: Hybrid EEG-EMG signals based approach for control of hand motions of a transhumeral prosthesis. In: 2019 IEEE 1st Global Conference on Life Sciences and Technologies (LifeTech) 2019, pp. 50–53 (2019). files/257/8883865.html.

13. Padfield, N., Zabalza, J., Zhao, H., Masero, V., Ren, J.: EEG-based brain-computer interfaces using motor-imagery: techniques and challenges. Sensors **19**, 1423 (2019)

14. Leeb, R., Sagha, H., Chavarriaga, R., del R. Millán, J.: A hybrid brain–computer interface based on the fusion of electroencephalographic and electromyographic activities. J. Neural Eng. **8**, 025011 (2011). https://doi.org/10.1088/1741-2560/8/2/025011

15. Ben Said, A., Mohamed, A., Elfouly, T., Harras, K., Wang, Z.J.: Multimodal deep learning approach for joint EEG-EMG data compression and classification. In: 2017 IEEE Wireless Communications and Networking Conference (WCNC), San Francisco, CA, USA, March 2017, pp. 1–6 (2017). https://doi.org/10.1109/WCNC.2017.7925709

16. Chowdhury, A., Raza, H., Meena, Y.K., Dutta, A., Prasad, G.: An EEG-EMG correlation-based brain-computer interface for hand orthosis supported neuro-rehabilitation. J. Neurosci. Methods **312**, 1–11 (2019)

17. Cisotto, G., Michieli, U., Badia, L.: A coherence study on EEG and EMG signals. ArXiv Prepr. ArXiv171201277 (2017)

18. Kawase, T., Sakurada, T., Koike, Y., Kansaku, K.: A hybrid BMI-based exoskeleton for paresis: EMG control for assisting arm movements J. Neural Eng. **14**, 016015 (2017). https://doi.org/10.1088/1741-2552/aa525f

19. Mudiyanselage, S.: A study of controlling upper-limb exoskeletons using EMG and EEG signals, p. 144 (2014)

20. Samuel, O.W., Li, X., Zhang, X., Wang, H.: A hybrid non-invasive method for the classification of amputees' hand and wrist movements, Haikou, China, p. 5 (2015)

21. Sarasola, A., et al.: A hybrid brain-machine interface based on EEG and EMG activity for the motor rehabilitation of stroke patients. In: 2017 International Conference on Rehabilitation Robotics (ICORR), London, July 2017, pp. 895–900 (2017). https://doi.org/10.1109/ICORR.2017.8009362.

22. Barachant, A., Bonnet, S., Congedo, M., Jutten, C.: Classification of covariance matrices using a Riemannian-based kernel for BCI applications. Neurocomputing **112**, 172–178 (2013). https://doi.org/10.1016/j.neucom.2012.12.039

23. Fu, R., Han, M., Tian, Y., Shi, P.: Improvement motor imagery EEG classification based on sparse common spatial pattern and regularized discriminant analysis. J. Neurosci. Methods **343**, 108833 (2020)

24. Park, Y., Chung, W.: Frequency-optimized local region common spatial pattern approach for motor imagery classification. IEEE Trans. Neural Syst. Rehabil. Eng. **27**(7), 1378–1388 (2019)

25. Roy, R., Sikdar, D., Mahadevappa, M., Kumar, C.: EEG based motor imagery study of time domain features for classification of power and precision hand grasps, pp. 440–443 (2017). https://doi.org/10.1109/NER.2017.8008384
26. Kiguchi, K., Hayashi, Y., Asami, T.: An upper-limb power-assist robot with tremor suppression control. IEEE (2011)
27. Biopac Systems, Inc.: EMG frequency signal analysis (2010)
28. Huang, G., Zhu, Q.-Y., Siew, C.-K.: Extreme learning machines: a new learning scheme of feedforward neural network. In: 2004 IEEE International Joint Conference on Neural Networks (IEEE Cat. No. 04CH37541), vol. 2, pp. 985–990 (2004)
29. Ribeiro, V.H.A., Reynoso-Meza, G., Siqueira, H.V.: Multi-objective ensembles of echo state networks and extreme learning machines for streamflow series forecasting. Eng. Appl. Artif. Intell. **95**, 103910 (2020)
30. Cene, V.H., Tosin, M., Machado, J., Balbinot, A.: Open database for accurate upper-limb intent detection using electromyography and reliable extreme learning machines. Sensors **19**, 20 (2019). https://doi.org/10.3390/s19081864
31. Kuncheva, L.I., Bezdek, J.C., Duin, R.P.W.: Decision templates for multiple classifier fusion: an experimental comparison. Pattern Recogn. **34**(2), 299–314 (2001)
32. Hastie, T., Tibshirani, R., Friedman, J.: The Elements of Statistical Learning: Data Mining, Inference and Prediction. Springer, New York (2009)
33. Japkowicz, N., Mohak, S.: Evaluating Learning Algorithms: A Classification Perspective. Cambridge University Press, New York (2011)
34. Hooda, N., Ratan, D., Neelesh, K.: Fusion of EEG and EMG signals for movements classification of unilateral foot Biomed. Signal Process. Control **60**, 8 (2020). https://doi.org/10.1016/j.bspc.2020.101990

Peripheral Nerve Segmentation in Ultrasound Images Using Conditioned U-Net

Harold Mauricio Díaz-Vargas[1]([✉]) [ID], Cristian Alfonso Jimenez-Castaño[1] [ID],
David Augusto Cárdenas-Peña[1] [ID], Oscar David Aguirre-Ospina[2],
and Alvaro Angel Orozco-Gutierrez[1] [ID]

[1] Automatics Research Group, Universidad Tecnológica de Pereira, Pereira, Colombia
{harold369,craljimenez,dcardenasp,aaog}@utp.edu.co
[2] Medicina Hospitalaria, Servicios Especiales de Salud, Manizales, Colombia
odaguirre@ses.com.co

Abstract. Peripheral Nerve Blocking (PNB) is a regional anesthesia procedure that delivers an anesthetic in the proximity of a nerve to avoid nociceptive transmission. Anesthesiologists have widely used ultrasound images to guide the PNB due to their low cost, non-invasivity, and lack of radiation. Due to the difficulties in visually locating the target nerve, automatic nerve segmentation systems attempt to support the specialist to perform a successful nerve block. This work introduces a deep neural network for automatic nerve segmentation in ultrasound images. The proposed approach consists of a conditioned U-Net model that includes the kind of target nerve as a second input allowing the network to learn new features to improve the segmentation. The model is trained and tested on a dataset holding four different peripheral nerves, achieving an average Dice coefficient of 0.70. Results show that the proposed C-UNet outperforms the conventional U-Net, benefiting the ultrasound-guided regional anesthesia.

Keywords: Nerve segmentation · U-Net · Deep learning ·
Ultrasound · Peripheral nerve blocking

1 Introduction

Regional anesthesia has different advantages over general anesthesia in medical procedures and surgeries, including improved post-operative mobility and reduced morbidity and mortality [1]. One of the most used procedures to perform regional anesthesia is the peripheral nerve blocking (PNB), which involves the administration of an anesthetic substance in the area surrounding a nerve structure to block the transmission of nociceptive information [2,3]. The PNB success depends on delivering the appropriate dose of anesthetic in the correct

Support information is omitted for blind review.

Y. Hernández Heredia et al. (Eds.): IWAIPR 2021, LNCS 13055, pp. 124–133, 2021.
https://doi.org/10.1007/978-3-030-89691-1_13

area, so avoiding adverse effects such as neurological damage or intoxication due to the flow of the anesthetic into the bloodstream [4,5].

In practice, ultrasonography (US) has become an attractive technique for image guidance to improve targeting accuracy because it enables real-time visualization of the nerve at a low cost, non-invasivity, and no radiation [6,7]. However, conventional 2D US has different drawbacks as image attenuation, artifacts, and speckle noise, which make the nerve location by visual inspection a challenging task for the specialist [8].

The automatic nerve-segmentation systems attempt to deal with such issues. Among the methods developed for US segmentation, traditional computer vision approaches preprocess images and extract local features that feed conventional machine learning pixel classifiers. For instance, a Bayesian approach modeled the distribution of superpixel-wise wavelet features to identify nerve structures [9]. However, designing an efficient feature set becomes a complex task that demands a deep knowledge of the echographic technique and tissue properties [10]. On the contrary, methods based on deep learning, mainly Convolutional Neural Networks (CNN), have emerged as powerful tools in the analysis of medical images from raw data [11]. Recently, the U-Net network allows an adequate semantic segmentation of various types of medical imaging systems, including US [12]. However, the varying echographic attributes across kinds of nerves hampers the segmentation results, so giving rise to varying architectures [13]. An automatic nerve segmentation approach firstly equalizes the histogram and applies a despeckling filter, to lastly segment with a modified version of the U-Net [14]. However, the introduced preprocessing increases both training and testing time. Another proposal replaces the encoder layers by recurrent convolution operations yielding the Recurrent Residual U-Net (R2U-Net) [15]. Despite a suitable performance on blood vessel segmentation, skin cancer, and lung classification, the R2U-Net misses spatial information and reduces the receptive field due to the backbone devoted to classification [16].

This work proposes a variation of the conventional U-Net, termed conditioned U-Net (C-UNet), that adds a new input at the deepest layer indicating the target nerve type to take advantage of the varying anatomical properties among nerves. Such additional information allows learning new features and enriches the latent space to improve the nerve delineation. Training and validation of the proposed C-UNet consider a dataset of US images holding sciatic, ulnar, median, and femoral nerves. The experimental comparison against the conventional U-Net in training convergence, performance metrics, and visual inspection validate the benefit of introducing the type of target nerve. Specifically, the C-UNet reached an average of 0.70, 0.73, 0.71, and 0.85 for Dice coefficient, precision, sensitivity, and AUC, respectively, in a validation subset of 372 images.

The paper is distributed as follows: Sect. 2 describes the dataset, preprocessing, and proposed network architecture. Section 3 presents and discusses the training and validation results for both the conventional U-Net and the C-UNet. Lastly, Sect. 4 concludes the work and declares future research directions.

2   Materials and Methods

2.1   Dataset and Data Augmentation

To train and validate the proposed approach, we consider a dataset of 619 US images from the sciatic, ulnar, median, and femoral nerve, recorded during the nerve blockage for orthopedic surgery. The dataset was acquired at the Santa Monica's Hospital (Dosquebradas, Colombia) using a Sonosite Nano-Maxx ultrasound system with a resolution of 360×279 pixels [9]. The same anesthesiologist performing the nerve blockage delineated the target nerve after the surgery. Top row of Fig. 1 exemplifies the four kinds of nerves in the dataset.

For reducing the natural overfitting of deep architectures, up-down and right-left flip transformations augment the dataset size by generating new ultrasound images to train and test the proposed network [17]. To this end, the OpenCV library applies the same transformation on both the ultrasound image and its respective segmentation mask, as shown in middle and bottom rows of Fig. 1. The final dataset holds 1857 image-segmentation pairs distributed as shown in Table 1. Lastly, the preprocessing resizes images and masks to 128×128 pixels to hasten the training while keeping the nervous structure.

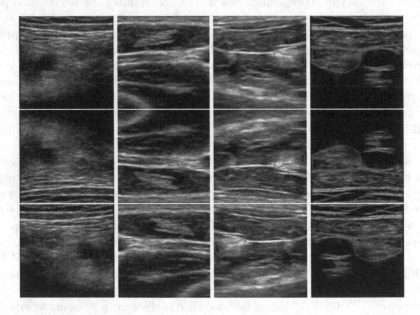

Fig. 1. Sample dataset images with their manual delineation. Left to right: sciatic, ulnar, median, and femoral nerves. Top to bottom: recorded image, up-down flipped, and left-right flipped.

Table 1. Number of images recorded and generated per nerve.

Nerve	Recorded	Generated	Total
Sciatic	287	574	861
Ulnar	221	442	663
Median	41	82	123
Femoral	70	140	210
Total	619	1238	1857

2.2   Conditioned U-Net for Nerve Segmentation

The proposed automatic nerve segmentation machine relies on a U-Net architecture, gaining attention in medical image analysis and holding an encoder and a decoder path. The encoder path extracts deep features through a convolutional neural network that downsamples the input image using learned linear filters. The decoder path, symmetrical to the encoder, reconstructs the image by concatenating a sequence of up-convolutions that upsample the deep feature vector. Corresponding layers in the encoder and decoder are connected via a copy-crop operation to recover spatial information lost during downsampling. The last layer of the U-Net predicts the probability of a pixel belonging to a nervous structure using the sigmoid function.

This work modifies the conventional U-Net network by introducing a second input layer that contains information about the kind of nerve to segment, yielding a Conditioned U-Net (C-UNet)[1]. The additional input corresponds to a tensor sizing the same $8 \times 8 \times 4$. The first two dimensions match the size of the deepest layer, while the third indicates the kind of nerve using one-hot encoding. Figure 2 illustrates the network conditioning as the red input concatenated to the deepest feature vector. As a result, the anesthesiologists can readily provide an image tag allowing the C-UNet to learn particular features of each nervous structure and improving the segmentation performance.

2.3   Training Procedure

We trained both networks, the conventional baseline U-Net and the proposed C-UNet, in a stratified hold-out scheme where 20% of the images compose the evaluation set and the remaining 80% the training set. Regarding the optimization procedure, the Adam algorithm with a learning rate of 5×10^{-6} minimizes the Dice loss computed as follows:

$$L_n = 1 - \frac{2\langle Y_n, \hat{Y}_n \rangle}{||Y_n|| + ||\hat{Y}_n||} \tag{1}$$

where Y_n and $\hat{Y}_n$ denote the ground-truth mask and the predicted nerve probability map for the n-th US image. $\langle \cdot, \cdot \rangle$ stands for the inner product between

---

[1] https://www.kaggle.com/harolddiaz1018/unet-cond.

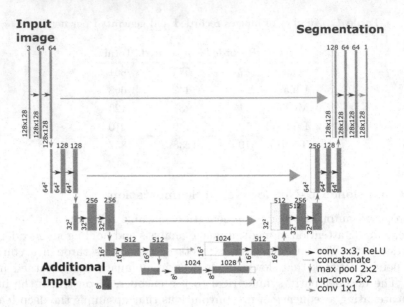

Fig. 2. Proposed C-UNet architecture. Blue boxes represent multi-channel feature maps. White boxes denote the copy of a feature map. The red box maps the target nerve label into a feature map. (Color figure online)

images and $|| \cdot ||$ the L2-norm for images. Image-wise losses are averaged over a batch to yield the epoch loss. The experiment fixed the batch size and number of the epochs to 32 and 300, respectively. Both the U-Net and the C-UNet were trained on the Kaggle platform using an NVIDIA TESLA P100 GPU. Table 2 summarizes the considered training hyper-parameters, previously tested on modified U-Nets [18,19].

Table 2. Training hyper-parameters for both networks

Hyper-parameter	Value
Input size	$128 \times 128 \times 3$
Epochs	300
Activation function	Sigmoid
Batch size	32
Learning rate	0.000005
Loss	Dice loss
Optimizer	Adam

2.4 Validation Approach

We evaluated the two models in terms of precision, sensitivity, the area under the ROC curve (AUC), and the Dice coefficient (DC) using a stratified subset of 20%

of the dataset. Precision assesses the fraction of positive nerve detections, being reduced by over-segmentations. Sensitivity describes the completeness of nerve predictions which diminishes when under-segmenting. The DC (also known as F1-score) is used in medical imaging to gauge the similarity between the ground truth and the predicted output. $DC = 1$ if and only if the manual delineation and the prediction perfectly match. On the contrary, $DC = 0$ in the absence of overlapping. These three measures depend on the number of correctly labeled nerve pixels (TP), mislabeled nerve pixels FP, and correctly labeled background pixels (TN). Lastly, the AUC measures the ability of the networks to distinguish nerve and background.

$$Precision = \frac{TP}{TP + FP} \tag{2}$$

$$Sensitivity = \frac{TP}{TP + FN} \tag{3}$$

$$DC = \frac{2TP}{2TP + FP + FN} \tag{4}$$

3   Results and Discussion

Figure 3 compares the validation losses during the training procedure. Note that both networks suitably converge before 300 epochs. Further, the behavior of the costs along the epochs proves the correct tune of hyper-parameters. Besides, the comparison of the two curves evidences that the U-Net and C-UNet share the loss descending rate. Such a fact indicates that training cost is also similar despite the C-UNet architecture is more complex than U-Net.

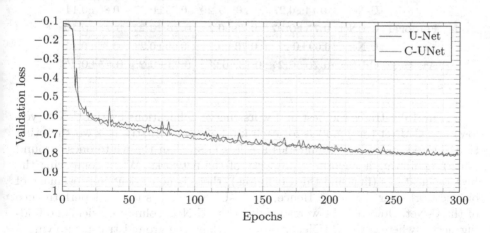

Fig. 3. Validation loss along the training epochs for the baseline and proposed networks.

After the training stage, we fed both networks with the evaluation images to obtain the class probabilities for each pixel. Then, a thresholding procedure at 0.5 provides binary images as the resulting segmentations. Then, the four performance metrics compare the segmentation and ground truth masks. Table 3 presents the performance metrics reached by both networks averaged over 372 evaluation images along with their standard deviation for each kind of nerve. The resulting scores evidence that the ulnar nerve is the most complex to segment, followed by the median, femoral, and sciatic as the less one. Also, the metrics prove that C-UNet outperforms U-Net at most of the metrics and nerves, which indicates a balanced segmentation enhancement. In particular, the Dice Coefficient increases for sciatic, median, and femoral nerves. Besides, the increment of 5% in the sensitivity of the median nerve remarks an improved segmentation for such nerve. On the contrary, the benefit is not evident for the ulnar since both models reach the same DC and precision scores. Consequently, the kind of nerve influences the segmentation results, and the C-UNet takes advantage of such information to improve its performance.

Table 3. Performance metrics for both networks. Average and standard deviation of 372 test images are reported.

		DC	Precision	Sensitivity	AUC
Sciatic	U-Net	0.79±0.15	0.80±0.16	0.81±0.18	0.90±0.09
	C-UNet	**0.80±0.13**	**0.81±0.15**	**0.83±0.16**	**0.91±0.08**
Ulnar	U-Net	0.55±0.32	0.61±0.36	0.55±0.34	0.77±0.17
	C-UNet	0.55±0.34	0.61±0.37	**0.56±0.36**	**0.78±0.18**
Median	U-Net	0.64±0.31	0.77±0.27	0.62±0.34	0.81±0.17
	C-UNet	**0.69±0.25**	**0.78±0.24**	**0.67±0.29**	**0.83±0.14**
Femoral	U-Net	0.74±0.27	**0.76±0.29**	0.73±0.27	0.86±0.14
	C-UNet	**0.75±0.27**	0.75±0.28	**0.76±0.27**	**0.87±0.14**
Average	U-Net	0.69±0.27	0.73±0.28	0.69±0.29	0.84±0.15
	C-UNet	**0.70±0.27**	0.73±0.28	**0.71±0.29**	**0.85±0.15**

Figure 4 illustrates the best and worst nerve delineations by the U-Net (yellow) and C-UNet (red) models for each kind of nerve. Firstly, it is worth noting that the red and yellow boundaries are less crisp than the white ones (ground truth), exhibiting a smoothing property of the networks. When comparing the best delineations (first and third columns), there is no evident improvement of one network over the other. Hence, the C-UNet matches the best performance of the U-Net. However, the worst result of the U-Net (column b) yields no finding nerve, whereas the C-UNet at least overlaps the ground truth, implying a benefit on nerve location. In fact, the worst delineations of the C-UNet (column d) for the sciatic, ulnar and median nerve confirm that the C-UNet attempts to locate the nerve despite missing the shape or including other regions. In those same images, the U-Net either misses the location or finds no nerve. Lastly, the hypothesis of a varying segmentation complexity across nerves is reinforced as the errors are also different for each of them. Consequently, adding information about the target nerve improves performance when a conventional U-Net network misses the nerve location.

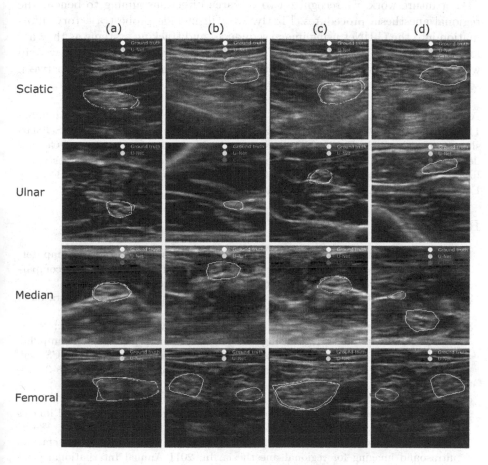

Fig. 4. Delineation results for each kind of nerve: Best (a) and worst (b) segmented images by the U-Net. Best (c) and worst (d) segmented images by the C-UNet. (Color figure online)

4   Concluding Remarks and Future Work

This work introduces a modified version of the U-Net for the automatic segmentation of nerve structures in ultrasound images. The main contribution lies in the network conditioning using the kind of target nerve. Numerical results in Table 3 prove that the C-UNet generally outperforms the conventional U-Net in most of the metrics proving a balanced improvement, meaning reduced over-segmentation and under-segmentation rates. Visual results in Fig. 4 make evident the varying segmentation complexity probably due to the echographic and morphological attributes of the target nerve and its neighborhood. Therefore, the C-UNet exploits the provided nerve label to enhance its location and delineation.

For future work, we recognize two research directions aiming to benefit the regional anesthesia procedures. Firstly, we will include probe trajectory information into the C-UNet using image sequences and tracking systems as they are known to enhance the delineation of complex structures [20]. Secondly, we will work on the exhaustive validation of the U-Nets to identify correlations between segmentation complexity and nerve properties.

Acknowledgments. This work was supported by the research project number 111084467950. And Cristian A. Jimenez C. was supported by the Doctorate Scholarship "Convocatoria del Fondo de Ciencia, Tecnología e Innovación del Sistema General de Regalías para la conformación de una lista de proyectos elegibles para ser viabilizados, priorizados y aprobados por el OCAD en el marco del Programa de Becas de Excelencia"–(Corte 2) funded by MinCiencias.

References

1. Hadjerci, O., Hafiane, A., Conte, D., Makris, P., Vieyres, P., Delbos, A.: Computer-aided detection system for nerve identification using ultrasound images: a comparative study. J. Inform. Med. Unlocked **3**, 2352–9148 (2016)
2. Philippona, C., et al.: Nervegps: a novel decision support system for ultrasound nerve block guidance, pp. 18–21 (2014)
3. Hadjerci, O., Hafiane, A., Makris, P., Conte, D., Vieyres, P., Delbos, A.: Nerve detection in ultrasound images using median Gabor binary pattern. In: Campilho, A., Kamel, M. (eds.) Image Analysis and Recognition. ICIAR 2014. LNCS, vol. 8815, pp. 132–140. Springer, Cham (2014). https://doi.org/10.1007/978-3-319-11755-3_15
4. Hadjerci, O., Hafiane, A., Morette, N., Novales, C., Vieyres, P., Delbos, A.: Assistive system based on nerve detection and needle navigation in ultrasound images for regional anesthesia. Expert Syst. Appl. **61**, 64–77 (2016)
5. Shi, J., Schwaiger, J., Lueth, T.C.: Nerve block using a navigation system and ultrasound imaging for regional anesthesia. In: 2011 Annual International Conference of the IEEE Engineering in Medicine and Biology Society, pp. 1153–1156 (2011)
6. Khan, A., Al-Asad, J., Latif, G.: Speckle suppression in medical ultrasound images through Schur decomposition. IET Image Process. **12**, 307–313 (2018)
7. Mwikirize, C., Nosher, J., Hacihaliloglu, I.: Convolution neural networks for real-time needle detection and localization in 2D ultrasound. Int. J. Comput. Assist. Radiol. Surg. **13**, 647–657 (2018)
8. Pesteie, M., Lessoway, V., Abolmaesumi, P., Rohling, R.: Automatic localization of the needle target for ultrasound-guided epidural injections. IEEE Trans. Med. Imaging **37**, 81–92 (2017)
9. Gil González, J., Álvarez, M., Orozco, A.: A probabilistic framework based on SLIC-superpixel and Gaussian processes for segmenting nerves in ultrasound images, vol. 2016, pp. 4133–4136 (2016)

10. Wang, R., Shen, H., Zhou, M.: Ultrasound nerve segmentation of brachial plexus based on optimized ResU-Net, pp. 1–6 (2019)
11. Litjens, G., et al.: A survey on deep learning in medical image analysis. Med. Image Anal. **42**, 60–88 (2017)
12. Ronneberger, O., Fischer, P., Brox, T.: U-Net: convolutional networks for biomedical image segmentation. In: Navab, N., Hornegger, J., Wells, W., Frangi, A. (eds.) Medical Image Computing and Computer-Assisted Intervention – MICCAI 2015. MICCAI 2015. LNCS, vol. 9351, pp. 234–241. Springer, Cham (2015). https://doi.org/10.1007/978-3-319-24574-4_28
13. Du, G., Cao, X., Liang, J., Chen, X., Zhan, Y.: Medical image segmentation based on U-Net: a review. J. Imaging Sci. Technol. **64**, 20508-1–20508-12(12) (2020)
14. Baby, M., Jereesh, A.: Automatic nerve segmentation of ultrasound images. In: 2017 International Conference of Electronics, Communication and Aerospace Technology (ICECA), vol. 1, pp. 107–112 (2017)
15. Alom, M.Z., Yakopcic, C., Hasan, M., Taha, T., Asari, V.: Recurrent residual u-net for medical image segmentation. J. Med. Imaging **6**, 014006 (2019)
16. Wang, B., Wang, S., Qiu, S., Wei, W., Wang, H., He, H.: CSU-Net: a context spatial U-Net for accurate blood vessel segmentation in fundus images. IEEE J. Biomed. Health Inform. **25**(4), 1128–1138 (2021)
17. Couedic, T., Caillon, R., Rossant, F., Joutel, A., Urien, H., Rajani, R.: Deep-learning based segmentation of challenging myelin sheaths, pp. 1–6 (2020)
18. Abraham, N., Illanko, K., Khan, N., Androutsos, D.: Deep learning for semantic segmentation of Brachial Plexus Nervesin ultrasound images using U-Net and M-Net, pp. 85–89 (2019)
19. Di Ianni, T., Airan, R.: Deep-fUS: functional ultrasound imaging of the brain using deep learning and sparse data (2020)
20. Horng, M.-H., Yang, C.-W., Sun, Y.-N., Yang, T.-H.: DeepNerve: a new convolutional neural network for the localization and segmentation of the median nerve in ultrasound image sequences. Ultrasound Med. Biol. **46**(9), 2439–2452 (2020)

Assessing the Relationship Between Binarization and OCR in the Context of Deep Learning-Based ID Document Analysis

Rubén Sánchez-Rivero[1]([✉]) [ID], Pavel Bezmaternykh[2,3] [ID],
Annette Morales-González[1] [ID], Francisco José Silva-Mata[1] [ID],
and Konstantin Bulatov[2,3] [ID]

[1] Advanced Technologies Application Center, CENATAV, Havana, Cuba
{rsanchez,amorales,fjsilva}@cenatav.co.cu
[2] Federal Research Center "Computer Science and Control" of Russian Academy
of Sciences, Moscow, Russia
bezmaternyh@isa.ru
[3] Smart Engines Service LLC, Moscow, Russia
kbulatov@smartengines.com

Abstract. Text recognition has been one of the areas greatly benefited from deep learning (DL) development, as well as the preprocessing methods contained in its workflow. Within the document analysis field, identity (ID) documents play a crucial role and should be studied in depth regarding this workflow. For this reason, we propose to analyze the relationship between DL-based binarization and recognition methods, specifically for this type of documents. We perform a review of four binarization and seven optical character recognition (OCR) algorithms, and present two sets of experiments assessing the influence of text size for binarization, and the impact of its output in the final text recognition. We show that DL-based binarization solutions are very sensitive to logical text size and they are still not effective in this domain, thus requiring major improvements. Among the evaluated text recognizers, the best performance over the binarization results was shown by the semantic reasoning network (SRN) method.

Keywords: Document image binarization · Identity document recognition · Optical character recognition · Deep learning

1 Introduction

Image segmentation is a common task in digital image processing and computer vision. An special case of segmentation, which consists in classifying image pixels in two groups, mainly known as background and foreground, is called binarization. This case is useful in document image analysis domain due to the document's binary nature itself. In some applications, the properly binarized document serves as a final result, e.g. in archival systems, but sometimes it is just a

© Springer Nature Switzerland AG 2021
Y. Hernández Heredia et al. (Eds.): IWAIPR 2021, LNCS 13055, pp. 134–144, 2021.
https://doi.org/10.1007/978-3-030-89691-1_14

preprocessing step for further stages. Among them, the most common is optical character recognition, or OCR, which converts the document's attributes into textual editable and transferable data.

The problem of document image binarization has been already studied for decades. The special Document Image Binarization Contest, or DIBCO [18,19], was established in 2009 and it is conducted to track the progress in this field. In presence of the well-established datasets in these contests, and due to the recent advances in supervised learning, the approach of training document image binarization from data have become widespread. Currently, the most successful approaches are mostly based on the usage of deep learning (DL) techniques. Among them, recurrent neural networks (RNN), fully convolutional networks (FCN), generative adversarial network (GAN), encoder-decoder architectures.

One drawback of these DIBCO contests is the low diversity of document types included in the datasets. The recently added DIB platform [6] eliminates these issues. First of all, it has gathered not only DIBCO datasets, but also LiveMemory, Nabuco and other photographed documents. Nevertheless, one of the most widespread and important class of documents, namely identity (ID) documents, is still missing there. It is difficult to collect a dataset for ID document analysis and recognition due to the presence of personal data in them. But recently such a dataset was finally published [1]. Thus, it opens the way for the exploration of ID document binarization problem. In identity document images, several issues can negatively interfere with the binarization and OCR output, for instance, special security objects and marks, diversity of colors and background, printing methods, diversity of sources and other special characteristics that depend on the country and its emission.

The main goal of this work is to investigate the influence of ID document image binarization on the accuracy of modern OCR solutions, most of which are based on deep learning techniques. The contributions of this work include a review of the most recent binarization and OCR techniques based on DL. Also, we propose a performance analysis of binarization techniques in the text recognition pipeline, specifically for the ID document domain, which have not been studied with these recent solutions. As complement, we introduce an analysis of the character size influence on the reviewed techniques, in order to showcase their advantages and limitations under different conditions.

2   Background

Most of the recent works dedicated to document image binarization address historical documents processing and target DIBCO datasets. A comprehensive review of this problem is outlined in [24]. This section contains a brief overview of deep neural networks which are ubiquitously used nowadays in document image binarization area and some aspects of their performance evaluation.

Fully convolutional networks [13], or FCN, are applied to semantic image segmentation. In [23], their adaptation to the binarization problem alongside with training details was proposed. The main feature of these networks is that they predict the class label for every pixel directly.

The frequently used U-Net CNN architecture [18,19] is derived in some way from FCN [21]. It is divided into two parts: the left one (encoder) helps capture the local image context, using a typical CNN architecture approach. The right one (decoder) helps to get precise pixel binarization via "up-convolutions". Recently, the integration of multiple pre-trained U-Net models was proposed in [9], to increase the binarization accuracy. Since the reduction of the required amount of computation is highly desirable, the special bipolar morphological CNN of U-Net architecture was presented in [11]. After applying the previously trained model, every pixel of the input image does not get a class label, but some selection level, normalized in the $[0,1]$ range. The binary image is obtained by applying some global threshold for the selection levels map. The convolutional autoencoders [5,17] follow similar principles and they display great performance in this domain. The resulting performance of these networks largely depends on the training data. Clearly, ID documents contain a number of challenges which differs in many aspects from the ones occurring on the historical document images. As a result, the applicability of such DL-based networks to the ID document recognition domain needs to be explored.

The choice of the binarization performance evaluation strategy depends on the final objective. In general, these strategies can be divided into two groups: the first one uses pixel-wise ground truth, while the second one, which is often called "indirect", does not. For the first group, a presence of well-established ground truth is crucial. Its construction is a very resource-consuming procedure which is mostly performed in a semi-manual way by domain experts. The second "indirect" group relies on the evaluation of binary document visual appearance or its recognition performance [15,20]. This was a dominant way to compare different binarization methods before datasets with annotated ground truth like DIBCO appeared. But to evaluate the recognition performance, an OCR engine is required. This is also often called end-to-end metric. To produce more objective results, several OCR engines should be used in this pipeline. For ID document binarization, the evaluation based on OCR performance is a good option because in the majority of applications a successful recognition is the final objective and there are no relevant datasets with established pixel-wise ground truth dedicated to this class of documents.

3   Algorithm Selection

Since our goal is to make an assessment of the influence of binarization algorithms for the ID document text recognition task, we present the algorithms selected for this study, along with a brief description and analysis of them.

Binarization Algorithms. In this section we describe three of the most relevant deep learning-based binarization algorithms to assess the impact of this step in the ID document analysis pipeline. The selection of these algorithms was made by having into account that two of them participated in the last two DIBCO competitions, and they have available source code for testing. The other one, even if it has not participated in any competition, has some well documented source code and community and it has been compared with other state-of-the-art methods in some recent works.

U-Net-bin [3]. This method was ranked first in DIBCO'17 [18]. It is a pure CNN-based solution which uses U-Net architecture. It operates on non overlapping tiles with size of 128×128 pixels of the source image. A special emphasis was placed on training data preparation and data augmentation techniques usage, including additional data to deal with the potential problems missing in the previous DIBCO datasets. It was shown that a better binarization accuracy can be obtained with this approach by choosing a proper activation function [7].

Gallego Autoencoder [5]. This deep learning-based method participated in the 2019 DIBCO competition [19] and ranked first in some sets of DocEng time-quality binarization competition [12]. This algorithm analyzes all the pixels in the image in a single pass. The architecture of the network is a convolutional autoencoder which makes downsampling and upsampling operations and it has a final layer with neurons that predict a value in the [0, 1] range.

Robin. It is another implementation of U-Net network. It does not have a published article with its description, but its source code is available[1]. This method is compared with existing state-of-the-art methods in several works.

Otsu Thresholding [16]. This method is based on a global thresholding approach and it is included in this study as a baseline of non-DL methods. It presents good performance in images with uniform backgrounds and it does not require parameter tuning. It is used in most competitions [12,19] and benchmarks [1] as baseline, but it presents some problems handling uneven illuminations, noise and non uniform backgrounds [24].

The main difference between both U-Net implementations is the training data preparation process and parameter tuning. All of the DL algorithms were trained mostly with the same datasets (DIBCO) and the same domains, because of the lack of binarization ground truth images due to the difficulty of this process.

Recognition Algorithms. In this section we present seven of the most recent and relevant recognition algorithms that we employ in this study to evaluate the accuracy of the binarization within the general pipeline. All of them are based on deep learning techniques. We selected these algorithms because of their presence in competitions and their ranks, also the novelty of the approaches, taking mostly recent works, that could contribute to an state-of-the-art review. Moreover, the availability of source codes and pretrained models was an important criterion for the selection.

Semantic Reasoning Networks (SRN) [26]. SRN is a four stage deep learning framework which obtained the best results in the ICDAR 2013 Competition. It uses a ResNet50 backbone network combined with Feature Pyramid Network,

---

[1] https://github.com/masyagin1998/robin.

and two transformer units to obtain a 2D feature map. They created a new attention mechanism called Parallel Visual Attention which improves the efficiency compared to other attention mechanisms.

Self-Attention Text Recognition Network (SATRN) [10]. SATRN is an autoencoder inspired by the work of [25], using some of its modules but introducing some new adaptations and modifications to the original ones.

Baek et al. [2]. This approach presents a Scene Text Recognition (STR) framework with 4 stages. In these 4 stages authors combine text normalization, feature extraction, sequence modeling and character sequence prediction.

Resnet CTC. This is a simple combination of deep learning methods, involving a ResNet backbone as feature extractor and a Connectionist temporal classification (CTC) module which employ the features to predict the characters of the text.

ResNet FC. A simple DL approach which involves a ResNet backbone for extraction and a fully connected layer (FC) for character prediction.

CSTR [4]. This is a classification-based method that uses a two network/stage approach: a backbone network to add hierarchical feature maps, and a second stage network for prediction, named separated convolutions with global average pooling prediction network (SPPN).

Tesseract [22]. This is an OCR engine maintained by Google with a long history in the text recognition task. It has been used as baseline and performance measure in some competitions [12] and surveys [14]. The version used in this work (4.1.1) utilizes an LSTM network for the recognition process. Its sensibility to the use of image preprocessing techniques [8] can help in the analysis of the influence of binarization as this is a preprocessing step.

It is important to note that only the Tesseract, SRN and SATRN models are trained for recognizing punctuation characters. This aspect must be taken into account, since slashes, commas and hyphens are regularly presented in the ID document images, thus affecting the recognition accuracy rate.

4   Proposed Pipeline Analysis and Capture Conditions

In order to determine the impact of the binarization algorithms on the ultimate text recognition task, we propose the following strategy. A first stage will be the analysis of the influence of the printed characters size and resolution on the binarization step. This will allow the selection of optimal sizes for every algorithm in the following stage. A second stage is related to determining the actual effect of the binarization process within the general OCR process.

Influence of Logical Symbol Size in Binarization. Previous studies of binarization algorithms in different contexts have shown a variability in their accuracy depending on the size of the characters for different types of documents [3]. This leads to the need of determining whether there is a relationship between the relative size of the characters and the results of the binarization step as a component of the recognition workflow. Since this type of algorithms are sensitive to the characteristics of the data used in the training step, testing different relative sizes and measuring accuracy values for the different resolutions can throw some light over this topic.

Influence of Binarization on OCR. Previous results have shown that there is an important relationship between the binarization step and OCR, observable in printed documents. However, there are current trends in the direct application of OCR without the presence of binarization, mainly based on deep learning. This is why we believe it is important to assess the role of binarization in these processes. To make this evaluation we will apply several recognition algorithms to the previously binarized images. We will take the best quality images and evaluate the OCR accuracy given their binary masks. Later, we will apply the same process to the raw images, without binarization, and evaluate the behaviour of the metrics in order to establish a relationship between these two steps.

5   Evaluation

We defined two sets of experiments corresponding to each of the proposals presented in Sect. 4. The details are given in this section.

Dataset. For our experiments, we employed the MIDV-500 dataset [1], one of the very few available datasets which focus on ID documents. This dataset contains 50 types of documents, each one with a corresponding source image (or template) with minimal distortions and capture problems (See Fig. 2a). It also contains 10 videos (for each type of document) of 30 frames each, captured with two different devices over 5 scenarios with variable conditions. Since the recognition algorithms surveyed in this work do not include other alphabet than the Latin one, 10 documents that were completely written in other alphabet were excluded from the raw template images in order to obtain a fair comparison.

Performance Metric. For the evaluation of the recognition algorithms, an OCR error rate based on the Normalized Levenshtein Distance was used (See Eq. 1), where r is the recognition result string, g t is the correct text field value provided in the ground truth and L_{Dist} is the Levenshtein Distance as in [15].

$$V(r, g) = \frac{2 * L_{\text{Dist}}(r, g)}{|r| + |g| + L_{\text{Dist}}(r, g)} \tag{1}$$

This distance (1) is computed for each text RoI (Region of Interest) of every document and then the mean of all the $V(r,g)$ of the RoIs is calculated.

Logical Symbol Size Experiments. We conducted an experiment to understand the relationship between the size of the input image and the binarization output. On the DIBCO datasets this size was set to 30 and 60 pixels. Since some binarization algorithms do not explicitly refer to this prescaling process, all the 40 template images were scaled so the character with the greater height match 30, 45 and 60 pixels. The three DL surveyed binarization methods were applied. Since Otsu is not influenced by the size of the images, it was not used in this experiment. The recognition method SRN was used in the resulting bi-tonal image. The evaluation was measured in terms of OCR error rate, according to Eq. 1 and we show the mean of this metric over all 40 documents in Table 1.

Table 1. Error rate of binarization algorithms with different scaling relative to logical symbol height in pixels. Lower is better.

Binarization algorithm	No resize	Symbol size = 30	Symbol size = 45	Symbol size = 60
Gallego et al.	14.77%	**10.49 %**	28.54%	51.99%
Robin	52.66%	21.56%	17.47%	**15.93%**
U-Net-bin	33.46%	15.48%	**14.56%**	27.83%

These results show how the scaling step, in accordance to the symbol size, drastically improves in all cases the result of the binarization as seen in Fig. 1, and consequently, the recognition. It can be seen that for each algorithm, different sizes impact the accuracy in different ways. With no resize, the difference between Gallego and the other algorithms is significant. When using the resize process, the gap among the three methods is greatly reduced. This support the conclusion that the symbol size have a direct relationship with the binarization and OCR pipeline accuracy, that is not proportional to the size itself, but with the size used in the training process of each algorithm.

(a)   (b)

Fig. 1. The result of U-Net-bin application to the image with (a) no prescaling (b) with prescaling to 45 relative symbol pixel height.

Influence of Binarization in OCR. This experiment was conducted in order to provide some insight about how well the selected binarization algorithms behave for ID document analysis in the MIDV-500 dataset, and how this affects the recognition process. For this experiment we employed the best symbol size for each algorithm obtained in the previous experiment, therefor all the template images, were resized in accordance before entering the binarization algorithms. The binarized images resulting from this process (See Fig. 2) were given as input to all the recognition algorithms mentioned in Sect. 3. We also considered the images without the binarization step to assess the recognition under this condition as well. The results were measured with Eq. 1 as the sum of this metric over all 40 documents as shown in Table 2.

Table 2. OCR error rate over the binarization results.

Recognition algorithm	w/o binarization	Binarization algorithm			
		Otsu	Gallego et al.	U–Net-bin	Robin
SRN	**5.97%**	07.15%	10.49%	14.56%	15.93%
Tesseract	**9.23%**	12.32%	13.88%	16.01%	18.24%
SATRN	**17.31%**	18.62%	20.60%	22.31%	24.61%
Baek et al.	**18.83%**	22.75%	24.38%	25.83%	27.34%
ResNet_CTC	**20.22%**	27.35%	26.67%	28.82%	30.02%
CSTR	**23.29%**	25.92%	28.26%	29.47%	30.83%
ResNet_FC	**28.41%**	31.95%	32.47%	33.87%	35.41%

It can be observed that all the recognition algorithms seem to behave better on non-preprocessed images. This can be caused by the nature of the training data, since all were trained for scene text recognition which is a task that has many complex images where the background is not uniform as in a binarized document. Also this may indicate that the binarization algorithms still have room for improvement in order to be useful with these new recognition algorithms in this domain. It can be seen that the Otsu algorithm outperformed all other DL methods. This can be due to the nature of the documents (good quality templates) which have mostly an uniform background, and do not present uneven illumination, blurring or other quality problems that normally affect the behaviour of Otsu. For the deep learning set, Gallego autoencoder approach displayed better performance than the other DL binarization algorithms even if it cannot reach the performance obtained by the non-binarized document image or Otsu's. Another observable result is that the SRN recognition algorithm outperformed by a huge difference all the other approaches, except for Tesseract, but it is important to state that the latter is not an algorithm but an engine, which performs some preprocessing steps (even its own binarization) within their pipeline.

The poor binarization impact in the text recognition pipeline shown in Table 2 may have two possible causes: either current DL-based binarization results are not good enough or current DL-based OCR algorithms are already good enough without the need of preprocessing their input. With the aim of clarifying this point, we created manual ground-truth (GT) binarization images for three templates of the dataset and we repeated the experiment, but just for these three specimens (see Table 3). Due to space limits, we report results only for the best three OCR methods in Table 2. This shows that the handcrafted binarized images obtained lower error rates than the non-binarized images, which means that binarization actually can improve the results of text recognition, but current algorithms still need to be enhanced to get closer to the performance of the GT.

Table 3. OCR error rate over the binarization results of three specimens, including their manual binarization ground truth (GT).

Recognition algorithm	w/o binarization	Binarization GT	Binarization algorithm			
			Otsu	Gallego et al.	U-Net-bin	Robin
SRN	4.97%	**3.55%**	7.15%	10.49%	14.56%	15.93%
Tesseract	9.23%	**8.49%**	12.32%	13.88%	16.01%	18.24%
SATRN	17.31%	**7.10%**	18.62%	20.60%	22.31%	24.61%

The images used in this experiment were the ID document templates. This means that their capture quality is the best possible for these documents, which do not depict capture problems in real-life scenarios. This raises the question of how well these algorithms will behave over video frames captured in uncontrolled environments.

(a)   (b)   (c)   (d)

Fig. 2. Well binarized result samples with different algorithms (a) Original template sample (b) Gallego et al. (c) Robin (d) U-Net-bin

6   Conclusions

In this work, we have reviewed some recent deep learning algorithms for document image binarization and their influence on the text recognition task in the field of identity document images. Our experimental results indicate that there is a direct relationship between character size with the obtained binarized image, and that this relationship depends mainly of the size used in the training stage of these algorithms. In order to make future methods more robust to this factor, we recommend either to include a resizing step in the binarization pipeline or to train the methods taking into account this variable and its possible behaviours. It was shown that for top quality ID document template images, the application of DL-based binarization solutions leads to lower recognition rates than without it. In a good quality scenario, the Otsu method obtains the best results, outperforming DL-based solutions. Thus, these solutions for ID document recognition domain still require major improvements since only the binarized GT outperforms the non-binarized images. For this domain, the SRN algorithm outperformed all the other evaluated methods in terms of recognition rate.

References

1. Arlazarov, V., Bulatov, K., Chernov, T., Arlazarov, V.: MIDV-500: a dataset for identity document analysis and recognition on mobile devices in video stream. Comput. Opt. **43**(5), 818–824 (2019)
2. Baek, J., et al.: What is wrong with scene text recognition model comparisons? Dataset and model analysis. In: International Conference on Computer Vision (ICCV) (2019)
3. Bezmaternykh, P., Ilin, D., Nikolaev, D.: U-Net-bin: hacking the document image binarization contest. Comput. Opt. **43**(5), 825–832 (2019)
4. Cai, H., Sun, J., Xiong, Y.: Revisiting classification perspective on scene text recognition. arXiv preprint arXiv:2102.10884 (2021)
5. Calvo-Zaragoza, J., Gallego, A.J.: A selectional auto-encoder approach for document image binarization. Pattern Recogn. **86**, 37–47 (2019)
6. DIB: Document image binarization. https://dib.cin.ufpe.br
7. Gayer, A., Sheshkus, A., Nikolaev, D.P., Arlazarov, V.V.: Improvement of U-Net architecture for image binarization with activation functions replacement. In: Thirteenth International Conference on Machine Vision. SPIE (2021)
8. Harraj, A.E., Raissouni, N.: OCR accuracy improvement on document images through a novel pre-processing approach. arXiv preprint arXiv:1509.03456 (2015)
9. Kang, S., Iwana, B.K., Uchida, S.: Complex image processing with less data-document image binarization by integrating multiple pre-trained U-Net modules. Pattern Recogn. **109**, 107577 (2021)
10. Lee, J., Park, S., Baek, J., Oh, S.J., Kim, S., Lee, H.: On recognizing texts of arbitrary shapes with 2D self-attention. In: Proceedings of the IEEE/CVF Conference on Computer Vision and Pattern Recognition Workshops, pp. 546–547 (2020)
11. Limonova, E.E., Nikolaev, D.P., Arlazarov, V.V.: Bipolar morphological u-net for document binarization. In: Osten, W., Zhou, J., Nikolaev, D.P. (eds.) Thirteenth International Conference on Machine Vision. SPIE (2021)
12. Lins, R.D., Simske, S.J., Bernardino, R.B.: DocEng'2020 time-quality competition on binarizing photographed documents. In: Proceedings of the ACM Symposium on Document Engineering 2020, pp. 1–4 (2020)
13. Long, J., Shelhamer, E., Darrell, T.: Fully convolutional networks for semantic segmentation. In: 2015 IEEE Conference on Computer Vision and Pattern Recognition (CVPR), pp. 3431–3440. IEEE (2015)
14. Michalak, H., Okarma, K.: Robust combined binarization method of non-uniformly illuminated document images for alphanumerical character recognition. Sensors **20**(10), 2914 (2020)

15. Milyaev, S., Barinova, O., Novikova, T., Kohli, P., Lempitsky, V.: Image binarization for end-to-end text understanding in natural images. In: International Conference on Document Analysis and Recognition, ICDAR, pp. 128–132 (2013)
16. Otsu, N.: A threshold selection method from gray-level histograms. IEEE Trans. Syst. Man Cybern. **9**(1), 62–66 (1979)
17. Peng, X., Cao, H., Natarajan, P.: Using convolutional encoder-decoder for document image binarization. In: 2017 14th IAPR International Conference on Document Analysis and Recognition (ICDAR), vol. 01, pp. 708–713 (2017)
18. Pratikakis, I., Zagoris, K., Barlas, G., Gatos, B.: ICDAR2017 Competition on Document Image Binarization (DIBCO 2017). In: 2017 14th IAPR International Conference on Document Analysis and Recognition (ICDAR). IEEE (2017)
19. Pratikakis, I., Zagoris, K., Karagiannis, X., Tsochatzidis, L., Mondal, T., Marthot-Santaniello, I.: ICDAR 2019 competition on document image binarization (DIBCO 2019). In: 2019 International Conference on Document Analysis and Recognition (ICDAR), pp. 1547–1556 (2019)
20. Rani, U., Kaur, A., Josan, G.: A new binarization method for degraded document images. Int. J. Inf. Technol., 1–19 (2019)
21. Ronneberger, O., Fischer, P., Brox, T.: U-Net: convolutional networks for biomedical image segmentation. CoRR abs/1505.04597 (2015)
22. Smith, R.: An overview of the Tesseract OCR engine. In: International Conference on Document Analysis and Recognition (ICDAR'07), vol. 2, pp. 629–633. IEEE (2007)
23. Tensmeyer, C., Martinez, T.: Document image binarization with fully convolutional neural networks. In: 2017 14th IAPR International Conference on Document Analysis and Recognition (ICDAR), pp. 99–104. IEEE (2017)
24. Tensmeyer, C., Martinez, T.: Historical document image binarization: a review. SN Comput. Sci. **1**(3), 1–26 (2020)
25. Vaswani, A., et al.: Attention is all you need. arXiv preprint arXiv:1706.03762 (2017)
26. Yu, D., et al.: Towards accurate scene text recognition with semantic reasoning networks. In: IEEE/CVF Conference on Computer Vision and Pattern Recognition, pp. 12113–12122 (2020)

Pattern Recognition and Applications

Pattern Recognition Strategies to Classify Traced Neurons

José D. López-Cabrera[1]([✉]) [iD], Leonardo A. Hernández-Pérez[1,2] [iD],
and Juan V. Lorenzo-Ginori[1] [iD]

[1] Informatics Research Center, Universidad Central "Marta Abreu" de Las
Villas, Villa Clara, 54830 Santa Clara, Cuba
josedaniellc@uclv.cu
[2] Empresa de Telecomunicaciones de Cuba S.A, Villa Clara, Santa Clara, Cuba

Abstract. This paper addresses two strategies for pattern recognition in high-dimension data sets, obtained from databases of digitally traced neurons. The first strategy has as distinctive characteristic that the features are obtained both from the whole neuron and from the axon and the dendrites as well. On the other hand, the second strategy is based in feature extraction from data sequences obtained from the decomposition of the traced neuron. Both strategies generate a wide variety of data which result in highly dimensional data sets. Two supervised pattern recognition alternatives were implemented for feature selection. When using the first strategy, the percentage of correctly classified cases raised up to 94.55% once the fusion of data extraction alternatives is performed and the feature selection methods are applied. These results are maintained for three different sets of traced neurons pertaining different regions of the cerebral cortex By means of the second strategy, a group or recursive feature elimination alternatives was evaluated. Using this strategy, the mean percentage of correctly classified cases achieved was 78.5% and 76.79% which are comparable to those obtained using multiple iterations and the computational time was reduced three to four times. The results obtained encourage the use of the proposed strategies to reduce the dimensionality of the data sets obtained from the traced neurons.

Keywords: Feature selection · Pattern recognition · Neuron classification · Traced neurons

1 Introduction

Neurons constitute the basic element of the nervous system and consequently they receive great attention from modern neuroscience. Successful application of digital processing of signals and images in neural morphology studies has been possible since the use of neural tracing techniques, which allow representing the neural structure in terms of spatial coordinates. Visual analysis of the neurons is very slow and prone to errors, which confer great importance to the automated classification of traced neurons [1]. This technique finds application in the study of pathologies or experiments capable of producing modifications in the neuron morphology.

© Springer Nature Switzerland AG 2021
Y. Hernández Heredia et al. (Eds.): IWAIPR 2021, LNCS 13055, pp. 147–157, 2021.
https://doi.org/10.1007/978-3-030-89691-1_15

Therefore, it is essential to find more effective features that allow discriminating different neuron classes improving the results of automated classification as well as the understanding of neural structures. However, the neuron tracing process is still slow and the sets of traced neurons available in the Internet do not contain large numbers of them. Furthermore, it is possible to obtain a high number of features from these structures, which result in high dimensionality data sets.

On the other hand, dealing with high dimensionality data sets is not an easy task. In order to avoid overfitting in the classifiers there is need of guarantee a cases-features ratio of at least 10:1 [2]. Therefore, the classification task should be preceded by an adequate feature selection, in order to satisfy the aforementioned ratio. Likewise, among the data sets dimensionality reduction techniques, feature selection addresses the problem of finding the most compact and informative set of features for a given problem.

The goal of this work is describing two of the strategies that have been used so far to perform an adequate feature extraction and selection in traced neurons data sets. In the first strategy the neuron tree is decomposed in axon and dendrites to extract morphological features based in the L-Measure software [3] as well as variants of the Sholl analysis [4] and based on angles [5]. The discriminating power of these features was determined through evaluation of various families of feature selection methods. On the other hand, in the second strategy data sequences are built from the neural structure, from which a wide set of features is extracted. This set of features is reduced afterwards by means of an iterative elimination of low importance features [6, 7]. Finally, both methods were evaluated by means of automated classifiers. The effectiveness measure employed was the accuracy (Acc) in terms of the percentage of correctly classified cases. When using the first strategy, the Acc values obtained reach 94.55% once the fusion of feature extraction alternatives is performed and the feature selection methods are applied. The second method demonstrated that it is not necessary to apply a procedure with multiple iterations in order to achieve an appropriate data selection: with two iterations, 78.53% and 78.72% mean Acc values are obtained respectively for the two data sets used. We stress the fact that with the two iterations experiment the computational time is reduced approximately four times. The maximum classification results were above 92.5% for both iteration methods and data sets. The application of the proposed strategies pursues making an improvement of the feature selection efficiency as well as to improve the classification indexes. These strategies work under the perspective of pattern recognition with supervised approach in high dimension data sets.

2 Materials and Methods

2.1 Data Bases

All the neurons used in this work were drawn from the NeuroMorpho.Org database [8]. To validate the first strategy the sets named C1, C2 and C3 were used, as shown in Table 1. C1 [9] contains 318 neurons divided in 192 interneurons and 126 pyramidal neurons, C2 [10] is composed by 220 neurons, 104 pertaining Layer 4 and 115 Layer 5 and C3 contains three classes divided in 87 pyramidal, 94 interneurons and 75 thalamocortical neurons.

In order to test the second strategy, two databases of traced neurons were used which were published in [6]. The first database (C4) comprises two sets of neurons: 20 control and 20 small interfering RNA (siRNA). The other database (C5) was also comprised by two groups: 21 controls and 21 nares occlusion (NO).

Table 1. Overview of the data bases used in this study. NM-ID corresponds to the NeuroMorpho.org identifier.

Species	Name	Region	Type	Neurons	Classes	NM-ID
Mouse	C1	Cerebral cortex	Pyramidal/ interneuron	318	2	21154911
Rat	C2	Cerebral cortex	Basket cells	220	2	27847467
Mouse	C3	Neocortex ventral thalamus	Pyramidal/ Interneuron/ Thalamortical	256	3	20141408 19065632
Mouse	C4	Olfactory bulb	Interneuron	40	2	21602912
Mouse	C5	Olfactory bulb	Interneuron	42	2	21602912

2.2 Methods and Tools to Extract and Select Features

In the first strategy the features are obtained directly from the neural structure. When using L-Measure [3] and NeuronCalc [4] the morphological features corresponding to C1, C2 and C3 data sets were obtained. In the second strategy the data sets were obtained from data sequences derived from the neuron structures. These sequences are formed by using Trees Toolbox [11]. Afterwards with the MATS tool [12] the features corresponding to the siRNA (C4) y NO (C5) data sets are extracted. Details on the methods used in both strategies can be found in [4]. The feature selection methods (FSM) used in this research are the same used in [7, 13]. These were divided in different families which were: filters, embedded, wrappers and ensembles. In the case of methods that need setting a threshold to determine the cardinality of the final feature set the approach followed in [14] was used. The threshold used was $\log2(n)$ and 5% of n, n being the cardinality of the feature set. This guaranteed the ratio needed between the numbers of cases and features in order to avoid overfitting [2].

2.3 Pattern Recognition Strategies

In the first strategy, decomposition of the neuron was performed by dividing the neural tree into axon and dendrites. This means that the features were calculated individually for the whole neuron, the axon and the dendrites. The first feature set (LM) was obtained by means of the L-Measure software [3]. When applying an FSM, lower dimension sets were obtained. The subsets obtained in this way were evaluated by means of supervised classification algorithms to determine the best combination classifier-FSM. The same procedure was performed for the remaining sets by using the NeuronCalc tool. In this way the feature sets based in the whole neuron (WN), the axon only (A) and the dendrites only (D) are obtained. Once the best features were determined from the previously mentioned individual feature sets (WN, A, D), a new feature set was created named U-WNAD as the union of these best features. The U-WNAD set was also evaluated to determine the most significant features through FSM. Finally, the union of the best features from both the LM and U-WNAD sets was performed and the new data set obtained was called U-LM-WNAD.

For the second strategy, the method used was conceived in similar way to that used in [4, 7]. An ordered sequence containing the topological information of the neuron was obtained. From this sequence a wide set of 500 features was obtained, and to reduce this dimension a procedure of iterative data elimination was implemented. This procedure employs low computational time evaluators of filtering type and ranker search algorithms. This procedure of iterative reduction eliminated 75, 50, 35 and 10% of the features. An alternative of only two iterations was also employed in which the first one leaves 75, 50, 25, 10 or 0.02% of the features and the second one leaves four features to guarantee the 10:1 cases-features relationship [2]. The computational time was obtained in terms of time consumption of the feature selection and classification algorithms. In this work, a DELL Optiplex 390 computer with Intel Pentium Processor G620 and 4 GB RAM memory was employed.

2.4 Classification Process

In order to evaluate the first pattern recognition strategy, the following classifiers were used: NaiveBayes (NB), DecisionTable (DT), LibSVM, IBk (Knn), C4.5, Logistic, RandomForest (RF) and DecisionStump (DS). Likewise, to evaluate the second strategy the methods employed were: BayesNet, SMO, IB1 and RF using a feature selection procedure which uses low computational time evaluators with ranker search algorithms. These feature evaluators were: ChiSquaredAttributeEval, FilteredAttributeEval, SVMAttributeEval, and ReliefFAttributeEval. All the nomenclature used corresponds to the evaluators and classifiers implemented in Weka [15].

3 Results

3.1 Results of Classification into Neuron Types Using the First Pattern Recognition Strategy

Figure 1 exhibits the mean Acc values and the corresponding standard deviations for each one of the feature subsets and classifiers for the C1 neuron set. The bar colors correspond to the feature extraction method as indicated in the legends. The FSM are grouped by families, as well as the results of no-application of FSM (No-FSM).

On the other hand, Fig. 2 presents the mean Acc values for the subsets that showed the best performance, divided by the alternatives used to extract and combine features. The bars correspond to the mean Acc values for the classifiers employed, as shown in the legends. The number of features used in the classification task is shown between parentheses, followed by the set name. For example, for the LM set the classification process used 12 features.

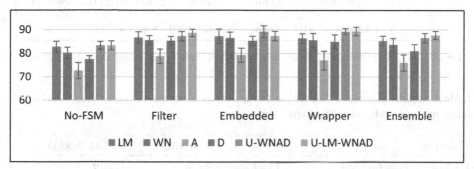

Fig. 1. Mean Acc obtained for the different FSM and classifier families, using the combinations of feature sets for the C1 neuron set.

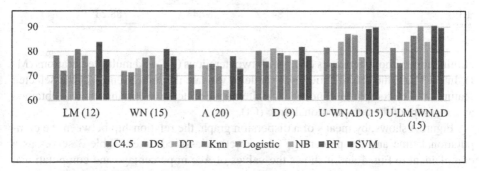

Fig. 2. Classifier performance for the best subsets in terms of Acc, using the C1 neuron set.

The same procedure was performed for the C2 neuron set. The results for the sets which showed the highest Acc are shown in Fig. 3. In this case only three alternatives were used to build the feature sets because these neurons do not have an axon.

Table 2 shows the Acc values for the C3 neuron set. Results are shown for two classifiers before selecting the best performance features and after this. This set of neurons was used only to verify that the best performing features found in the previous tasks maintained their discriminative properties for a multiclass classification problem.

3.2 Results of Classification into Neuron Types Using the Second Pattern Recognition Strategy

When using two traced neurons data sets the purpose was evaluating the percentage of correctly classified cases and the computational time for each alternative of iterative

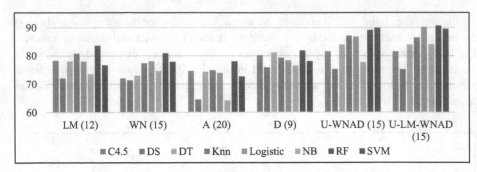

Fig. 3. Classifier performance for the best subsets in terms of Acc, using the C2 neuron set.

Table 2. Results in terms of Acc for the C3 neuron set using the tree-based classifiers family, before reducing the feature set and after doing that.

Classifier		LM	U-WNAD	U-LM-WNAD
C4.5	No-FSM	73.49	74.54	74.79
RF		78.92	79.32	80.13
C4.5	Reduced Set	79.71	80.76	83.42
RF		84.32	87.43	88.24

elimination: without iterations (WI), with two iterations (2-I) and multiple iterations (M-I). In each case the classification was made to validate the effectiveness of the selected feature set. The computing time for each alternative of iterative elimination was obtained as a measure of the computational time (Ct).

Figure 4 shows, by means of a dispersion graph, the relationship between the computational time and the percentage of correctly classified cases. Table 3 serves as a complement to Fig. 4 and it shows the values of Acc in percentage and computational time Cc in seconds. The result obtained when eliminating 10% of the features in each iteration when applying the M-I process is included. This result is not included in Fig. 4 to allow a better visual effect on the rest of the represented values.

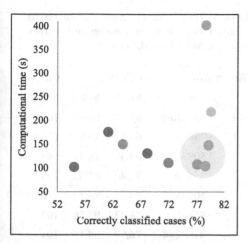

Fig. 4. Dispersion plot relating the computational time with the percentage of correctly classified cases, for the siRNA (C4) data set.

Table 3. Outline of the results for each alternative when using the siRNA neuron set.

Alternative		Acc(%)		Ct(s)
		Mean	Max	
S-I	4 Features	55,00	65	102
2-I	75%-4	61,09	70	175
	50%-4	63,75	77,5	149
	25%-4	68,13	77,5	130
	10%-4	71,88	85	110
	5%-4	77,03	82,5	107
	0.02%-4	78,50	92,5	104
M-I	75%	79,06	95	147
	50%	79,53	95	217
	25%	78,59	87,5	402
	10%	78,91	87,5	990

Table 3 shows the Acc percentage for each one of the alternatives analyzed for the siRNA database. The best results are highlighted in bold, these correspond to the results circled in the scatter plot. The first row shows the result of ranking the set of 500 features and classify using the four best, without a previous iterative selection (S-I). The following six results have in common that they represent the outcome of classifying in only two iterations (2-I). The first of them (75%-4) means that in the first iteration 25% of all features are discarded and the remaining 75% are taken to rank and classify with the four best ones. The remaining five cases of the two-iterations group receive a similar treatment. Finally, the last four rows of the table: 10%, 25%, 50% and 75% represent the result of classifying with four features after eliminating in an M-I process the above mentioned percentage of features (in each iteration) until reaching four features. Each mean value is the result of 16 classifications.

In order to discard the influence of the data set in the results obtained, the same procedure was applied to the NO neuron database. Similarly to the previous data set, C5 data set has 500 features in total. Figure 5 and Table 4 are obtained using the NO neuron data base. These are in correspondence to the previously described for the siRNA neuron data base.

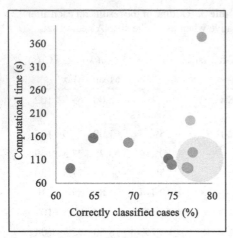

Fig. 5. Dispersion plot relating the computational time with the percentage of correctly classified cases, for the NO neuron data set (C5).

Table 4. Outline of the experimental results obtained for each one of the alternatives when using the NO neuron data set.

Alternative		CCC(%)		Ct(s)
		Mean	Max	
S-I	4 Features	61.90	66,67	102
2-I	75%-4	64.88	73,81	175
	50%-4	69.35	78,57	149
	25%-4	74.40	83,33	130
	10%-4	74.85	88,10	110
	5%-4	**76.93**	**92,86**	**107**
	0.02%-4	**76.79**	**88,10**	**104**
M-I	**75%**	**77.53**	**92,86**	**147**
	50%	77.23	92,86	217
	25%	78.72	88,10	402
	10%	78.27	90,48	990

4　Discussion

From the results shown in Fig. 1 it is observed that the use of FSM improves significantly the Acc values in the classification tasks. Notice that in all cases the mean Acc per FSM family surpass that obtained without applying FSM which evidences the importance of reducing the feature set to use one of greater discriminating power. Likewise, it was evidenced that for the wrappers and embedded FSM families the best global performance is attained, reaching mean Acc values above 86%. The best FSM per family were CFS for filters, SVMattributeval for embedded, RF for wrappers and InformationGain for ensemble along with 15 features. Notice the significant decrement in the final number of features used for classification: subsets of less than 20 features were obtained in most cases. This fact reduces the computational time in the training phase and improves the performance of the classifiers.

From the viewpoint of the feature extraction alternatives, it was observed that the A set showed the worst performance in all cases. Additionally, set LM was surpassed by set D, which evidences the power of the latter to separate these neurons. Notice also that the union of these features increases the performance indexes of the classifiers: the best subsets were obtained for U-WNAD y U-LM-WNAD. In regard of classifier behavior, the Friedman test (0.05 significance) showed that there exist differences among some of the classifiers being compared. The Finner post-hoc test showed that RF attained the best results, exhibiting statistically significant differences which reveal advantages of it when compared to the rest of the classifiers employed here.

An experiment similar to that performed with the C1 neuron set was made for the C2 neuron set. Notice that in this case the traced neurons do not exhibit an axon and therefore in this case there were not features WN or A. Figure 2 shows the results, which agree with those obtained for the C1 set: again, the RF classifier obtained the best results. Likewise, the combination of strategies to obtain the best features showed better results than the individual use of them. Particularly, the strategy of combining features from L-Measure and NeuronCalc and then applying FSM increased the classification effectiveness.

Finally, the effect of using the best performance features in a three-class classification task using the C3 neuron set was evaluated. Table 2 shows the advantage of applying the RF and C4.5 classifiers before and after reducing the feature set. Again, there is an Acc increment for the union of features U-LM-WNAD. This reaffirms the importance of the features selected in previous tasks to contribute in the classification.

On the other hand, some considerations are made on the iterative feature elimination to reduce the dimension of large sets and their computational time. The feature selection tools frequently fail when dealing with high dimensional data sets and this is evidenced here by the results of classification without iterations (S-I), which barely attains 55% Acc and 102 s for the best computational time.

The experiment performed with 2-I demonstrated that when a larger proportion of features is eliminated in the first iteration there is an improvement both in Acc and computer time (see Table 3). This result suggests that the ranker methods do not achieve an appropriate ordering in a large feature set but are capable of discriminating correctly those features that do not carry useful information. This is evidenced by the classification outcome, where 99.98% of the features are discarded in the first iteration leaving only 10 for the second one. This is apparent in the result 0.02%-4 shown in Table 3 which reveals a better result in 23.5% - compared to the no-iterations case- with computation time incremented in only two seconds.

Iterative elimination of features was found as the most reported method in the literature, named here M-I to differentiate it from the other two alternatives mentioned. This method obtained the best results in the present study, however the advantage was only one percent when compared to 2-I (see Table 3).

A significant increment of the computational time is evidenced for the three experiments of the group M-I, which is inversely proportional to the amount of iterations required to eliminate useless features. It is evident that eliminating 75% of the features reduces significantly the number of iterations needed and improves the computational efficiency, and the opposite happens when only 10% of the features are eliminated.

The results obtained using the NO neuron database suggest that the effects of the iterative feature elimination strategy do not depend upon the database. In this case the best result was Acc $= 76.93\%$ with only two iterations and elimination of 95% of the features in the first iteration. On the other hand, the best result using M-I (Acc $= 78.72\%$) was obtained eliminating 25% of the features, which is better than the previously mentioned in 1.79%, but at the price of fourfold computation time.

5 Conclusion

Obtaining a reliable classification of traced neurons is of paramount importance for the efforts made to understanding the brain functioning. There is not currently a definitive solution to this problem, leaving a wide margin to define new pattern recognition strategies capable of improving the computational classification of traced neurons.

The subsets obtained by means of FSM in the task of classification the cerebral cortex by regions evidenced a substantial improvement in terms of Acc in three evaluated classification tasks, in which the RF classifier attained the best results. Moreover, it was shown that the union among distinct methods to extract features makes a significant contribution to the automated classification of traced neurons.

The use of a two iterations process employing low computational time filtering evaluators and ranker-type search algorithms, results can be achieved which are comparable to those obtained using a multiple feature elimination process with a reduction in 3.6 to 4 times in the computation time.

References

1. Zeng, H., Sanes, J.R.: Neuronal cell-type classification: challenges, opportunities and the path forward. Nat. Rev. Neurosci. **18**, 530–546 (2017). https://doi.org/10.1038/nrn.2017.85
2. Foster, K.R., Koprowski, R., Skufca, J.D.: Machine learning, medical diagnosis, and biomedical engineering research-commentary. Biomed. Eng. OnLine **13**, 94 (2014)
3. Scorcioni, R., Polavaram, S., Ascoli, G.A.: L-measure: a web-accessible tool for the analysis, comparison and search of digital reconstructions of neuronal morphologies. Nat. Protoc. **3**, 866–876 (2008)
4. López-Cabrera, J.D., Hernández-Pérez, L.A., Orozco-Morales, R., Lorenzo-Ginori, J.V.: New morphological features based on the Sholl analysis for automatic classification of traced neurons. J. Neurosci. Methods **343**, 108835 (2020). https://doi.org/10.1016/j.jneumeth.2020.108835
5. López-Cabrera, J.D., Lorenzo-Ginori, J.V.: Automatic classification of traced neurons using morphological features. Comput. Sist. **21**, 537–544 (2017). https://doi.org/10.13053/cys-21-3-2495
6. Hernández-Pérez, L.A., Delgado-Castillo, D., Martín-Pérez, R., Orozco-Morales, R., Lorenzo-Ginori, J.V.: New features for neuron classification. Neuroinformatics 1–21 (2018). https://doi.org/10.1007/s12021-018-9374-0
7. Hernández-Pérez, L.A., López-Cabrera, J.D., Orozco-Morales, R., Lorenzo-Ginori, J.V.: Classification of neuron sets from non-disease states using time series obtained through non-linear analysis of the 3D dendritic structures. In: Hernández Heredia, Y., Milián Núñez, V., Ruiz Shulcloper, J. (eds.) Progress in Artificial Intelligence and Pattern Recognition, pp. 17–25. Springer, Cham (2018)
8. Ascoli, G.A., Donohue, D.E., Halavi, M.: NeuroMorpho. Org: a central resource for neuronal morphologies. J. Neurosci. **27**, 9247–9251 (2007)
9. Guerra, L., McGarry, L.M., Robles, V., Bielza, C., Larrañaga, P., Yuste, R.: Comparison between supervised and unsupervised classifications of neuronal cell types: a case study. Dev. Neurobiol. **71**, 71–82 (2011). https://doi.org/10.1002/dneu.20809
10. Vasques, X., Vanel, L., Villette, G., Cif, L.: Morphological neuron classification using machine learning. Front. Neuroanat. **10**, 102 (2016)

11. Cuntz, H., Forstner, F., Borst, A., Häusser, M.: The TREES toolbox—probing the basis of axonal and dendritic branching. Neuroinformatics **9**, 91–96 (2011). https://doi.org/10.1007/s12021-010-9093-7
12. Kugiumtzis, D., Tsimpiris, A.: Measures of Analysis of Time Series (MATS): A MATLAB toolkit for computation of multiple measures on time series data bases. ArXiv10021940 Stat (2010)
13. López-Cabrera, J.D., Lorenzo-Ginori, J.V.: Feature selection for the classification of traced neurons. J. Neurosci. Methods **303**, 41–54 (2018). https://doi.org/10.1016/j.jneumeth.2018.04.002
14. Seijo-Pardo, B., Bolón-Canedo, V., Alonso-Betanzos, A.: Testing different ensemble configurations for feature selection. Neural Process. Lett. **46**, 857–880 (2017). https://doi.org/10.1007/s11063-017-9619-1
15. Bouckaert, R.R., et al.: WEKA manual for version 3-9-1. Univ. Waikato Hamilt. N. Z. (2016)

Evaluation of Hepatic Fibrosis Stages Using the Logical Combinatorial Approach

Nathalie Alemán-García[1] and Martha R. Ortiz-Posadas[2](✉) ⓘ

[1] Post-graduate Biomedical Engineering Program, Universidad Autónoma Metropolitana Iztapalapa, Mexico, Avenue San Rafael Atlixco No. 186, Col. Vicentina, 09340 Alcaldía Iztapalapa, Ciudad de México, CP, México
[2] Electrical Engineering Department, Universidad Autónoma Metropolitana Iztapalapa, Mexico, Avenue San Rafael Atlixco No. 186, Col. Vicentina, 09340 Alcaldía Iztapalapa, Ciudad de México, CP, México
posa@xanum.uam.mx

Abstract. A mathematical model is presented to determine the stage of hepatic fibrosis, applying the logical combinatorial approach of pattern recognition theory. A similarity function was designed to discriminate rats according to their liver tissue characteristics, and a partial precedence algorithm called ALVOT was applied to classify the fibrosis stage. A set of data obtained from the thermal behavior of liver tissue and the identification of the fibrosis stage according to the Metavir score was used. The model was applied to a sample of 16 rats from the reported fibrosis induction animal model, and a comparative analysis was made between the classification made by the Metavir scoring system and the mathematical model presented here. The algorithm correctly classified 75% of the cases.

Keywords: Hepatic fibrosis stages · Supervised classification · Logical-combinatorial pattern recognition

1 Introduction

Hepatic fibrosis is a condition that alters normal structure and composition of the liver. Long term, it leads to complications such as cirrhosis; an advanced stage of chronic liver diseases, which in turn can drive to liver cancer. Hence, knowing the fibrosis degree is an important clinical data that can help in the prognosis and treatment of liver diseases. Because fibrosis implies morphological damage, liver biopsy has come to be the natural gold standard for staging the disease. This procedure carries potential limitations including sampling errors and interobserver variations. Although several means exist for minimizing these risks, such as procurement of biopsies of sufficient length and interpretation of biopsies by experienced liver pathologists [1]. The cost and constraints generated by this invasive procedure has triggered an intensive search for alternative non-invasive methods for staging the disease. In this work we present a noninvasive method for the evaluation of liver fibrosis, by a mathematical model applying the logical combinatorial approach of pattern recognition theory [2]. Data

© Springer Nature Switzerland AG 2021
Y. Hernández Heredia et al. (Eds.): IWAIPR 2021, LNCS 13055, pp. 158–166, 2021.
https://doi.org/10.1007/978-3-030-89691-1_16

obtained from the thermal behavior of liver tissue and the identification of the fibrosis stage according to the Metavir score were [3, 4]. A similarity function was designed to discriminate individuals according to liver tissue characteristics, and a partial precedence algorithm called Voting algorithm [2] was applied to classify the fibrosis stage. Finally, a comparative analysis was made between the classification made by the Metavir score and the logical combinatorial approach.

2   Mathematical Model

Let U be a universe of objects and let us consider a given finite sample $O = \{O_1, \ldots, O_m\}$ of such (descriptions of the) objects. We shall denote by $X = \{x_1, \ldots, x_n\}$ the set of variables used to study these objects. Each of these features has associated a set of admissible values (domain) M_i, $i = 1, \ldots, n$.

Definition 1. An object description O is an n-tuple $I(O) = (x_1(O), \ldots, x_n(O))$, where $x_i: M \to M_i$, for $i = 1, \ldots, n$ are the variables of features used for describing it. Over M_i no algebraic or topologic structure is assumed.

Definition 2. Let $C = \{C_1, \ldots, C_n\}$ be a set of functions called comparison criterion for each variable $x_i \in X$ such as: $C_i: M_i \times M_i \to \Delta_i$; $i = 1, \ldots, n$ where Δ_i can be of any nature; it is an ordered set and can be finite or infinite. The comparison criterion can denote similarity or difference. It is important to remark that every C_i is designed individually to reflect the nature and interpretation of each variable x_i. All comparison criteria must be defined jointly with the experts, in order to incorporate his/her expertise.

2.1   Voting Algorithm

Many problems in Medicine, such as differential diagnosis of diseases, to determine the patient's treatment, or to prognosticate the patient's rehabilitation, are problems of supervised classification. In general, physicians reach their conclusions for diagnosis or prognosis based on the analogies found between medical cases by accumulated knowledge through their experiences and observations. Thus, the analogy concept is present in almost all the reasoning of the medicine specialists. In the logical combinatorial approach, most algorithms of supervised classification are based on partial precedence, and that is why in this work was used the Voting algorithm [2]. This algorithm comprises six steps: 1) Defining the system of support sets; 2) Defining the similarity function; 3) Row evaluation, given a fixed support set; 4) Class evaluation for a fixed support set; 5) Class evaluation for all the system of support sets; and 6) Resolution rule. Thus, to define a voting algorithm, is to define a set of parameters for each of the above six steps.

2.2   Metavir Scoring System

The Metavir scoring is a system used to assess the extent of inflammation and fibrosis by histopathological evaluation in a liver biopsy. The grade indicates the activity or degree of inflammation while the stage represents the amount of fibrosis. Metavir score defines five stages for the disease: F_0: no fibrosis; F_1: Portal fibrosis without septa; F_2:

Portal fibrosis with few septa; F_3: Numerous septa without cirrhosis; F_4: Cirrhosis. The use of this score yields an ordinal qualitative variable so, the mean and standard deviation (σ) of the evaluations were calculated mapping the values as $F_1 = 1, F_2 = 2$ to $F_4 = 4$ progressively [5].

3 Mathematical Model Applied to Hepatic Fibrosis Diagnostic

We defined the variables and their domains, as well as their weights to determine the relative valuations of a shift between the top and bottom of a defined domain. Afterwards, we developed a similarity function to compared different samples of hepatic tissue, and for classifying the stages of the fibrosis we use the Voting algorithm [2].

3.1 Variables

Seven variables were defined for the description of liver tissue (Table 1). The variable x_1 = induction time, was defined with four groups of rats according to the number of weeks of induction (4, 8, 12, 18 weeks). The variable x_2 = weight gain, was determined with the upper weight limit of each of these four groups: 35, 70, 105 and 140 [g]. For fibrosis percentage (x_3), three groups with upper limits were defined: 2, 4 and 6 percent. For x_4 = referenced power, we calculated the average of the difference between the sensor response, in the warm-up period for each individual with respect to the control group. For this variable, six groups were determined, and their upper limits were used: [7.5, 15, 22.5, 30, 37.5, 45]$\times 10^{-3}$. The variable x_5 = fat percentage, was defined with three groups with their upper limits (0.4, 1.2 and 10). For x_6 = standard deviation (SD) of the fibrosis percentage (σ_F), it was expressed by three groups with their upper limits (0.5, 1 and 1.5). The variable x_7 = SD of fat percentage (σ_G), was grouped into three intervals with upper limits at 0.35, 0.7 and 1.75.

3.2 Comparison Criteria

A comparison criterion (C_i) was defined for denoting the difference between two admissible values (M_i) of each variable x_i (Table 1). Observe that for some variables, the maximum difference between them is not one. For example, the induction time (x_1) has a maximum difference of 0.69 between the values 1 (four weeks of induction) and 4 (13 weeks) —data was collected at the 13 weeks of fibrosis induction—, because there are nine weeks of difference (9 (1/13) = 0.69). For the referenced power (x_4), the maximum difference is 0.83 since there is a group of rats within the animal model without fibrosis (control group) that represents the maximum difference $x_4 = 1$. In the same manner, the maximum difference for the variables x_6 = mean of the fat percentage, and x_7 = deviation of the fat percentage, is not one since there is the possibility of finding a lower value (a minimum) for these variables in the control group.

On the other hand, the relevance factor of each variable (ρ_i) was defined jointly with the work team that consisted of three experts in liver structure and function, and two

Table 1. Variables, relevance, domain and comparison criteria for Hepatic Fibrosis

x_i	ρ_i	M_i	C_i					

| x_1. Induction time | 0.25 | [1,4] |

C_1	1	2	3	4
1	0	0.15	0.46	0.69
2		0	0.31	0.54
3			0	0.23
4				0

| x_2. Weight gain | 0.25 | [1,4] |

C_1	1	2	3	4
1	0	0.3	0.7	1
2		0	0.3	0.7
3			0	0.3
4				0

| x_3. Fibrosis percentage (mean) | 0.2 | [1,3] |

C_3	1	2	3
1	0	0.5	1
2			0.5
3			0

| x_4. Referenced power (sensor) | 0.1 | [1,6] |

C_4	1	2	3	4	5	6
1	0	0.17	0.33	0.5	0.67	0.83
2		0	0.17	0.33	0.5	0.67
3			0	0.17	0.33	0.5
4				0	0.17	0.33
5					0	0.17
6						0

| x_5. Fat percentage (mean) | 0.1 | [1,3] |

C_5	1	2	3
1	0	0.08	0.96
2		0	0.92
3			0

| x_6. SD fibrosis percentage (σ_F) | 0.05 | [1,3] |

C_6	1	2	3
1	0	0.5	1
2		0	0.5
3			0

| x_7. SD Fat percentage (σ_G) | 0.05 | [1,3] |

C_7	1	2	3
1	0	0.2	0.8
2		0	0.4
3			0

experts in the measurement and sensing of physical variables. The variables with the greatest relevance were x_1 = induction time and x_2 = weight gain, as they were the independent variables. The fibrosis percentage (x_3) also obtained a high value (ρ_4 = 0.2) because it is a parameter directly related to liver fibrosis. The description of each rat ($D(R_j)$) was expressed in accordance with (4):

$$D(R_j) = (x_1, x_2, x_3, x_4, x_5, x_6, x_7) \tag{4}$$

$D(R_j)$= (induction time, weight gain, fibrosis percentage, referenced power, fat per. centage, SDFibrosis, SDFat).

3.3 Similarity Function

Comparison criteria as well as similarity function can denote similarity or difference. In this work, the comparison criteria (C_i) were defined for denoting difference. The greater the difference, the greater the value (Table 1). Since the similarity function is defined by the comparison criteria and these are of difference, it was necessary to calculate the symmetric value to find the similarity between the two descriptions of liver tissue compared. The similarity function was defined with (5).

$$\begin{aligned}
\beta(I(R_j)I(R_r)) = 1 - [&0.25C_1(x_1(R_j), x_1(R_r)) + 0.25C_2(x_2(R_j), x_2(R_r)) \\
&+ 0.20C_3(x_3(R_j), x_3(R_r)) + 0.10C_4(x_4(R_j), x_4(R_r)) \\
&+ 0.10C_5(x_5(R_j), x_5(R_r)) + 0.05C_6(x_6(R_j), x_6(R_r)) \\
&+ 0.05C_7(x_7(R_j), x_7(R_r))]
\end{aligned} \tag{5}$$

3.4 Fibrosis Hepatic Evaluation Using the Metavir Score as Classification Criterion

The Metavir evaluations used in this work were made on 40 images acquired from the liver of 16 rats from the reported fibrosis induction animal model [4, 5]. Three Metavir evaluations were performed blindly and independently by three experts from the Liver, Pancreas and Motility Laboratory (HIPAM, its Spanish acronym), of the Experimental Medicine Unit of the General Hospital of Mexico. The final evaluation of the fibrosis stage for each rat was made by estimating the mode of the three evaluations (Table 2).

The 16 fibrosis-induced rats were divided into two groups. The learning matrix (LM) was constructed with 12 rats distributed in four classes corresponding to the four phases of liver fibrosis according to the Metavir scale (Table 3). The four rats to be classified (control sample) were those that presented inconsistencies between the actual fibrosis progress and the expected one: R_{1B}, R_{2C}, R_{3D} and R_{4C}, [4, 5]. R_{1B} was diagnosed by experts as F_3 but an F_1 stage was expected, and R_{2C} had an F_1 diagnosis, although it received an induction to the F_2 stage.

The Voting algorithm classification was correct only for the R_{2C} in F_1. In the other three rats there was no coincidence: R_{1B} was classified in F_2, and it was diagnosed by

Table 2. Rats data and metavir evaluation for Hepatic Fibrosis

	Rat data		Metavir evaluation		
Group	Rat name	Weigth [g]	Fibrosis stage	Mean	Standard deviation
T1	A	311	F1	1.1	0.316
	B	321	F3	2.5	0.707
	C	335	F1	1.3	0.483
	D	345	F1	1.3	0.675
T2	A	311	F2	1.7	0.483
	B	287	F2	1.7	0.483
	C	315	F1	1.2	0.422
	D	340	F2	2.1	0.568
T3	A	300	F2	2.0	0.471
	B	352	F4	3.9	0.316
	C	378	F3	3.3	0.483
	D	342	F4	3.7	0.483
T4	A	372	F4	4.0	0
	B	382	F4	4.0	0
	C	386	F3	2.9	0.316
	D	384	F4	3.7	0.483

Table 3. Classification results considering the metavir evaluation as classification criteria

Class (Fibrosis stage)	Rats for classification				
	Classified rats	R1B	R2C	R3D	R4C
F_1	R_{1A}	0.78	0.84	0.54	0.28
	R_{1C}	0.86	**0.96**	0.62	0.33
	R_{1D}	0.83	0.88	0.58	0.37
F_2	R_{2A}	0.78	0.88	0.62	0.29
	R_{2B}	0.76	0.86	0.60	0.31
	R_{2D}	**0.90**	0.83	0.79	0.54
	R3A	0.75	0.68	0.79	0.51
F_3	R3C	0.68	0.57	**0.92**	0.76
F_4	R3B	0.88	0.78	0.88	0.55
	R4A	0.59	0.49	0.84	**0.80**
	R4B	0.54	0.47	0.73	0.73
	R4D	0.50	0.43	0.74	0.77

the experts in F_3. Its description with the original values of the variables was: $R_{T1B} = (46, 1, 0.0312, 2.79, 0.78, 0.068, 0.027)$ Mapping the variables to the established ranges:

$$R_{T1B} = (2, 1, 5, 2, 2, 1, 1)$$

This rat had an induction time of 4 weeks. Note that the first two variables of greatest relevance correspond to the values in the first weeks of induction, so their contribution suggests a lower classification (few time and little weight gain).

R_{3D} was classified at F_3 and was diagnosed at F_4. Its description was: $R_{T3D} = (62, 3, 0.0335, 4.633, 1.115, 0.1823, 0.1335)$, Mapping the variables in the established ranges:

$$R_{T3D} = (2, 3, 5, 3, 3, 1, 1).$$

As with R_{B1}, the variables x_1 and x_2 indicate membership in a lower class.

The rat R_{4C} obtained the most significant vote for class F_4 and was diagnosed in F_3. The description of the rat was:
$R_{T4C} = (101, 4, 0.0104, 4.337, 1.1925, 9.763, 1.6045)$ Mapping the variables in the established ranges:

$$R_{T4C} = (3, 4, 2, 3, 3, 3, 3).$$

The percentage of fat observed in this rat is completely atypical. The average of the rats in the T4 group, without considering this case, is 0.53% fat, and R_{4C} has almost 19 times faster than the rest of the rats that shared the same induction time. It is likely that this fact affected the rest of the parameters. It is important to mention that commonly, in cases with abundant steatosis (intrahepatic fat), a peri-cellular fibrosis pattern is found (colloquially called "chicken wire") that could influence the fibrosis quantification.

The results obtained so far indicate that the seven defined variables do not provide sufficient information to correctly discriminate the evolution of liver fibrosis, since there was a 25% success rate in the classification. On the other hand, it should be noted that the diagnosis based on the Metavir score is based on distinguishing morphological patterns by experts, which are not necessarily related to the amount of fibrosis and therefore, could not be a good parameter to define the classes of the Learning Matrix, given the physical nature of the variables considered for the design of the similarity function. Therefore, a different way of defining classes is proposed, as described below.

3.5 Fibrosis Hepatic Evaluation Using Fibrosis Percentage as Classification Criterion

A modified Learning Matrix (LM') was constructed, using the variable $x_3 = $ percentage of fibrosis as a criterion to conform the classes. It is a quantitative variable directly related to the problem to be studied and is measured on a continuous scale. This variable is 3-valued (Table 1), and each value corresponds to a stage of fibrosis: low, medium, and high. It should be clear that these classes are not the same as those considered in the Metavir scale (Table 2). The objective of these three proposed classes is to provide a new criterion for the classification of the liver fibrosis stage. The classes intervals were defined with the liver pathologists, and it correspond to the average percentage of fibrosis per rat, were: Class 1 corresponds to the interval [0, 2%], Class 2 to [2.1, 4%] and, Class 3 to [4.1, 6%]. The mode of the Metavir evaluation and its $SD_{Metavir}$ were incorporated to the LM'. Thus, the description of each rat was expressed with (4) changing the variables related to fibrosis for those related to Metavir:

$D(R_j)$ = (induction time, weight gain, referenced power, **Metavir mode**, fat percentage, $\mathbf{SD_{Metavir}}$, SD_{Fat}).

The same four rats were classified: R_{1B}, R_{2C}, R_{3D} and R_{4C}, and the rest were used to construct the second proposed LM'. The ALVOT algorithm correctly classified 75% of the cases. Table 4 shows the results obtained by the similarity function β (5). The rats R_{1B}, R_{2C} and R_{4C} were classified in their class: Class 2, Class 1 and Class 3, respectively. R_{3D} obtained the most significant vote for Class 2, but it belongs to Class 3 according to its mean of percentage of fibrosis (4,633). The description of this rat was:

R_{R3D} = (62, 3, 4, 0.483, 0.0335, 0.1823, 0.1335) Mapping the variables in the established ranges:

$$R_{R3D} = (2, 3, 4, 3, 5, 1, 1)$$

Table 4. Classification results considering fibrosis percentage as classification criteria

Class	Classified rat	Rat for classification			
		R1B	R2C	R3D	R4C
Low fibrosis [0,2%]	R_{1A}	0.71	0.85	0.55	0.37
	R1C	0.83	**0.96**	0.67	0.42
	R1D	0.79	0.89	0.59	0.42
	R_{2A}	0.80	0.82	0.72	0.44
	R_{2B}	0.78	0.80	0.70	0.46
Medium fibrosis [2.1, 4%]	R_{2D}	**0.85**	0.90	0.77	0.56
	R3A	0.70	0.75	0.77	0.54
	R3B	0.77	0.69	**0.98**	0.59
High fibrosis [4.1, 6%]	R3C	0.79	0.68	0.84	**0.74**
	R4A	0.59	0.51	0.80	0.70
	R4B	0.51	0.46	0.72	0.66
	R4D	0.52	0.48	0.74	0.67

Comparing the results with the previous classification by Metavir score, there are two elements that must be highlighted. First, choosing a physical parameter to form the classes is better, since the identification of the fibrosis phase in which a certain rat is related to this type of parameter. The description of the rats in terms of the physical parameters and the classification strategy based on the similarity between the rats already classified, also results in a different perspective and better attached to reality. That is, the model with the logical-combinatorial approach improved the initial classification. In this sense, it would be interesting not to consider the Metavir qualitative classification, and only involve quantitative parameters in the model. Second, the weights of the variables and of the comparison criteria depend on the relevance that the experts have defined for each of them, and this is reflected in the final score obtained by the similarity function as well.

4 Conclusion

The results of this work represent a contribution, not only for the development of new non-invasive methods for the diagnosis of liver fibrosis, but also in the characterization of the tissue with physical parameters, in such a way that there is more information that, in turn, contribute to new treatment and prevention alternatives.

It is important to say that these are preliminary results. We realize that the sample studied was small. It would be advisable to use a greater number of rats, whose biopsy results allow a more representative statistic to be made.

This is the first approximation in the use of the logical-combinatorial approach of pattern recognition theory in identifying the stage of liver fibrosis so, as future work, we intend to carry out sensitivity and reliability tests on the model.

References

1. Bedossa, P., Carrat, F.: Liver biopsy: the best, not the gold standard. J Hepatol. **50**(1), 1–3 (2009). https://www.journal-of-hepatology.eu/article/S0168-8278(08)00707-1/fulltext, https://doi.org/10.1016/j.jhep.2008.10.014. Epub 2008 Nov 6. PMID: 19017551
2. Ortiz-Posadas, M.R.: The logical combinatorial approach applied to pattern recognition in medicine. In: Toni, B. (ed.) New Trends and Advanced Methods in Interdisciplinary Mathematical Sciences. SSTEAMH, pp. 169–188. Springer, Cham (2017). https://doi.org/10.1007/978-3-319-55612-3_8
3. Bedossa, P., Poynard, T.: An algorithm for the grading of activity in chronic hepatitis C. Metavir Coop. Study Group. Hepatol. **24**(2), 289–293 (1996)
4. Aleman-García, N., et al.: Fibrosis evaluation of animal liver tissue by thermal conduction. In: Torres, I., Bustamante, J., Sierra, D. (eds) VII Latin American Congress on Biomedical Engineering, CLAIB 2016, IFMBE Proceedings, vol. 60, pp. 884–887. Springer, Singapore (2016).https://doi.org/10.1007/978-981-10-4086-3_169
5. Alemán-García, N.: Study of hepatic alterations due to fibrosis with photo-thermal characterization techniques. Thesis of Master's in Sciences in Biomedical Engineering. Universidad Autónoma Metropolitana Iztapalapa, Mexico City (In Spanish) (2017)

A Proposal of Condition Monitoring with Missing Data and Small-Magnitude Faults in Industrial Plants

José M. Bernal-de-Lázaro[1] ⓘ, Carlos Cruz Corona[2] ⓘ,
Marcelo Lisboa Rocha[3] ⓘ, Antônio J. Silva Neto[4] ⓘ,
and Orestes Llanes-Santiago[1](✉) ⓘ

[1] Universidad Tecnológica de La Habana José Antonio Echeverría, La Habana, Cuba
jbernal@automatica.cujae.edu.cu, orestes@tesla.cujae.edu.cu
[2] Universidad de Granada, Granada, Spain
[3] Universidade Federal do Tocantins, Palmas, TO, Brazil
[4] Universidade do Estado do Rio de Janeiro, Nova Friburgo, RJ, Brazil

Abstract. The patterns of incipient and small-magnitude faults are easily masked by the effect of interferences, missing data, and noisy measurements which are common in the industrial environments. Therefore, a smart data analysis of these patterns is needed for effectively minimizing the false and missing alarm rates resulting from noise, uncertainty, and unknown disturbances with the goal to achieve high detection performances, even in presence of missing data in the observations. This paper provides a novel methodology for the on-line imputation of missing data by using three techniques: Fuzzy C-means (FCM), Singular Value Decomposition (SVD), and Partial Least Squares regression (PLSr). Afterward, a data preprocessing stage using the KPCA and Exponentially Weighted Moving Average (EWMA-ED) is developed. The effectiveness of the proposal to obtain satisfactory results in the detection of small-magnitude faults was validated by using the Tennessee Eastman (TE) process benchmark.

Keywords: Incipient faults · Missing data · EWMA-ED · KPCA

1 Introduction

There is an increasing interest in the development of data-based techniques for the fault detection in production plants [9,19]. However, the performance of these techniques can be seriously affected by outliers, noisy measurements, and missing data, which are very common in industrial environments [7]. The observations with incomplete values can result from the occasional disrupt of data acquisition systems, sensor failure, merging data from different systems, inconsistent

National Program of Research and Innovation - ARIA, Project No. 27, CITMA, Cuba and CAPES-PRINT, Process No. 88881.311758/2018-01, from Brazil.

Y. Hernández Heredia et al. (Eds.): IWAIPR 2021, LNCS 13055, pp. 167–176, 2021.
https://doi.org/10.1007/978-3-030-89691-1_17

sampling rates, possible errors in transmission networks and communication protocols among other reasons [23]. It is known that missing data could hide relevant information about possible relations between variables and abnormal operating conditions [14]. Then, the imputation procedures should be part of the fault diagnosis systems for handling the missing data.

Some advanced procedures for handling the missing data problem include the use of the Moving-average models, regression approaches [6], statistical methods such as the mean substitution [1], and Expectation-maximization algorithms [29]. Likewise, imputation procedures based on the Artificial Neural Network [17], Bayesian networks [2], and Fuzzy Inference System [15] have also been successfully utilized. However, these approaches have been mainly evaluated in areas where the computational complexity is not high, and the real time concept are not strictly relevant such as biological researches [22], social sciences [24], and clinical studies [3]. For complex industrial processes such as chemical and pharmaceutical industries where the demands of efficiency, quality, and safety are very high, the typical procedures to deal with the missing data imply a hard limitation [14]. Moreover, in the monitoring of incipient faults, it is necessary to minimize the bias added by the imputation procedures for not distort the behavior of the variables, and to take into account that slow changes in the processes due to faults can be masked by the effect of control procedures, disturbances and noise.

The main objective of this paper and its main contribution is to propose a fault diagnosis methodology wherein the on-line imputation of the missing data patterns is considered with the aim to improve the performance of the fault diagnosis systems even in presence of small-magnitude faults. Three imputation methods to deal with the missing values are evaluated in the proposal: Fuzzy C-means (FCM), Singular Value Decomposition (SVD), and Partial Least Squares Regression (PLSr). These algorithms are powerful computational tools for imputation tasks, but other approaches could also be utilized [5,8,22].

This paper is organized as follows, Sect. 2 presents the proposed methodology, the TE benchmark and the main characteristics of the missing data mechanisms used in the paper. The results are discussed in Sect. 3. Finally, the conclusions and future works are given in Sect. 4.

2   Materials and Methods

2.1   Description of the Proposed Methodology

The proposed methodology is summarized in Fig. 1. Notice that this procedure requires an off-line phase where by using a historical data set, all parameters of the algorithms used in the fault detection system are tuned and the mean vector of each class is determined. In the proposal $X = \{x_1, x_2, \cdots, x_i\} \subset \mathbf{R}^{i \times j}$ denotes the historical data set obtained from an industrial process, where $i = 1, 2, ..., c * m$, $j = 1, 2, .., p$, c represents the number of operation states or classes (normal operation state and fault states), m identifies the number of observations without missing values that belong to each operation state and p represents the number of variables in each observation.

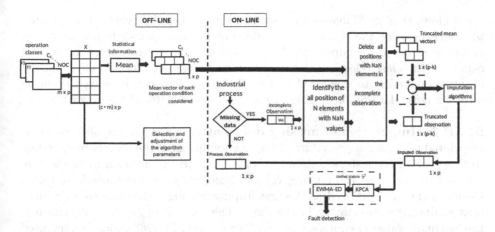

Fig. 1. Procedure proposed for handling incomplete observations and fault detection.

STEP 1: (Finding the missing data positions). Missing data patterns are successive observations where one or more variables are temporarily unavailable, which result in inconsistent values that not reflect the actual state of the measured physical quantity [13]. As it is shown in Fig. 1, the procedure begins with the location of missing variables in the observation acquired. If the observation does not have missing variables, it is directly analyzed to decided if it belongs to the normal operation state or not. If there are k missing variables, they are removed to obtain a modified vector $\tilde{x}_{1 \times (p-k)}$, where only the available variables are considered.

STEP 2: (Classification of the partial information). In the second step, the same k variables missed in the observation are removed in the mean vector of each class. The modified observation $\tilde{x}_{1 \times (p-k)}$ and the mean vectors $\bar{x}_{i \times (p-k)}$ for $i = 1, .., c$ are compared. To determine a possible class to which the observation $\tilde{x}_{1 \times (p-k)}$ may belong, a majority vote decision and three similitude metrics are considered:

$$d_1(\tilde{x}', \bar{x}') = \langle \tilde{x}', \bar{x}' \rangle_{\mathrm{F}} \left[\langle \tilde{x}', \tilde{x}' \rangle_{\mathrm{F}} \langle \bar{x}', \bar{x}' \rangle_{\mathrm{F}} \right]^{-\frac{1}{2}} \tag{1}$$

$$d_2(\tilde{x}', \bar{x}') = \left[\frac{1}{(p-k)} \sum_{i=1}^{p-k} (\bar{x}'_i - \tilde{x}'_i)^2 \right]^{-\frac{1}{2}} \tag{2}$$

$$d_3(\tilde{x}', \bar{x}') = \frac{2}{\sqrt{\pi}} \int_{\psi}^{\infty} e^{-t^2} \, dt \tag{3}$$

The metric in Eq. (1) is defined as the normalized Frobenius inner product between the imputed data and the covariance matrix of the mean vector [16]. The second metric (Eq. (2) is the inverse of the Root Mean Square Error (RMSE). The third metric is a similarity factor represented by Eq. (3), and proposed in [25], which can be understood as the probability that the center of each cluster is not closer than its Mahalanobis distance. Finally, the observation is associated to a class by using the majority vote rule. The purpose of associating the observation to a class is for improving the subsequent imputation process. If an error occurs in the class selection, the imputation process produces an effect on the observation similar to that produced by the noise. This can be solved by using a robust noise data preprocessing mechanism as the Kernel-PCA algorithm.

STEP 3: (Imputation of missing data patterns). After the observation is associated to a class, a procedure of imputation by using the data corresponding to this class in the historical data set is made. Three imputation methods were selected to deal with the missing values in this stage of the procedure. Fuzzy C-Means (FCM) is utilized as the first imputation algorithm due to its robustness against the uncertainty in the data. The second imputation algorithm is the Singular Value Decomposition (SVD) proposed by [26] which is very used in these issues because of its satisfactory results. The last imputation method is the NIPALS-PLSr algorithm, which replaces the missing values with predicted scores using a regression approach [20]. To evaluate the performance of these imputation methods, the RMSE is always used.

STEP 4: (Dimensionality reduction of the imputed observations). After the imputation of missing values, the Kernel PCA (KPCA) and EWMA with enhanced dynamic (EWMA-ED) are used to remove the irrelevant information (i.e., outliers, noise, and correlate variable process) that may hide the faults in development or overload the system's management. In this case, the RBF kernel was selected by its good results in similar applications.

STEP 5: (Dynamic smoothing of the detection statistics). In order to detect small changes resulting from the abnormal conditions of the process, the Squared Prediction Error (SPE) and Hotelling's T^2 are integrated by using the unified index (φ) in Eq. (4) [28]. Afterward, the smoothing through an EWMA scheme with reinforcing dynamic is applied.

$$\varphi_\delta(t) = \frac{\text{SPE}}{\text{UCL}_{\text{spe}}} + \frac{T^2}{\text{UCL}_{T^2}} \tag{4}$$

$$\varphi_\delta(t) = \delta\lambda\varphi_\delta(t) + (1-\lambda)\varphi_\delta(t-1) \tag{5}$$

The EWMA-ED given in Eq. (5) uses an enhanced factor (δ) to emphasize the current value of the statistics, without ignoring the previous observations [12]. Note that λ is a constant ($0 < \lambda \leq 1$) that determines the depth of memory used on the statistics and δ is an enhanced parameter, such that $0 < \delta \cdot \lambda \leq 1$. In each case, the confidence limits of statistics are also determined by using their conventional version. The confidence limit of UCL_{T^2} can be calculated by the data probability distribution. The confidence limit for UCL_{spe} is given by

$$\begin{cases} \text{UCL}_{\text{spe}} = \theta_1 \left[\frac{h_0 c_\alpha \sqrt{2\theta_2}}{\theta_1} + \frac{\theta_2 h_0(h_0-1)}{\theta_1^2} + 1 \right]^{1/h_0} \\ \theta_i = \sum_{j=\alpha+1}^n \zeta_j^i \qquad h_0 = 1 - \frac{2\theta_1\theta_3}{3\theta_2^2} \end{cases} \tag{6}$$

For both statistics, the 95% confidence limit is adopted. The upper control threshold for the φ_δ statistic is obtained through kernel density estimation (KDE). The Fault detection rate (FDR) is also calculated by using Eq. (7) in order to evaluate the fault detection process tasks.

$$FDR = \frac{\text{No. of samples } (\varphi > \varphi_{lim} | fault \neq 0)}{\text{total samples } (fault \neq 0)} \times 100\% \qquad (7)$$

2.2 Case of Study: Tennessee Eastman Process

The Tennessee Eastman is a chemical benchmark used extensively in the process monitoring research. This benchmark process , consists of five interconnected units: a reactor, a vapor-liquid separator, a product condenser, a recycle compressor, and a product stripper [4]. In this paper, three faults F1, F3, and F15 are used to validate the effectiveness of the proposal. The fault F1 was selected because of it is an abrupt fault, while F3 and F15 are small-magnitude faults for which high detection performances are not usually achieved in the specialized literature. The variables affected by the fault F3 have very similar behaviors in terms of the mean and variance with the normal operating condition of the process. The fault F15 results from an unexpected increase in the inlet temperature of the condenser cooling water. Such variation causes a shift on the mean condenser cooling flow, which produces an out-of-control for other operation variables. However, as a result of the control loops, the affected variables can be returned to their set-point excepting the temperature of the condenser cooling water.

It is important to highlight that this benchmark has no natural incomplete measurements. Therefore, missing values were artificially induced into the historical data sets by using three standard mechanisms for planned missing data designs [2, 14, 23]. Missing at Random (MAR) mechanism that occurs when the probability that the variable x_{ij} is missing depends on the other observed variables, but not on the value of the missing variable itself. Missing Completely at Random (MCAR) mechanism that occurs when the probability that the variable x_{ij} is missing is unrelated to the value of x_{ij} itself or any other variable in the data set X. Finally, non-ignorable case, also known as Missing not at Random (NMAR) mechanism that occurs when the probability that the variable x_{ij} is missing is related to the value of x_{ij} itself even if the other variables are controlled in the analysis. Based on the study developed by [23], four types of missing data patterns were considered in the present paper: Drop-out missingness and Patterned missingness representing the MCAR mechanism, Random missingness representing the MAR mechanism and Censor missingness as an example of the NMAR mechanism. Moreover, in this study different percentages of missing measurements varying from 1% to 20% are considered. The aim is to evaluate the behavior of the proposed methodology against several types missing data patterns.

3   Experimental Results

The parameters values of the above algorithms should be adjusted before to use the procedure proposed. In this case, the number of eigenvalues for KPCA is selected by using the criterion $\lambda_i/sum(\lambda_i) > 0.0001$. Consequently, the dimension of the feature space for the TE data sets is reduced to $\mathbf{R}^{33} \rightarrow \mathbf{R}^{19}$, according to the cutoff value selected. Meanwhile, the parameter values of the kernel function and EWMA-ED are chosen according to the suggested values in [12], such that: $\sigma = 1276.22911$, $\lambda = 0.00666$, and $\delta = 3.04656$.

3.1   Classification of Incomplete Observations

A qualitative comparison of the results of the second step of the proposal are provided in Fig. 2. These results are analyzed by using four graphical blocks representing how the partial observations without the missing values generated by different missingness are classified in one of possible operating condition of the process.

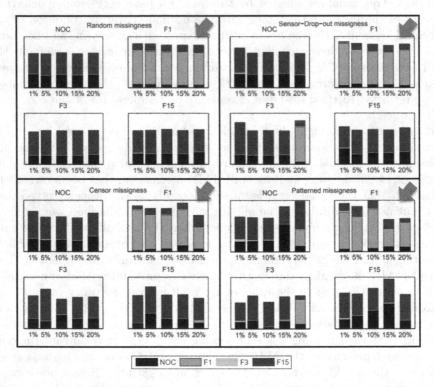

Fig. 2. Qualitative comparison of the results from the second step of the proposal.

In each block, four bar graphs show the results for the operating conditions that are studied. The title of each bar graphs shows the target class expected in the output of the classification procedure (i.e., NOC, F1, F3, F15). The colored and individual length of the bar graphs are used to reveal the proportion of the partial observations misclassified with respect to the target class expected. As can be appreciated in marked graphs most of the observations corresponding to the fault F1 are correctly recognized. Notice that a successful data classification is given by graphs where the mainly color and the length of the bars are associated with the target class expected. In contrast to the fault F1, the faults F3 and F15 show high confusion levels with respect the NOC class.

3.2 Results of the Imputation and Detection Stages

The results for the third step of the proposal are shown in Fig. 3. In this case, no significant differences between the imputation results made for the different algorithms for the normal operation condition (NOC), F3, and F15 were found.

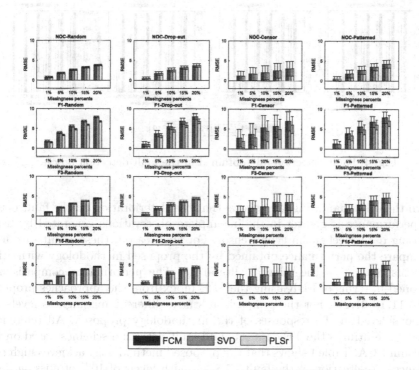

Fig. 3. Imputation performances obtained from the FCM, SVD, and PLSr algorithms.

For the first two cases, the RMSE values are always less than 5% regardless of the missing data mechanisms evaluated. Further analysis shown that the worst results during the imputation procedure are obtained for the fault F1. As shown in Fig. 3, a performance greater than 90% for the three imputation algorithms was achieved. The results obtained show an expected decrease in the performance of the algorithms due to the increased percentages of missing data in the simulations. The impact of the imputation stage was further analyzed considering the non-parametric Wilcoxon test, where no imputation algorithm was the winner for a level of significance $\alpha = 0.05$.

Based on these results, Fig. 4 depicts a comparison between the fault detection performances obtained for the different missing data mechanisms when the PLSr algorithm is utilized for the missing data treatments. Meanwhile, Fig. 4 reveals that higher fault detection performances are obtained for the Drop-out and Patterned missingness. Notice that for the fault F1, a detection performance greater than 98% is always achieved. For the fault F3, the detection performance overcomes the 80% only in the simulations with 1% and 5% of missing values. Besides, the detection of the fault F15 is seriously affected by the imputation of the incomplete observations of the process.

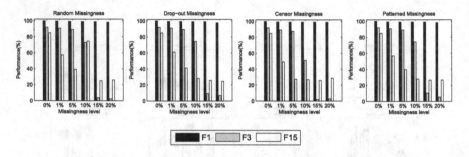

Fig. 4. Fault detection rate obtained in the fault detection process

On the other hand, Fig. 4(c) shows that the deterioration on the fault detection performance is greater in the incomplete observations generated by using a missing data mechanism type Censor. For this reason, these results are used to compare the performance obtained by the proposed methodology with other proposals present in the scientific literature. The performance comparison is developed in terms of FDR using the SPE index from the approaches proposed by [10, 11, 18, 21, 27]. For the comparison study, different missingness levels are also considered in the responses of the methodology proposed. All referenced works above utilizes the TE data sets and fault detection schemes based on the algorithm PCA. Table 1 shows that the proposed methodology achieves high performances of detection of the fault F1 even with levels of 10% of missing data. In the case of the faults F3 and F15, the performance of the proposed methodology decreases when the percentage of missing data is increased. However, the performance of the proposed methodology is better than the other techniques even when they are not affected by the missing variables. These results confirm the validity of the proposed scheme for the detection of the incipient faults in the industrial plants even in presence of missing data.

Table 1. Fault detection rate (FDR %) based on the SPE statistics for the faults

	Rato et al., 2016	Yu et al., 2017	Sánchez et al., 2018	Harkat et al., 2019	Hamrouni et al., 2020	Results obtained with the methodology proposed considering a Censor missigness			
Faults	MWPCA	NDPCA	PCA_{RES}	$IKPCA_{UL}$	$IKPCA_{CR}$	PMV 0%	PMV 1%	PMV 5%	PMV 10%
F1	99.60	99.50	99.88	100	98.96	100.0	99.70	99.68	99.50
F3	0.40	3.26	6.20	22.40	8.89	92.02	89.68	87.90	50.90
F15	0.20	28.16	9.10	27.20	6.95	85.04	49.21	28.03	25.10

4 Conclusions

In this paper, a new methodology to improve the detection of small-magnitude faults with missing data was proposed. The proposal was evaluated by using the TE process. In the analysis, it was evidenced that the detection of small-magnitude faults is affected by the bias added in the imputation procedures. However, the proposed methodology achieves better results than recent fault detection systems proposed in the scientific literature even when the data used by those proposals were not affected by missing values. These results confirm the validity of the proposed methodology. In future works, it is necessary to continue working on improving the performance levels achieved in the detection process in the presence of missing variables by evaluating other variants of detection tools.

References

1. Ardakani, M., Shokry, A., Saki, G., Escudero, G., Graells, M., Espuña, A.: Imputation of missing data with ordinary kriging for enhancing fault detection and diagnosis. In: Computer Aided Chemical Engineering, vol. 38, pp. 1377–1382. Elsevier (2016)
2. Askarian, M., Escudero, G., Graells, M., Zarghami, R., Jalali-Farahani, F., Mostoufi, N.: Fault diagnosis of chemical processes with incomplete observations: a comparative study. Comput. Chem. Eng. **84**, 104–116 (2016)
3. Davis, D., Rahman, M.: Missing value imputation using stratified supervised learning for cardiovascular data. J. Inf. Data Mining **1**(2), 1–11 (2016)
4. Downs, J.J., Vogel, E.F.: A plant-wide industrial process control problem. Comput. Chem. Eng. **17**(3), 245–255 (1993)
5. Dray, S., Josse, J.: Principal component analysis with missing values: a comparative survey of methods. Plant Ecol. **216**, 657–667 (2015)
6. Folch-Fortuny, A., Arteaga, F., Ferrer, A.: PLS model building with missing data: new algorithms and a comparative study. J. Chemometr. **31**(7), 1–12 (2017)
7. Garces, H., Barbaro, D.S.: Outliers detection in environmental monitoring databases. Eng. App. Artif. Intell. **24**(2), 341–349 (2011)
8. García-Laencina, P., Sancho-Gómez, J., Figueiras-Vidal, A.: Pattern classification with missing data: a review. Neural Comput. App. **19**(2), 263–282 (2010)
9. Ge, Z.: Review on data-driven modeling and monitoring for plant-wide industrial processes. Chemometr. Intell. Lab. Syst. **171**, 16–25 (2017)

10. Hamrouni, I., Lahdhiri, H., ben Abdellafou, K., Taouali, O.: Fault detection of uncertain nonlinear process using reduced interval kernel principal component analysis (RIKPCA). Int. J. Adv. Manuf. Technol. **106**(9), 4567–4576 (2020)
11. Harkat, M.F., Mansouri, M., Nounou, M., Nounou, H.: Fault detection of uncertain nonlinear process using interval-valued data-driven approach. Chem. Eng. Sci. **205**, 36–45 (2019)
12. Bernal-de Lázaro, J., Llanes-Santiago, O., Prieto-Moreno, A., Knupp, D., Silva-Neto, A.: Enhanced dynamic approach to improve the detection of small-magnitude faults. Chem. Eng. Sci. **146**, 166–179 (2016)
13. Little, R., Rubin, D.: Statistical Analysis with Missing Data. John Wiley & Sons, New York (2014)
14. Llanes-Santiago, O., Rivero-Benedico, B., Gálvez-Viera, S., Rodríguez-Morant, E., Torres-Cabeza, R., Silva-Neto, A.: A fault diagnosis proposal with online imputation to incomplete observations in industrial plant. Revista Mexicana de Ingeniería Química **18**(1), 83–98 (2019)
15. Luengo, J., Saéz, J.A., Herrera, F.: Missing data imputation for fuzzy rule-based classification systems. Soft Comput. **16**, 863–881 (2012)
16. Nguyen, C.H., Ho, T.B.: An efficient kernel matrix evaluation measure. Pattern Recogn. **41**(11), 3366–3372 (2008)
17. Ortiz Ortiz, F., Llanes-Santiago, O.: A proposal of robust fault diagnosis system in presence of missing data and noise in mechanical systems. Revista Politécnica **48**(1), 7–18 (2021). https://doi.org/10.33333/rp.vol48n1.01
18. Rato, T., Reis, M., Schmitt, E., Hubert, M., De Ketelaere, B.: A systematic comparison of pca-based statistical process monitoring methods for high-dimensional, time-dependent processes. AIChE J. **62**(5), 1478–1493 (2016)
19. Rodríguez-Ramos, A., et al.: A novel fault diagnosis scheme applying fuzzy clustering algorithms. Appl. Soft Comput. **58**, 605–619 (2017)
20. Rosipal, R., Trejo, L.J.: Kernel partial least squares regression in reproducing kernel hilbert space. J. Mach. Learn. Res. 97–123 (2001)
21. Sánchez-Fernández, A., Baldán, F., Sainz-Palmero, G., Benítez, J., Fuente, M.: Fault detection based on time series modeling and multivariate statistical process control. Chemom. Intell. Lab. Syst. **182**, 57–69 (2018)
22. Schmitt, P., Mandel, J., Guedj, M.: A comparison of six methods for missing data imputation. J. Biom. Biostat. **6**(1), 1–6 (2015)
23. Severson, K.A., Molaro, M.C., Braatz, R.D.: Principal component analysis of process datasets with missing values. Processes **5**, 1–18 (2017)
24. Silva-Ramírez, E., López-Coello, M., Pino-Mejías, R.: An application sample of machine learning tools, such as SVM and ANN, for data editing and imputation. In: Soft Computing for Sustainability Science, pp. 259–298. Springer (2018)
25. Singhal, A., Seborg, D.E.: Matching patterns from historical data using PCA and distance similarity factors. In: Proceedings of the American Control Conference, vol. 2, pp. 1759–1764 (2001)
26. Troyanskaya, O., et al.: Missing value estimation methods for DNA microarrays. Bioinformatics **17**, 520–525 (2001)
27. Yu, H., Khan, F.: Improved latent variable models for nonlinear and dynamic process monitoring. Chem. Eng. Sci. **168**, 325–338 (2017)
28. Yue, H.H., Qin, S.J.: Reconstruction-based fault identification using a combined index. Indust. Eng. Chem. Res. **40**(20), 4403–4414 (2001)
29. Zhang, K., Gonzalez, R., Huang, B., Ji, G.: Expectation-maximization approach to fault diagnosis with missing data. IEEE Trans. Indust. Elect.**62**(2), 1231–1240 (2015)

A Proposal of Metric for Improving Remaining Useful Life Prediction in Industrial Systems

Adriana Villalón-Falcón[1], Alberto Prieto-Moreno[1],
Marcos Quiñones-Grueiro[2], and Orestes Llanes-Santiago[1](✉)

[1] Universidad Tecnológica de La Habana José Antonio Echeverría, CUJAE,
Marianao, La Habana, Cuba
{avillalon,albprieto}@automatica.cujae.edu.cu,
orestes@tesla.cujae.edu.cu
[2] Institute for Software Integrated Systems, Vanderbilt University,
Nashville, TN, USA
marcos.quinones.grueiro@vanderbilt.edu

Abstract. The deterioration of engineering systems due to wear and working conditions impact directly on their performance, requiring more efficient maintenance programs to prevent unexpected stops and increase production quality. Neural networks have shown significant results in predicting the remaining useful life (RUL) of systems. A neural network for prognostic is generally trained to minimize the mean square error (MSE) between the RUL prediction and its true value. This metric gives equal importance to the error at the beginning and at the end of a system's useful life. However, the prediction of the RUL is more critical as a system approaches the end of its useful life. Therefore, making an accurate evaluation of prognostic models requires to take this into account. In this paper, a new performance metric for the evaluation of prognostic models is proposed with the objective of establishing a direct relation between RUL prediction and maintenance planning. In addition, a procedure to use this metric for training a multilayer perceptron (MLP) network is proposed to improve the network's capacity to learn degradation patterns near the end of the useful life. The procedure is applied to NASA Commercial Modular Aero-Propulsion System Simulation (C-MAPSS) dataset, improving the prediction results significantly.

Keywords: Remaining useful life · Prognostics · Multilayer perceptron · Performance metric · Pattern recognition

1 Introduction

Engineering systems are the core of modern production systems, that are constantly on demand for higher quality and lower costs. The deterioration due

Project No. 27 of National Program of Research and Innovation ARIA of CITMA, Cuba.

to time, wear, and working conditions impacts directly the performance of the system, causing unexpected stops and affecting production quality [1]. More efficient maintenance programs including equipment condition-based monitoring and prognostic of the system are required to allow an improvement of the productivity and safety.

Prognostic methods based on machine learning are appropriate when a system is complex enough that is difficult to develop precise physics-based models [1]. The objective is to use the measurements of system variables as data to create a model that learns the degradation patterns with the objective of predicting the RUL. In this direction, a wide variety of machine learning models have risen as models with significant performance on the prediction task. With the considerable amount of models, therefore, it becomes crucial selecting the best to support decision making. Thus, metrics have been designed to measure prediction accuracy giving greater importance to error made near the end of the useful life of a system [7, 10, 14].

Although many metrics have been widely used to measure prognostic performance, literature does not report its use during the training of prediction models. Using machine learning for prognostics, particularly neural networks, implies that an optimization algorithm is used to fit model parameters with the objetive of minimizing the prediction error. Generally, the mean square error (MSE) metric is used as objective function during training [3, 9]. MSE measures the prediction error by giving the same importance to each prediction instant. Therefore, prediction error evolution is masked and a lower error for RUL prediction near the end of useful life cannot be guarantee.

In this paper, a methodology for training neural network models for RUL prediction, with the objetive of minimizing the prediction error giving greater importance to error near the end of the useful life of a system, is proposed. A new performance metric is also presented in order to have a better representation of prognostic performance. This proposal is validated by using the NASA Commercial Modular Aero-Propulsion System Simulation (CMAPSS) benchmark [10].

2   Preprocessing

Data Labelling: In order to train a model for RUL prediction, it is necessary a set of input and output data. The input data is the information from several sensors and the output data is the RUL. In this paper, a piece-wise function (1) that represents the behavior of a system that begins to degrade after a certain time of operation, when some failure has occurred, is used to label the data [4, 9]

$$l = \begin{cases} R_c, & \text{if } 0 \quad \le c \le SOF \\ EOL - c, & \text{if } SOF < c \le EOL \end{cases} \tag{1}$$

where l is the label which corresponds to the RUL in the time unit corresponding to system operation; EOL is the last time instant or end of life of the system; c is the current time instant; R_c is the initial constant value of RUL; and SOF is the start of failure which is equal to $EOL - R_c$.

Data Normalization: One of the most commonly used normalization techniques is called Z-Score, which is based on the mean and the standard deviation of the data to scale it. When working with different operating regimes, in order to ensure an equal contribution of each sensor in all regimes, it is better for the prediction task to incorporate the information of each regime in the normalization [1]. Thus, the normalization of the samples corresponding to each sensor f is performed according to Eq. (2).

$$N(x^{(r,f)}) = \frac{x^{(r,f)} - \mu^{(r,f)}}{\sigma^{(r,f)}} \tag{2}$$

For the sensor f, $x^{(r,f)}$ represents the data, $\mu^{(r,f)}$ and $\sigma^{(r,f)}$ are the mean and standard deviation of the data set in the operating regimen r, respectively.

3   Performance Metrics

Accuracy metrics quantify the closeness between the model prediction and true measured values [14]. Generally, metrics compute this closeness as the difference between the RUL predicted values (RUL^*) and true values (RUL), $\Delta = RUL^* - RUL$, also called prediction error. Accuracy metrics are created by modifying the prediction error equation, to add desired features for metrics, based on prognostic methods capability for supporting maintenance decision. The most relevant features that metrics include, according to their recurrence and ordered by their importance, are:

1. *Overall performance.* Accuracy must be measured over the entire lifetime, capturing the prediction error behavior. Some metrics have been used to measure the prediction error in an instant of the system degradation (Exponential Transformed Accuracy (ETA) [7], Relative Accuracy (RA) [10]). RUL prediction is a continuous process, thus the evaluation of methods for this purpose requires measuring how the error changes over time (Mean Absolute Error (MAE) [15], Cumulative relative accuracy (CRA) [10], Root Mean Square Error (RMSE) [7,14], Mean Absolute Percentage Error (MAPE) [14,15], Timeliness Weighted Error Bias (TWEB) [2,14]). It is not enough to consider the error at specific time instants as unique evaluation measure.

2. *Metric value in time units.* Accuracy value must be given in the time units of the RUL measurement (i.e. hour, day, cycle). The time unit of the prediction is key for measuring prognostic methods accuracy, allowing to establish a connection to equipment operation and maintenance planning. Some metrics provide normalized values, generally in the range $[0, 1]$, masking the prediction time unit (ETA, RA, CRA, MAPE, TWEB). Measures such as mean and median are commonly used to summarize the error made at each prediction time (MAE, RMSE).

3. *Time based penalization.* Decision making is critical towards the end of life. Therefore, penalization factor must be added that gives greater importance to prediction errors made near the end of life. Usually, a function is defined

to penalize the error given the time instant at which the prediction was made (TWEB, CRA). A linear function (3) and a gaussian kernel (4) have been used as penalization functions.

$$\alpha(t) = \frac{t}{\sum_{t=t_0}^{T} t} \tag{3}$$

$$\alpha(t) = e^{-\frac{(t-T)^2}{\frac{T^2}{2}}} \tag{4}$$

where t_0 and T are the start and end of life, respectively.

4. *Late prediction based penalization.* Late predictions (positive Δ) are penalized over early predictions (negative Δ), due to the impact on maintenance. Positive errors are made for predicting a higher RUL value than the true RUL, causing the system to reach the end of life before maintenance. Conversely, negative errors favor the execution of maintenance tasks before the end of the useful life of the systems. Commonly, a function is defined to penalize the error. This function is used as conversion function that receive a prediction error and retrieve a value related to its magnitud and sign. An exponential function (5) has been used as penalization function (ETA, TWEB).

$$\zeta(t) = \begin{cases} e^{-\frac{\Delta}{\varphi_1}} - 1, \text{ if } \delta < 0 \\ e^{\frac{\Delta}{\varphi_2}} - 1, \quad \text{if } \delta \geq 0 \end{cases} \tag{5}$$

Although penalization functions presented in equations (3) and (4) give a larger value as time approaches to the end of life, they do not include information about the critical moment for decision making in a particular application. It is expected that a prognostic performance metric holds some physical significance such as a time index that provides a required prediction horizon, or time required to apply a corrective action [10]. Therefore, a new accuracy metric to evaluate the performance of RUL prediction methods, that includes the first three features presented, and capture knowledge for supporting decision making, is proposed.

In order to achieve a better evaluation of the performance of RUL prediction models, this metric periodically measures the error during the degradation process and includes time-based penalization, keeping values time unit.

3.1   Proposed Performance Metric

The proposed metric is defined as follows:

Definition 1. *(**Root Weighted Mean Squared Error**) Given a set $\{E_i\} \in \mathbf{E}$ with $i = 1, 2, ..., N$ of representative systems of the same type of system $\mathbf{E}$, the **Root Weighted Mean Squared Error** (RWMSE) for $\mathbf{E}$ is obtained as:*

$$RWMSE = \frac{\sum_{i=1}^{N} RWMSE_i}{N} \tag{6}$$

where

$$RWMSE_i = \sqrt{\frac{\sum_{t=1}^{T} \alpha_{RUL_{i,t}} * \left(RUL_{i,t}^* - RUL_{i,t}\right)^2}{\sum_{t=1}^{T} \alpha_{RUL_{i,t}}}} \tag{7}$$

is a weighted average of the prediction errors during the degradation of system i, $RUL_{i,t}^*$ and $RUL_{i,t}$ are the predicted and true RUL at instant t during the degradation of system i, respectively, T is the time frame over which the deviation is measured, $\alpha_{RUL_{i,t}}$ is the weight assigned to the RUL prediction error of system i when it is calculated for each instant t, and N is the number of systems.

Several types of functions could be used to determine $\alpha_{RUL_{i,t}}$. In this paper, the exponential function given in Eq. (8) is selected. Considering that, as the system approaches the end of its useful life, the importance of accurately estimating the value of the RUL grows exponentially. This function places greater weight on prediction errors near the end of the systems life.

$$\alpha_{RUL_{i,t}} = a * e^{bx} + c \tag{8}$$

where x is defined as $RUL_{i,t} - RUL_{warning}$, and $RUL_{warning}$ is the value of RUL from which the precision of the RUL prediction is considered critical, such that the weight assigned to the error is greater from that moment on. Parameters $a, c \geq 0$ such that the effects of errors do not cancel each other and each error contributes to the average. Moreover, $a = 1$ to differentiate the error weights assigned to both sides of $RUL_{warning}$. Parameter $b \in \mathbb{R}^-$ because of $\alpha_{RUL_{i,t}}$ should increase as the RUL decreases. Function $\alpha_{RUL_{i,t}}$ should present a smooth shape, gradually varying as it approaches to $RUL_{i,t} = 0$. Therefore, the smooth shape is guaranteed by selecting $b = \frac{-1}{RUL_{warning}}$. In practice, $RUL_{warning}$ value can be defined by experts in the maintenance area or it can be assigned based on the knowledge acquired from the data.

Substituting the values assigned to the parameters in Eq. (8), the weight function obtained is:

$$\alpha_{RUL_{i,t}} = e^{1 - \frac{RUL_{i,t}}{RUL_{warning}}} \tag{9}$$

4   Prognostic Model and Model Training

Prognostic Model: Neural networks are one of the most widely used data-driven methods, due to their ability to model complex nonlinear relationships among the variables. Convolutional neural network (CNN) [6,8,9], auto-encoder (AE) [12,13], and recurrent neural network (RNN) [3,11] are some of the most common network architectures used for RUL prediction. In this paper, a multi-layer perceptron architectures is selected for testing the proposed procedure due to its simplicity and the promising results shown in [1]. The MLP architecture for RUL prediction, generally, consists of three layers: (1) input layer, where sensor data is received; (2) a hidden layer with n neurons containing an activation function; (3) and an output layer with one neuron and an activation function.

Model Training: For neural networks, a loss function is generally used to compute and retro-propagate this error, working as the objective function of the optimization algorithm. The MLP model is trained using mean square error (10) and weighted mean square error (11) to demonstrate the influence of training with these loss functions on the RUL prediction. RMSProp optimizer is used to update the network parameters during training [5], with a mini-batch approach to optimize the loss function by iteratively updating the network weights and biases.

$$MSE = (RUL_{i,t}^* - RUL_{i,t})^2 \qquad (10)$$

$$WMSE = \alpha_{i,t} * (RUL_{i,t}^* - RUL_{i,t})^2 \qquad (11)$$

Mini-batches configuration depends on the distribution of the data for training. The overall training process is shown in Algorithm 1.

Algorithm 1. Training algorithm

Parameters: *optimizer*: method to update network parameters (weights and biases), *lr*: learning rate, *minibatchsize*: size of the mini-batch to update network parameters, *epochs*: number of times that the data is passed through the network
Inputs: M: training measurements, RUL: training RUL

Initialization: $w \leftarrow initialization()$
for *epoch* $\in 1 : epochs$ **do**
    for *batch* $\in 1 : minibatchsize$ **do**
        Obtain batch data M_b and RUL_b
        Obtain network output $RUL_b^* = model(M_b)$
        Obtain prediction error $l_b = loss(RUL_b, RUL_b^*)$
        Update network parameters $w \leftarrow optimizer(lr, l_b, w)$
    end for
end for

Generally, when training with MSE, the data for each batch is randomly selected from all the data. However, when training with WMSE, the goal is to recognize the degradation pattern by applying the weights according to the metric configuration. Thus, each batch is created selecting degradation trajectories that show entire degradation patterns, instead of randomly selected samples that can be located in different trajectories, not showing the degradation pattern.

5   Dataset Description

In this paper, the NASA Commercial Modular Aero-Propulsion System Simulation (CMAPPS) dataset is used for training and validating the proposal [10]. The C-MAPPS dataset is formed by four distinct datasets. Each dataset contains a number of training engines (Engines: Training (N)) with run-to-failure information and a number of testing engines (Engines: Testing) with information terminating before a failure is observed (See Table 1). There are two failure modes: high-pressure compressor degradation and fan degradation. Each engine provides the following information: engine identifier, operation time (in flight cycles), 3 operating condition parameters (altitude, mach number and throttle resolver angle), and 21 sensor signals (4 temperatures, 4 pressures, 6 speeds and 7 others).

Engines start operating with various degrees of initial wear but are considered healthy. As the number of cycles increases, the engines begin to deteriorate until they can no longer function. At this point, engines are considered unhealthy. The training dataset has run-to-failure information collected over the entire life of the engines until failure. Unlike training dataset, the testing dataset contains temporal data that terminates some time before a system failure. The objective is to predict the RUL of test engines [10].

Table 1. C-MAPSS dataset description.

Data	FD001	FD002	FD003	FD004
Engines: Training	100	260	100	249
Engines: Test	100	259	100	248
Operating conditions	1	6	1	6
Number of failure modes	1	1	2	2

5.1 Preprocessing

Data Labelling: For these datasets, Eq. (1) is used to label the data. In this paper, R_c is set to 130 since it is the value generally used in the literature [4].

Data Normalization: In the dataset, there are three variables (altitude, mach number, and throttle resolver angle) that refer to the operating conditions of the turbines and these have a strong impact on the performance of the system. In the datasets, where the six operating regimes are present, Eq. (2) is used to normalize the data.

6 Results

The MLP model defined in Sect. 4 is configured as follow: (1) input layer, where the input neurons receive data corresponding to the flight cycle, 3 operating conditions and 21 sensor signals; (2) a hidden layer with 10 neurons containing a sigmoid activation function; (3) and an output layer with one neuron and a linear activation function. The model is trained following Algorithm 1 using MSE and WMSE as loss functions. Training hyper-parameters (learning rate, mini-batch size and number of epochs) are tuned by grid search. The value range of learning rate is { 0.001, 0.01, 0.1, 0.2 }, the value range of mini-batch size for

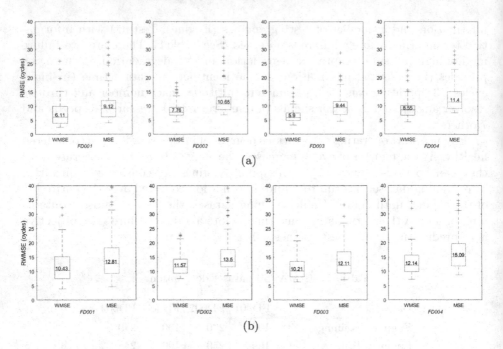

Fig. 1. (a) RMSE from the last 30 cycles of life (b) RWMSE from the last 130 cycles of life

MSE training is { 100, 150, 200, 250 } and for WMSE training is { 1, 5, 10 }, and the value range of the number of epochs is { 30, 40, 50 }. After a comparative analysis, the learning rate is set to 0.2, the mini-batch size for MSE training is set to 200 samples and for WMSE is set to 1 trajectory, and the number of epochs is set to 50.

In experiments, the training set in each dataset is used to train and validate the procedure, since the test set does not contain information on the operation of the engines until failure. This information is necessary to evaluate the prediction models throughout the degradation process. For training with WMSE loss function, the value of $RUL_{warning}$ is set to 30, considering the windows size generally used to process data for this dataset. A k-fold cross validation procedure has been used on the datasets with $k = 10$, in order to compare loss functions influence on the training process. The prediction errors of each model in each partition are compared using the Wilcoxon statistical test. The significance level (α) of the test is 0.05.

Since the goal is to minimize the prediction error near the end of the useful life, a first error estimation is made by obtaining the RMSE over last 30 cycles of each engine. Test results show a significant difference between the prediction errors when training with MSE and WMSE, in which the proposed approach in this paper presents the smallest error (See Fig. 1(a)). The test results demonstrate that the proposed approach has lower error in the prediction of the RUL as the engines approach the end of their useful life. In order to demonstrate that

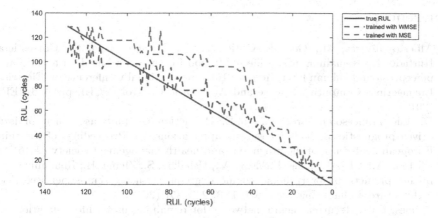

Fig. 2. RUL prediction from engine 79 in dataset FD001.

RWMSE can also be used as a metric to compare prognostic models, the prediction error over the last 130 cycles of each engines is calculated with this metric. Test results also show that the proposed approach in this paper has the smaller error (See Fig. 1(b)), which is consistent with the results from calculating RMSE over last 30 cycles.

The predicted RUL for engine 79 throughout the degradation process obtained from models trained using MSE and WMSE is presented in Fig. 2 to show the how with the proposed approach the RUL predicted gets closer to the true RUL towards the end of the life of the engine.

7   Conclusions and Future Work

In this paper, a new procedure is proposed to train a neural network model to learn degradation pattern near the end of the useful life of a system. To evaluate its effectiveness, a multilayer perceptron architecture was trained for predicting the RUL of turbofan engines from the C-MAPSS dataset. Using this approach, a simple model is obtained that improves the prediction the RUL of a turbofan engine.

The new performance metric, RWMSE, proposed to evaluate RUL prediction models, allows characterizing the evolution of the prediction error of the models and links the prediction of the RUL with the planning of the maintenance tasks from the term $RUL_{warning}$. This metric is a first step for generalizing prognostic metrics with a goal on unifying their strengths and removing their limitations in their understanding and better use in evaluating how well does a model perform towards predictive maintenance.

In further research, the proposal will be applied to other neural network architectures used to analyze time series as recurrent networks.

References

1. Alberto-Olivares, M., Gonzalez-Gutierrez, A., Tovar-Arriaga, S., Gorrostieta-Hurtado, E.: Remaining useful life prediction for turbofan based on a multilayer perceptron and kalman filter. In: 2019 16th International Conference on Electrical Engineering, Computing Science and Automatic Control (CCE), pp. 1–6. IEEE (2019)
2. Di Maio, Franceso an Turati, P., Zio, E.: Prediction capability assessment of data-driven prognostic methods for railway applications. In: Proceedings of the third European conference of the prognostic and health management society (2016)
3. Ellefsen, A.L., Bjørlykhaug, E., Æsøy, V., Ushakov, S., Zhang, H.: Remaining useful life predictions for turbofan engine degradation using semi-supervised deep architecture. Reliab. Eng. Syst. Saf. **183**, 240–251 (2019)
4. Heimes, F.O.: Recurrent neural networks for remaining useful life estimation. In: 2008 International Conference on Prognostics and Health Management, pp. 1–6. IEEE (2008)
5. Hinton, G., Srivastava, N., Swersky, K.: Neural networks for machine learning lecture 6a overview of mini-batch gradient descent. Cited on 14(8) (2012)
6. Huang, C.G., Huang, H.Z., Li, Y.F., Peng, W.: A novel deep convolutional neural network-bootstrap integrated method for RUL prediction of rolling bearing. J. Manuf. Syst. (2021)
7. Lei, Y., Li, N., Guo, L., Li, N., Yan, T., Lin, J.: Machinery health prognostics: a systematic review from data acquisition to RUL prediction. Mech. Syst. Signal Process. **104**, 799–834 (2018)
8. Li, H., Zhao, W., Zhang, Y., Zio, E.: Remaining useful life prediction using multi-scale deep convolution neural network. Appl. Soft Comput. **89**, 106–113 (2020)
9. Li, X., Ding, Q., Sun, J.Q.: Remaining useful life estimation in prognostics using deep convolution neural networks. Reliab. Eng. Syst. Saf. **172**, 1–11 (2018)
10. Saxena, A., Goebel, K., Simon, D., Eklund, N.: Damage propagation modeling for aircraft engine run-to-failure simulation. In: 2008 International Conference on Prognostics and Health Management, pp. 1–9. IEEE (2008)
11. Shi, Z., Chehade, A.: A dual-LSTM framework combining change point detection and remaining useful life prediction. Reliab. Eng. Syst. Saf. **205**, 107257 (2021)
12. Song, Y., Shi, G., Chen, L., Huang, X., Xia, T.: Remaining useful life prediction of turbofan engine using hybrid model based on autoencoder and bidirectional long short-term memory. J. Shanghai Jiatong Univ. (Sci.) **23**(1), 85–94 (2018)
13. Wang, H., Peng, M.j., Miao, Z., Liu, Y.k., Ayodeji, A., Hao, C.: Remaining useful life prediction techniques for electric valves based on convolution auto encoder and long short term memory. ISA Trans. **108**, 333–342 (2021)
14. Zeng, Z., Di Maio, F., Zio, E., Kang, R.: A hierarchical decision-making framework for the assessment of the prediction capability of prognostic methods. Proc. Inst. Mech. Eng. Part 0. J. Risk Reliab. **231**(1), 36–52 (2017)
15. Zhang, H., Mo, Z., Wang, J., Miao, Q.: Nonlinear-drifted fractional Brownian motion with multiple hidden state variables for remaining useful life prediction of lithium-ion batteries. IEEE Trans. Reliab. **69**(2), 768–780 (2019)

A Fuzzy Logic Proposal for Diagnosis Multiple Incipient Faults in a Power Transformer

J. C. Fernández[1]([⊠]) [iD], L. B. Corrales[2]([⊠]) [iD], F. H. Hernández[3]([⊠]) [iD],
I. F. Benítez[4]([⊠]) [iD], and J. R. Núñez[5]([⊠]) [iD]

[1] Department of Operations, Generating Sets and Electric Services,
85100 Bayamo, Granma, Cuba
jcfernandez@grm.geysel.une.cu
[2] Faculty of Electromechanics, Department of Electrical Engineering,
University of Camagüey, 70100 Camagüey, Cuba
luis.corrales@reduc.edu.cu
[3] Stainless Steel, Department of Electrical Engineering, ACINOX, 75100 Tunas, Cuba
felix@acinoxtunas.co.cu
[4] Faculty of Electrical Engineering, Department of Automatic Control Engineering,
University of Oriente, 90500 Santiago of Cuba, Cuba
ibenitez@uo.edu.cu
[5] Faculty of Engineering, Department of Electrical Engineering, University of the Costa,
080002 Barranquilla, Colombia
jnunez22@cuc.edu.co

Abstract. For the safety and continuity of service in industrial electrical systems, the availability of transformers is essential. For this reason, it is necessary to develop intelligent fault diagnosis techniques to reduce repair and maintenance costs. Recently, several methods have been developed that use artificial intelligence techniques such as neural networks, support vector machines, hybrid techniques, etc., for the diagnosis of faults in power transformers using gas analysis. These methods, although they present very good results, encounter restrictions to determine the precise moment before the occurrence of multiple fault of small magnitude and are difficult to implement in practice. This document proposes a method to diagnose multiple incipient faults in a power transformer using fuzzy logic. The proposal, based on historical data from the composition of the gases dissolved in the oil, achieves a performance in the classification of multiple incipient fault of 98.3%. With reliable samples of dissolved gas, it guarantees an overall rate of accuracy in detecting incipient faults that is superior to that obtained by the most successful conventional methods in the industry. The proposal does not encounter generalization difficulties and constitutes a simple solution that allows determining the state of the transformer in service without affecting the continuity of the electricity supply.

Keywords: Power Transformer · Fault diagnosis · Fuzzy logic · Dissolved gas analysis

© Springer Nature Switzerland AG 2021
Y. Hernández Heredia et al. (Eds.): IWAIPR 2021, LNCS 13055, pp. 187–198, 2021.
https://doi.org/10.1007/978-3-030-89691-1_19

1 Introduction

A transformer is considered to have stopped operating correctly when, due to damage, it becomes unable to provide the service required by its design. When this defect prevents it from functioning normally, putting it at risk of deterioration, a failure is said to have occurred [1]. The availability of power transformers is critical to the continuity of power supply in industrial and power electrical systems. For this reason, it is essential that fault diagnosis systems are incorporated into electrical systems that allow maintaining a satisfactory operation by compensating for the effects of disturbances and changes that occur in industrial processes.

In [2] a diagram showing the main fault diagnosis methods FDI (Fault Detection and Isolation) is presented. These are divided into two large groups: methods based on models and those based on historical data of the process. FDIs that use historical data are considered an issue of great importance for today's industries since they constitute an advantage in very complex systems, where the relationships between variables are non-linear and where it is very difficult to determine a model efficiently.

In [3–6] multiple analyzes and applications have been carried out, based on the history of the process, which use artificial intelligence techniques to detect failures in power transformers. In these works, the study of dissolved gas chromatography in oil (DGA) is considered the most successful technique in the diagnosis of incipient failures. In [7–9] Artificial Neural Networks and in [10–12] Vector Support Machines (SVM) are used as the most used fault classification techniques in FDI methods. The authors [13–16] have combined different artificial intelligence techniques with fuzzy logic to achieve better results in the identification of failures. Although these diagnostic techniques are the ones that have demonstrated the most success in electrical systems, they encounter restrictions in the ability to determine the precise moment for the intervention of the equipment before the occurrence of multiple incipient faults of small magnitude.

Making an analysis of the different techniques approached in recent years, within the fault diagnosis methods oriented to power transformers, an increase in fuzzy logic can be seen [17–20]. The application of fuzzy logic has been widely accepted for contributing to eradicate the inconveniences to establish the conditions of the limits in the proportions of the gases dissolved in the oil of the electrical transformers.

The main contribution is the development of a method based on historical data that is aimed at solving the problems presented by current fault diagnosis systems to determine the precise moment of occurrence of multiple incipient faults of small magnitude using fuzzy logic from the analysis DGA. The proposal is a simple solution that is easy to implement in practice that will allow determining the condition of the transformer, without affecting the continuity of the service and reducing the number of unplanned shutdowns in power transformers that affect the availability of electrical systems.

2 Materials and Methods

This study is carried out in the Stainless-Steel Company (ACINOX, spanish translation), Las Tunas. In this place, the electrical effects are classified according to an order of priority using categories for each case. This means that, among the breakdowns to be solved, those of first necessity are those that most affect steel production. In this sense, the 63 MVA transformer located in the 220 kV ACINOX The Tunas substation constitutes a fundamental element within the electrical system.

This equipment that feeds the 34.5 kV bar to serve the ACINOX Stainless Steel Plant is designed to work under the following technical specifications: nominal power 63/63/10MVA at 60Hz; primary voltage $230 \pm 10 \times 1\%$ kV; secondary voltage $35 \pm 2 \times 2.5\%$ kV and tertiary voltage 6.28 kV. The primary current is 157.7/158.1/143.8A; secondary current 1093.9/1039.2/989.7A and tertiary current 919.4A. Its cooling system is OFAF, which means that the oil is forced to circulate within the closed circuit of the transformer tank by means of oil pumps. As internal protection for small faults, a Buchholz Custos type RR-RRF-GQ gas and/or pressure relay is installed. It incorporates a Hydrocal 1008-type gas dissolved in oil analyzer, which facilitates real-time gas diagnosis.

2.1 Analysis of the Main Electrical Interruptions that Occurred in the Steel Mill

This section presents the statistical result of the main failures in power transformers and the particular case of the 63 MVA transformer. In the world, the statistics of failures in power transformers up to 700 kV indicate that 38% of these are related to the windings; 31% with on-load tap-changers (OLTC); 17% in bushings, 8% in insulation and 6% in accessories [21]. In Cuba, the statistics of typical failures for transformers of the National Electroenergetic System (SEN, spanish translation) show that the main failure points and, therefore, those that must be monitored with the highest priority are the windings and OLTC.

For the study, all the electrical failures that occurred in the last five years in the main areas of the ACINOX the Tunas Stainless Steel Plant were analyzed: The Electric Arc Furnace (EAF) and the Spoon Furnace (LF) [22].

The study carried out shows that there were 272 electrical interruptions in the EAF area, equivalent to 25.8% of the total interruptions. In LF, it occurs 21.5% and in other areas, the interruptions do not exceed 20%. As can be seen, the EAF circuit has a higher incidence than the other areas. Taking into account the superiority of the electrical affectations in the EAF area and the unacceptability of the interruption of the supply in steel production, it was decided to choose the 63 MVA transformer as the object for the design of the proposed fault diagnosis method. The importance of the choice lies in the fact that the failures that occurred in this transformer affect the continuity of the electrical supply in the 34.5 kV bus that feeds the EAF circuit, which implies great economic losses in the country [22].

Therefore it was decided to diagnose the following faults: Partial Discharges (PD), Partial Low Energy Discharges (D1), Partial High Energy Discharges (D2), Thermal Failure <300 °C (T1), Thermal Failure Between 300 °C and 700 °C (T2), high energy thermal failure >700°C (T3) and F7: multiple faults obtained through the combinations between Duval methods and the extended thermal and electrical fault mixing zone (DTe). In this document the T1 and T2 faults will not be diagnosed separately as in the experiments of current fault diagnosis systems both are considered low energy thermal faults <700 °C (LTF).

2.2 Description of the Design Proposal

The proposed fault diagnosis method uses gas data that is extracted through the Hydrocal 1008 allowing electrical and mechanical faults to be detected online. This method guarantees a real-time diagnosis without affecting the continuity of the transformer's service, which facilitates efficient maintenance management. For the detection of incipient faults in power transformers from the DGA analysis, the conventional diagnostic methods most used in the industry are the following: Key Gas Method, Doernenburg Method (DRM), Rogers Method (RRM), IEC Method (IRM) and Duval Methods [22].

According to what has been studied in previous investigations [23–25], a design proposal is made to diagnose multiple incipient faults in the 63 MVA transformer that feeds the 34.5 kV bus of the 220 kV ACINOX the Tunas Substation. This bar feeds the electrical circuit of the EAF of the Tunas steel production plant. The proposal uses the gas thresholds obtained from the knowledge of experts and the analysis of the historical behavior of the concentrations of the gases dissolved in the mineral oil of power transformers of the steel mill that have switching under load. With this, a simple solution is offered to determine the normal condition of the transformer during service.

The method proposed in this work uses the Duval Pentagon (DPM) interpretation method and combines it with an extension of the triangle 1 method or the classical Duval method (DTM), which guarantees good results in the identification of multiple incipient faults.

The method consists of determining the problem that affects a transformer using the center of symmetry or centroid of the geometric figure formed by the coordinates of each dissolved gas. For the calculation, the summation of the relationships of its vertices is used to find the area of the Duval polygon and subsequently the values of the coordinates of the centroid C_x and C_y as indicated by the following equations in [26]:

$$A = \frac{1}{2} \sum_{i=0}^{n-1} (x_i y_{i+1} - x_{i+1} y_i) \tag{1}$$

$$C_x = \frac{1}{6A} \sum_{i-0}^{n-1} (x_i + x_{i+1})(x_i y_{i+1} - x_{i+1} y_i) \tag{2}$$

$$C_y = \frac{1}{6A} \sum_{i-0}^{n-1} (y_i + y_{i+1})(x_i y_{i+1} - x_{i+1} y_i) \tag{3}$$

Where, i is the lower limit and takes the values of 0, 1, 2, 3 and 4, n the number of vertices of the polygon and x_i and y_i are the coordinates of the vertices.

The proposed method consists of identifying the faults of the Coordinates C_x and C_y and the extension that is made of DTM for the DT zone based on previous investigations. Then, both results from the interpretation of the DPM zones and the classic Duval triangle are compared for the identification of simple faults. In this way, if the diagnoses of both Duval methods are different, they are taken into account as multiple failures since both methods are autonomous in identifying the failures. Finally, this result is added to those identified by the extended DT zone. In this way the multiple failures will be identified as DT or they can be any of the combinations between the single failures of both Duval methods.

Initially, this document proposes a method that uses the limit thresholds of the key gases that appear in the database of the International Electrotechnical Commission (IEC TC 10) referred to in [27]. These data were obtained through the analysis of IEC experts for normal DGA cases, which constitutes a low complexity solution to improve fault identification. The IEC TC 10 data in suitable range used by the proposed diagnostician is from IEC normal gas statistics for OLTC transformers in service.

In addition to using the symptoms or input variables $\%H_2$, $\%CH_4$, $\%C_2H_2$, $\%C_2H_4$, and $\%C_2H_6$, individual amounts of gases are monitored in parts per million (ppm)v. The symptoms do not make sense if the concentrations of the individual gases belong to the DGA ranges considered normal (N) of IEC TC 10. This means that the transformer is in good condition and the DGA cases are considered out of danger.

Figure 1 shows the structure of the fault diagnosis system that is proposed from the chromatographic analysis of gases. First, it is checked that the quantities of the key gases do not exceed the limits of IEC TC 10 considered normal. In case of being exceeded, the fuzzification process is carried out, where each of the symptom variables are converted into qualitative variables.

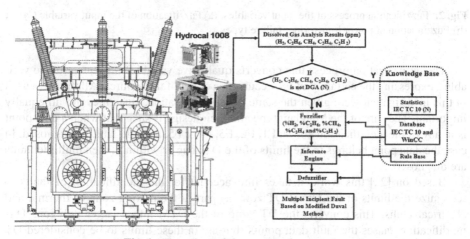

Fig. 1. Flow chart of the proposed approach.

The fuzzification process in the input variables of the proposal is carried out through the construction of trapezoidal membership functions since it has proven to be the most accurate function in the detection of incipient failures [22]. Then, with a rule base, the relationship between the symptoms that are manifested in the measured variables and the occurrence of the failures is expressed.

Based on [22] the extension of DTM in the design proposal it is taken into account when adding 0.85% to all the limits of the DT zone. For example: The $\%C_2H_2$ limits are located at 4.85, 13.85, 15.85 and 29.85 with the new proposal. This increase means that the fault data points that are in these limits are considered DT and that the border limits of the neighboring polygons are modified to avoid redundancy during the classification of simple faults.

The FDIp input variables are represented by membership functions that are defined through the set of linguistic variables (Mf1, Mf2, Mf3, Mf4 and Mf5) as shown in the example in Fig. 2 a) for the case of acetylene. Figure 2 b) shows the fuzzification of all the faults to be diagnosed. In these output variables, five types of incipient failures are considered in the category of simple failures (F1: PD, F2: D1, F3: D2, F4: LTF and F5: T3) and one failure in the category of multiple failures (F6: Fm). The latter represents the mixture of thermal and electrical faults in Duval's DT polygon with the extension of the boundary limits of this area. The six linguistic variables that represent the output of the proposed method are located in the range from 0 to 12 as shown in Fig. 2 b).

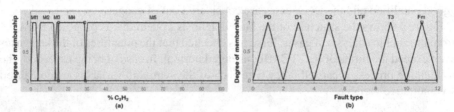

Fig. 2. Fuzzification process of the input variables. (a) Fuzzification of the input variable C_2H_2; (b) Fuzzification of power transformer failure types.

The defuzzication process that converts qualitative variables into quantitative variables, expressing the certainty of the occurrence or not of the failures. All the rules used in this investigation were given the same order of operation, since they are all equally important. They are of the Mandani type and their design is such that when a data point is in any of the identification zones: F1, F2, F3, F4 or F5, a single fault is diagnosed. In case the data point belongs to the limits of the DT zone or within it, then multiple faults are diagnosed.

Based on [22] this work, it takes into account for the identification of faults to recognize the limits of the Duval DT zone as part of the mixing zone of thermal and electrical faults. This converts the DT zone of the DTM into a larger polygon. This modification causes the fault data points that are in these limits to be considered DT and the boundary limits of the neighboring polygons are modified to avoid redundancy during the classification of simple faults. All the rules used in this stage were given the same order of operation, since they are all equally important. They are of the Mandani type and their design is such that when a data point is in any of the identification zones: D1, D2, T1, T2, T3, and PD, a single fault is diagnosed by DTM. In case the data point belongs to the limits of the DT zone or within it, then multiple faults are diagnosed (Fm).

3 Results and Discussion

To validate the FDIp, MATLAB software was used. For this, several samples of DGA cases were used, distributed as follows: 80 (PD), 22 (D1), 58 (D2), 21 (LTF), 44 (T3), 118 multiple fault (Fm) and 238 (N). The data for validation come from two fundamental sources. The first source belongs to the data on the operation of two 63MVA electrical transformers, corresponding to the 220 kV Substation, which serve the ACINOX Las

Tunas steel plant. In this data set, the cases of DGA analysis of the maintenance reports made by experts from the Electrical Department in the company ACINOX and the historical record of the WinCC SCADA were chosen.

These data correspond to daily DGA samples that were chosen through the SCADA link with the Hydrocal 1008 type gas analyzers that are installed in the selected 63MVA power transformers. The other source comes from the database of the IEC TC 10 taken from, through which cases that were used for the analysis of results were analyzed. In all identified failure cases, the transformers were withdrawn from service.

In [28–30] have investigated the precision of conventional DGA techniques: DRM, RRM, IRM, DTM and DPM. In these works, the results of the Duval methods in the classification of failures are superior to the rest of the conventional interpretation guides. For this reason, both methods have been selected for comparison against FDIp, as they have been the most reliable power transformer fault diagnosis techniques in the industry. Table 1 shows the comparison of the conventional Duval methods analyzed against the proposed FDIp method.

Table 1. Accuracy comparison of the proposed method against Duval's methods

Method	Correct rate of each fault (cases number)					
	PD (80)	D1 (22)	D2 (58)	LTF (21)	T3 (44)	Fm (118)
DTM	77.5%	86.4%	91.4%	81.0%	84.1%	93.2%
DPM	93.8%	77.3%	89.7%	85.7%	93.2%	-
FDIp	91.3%	81.8%	96.6%	90.5%	95.3%	98.3%

This method identifies the types of low and high temperature overheating failures with an accuracy of 90.5% and the very high temperature overheating failures with 95.3%. Low energy discharges are interpreted by 81.8%, high intensity discharges by 96.6% and partial discharges by 91.3%.

The FDIp simulation not only demonstrates the method's accuracy in diagnosing small and incipient faults in power transformers, but also achieves 98.3% accuracy in identifying multiple incipient faults.

The results of the design of the experiment demonstrated that combining the Duval guidelines in the FDIp provided useful information on the identification of multiple incipient failures, as only two cases were incorrectly interpreted, indicating the feasibility of the proposal.

Figure 3 shows an example in the software MATLAB® (R2018a) of a DGA (C1) case where the DPM diagnosis identifies a simple T3 fault at the coordinates $C_x = 3.552$ and $C_y = -9.129$. For this type of failure, the results of the gas analysis were the following: $H_2 = 43$ ppm, $CH_4 = 47$ ppm, $C_2H_2 = 33$ ppm, $C_2H_4 = 53$ ppm and $C_2H_6 = 9$ ppm. While the C1 in DPM found only a single fault, the proposed system placed this sample in the DTe zone, which improves the fault classification results.

Although the superiority of the DPM method was demonstrated in the diagnosis of incipient faults in power transformers compared to DTM and the other conventional

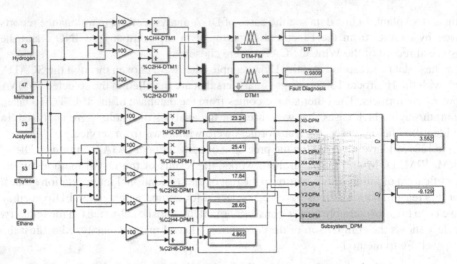

Fig. 3. Simulink model for the fuzzy proposed approach

methods [31]. The results in Fig. 3 during validation demonstrate the inability of the DPM method to identify multiple failures. However, using it in conjunction with the Duval Multiple Fault Extension (DTM-FM) allows you to better identify faults.

Figure 4 shows all the results of the PMD diagnosis against all the DGA data used in the validation. In her, it is appreciable how the diagnosis the normal DGA data can appear in any interior polygon, which demonstrates its inability to detect normal DGA cases. In our case, they were located in the T1, T2 and S areas of the pentagon. Although DPM demonstrated the highest success rate in diagnosing incipient faults, it is not a suitable method for identifying multiple faults. Another difficulty is that the faults found at the limits of interior borders are located in areas of fuzzy transition; they are so strict that they are difficult to interpret because they share information between one and another fault [31].

The misinterpreted cases are due to data samples belonging to the fuzzy transition areas between the fault zones of the pentagon, which interfere with the diagnosis. The authors are investigating this topic. With the proposed design strategy, the method fulfills the objective of an easy-to-implement solution to improve results in identifying the precise moment of occurrence of multiple small-magnitude incipient faults. It is necessary to emphasize that, in electrical processes, the statistical analysis of symptom variables and the fuzzy logical contribution is fundamental for the design of fault diagnosis methods in industrial electrical systems.

The use of artificial intelligence techniques such as fuzzy logic, together with the available equipment, are useful tools to solve the problems of incipient multiple faults of small magnitude in power transformers in real time.

The results of the proposed system constitute a continuity for future studies in the diagnosis of power transformer failures based on the analysis of gases dissolved in the oil. The FDIp does not encounter implementation difficulties in practice, so the generalization of this method is the object of study in the rest of the steel process

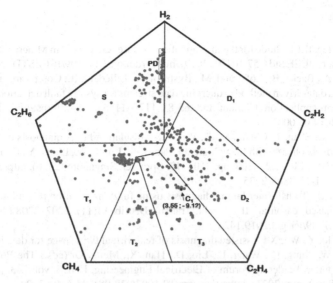

Fig. 4. Distribution of data DGA in Duval pentagon.

transformers in ACINOX and any power transformer immersed in mineral oil installed in the national system of electro energy.

The cases misinterpreted by the presented proposal are due to data samples that belong to the fuzzy transition areas between the fault zones of the pentagon. This difficulty, which interferes with the result of the diagnosis, is being investigated by the authors.

4 Conclusions

The FDI methods based on historical data using gas chromatography, the use of fuzzy logic is essential to improve the precision of the analysis of dissolved gases in the oil and to increase the detection capacity of multiple incipient failures in the power transformers.

It was possible to design an incipient failure diagnosis method, based on historical data, which obtained a total accuracy rate that demonstrated its superiority over conventional Duval methods.

The proposal offered a method to determine the condition of the transformer in service without having to affect the continuity of the power supply and achieved the classification of multiple small-magnitude faults by 98.3%.

The results of the work show that there is a simple, low-complexity and easy-to-implement solution for any power transformer of the national electrical energy system.

Acknowledgements. The authors appreciate the collaboration of the members of the Research Project: Advanced Automation for the Elaboration and Refinement of Steels (AA-ELACERO) -Code: P211LH021–023 financed by the Stainless Steel Company, ACINOX, Las Tunas in Cuba. We thank the specialists of the Electric and Automatic Group at ACINOX. We are very grateful to the University of Oriente (UO) for guaranteeing the necessary resources to carry out this research.

References

1. T. Committee. IEEE Guide for the Interpretation of Gases Generated in Mineral Oil-Immersed Transformers, IEEE Std C57.104™ (2019). https://doi.org/10.1109/IEEESTD.2019.8890040
2. Alzghoul, A., Backe, B., Löfstrand, M., Byström, A., Liljedahl, B.: Comparing a knowledge-based and a data-driven method in querying data streams for system fault detection: a hydraulic drive system application. Comput. Ind. **65**(8), 1126–1135 (2014). https://doi.org/10.1016/j.compind.2014.06.003
3. Chang, C.-K., Shan, J., Chang, K.-C., Pan, J.-S.: Insulation faults diagnosis of power transformer by decision tree with fuzzy logic. In: Pan, J.-S., Lin, J.-W., Liang, Y., Chu, S.-C. (eds.) ICGEC 2019. AISC, vol. 1107, pp. 310–317. Springer, Singapore (2020). https://doi.org/10.1007/978-981-15-3308-2_35
4. Guo, C., et al.: Transformer failure diagnosis using fuzzy association rule mining combined with case-based reasoning. IET Gener. Transm. Distrib. **14**(11), 2202–2208 (2020). https://doi.org/10.1049/iet-gtd.2019.1423
5. Duan, J., He, Y., Wu, X.: Assisted diagnosis of real-virtual twin space for data insufficiency. In: Chen, W., Yang, Q., Wang, L., Liu, D., Han, X., Meng, G. (eds.) The Proceedings of the 9th Frontier Academic Forum of Electrical Engineering. LNEE, vol. 743, pp. 387–395. Springer, Singapore (2021). https://doi.org/10.1007/978-981-33-6609-1_34
6. Singh, A.K., Saxena, A., Roy, N., Choudhury, U.: Inter-turn fault stability enrichment and diagnostic analysis of power system network using wavelet transformation-based sample data control and fuzzy logic controller. Trans. Inst. Measur. Control, 01423312211007006 (2021). https://doi.org/10.1177/01423312211007006
7. Sahoo, S., Chowdary, K.V.V.S.R., Das, S.: DGA and AI technique for fault diagnosis in distribution transformer. In: Sherpa, K.S., Bhoi, A.K., Kalam, A., Mishra, M.K. (eds.) ETAEERE 2020. LNEE, vol. 691, pp. 35–46. Springer, Singapore (2021). https://doi.org/10.1007/978-981-15-7511-2_4
8. Tahir, M., Tenbohlen, S.: Transformer winding condition assessment using feedforward artificial neural network and frequency response measurements. Energies **14**(11), 3227 (2021). https://doi.org/10.3390/en14113227
9. Tao, L., Yang, X., Zhou, Y., Yang, L.: A novel transformers fault diagnosis method based on probabilistic neural network and bio-inspired optimizer. Sensors **21**(11), 3623 (2021). https://doi.org/10.3390/s21113623
10. Mo, W., Kari, T., Wang, H., Luan, L., Gao, W.: Power transformer fault diagnosis using support vector machine and particle swarm optimization. In: 2017 10th International Symposium on Computational Intelligence and Design (ISCID), 2017, vol. 1, pp. 511–515: IEEE. Hangzhou, China (2017). https://doi.org/10.1109/ISCID.2017.165
11. Kazemi, Z., Naseri, F., Yazdi, M., Farjah, E.: An EKF-SVM machine learning-based approach for fault detection and classification in three-phase power transformers. IET Sci. Meas. Technol. **15**(2), 130–142 (2021). https://doi.org/10.1049/smt2.12015
12. Velásquez, R.M.A.: Support vector machine and tree models for oil and Kraft degradation in power transformers. Eng. Fail. Anal. **127**, 105488 (2021). https://doi.org/10.1016/j.engfailanal.2021.105488
13. Hoballah, A., Mansour, D.-E.A., Taha, I.B.: Hybrid grey wolf optimizer for transformer fault diagnosis using dissolved gases considering uncertainty in measurements. IEEE Access **8**, 139176–139187 (2020). https://doi.org/10.1109/ACCESS.2020.3012633
14. Shiling, Z.: Application of joint immune ant colony algorithm and fuzzy neural network to path planning and visual image processing of inspection robot in substation. In: 2020 3rd International Conference on Artificial Intelligence and Big Data (ICAIBD), 2020, pp. 142–148. IEEE, Chengdu, China (2020). https://doi.org/10.1109/ICAIBD49809.2020.9137437

15. Taha, I.B., Hoballah, A., Ghoneim, S.S.: Optimal ratio limits of rogers' four-ratios and IEC 60599 code methods using particle swarm optimization fuzzy-logic approach. IEEE Trans. Dielectr. Electr. Insul. **27**(1), 222–230 (2020). https://doi.org/10.1109/TDEI.2019.008395

16. Tightiz, L., Nasab, M.A., Yang, H., Addeh, A.: An intelligent system based on optimized ANFIS and association rules for power transformer fault diagnosis. ISA Trans. **103**, 63–74 (2020). https://doi.org/10.1016/j.isatra.2020.03.022

17. Malik, H., Sharma, R., Mishra, S.: Fuzzy reinforcement learning based intelligent classifier for power transformer faults. ISA Trans. **101**, 390–398 (2020). https://doi.org/10.1016/j.isatra.2020.01.016

18. Palke, R., Korde, P.: Dissolved Gas Analysis (DGA) to diagnose the internal faults of power transformer by using fuzzy logic method. In: 2020 International Conference on Communication and Signal Processing (ICCSP), 2020, pp. 1050–1053. IEEE, Chennai, India (2020). https://doi.org/10.1109/ICCSP48568.2020.9182279

19. Prasojo, R.A., Gumilang, H., Maulidevi, N.U., Soedjarno, B.A.: A fuzzy logic model for power transformer faults' severity determination based on gas level, gas rate, and dissolved gas analysis interpretation. Energies **13**(4), 1009 (2020). https://doi.org/10.3390/en13041009

20. Abdo, A., Liu, H., Zhang, H., Guo, J., Li, Q.: A new model of faults classification in power transformers based on data optimization method. Electric Power Syst. Res. **200**, 107446 (2021). https://doi.org/10.1016/j.epsr.2021.107446

21. Tenbohlen, S., Jagers, J., Vahidi, F., Standardized survey of transformer reliability: on behalf of CIGRE WG A2. 37. In: 2017 International Symposium on Electrical Insulating Materials (ISEIM), 2017, vol. 2, pp. 593–596. IEEE, Toyohashi, Japan (2017). https://doi.org/10.23919/ISEIM.2017.8166559

22. Blanco, J.C.F., González, F.H.H., Barrios, L.B.C.: Método de lógica difusa para el diagnóstico de fallos incipientes en un transformador de 40MVA. Rev. Ing. Electrón. Autom. y Com. **42**(2), 76–88 (2021). 1815-5928

23. Li, E., Wang, L., Song, B.: Fault diagnosis of power transformers with membership degree. IEEE Access **7**, 28791–28798 (2019). https://doi.org/10.1109/ACCESS.2019.2902299

24. Mohamad, F., Hosny, K., Barakat, T.: incipient fault detection of electric power transformers using fuzzy logic based on roger's and IEC method. In: 2019 14th International Conference on Computer Engineering and Systems (ICCES), 2019, pp. 303–309. IEEE, Cairo, Egypt (2019). https://doi.org/10.1109/ICCES48960.2019.9068132

25. Niţu, M.-C., Aciu, A.-M., Nicola, C.-I., Nicola, M.: Power transformer fault diagnosis using fuzzy logic technique based on dissolved gas analysis and furan analysis. In: 2017 International Conference on Optimization of Electrical and Electronic Equipment (OPTIM) and 2017 Intl Aegean Conference on Electrical Machines and Power Electronics (ACEMP), 2017, pp. 184–189. IEEE, Brasov, Romania (2017). https://doi.org/10.1109/OPTIM.2017.7974968

26. Duval, M., Lamarre, L.: The duval pentagon-a new complementary tool for the interpretation of dissolved gas analysis in transformers. IEEE Electr. Insul. Mag. **30**(6), 9–12 (2014). https://doi.org/10.1109/MEI.2014.6943428

27. Duval, M., DePabla, A.: Interpretation of gas-in-oil analysis using new IEC publication 60599 and IEC TC 10 databases. IEEE Electr. Insul. Mag. **17**(2), 31–41 (2001) %@ 0883-7554. https://doi.org/10.1109/57.917529

28. Faiz, J., Soleimani, M.: Dissolved gas analysis evaluation in electric power transformers using conventional methods a review. IEEE Trans. Dielectr. Electr. Insul. **24**(2), 1239–1248 (2017). https://doi.org/10.1109/TDEI.2017.005959

29. Mahmoudi, N., Samimi, M.H., Mohseni, H.: Experiences with transformer diagnosis by DGA: case studies. IET Gener. Transm. Distrib. **13**(23), 5431–5439 (2019). https://doi.org/10.1049/iet-gtd.2019.1056

30. Rahman, O., Wani, S.A., Parveen, S., Khan, S.A.: Detection of incipient fault in transformer using DGA based integrated intelligent method. In: 2019 International Conference on Power Electronics, Control and Automation (ICPECA), 2019, pp. 1–6. IEEE, New Delhi, India (2019). https://doi.org/10.1109/ICPECA47973.2019.8975638
31. Pattanadech, N., Wattakapaiboon, W.: Application of Duval pentagon compared with Other DGA interpretation techniques: case studies for actual transformer inspections including experience from power plants in Thailand. In: 2019 5th International Conference on Engineering, Applied Sciences and Technology (ICEAST), 2019, pp. 1–4. IEEE, Luang Prabang, Laos (2019). https://doi.org/10.1109/ICEAST.2019.8802523

A Robust Fault Diagnosis Strategy in Mechanical Systems Using Pythagorean Fuzzy Sets

Adrián Rodríguez Ramos[1], José Luís Verdegay Galdeano[2],
and Orestes Llanes-Santiago[1]([⊠]) (iD)

[1] Universidad Tecnológica de La Habana José Antonio Echverría, CUJAE, Marianao,
La Habana, Cuba
adrian.rr@automatica.cujae.edu.cu, orestes@tesla.cujae.edu.cu
[2] Universidad de Granada, Granada, Spain
jlverdagay@decsai.ugr.es

Abstract. A robust fault diagnosis strategy in mechanical systems based on the use of Pythagorean fuzzy sets is presented. A variant of the FCM algorithm called Pythagorean Fuzzy C-Means (PyFCM) is obtained modifying the original FCM algorithm by using Pythagorean fuzzy sets. Furthermore, with the aim to obtain greater separability among classes, and reduce classification errors a kernel version of PyFCM (KPyFCM) is obtained. The proposed strategy is applied to the Development and Application of Methods for Actuator Diagnosis in Industrial Control Systems (DAMADICS) benchmark. A comparative analysis with other algorithms that use standard and non-standard membership grades is made. The satisfactory results obtained by the proposal indicates its feasibility.

Keywords: Fault diagnosis · Pythagorean fuzzy sets · Mechanical systems

1 Introduction

In modern industries is a requirement to obtain high level of efficiency, quality of the products, industrial safety, and to accomplish with environmental regulations. Faults in affect the productivity of the industrial plants, in several cases compromises the safety of the operators and they can affect the environment [8].

Mechanical systems represent a fundamental part of the most industrial plants and a significant number of faults in these plants are associated to this type of systems. It is the main reason for which the scientific community dedicate an special attention in the develop of fault diagnosis strategies to mechanical systems [10,12,16,20].

National Program of Research and Innovation - ARIA, Project No. 27, CITMA, Cuba.

Y. Hernández Heredia et al. (Eds.): IWAIPR 2021, LNCS 13055, pp. 199–210, 2021.
https://doi.org/10.1007/978-3-030-89691-1_20

In general, fault diagnosis methods are classified in two large groups: those based on models [3,5] and those based on historical data [4,9]. The strategies in the first group are based on residuals obtained from the difference between the measurable signals from the real process and the values obtained from a model of the process. However, obtaining an adequate model for this aim in complex processes is very difficult. In the case of the approaches based on historical data, they do not need a mathematical model, and neither require much prior knowledge of the process parameters [15]. This is an advantage in complex systems, where relationships among variables are nonlinear, and not totally known.

Techniques based on fuzzy tools are increasingly being applied in several scientific areas. Some examples are: image processing [14], control strategies [13], classification [6], and condition monitoring applications [11].

A main aspect in the use of fuzzy sets is the provision of membership grades. In order to enhance the capability of fuzzy sets for capturing and model user provided membership information, researchers have introduced non-standard second order fuzzy sets such as intuitionistic [1] and interval type-2 fuzzy sets [7]. These non-standard fuzzy sets allow the inclusion of imprecision and uncertainty in the specification of membership grades.

In 2013, Prof. Ronald R. Yager introduced another class of non-standard fuzzy subset named Pythagorean fuzzy subset [17]. In [18], it is shown that the space of Pythagorean membership grades is greater than the space of intuitionistic membership grades. This allows the use of the Pythagorean fuzzy sets in a greater set of applications than the intuitionistic fuzzy sets.

The data obtained by the Supervisory Control and Data Acquisition (SCADA) systems from complex industrial processes are frequently corrupted by noise. This introduces uncertainties in the observations which seriously affect the performance of the fault diagnosis systems by increasing the number of false alarms (fault diagnosis system confuses the Normal Operation Condition (NOC) with a fault), and by deteriorating the correct identification and location of faults.

In order to overcome these problems, and to obtain a robust fault diagnosis strategy applied in mechanical systems, an approach based on the use of Pythagorean membership grades is proposed which constitutes the main contribution of this paper. In this sense, a new variant of the Intuitionistic Fuzzy C-Means algorithm, called Pythagorean Fuzzy C-Mean algorithm (PyFCM), and it's kernel version (KPyFCM), which permits to achieve greater separability among classes and reduce classification errors, are obtained.

The organization of the paper is the following: in Sect. 2, the general characteristics of the tools used in the proposed methodology are presented. In Sect. 3, a description of the classification methodology using fuzzy clustering techniques is presented. In Sect. 4 the proposed methodology is evaluated with the Development and Application of Methods for Actuator Diagnosis in Industrial Control Systems (DAMADICS) benchmark. Next, an analysis of the results obtained and a comparison with other computational tools is developed in Sect. 5. Finally, the conclusions are presented.

2   Materials and Methods

In this section are firstly presented the general characteristics of Intuitionistic FCM (IFCM) algorithm. Next, the general characteristics of the Pythagorean membership grades, the Pythagorean FCM algorithm (PyFCM), and its kernel version (KPyFCM) are also presented.

2.1   Intuitionistic Fuzzy C-Means Algorithm

Intuitionistic fuzzy c-means clustering algorithm is based upon intuitionistic fuzzy set theory given by Atanassov [1] where membership $\mu(x)$ and nonmembership $v(x)$ functions are considered. An intuitionistic fuzzy set A in X, is written as:

$$A = \{x, \mu_A(x), v_A(x) \,|x \in X \} \tag{1}$$

where $\mu_A(x) \longrightarrow [0,1]$, $v_A(x) \longrightarrow [0,1]$ are the membership and non-membership degrees of an element in the set A with the condition: $0 \leq \mu_A(x) + v_A(x) \leq 1$. For all intuitionistic fuzzy sets, a hesitation degree $\pi_A(x)$ is also indicated [1]. It express the lack of knowledge in defining of whether x belongs to IFS or not and it is given by:

$$\pi_A(x) = 1 - \mu_A(x) - v_A(x); 0 \leq \pi_A(x) \leq 1 \tag{2}$$

Intuitionistic fuzzy c-means objective function contains two terms: (i) modified objective function of conventional FCM using Intuitionistic fuzzy set and (ii) intuitionistic fuzzy entropy (IFE). IFCM minimizes the objective function 3:

$$J_{IFCM} = \sum_{i=1}^{c} \sum_{k=1}^{N} \mu_{ik}^{*m} d_{ik}^2 + \sum_{i=1}^{c} \pi_i^* e^{1-\pi^*} \tag{3}$$

$\mu_{ik}^* = \mu_{ik}^m + \pi_{ik}$, where μ_{ik}^* denotes the intuitionistic fuzzy membership and μ_{ik} denotes the conventional fuzzy membership of the kth data in the ith class. π_{ik} is the hesitation degree, which is defined as:

$$\pi_{ik} = 1 - \mu_{ik} - (1 - \mu_{ik}^\alpha)^{1/\alpha}, \alpha > 0 \tag{4}$$

and it is calculated from Yager's intuitionistic fuzzy complement as

$$N(x) = (1 - x^\alpha)^{1/\alpha} , \ \alpha > 0 \tag{5}$$

thus, with the help of Yager's intuitionistic fuzzy complement, intuitionistic fuzzy set becomes:

$$A = \left\{x, \mu_A(x), (1 - \mu_A(x)^\alpha)^{1/\alpha} \,|x \in X \right\} \tag{6}$$

and

$$\pi_i^* = \frac{1}{N} \sum_{k=1}^{N} \pi_{ik}, k \in [1, N] \tag{7}$$

The second term in the objective function is called intuitionistic fuzzy entropy (IFE) and it is the measure of fuzziness in a fuzzy set [19]. For intuitionistic fuzzy cases, if $\mu_A(x_i)$, $v_A(x_i)$, $\pi_A(x_i)$ are the membership, non-membership, and hesitation degrees of the elements of the set $X = x_1, x_2, ..., x_n$, then intuitionistic fuzzy entropy, IFE that denotes the degree of intuitionism in fuzzy set, may be given as:

$$IFE(A) = \sum_{i=1}^{n} \pi_A(x_i)e^{[1-\pi_A(x_i)]} \tag{8}$$

where $\pi_A(x_i) = 1 - \mu_A(x_i) - v_A(x_i)$ IFE is introduced in the objective function to maximize the good points in the class. The goal is to minimize the entropy. Modified cluster centers are:

$$v_i^* = \frac{\sum_{k=1}^{n} \mu_{ik}^* x_k}{\sum_{k=1}^{n} \mu_{ik}^*} \tag{9}$$

2.2   Pythagorean Fuzzy C-Means Algorithm (PyFCM)

A new class of nonstandard fuzzy sets called Pythagorean fuzzy sets (PFS) is presented in [18]. The membership grades associated with these sets will be named as Pythagorean membership grades.

For expressing the Pythagorean membership grades a pair of values $r(x)$ and $d(x)$ for each $x \in X$ are assigned. Both values will be called as the strength of commitment at x in the case of $r(x) \in [0,1]$ and the direction of commitment in the case of $d(x) \in [0,1]$. The values $r(x)$ and $d(x)$ are associated with a pair of membership grades $A_Y(x)$ and $A_N(x)$. These memberships grades indicate the support for membership of x in A and the support against membership of x in A respectively. Next, it is shown that $A_Y(x)$ and $A_N(x)$ are related using the Pythagorean complement with respect to $r(x)$. More specially, the values of $A_Y(x)$ and $A_N(x)$ are defined from $r(x)$ and $d(x)$ as

$$A_Y(x) = r(x)cos(\theta(x)) \tag{10}$$

$$A_N(x) = r(x)sin(\theta(x)) \tag{11}$$

where

$$\theta(x) = (1 - d(x))\frac{\pi}{2} \tag{12}$$

and $\theta(x) \in [0, \frac{\pi}{2}]$ is expressed in radians.

In [18] is shown that $A_Y(x)$ and $A_N(x)$ are Pythagorean complements with respect to $r(x)$ and that

$$A_Y^2(x) + A_N^2(x) = r^2(x)(cos^2(\theta) + sin^2(\theta)) \tag{13}$$

In a general form, a Pythagorean membership grade is represented by a pair of values (a, b) such that $a, b \in [0, 1]$ and $a^2 + b^2 \leq 1$. In this case, $a =$

$A_Y(x)$, indicates the degree of support for membership of x in A and, $b = A_N(x)$ indicates the degree of support against membership of x in A. Taking into account the pair (a, b), the Eq. (13) can be expressed as $a^2 + b^2 = r^2$. This indicates that a Pythagorean membership grade is a point of a circle of radius r.

An intuitionistic membership grade presented in [1] is also a pair (a, b) that satisfies $a, b \in [0, 1]$ and $a + b \leq 1$. In [18] was demonstrated that the set of Pythagorean membership grades is greater than the set of intuitionistic membership grades. That result is clearly shown in Fig. 1 taken from [18]. Here, it is possible to observe that intuitionistic membership grades are all points under the line $x + y \leq 1$ and the Pythagorean membership grades are all points with $x^2 + y^2 \leq 1$.

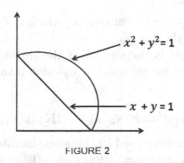

FIGURE 2

Fig. 1. Comparison of space of Pythagorean and intuitionistic membership grades.

Taking into account the theory of Pythagorean fuzzy sets, it can be said that the objective function on the Pythagorean Fuzzy C-Means algorithm (PyFCM) is similar to the one obtained for the IFCM algorithm according Eq. 3. In this case, a hesitation degree, $\pi_A(x)$, is given by:

$$\pi_A(x) = 1 - \mu_A^2(x) - v_A^2(x); 0 \leq \pi_A(x) \leq 1 \tag{14}$$

Therefore, in Eq. 3, π_{ik} is defined as:

$$\pi_{ik} = 1 - u_{ik}^2 - (1 - u_{ik}^\alpha)^{2/\alpha}, \alpha > 0 \tag{15}$$

The most important implication of this result is the possibility of using the Pythagorean fuzzy sets in a larger set of situations than intuitionistic fuzzy sets. In the case of fault diagnosis, this result allows to improve the classification process.

Pythagorean membership functions allow the use of a larger set of numeric values and greater in absolute value than those allowed by institutionistic membership functions for assigning the membership degree to an observation. In the classification process, the membership degree to a class is maximized. If there is a larger number of values in the search space and these values are greater in absolute value than the institutionistic case, then, this allows to improve the classification process due to a better separation of classes.

2.3 Pythagorean Fuzzy C-Means Algorithm Based on a Kernel Approach

Kernel version of the PyFCM (KPyFCM) is obtained in order to achieve greater separability among classes, and reduce the classification errors. KPyFCM minimizes the objective function:

$$J_{KPyFCM} = \sum_{i=1}^{c} \sum_{k=1}^{N} \mu_{ik}^{*m} \left\| \mathbf{\Phi}(\mathbf{x_k}) - \mathbf{\Phi}(\mathbf{v_i}) \right\|^2 + \sum_{i=1}^{c} \pi_i^* e^{1-\pi^*} \tag{16}$$

where $\mu_{ik}^* = \mu_{ik}^m + \pi_{ik}$, π_{ik} hesitation degree, which is defined according to Eq. (15) and π_i^* is defined as the Eq. (7).

Also, $\left\| \mathbf{\Phi}(\mathbf{x_k}) - \mathbf{\Phi}(\mathbf{v_i}) \right\|^2$ is the square of the distance between $\mathbf{\Phi}(\mathbf{x_k})$ and $\mathbf{\Phi}(\mathbf{v_i})$. The distance in the feature space is calculated through the kernel in the input space as follows:

$$\left\| \mathbf{\Phi}(\mathbf{x_k}) - \mathbf{\Phi}(\mathbf{v_i}) \right\|^2 = \mathbf{K}(\mathbf{x_k}, \mathbf{x_k}) - 2\mathbf{K}(\mathbf{x_k}, \mathbf{v_i}) + \mathbf{K}(\mathbf{v_i}, \mathbf{v_i}) \tag{17}$$

One of kernel function more used in the scientific literature is the Gaussian kernel because of it's easy implementation and satisfactory results. If the Gaussian kernel is used, then $\mathbf{K}(\mathbf{x}, \mathbf{x}) = 1$ and $\left\| \mathbf{\Phi}(\mathbf{x_k}) - \mathbf{\Phi}(\mathbf{v_i}) \right\|^2 = 2\left(1 - \mathbf{K}(\mathbf{x_k}, \mathbf{v_i})\right)$. Thus, Eq. (16) can be written as:

$$J_{KPyFCM} = 2\sum_{i=1}^{c} \sum_{k=1}^{N} \mu_{ik}^{*m} \left\| 1 - \mathbf{K}(\mathbf{x_k}, \mathbf{v_i}) \right\|^2 + \sum_{i=1}^{c} \pi_i^* e^{1-\pi^*} \tag{18}$$

where,
$$\mathbf{K}(\mathbf{x_k}, \mathbf{v_i}) = e^{-\|\mathbf{x}_k - \mathbf{v}_i\|^2 / \sigma^2} \tag{19}$$

Minimizing Eq. (18) under the constraint $\sum_{i=1}^{l} u_{ik} = 1, k = 1, 2, ..., N$, yields:

$$\mu_{ik}^* = \frac{1}{\sum_{j=1}^{c} \left(\frac{1 - \mathbf{K}(\mathbf{x_k}, \mathbf{v_i})}{1 - \mathbf{K}(\mathbf{x_k}, \mathbf{v_j})} \right)^{1/(m-1)}} \tag{20}$$

$$\mathbf{v}_i = \frac{\sum_{k=1}^{N} \left(\mu_{ik}^{*m} \mathbf{K}(\mathbf{x_k}, \mathbf{v_i}) \mathbf{x_k} \right)}{\sum_{k=1}^{N} \mu_{ik}^{*m} \mathbf{K}(\mathbf{x_k}, \mathbf{v_i})} \tag{21}$$

KPyFCM algorithm is presented in Algorithm 1.

Algorithm 1. Pythagorean Fuzzy C-Means algorithm based in a kernel approach (KPyFCM)

Input: data, c, $\epsilon > 0$, $m > 1$, σ, Itr_{max} (number of iterations)
Output: fuzzy partition **U**, class centers **V**
1. Initialize **U** to random fuzzy partition
2. $t \leftarrow 1$
3. **repeat**
4. Update the center of each class according to (21) for Gaussian kernels
5. Calculate the distances according to (17)
6. Update **U** according to (20).
7. $t \leftarrow t + 1$
8. **until** $\|U_t - U_{t-1}\| < \epsilon \wedge t \geq Itr_{max}$
9. **return** fuzzy partition **U**, class centers **V**

---

3   Description of the Proposal

The classification scheme proposed in this paper is shown in Fig. 2. It presents an offline training stage and an online recognition stage. In the training stage, the historical data of the process are used to train (modeling the functional stages through the clusters) a fuzzy classifier. After the training, the classifier is used online (recognition) in order to classify every new sample taken from the process. In this stage, the observations obtained by the SCADA system are classified one by one. In the classification process, the distance between the received observation and each one of the class centers is calculated. Next, the fuzzy membership degree of the observation to each one of the c classes is obtained. The observation will be assigned to the class with highest membership degree. The result intends to offer information about the system state in real-time for the operator.

4   Benchmark Case Study: DAMADICS

In order to apply the proposed methodology to fault diagnosis in the mechanical systems the DAMADICS benchmark was selected. This benchmark represents an actuator [2] belonging to the class of intelligent electro-pneumatic devices widespread in industrial environment. This actuator is considered as an assembly of devices consisting of:

- Control valve
- Spring-and-diaphragm pneumatic servomotor
- Positioner

The general structure of this actuator is shown in Fig. 3

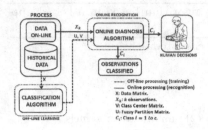

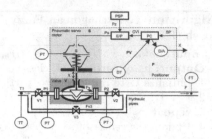

Fig. 2. Classification scheme using fuzzy clustering.

Fig. 3. Structure of benchmark actuator system.

The control valve acts on the flow of the fluid passing through the pipeline installation. A servomotor carries out a change in the position of the control valve plug, by acting on fluid flow rate. A spring-and-diaphragm pneumatic servomotor is a compressible fluid powered device in which the fluid acts upon the flexible diaphragm, to provide linear motion of the servomotor stem. The positioner is a device applied to eliminate the control-valve-stem miss-positions produced by the external or internal sources such as: friction, clearance in mechanical assemblies, supply pressure variations, hydrodynamic forces, among others. The set of measurements of 6 process variables were stored with a sample time of 1 s. For each one of the six process states (Normal operation and the five faults) 300 observations were stored for a total of 1800 observations. To this data set were added 300 new observations evenly distributed among the classes in order to represent the possible outliers for each class. Furthermore, white noise was added in the simulation to the measurement and process variables in order to simulate the variability present in real world processes. A description of the simulated faults and the measured process variables is shown in Table 1.

Table 1. Faults simulated and measured process variables in DAMADICS

Faults simulated in the DAMADICS		Measured process variables
Fault	Description	Description
1	Valve clogging	Process control external signal
7	Critical Flow	Inlet liquid pressure
12	Electro-pneumatic transducer fault	Oulet liquid pressure
15	Positioner spring fault	Stem displacement
19	Flow rate sensor fault	Liquid flow rate
		Process value

5   Analysis of Results

Table 2 shows the confusion matrix for experimental dataset where F1: Fault 1, F7: Fault 7, F12: Fault 12, F15: Fault 15 and F19: Fault 19. The main diagonal is associated with the number of observations successfully classified. Since the total number of observations per class is known, the accuracy (TA) can also be computed. The last row shows the average (AVE) of TA.

Table 2. CM for the DAMADICS process (F1: 300, F7: 300, F12: 300, F15: 300, F19: 300).

FCM	F1	F7	F12	F15	F19	TA (%)
F1	182	23	20	14	61	60.67
F7	21	211	26	24	18	70.33
F12	28	41	191	22	18	63.67
F15	67	61	11	149	12	49.67
F19	30	35	20	16	199	66.33
AVE						62.13

KFCM	F1	F7	F12	F15	F19	TA (%)
F1	230	12	9	2	47	76.67
F7	9	265	12	11	3	88.33
F12	10	13	260	9	8	86.67
F15	46	44	8	192	10	64.00
F19	14	17	7	8	254	84.67
AVE						80.07

IFCM	F1	F7	F12	F15	F19	TA (%)
F1	208	19	15	4	54	69.33
F7	14	239	18	23	6	79.67
F12	18	24	221	21	16	73.67
F15	51	48	14	166	21	55.33
F19	24	28	13	10	225	75.00
AVE						70.60

KIFCM	F1	F7	F12	F15	F19	TA (%)
F1	263	7	3	1	26	87.67
F7	10	276	8	6	0	92.00
F12	9	10	269	7	5	89.67
F15	33	30	11	210	16	70.00
F19	12	15	4	4	265	88.33
AVE						85.53

PyFCM	F1	F7	F12	F15	F19	TA (%)
F1	215	16	13	6	50	71.67
F7	11	253	15	16	5	84.33
F12	17	22	244	11	6	81.33
F15	50	47	9	180	14	60.00
F19	18	23	9	11	239	79.67
AVE						75.40

KPyFCM	F1	F7	F12	F15	F19	TA (%)
F1	270	5	2	1	22	90.00
F7	5	289	4	2	0	96.33
F12	6	8	281	4	1	93.67
F15	23	17	7	244	9	81.33
F19	10	12	0	1	277	92.33
AVE						90.73

As several algorithms are presented, it is necessary to analyze if there are significant differences among the results of them. To achieve this, it is necessary to apply statistical tests.

5.1 Statistical Tests

In our case, for six experiments ($k = 6$) and 10 datasets ($N = 10$), the value of statistical Friedman $F_F = 340$ was obtained. With $k = 6$ and $N = 10$, F_F is distributed according to the F distribution with $6 - 1 = 5$ and $(6 - 1) \times (10 - 1) = 45$ degrees of freedom. The critical value of $F(5,45)$ for $\alpha = 0.05$ is 2.4221, so the null-hypothesis is rejected ($F(5,45) < F_F$) which means that at least the average performance of at least one algorithm is significantly different from the average value of the performance of other algorithms and the Wilcoxon test is applied to determine it.

Table 3 shows the results of the comparison in pairs of the algorithms (1: FCM, 2: IFCM, 3: PyFCM, 4: KFCM, 5: KIFCM, 6: KPyFCM) using the Wilcoxon test. The first two rows contain the values of the sum of the positive (R^+) and negative (R^-) rank for each comparison established. The next two rows show the statistical values T and the critical value of T for a level of significance $\alpha = 0.05$. The last row indicates which algorithm was the winner in each comparison.

Table 3. Results of the Wilcoxon test

	1 vs 2	1 vs 3	1 vs 4	1 vs 5	1 vs 6	2 vs 3	2 vs 4	2 vs 5	2 vs 6	3 vs 4	3 vs 5	3 vs 6	4 vs 5	4 vs 6	5 vs 6
$\sum R^+$	0	0	0	0	0	0	0	0	0	0	0	0	0	0	0
$\sum R^-$	55	55	55	55	55	55	55	55	55	55	55	55	55	55	55
T	0	0	0	0	0	0	10	0	0	0	0	0	0	0	0
$T_{\alpha=0.05}$	8	8	8	8	8	8	8	8	8	8	8	8	8	8	8
Winner	2	3	4	5	6	3	4	5	6	4	5	6	5	6	6

As can be seen, among the FCM, IFCM and PyFCM algorithms, the PyFCM algorithm obtains the better results. In the analysis with the Kernel algorithms, the KPyFCM algorithm obtains the better results. Taking into account all algorithms, it is shown that the KPyFCM algorithm obtains the best results.

6   Conclusions

The main contribution of this work is the development of a robust scheme for condition monitoring in industrial systems by using Pythagorean membership grades. The fundamental motivation for this proposal is based on the fact that the space of Pythagorean membership grades is greater than the space of the standard and intuitionistic membership grades. This allows for a better assignation of the membership grade to the observations obtained from complex industrial processes that are corrupted by noise which introduce high uncertainties, and this seriously affects the performance of the condition monitoring systems.

In the proposal, the FCM algorithm is modified by using Pythagorean fuzzy sets, and a new variant of that algorithm called Pythagorean Fuzzy C-Mean (PyFCM) algorithm is obtained. In addition, a kernel version of the PFCM algorithm (KPyFCM) is obtained in order to achieve greater separability among the classes, for reducing the classification errors. The approach proposed was validated using synthetic datasets and the DAMADICS process benchmark. The promising results obtained indicate the feasibility of the proposal.

References

1. Atanassov, K.: On Intuitionistic Fuzzy Sets Theory. Springer, Heidelberg (2012). https://doi.org/10.1007/978-3-642-29127-2
2. Bartys, M., Patton, R., Syfert, M., de las Heras, S., Quevedo, J.: Introduction to the DAMADICS actuator FDI benchmark study. Control Eng. Pract. **14**, 577–596 (2006)
3. Camps-Echevarría, L., Llanes-Santiago, O., Silva Neto, A.: An approach for fault diagnosis based on bio-inspired strategies. In: IEEE Congress on Evolutionary Computation, pp. 1–7 (2010). https://doi.org/10.1109/CEC.2010.5586357
4. Cerrada, M., Sánchez, R.-V., Pacheco, F., Cabrera, D., Zurita, G., Li, C.: Hierarchical feature selection based on relative dependency for gear fault diagnosis. Appl. Intell. **44**(3), 687–703 (2015). https://doi.org/10.1007/s10489-015-0725-3
5. Isermann, R.: Fault-Diagnosis Applications: Model-Based Condition Monitoring: Actuators, Drives, Machinery, Plants, Sensors, and Fault-Tolerant Systems. Springer, Heidelberg (2011). https://doi.org/10.1007/978-3-642-12767-0
6. Liu, L., Yang, A., Zhou, W., Zhang, X., Fei, M., Tu, X.: Robust dataset classification approach based on neighbor searching and kernel fuzzy c-means. IEEE/CAA J. Autom. Sin. **2**, 235–247 (2015)
7. Mendel, J.M., John, R.I., Liu, F.: Interval type-2 fuzzy sets made simple. IEEE Trans. Fuzzy Syst. **14**, 808–821 (2006)
8. Park, Y., Fan, S., Hsu, C.: A review on fault detection and process diagnostics in industrial processes. Processes **8**(1123), 1–26 (2020). https://doi.org/10.3390/pr8091123
9. Prieto-Moreno, A., Llanes-Santiago, O., García Moreno, E.: Principal components selection for dimensionality reduction using discriminant information applied to fault diagnosis. J. Process Control **33**, 14–24 (2015)
10. Rodríguez Ramos, A., Bernal de Lázaro, J.M., Prieto Moreno, A., da Silva Neto, A.J., Llanes-Santiago, O.: An approach to robust fault diagnosis in mechanical systems using computational intelligence. J. Intell. Manuf. **30**(4), 1601–1615 (2017). https://doi.org/10.1007/s10845-017-1343-1
11. Rodríguez Ramos, A., Llanes-Santiago, O., Bernal de Lázaro, J.M., Cruz Corona, C., Silva Neto, A., Verdegay Galdeano, J.: A novel fault diagnosis scheme applying fuzzy clustering algorithms. Appl. Soft Comput. **58**, 605–619 (2017)
12. Rodríguez Ramos, A., et al.: An approach to multiple fault diagnosis using fuzzy logic. J. Intell. Manuf. **30**(1), 429–439 (2016). https://doi.org/10.1007/s10845-016-1256-4
13. Tong, S., Liu, W., Quian, D., Yan, X., Fang, J.: Design of a networked tracking control system with a data-based approach. IEEE/CAA J. Autom. Sin. **6**, 1261–1267 (2019)
14. Wang, C., Pedrycz, W., Zhou, M., Li, Z.: Sparse regularization-based fuzzy c-means clustering incorporating morphological grayscale reconstruction and wavelet frame. IEEE Trans. Fuzzy Syst. (2020). https://doi.org/10.1109/TFUZZ.2020.2985930
15. Wang, J., Hu, H.: Vibration-based fault diagnosis of pump using fuzzy technique. Measurement **39**, 176–185 (2009)
16. Xu, X., Cao, D., Zhou, Y., Gao, J.: Application of neural network algorithm in fault diagnosis of mechanical intelligence. Mech. Syst. Signal Process. **141**, 106625 (2020). https://doi.org/10.1016/j.ymssp.2020.106625
17. Yager, R.R.: Pythagorean membership grades in multi-criteria decision making. Technical report, Iona College, New Rochelle, NY (2013)

18. Yager, R.R.: Pythagorean membership grades in multicriteria decision making. IEEE Trans. Fuzzy Syst. **22**, 958–965 (2014)
19. Zadeh, L.: Probability measures of fuzzy events. J. Math. Anal. Appl. **23**, 421–427 (1968)
20. Zhang, X., Zhang, G., Li, Y.: A novel fault diagnosis approach of a mechanical system based on meta-action unit. Adv. Mech. Eng. **11**(2), 1–15 (2019). https://doi.org/10.1177/1687814019826644

Prediction of Diabetes Mortality in Mexico City Applying Data Science

Joaquín Pérez-Ortega[1]([✉]) [iD], Andrea Vega-Villalobos[1] [iD],
Nelva Nely Almanza-Ortega[2] [iD], Rodolfo A. Pazos-Rangel[3],
José Crispín Zavala-Díaz[4] [iD], José María Rodríguez-Lélis[1] [iD],
and Yazmín Hernández[1] [iD]

[1] Tecnológico Nacional de México/CENIDET, 62490 Cuernavaca, MOR, Mexico
[2] Tecnológico Nacional de México/IT de Tlalnepantla, 54070 Tlalnepantla de Baz,
EDOMEX, Mexico
[3] Tecnológico Nacional de México/IT de Cd. Madero, Cd, 89440 Madero, TAM, Mexico
[4] Administración E Informática, Universidad Autónoma de Morelos/Facultad de Contaduría,
62209 Cuernavaca, MOR, Mexico

Abstract. Around the world, diabetes is a disease that in recent years has had a significant increase in mortality rates. Currently, several countries consider diabetes
an important public health problem, particularly Mexico. In this research work, the
problem of mortality forecasting for the next 5 years in Mexico City was addressed
by applying Data Science. For developing the application, an extension of the IBM
methodology called Batch MFCD was used, which is oriented to the epidemiology domain. All the mortality and other data used in the research are from public
and official databases and belong to the 1990–2019 interval. For forecasting we
selected the Support Vector Regression (SVR) model, which allowed forecasting
the mortality rates for Mexico City in the 2020–2024 interval. A decrease of the
mortality rate for the 2017–2019 interval was observed for the actual data, and for
the 2020–2024 interval it is forecasted that mortality will continue to decrease at
a similar rate. It is worth mentioning that 2020 was an atypical year, because of
the COVID-19 pandemic; therefore, it is foreseeable that its effect may affect the
actual mortality rates in subsequent years.

Keywords: Data Science · Data Mining · Prediction · Epidemiology · Diabetes

1 Introduction

Data Science is an emerging field in Computer Science, of multi-disciplinary nature,
which is oriented to obtain knowledge from large volumes of data for answering questions
useful for decision making [1–3]. It uses tools and principles from other fields such as
Data Mining, Artificial Intelligence and Statistics, among others.

Diabetes mellitus is a disease that has increased significantly its morbidity and mortality rates in recent years. Worldwide many governments consider it as a public health
problem, including Mexico. According to the World Health Organization, in the year
2014 the diabetic population was 422 million [4].

© Springer Nature Switzerland AG 2021
Y. Hernández Heredia et al. (Eds.): IWAIPR 2021, LNCS 13055, pp. 211–218, 2021.
https://doi.org/10.1007/978-3-030-89691-1_21

Diabetes is a chronical degenerative disease and its treatment is expensive. Families of diabetic people are affected, both concerning the financial aspect, because of the cost of medication, as well as health care, especially in the late phases of the disease [5].

In recent years, Data Science has been successfully used in the health field. It has been remarkable its application in numerous clinical and epidemiological studies of the pandemic caused by SARS-CoV-2 and the COVID-19 disease [6]. In particular in the case of diabetes, Data Science has been used mainly in research with a clinical emphasis [7, 8].

In Mexico the morbidity and mortality by diabetes have grown at an alarming rate; therefore, the Health Ministry has declared an epidemiology emergency since 2016 [9, 10]. Generally, it has been observed that the districts of Mexico City have had some of the largest increases in their rates nationwide [5, 11]. The objective of this research is to find estimates of mortality rates for diabetes for the following five years. Based on mortality and population data of Mexico City districts for the 1990–2019 interval, we think that the results obtained may be useful for the medical field to increase its knowledge on the disease and for the health authorities to implement strategies for preventing and mitigating the disease effects, as well as for using resources efficiently.

2   Data Science Methodology

For the development of this application, we used Batch FMDS (see Fig. 1) as an extension of the methodology proposed by IBM [12]. Batch FMDS is oriented to the epidemiological domain through Phase 1, which involves one of the main advantages of the proposed methodology. The objective of "Business understanding" consists in formulating a research question, which satisfies the characteristics of epidemiological studies. This question is directly related to a solution method, established in "Analytic approach" of the IBM methodology [12], in order to achieve a precise and correct answer. After that, Phase 2 involves a series of tasks related to the data, such as collecting, understanding, and cleaning, among others. Finally, modeling the selected method, evaluating it and presenting its results are performed during Phase 3.

The questions that guided the development of this research were the following: How do the mortality rate for diabetes mellitus has evolved in Mexico City (CDMX) and the State of Mexico? How will this rate behave for the interval 2020–2024? The questions, according to the proposed methodology, can be answered by using the Support Vector Regression (SVR) model.

2.1   Source of Data

The data were collected from different official information sources from Mexico. Those sources and the data description are listed below:

- Mortality database: records of deaths that occurred between 1990 and 2019 for different causes of deaths were extracted from the General Directorate of Health Information (DGIS) [13].

Phase 1: Problem definition

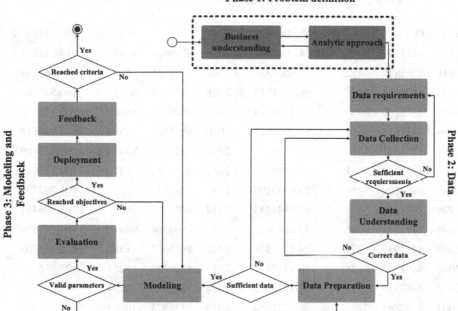

Fig. 1. Batch FMDS methodology

- Population database: records of the total population in Mexico for 1990, 1995, 2000, 2005, 2010, 2015 and 2019 were extracted from the National Institute of Statistics and Geography (INEGI) [14].
- Population estimates: records from 2016 to 2024, extracted from the National Population Council (CONAPO) [15].
- International catalogue of diseases (CIE-10): classification codes and names of diseases, extracted from the Collaborating Center for the Family of International Classifiers (CEMECE) [16].

2.2 Data Warehouse Description

According to Phase 2 of the methodology a Data warehouse was generated. Databases were analyzed in order to understand the information provided, to select and understand the attributes of interest, and to identify attributes with errors, which should be corrected or deleted. All data are integrated in a data warehouse with the following schema: Year (when the deaths occurred), Population (inhabitants of Mexico City), Incidence (number of deaths) and Mortality Rate (per 100,000 inhabitants). The mortality rate is the result of dividing the number of incidences by the population and finally multiplying by 100,000.

This generates the final data set integration for Diabetes in Mexico City shown in Table 1.

Table 1. Data for diabetes for Mexico City in the interval 1990–2019.

Year	PCM	Incidence	Mortality rate	Year	PCM	Incidence	Mortality rate
1990	8213181	4493	54.7047484	2006	8510826	9705	114.031235
1991	8265854	4452	53.8601335	2007	8547515	8440	98.742149
1992	8318527	4968	59.7221119	2008	8584204	8631	100.545141
1993	8371200	4644	55.4759174	2009	8620893	8808	102.17039
1994	8423873	4659	55.3071016	2010	8657589	10564	122.020114
1995	8476542	5017	59.1868713	2011	8928401	8743	97.9234692
1996	8480420	5067	59.7493992	2012	8911663	9107	102.191925
1997	8484298	5058	59.6160107	2013	8893742	9320	104.792786
1998	8488176	5690	67.0344253	2014	8874725	9619	108.386457
1999	8492054	6205	73.068306	2015	8854598	9499	107.277598
2000	8495935	6339	74.6121528	2016	8925667	11580	129.738203
2001	8491577	6638	78.1715811	2017	8996736	11251	125.056465
2002	8487219	6971	82.1352672	2018	9067805	10214	112.64027
2003	8482861	7488	88.2721054	2019	9138874	10203	111.643951
2004	8478503	7765	91.5845639				

2.3 Data Model

According to Phase 3 of the methodology a Data Model was generated. The forecasting model selected was Support Vector Regression (SVR), which has proven to be highly effective in solving non-linear problems, even with a small sample of training dataset [17–19]. This technique is a modification of the Support Vector Machine (SVM) [20, 21]. In SVR the support vectors are the closest points towards the generated hyperplane in a n-dimensional space which divides, as wide as possible, the data points on the hyperplane and return as output a real number [20–22]. Another important feature of SVR is to choose the right kernel such as linear, polynomial, sigmoid, and radial basis function (RBF) [23]. The RBF kernel combined with parameters $\varepsilon = 0.1$ and $c = 5000$ has shown to work better for this particular case. The other parameters where automatically adjusted by some assistance tools of the Python language, through the scikit-learn library, as it is shown next.

class sklearn.svm.SVR(*, kernel = 'rtf', degree = 3, gamma = 0.00044494, coef0 = 0.0, tol = 0.001, C = 5000, epsilon = 0.1, shrinking = True, cache_size = 200, verbose = False, max_iter = −1).

We evaluated the model and forecasting accuracy with the R-squared metrics. The result for Mexico City was R-squared = 0.9082278496408016, while for the State of Mexico it was R-squared = 0.9882537570515627.

3 Results and Discussion

When analyzing the actual data of mortality rate for Mexico City in the interval 1990–2019, it was observed atypical data for the years 2006, 2010, 2016 and 2017 with high mortality rates. It is known that atypical data affect the effectiveness of forecasting models. Then, there are two alternatives: eliminate them or adjust the parameters for generating the model by considering the influence of the atypical data. For validating our model, additional information was included from the problem context. Specifically, we obtained data of the same time interval for all the municipalities of the State of Mexico, which are adjacent to Mexico City. The parallel analysis of actual data and those of the forecast model for Mexico City and the State Mexico was very useful for fine-tuning the model parameters and for interpreting the results.

Table 2 shows the results of the forecast for the interval 2020–2024 for Mexico City and the State of Mexico. Notice that the figures of the State of Mexico are smaller than those of Mexico City. It is worth mentioning that for the State of Mexico the rate increases from year to year, while the one for Mexico City decreases. It is remarkable that the actual rate for Mexico City decreased in the years 2017, 2018 and 2019, and according to the forecast it will continue to decrease (Table 2 and Fig. 2). It is important to mention that the largest actual rate for Mexico City occurred in 2016, and at the end of this year the health authorities issued an emergency epidemiological declaration for diabetes. This forced to establish prevention and control measures for the disease by government institutions. A possible causal explanation for the mortality rate decreases in Mexico City is that the adopted measures have been effective.

Table 2. Forecast of the mortality rate for Mexico City and the State of Mexico for the interval 2020–2024.

Year	State Mex	CDMX
2020	88.01866629	111.672886
2021	88.78104835	110.7711468
2022	89.41172035	109.558978
2023	89.91201511	108.0400954
2004	90.28400679	106.2201814

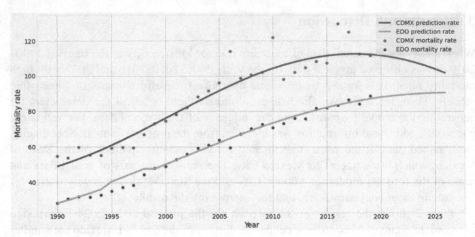

Fig. 2. Forecast of the mortality rate for Mexico city (CDMX) and the State of Mexico (EDO) for the interval 2020–2024.

4 Conclusions

One of the contributions of this research is the development of a data warehouse for diabetes from official data, which integrates population data and mortality statistical data for the interval 1990–2019.

The use of the Batch FMDS methodology by IBM shown to be an adequate option for developing the application, because of its orientation to the epidemiology field. In particular, its approach for associating the research question with the Data Science technique applied.

The main contribution of the research was the development of a Support Vector Regression (SVR) model, which allowed forecasting the mortality rates for Mexico City in the 2020–2024 interval. A decrease of the mortality rate for the 2017–2019 interval was observed for the actual data, and for the 2020–2024 interval it is forecasted that mortality will continue to decrease at a similar rate. It is worth mentioning that 2020 was an atypical year, because of the COVID-19 pandemic; therefore, it is foreseeable that its effect may affect the actual mortality rates in subsequent years.

Finally, we think that the results of this research may contribute to decision making by public health authorities in Mexico. In particular, for implementing strategies for preventing and mitigating the disease effect on the population.

An interesting future work will be to study the population-wise morbidity caused by COVID-19 and one of its main co-morbidities: diabetes. Additionally, it will be interesting to investigate the effects of mobility restrictions during the pandemic and its effect on the diabetic population.

Acknowledgements. This work was supported by TecNM (grant 10108.21-P) and by PRODEP (grant 28022). PhD student Andrea Vega Villalobos acknowledge her scholarship (Grantee No. 576646) by the Consejo Nacional de Ciencia y Tecnología, Mexico.

References

1. Ozdemir, S.: Principles of Data Science. Packt Publishing Ltd, Birmingham UK (2016)
2. Igual, L., Seguí, S.: Introduction to Data Science. Springer, Cham, Switzerland (2017). https://doi.org/10.1007/978-3-319-50017-1
3. VanderPlas, J.: Python Data Science Handbook: Essential Tools for Working with Data. O'Reilly Media Inc, California USA (2016)
4. OMS. https://www.who.int/health-topics/diabetes#tab=tab_1. Accessed 28 May 2021
5. Dávila-Cervantes, C.A., Pardo Montaño, A.M.: Diabetes mellitus: Aporte al cambio en esperanza de vida en México 1990, 2000 y 2010. Revista de Salud Pública **16**(6), 910–923 (2014)
6. Selvin, E., Juraschek, S.P.: Diabetes epidemiology in the COVID-19 pandemic. Diabetes Care **43**(8), 1690–1694 (2020)
7. Mehdi, M.J., Srinivasrao, N., Sireesha, A.: Detection and prognosis of diabetes based on data science techniques. Mater. Today: Proc. **33**, 4814–4818 (2020)
8. Davis, J.A., Burgoon, L.D.: Can data science inform environmental justice and community risk screening for type 2 diabetes? PLoS ONE **10**(4), e0121855 (2015)
9. Castellanos, J.L.V., Cerda, A.P.: Diabetes mellitus tipo 2: un problema epidemiológico y de emergencia en México. Investigación en Salud **150**(99), 18–26 (2001)
10. CENAPRECE Declaratoria de Emergencia. http://www.cenaprece.salud.gob.mx/programas/interior/emergencias/descargas/pdf/DeclaratoriaEmergenciaEpidemiologicaEE-4-16.pdf. Accessed 28 May 2021
11. Soto-Estrada, G., Moreno-Altamirano, L., Pahua Díaz, D.: Panorama epidemiológico de México, principales causas de morbilidad y mortalidad. Revista de la Facultad de Medicina (México) **59**(6), 8–22 (2016)
12. IBM Analytics Metodología fundamental para la ciencia de datos. https://www.ibm.com/downloads/cas/WKK9DX51. Accessed 28 May 2021
13. DGIS Defunciones. http://www.dgis.salud.gob.mx/contenidos/basesdedatos/da_defunciones_gobmx.html. Accessed 28 May 2021
14. INEGI Serie historica censal e intercensal (1990–2010). https://www.inegi.org.mx/programas/ccpv/cpvsh/. Accessed 28 May 2021
15. CONAPO Tabulados básicos. http://www.conapo.gob.mx/es/CONAPO/Tabulados_basicos. Accessed 28 May 2021
16. CEMECE Clasificación de enfermedades. http://www.dgis.salud.gob.mx/contenidos/intercambio/diagnostico_gobmx.html. Accessed 28 May 2021
17. Trzciński, T., Przemysław, R.: Predicting popularity of online videos using support vector regression. IEEE Trans. Multimedia **19**(11), 2561–2570 (2017)
18. Jain, R.K., Smith, K.M., Culligan, P.J., Taylor, J.E.: Forecasting energy consumption of multifamily residential buildings using support vector regression: Investigating the impact of temporal and spatial monitoring granularity on performance accuracy. Appl. Energy **123**, 168–178 (2014)
19. Khan, F.M., Zubek, V.B.: Support vector regression for censored data (SVRc): a novel tool for survival analysis. In: 2008 Eighth IEEE International Conference on Data Mining. pp. 863–868. IEEE, USA (2008)
20. Drucker, H., Burges, C.J., Kaufman, L., Smola, A., Vapnik, V.: Support vector regression machines. Adv. Neural. Inf. Process. Syst. **9**, 155–161 (1997)
21. Vapnik, V.N.: The nature of statistical learning theory. 2nd. Springer Science and Business Media, Berlin, Germany (2000).https://doi.org/10.1007/978-1-4757-2440-0

22. Awad, M., Rahul, K.: Efficient Learning Machines: Theories, Concepts, and Applications for Engineers and System Designers. Springer Nature, Basingstoke UK (2015). https://doi.org/10.1007/978-1-4302-5990-9

23. Guo, Y., Bartlett, P.L., Shawe-Taylor, J., Williamson, R.C.: Covering numbers for support vector machines. In: Proceedings of the Twelfth Annual Conference on Computational Learning Theory, pp. 267–277. ACM, NY USA (1999)

Balancing of Samples in Class Hierarchy

Shuhei Aoki$^{(\boxtimes)}$ and Mineichi Kudo

Hokkaido University, Sapporo 060-814, Japan
{shuhei_aoki,mine}@ist.hokudai.ac.jp

Abstract. In real-world classification problems, it is often the case that some classes (head classes) have large numbers of samples and the other classes (tail classes) have small numbers of samples. Such imbalance problems have been widely studied for a long time, and various methods have been proposed, such as oversampling from tail classes or heavy weighting to tail classes. However, these approaches lose the effectiveness when the number of classes is very large and imbalance is remarkable. Such a problem is called a long-tailed problem where there are a few head classes and many tail classes. In this paper, we construct a class hierarchy (a binary tree) where the numbers of samples are almost balanced in left and right children of each node. Some experiments demonstrated the effectiveness of the proposed approach.

Keywords: Imbalance problems · Long-tailed problems · Hierarchical classification · Class hierarchy · Class decision trees

1 Introduction

An *Imbalanced Dataset* is a dataset that has a large difference in the number of samples between head classes and tail classes. It is well known that classifiers trained from such a dataset underestimate tail classes because misclassification of them does not give a large impact on the total accuracy [1]. Recently many practical problems are largely imbalanced such as anomaly detection, medical diagnosis and e-mail filtering. Imbalance problems have been widely studied for a long time [1–3,8,14]. However, when the number of classes is very large and many tail classes have extremely small numbers of samples, conventional methods such as cost-sensitive learning [3] or re-sampling [14] cannot work well because of the difficulty of tuning the parameters. Extremely imbalanced problems are also called *long-tailed problems*. An example is shown in Fig. 1. A class hierarchy [5,6] is a promising approach for dealing with many-class, but not always imbalance, problems, and is typically realized as a binary tree with nodes consisting of a class subset. A class hierarchy can be constructed in top down manner by dividing a class set into its two disjoint subsets and repeat the procedure until each subset consists of only one class [5,6,15]. However, much attention has not been paid for the imbalance of samples so far in those trees. In this paper, we propose a construction algorithm of such a binary tree that the numbers of samples of left

© Springer Nature Switzerland AG 2021
Y. Hernández Heredia et al. (Eds.): IWAIPR 2021, LNCS 13055, pp. 219–228, 2021.
https://doi.org/10.1007/978-3-030-89691-1_22

and right children are well balanced in each node. It is, therefore, expected to mitigate the imbalance in long-tailed problems at least in each node, bringing a higher accuracy on tail classes.

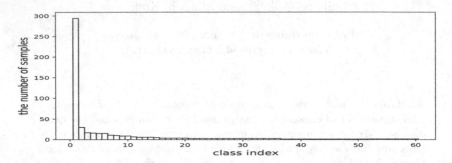

Fig. 1. Long-tailed distribution of dataset `birds` (the classes are sorted in descending order of sample sizes (see Table 1)).

2   Related Works

There are mainly three approaches for coping with imbalance problems: 1) Data level approaches: re-sample, that is, conduct over-sampling from tail classes or under-sampling from head classes [14], 2) Algorithm level approaches: remodel existing classification algorithms to bias tail classes [3] and 3) Ensamble-based approaches: combine ensemble learning algorithms with cost-sensitive learning or re-sampling [8]. Some of them consider the cases including classes with extremely small numbers of samples [2]. However, few methods have paid sufficient attention to long-tailed datasets where a very large number of classes exists.

On the other hand, hierarchical classification has gained a significant attention in dealing with multi-class problems [12,13]. Two well-known methods are decision directed acyclic graphs (DDAGs) [13] and binary hierarchical decision trees (BHDTs) [12]. DDAGs train $\binom{C}{2}$ classifiers (C: the number of classes) and use a directed acyclic graph (DAG) to compare a class pair at a node. The classes other than the chosen pair of classes are ignored at that node, so that the samples of those classes are passed into both of children nodes, resulting in the existence of some merge nodes to recombine the separated samples of the same class. BHDTs use a decision tree that divides a class set into two class subsets at a node. As a result, it has C leaves of a single class. In general, BHDTs are more efficient than DDAGs in the number of comparison times [12]. One of the BHDT methods is Class Decision Tree (CDT) [5,6]. In this paper, we focus on CDT and modify it so as to have a good balance in sample sizes at each node.

2.1   Class Decision Trees (CDTs)

The top-down construction of a CDT [5] starts with the entire class set at the root node, and repeats a division of a class set into its disjoint two subsets until each node has one class only. Although there is a bottom-up method shown in [6], in this paper, we adopt a top-down way since we can control better the balance of samples in a top-down way.

3   Sample Balanced Class Hierarchy (SBCH)

Here, we propose the idea of Sample Balanced Class Hierarchy (SBCH). In long-tailed distributions, tail classes occupy the majority in number, but their samples are extremely small, typically one, two or three (see Fig. 1). On the contrary, head classes are only a few but cover a majority of samples. Thus, even classifiers with a high total accuracy often perform poorly for tail classes. Our idea to cope with such a large imbalance is to divide the entire set of classes into two class subsets having almost equal number of samples, and repeat this division so as to construct an SBCH. Unfortunately, the problem to partition a class set of different numbers of samples into two disjoint subsets such that their numbers of samples are as close as possible is NP-complete (two-partition problem) [4]. Therefore, we propose a heuristic way.

3.1   Evaluation of Class Set Pairs

Consider a completely undirected graph $G = (V, E)$ where $V = \{c_i\}$ is a set of nodes corresponding to classes c_i and $E = \{e_{ij}\}$ is a set of edges e_{ij} with weight w_{ij} defined by

$$w(c_i, c_j) = \lambda s(c_i, c_j) + (1 - \lambda) b(c_i, c_j), \tag{1}$$

where $s(c_i, c_j)$ $(0 \leq s \leq 1)$ is the degree of separability between classes c_i and c_j and $b(c_i, c_j)$ $(0 \leq b \leq 1)$ is the degree of sample size balance between them. We conduct a Max-Min cut [5] in the graph G. Concretely, with a parameter λ $(0 \leq \lambda \leq 1)$, we find a partition (V_1^*, V_2^*) of V satisfying

$$(V_1^*, V_2^*) = \arg\max_{(V_1, V_2)} \min_{c_1 \in V_1, c_2 \in V_2} w(c_1, c_2), \; 0 \leq \lambda \leq 1. \tag{2}$$

For the degree $s(c_1, c_2)$ of separability, we use the value of the classification accuracy estimated by the leave-one-out (LOO) technique with 1-nearest neighbor (1-NN) classifier applied to c_1 and c_2. For the degree $b(c_1, c_2)$ of sample balance, we use a weighted entropy:

$$b(c_1, c_2) = \frac{n_1 + n_2}{N} H\left(\frac{n_1}{n_1 + n_2}, \frac{n_2}{n_1 + n_2}\right), \tag{3}$$

where n_1 and n_2 are the numbers of samples in classes c_1 and c_2 and N is the total number of samples $(N \geq n_1 + n_2)$. This value becomes smaller when classes c_1 and c_2 have smaller numbers of samples and are more imbalanced.

3.2   Max-Min Algorithm

Our max-min criterion for 2-partition (U, W) of a node set V:

$$\max_{U,W} \min_{i \in U, j \in W} w_{ij}$$

is easily solvable by the minimum-cost spanning tree.

Theorem 1. *The solution of* **Max-Min problem** *is given by cutting the edge of the maximum weight in the minimum-cost spanning tree.*

Proof. As well known, the minimum-cost spanning tree has the MST (Minimum-cost Spanning Tree) property [16], that is, for any 2-partition (U, W) of the node set V, if e is the edge between U and W having the smallest weight, then e is necessarily included in the minimum-cost spanning tree M. Therefore, the 2-partition (U, W) obtained by cutting the largest weight e' of M gives the solution of the max-min criterion.

For construction of the minimum-cost spanning tree, we could use Prim's algorithm of $O(|V|^2)$ time or Kraskal's algorithm of $O(|E| \log |E|)$ time. For a complete graph, therefore, Prim's algorithm has an advantage in time.

Max-Min algorithm using a minimum-cost spanning tree

1. Construct the minimum-cost spanning tree M of graph $G = (V, E)$
2. Find the edge $e \in M$ with the largest weight.
3. Separate M into M_1 and M_2 by cutting e.
4. Gathering all nodes connected to M_1 (M_2), make U (W).

Repeating **Max-Min algorithm** starting from a whole set V of classes, we can construct a SBCH. The algorithm is shown in Fig. 2. First we construct a complete graph $G = (V, E)$ and give weights on all the edges according to (1). Then, we construct a minimum-cost spanning tree M over G. Furthermore, we sort the $|V| - 1$ edges of M in decreasing order of the weights. Last, by cutting the largest-weight edge of M, we divide M into M_1 and M_2, smaller minimum-cost spanning trees. Repeating this division, we construct a SBCH. Here, two class subsets U and W of V are given such that U is of nodes connected to M_1 and W is of nodes connected to M_2. Note that we used a static graph with weights unchanged even after merging. It would be better to recalculate the entropy and the separability in a dynamic way at the expense of computation cost.

Lorena and Carvalho [15] have shown a similar algorithm in a bottom-up way, that is, building a class decision tree by repeating a merging process of two sets of classes according to Kruskal's algorithm. In fact, SBCH is the same as theirs as a result, except for the contents of the weights. However, our construction is made in a top-down way, repeating divisions from a whole set of classes. This contributes to the reduction of time complexity because Prim's algorithm of $O(n^2)$ for constructing a minimum-cost spanning tree is superior to Kruskal's algorithm of $O(n^2 \log n^2)$ for a complete graph of size n. Although we need more cost to sort $n - 1$ edges and $n - 1$ divisions, they are carried out in $O(n \log n)$ and

$O(n)$. More important difference from Lorena and Carvalho's approach is that they use Kruscal's algorithm as a clustering method without a clear optimization criterion, while we developed our algorithm to solve **Max-Min problem** with the equivalence proof with a minimum-cost spanning tree. Note that Prim's algorithm does not give a correct solution when it is used in a bottom-up way.

Procedure main

Input: $V = \{c_i\}_{i=1}^C$:a class set
   $S = \{(x_i, y_i)\}_{i=1}^n$:a sample set
   λ: a balance parameter $(0 \leq \lambda \leq 1)$
Output: T: a class decision tree

$W = \textbf{Weighting}(V, \lambda, S)$;
Make a complete graph $G = (V, E, W)$;
// Construct a minimum-cost spanning tree
$M = \textbf{Prim}(G)$;
$F = $ (the set of edges (u, v) of M);
// Sort F in decreasing order of weights
$F = \textbf{Sort}(F)$;
$T.set \leftarrow V$; // root node
$\textbf{Division}(T, V, F, M)$;
return;

Procedure Weighting (V, λ, S)

Input: $V = \{c\}$: a vertex set
   λ: a balance parameter $(0 \leq \lambda \leq 1)$
   $S = \{(x_i, y_i)\}_{i=1}^n$:a sample set
Output: $\{w(c, c')\}$: edge weights

$N \leftarrow |S|$;
for every pair $(c, c') \in V \times V (c \neq c')$ **do**
   $s(c, c') \leftarrow $ (LOO accuracy between c and c');
   $n \leftarrow$ (the number of samples of c);
   $m \leftarrow$ (the number of samples of c');
   $b(c, c') \leftarrow \frac{(n+m)}{N} H\left(\frac{n}{n+m}, \frac{m}{n+m}\right)$;
   $w(c, c') \leftarrow \lambda \cdot s(u, v) + (1 - \lambda) \cdot b(u, v)$;
return $\{w(c, c')\}$;

Procedure Division(T, V, F, M)

Input: T: a tree V: a vertex set
   F: an edge set M: a spanning tree
Output: T: an updated tree

$(u^*, v^*) = \arg \max_{(u,v) \in M} w(u, v)$;
$F \leftarrow F \setminus \{(u^*, v^*)\}$;
$M_1, M_2 \leftarrow M \setminus \{(u^*, v^*)\}$;
$U \leftarrow \{u \in V \mid u \in M_1\}$;
$W \leftarrow \{w \in V \mid w \in M_2\}$;
$T_1.set \leftarrow U$;
$T_2.set \leftarrow W$;
$T.leftson \leftarrow T_1$;
$T.rightson \leftarrow T_2$;
if $|U| > 1$
   $\textbf{Division}(T.leftson, U, F, M_1)$;
if $|W| > 1$
   $\textbf{Division}(T.rightson, W, F, M_2)$;
return ;

Fig. 2. Algorithm SBCH.

Table 1. Datasets. Here, #C: the number of classes, #F: the number of features and #S: the distribution of sample numbers. *Imbalance Ratio* is the average ratio of n_-/n_+ where n_+ is the number of samples in a class and n_- is the number of samples in the other classes.

Name	#C	#F	#S	Imbalance ratio
Glass	6	9	76,70,29,17,13,9	10.0
Yeast	10	8	463,429,244,163,51,44,37,30,20,5	53.6
Birds	60	260	294,30,17,16,15,15,11,10,9,9,7,6,6,6, 5,4,...,4,3,...,3,2,...,2	190.9

4   Experiments

We used two imbalanced datasets `glass` and `yeast` taken from UCI Machine Learning Repository [7] and one multi-label imbalanced dataset `birds` taken from A Java Library for Multi-Label Learning (Mulan) [10]. This multi-label dataset (`birds`) was translated into a single-label dataset by regarding a distinct subset of labels as a single meta-class. Each dataset is standardized to mean zero and variance one in each feature. The statistics are shown in Table 1. We adopted Support Vector Machine (with an RBF kernel) as a classifier in each node of the constructed tree. The regularization parameter C is set to 1000. Other hyper-parameters of SVM were set to the default values given by the python library scikit-learn [11]. We examined several values of the balance parameter λ in SBCH from 0 (sample balance only) to 1 (separability only) [5] in steps of 0.1. We used three metrics of classification performance calculated by LOO: the *balanced accuracy* (the average of accuracies of individual classes) and the accuracy of the latter half of all classes (Tail-1/2) and the latter quarter of them (Tail-1/4). As a baseline classifier, we adopted SVM in a standard one-versus-rest strategy. This way of classification is denoted as Flat. In the proposed class hierarchy, SVM is used in common to all nodes but is trained differently according to the samples of left and right children. For reducing the training time, the class hierarchy is constructed only once from all the training samples and fixed for training with different sets of data in LOO.

4.1   Results

The constructed class hierarchies by CDT [5] and by SBCH on `glass`, `yeast` and `birds` are shown in Figs. 3 and 4. We notice that the class hierarchies by SBCH are extremely one-sided (imbalance in tree form) but are well balanced in sample number at each node, compared with the trees by CDT (see the values of the entropy in nodes). This imbalance is often natural in long-tailed datasets because the number of samples decreases exponentially in many of such datasets. Suppose that ith class c_i has $k \cdot 2^{-i}$ samples for a constant k. In such a dataset, the largest class is left out first at the root node (because $2^{-1} > \sum_{i \geq 2} 2^{-i}$), and the second largest class follows to achieve the best balance at each node (Fig. 3

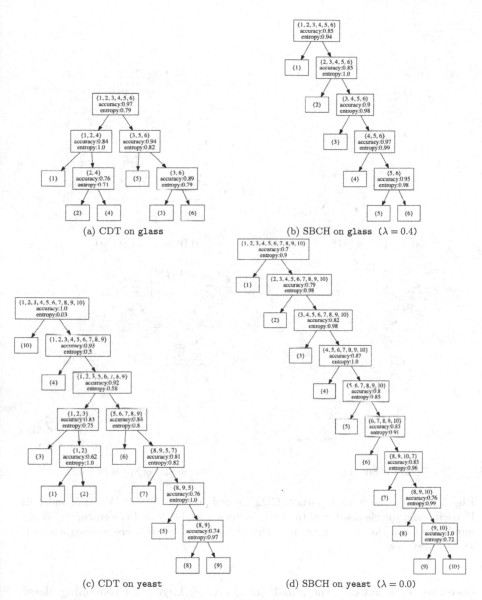

(a) CDT on glass

(b) SBCH on glass ($\lambda = 0.4$)

(c) CDT on yeast

(d) SBCH on yeast ($\lambda = 0.0$)

Fig. 3. CDT [5] and proposed SBCH ($\lambda = 0.4$ on glass and $\lambda = 0.0$ on yeast). In each node, the class subsets, the LOO accuracy by 1-NN and the entropy of sample numbers of two children are given in the order. The class IDs are re-assigned in the sample size order.

(b)(d) and Fig. 4 (e)(f)). As a result, tail classes are located in a bottom part of the tree, resolving the imbalanced problem among tail classes. Note that in **birds**, only the first class has an extremely large number of samples, so that

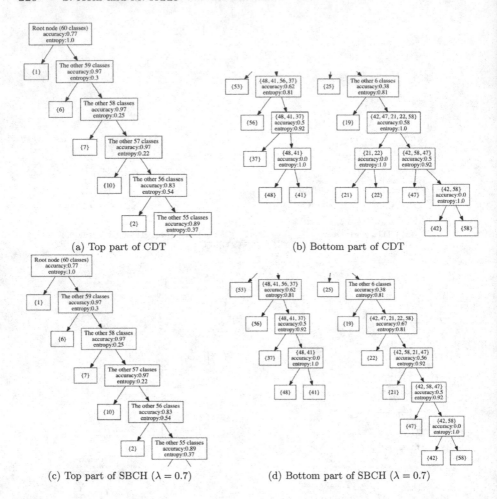

Fig. 4. The top and bottom parts of CDT [5] and proposed SBCH ($\lambda = 0.7$) on birds. In each node, the class subsets, the LOO accuracy by 1-NN and the entropy of sample numbers of two children are given in the order. The class IDs are re-assigned in the sample size order.

once class c_1 is left out, the imbalance decreases largely for remaining classes. This is the reason the tree of SBCH ($\lambda = 0.7$) is close to CDT. On the contrary, the accuracy of SBCH decreases in the upper part of the trees compared with CDT (see the accuracy in each node). In Table 2, SBCH gains the best scores in the balanced accuracy and Tail-1/4, but the second best score in Tail-1/2 on birds. From the values of Tail-1/4, it is clear that the proposed SBCH is the most effective for tail classes, but not so effective for head to body classes.

Table 2. Comparison of three approaches of Flat, CDT [5] and SBCH (proposed). In SBCH, the best value of λ is chosen ($\lambda^* = 0.4$ for glass, 0.0 for yeast and 0.7 for birds).

Dataset	Balanced Accuracy(%)			Tail-1/2(%)			Tail-1/4(%)		
	Flat	CDT	SBCH	Flat	CDT	SBCH	Flat	CDT	SBCH
Glass	50.57	53.71	**57.39**	48.53	54.41	**61.76**	23.08	28.21	**46.15**
Yeast	53.78	**54.59**	**54.59**	55.74	54.05	**60.64**	57.76	57.47	**62.07**
Birds	10.90	**11.79**	**11.79**	**18.35**	16.91	16.91	9.20	**11.04**	**11.04**

5 Discussion

The proposed SBCH is an extension of CDT [5]. Indeed, CDT is a special case of SBCH for $\lambda = 1.0$. The other extreme is the case of $\lambda = 0.0$ in which we do not pay attention to the separability at all. Therefore, the best value $\lambda = 0.0$ for yeast might give us a strange impression. However, this is a case that we should put a large priority on the sample balance because every class pairs have a similar degree of separability between them. Indeed, in yeast, the separabilities are in the range of $[0.80, 1.0]$ except for 2 pairs. In general, a middle value of λ exists as an optimal value in SBCH. We could use cross-validation to find it. In a long-tailed data, feature selection is also effective for improving the classification accuracy of tail classes. Indeed, another research of us demonstrates the effectiveness [9]. Therefore one of future directions of this research would be to incorporate feature selection with balancing of sample numbers. In addition, there is still room for improvement in computational complexity and in application to multi-label problems.

6 Conclusion

We have proposed an SBCH for improving the accuracy of tail classes in long-tailed problems. Experimentally we confirmed that the constructed sample-balance based class hierarchy outperformed the accuracy-based class decision tree [5] in classification of tail classes. In order to balance the number of samples of them more appropriately, we will discuss dynamic re-calculation of separability and entropy at a node in the future.

Acknowledgement. This work was partially supported by JSPS KAKENHI Grant Number 19H04128.

References

1. He, H. et al.: Learning from imbalanced data. IEEE Trans. Knowl. Eng. **21**, 1263–1284 (2009)

2. Yin, X., et al.: Feature transfer learning for face recognition with under-represented data. In: Proceedings of 2019 Conference on Computer Vision and Pattern Recognition(CVPR2019), 2019, Long Beach, USA, pp. 5704–5713 (2019)
3. Jiang, L., Li, C., Wang, S.: Cost-sensitive Bayesian network classifiers. Pattern Recogn. Lett. **45**, 211–216 (2014)
4. Hayes, B.: The easiest hard problem. Comput. Sci. **90**(2), 113–117 (2002)
5. Aoki, K., Kudo, M.: A top-down construction of class decision trees with selected features and classifiers. In: Proceedings of HPCS 2010, Caen, France, 390–398 (2010)
6. Aoki, K., Kudo, M.: Decision tree using class-dependent feature subsets. In: Proceedings of the: Joint IAPR Workshop on Structural, Syntactic, and Statistical Pattern Recognition(SSPR2002), 2396, pp. 761–769. Springer, Berlin, Heidelberg (2002)
7. Duaand, D., Graff, C.: UCI machine learning repository. [http://archive.ics.uci.edu/ml]. Irvine, University of California, School of Information and Computer Science, CA (2019)
8. Galar, M., et al.: A review on ensembles for the class imbalance problem: bagging-, boostiong-, and hybrid-based approaches. IEEE Trans. Syst. Man Cybern. Part C (App. Rev.), **42**(4), 463–484 (2012)
9. Horio, T., Kudo, M.: Feature Selection with Class Hierarchy for Imbalance Problems. In: IWAIPR 2021 (under review)
10. Tsoumakas et al., G.: Mulan: a java library for multi-label learning. J. Mach. Learn. Res. **12**, 2411–2414 (2011)
11. Pedregosa, et al.: Scikit-learn: machine learning in python. JMLR **12**, 2825–2830 (2011)
12. Cevikalp, H.: New clustering algorithms for the support vector machine based hierarchical classification. Pattern Recogn. Lett. **31**(11), 1285–1291 (2010)
13. Platt, J.C., Cristianini, N., Taylor, J.S.: Large Margin DAGs for Multiclass Classification. In: Proceedings of the 12th International Conference on Neural Information Processing Systems, pp. 547–553 (1999)
14. Chawla, N.V., et al.: SMOTE: synthetic minority over-sampling technique. J. Artif. Intell. Res. **16**, 321–357 (2002)
15. Lorena, A.C., Carvalho, A.C.P.L.F.: Building binary-tree-based multiclass classifiers using separability measures. Neurocomputing, **73**(16-18), 2837–2845 (2010)
16. Aho, A.V., Hopcroft, J.E., Ullman, J.D.: Data Structures and Algorithms. Addison-Wesley Publishing Company Inc., Reading, Mass, USA (1983)

Feature Selection with Class Hierarchy for Imbalance Problems

Tomoya Horio[✉] and Mineichi Kudo

Hokkdaido University, Sapporo 060-814, Japan
{horio,mine}@ist.hokudai.ac.jp

Abstract. In this paper, we aim to improve the classification performance in imbalance data by mitigating the impact of the curse of dimensionality especially in minority classes of a few samples. We exploit a class hierarchy realized as a binary tree whose node has a subset of classes. We construct such a binary tree in a top-down way by taking into consideration the separability of classes and the size of the feature subset. It is expected that the generalization performance is improved, especially in minority classes having a small number of samples, and that the interpretability of the decision rule is enhanced by the smallness of the number of features. Experimental results showed a remarkable improvement is by the proposed method in large-scale problems with many classes, e.g. from 48% to 62% in the balanced accuracy. In addition, only one feature was chosen in every node of the class hierarchy in all the four datasets, bringing a high interpretability of the classification rules.

Keywords: Imbalanced problems · Class-dependent feature selection · Class hierarchy

1 Introduction

Recently, many practical problems are *class-imbalanced*, that is, there are some *head classes* having a large number of samples and *tail classes* having only a small number of samples. In class imbalance problems, classifiers trained by imbalanced data tend to put a priority on the head classes to gain a higher overall accuracy. Nevertheless, it is often the case that tail classes are more important than head classes in classification. Examples are the diagnosis of rare diseases and marketing of novel products. To mitigate the bad effect of class imbalance, over/under-sampling and class-sensitive cost functions [1–3] have been adopted. However, their effects are limited especially for problems of a very large number of classes. More importantly, we have to face more seriously the curse of dimensionality [4] that affects much on tail classes where the ratio of the number of samples to the number of features decreases dramatically. In this study, we tackle above two problems, i.e., imbalance problems with a large number of classes and the curse of dimensionality on tail classes. In addition, interpretability of classification rules is one of our concerns. To cope with these problems we construct a class hierarchy with only a few number of features in each node.

© Springer Nature Switzerland AG 2021
Y. Hernández Heredia et al. (Eds.): IWAIPR 2021, LNCS 13055, pp. 229–238, 2021.
https://doi.org/10.1007/978-3-030-89691-1_23

2   Related Works

2.1   Algorithms Against Class Imbalance

Typical approaches to the problem of class imbalance are three of 1) over-sampling from tail classes, 2) under-sampling from head classes, 3) cost-modification in criteria [1–3]. The first approach is to oversample until the sample sizes of the tail classes are almost equal to those of the other classes. Depending on whether the sampling rules are random or deterministic, they are classified into *random oversampling* and *focused oversampling* [1]. On the contrary, the second approach undersamples from head classes. The final approach is to vary the relative costs of misclassification depending on the sample sizes of classes in minimizing the total cost. Resampling from the same training sample set is problematic. Therefore, for example, SMOTE (Synthetic Minority Oversampling Technique) [2] generates synthetic samples in the minority classes to overcome over-fitting [3]. However both of sampling and cost adjustments have the difficulty in setting of the parameters for problems of a large number of classes.

2.2   Class Hierarchy

In order to deal with a large number of classes and to mitigate the curse of dimensionality on tail classes, we use the concept of class hierarchy [5–7]. When a class hierarchy is realized as a binary tree, a multi-class problem is divided into a set of two-class-subset problems. In a binary tree realization, a leaf is of one class, and reversely a class appears at only one leaf. To construct a tree, starting from the root node containing all the classes, each node is divided into two children nodes of disjoint class subsets, and the leaves are used for final decision. There are two phases: designing of a class hierarchy (training) and exploiting of the hierarchy (testing or classification).

We carry out feature selection in the middle of construction of the hierarchy. More precisely, for the division at each node we determine two class subsets so as to be separated sufficiently from each other in a space of a smaller number of features. Note that such a feature selection depends on those two class subsets, that is, it is class-dependent feature selection [6,7]. It is clear that a feature subset effective for a class subset pair is not always effective for another pair.

3   Construction of Class Hierarchy

This section describes the training phase, that is, the design of a class hierarchy. There are two typical strategies. One is a bottom-up strategy that designs a hierarchy by merging the closest two class subsets into one, starting from leaves of a single class [5,6]. The other is a top-down strategy that designs a hierarchy by repeating a division of a class set into the furthest two class subsets at each node, starting from the root node, to the leaves [7]. Since the classification of a test sample starts from the root node, there is an error propagation downward. We take a top-down strategy, paying more attention to the error propagation than easiness of construction.

3.1   Class Decision Tree (CDT)

We put our basis on a top-down way, called Class Decision Tree (CDT) [7]. We also call the constructed trees CDTs. In CDT, we partition a class set into two class subsets so as to achieve a minimum graph cut of $G = (V, E)$ where node $v_i \in V$ corresponds to class i, and edge $e_{ij} \in E$ has a weight $S_{ij} = S(v_i, v_j)$ showing the degree of separability between classes i and j. For S_{ij}, we assign the value of Leave-One-Out (LOO) correct classification rate of the nearest neighbor (NN) applied to the samples of classes i and j. However, in a complete graph of which edges have similar weights, such a minimum cut tends to separate a single class from the other classes because of the minimum number of edges connected to a single class. In order to cope with this problem, [7] proposes to maximize $\min_{v_1 \in V_1, v_2 \in V_2} S(v_1, v_2)$ instead of minimizing $\sum_{v_1 \in V_1, v_2 \in V_2} (1 - S(v_1, v_2))$. Alternative way for CDT construction is to use the normalized minimum cut [8], but we do not consider that way in this paper. In [7], feature selection is also proposed to carry out in each node of a CDT, but it is after construction of the tree, not in the middle of tree construction as adopted in this paper. We compare the difference in the experiments.

3.2   Proposed Method: Feature Selection Based CDT

Unlike CDT, we conduct feature selection in the middle of construction of a CDT, that is, we decide the partition of a class set at a node by taking into consideration the number of features in addition to the separability of two candidate class subsets. Specifically, we use as a criterion the classification rate measured in the space of selected features and the number of the features. We find two disjoint class subsets V_1 and V_2 as a partition of a parent class set V to maximize the following criterion:

$$(1 - \lambda) S_F(V_1, V_2) - \lambda \frac{|F(V_1, V_2)|}{|F_0|}, \quad 0 \le \lambda \le 1. \tag{1}$$

Here, $F(V_1, V_2)$ is a feature subset used to separate V_1 and V_2, $S_F(V_1, V_2)$ is the separability between V_1 and V_2 using $F(V_1, V_2)$, F_0 is the set of all features, and λ is a parameter to balance separability and feature number (in the experiments, we use $\lambda = 0.5$). It is intractable in complexity to find the optimal solution of (1), so, in this study, we consider the following heuristics. First, we find the initial partition $(V_1^{(0)}, V_2^{(0)})$ according to [7] to maximize the separability suboptimally with the full set of features. Then conduct feature selection for the two-class problem of $V_1 = V_1^{(0)}$ and $V_2 = V_2^{(0)}$, considering each of them as a meta-class. Next, move one class from V_1 to V_2, or V_2 to V_1, to find a better partition in (1). If no move is found to improve (1), we terminate the procedure. Otherwise, we continue this procedure on the updated partition (V_1, V_2). Here, Sequential Forward Search (SFS) [9] is used for searching of a better feature subset $F(V_1, V_2)$ in a candidate partition (V_1, V_2), and the searching is terminated when a chosen subset shows a better or equal accuracy to that with the full set of features. This way guarantees that the performance after feature selection is necessarily better than that of the case without feature selection, in the training error. We avoid a duplicate examination of the same partition with a flag array. Figure 1 shows the algorithm. We call this algorithm Feature Selection based Class Decision Tree, shortly FS-CDT.

By CDTwFS [7], we denote the procedure that constructs a tree on the separability only and conducts feature selection in each node after tree construction. Assuming that n samples of m-dimensional vectors belonging to one of k classes are given as input, the computational complexity in the training phase of CDTwFS is $O(n^2m^2)$, whereas that of the proposed FS-CDT is $O(Tkn^2m^2)$ where T is the total number of examined partitions.

A test sample is classified in top-down manner. Note that different classifiers can be used at different nodes, while the classification problem (V_1 and V_2) and the feature subset (F) is fixed at every node in FS-CDT.

4   Experiments

4.1   Experimental Method

We compared four methods of Class Decision Tree (CDT) [7], CDT with feature selection (CDTwFS) [7], Feature Selection based CDT (FS-CDT) (the proposed method) and classification without class hierarchy (Flat). The classifier used in common for all the four approaches is k-NN classifier with $k = 1, 3$. The metrics for evaluation are the over-all accuracy and the *balanced accuracy*, the average of class-wise classification accuracies, both measured by LOO procedure. The balanced accuracy is used for leveraging the performance of the tail classes. The number of features is also used as a metric for interpretability. For economizing time, we used a class decision tree designed from all the training samples in common to different sample partition of LOO, in three methods of CDT, CDTwFS and FS-CDT.

4.2   Data Set

Experiments were performed on four datasets taken from the UCI Machine Learning Repository [10] and Mulan: A Java Library for Multi-Label Learning [11]. The details of the datasets are shown in Table 1. The class IDs are reassigned according to their sample numbers (in decreasing order). As shown in Table 1 and Fig. 2, all datasets are class-imbalanced. The birds dataset is a multi-label dataset, but was treated it as a single-label dataset by regarding a distinct label set as one meta-class.

4.3   Class Hierarchy

Figures 3 and 4 show the class hierarchies designed by CDTwFS and that by the proposed FS-CDT on the two large datasets arrhythmia and birds. In addition, some statistics of those trees are shown in Tables 2 and 3.

Procedure **main**

Input: $V = \{c_i\}_{i=1}^{C}$: a class set
  λ : parameter $(0 \le \lambda \le 1)$
  F : a feature set
Output: T : a class decision tree

$T.set \leftarrow V$;   (root node)
Division(T, F, λ)
return;

Procedure **SFS**(U, W, F)

Input: U, W : disjoint class subsets $(n = |u|, m = |v|)$
  F : a feature set
Output: G: selected feature subset

$G \leftarrow \emptyset$; $H \leftarrow F \setminus G$;
$w_0 \leftarrow$ (LOO accuracy for (U, W) attained with F);
$w \leftarrow 0.0$;
do
  for every feature subset $G' \leftarrow G \cup \{f \mid f \in H\}$ **do**;
    Remain G' with the highest LOO accuracy w'.
    if $w' > w$;
      Update G with G' and recalculate $H \leftarrow F \setminus G$;
      $w \leftarrow w'$;
  while $(w < w_0)$
  return G ;

Procedure **Division**(T, F, λ)

Input: T : a tree
  F : a feature set
  λ : parameter $(0 \le \lambda \le 1)$
Output: T: an updated tree

$V \leftarrow T.set$;
$(V_1, V_2, G) = \mathbf{Partition}(V, F, \lambda)$
$T.fset \leftarrow G$;
$T_1.set \leftarrow V_1$;
$T_2.set \leftarrow V_2$;
$T.leftson \leftarrow T_1$;
$T.rightson \leftarrow T_2$;
if $|V_1| > 1$
  Division$(T.leftson, F, \lambda)$
if $|V_2| > 1$
  Division$(T.rightson, F, \lambda)$
return ;

Procedure **Partition**(V, F, λ)

Input: $V = \{c_i\}_{i=1}^{k}$: a class subset at a node
  F : a feature set
Output: U, W: class subsets
  G: selected feature subset

if $k = 2$ **then**
  return $(U = \{c_1\}, W = \{c_2\}, \mathbf{SFS}(U, W, F))$;
$(U_0, W_0) \leftarrow$ the partition by CDT [6]   (Initialization)
$G \leftarrow \mathbf{SFS}(U_0, W_0, F)$;
$w_0 \leftarrow (1 - \lambda)S_G(U_0, W_0) - \lambda|G|/|F|$;
do about (U_0, W_0)
  for every move of a class from one set to another **do**
    Remain (U, W) with G attained the largest w in
    $G \leftarrow \mathbf{SFS}(U, W, F)$;
    $w \leftarrow (1 - \lambda)S_G(U, W) - \lambda|G|/|F|$;
    if $w > w_0$
      Update (U_0, W_0) with (U, W)
  while $(w > w_0)$
  return $(U_0, W_0, \mathbf{SFS}(U_0, W_0, F))$;

Fig. 1. Algorithm FS-CDT. In procedure Partition, $S_G(U, W)$ is the separability between U and V in the feature space of G.

Table 1. Data set. #C, #F, and #S are the number of classes, the number of features, and the number of samples, respectively.

Name	#C	#F	#S
glass	6	9	76, 70, 20, 17, 13, 9
dermatology	6	34	111, 71, 60, 48, 48, 20
arrhythmia	13	279	243, 50, 39, 25, 21, 15, 14, 13, 9, 5, 4, 2, 2
birds	60	260	294, 30, $[17-7] \times 9$, 6×3, 5, 4×5, 3×16, 2×24

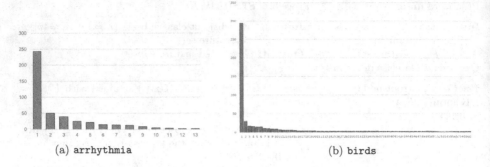

(a) arrhythmia   (b) birds

Fig. 2. Sample numbers in two large datasets. The class IDs are reassigned according to the sample numbers.

First we notice that the training accuracy at each node is better in FS-CDT than CDT, producing a difference in the upper part of those trees, although the shapes are similar in arrhythmia (Fig. 3). Second we see that feature selection is very effective at least in training phase regardless of the timing, i.e., independent of whether after or in the middle of tree construction (CDT vs. CDTwFS and FS-CDT). Third, the number of features selected at each node is very small but the degree of separation is high enough in FS-CDT (Tables 2 and 3). Indeed, only one feature is chosen at every node in FS-CDT, meaning that a single feature is sufficient to attain the same classification performance as the case of the whole set of features.

4.4   Over-All Accuracy and Balanced Accuracy

The over-all and balanced accuracies obtained LOO with k-NN ($k = 1, 3$) are shown in Tables 4 and 5. First we notice that class hierarchy alone does not contribute to the improvement of accuracy (CDT vs. Flat), although it is partly because the classifier is k-NN (without feature selection, 1-NN brings the same accuracy to Flat and CDT). Feature selection in the middle of tree construction is the key of improvement (see the accuracy of FS-CDT in Table 4). Feature selection is also applied to CDTwFS, but feature selection after tree construction is not so effective. This is because the training accuracy is improved by feature selection in general. Especially, feature selection in FS-CDT is most effective to classification of tail classes (Table 5).

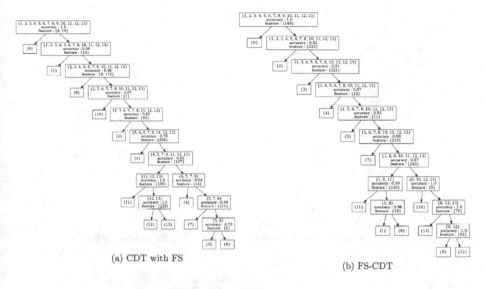

(a) CDT with FS

(b) FS-CDT

Fig. 3. Class hierarchy of `arrhythmia` dataset. Information in a node is the class subset, the training accuracy, and the feature subset.

Table 2. Average separability on training data over nodes

Dataset	CDT	CDTwFS	FS-CDT
glass	0.88	**0.99**	**0.99**
dermatology	0.94	**0.96**	0.95
arrhythmia	0.70	0.90	**0.97**
birds	0.76	0.96	**0.98**

Table 3. Average number of features over nodes. #F is the number of features.

Dataset	#F	CDTwFS	FS-CDT
glass	9	**1.0**	**1.0**
dermatology	34	1.6	**1.0**
arrhythmia	279	1.16	**1.0**
birds	260	**1.0**	**1.0**

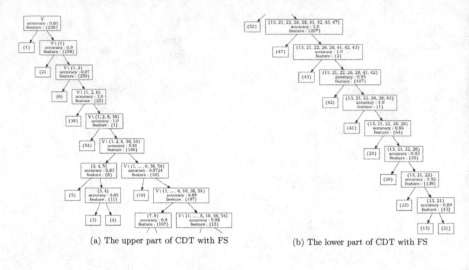

(a) The upper part of CDT with FS

(b) The lower part of CDT with FS

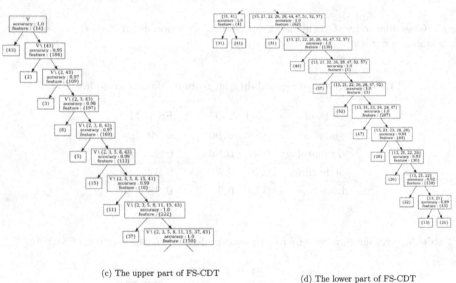

(c) The upper part of FS-CDT

(d) The lower part of FS-CDT

Fig. 4. Class hierarchy of `birds` data set. Information in a node is the class subset, the training accuracy, and the feature subset.

Table 4. Total accuracy. The best score is shown with the corresponding value of k^* in k-NN.

Dataset	Flat(k^*)	CDT(k^*)	CDTwFS(k^*)	FS-CDT(k^*)
glass	0.73(1)	0.73(1)	**0.98**(1)	**0.98**(1)
dermatology	0.90(1)	0.90(1)	**0.93**(1)	0.90(3)
arrhythmia	0.64(3)	0.61(3)	0.51(3)	**0.72**(3)
birds	0.53(3)	0.47(3)	0.65(1)	**0.67**(1)

Table 5. Balanced accuracy. The best score is shown with the corresponding value of k^* in k-NN.

Dataset	Flat(k^*)	CDT(k^*)	CDTwFS(k^*)	FS-CDT(k^*)
glass	0.71(1)	0.71(1)	**0.95**(1)	**0.95**(1)
dermatology	0.90(1)	0.90(1)	**0.92**(1)	0.90(3)
arrhythmia	0.32(3)	0.32(3)	0.24(3)	**0.43**(3)
birds	0.07(1)	0.07(1)	0.48(1)	**0.62**(3)

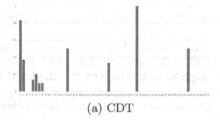

(a) CDT

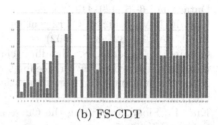

(b) FS-CDT

Fig. 5. Classification accuracy for individual classes in `birds` by CDT and FS-CDT. The horizontal axis shows the class ID (sorted by the sample numbers), and the vertical axis shows the accuracy. Note that only two samples are given after class #37.

5   Discussion

The effectiveness of feature selection was confirmed in the examined four imbalance data, especially in a large-scale dataset `birds` of 60 classes. In the proposed method, the number of selected features is always one at every node for all the datasets. This is desirable in generalization performance, the difference between training and testing errors, and interpretability. Especially, it would be most effective to conquer the curse of dimensionality on tail classes as shown in Table 5 and Fig. 5. We need to investigate more datasets to make clear whether this is a typical case or not.

In addition, though it was not our principal goal, the class imbalance problem was partially solved in those datasets. Indeed, the class IDs assigned the trees tend to increase from top to down (Figs. 3 and 4), resulting in the numbers of samples in left and right children of a node are well balanced.

6   Conclusion

We have proposed a novel class hierarchy (a binary tree) called FS-CDT whose nodes have a very small number of features but a sufficient separability of two children class subsets. The smallness of the selected feature subset brought a significant improvement on classification of tail classes with a small number of samples, because it mitigates the curse of dimensionality. In the future, we will discuss some ways to take a sample balance more directly and to reduce the computational cost to make this approach scale to larger imbalance data.

Acknowledgment. This work was partially supported by JSPS KAKENHI Grant Number 19H04128.

References

1. Japkowicz, N., Stephen, S.: The class imbalance problem: a systematic study. Intell. Data Anal. **6–5**, 429–449 (2002)
2. Chawla, N.V., et al.: SMOTE: synthetic minority over sampling technique. J. Artif. Intell. Res. **16**, 321–357 (2002)
3. Gosain, A., Sardana, S.: Handling class imbalance problem using oversampling techniques: a review. In: Proceedings of IEEE 2017 International Conference on Advances in Computing, Communications and Informatics (ICACCI), Udupi, India (2017)
4. Kuo, F., Sloan, L.: Lifting the Curse of Dimensionality. American Mathematical Society, US (2005)
5. Lorena, A., Carvalho, A.: Building binary-tree-based multiclass classifiers using separability measures. Neurocomputing **73**, 2837–2845 (2010)
6. Aoki, K., Watanabe, T., Kudo, M.: Design of decision tree using class-dependent feature subsets. Trans. Inst. Electron. Inf. Commun. Eng. **J86-D2**(8), 1156–1165 (2003)
7. Aoki, K., Kudo, M.: A top-down construction of class decision trees with selected features and classifiers. In: Proceedings of the 2010 International Conference on High Performance Computing and Simulation (HPCS 2010), Caen, France, pp. 390–398 (2010)
8. Shi, J., Malik, J.: Normalized cuts and image segmentation. IEEE Trans. Pattern Anal. Mach. Intell. **22**(8), 888–905 (2000)
9. Pudil, P., Novovičová, J., Kittler, J.: Floating search methods in feature selection. Pattern Recogn. Lett. **6**(1), 1119–1125 (1994)
10. Dua, D., Graff, C.: UCI Machine Learning Repository. http://archive.ics.uci.edu/ ml. University of California, School of Information and Computer Science, Irvine, CA (2019)
11. Tsoumakas, G., Spyromitros-Xioufis, E., Vilcek, J., Vlahavas, I.: MULAN: a Java library for multi-label learning. J. Mach. Learn. Res. **12**, 2411–2414 (2011)

SVM Based EVM for Open Space Problems

Yasuyuki Kaneko$^{(\boxtimes)}$ and Mineichi Kudo

Hokkaido University, Sapporo 060-814, Japan
{yasuyuki,mine}@ist.hokudai.ac.jp

Abstract. In this paper, we consider a multi-class classifier for problems where unknown classes are included in testing phase. Previous classifiers consider the "closed-set" case where the classes used for training and the classes used for testing are the same. A more realistic case is the "open-set" recognition, in which only a limited number of classes appear at training time, and unknown classes appear during testing. To handle such problems, we need classifiers that accurately classify data belonging to not only known classes but also unknown classes. In this paper, We introduce a Support Vector Machine (SVM) based Extreme Value Machine (EVM) to determine a compact class region. Any data outside of such class regions is rejected as being in unknown classes. To construct a class region, we approach the class decision boundary found by SVM towards the samples, by removing some support vectors close to the boundary. This SVM based EVM resolves the three problems that EVM possesses: unfair size of class regions, excessive sensibility to certain points and fragmentation of a class region.

Keywords: Extreme value theory · Support vector machines · Open set recognition · Anomal detection

1 Introduction

A lot of high performance classifiers such as deep neural networks have been developed so far. These classifiers work most under a *closed condition* where classes to appear are known already in training time. A more realistic scenario is an *open condition* where unknown classes appear in testing time. Such a situation is also called Open Set Recognition (OSR) [10]. Examples are rare disease diagnosis and web application services where newly discovered diseases and newly released applications appear day by day.

A pioneer work in OSR was made by Scheirer *et al.* [10] who formalized OSR and proposed a 1-vs-set machine, using a linear SVM, by considering an open space risk in addition to an empirical risk. Although 1-vs-set machine reduces the region of a known class compared with that of the original SVM, the region is

© Springer Nature Switzerland AG 2021
Y. Hernández Heredia et al. (Eds.): IWAIPR 2021, LNCS 13055, pp. 239–248, 2021.
https://doi.org/10.1007/978-3-030-89691-1_24

still unbounded because of the linearity. The difficulty of OSR is that classifiers have to deal with samples belonging to unknown classes, that is, they have to be trained by no sample of the classes. There are some approaches to cope with this difficulty such as one-class SVM [11] and classifiers with a reject option [1,3,4,13]. Among them, Extreme Value Machine (EVM) [8] is one of the most promising ones. EVM determines a class region as a set of hyper-balls centered at each of the samples. The radius of a ball is determined by Extreme Value Theorem (EVT) [6] applied to the nearest samples belong to the other classes. The region is now bounded but still suffers from several problems that will be introduced later.

2   Related Work

2.1   Algorithm for Open Space Recognition

Scheirer *et al.* proposed Weibull-calibrated SVM (WSVM) [9] for OSR. WSVM introduces a Compact Abating Probability (CAP) model that guarantees that the probability of samples becomes zero if they are away at a certain distance from any training sample of a class.

Junior *et al.* proposed Open Space Nearest Neighbor (OSNN) [7]. In OSNN, for an input sample s, we find the nearest two samples t,u belonging to different classes, if ratio $d(s,t)/d(s,u) > T$ holds for a threshold T, then the input sample s is assigned to an unknown class, otherwise recognized as the class of t or u.

2.2   EVT Based Algorithm

We explain the outline of EVM that we put our basis on. In EVM [8], we select one sample x_1 from the positive class, a *positive* class of interest (Fig.1(a)). Then, as statistics, we consider the half distance m's from x_1 to all the negative samples (Fig.1(b)(c)). By multiplying -1 to these distances, we consider the max value. To estimate a distribution (EVD) of the extreme value of m's, we collect τ maximum values (Fig.1(d)). According to EVT [6], we use a Weibull distribution as the extreme value distribution because the values are upper-bounded by zero (Fig.1(e)). With a parameter δ as a percentile (Fig.1(e)), we determine the radius m_{ex} of the ball centered at x_1 (Fig.1(f)). The ball centered at x_1 shows a local domain of x_1 (Fig.1(e)). Collecting these local balls over all positive samples, we have a positive class region.

Applying this procedure to all classes in turn, we have their class regions. Classification is made by whether a test sample falls into one of the class regions (to be assigned to a known class) or not (to reject). EVM is a kernel-free nonlinear classification.

Unfortunately, EVM suffers from three problems (Fig. 2). First, a class can have a larger region than those of the other classes when it is apart from the other classes (*the problem of unfair size of class regions*). Second, a samples far from the other samples of the same class can dominate the class region) (*the problem of excessive sensibility of individual samples*). Third, a class region can be divided into small connected regions (*the problem of fragmentation of a class region*). These problems are due to the independency of radii of balls and the isotropy by a ball.

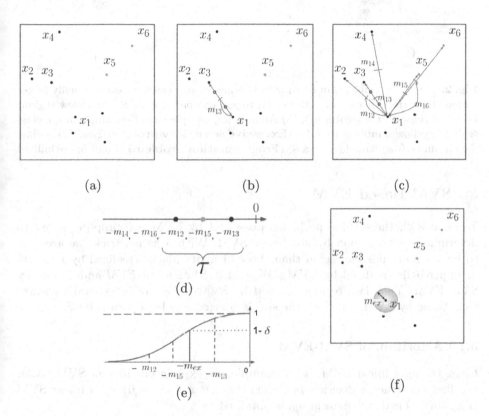

(a)   (b)   (c)

(d)

(e)   (f)

Fig. 1. Working flow of EVM. We consider to enclose a positive sample x_1 by a ball as a component of the class region. There are three classes (black, yellow and blue) in Fig. 1(a). We calculate distances between x_1 and all negative samples (x_2 to x_6) (samples of blue and orange), e.g., $m_{13} = \|x_1 - x_3\|/2$. To find the max value of m's, we multiply -1 and sort these values (Fig. 1(d)). We estimate an extreme value distribution by the maximum τ values, and obtain m_{ex} with a percentile δ (Fig. 1(e)). Finally, we build a ball around x_1 with radius of m_{ex} (Fig. 1(f)). (Color figure online)

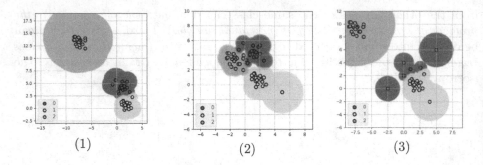

Fig. 2. The three problems in EVM [8]: (1) Some classes can have exceptionally larger regions than the other classes (the green region compared with red or yellow region) (**Unfair region size problem**), (2) An anomaly sample can affect much on the class region (a yellow sample at $(5, -1)$) (**Excessive sensibility problem**), and (3) A class region can be fragmented (red class) (**Fragmentation problem**) (Color figure online)

3   SVM Based EVM

To cope with these three problems possessed by EVM, we propose a way to determine a class region by non-linear SVM. With a kernel trick, we are able to have a more flexible region than those of hyper-planes (realized by 1-vs-set) or hyper-balls (realized by EVM). We call it *SVM based EVM* and denote by SVM-EVM. The class regions learned by SVM-EVM are in general narrower than those by EVM, although the size is controllable by a parameter δ.

3.1   Algorithm of SVM-EVM

First, taking a linear SVM as an example, we explain our idea of SVM-EVM. We first construct a decision boundary $\{x \mid \omega^T x + \omega_0 = 0\}$ by a linear SVM (Fig. 3(a)). Then, the margin m_0 is obtained as

$$m_0 = \frac{1}{\sqrt{\sum_{i \in SV}^n \lambda_i}}, \tag{1}$$

where λ_i is Lagrange multipliers determined by the formulation of SVM (for example, see [2]), and SV is the set of support vectors. As a next step, we estimate an Extreme Value Distribution (EVD) of $-m_0$ (the minimum distance of the positive samples to the decision). To collect another candidate extreme value, we remove one of the *positive* support vectors and reconstruct another SVM to have the second margin m_1 (Fig. 3(b)). We repeat this procedure according to a deletion ordering of samples (Fig. 4) to obtain a necessary number τ of margins. All these margins multiplied by -1 are dealt as extreme values for estimation of an EVD. We can think of Weibull distributions for because the values of $-m's$ is upper-bounded by zero. The parameter estimation is made

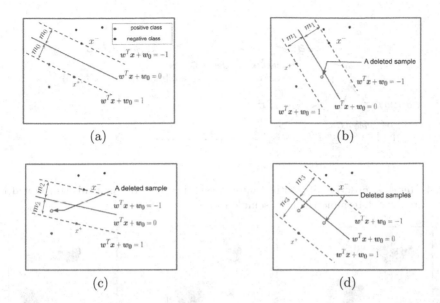

Fig. 3. Procedure for deleting support vectors (SVs) to obtain an extreme value and semi-extreme values. Positive class SVs are deleted one by one. First we find a decision boundary with margin m_0 by linear-SVM in (a). In (b), we delete a positive SV and construct another linear-SVM to find a new margin m_1, then $m_2, m_3, \ldots$. We continue this procedure until τ m's are obtained. The removing order is shown in Fig. 4.

by Maximum Likelihood Estimate implemented in SciPy [14]. Last, with a user-specified percentile δ, we determine the values of m_{ex}. With this m_{ex}, we define the class region as the positive region:

$$R = \left\{ x \mid \sum_{i \in SV}^{n} \lambda_i y_i K(x_i, x) + w_0 - \frac{m_{ex}}{m_0} \geq 0 \right\}, \tag{2}$$

where $K(x_i, x)$ is an RBF kernel. In our method, we set τ to 1% or less of total number of samples.

3.2 An Achievement of SVM-EVM

A simple experiment was conducted. In a two-dimension space, we considered three classes of 20 samples each. In Fig. 5, the class regions by SVM-EVM with $\delta \in \{0.0, 0.01, 0.5\}$ are shown.

3.3 Solving Three Problems

Here, we show some examples to demonstrate that the proposed SVM-EVM resolves three problems of EVM (Fig. 6). The proposed SVM-EVM obtains the class regions surrounded by nonlinear functions that are determined by a whole set of the training samples.

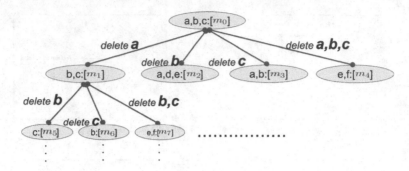

Fig. 4. Removal ordering of positive support vectors. By traversing this tree in width-first search, we determine the next sample to remove.

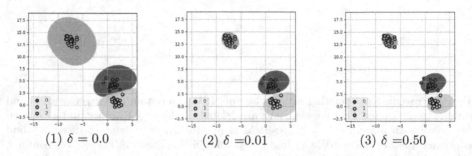

Fig. 5. Class regions obtained by SVM-EVM for $\delta = 0.0$, 0.5 and 0.01. The case of $\delta = 0.0$ is equal to SVM.

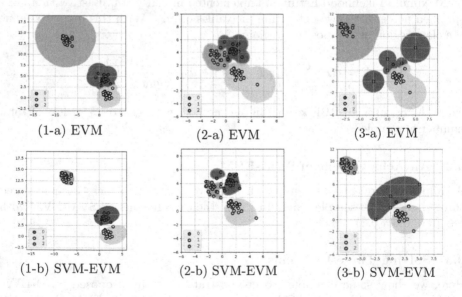

Fig. 6. Solutions by SVM-EVM to three problems in EVM (Fig. 2). From top to down, (1) **unfair region size problem**, (2) **Excessive sensibility problem** and (3) **Fragmentation problem**.

4   Experiments

An experiment was conducted to confirm the effectiveness of the proposed method. We used OLETTER dataset which is generated for an open space recognition problem and is made by modifying Letter dataset [5]. This data is of 20 000 black and white images of N =26 capital letters in 16 different styles (Fig. 7).

4.1   Experimental Procedure

We carried out the following, referring to [7].

1. Choose $n \in \{3,6,9,12\}$ known classes randomly from $N = 26$ classes and leave $N - n$ classes as unknown classes.
2. Choose randomly a half of all training samples from known classes to make a training set S_{tr_known}. By collecting the remaining samples of known classes we make a set S_{te_known}. With the set $S_{unknown}$ of samples of $N - n$ unknown classes, we make a test set S_{te_both} by $S_{te\_both} = S_{te\_known} \cup S_{unknown}$.
3. Apply EVM or SVM-EVM: training with S_{tr_known} and testing with S_{te_both}.
4. Repeat 10 times Steps 1 to 3.

We compared the proposed SVM-EVM with EVM. The RBF kernel $K(x_i, x_j) = \exp(-\gamma||x_i - x_j||^2)$ is used in SVM-EVM and the kernel parameter γ is chosen from $\{0.10, 0.11, ..., 10.00\}$. We set the restriction parameter δ to 0.5 to determine m_{ex} as shown in Fig. 1(e). The larger δ is, the smaller the area is as shown in Fig. 5. The number τ of candidate extreme values was set to 2. This is less than 1% of the number of training samples in each class. In addition, SVM was forcibly set so as to have a hard margin. The parameters τ and δ of EVM, we used the author's setting [8].

As a metric for evaluation, we used "micro" f-measure denoted by f_μ [12] and defined by,

$$f_\mu = \frac{2 \times precision_\mu \times recall_\mu}{precision_\mu + recall_\mu}, \tag{3}$$

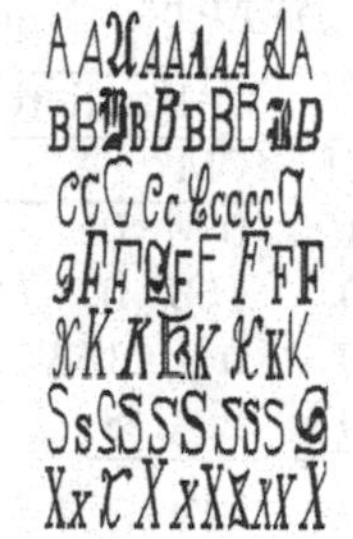

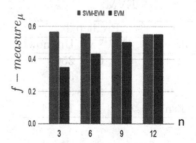

Fig. 7. Different font styles in OLET-TER (10 styles in one letter)

Fig. 8. Comparison between EVM and SVM-EVM in f-measure$_\mu$. The horizontal axis shows the number n of known classes. The vertical axis is the average f_μ value in 10 times.

where

$$precision_\mu = \frac{\sum_{i=1}^n TP_i}{\sum_{i=1}^n (TP_i + FP_i)}, \ recall_\mu = \frac{\sum_{i=1}^n TP_i}{\sum_{i=1}^n (TP_i + FN_i)}, \qquad (4)$$

where FP_i and FN_i are "False Positive" and "False Negative" when class i is regarded as the positive class and the other classes including unknown classes as the negative class as a whole. The micro f-measure is the accuracy on known classes taking into consideration unknown classes (note that FP_i or FN_i (i=1, 2, ..., n) includes the samples from or to unknown classes ($n + 1$th class)).

4.2   Result

The result is shown in Fig. 8. SVM-EVM is better than EVM regardless of the number n of known classes. It is more advantageous when n is small. We also show their confusion matrices in Table 1. These matrices are for when letters 'L', 'M' and 'K' are known classes ($n = 3$). The parameters were chosen in such a way that the same degree of correct prediction is made for samples of unknown classes: $\tau = 75$ (the recommended value in [8]), $\delta = 1.0 - 1.0^{-14}$ for EVM, and $\tau = 2$, $\delta = 0.5$ for SVM-EVM. The values of δ and γ are chosen so as to attain the best *f-measure* value. A large difference of δ between EVM and SVM-EVM comes from the difference of distances: the Euclidean distance in the former, while a distance in a reproducing kernel space in the latter. From this comparison, we see that the class regions found by SVM-EVM are more appropriate than those of EVM. We also examined the sensitivity of δ. As a result, it was revealed that δ is insensitive to the result, so that the authors recommend to use $\delta = 0.5$ in general.

Table 1. Confusion matrices of EVM and SVM-EVM for three known classes of "L", "M", "X" ($n = 3$), and other 23 unknown classes. The parameters for EVM are chosen so as to show a comparable performance on unknown classes.

EVM

Actual	Predicted "L"	"M"	"X"	Unknown
"L"	46	0	0	350
"M"	0	73	0	319
"X"	0	0	39	354
Unknown	0	0	15	17624

SVM-EVM

Actual	Predicted "L"	"M"	"X"	Unknown
"L"	125	0	0	271
"M"	0	153	0	239
"X"	0	0	153	240
Unknown	0	2	8	17629

5   Discussion

SVM-EVM is superior to 1-vs-set machine in the shape of class regions, because a class region by the latter is a half-space, while that by the former has a non-linearly enclosed shape. SVM-EVM is superior to EVM in the treatment of data because a class region by the latter is a collection of local regions associated to individual samples, while that by the former is a single region associated to all the samples. The reason why SVM-EVM does not depend on the value of the percentile δ so much is because the estimated EVD on the minus margins is so steep around a point, that the margin specified by a percentile δ does not change even if δ has changed. The steepness means that many samples are the support vectors due to the nonlinearity of SVM with RBF kernels.

6 Conclusion

We have presented a novel algorithm for open set classification. This algorithm, called SVM-EVM, determines a class region by a decision boundary generated by SVM but in such a way that the boundary is closer to the samples of the positive class than the original boundary. The extreme value theory is used to determine the degree to what the boundary is close to the samples. SVM-EVM has solved three problems that EVM held, and showed a better performance in an experiment. We will investigate more datasets to confirm the effectiveness of SVM-EVM.

Acknowledgment. This work was partially supported by JSPS KAKENHI Grant Number 19H04128.

References

1. Bartlett, P.L., Wegkamp, M.H.: Classification with a reject option using a hinge loss. J. Mach. Learn. Res. **9**(59), 1823–1840 (2008)
2. Bishop, C.M.: Pattern Recognition and Machine Learning (Information Science and Statistics). Springer, Heidelberg (2006)
3. Chow, C.: On optimum recognition error and reject tradeoff. IEEE Inf. Theory **16**(1), 41–46 (1970)
4. Fischer, L., Hammer, B., Wersing, H.: Optimal local rejection for classifiers. Neurocomputing **214**, 445–457 (2016)
5. Frey, P.W.: Letter recognition using Holland-style adaptive classifiers. Mach. Learn. **6**, 161–182 (1991). https://doi.org/10.1007/BF00114162
6. Kotz, S., Nadarajah, S.: Extreme Value Distributions: Theory and Applications. Imperial College Press, London (2000)
7. Mendes Júnior, P.R., et al.: Nearest neighbors distance ratio open-set classifier. Mach. Learn. **106**(3), 359–386 (2017)
8. Rudd, E.M., Jain, L.P., Scheirer, W.J., Boult, T.E.: The extreme value machine. IEEE Pattern Anal. Mach. Intell. **40**(3), 762–768 (2018)
9. Scheirer, W.J., Jain, L.P., Boult, T.E.: Probability models for open set recognition. IEEE Pattern Anal. Mach. Intell. **36**(11), 2317–2324 (2014)
10. Scheirer, W.J., de Rezende Rocha, A., Sapkota, A., Boult, T.E.: Toward open set recognition. IEEE Pattern Anal. Mach. Intell. **35**(7), 1757–1772 (2012)
11. Schölkopf, B., Platt, J.C., Shawe-Taylor, J.C., Smola, A.J., Williamson, R.C.: Estimating the support of a high-dimensional distribution. Neural Comput. **13**(7), 1443–1471 (2001)

12. Sokolova, M., Lapalme, G.: A systematic analysis of performance measures for classification tasks. Inf. Process. Manag. **45**(4), 427–437 (2009)
13. Tax, D., Duin, R.: Growing a multi-class classifier with a reject option. Pattern Recogn. Lett. **29**(10), 1565–1570 (2008)
14. Virtanen, P., Gommers, R., et al.: SciPy 1.0: fundamental algorithms for scientific computing in Python. Nat. Methods **17**, 261–272 (2020)

Data Drive Fuzzy Cognitive Map for Classification Problems

Jairo A. Lefebre-Lobaina[✉] and María M. García[✉]

Universidad Central "Marta Abreu" de Las Villas, Villa Clara, Cuba
jairo@uclv.cu, mmgarcia@uclv.edu.cu

Abstract. In recent years Fuzzy Cognitive Maps had become an important tool for expert knowledge representation due to the flexibility and interpretability of modeled maps. Its construction frequently requires an expert's intervention but, there are situations when only the data is available or is required to extract the contained implicit knowledge for analysis or decision making proposes. Several studies have been developed to improve or find causal relation values between the map concepts but usually require a previous concept definition step carried out by experts. The frequent pattern mining techniques show a way for non-trivial relations extraction from datasets, and those relations may represent a causality degree. In this paper, a strategy to extract concepts from continuous and discrete features for supervised classification problems is proposed. Additionally, to estimate the causality degree between defined map concepts is proposed to use association rule mining techniques. Finally, the strategy is evaluated to show the interpretability and accuracy of generated Fuzzy Cognitive Maps.

Keywords: Fuzzy Cognitive Maps · Association · Causal relations

1 Introduction

Due to Fuzzy Cognitive Map (FCM) high interpretability degree, several researchers had used this technique for modeling systems with interesting results. In several works the FCMs had being used to solve problems related to medical diagnosis [2,3], time series forecasting [20], futuristic scenario building [10], and pattern recognition [14]. For modeling problems using FCM, during the knowledge engineering steps [18] is required the intervention of domain experts to define the map concepts and causal relations value. Previous studies [19] show the effectiveness and characteristics of these well-established deductive methods for model FCMs. But, at least the experts are required to define the concepts, and generated models are affected by subjective criteria, the main leaks of expert-based methods.

More recently, researchers have developed several works where they propose learning algorithms for FCMs [14] using historical data. The main idea in these papers is to fit the weight of values corresponding to the FCM causal relation matrix, but some approaches have severe limitations to be applied over

© Springer Nature Switzerland AG 2021
Y. Hernández Heredia et al. (Eds.): IWAIPR 2021, LNCS 13055, pp. 249–259, 2021.
https://doi.org/10.1007/978-3-030-89691-1_25

large-scale data [15]. Several unsupervised and supervised algorithms have been
proposed to generate or update the FCM topology generally grouped in three
main categories [14]: Hebbian-type, error-based, and hybrid methods, but other
approaches can also be found [7]. The proposed strategies require a prior definition of the map concepts by experts and are focused on updating or defining the causal relations, which means that without some domain knowledge
those strategies are difficult to apply. Additionally, [10] presents a strategy for
FCM construction from text data, but is applied only in future-oriented opin-
ions extracted from websites and is difficult to extend for another type of data.
Also, in [15] is presented a hybrid approach with a deterministic learning rule
to compute the weights among input and output concepts presents the same
limitations mentioned.

Defining FCM's concepts and causal relations from data requires a concept
definition strategy and the evaluation of causality between them. This work proposes an automatic method for the definition of concepts and the identification
of causal relations from stored data, also reducing the human intervention to
a minimum degree and preserving the FCM interpretability and accuracy for
classification problems.

The rest of this paper is structured in the following way. In Sect. 2, is presented the theoretical background for FCMs and the methods used. Section 3
describes the strategy used for FCM's construction and the algorithms that intervene in the process. Section 4 covers the interpretation of the generated topology,
the experiments carried out between different FCM construction strategies and
the comparisons with other classification algorithms. Finally, some relevant conclusions are presented in Sect. 5.

2   Theoretical Background

2.1   Fuzzy Cognitive Maps

In 1986 B. Kosko introduced the Fuzzy Cognitive Maps theory [11] that defines
the nodes or concepts and their connections as basic elements to build the cognitive map structure. B. Kosko also introduced some elements of the fuzzy logic
approach giving a value for each link between two nodes in the range $[-1, 1]$,
representing the causation degree that may represent the result of a linguistic
variable quantification [11]. The sign of the arcs represents the relation behavior
in nodes, a positive relation $(+)$ between nodes A and B means that the value
of node B changes in the same change direction value of node A; a negative
relation $(-)$ between nodes A and B means that the value of node B change in
opposite change direction value of node A. Change proportion between nodes in
both cases is defined by the causality degree value.

Mathematically it can be defined as the 4-tuple (C, W, A, f), where $C = (c_1, c_2, c_3, \ldots c_n)$ is the set of nodes of the graph, $W : (c_i, c_j) \rightarrow w_{ij}$ is the
function that determines the value of the causal relation between the nodes c_i
and c_j [11]. To determine the activation degree of each system concept over time
$t = (1, 2, 3, \ldots T)$ the function $A : (c_i, t) \rightarrow A_i^t, A \in \mathbb{R}$ is used. In addition,
the map uses a function $f \in \mathbb{R}$ to limit each concept activation range in a

desired interval $[-1, 1]$. Structurally a FCM can be represented as a graph where the value of the causal relation between two nodes c_i and c_j is represented in component w_{ij} that belongs to weight matrix W.

To define the FCM starting only from a set of data requires identifying the concepts (nodes) and causal relations (connections between nodes) existing between them. A definition of the causality concept is the basis for applying any technique to find causal relations.

2.2   Causality and Statistical Association Analysis

To define the FCM structure is required the identification of causal relation between features that describe the dataset. A starting point for the identification of causal relations is the statistical association analysis, which includes correlation analysis and frequent pattern mining techniques [13].

Correlation analysis, more specific correlation coefficient is a summary measure that describes the statistical relationship between two variables, scaled in the range $[-1, 1]$, where values close to 0 means weak relation and farther away from 0, the relation is positive if close to 1 and negative if close to -1 [6]. Nevertheless, correlation it is a symmetric function and implies that the data must have a monotonous relationship between its values [6].

Frequent pattern mining techniques can find relations among items and the problem of finding association rules is closely related to that of frequent patterns. The original motivation for searching association rules came from the need to analyze supermarket transaction data and determine customer behavior [1]. A rule $X \Rightarrow Y$ is considered an association rule at minimum support $supp_m$, and minimum confidence $conf_m$ when the following two conditions hold true:

- The set $X \cup Y$ is a frequent pattern
- The ratio of the $supp_m$ of $X \cup Y$ to that of X is at least $conf_m$

The minimum confidence $conf_m$ is always a fraction less than 1 because the support of the set $X \cup Y$ is always less than that of X [1]. These techniques do not require monotonous relationships in data and use non-symmetric coefficients like rule confidence, which makes them an interesting strategy for causal relation value definition.

Nevertheless, statistical association analysis not necessarily represent causality since these relations may be accidental, spurious and conditional [13]. An association is a necessary but not sufficient condition to ensure causality, however the associations identified can be considered as a hypothesis of causal relations.

3   Data Drive FCM Construction

As mentioned earlier, an FCM is essentially a directed graph, where the nodes denote concepts and edges relations between them. The FCM construction from data is divided into two main steps: the definition of the map concepts and the definition of the relations between concepts identified. Since inside the dataset may appear many kinds of data, the proposed strategy is applied to continuous and discrete features and does not handle missing values.

3.1   Concepts Definition

To define the concepts for an FCM is required a strategy for each kind of feature according to the stored data type.

For discrete features, it is proposed to carry out a concatenation between the name of the attribute and each possible value. For example, if the temperature attribute contains the values *high*, *medium* and *low*, the concepts for this feature would be like: *temperature-high*, *temperature-medium* and *temperature-low*. This strategy results in a binary activation for implied concepts in generated FCM inference process. The concepts associated with the class feature will be the output layer of the neural network after the inference process.

For continuous data, a similar strategy may be used but the representation of the feature as concepts is required. To use the feature name only and represent it with some data partitions makes it hard to differentiate and name the values associated with any sub-division. A discretization or fuzzification process allows to model linguistic terms as concepts, preventing information leaks and preserving an interpretable output model.

Fuzzy clustering is a method used to identify groups from data where each element is associated with all clusters and each association value $v \in [0,1]$. The Fuzzy c-means algorithm was proposed by Dunn, and Bezdek presented an update in [4]. The algorithm objective function is defined as:

$$ J = \sum_{i=1}^{c} \sum_{k=1}^{n} u_{ik}^{m} \|x_k - v_i\|^2 \tag{1} $$

Since fuzzy clustering usually is better to fit natural partitions than crisp ones and to preserve the interpretability in generated FCM, the clustering algorithm Fuzzy c-means is used.

The first step of the algorithm requires to estimate the appropriate number of clusters n by executing the algorithm to $k = [2,7]$ times because the best n value found will be the number of concepts generated from that feature and too many fuzzy concepts are hard to understand, and affect the interpretability [5] in generated FCM. After applying the efficient criteria-validity index CFE [9] is obtained the best value of n, defining the fuzziness index $m = 2$ and executing the Fuzzy c-means algorithm [4] over the list of values V, associated to the corresponding feature, is obtained a $M \times N$ matrix. Where M is the length of V and N the number of clusters. Each value m_{ij} with $i = 1, ... M$ and $j = 1, ... N$ in the matrix represents the degree of membership for corresponding value $v_i \in V$ for each cluster n_j. After generating the fuzzy cluster, each cluster may be associated with a linguistic term by experts, resulting in a concept name structure similar to discrete concepts preserving the interpretability of the generated FCM.

To select the final decision node in the generated FCM is required to compare the average activation for each output neuron during the inference process. Finally, the output node with the highest activation average is the selected to retrieve the result from the concept name.

3.2   Relation Value Definition

To define a causal relation, the degree of causality defined between the concepts involved is not necessarily symmetric, also the variables present in classification problems do not necessarily have a monotonous relationship in their values.

Table 1. Contingency table of relation $p \rightarrow q$

$p \rightarrow q$	q	$\bar{q}$	
p	n_{11}	n_{12}	p_t
$\bar{p}$	n_{21}	n_{22}	$\bar{p}_t$
	q_t	$\bar{q}_t$	T

In consideration of the requirements and behavior of the correlation coefficient, it is not recommended to use it to define causal relations. In this proposal, a pattern mining technique based on Apriori [1] to extract association between defined feature concepts is used.

The contingency table of relations between two concepts and the values that characterize them are presented in Table 1. The table represent the relation between the values p_i and q_j concerning two different features F_i and F_j respectively. The values $p \in F_i$ and $\bar{p} \in F_i$ represents the set of positions where $p \in F_i$, $\bar{p} \in F_i$ and $p \cap \bar{p} = \emptyset$. The values $q \in F_j$ and $\bar{q} \in F_j$ represents the set of positions where $q \in F_j$, $\bar{q} \in F_j$ and $q \cap \bar{q} = \emptyset$. The coefficients n_{11} represents amount of times that p and q appear together according to table, n_{12} represents the amount of times that p appears with any element of $\bar{q}$, n_{21} represents the amount of times that q appears with any element of $\bar{p}$ and n_{22} represents the amount of times that any element of $\bar{q}$ appears with any element of $\bar{p}$. In addition $T = p_t + \bar{p}_t = q_t + \bar{q}_t$ where p_t is the amount of times is that p_i appears in F_i and $\bar{p}_t = |F_i| - p_t$, the same applies to q_t and $\bar{q}_t$ respect to F_j.

The values of coefficients presented in Table 1 are intuitive to calculate when p and q are concepts related to discrete features. But, for concepts related to continuous features that are described by a membership degree, is presented a generalization of coefficients functions in Eqs. (2) to (5).

$$n_{11} = \sum_{i=1}^{T} p_i * q_i \qquad (2) \qquad n_{12} = \sum_{i=1}^{T} p_i * (1 - q_i) \qquad (3)$$

$$n_{21} = \sum_{i=1}^{T}(1 - p_i) * q_i \qquad (4) \qquad n_{22} = \sum_{i=1}^{T}(1-p_i)*(1-q_i) \qquad (5)$$

For the concepts related to the same discrete feature is defined a default -1 causal value among them, due to the presence of a concept means the absence of the others. No default relation value is proposed for concepts associated with continuous features. The remaining relations are estimated using the first step of the Apriori algorithm to identify relations between each pair of nodes related to different features. The algorithm uses only the first step of the Apriori algorithm because the relations between more than two nodes are hard to represent in the FCM topology and affect the interpretability of generated map. Finally, the FCM ends with the relations with support (6) higher than a previously defined minimum support $supp_m$ and with a causality evaluation higher than a previously defined minimum causality value.

$$supp(q,p) = \frac{n_{11}}{T} \qquad (6) \qquad conf(q,p) = \frac{n_{11}}{p_t} \qquad (7)$$

However, to define the causality value in the relations, several functions can be used, as long as they comply with the following properties. For $f(a,b)$ as function to determine the relation value between the nodes a and b, $f(a,b) \in [-1,1]$, and it's no required that $f(a,b) = f(b,a)$. That behavior is defined due to the causal relations that are represented on the map are bound for the interval $[-1,1]$, and the fact that a cause b in a given value does not necessarily imply that b cause a in the same value.

$$pinf(q,p) = \frac{n_{11}/(n_{12} * n_{21})}{p_t} \qquad (8)$$

According to the causality function characteristics, confidence (7) or positive influence (8) functions described can be used. The main difference between these functions is that influence gives an important weight to target concept elements that are not implied by the origin concept. It is the decision of the specialists which function to use according to the characteristics of the application domain.

4   Experimental Results

The proposed method is a different approach due it requires human intervention only to define concept names associated with continuous features. Each continuous concept is associated with a fuzzy set found in the clustering process. This step is very important because it allows achieving a high interpretability degree in the generated FCM.

The proposed topology is defined by a set of concepts that characterize the training dataset and a set of relations associated with the observed behavior in data. The generated FCM topology for the dataset presented in Table 2 is represented in Fig. 1 without evaluating any causality function. To preserve the generated model simplicity the feature names are not used to name the concepts, instead are represented with colors in the way: blue represents F1, yellow represents F2 and red represents the Class feature. Also, is assumed that the

Table 2. Simple example dataset

F1	F2	Class
x	9.8	a
x	7.3	a
y	1.1	r
y	3.6	r

continuous feature F2 have two associated clusters: Best (B) and Low (L). The values W_{ij} represents the relation weight defined by the selected function, and the default relation value for discrete features (-1) are also represented.

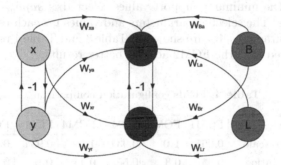

Fig. 1. Example topology (Color figure online)

From the data presented in Table 2 can be appreciated that independently of the causal coefficient used, exist a strong relationship between the concepts x and a with a similar degree to y and r. Also, if the causal coefficients $conf$ or $pinf$ are used, the causality value between concepts y and a will be zero, but the appreciated "causal negation" is preserved during the inference process due to defined -1 value between discrete concepts of the same feature. Although the fuzzy concepts B and L have no explicit negation between them, if a concept is activated to a certain degree d implies that the other will be activated in a $1-d$ degree. In that way, an implicit relation in the generated topology is defined and preserves the higher activation values during the inference process.

The proposed method can also be defined as a data-driven type, due is not required to define the fuzzy concept names to use the generated FCM as a classification tool. To show the results achieved by the generated FCMs several experiments were carried out.

According to the proposed strategy and the diversity of parameters that may be used in the FCM generation, several configurations were tested, highlighting the best results for each test. The algorithms were tested using a random data partition for each configuration and algorithm compared. Also, eight datasets of the UCI ML repository were used for the tests.

Table 3. FCMs configuration tested

Function	FCM1	FCM2	FCM3	FCM4	FCM5	FCM6
Activation	tanh	tanh	sigmoid	sigmoid	relu	relu
Causality	conf	pinf	conf	pinf	conf	pinf

Several configurations for the FCM generation were tested to finally select the best configuration according to obtained results and compare it with other algorithms. For the FCM generation test, three main parameters were selected: activation function, like *sigmoid* and *tanh* [12], also the rectified linear function (*relu*) [16] is tested in this step. The relation functions tested were the previously presented confidence (*conf*) and positive influence (*pinf*) coefficients. In all experiments the minimum support values selected is $supp_m = 0$, to test all possible relations. The selected parameters and values for each tested configuration and the accuracy results are shown in Table 3 and Table 4 respectively, also can be appreciated that the FCM2 achieve better results.

Table 4. FCMs configuration comparison

Dataset Tested	FCM1	FCM2	FCM3	FCM4	FCM5	FCM6
balance-scale	0.065	**1.0**	0.934	**1.0**	0.934	0.978
heart-statlog	0.45	0.8	0.55	0.45	**0.9**	0.8
SPECT	0.352	**0.823**	**0.823**	**0.823**	**0.823**	**0.823**
dermatology	0.222	**0.814**	0.296	0.074	0.481	0.555
lymph	0.272	**0.909**	0.545	0.0	0.818	0.818
tic-tac-toe	0.859	**1.0**	**1.0**	**1.0**	0.661	0.845
solar.flare1	0.214	**0.5**	0.357	0.142	0.357	0.428
monks2	0.468	**1.0**	**1.0**	**1.0**	0.656	0.656
zoo	**0.857**	**0.857**	0.428	0.428	0.714	**0.857**

In addition, comparisons were made between some of the well-known classifiers [8] with same test strategy and over same datasets, according to the results of Table 4 the configuration selected is FCM2. The algorithms tested are implemented in scikit-learn [17] and the parameters set for each one in the test are:

- KNN ($k = 5$)
- L. SVM ($C = 0.025$)
- RBF SVM ($gamma = 2, c = 1$)
- Dec. Tree ($max\_depth = 5$)
- R. Forest ($max\_depth = 5, n\_estimators = 10, max\_features = 1$)
- AdaBoost ()
- Gaussian Naive Bayes ()

In Table 5 the results of comparison between generated FCM and other algorithms show that the proposed strategy for FCM generation reaches acceptable results values preserving the interpretability of the generated model. Additionally, the results of the generated map can be improved using any of the other existent methods [7].

Table 5. FCM and estimators comparison

Dataset	FCM	KNN	L. SVM	RBF SVM	Dec. Tree	R. Forest	Ada Boost	G.N. Bayes
balance-scale	**1.0**	0.978	0.934	0.934	**1.0**	0.934	**1.0**	**1.0**
heart-statlog	0.8	0.35	0.8	0.55	0.6	0.75	0.75	**0.85**
SPECT	0.823	0.823	0.823	0.823	0.823	0.823	**0.882**	0.588
dermatology	0.814	0.666	**0.962**	0.296	**0.962**	0.888	0.407	0.925
lymph	0.909	0.818	0.909	0.545	**1.0**	0.818	0.727	0.909
tic-tac-toe	**1.0**	0.901	**1.0**	0.661	**1.0**	0.985	**1.0**	**1.0**
monks2	**1.0**	0.93	**1.0**	0.875	**1.0**	**1.0**	**1.0**	**1.0**
solar.flare1	0.5	**0.571**	0.357	0.214	**0.571**	0.428	0.428	0.071
zoo	0.857	0.571	0.714	0.428	**1.0**	**1.0**	0.857	**1.0**

5 Conclusions

In this work, we have presented a strategy to build FCMs from discrete and continuous data for classification problems. The map topology is defined by extracting concepts from data, and the relations between every pair of concepts are defined using statistical association coefficients. Functions like confidence and the proposed positive influence coefficient were tested.

The proposed method builds FCMs with the minimum human intervention and without affecting the output model accuracy, using the Apriori and Fuzzy c-means algorithms to define the map concepts. Also, comparisons made between FCMs generated with different parameters show that they have different behavior depending on the data set used, and the positive influence coefficient with a tanh activation function usually performs better than other configurations. The results obtained comparing over well-known datasets show that the proposal generates an interpretable model that achieves acceptable accuracy results. Finally, the proposed generation strategy opens a field for association based learning algorithms for FCM.

Posterior studies will be focused on reducing mentioned undesired effects in association based relations, test other association rules coefficients like odds ratio and their relation with functions to determine the relation sign. Also, review the impact of different clustering algorithms in the construction process. Further will propose an adaptation for handling missing values and multivalued features for process datasets closer to reality.

References

1. Aggarwal, C.C., Bhuiyan, M.A., Al Hasan, M.: Frequent pattern mining algorithms: a survey. In: Aggarwal, C., Han, J. (eds.) Frequent Pattern Mining, pp. 19–64. Springer, Cham (2014). https://doi.org/10.1007/978-3-319-07821-2_2
2. Amirkhani, A., Mosavi, M.R., Mohammadi, K., Papageorgiou, E.I.: A novel hybrid method based on fuzzy cognitive maps and fuzzy clustering algorithms for grading celiac disease. Neural Comput. Appl. **30**(5), 1573–1588 (2018)
3. Amirkhani, A., Papageorgiou, E.I., Mohseni, A., Mosavi, M.R.: A review of fuzzy cognitive maps in medicine: taxonomy, methods, and applications. Comput. Methods Programs Biomed. **142**, 129–145 (2017)
4. Bezdek, J.C.: Fuzzy-Mathematics in Pattern Classification. Cornell University, Ithaca (1973)
5. Casillas, J., Cordón, O., Triguero, F.H., Magdalena, L.: Interpretability Issues in Fuzzy Modeling, vol. 128. Springer, Heidelberg (2013). https://doi.org/10.1007/978-3-540-37057-4
6. Cohen, J., Cohen, P., West, S.G., Aiken, L.S.: Applied Multiple Regression/Correlation Analysis for the Behavioral Sciences. Routledge, Abingdon (2013)
7. Felix, G., Nápoles, G., Falcon, R., Froelich, W., Vanhoof, K., Bello, R.: A review on methods and software for fuzzy cognitive maps. Artif. Intell. Rev. **52**(3), 1707–1737 (2019)
8. Fernández-Delgado, M., Cernadas, E., Barro, S., Amorim, D.: Do we need hundreds of classifiers to solve real world classification problems? J. Mach. Learn. Res. **15**(1), 3133–3181 (2014)
9. He, H., Tan, Y., Fujimoto, K.: Estimation of optimal cluster number for fuzzy clustering with combined fuzzy entropy index. In: 2016 IEEE International Conference on Fuzzy Systems (FUZZ-IEEE), pp. 697–703. IEEE (2016)
10. Kim, J., Han, M., Lee, Y., Park, Y.: Futuristic data-driven scenario building: incorporating text mining and fuzzy association rule mining into fuzzy cognitive map. Expert Syst. Appl. **57**, 311–323 (2016)
11. Kosko, B.: Fuzzy cognitive maps. Int. J. Man-Mach. Stud. **24**(1), 65–75 (1986)
12. Kottas, F., Boutalis, Y.S., Devedzic, G., Mertzios, B.G.: A new method for reaching equilibrium points in fuzzy cognitive maps. In: 2004 2nd International IEEE Conference on 'Intelligent Systems'. Proceedings (IEEE Cat. No. 04EX791), vol. 1, pp. 53–60. IEEE (2004)
13. Li, J., Liu, L., Le, T.D.: Practical Approaches to Causal Relationship Exploration. Springer, Cham (2015). https://doi.org/10.1007/978-3-319-14433-7
14. Nápoles, G., Leon Espinosa, M., Grau, I., Vanhoof, K., Bello, R.: Fuzzy cognitive maps based models for pattern classification: advances and challenges. In: Pelta, D., Cruz Corona, C. (eds.) Soft Computing Based Optimization and Decision Models, vol. 360, pp. 83–98. Springer, Cham (2018). https://doi.org/10.1007/978-3-319-64286-4_5
15. Nápoles, G., Jastrzebska, A., Mosquera, C., Vanhoof, K., Homenda, W.: Deterministic learning of hybrid fuzzy cognitive maps and network reduction approaches. Neural Netw. **124**, 258–268 (2020)
16. Oostwal, E., Straat, M., Biehl, M.: Hidden unit specialization in layered neural networks: ReLU vs. sigmoidal activation. Phys. A: Stat. Mech. Appl. **564**, 125517 (2021)
17. Pedregosa, F., et al.: Scikit-learn: machine learning in Python. J. Mach. Learn. Res. **12**, 2825–2830 (2011)

18. Studer, R., Benjamins, V.R., Fensel, D.: Knowledge engineering: principles and methods. Data Knowl. Eng. **25**(1–2), 161–197 (1998)
19. Stylios, C.D., Bourgani, E., Georgopoulos, V.C.: Impact and applications of fuzzy cognitive map methodologies. In: Kosheleva, O., Shary, S., Xiang, G., Zapatrin, R. (eds.) Beyond Traditional Probabilistic Data Processing Techniques: Interval, Fuzzy etc. Methods and Their Applications. SCI, vol. 835, pp. 229–246. Springer, Cham (2020). https://doi.org/10.1007/978-3-030-31041-7_13
20. Yuan, K., Liu, J., Yang, S., Wu, K., Shen, F.: Time series forecasting based on kernel mapping and high-order fuzzy cognitive maps. Knowl.-Based Syst. **206**, 106359 (2020)

Extracting Composite Summaries
from Qualitative Data

Carlos R. Rodríguez Rodríguez[1,2](✉) (iD), Marieta Peña Abreu[1] (iD),
and Denis Sergeevich Zuev[2] (iD)

[1] University of Informatics Sciences, Havana, Cuba
crodriguezr@uci.cu
[2] Kazan Federal University, Tatarstan, Russia

Abstract. The paper proposes a model combining association rules and elements of Rhetorical Structure Theory (RST) to generate composite linguistic summaries from qualitative data. The specifications of three new abstract forms of composite linguistic summaries for qualitative data are presented. The proposed abstract forms represent relations of Evidence, Contrast, and Emphasis inspired by RST, consisting of at least two semantically related constituent statements linked by a connector specific to each relation. The constituent statements have the structure of the classical protoforms of linguistic summaries, which in this paper are built from an association rule, to which a fuzzy linguistic quantifier is assigned. Moreover, the definitions of truth degree, relation strength, and coverage degree for composite relations are presented. The model applicability was checked through a use case performed with a database of 2128 cases of the Economic Chamber of the Provincial People's Court of Havana.

Keywords: Association rules · Linguistic descriptions of data · Linguistic data summarization · Rhetorical structure theory

1 Introduction

Linguistic Data Summarization (LDS) [1] is a widespread data mining approach [2–11]. Its mainstream consists of modeling numerical variables using fuzzy logic. At the same time, there are problems whose variables are qualitative, which have received little attention from researchers. However, some authors [5, 8] have proposed approaches that allow working with mixed data.

There are two key user-oriented issues: usability and interpretability of the summaries. Zadeh's concept of protoform [12], and its extension as a hierarchy of abstract forms for LDS [13], have been widely used to deal with these issues. However, several studies cited in [10] point out two main limitations of LDS. The first one concerns the inappropriateness of protoforms to be provided directly to users. The second one is related to the lack of expressiveness of protoforms beyond standard quantified sentences. Some proposals that improve the expressiveness of linguistic summaries are [2, 10], but again they are not oriented to problems with qualitative information.

© Springer Nature Switzerland AG 2021
Y. Hernández Heredia et al. (Eds.): IWAIPR 2021, LNCS 13055, pp. 260–269, 2021.
https://doi.org/10.1007/978-3-030-89691-1_26

This paper proposes an extension for qualitative variables of the framework presented in [10], combining association rules and elements of Rhetorical Structure Theory (RST). For this purpose, some basic notions about linguistic summarization, association rules, and RST are introduced. Next, the proposed extension is discussed. Section 3 describes a use case developed to verify the applicability of the model.

1.1 Some Preliminary Concepts

Let $D = \{[v_1(y_1), \ldots, v_m(y_1)], \ldots, [v_1(y_n), \ldots, v_m(y_n)]\}$ be a dataset of n objects $Y = \{y_1, \ldots, y_n\}$ characterized by m attributes $V = \{v_1, \ldots, v_m\}$ taking values in $X = \{X_1, \ldots, X_m\}$; $v_j(y_i)$ denotes the value of attribute v_j for object y_i, and v_j takes on its values from a set X_j. A linguistic summary is a statement of the form (1) or (2):

$$T(Qy' \text{ are } S) \tag{1}$$

$$T(QFy' \text{ are } S) \tag{2}$$

where S is a summarizer (*e.g., are paid*), a label representing a specific value of v_j; Q is a quantity in an agreement given as a fuzzy linguistic quantifier (*e.g., most*); and T is the truth degree of the summary (*e.g., 0.85*), which takes values in $[0, 1]$. In (Eq. 2), a qualifier F (*e.g., for delay*) is added. F is a filter to obtain a specific subset of Y. The following is a statement like (Eq. 2): **T(Most claims for delay are paid) = 0.85.**

In order to evaluate the summaries we will use the truth degree and the relation strength proposed in [10], and also we will extend the traditional coverage degree.

Association Rules Mining (ARM). ARM deals with finding relations between frequent attributes in a database [14]. Let $A = \{a_1, \ldots, a_m\}$ be a set of m binary attributes and $R = \{r_1, \ldots, r_n\}$ a set of n transactions where r_j is a binary vector representing the membership of each attribute a_i to the transaction. Let be $B \subset A$, a transaction r_j supports B if $\forall b_i \in B : b_i = 1$. An association rule is an implication (Eq. 3), where $B \subset A, C \subset A$, and $B \cap C = \emptyset$:

$$B \Rightarrow C \tag{3}$$

Kacprzyk and Zadrożny state that the association rules may be interpreted as a special case of the linguistic summaries [3]. Some authors have used fuzzy association rules [3, 7] or Apriori inspired algorithms [4, 5] to obtain linguistics summaries. Clearly, the association rule mining algorithms are efficient tools for finding linguistic summaries with a certain level of validity in any of the protoforms proposed in [13].

Mapping the rule (3) into the summary (2), we would have $T(QB \Rightarrow C)$, where the value of T is obtained by evaluating the confidence of the rule on the fuzzy set of Q.

Rhetorical Structure Theory (RST). RST is a comprehensive theory of textual organization, which was first proposed in [15]. The core of RST is the set of mononuclear and multi-nuclear rhetorical relations. In the former ones, one of the text spans is more important than the other one, which play the role of nucleus and satellite respectively. All text spans are equally salient in multi-nuclear ones, all are nucleus [16].

RST has been widely used in chatbots, text summarization, sentiment analysis, machine translation, text generation, and information retrieval [16]. In [10], a framework for composite protoforms of linguistic descriptions of numeric data based on semantic relations among simpler protoforms is proposed. Besides, a taxonomy of three composite relations (Evidence, Contrast, and Emphasis) is defined.

2 Extracting Composite Summaries from Qualitative Data

This section presents an extension of the framework proposed in [10] to generate composite summaries from association rules of qualitative variables. We first adopt some previous definitions given in [10] and discuss the necessary elements for this paper. Then we introduce the coverage degree of a composite protoform. Finally, we discuss the extensions of the Evidence, Contrast, and Emphasis relations.

Definition 1. A composite protoform P^r is the composition of two or more protoforms, which can function as nuclei (P^N) or satellites (P^S) of P^r, and which are semantically related through a relation r. P^r is constrained by C_{PN} (the constraints on the nucleus), C_{PS} (the constraints on the satellites), and C_{PN+PS} (the constraints on the combination of both roles). Constraints C_{PN}, C_{PS} and C_{PN+PS} allow to specify the type of protoforms to be used or more detailed conditions in a specific type of protoform.

$$P^r \rightarrow \{P^N r\{P^S, ..., P^S\}, C_{PN}, C_{PS}, C_{PN+PS}\} \tag{4}$$

Remark. In our case, P^N and P^S are type-I (Eq. 1) or type-II (Eq. 2) protoforms, which take the form $QX \Rightarrow Y$, where X and Y can be simple (one attribute) or complex (two or more attributes) predicates. In type-I protoforms, X comprises all transactions.

Definition 2. The truth degree of a composite protoform $T(P^r)$ is computed by aggregating the truth degree of its constituents. The aggregation can be performed using a t-norm (minimum, product, Lukasiewicz, etc.).

$$T(P^r) = T\left(P^N\right) \otimes \otimes_{i=1}^n T\left(P_i^S\right) \tag{5}$$

Definition 3. The relation strength μ_r is defined as the membership degree of a pair of protoforms (nucleus and satellite) against the relation r.

$$\mu_{r^s} : \left\{P^N, P^S\right\} \rightarrow [0, 1] \tag{6}$$

Definition 4. The relation strength of a composite protoform $S(P^r)$ is calculated by aggregating the values of μ_r between the nucleus and each satellite.

$$S(P^r) = \otimes_{i=1}^n \mu_r\left(P^N, P_i^S\right) \tag{7}$$

Remark. In the taxonomy of composite protoforms [10], the μ_r is calculated based on relation strength matrices defined on linguistic variables. Besides, the summarizers for the constituent protoforms are composed of properties that belong to the same linguistic variables. $S(P^r)$ considers only the value of μ_r between the summarizers.

However, in RST, most of the relations are mononuclear, in which the satellite complements the nucleus. In such cases, it seems advisable to define the relation strength considering how well the satellite fulfills its role. On the other hand, in multi-nuclear relations (e.g., Contrast), it is advisable to define the relation strength holding all the attributes of the constituent protoforms instead of considering only the summarizers. Therefore, our proposal adopts the definitions of μ_r and $S(P^r)$ but, μ_r will be defined in the most appropriate way for each relation. Moreover, the aggregation operations will be performed using the most suitable operator for each case.

Several authors consider that the coverage degree is a useful measure of a linguistic summary. Coverage degree describes how representative the summary is regarding the data set. In this paper, the traditional coverage degree is extended as follows.

Definition 4. The coverage degree of a composite protoform $C(P^r)$ denotes the number of transactions covered by at least one of the constituent statements. $C(P^r)$ is derived from the aggregation of the coverage degrees of those constituents.

$$C(P^r) = C\left(P^N\right) \otimes \otimes_{i=1}^n C\left(P_i^S\right) \tag{8}$$

3 Evidence Composite Relation

The Evidence composite relation P^e is based on the evidence relation defined in RST. P^e provides one main statement (the nucleus) and one or more auxiliary statements (the satellites), which supply finer-grained information that validates the nucleus.

Table 1 shows the extended specification of P^e, whose structure is P^N, $since P^S$. The nucleus can now be a type-I or type-II statement, which allows building more enriched Evidence relations. The satellite can be one or more non-overlapping type-II statements. In P^e, the satellites must semantically support the nucleus. This means that all constituents must share the same summarizer. In addition, the relation strength will depend on the degree to which the satellites support the nucleus.

Relation Strength of P^e. In the RST the satellite of an Evidence relation aims to increase the reader's belief in the nucleus assertion. Therefore, the relation strength be given by the degree to which the satellite supports the nucleus. Thus, $\mu_r(P^N, P^S) = C(P^S)/C(P^N)$, i. e., the relation strength will increase as the satellites' support to the nucleus increases. When $S(P^e) = 1$, P^e will be a full Evidence relation. Relation strength of P^e is defined as follows:

$$S(P^e) = \sum_{i=1}^n \mu_r\left(P^N, P_i^S\right) \tag{9}$$

Coverage Degrees of P^e. Since in the Evidence relation, all possible satellites will always be subsets of the nucleus, the coverage degree of P^e is expressed as follow:

$$C(P^e) = C(P^N) \tag{10}$$

Table 1. Specification of the Evidence relation

relation: Evidence	Examples
protoform: P^N, sinceP^S expanded protoform-1: $QX \Rightarrow A$, **since** $QCX \Rightarrow A, \ldots, QZX \Rightarrow A$ $C_{PN} : P^N$ is a type-I quantified statement $C_{PS} : P^S$ is a type-II quantified statement $C_{PN+PS} : (CX, \ldots, ZX \subset X) \wedge (CX \cap \cdots \cap ZX = \emptyset)$ expanded protoform-2: $QBX \Rightarrow A$, since$QCX \Rightarrow A, \ldots, QZX \Rightarrow A$ $C_{PN} : P^N$ is a type-II quantified statement $C_{PS} : P^S$ is a type-II quantified statement $C_{PN+PS} : (CX, \ldots, ZX \subset BX) \wedge (CX \cap \cdots \cap ZX = \emptyset)$	1. *Many* claims have amounts less than 414,300 pesos, **since** *most* claims that are paid have amounts less than 414.300 pesos 2. *Most* claims that are paid have amounts less than 414.300 pesos, **since** *most* claims that MITRANS does pay have amounts less than 414,300 pesos

3.1 Contrast Composite Relation

The contrast relation defined in RST consists of no more than two nuclei that are the same in many respects and different in others regarding which they are compared. In [10], a Contrast composite protoform consisting of a nucleus and several satellites is proposed. Within it, the authors distinguish two sub relations: deviation and opposition. Based on the above, we introduce our Contrast composite relation approach.

A Contrast composite relation P^c consists of two nuclei, which provide contrasting information about the same attributes of the analyzed problem. The general structure of P^c isN^1, **but**N^2. Table 2 shows its specification. The nuclei can now be type-I or type-II statements, which allows building more enriched Contrast relations. Both N^1 and N^2 can have complex predicates in their antecedents and consequents, but at least one pair of predicates must be different. The constraint $P\_Dif(K, L)$ ensures that, given the predicates $K \in N^1$ and$L \in N^2$, they have at least one attribute that is the same but with different values. For example: K={causal=*delay*, plaintiff=MES}, L={causal=*non-payment*, plaintiff=MES}.

$$P\_Dif(K, L) = \exists (k_i \in K, l_j \in L) | att_{k_i} = att_{l_j}; val_{k_i} \neq val_{l_j};$$
$$i = 1, 2, \ldots, n; j = 1, 2, \ldots, n \tag{11}$$

We do not adopt the distinction of contrast sub relations proposed in [10]. Its restrictions do not admit representing attributes with an even number of labels having progressive contrast degrees. Instead, we believe that a single type of relations that allows the designer to freely specify the degree of contrast between each pair of labels offers greater expressiveness. For example, Fig. 1 models the contrast degree between the labels of the attribute "claim amount".

Table 2. Specification of the Contrast composite relation

relation: Contrast	Examples
protoform: N^1, **but** N^2 expanded protoform-1: $QX \Rightarrow A,$ **but** $QY \Rightarrow B$ $C_{N1} : N^1$ is a type-I quantified statement $C_{N2} : N^2$ is a type-I quantified statement $C_{N1+N2} : (X = Y) \wedge (att_A = att_B) \wedge P\_Dif(A, B)$ expanded protoform-2: $QX \Rightarrow A,$ **but** $QY \Rightarrow B$ $C_{N1} : N^1$ is a type-I quantified statement $C_{N2} : N^2$ is a type-II quantified statement $C_{N1+N2} : (Y \subset X) \wedge (att_A = att_B) \wedge P\_Dif(A, B)$ expanded protoform-3: $QX \Rightarrow A,$ **but** $QY \Rightarrow B$ $C_{N1} : N^1$ is a type-II quantified statement $C_{N2} : N^2$ is a type-II quantified statement $C_{N1+N2} : (((att_A = att_B) \wedge (att_X = att_Y)) \wedge (P\_Dif(A, B) \vee P\_Dif(X, Y))) \vee$ $(((att_A = att_Y) \wedge (att_X = att_B)) \wedge (P\_Dif(A, Y) \vee P\_Dif(X, B)))$	1.*Many* claims are for non-payment, **but** *some* are for delay 2. *About half* of the claims are paid, **but** *about half* of the claims for non-payment are not paid afterwards 3. *Many* claims for non-payment have amounts less than 414,300 pesos, **but** *most* claims for delay also have amounts less than 414,300 pesos

$$R^c_{amount} = \begin{matrix} & i1 & i2 & i3 & i4 & i5 & i6 \\ i1 & 0 & 0.25 & 0.5 & 1 & 1 & 1 \\ i2 & 0.25 & 0 & 0.25 & 0.5 & 1 & 1 \\ i3 & 0.5 & 0.25 & 0 & 0.25 & 0.5 & 1 \\ i4 & 1 & 0.5 & 0.25 & 0 & 0.25 & 0.5 \\ i5 & 1 & 1 & 0.5 & 0.25 & 0 & 0.25 \\ i6 & 1 & 1 & 1 & 0.5 & 0.25 & 0 \end{matrix}$$

Legend
$i1$='(-inf–414300]'
$i2$='(414300–506830.5]'
$i3$='(506830.5–658558]'
$i4$='(658558–1230603]'
$i5$='(1230603–1243984]'
$i6$='(1243984–1361474]'

Fig. 1. Matrix of contrast degrees between the labels of the attribute "claim amount".

Relation Strength of P^c. Since P^c provide contrasting information, its relation strength will depend on the contrast degree between the labels of each pair of equal attributes in the constituent statements. This value must be specified by the designer. So given an attribute $U = [u_1, u_2, \ldots, u_n]$, a relation strength set is defined on $U \times U$ by Eq. (12), where x_{ij} represents the contrast degree between u_i and u_j. See Fig. 1.

$$R_U = (x_{ij}/u_i, u_j) | u_i, u_j \in U \times U; x_{ij} \in [0, 1]; i \leq m; j \leq m \qquad (12)$$

The relation strength evaluation function between a pair of values is defined as:

$$\mu_{R_U}(u_i, u_j) = x_{ij} | x_{ij} \in (x_{ij}/u_i, u_j); (x_{ij}/u_i, u_j) \in R_U \qquad (13)$$

There are two particular cases: in the expanded protoform-1, since $X = Y$, then $\mu_{R_U}(X, Y) = 0$, while for the expanded protoform-2, where $Y \subset X$, $\mu_{R_U}(X, Y) = 0.5$.

Then, the relation strength of P^c is calculated as the arithmetic mean of the x_{ij} values for each pair of equal attributes:

$$S\left(P^c\right) = \mu_r\left(N^1, N^2\right) = \frac{1}{n}\sum_{k=1}^{n}\mu_{RU_k}\left(u_i^k, u_j^k\right) \tag{14}$$

Coverage Degrees of P^c. The coverage degree of P^c is obtained by adding the coverage degree of its constituent statements since they are mutually exclusive.

$$C\left(P^c\right) = C\left(N^1\right) + C\left(N^2\right) \tag{15}$$

3.2 Emphasis Composite Relation

The emphasis relation is not considered in the RST. However, in [10], it is defined as "a cross-relation frequently found in domains with narratives based on numeric variables". Those authors model it as a relation between the labels at the extremes of a fuzzy linguistic variable (FLV) and their adjacent labels. This approach is useful in summarization problems with FLV and some cases of ordinal qualitative variables. But it does not apply to summarization problems with nominal qualitative variables.

Emphasis means special importance, value, or prominence given to something. Under this concept, we introduce another approach of Emphasis composite relation.

The new Emphasis composite relation P^h combines two similar statements in which the second one (the satellite) has an additional predicate that specifies the main feature of the objects described by the first one (the nucleus). P^h could be considered a special type of the Elaboration relation defined in RST ("generalization – specific" subtype). The difference lies in the fact that, in P^h, the satellite highlights the most representative "specification" of the "generalization" that describes the nucleus.

An Emphasis relation adopts the structure P^N, *especially* P^N, and its features are specified in Table 3. In this relation, the statement that functions as the nucleus constitutes the antecedent of the satellite. In turn, the consequent of the satellite contains a different predicate that emphasizes a feature of the nucleus. The nucleus can now be a type-I or type-II statement, which allows building more enriched Emphasis relations. Meanwhile, the satellite has been constrained to only one type-II statement.

Example. Consider the assertion: "Many claims have amounts less than \$414,300, and especially many of them are paid". Here, the predicate "are paid" is the most frequent among the claims for amounts not exceeding \$414,300. Therefore, the locution "especially many of them are paid" emphasizes the prevalent property in the claims covered by the statement: "Many claims have amounts less than \$414,300".

Strength Relation of P^h. Since in P^h, the satellite highlights the most frequent feature of the nucleus, it seems advisable that the relation strength be given by the level of representativeness that the satellite achieves concerning the nucleus. Thus, $\mu_r(P^N, P^S) = C(P^s)/C(P^N)$, i.e., the relation strength increases as the representativeness increases. As P^h has only two statements, $S\left(P^h\right)$ is calculated as follow:

$$S\left(P^h\right) = \mu_r\left(P^N, P^S\right) = C(P^s)/C(P^N) \tag{16}$$

Table 3. Specification of the Emphasis composite relation

relation: Emphasis	Examples
protoform: P^N, *especially* P^S *expanded protoform-1*: $QX \Rightarrow A$, *especially* $QXA \Rightarrow C$ $C_{PN} : P^N$ is a type-I quantified statement $C_{PS} : P^S$ is a type-II quantified statement $C_{PN+PS} : XA = XareA$ *expanded protoform-2*: $QBX \Rightarrow A$, *especially* $QBXA \Rightarrow C$ $C_{PN} : P^N$ is a type-II quantified statement $C_{PS} : P^S$ is a type-II quantified statement $C_{PN+PS} : BXA = BXareA$	1. *Many* claims have amounts less than \$414,300, *especially* *most* claims for amounts less than \$414.300 are paid 2. *Almost all* claims of MICONS have amounts less than \$414.300, *especially* *most* claims of MICONS for amounts less than \$414,300 are for non-payment

Coverage Degrees of P^e. The coverage degree of P^h is calculated as in Eq. (10).

4   Use Case

We developed a use case to illustrate how the method works. The task consisted of extracting composite summaries from a database of 2128 cases of the Economic Chamber of the Provincial People's Court of Havana. The database records consist of five nominal attributes, collected from 2013 to 2015, and have no missing values.

To obtain the composite summaries, we perform the following procedure:

1. Generate type-II summaries using Apriori and the quantifiers defined below.
2. Generate type-I summaries using the L1 itemsets obtained with Apriori, which have the support ≥ 0.5, and the quantifiers defined below.
3. Generate all possible composite relations by combining the above summaries. Discard relations with $T(P^e) < 0.5$ and $S(P^e) < 0.5$. Eliminate redundant relations.
4. Eliminate type-I and type-II summaries that are not part of any composite relation.

The Apriori algorithm (Weka version) was used with the following parameters: *numRules=100, metricType=Confidence, minMetric=0.5, delta=0.05, minSupport=0.1*.

Four linguistic quantifiers were modeled with trapezoidal fuzzy sets: *About_half* =[0.42, 0.48, 0.52, 0.58], *Many*=[0.52, 0.58, 1, 1], *Most*=[0.72, 0.78, 1, 1], *Almost_all*=[0.92, 0.98, 1, 1]. In each case, the most specific quantifier for which the summary retained a value of $T \geq 0.5$ was assigned.

First, 34 type-II and three type-I summaries with $T \geq 0.5$ and $C \geq 0.1$ were obtained. Combining them to generate composite relations yielded the results shown in Table 4. The minimum, maximum, mean, and standard deviation values correspond to the non-redundant relations, which are the final set of relations. Those results are consistent with the definition of each type of relation. Evidence relations have the highest mean of $S(P)$ since P^e involves a summary and as many of its non-overlapping subsets as possible. Emphasis relations also have a high value of $S(P)$, although lower than that of P^e, because P^h has only one satellite, which will rarely fully support the nucleus. Also, it is reasonable that the Contrast relations are those of higher $C(P)$ and lower $S(P)$. The mean of $T(P)$ is high in all cases, although the maximum membership principle was not adopted to assign the quantifiers.

Table 4. Statistical results of the use case

Composite relations	Measures	$T(P)$	$S(P)$	$C(P)$
Evidence, P^e Initially generated: 42 Exceeded thresholds: 23 *No redundancy: 18======>*	Min	0.6	0.57	0.11
	Max	1	1	0.73
	Mean	0.9050	0.8433	0.3083
	StdDev	0.1395	0.1303	0.1806
Contrast, P^c Initially generated: 19 Exceeded thresholds: 14 *No redundancy: 11======>*	Min	0.54	0.5	0.24
	Max	1	1	0.84
	Mean	0.8382	0.5973	0.4973
	StdDev	0.1578	0.1536	0.1854
Emphasis, P^h Initially generated: 19 Exceeded thresholds: 19 *No redundancy: 16======>*	Min	0.6	0.5	0.11
	Max	1	0.97	0.73
	Mean	0.9119	0.7425	0.2944
	StdDev	0.1298	0.1434	0.1868

5   Conclusions

This contribution proposes an extension of the framework presented in [10]. Our model focuses on those real decision-making problems where the primary data are qualitative. For those cases, mainstream LDS, based on fuzzy sets modeling numerical variables, is not applicable. However, with the approach proposed in this paper, summaries of numerical variables can be built using the linguistic labels of the fuzzy sets.

The summaries generated by the model are semantic relations that enrich the interpretation of the information contained in the dataset. They make it possible to identify different types of underlying behaviors in the same set of constituent statements. Thus, this approach seems to be more useful than the traditional one in which constituent statements are analyzed independently.

The constraints of the protoform subtypes of each type of relation allow modeling many behaviors of the problem attributes. However, some problems may require the modification of these constraints or the creation of new protoform subtypes.

As future work, the acceptance of the summaries generated with the model will be evaluated among decision-makers from different levels of the legal domain, exploring the legal activities in which the types of summaries proposed are potentially helpful.

References

1. Yager, R.R.: A new approach to the summarization of data. Inf. Sci. **28**, 69–86 (1982)
2. Trivino, G., Sugeno, M.: Towards linguistic descriptions of phenomena. Int. J. Approx. Reason. **54**, 22–34 (2013). https://doi.org/10.1016/j.ijar.2012.07.004
3. Kacprzyk, J., Zadrozny, S.: Derivation of linguistic summaries is inherently difficult: Can association rule mining help? (2013). https://doi.org/10.1007/978-3-642-30278-7_23
4. Wilbik, A., Kaymak, U., Dijkman, R.M.: A method for improving the generation of linguistic summaries. In: IEEE International Conference on Fuzzy Systems (2017). https://doi.org/10.1109/FUZZ-IEEE.2017.8015752
5. Smits, G., Nerzic, P., Pivert, O., Lesot, M.J.: Efficient generation of reliable estimated linguistic summaries. In: IEEE International Conference on Fuzzy Systems (2018). https://doi.org/10.1109/FUZZ-IEEE.2018.8491604
6. Kacprzyk, J., Yager, R., Merigo, J.M.: Towards human-centric aggregation via ordered weighted aggregation operators and linguistic data summaries: a new perspective on Zadeh's inspirations. IEEE Comput. Intell. Mag. **14**, 16–30 (2019). https://doi.org/10.1109/MCI.2018.2881641
7. Pupo, I., Vacacela, R., Pérez, P.Y., Mahdi, G.S., Peña, M.: Experiencias en el uso de técnicas de softcomputing en la evaluación de proyectos de software. Investigación Oper. **41**, 108–119 (2020)
8. Pérez Pupo, I., Piñero Pérez, P.Y., Bello, R., Acuña, L.A., García Vacacela, R.: Linguistic summaries generation with hybridization method based on rough and fuzzy sets. In: Bello, R., Miao, D., Falcon, R., Nakata, M., Rosete, A., Ciucci, D. (eds.) IJCRS 2020. LNCS (LNAI), vol. 12179, pp. 385–397. Springer, Cham (2020). https://doi.org/10.1007/978-3-030-52705-1_29
9. Yager, R.R.: An introduction to linguistic summaries. In: Lesot, M.-J., Marsala, C. (eds.) Fuzzy Approaches for Soft Computing and Approximate Reasoning: Theories and Applications. SFSC, vol. 394, pp. 151–162. Springer, Cham (2021). https://doi.org/10.1007/978-3-030-54341-9_13
10. Ramos-Soto, A., Martin-Rodilla, P.: Enriching linguistic descriptions of data: a framework for composite protoforms. Fuzzy Sets Syst. **407**, 1–26 (2021). https://doi.org/10.1016/j.fss.2019.11.013
11. Moreno-Garcia, J., Jimenez-Linares, L., Liu, J., Rodriguez-Benitez, L.: Generation of linguistic descriptions for daily noise pollution in urban areas. In: 2021 IEEE International Conference on Fuzzy Systems (FUZZ-IEEE), pp. 1–6 (2021). https://doi.org/10.1109/FUZZ45933.2021.9494388
12. Zadeh, L.A.: A prototype-centered approach to adding deduction capability to search engines - The concept of protoform. In: Annual Conference of the North American Fuzzy Information Processing Society - NAFIPS (2002). https://doi.org/10.1109/NAFIPS.2002.1018115
13. Kacprzyk, J., Zadrozny, S.: Linguistic database summaries and their protoforms: towards natural language based knowledge discovery tools. Inf. Sci. **173** (2005). https://doi.org/10.1016/j.ins.2005.03.002
14. Agrawal, R., Imieliński, T., Swami, A.: Mining association rules between sets of items in large databases. ACM SIGMOD Rec. **22** (1993). https://doi.org/10.1145/170036.170072
15. Mann, W.C., Thompson, S.A.: Rhetorical structure theory: toward a functional theory of text organization. Text-Interdiscip. J. Study Discourse **8**, 243–281 (1988)
16. Hou, S., Zhang, S., Fei, C.: Rhetorical structure theory: a comprehensive review of theory, parsing methods and applications. Expert Syst. Appl. **157** (2020). https://doi.org/10.1016/j.eswa.2020.113421

A Novel Initial Population Construction Heuristic for the DINOS Subgroup Discovery Algorithm

Lisandra Bravo-Ilisástigui[ID], Lenier Reyes-Morales[ID], Diana Martín, and Milton García-Borroto[(✉)][ID]

Universidad Tecnológica de la Habana José Antonio Echeverría, CUJAE, Havana, Cuba
{lbravo,lreyes,diana,mgarciab}@ceis.cujae.edu.cu

Abstract. Evolutionary algorithms for subgroup discovery usually randomly initialize the population, which often causes them to spend part of their time evaluating unpromising solutions. This situation causes the algorithm to take more time to converge to good solutions. In this paper, we present a new initial population construction heuristic for DINOS, a genetic subgroup discovery algorithm that mines non-redundant subgroups with high quality in a short time. The proposed heuristic is based on the generation of a collection of decision trees, allowing to obtain an initial population in which all the rules are valid and with a large coverage of the database. The quality of these rules is also high and they contain a large diversity in the attributes used, allowing to deal with problems having a large number of dimensions. The experiments carried out show that the new method allows mining more high-quality and diverse subgroups in a slightly higher computational time.

Keywords: Subgroup discovery · DINOS · Evolutionary algorithm · Initialization

1 Introduction

Subgroup discovery aims to identify a set of rules of interest according to their unusualness from a property of interest. It is one of the most well-known techniques for mining descriptive patterns on data [16]. Subgroup discovery allows from finding properties in patients that impact survival in COVID19 [19] to automatic sentiment detection in a textual corpus [21].

There are many different methods for subgroup discovery. In recent years, algorithms based on evolutionary approaches have received a significant attention [3,5,9,15]. Evolutionary algorithms imitate the principles of natural evolution to guide the rule search process [6]. They start from an initial population, which evolves in each iteration to better adapt to the constraints and performance functions [8].

© Springer Nature Switzerland AG 2021
Y. Hernández Heredia et al. (Eds.): IWAIPR 2021, LNCS 13055, pp. 270–279, 2021.
https://doi.org/10.1007/978-3-030-89691-1_27

As with most evolutionary approaches, the quality of the result is usually dependent on the initial solution, which is usually randomly generated. The quality of this initial population can directly influence not only the quality of the result but the speed of convergence to the final solution, as well [8]. This happens because evolutionary algorithms frequently stagnate at local optima, so the algorithm needs to be re-started to explore another part of the search space. Although other optimization problems where the generation of good initial solutions have been deeply explored, in subgroup discovery tasks this problem has received limited attention [1].

DINOS [15] is a multi-objective evolutionary algorithm, for mining non-redundant subgroups in mixed databases without prior pre-processing. It obtains state-of-the-art results, usually in significantly smaller execution times. Its initialization procedure has a semi-algebraic construction heuristic based on covering. This heuristic, while ensuring that initial solutions are feasible (covering at least one example), does not guarantee a quality initial population.

In this paper, we present an initial population construction heuristic for DINOS based on a random collection of binary trees, induced with the C4.5 method [17]. To adapt the procedure to the subgroup task, we incorporate a stopping condition based on the unusualness of the rules. All this allows obtaining an initial population in which all the rules are valid, with large coverage of the database, and with the unusualness of the rules having large values. Another important aspect is the diversity in the attributes present in the rules because it allows analyzing the problem from different dimensions. To the best of our knowledge, this is the first time that a decision tree-based procedure is used for this purpose.

The structure of the paper is the following: Sect. 2 presents some important definitions and a review of the state of the art in heuristics to generate initial populations in evolutionary algorithms for subgroups discovery. Then, Sect. 3 introduces the new initialization procedure. Finally, the experimental results are presented in Sect. 4 and the conclusions appear in Sect. 5.

2 Background

The main objective of the subgroup discovery is to identify an interesting group of individuals, where interestingness is defined as a distributional unusualness for a certain property of interest. Evolutionary algorithms have been successfully applied for the Subgroup Discovery task [6]. The construction of the initial population in evolutionary algorithms "plays a crucial role in the effectiveness of the algorithm and its efficiency" [20]. In the generation of the initial population, three criteria to be handled are diversification, computational cost, and quality of the solutions [20].

MESDIF [7] and NMEEF-SD [4] are multiobjective evolutionary algorithms that use some form of Pseudo-Random Number Generator technique to initialize their starting populations. Both algorithms generate rules containing all possible variables and use randomness to select the corresponding values. However, because of MESDIF and NMEEF-SD's choice for the sizes of individuals in the starting population, the generated rules have too many attribute-value pairs when the dataset has too many attributes. Therefore, the generated initial population provides bad quality starting points for the search phase. NMEEF-SD remedies that situation to a certain degree by limiting the number of attribute-value pairs, in 75% of the initial population, to just 25% of the available attributes. For a dataset with tens of thousands of features, 25% may still be too high a number. Therefore, for a high enough value of available attributes, NMEEF-SD is expected to suffer the same problem as MESDIF. Furthermore, the tweaks made by their crossover and mutation operators may not be enough to lead the search process away from these enormous, useless, rules and the convergence of the evolutionary process is questionable [1].

In [1], the authors propose a new form of initialization that improves the performance of these algorithms in databases with high dimensionality. This population initialization operator generates each individual independently using a randomly generated number from a beta distribution with predetermined α and β values to define the rule size. Which attributes are selected and their correspondent values are determined at random using a uniform distribution. The generated rule is added to the population, whose size needs to be provided by the user as a parameter.

DINOS [15] is a multi-objective evolutionary algorithm that can extract quantitative rules for the description of non-redundant subgroups without previews discretization, and with a good balance between unusualness [2], accuracy [12], and sensitivity [13]. To achieve this, DINOS performs evolutionary learning of the rules. To avoid stagnation and promote diversity, the population is restarted to search in other areas of the search space, and the best rule of each subgroup found in the evolutionary process is kept in an External Population (EP).

DINOS include a heuristic to obtain the initial population. It ensures a set of rules in the algorithm where each one covers at least one instance of the database. To do this, first, the attributes involved in the rule are randomly selected. Next, it is randomly determined whether the interval will be positive or negative. Then an instance is randomly chosen from the DB to create the intervals corresponding to each attribute, such that the value of the selected instance is in the center of the interval, with a size for the interval equal to 50% of the domain of its attribute. Also, if any of the interval limits exceed the limit of the domain of its attribute, then the interval limit is replaced by the limit of the attribute's domain. Finally, the DB examples covered by the rule are marked. This process is repeated until the initial population is completed using the DB examples that have not been marked. If all the DB examples have been marked and the initial population has not been completed, the examples are unmarked again and the process is repeated until the initial population is completed.

A reinitialization process is applied whenever in a generation the amount of new solutions does not exceed $\alpha\%$ since it means that a stable state in the quality of the population has been reached. The first step is to update the EP. Then a new population is generated, whose main characteristic is that the rules cover examples that have not been previously covered by the solutions stored in the EP. For this purpose, is applied the same heuristic for the construction of the initial but taking as reference the examples not covered by the solutions in the EP.

DINOS obtains subgroups in the form of interval rules, in which the class attribute at the head of the rule is always nominal. The values of the variables present in the body of the rule may appear negated. In the coding of rules for the evolutionary process, each rule is represented as a chromosome, which is a vector of n genes representing the attributes and intervals of the rule, where n is the number of attributes of the database where the gene on index i represents the attribute on the same position. In the learning process, the attributes present in each rule are determined, as well as the intervals in which the rule is valid.

The initialization strategy of DINOS has no control over the size of new solutions. So it presents similar drawbacks as NMEEF and MESDIF.

3   Initial Population Construction Heuristic Based on Random Decision Forests

The construction heuristic for an evolutionary subgroup discovery algorithm must guarantee an initial population in which all the rules are valid, the largest possible coverage of the database, and that the unusualness of the rules is as high as possible. Another important aspect is the diversity in the attributes present in the rules because it allows analyzing the problem from different dimensions. In the case of DINOS, which mines non-redundant rules, the overlapping in the coverage of the rules must be also taken into account.

For this purpose, we propose the construction of a collection of trees, which promotes diversity and quality in the rules generated, as well as a high coverage of the database. The method employs two diversity generation mechanisms. First, each tree is trained with a bootstrap sample of the objects with replacement. Second, the attributes to be used in each tree are randomly selected, taking into account that they are not repeated between trees. To increase the speed, the procedure of calculating the best attributes, which usually implied a sorting of the attributes, is eliminated. Post-pruning methods are also eliminated to achieve greater variability in the rules obtained from each tree and decrease execution time.

The forest trees are generated with a modified version of C4.5 [18]. Two main modifications to the algorithm were included, the first is in the branching stop condition. When a child node has the same predominant class as the parent and the unusualness value is less, the growth of that path is stopped. Branch development also stops when less than 1% of the DB is left in the node. The second modification involves the way the node is divided so that rules with negated conditions can be generated. In the case of numerical attributes, a binary division is used, we search for the two best cut-off points and divide the set into those examples that fall between the points and the ones that are not. For nominal attributes, a partition is created for each attribute value and its negation.

The rules are extracted from the trees by applying a depth-first search, which obtains as many rules as leaves in the tree. The construction of the trees is performed in parallel and stops when the number of rules of the initial population is reached. The number of trees varies according to the problem and the execution due to the randomness of the process.

4   Experimental Results

This section presents a comparative analysis of DINOS using the original heuristic (DINOS) and the new construction heuristics (DINOS-F). We will analyze the final quality of the solutions, as well as the execution time. The experiments were carried out using 20 DBs frequently used in subgroup discovery papers from the UCI-ML repository [10]. Table 1 resumes the DBs characteristics.

Table 1. Database characteristics.

Name	Var	Disc	Cont	Cla	Inst	Abbrev	Name	Var	Disc	Cont	Cla	Inst	Abbrev
Appendicitis	7	0	7	2	106	Apen	Glass	9	0	9	6	214	Glass
Australian	14	8	6	2	690	Aust	Haberman	3	0	3	2	306	Habe
Balance	4	0	4	3	625	Blce	Heart	13	6	7	2	270	Heart
Brest Cancer	8	7	1	2	256	BrCr	Hepatitis	19	13	6	2	155	Hepa
Bridges	7	4	3	2	102	Brdg	Ionosphere	34	0	34	2	351	Ionos
Bupa	6	0	6	2	309	Bupa	Iris	4	0	4	3	150	Iris
Cleveland	13	0	13	5	303	Clev	Led	7	0	7	10	500	Led
Diabetes	8	0	8	2	768	Diab	Primary Tumor	17	17	0	21	303	PryTmr
Echo	6	1	5	2	131	Echo	Vehicle	18	0	18	4	846	Veh
German	20	13	7	2	1000	Germ	Wine	13	0	13	3	178	Wine

The experimental study measures the unusualness, sensitivity, and confidence metrics, which are the most commonly used quality parameters for subgroups. Ten-fold cross-validation is performed for each algorithm, repeating each execution tree times.

In the first experiment, we compute the average of the metrics of all the mined rules [11]. Then, the values of the models obtained for all databases are averaged. According to results, appearing in Table 2, DINOS obtains higher average results than DINOS-F. Nevertheless, since comparing methods using metric average can be biased toward the one that returns lesser patterns [14], we perform another experiment.

The second experiment, following a methodology proposed in [14], allows observing behaviors that might be hidden by the mean aggregation. It performs a pairwise comparison between algorithms, analyzing the model's quality based on the individual subgroup's quality distribution. In this way, is possible to evaluate the individual contribution of the subgroups to the model quality. It also allows evaluating how much the subgroup models obtained resemble each other. Besides, it proposes a set of bar charts that visually support the comparison. This method works over cross-validation and averages the observations of each model with those obtained from the same DB.

Table 2. Average of metrics for each algorithm per DB. Best results appear bolded.

BD	Confidence		Unusualness		Sensitivity	
	DINOS	DINOS-F	DINOS	DINOS-F	DINOS	DINOS-F
Apen	0.731	**0.792**	0.067	**0.084**	0.597	**0.659**
Aust	**0.685**	0.626	0.069	0.035	0.466	0.271
Blce	**0.573**	0.538	**0.056**	0.046	**0.499**	0.347
BrCr	0.687	**0.775**	**0.014**	0.013	**0.576**	0.459
Brdg	**0.797**	0.787	0.03	**0.04**	0.548	**0.652**
Bupa	**0.766**	0.617	0.005	**0.017**	0.44	**0.519**
Clev	**0.438**	0.298	**0.043**	0.024	**0.477**	0.35
Diab	**0.697**	0.65	**0.051**	0.036	**0.559**	0.352
Echo	**0.693**	0.666	0.038	**0.046**	**0.485**	0.404
Germ	**0.689**	0.6	**0.012**	0.011	**0.614**	0.4
Glass	**0.472**	0.363	**0.043**	0.033	**0.497**	0.461
Habe	**0.708**	0.672	0.017	**0.027**	**0.614**	0.601
Heart	**0.695**	0.633	**0.059**	0.039	**0.419**	0.29
Hepa	**0.752**	0.659	0.047	**0.051**	**0.527**	0.502
Ionos	**0.757**	0.648	**0.055**	0.037	**0.332**	0.226
Iris	**0.716**	0.662	**0.112**	0.096	**0.611**	0.543
Led	0.542	**0.565**	0.053	**0.061**	0.639	**0.744**
PryT	0.36	0.36	0.018	**0.02**	0.511	**0.528**
Veh	**0.463**	0.414	**0.045**	0.027	**0.439**	0.258
Wine	**0.561**	0.508	**0.063**	0.042	**0.443**	0.336

Figure 1 presents the results. First, Fig. 1(a) shows how similar the models are by observing the number of subgroups that are common, i.e. that both algorithms can detect (gray bar) concerning the number of subgroups mined by every single algorithm (white and black bars). The figure shows that DINOS-F mines more unique patterns in most databases.

The second aspect of the comparison is to measure the quality distribution. To do this, the minimum and maximum values of the observed metric are determined among the rules of both algorithms. After, this interval is divided into three subintervals of the same amplitude. Then we count for each algorithm how many rules are found in each subinterval. The method that presents a higher rules percentage in the upper subintervals (white bar) has a distribution that favors the quality of the models. Figures 1(b), 1(c), and 1(d) show the results for the metrics Confidence, Unusualness, and Sensitivity, respectively. Since the white and gray bars of DINOS-F are usually larger than those in DINOS, we can conclude that DINOS-F mines more high-quality patterns than DINOS.

To explain the results in experiments 1 and 2, we performed a third experiment. In this experiment, we joined the rules mined by both algorithms, removing duplicates, and calculating the ratio of rules find by each method. Before

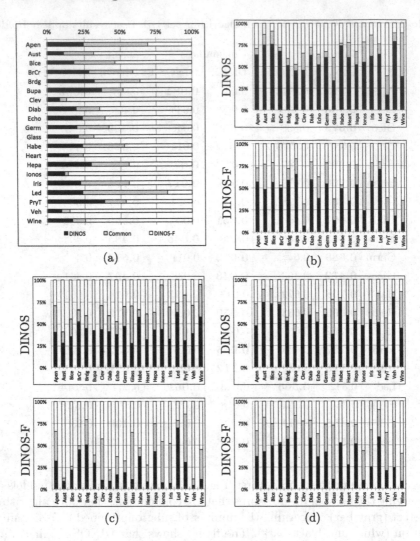

Fig. 1. Paired comparison DINOS and DINOS-F (a) Analysis of the number and similarity of the subgroups found, b) Quality distribution Confidence, c) Quality distribution Unusualness, d) Quality distribution Sensitivity.

that, we split all the rules into three equal-width intervals, calculated using the maximum and minimum value of the metric. In this way, we can alleviate the problem of averaging the metric value of many rules of different quality values.

Results, appearing in Table 3, show that DINOS-F can find a larger fraction of the best patterns, considering confidence and WRACC, while finding a little fewer patterns for sensitivity. On the other hand, DINOS-F find a significantly larger collection of middle and low-quality patterns. In conclusion, the initialization procedure introduced in this paper improves the original DINOS algorithm, allowing it to find a significantly larger collection of patterns of all qualities.

Table 3. Averages of the ratio of found rules of high, middle, and low quality of DINOS and DINOS-F. Higher results appear bolded.

Metric	Quality	DINOS	DINOS-F
Conf	high	0.74	**0.86**
	mid	0.51	**0.75**
	low	0.50	**0.75**
WRACC	high	0.74	**0.81**
	mid	0.64	**0.68**
	low	0.53	**0.78**
Sens	high	**0.90**	0.86
	mid	0.57	0.57
	low	0.45	**0.77**

Table 4. Averages of the standard deviation of the number of found rules of high, middle, and low quality of DINOS and DINOS-F. Higher results appear bolded

Metric	Quality	DINOS	DINOS-F
Conf	high	1.13	**1.67**
	mid	1.07	**2.38**
	low	1.68	**3.92**
WRACC	high	**0.62**	0.54
	mid	0.65	**0.89**
	low	2.19	**5.48**
Sens	high	**0.76**	0.70
	mid	1.02	**1.60**
	low	1.95	**4.90**

Finally, Table 4 presents the average of the standard deviation of the number of patterns mined per DINOS and DINOS-F of every given quality. Since the deviation of DINOS-F is larger in most cases, it shows that the variability of the results per execution of DINOS is also larger, and it is associated with the improvement in the diversity of the initialization procedure.

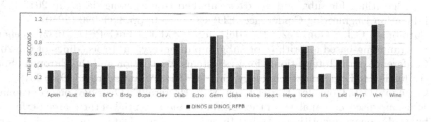

Fig. 2. Execution time of DINOS and DINOS-F per database

The execution time of DINOS-F is only somewhat higher than the original DINOS, as can be seen in Fig. 2.

5   Conclusions

In this paper, we propose a novel initial population construction heuristic for DINOS, a fast and accurate non-redundant subgroup discovery algorithm. The proposed procedure, on the contrary to traditional individual-based generators, is based on the induction of a collection of random decision trees. For this purpose, two new features are introduced to the tree construction model: a new stopping condition based on the unusualness of the rule, and a new way of partitioning the space for decision trees that allows generating rules with negated attributes.

The experimental study shows that our proposal improve the performance of the original algorithm in different ways. First, it allows DINOS to mine significantly more amounts of subgroups. Second, the mined subgroups are better in terms of WRACC and confidence, and only somewhat worst in terms of sensitivity. Finally, DINOS-F has more variability in the number of mined rules per execution, which is associate with the increase in the diversity induced by the initialization procedure. These improvements are obtained using only a slightly higher computer time.

Since the idea of using random decision trees as a construction heuristic for subgroup discovery based on evolutionary algorithms has been proved to generate good results for DINOS, we are planning to expand it to similar algorithms.

References

1. de Albuquerque Torreao, V., Vimieiro, R.: Effects of population initialization on evolutionary techniques for subgroup discovery in high dimensional datasets. In: 2018 7th Brazilian Conference on Intelligent Systems (BRACIS), pp. 25–30 (2018)
2. Carmona, C., del Jesus, M., Herrera, F.: A unifying analysis for the supervised descriptive rule discovery via the weighted relative accuracy. Knowl.-Based Syst. **139**, 89–100 (2018)
3. Carmona, C.J., González, P., Del Jesus, M.J., Herrera, F.: NMEEF-SD: non-dominated multiobjective evolutionary algorithm for extracting fuzzy rules in subgroup discovery. IEEE Trans. Fuzzy Syst. **18**, 958–970 (2010)
4. Carmona, C.J., González, P., Del Jesus, M.J., Romero, C., Ventura, S.: Evolutionary algorithms for subgroup discovery applied to e-learning data. In: 2010 IEEE Education Engineering Conference, EDUCON 2010, pp. 983–990 (2010)
5. Carmona, C.J., González, P., del Jesús, M.J.: FuGePSD: fuzzy genetic programming-based algorithm for subgroup discovery. In: Proceedings of the 2015 Conference of the International Fuzzy Systems Association and the European Society for Fuzzy Logic and Technology, pp. 447–454. Atlantis Press (2015/2016)
6. Carmona, C.J., González, P., del Jesus, M.J., Herrera, F.: Overview on evolutionary subgroup discovery: analysis of the suitability and potential of the search performed by evolutionary algorithms. Wiley Interdiscip. Rev.: Data Min. Knowl. Discov. **4**(2), 87–103 (2014)

7. Carmona, C.J., González, P., del Jesus, M.J., Navío-Acosta, M., Jiménez-Trevino, L.: Evolutionary fuzzy rule extraction for subgroup discovery in a psychiatric emergency department. Soft Comput. **15**(12), 2435–2448 (2011)
8. De Jong, K.: Evolutionary computation: a unified approach. In: Proceedings of the 2016 on Genetic and Evolutionary Computation Conference Companion, GECCO 2016 Companion, pp. 185–199. Association for Computing Machinery, New York (2016)
9. Del Jesus, M.J., Gonzílez, P., Herrera, F.: Multiobjective genetic algorithm for extracting subgroup discovery fuzzy rules. In: Proceedings of the 2007 IEEE Symposium on Computational Intelligence in Multicriteria Decision Making, MCDM 2007, pp. 50–57 (2007)
10. Dheeru, D., Karra Taniskidou, E.: UCI machine learning repository (2017)
11. García, S., Fernández, A., Luengo, J., Herrera, F.: Advanced nonparametric tests for multiple comparisons in the design of experiments in computational intelligence and data mining: experimental analysis of power. Inf. Sci. **180**(10), 2044–2064 (2010). Special Issue on Intelligent Distributed Information Systems
12. García-Borroto, M., Loyola-González, O., Martínez-Trinidad, J.F., Carrasco-Ochoa, J.A.: Evaluation of quality measures for contrast patterns by using unseen objects. Expert Syst. Appl. **83**, 104–113 (2017)
13. García-Vico, A., Carmona, C., Martín, D., García-Borroto, M., del Jesus, M.: An overview of emerging pattern mining in supervised descriptive rule discovery: taxonomy, empirical study, trends, and prospects. WIREs Data Min. Knowl. Discov. **8**(1), e1231 (2018)
14. Bravo Ilisástigui, L., Martín Rodríguez D., García-Borroto M.: A new method to evaluate subgroup discovery algorithms. In: Nyström I., Hernández Heredia, Y., Milián Núñez, V. (eds.) CIARP 2019. LNCS, vol. 11896, pp. 417–426. Springer, Cham (2019). https://doi.org/10.1007/978-3-030-33904-3_39
15. Ilisástigui, L.B., Rodríguez, D.M., García-Borroto, M.: A new method for non-redundant subgroup discovery (in Spanish). Revista Cubana de Ciencias Informáticas **14**, 18–40 (2020)
16. Luna, J.M., Carmona, C.J., García-Vico, A., del Jesus, M.J., Ventura, S.: Subgroup discovery on multiple instance data. Int. J. Comput. Intell. Syst. **12**(2), 1602–1612 (2019)
17. Quinlan, J.R.: C4.5: Programs for Machine Learning. Morgan Kaufmann Publishers Inc., San Francisco (1993)
18. Quinlan, J.R.: Bagging, Boosting, and C4.5, vol. 1, pp. 725–730. AAAI Press (1996)
19. Sáez, C., Romero, N., Conejero, J.A., García-Gómez, J.M.: Potential limitations in COVID-19 machine learning due to data source variability: a case study in the nCov2019 dataset. J. Am. Med. Inform. Assoc. **28**(2), 360–364 (2020)
20. Talbi, E.G.: Metaheuristics: From Design to Implementation, vol. 74. Wiley, Hoboken (2009)
21. Valmarska, A., Cabrera-Diego, L.A., Linhares Pontes, E., Pollak, S.: Exploratory analysis of news sentiment using subgroup discovery. In: Proceedings of the 8th Workshop on Balto-Slavic Natural Language Processing, pp. 66–72. Association for Computational Linguistics, Kiyv (2021)

A Survey on the Methods to Determine the Sensitivity of Textual Documents: Solutions and Problems to Solve

Saturnino Job Morales Escobar[1]([✉]), José Ruiz Shulcloper[2], Cristina Juárez Landín[3], Osvaldo Andrés Pérez García[4], and José Sergio Ruiz Castilla[5]

[1] Centro Universitario UAEM Valle de México, Universidad Autónoma del Estado de México (UAEM), Atizapán de Zaragoza, Estado de México, México
[2] Head of the Research Group on Logical Combinatorial Pattern Recognition, Vice Rectory of Investigations, University of Informatics Sciences, Havana, Cuba
jshulcloper@uci.cu
[3] Centro Universitario UAEM Valle de Chalco, Universidad Autónoma del Estado de México (UAEM), Valle de Chalco Solidaridad, Estado de México, México
[4] Equipo de Investigaciones de Minería de Datos, CENATAV - DATYS, La Habana, Cuba
osvaldo.perez@cenatav.co.cu
[5] Centro Universitario UAEM Texcoco, Universidad Autónoma del Estado de México (UAEM), Texcoco, Estado de México, México
jsruizc@uaemex.mx

Abstract. The identification of sensitive information, whether personal or institutional, is a fundamental step when dealing with the problem of information leakage. This problem is one of the most pressing to which companies and research centers dedicate a considerable amount of material and intellectual resources, as a particular case, to the development of methods or the application of some already known ones to the identification of sensitive information. This increased the proposals with promising results, but without yet offering a totally satisfactory solution to the problem. Under these conditions, it is considered necessary to make a critical analysis of the existing methods and techniques and their future projections. In this paper, a review of the proposals for the determination of sensitivity in textual documents is presented and a taxonomy is introduced to better understand the approaches with which this problem has been approached in the context of information leakage. Starting from the critical analysis and the practical needs raised by experts in the areas of possible application, lines of research on this subject are outlined that include the development of methods for the automation of the classification of sensitive textual documents. Possible extensions that these studies may have in similar application areas are proposed based on other information carriers, such as the cases of images, recordings and other forms of information object, each of which entails levels of complexity that merit studies analogous to the one carried out in this work.

Keywords: Information leakage · Document sensitivity · Information protection systems · Information objects · Supervised classification

© Springer Nature Switzerland AG 2021
Y. Hernández Heredia et al. (Eds.): IWAIPR 2021, LNCS 13055, pp. 280–289, 2021.
https://doi.org/10.1007/978-3-030-89691-1_28

1 Introduction

One of the most valuable resources for any organization is undoubtedly the information contained in its information objects, a concept presented in [1], which correspond to data, documents, images, videos, audio, etc. These information objects, due to the very nature in which they are presented, processed, sent or stored, must be treated in different ways.

Obviously, each information object will possess, either intrinsically or because of the context where it is generated, or in combination of both, a different valuation. It is from this assessment that pertinent actions must be taken for its protection, both to preserve it and prevent its loss, and to prevent its dissemination or access by unauthorized instances.

Textual information objects or documents that can be considered sensitive are of particular interest, but what should be understood by a sensitive document? A document will be sensitive if it contains sensitive information and sensitive information "is that which cannot be made public" [2], or "the sensitivity of the information can be evaluated based on the impact that may result from its leakage" [3]. In the previous definitions it is assumed that once the sensitivity is determined it will not be modified, however, it is common for it to occur. Therefore, for the authors of this work, *the sensitivity of a document is an assessment of its importance, privacy and confidentiality at a given moment.*

Based on the above, given the sensitivity of some information objects, they should be restricted to use, however, due to practical needs, they are used in daily activities, automated or not, making them vulnerable to their theft or inappropriate use.

On the other hand, in the processes of generation, handling or storage of sensitive information objects, there is no certainty that all the organization's personnel follow the security policies and/or that, when using assurance applications, Users comply with the instructions to prevent and avoid unauthorized access. In the case of information leakage, many incidents have been reported in the specialized and dissemination literature. From, for example, the filtering of emails presented in [3], social engineering attacks [4], to the dissemination in the international press and on the internet site of information classified as secret from governments and organizations, negatively impacting them on a social level, economic and political.

According to what is expressed in [5–7], the leakage of information can be the result of deliberate actions or spontaneous errors, which can be increased by its internal or external transmission via email, instant messages, web page forms, among other means and even more, the risk increases when sensitive information objects are shared by customers, business partners, external employees, cloud storage, etc.

In [8] the authors define data leakage as the accidental or inadvertent distribution of sensitive data to an unauthorized entity. Sensitive data for an organization includes intellectual property, financial information, patient information, personal data, among others.

Under these conditions, with the intention of solving this problem, methods have been proposed to ensure data privacy [9], developed systems such as those aimed at Data Leakage Prevention (DLP), detection of data leakage [10], among others, which are designed to detect, monitor and protect confidential data and detect its misuse based on predefined rules. DLP systems are added to traditional security measures such as

Intrusion Detection Systems IDS, which work adequately for well-defined, structured and constant data, as expressed in [5].

Motivated by the relevance, timeliness and complexity of the problem of determining the sensitivity of information objects to face the problem of information leakage, this work presents a critical analysis of the methods for determining the sensitivity of a type of information objects: documents, and we introduce a taxonomy that will help to better understand the approaches with which this problem has been approached and to envision possible lines of work on the subject.

2   Systems for Data Leakage Prevention (DLP)

It is in DLP systems, where most work has been done on the problem of determining data sensitivity and the development of tools that detect and protect sensitive information continues, automatic methods capable of detecting sensitive data and determine the relevant mechanisms to protect them based on their sensitivity are required. Currently, the leakage of sensitive information objects is considered an emerging problem of threat to the security of organizations given that the number of incidents continues to grow.

DLP systems belong to the set of security technologies designed with the purpose of automatically preventing the leakage or loss of sensitive data in any of its three states: in use, in transit or at rest, in the event of problems related to threats [5].

The basic architecture of DLP systems is made up of three modules (see Fig. 1). The first detects whether a document is being sent, created or accessed (for printing, copying, editing, sending over the network, etc.) regardless of its content. The second module analyzes the document detected in the filter, reviews it and sends it to the third module for an assessment in accordance with the established policy. This last module responds by allowing or blocking, if necessary, actions on the information to be protected, issuing the corresponding alert.

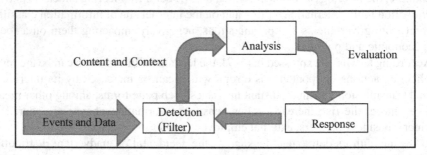

Fig. 1. Basic DLP architecture

The most important characteristics of each module are defined by the policy of the entity that applies the DLP solution to protect its information. For example, the filtering of documents will consider the Threat Model (representation of everything that affects the security of a system) and the Attack Vectors (possible entry gates that can be used for attack) identified entry, information that is domain dependent. The analysis of the detected documents is carried out at the content or context levels, both aspects are closely related to the owner of the information and the files. Finally, the responses that the system

Table 1. Taxonomy of methods used to determine the sensitivity of documents.

Methods and Description
Contextual Approach
Use of metadata associated with sensitive data, e.g., in data submission, source, destination, time, size, format, frequency, topic registration. The metadata can be used in processes or in transaction patterns and is based on defined policies. Examples of proposed algorithms to obtain characteristics that detect misdirected emails can be found in [12, 13] or algorithms based on file sharing between peers [15].
Content Approach
Regular expressions: Set of terms or characters used to form detection patterns, typically used for partial or exact detection in social security numbers, credit cards, personal and corporate records. Specific dictionary-based techniques can speed up and improve detection significantly [14,15].
Classifiers: They depend considerably on an adequate classification of the data. Typically, the owner of the data is responsible for determining the sensitivity of the data and whether it should be protected. Most solutions are based on tag and dirty word list. It is also assumed that to allow access to sensitive data or move it between different domains, all data must be well labeled with its corresponding classification [16-18, 25].
Information object fingerprinting: They are used especially in unstructured data to detect partial or exact coincidence. It is the most common technique used to detect information leakage, DLP with hashing functions such as MD5 and SHA1 can achieve up to 100% accuracy if the files are not altered [19]. Proposals have been made to overcome human or application oversights and maintain detection of sensitive data in transit, using a fuzzy marking algorithm discussed in [20].
N-grams: They are widely used in natural language processing, in machine learning and in information retrieval by weight of terms. It mainly depends on the frequency analysis of terms and n-grams in the documents. The first to use it on DLP were Hart and Johnson to classify business documents into sensitive and non-sensitive; They use Support Vector Machines (SVM) to classify three types of data: private business, public and non-business [15,19, 21].
Weighing of terms: The weighing of terms is a statistical method that indicates the importance of a term in a document, used in text classification and models of vector spaces where documents are treated as vectors and functions are used to determine the frequencies of the terms [22,23].
Machine learning: They use a characteristic space model, where a text sample is transformed into a representation by means of a vector. They use a parameterized function on the training set to make the classification decision. The training sample is divided into groups (clusters) and a classification model based on each of these groups is constructed based on the paragraphs of the document [3, 24].

must issue will be nuanced by the level of security that you want to obtain with the DLP application, which is expressed in the security policy defined for the system.

From the technical point of view, the complexities associated with the Detection and Response modules have been identified [11] and are closely linked to the technological support of the computer system on which the DLP is implemented. It is in the Analysis module where the theoretical problems related to determining the sensitivity of the information to be protected are located.

From the analysis of the DLP systems studied and published methods, the methods can be grouped for study according to the approach assumed by DLP. In Table 1, we present a taxonomy of the methods under these considerations. These methods, for the most part, have been developed with the aim of evaluating the sensitivity level of the information, regardless of when the event that links the document to a security threat occurs. They are oriented to process all the content, assuming that the classification will be Boolean: Yes or No.

3   Analysis of Methods for Determining the Sensitivity of Documents: Advantages and Limitations

Regarding the main context and content methods mentioned, an analysis is presented below with the intention of identifying the advantages and limitations of each of them. In the following section, on this basis, the problems that we consider are pending to be addressed are described.

3.1   Context Analysis

In the development of analysis methods based on the context [12, 15], features such as: file name, file owner and assigned permissions, network protocols, encrypted file formats, user role are used, web services used, web addresses, information associated with the USB type devices used (example: manufacturer, model number) or the desktop application used to edit, read or send the information. With this knowledge, the work of discovering possible channels of information leakage can be guided by applying anomaly detection.

Generally, in this anomaly-based approach, data on the behavior of legitimate users are collected, and then statistical tests are applied to compare it to observed behavior. Based on this comparison, it is determined whether it is legitimate or not. The main element of this approach is the generation of rules that can reduce the proportion of false alarms, both in the detection of new attacks and of already known attacks.

Among the advantages of the approach is the use of features in the description of the information object to determine its sensitivity. But what we consider its greatest disadvantage is that the sensitivity of the document is not determined, it focuses on characterizing the users.

3.2   Content Analysis

Sensitivity based on content is linked to the meaning that the data may have. Each piece of data can contain a large amount of information, however, it can be increased or decreased if it is related to other data. The authors of this work consider that the content of an information object must be closely related to the environment in which said object originates, for example, in a banking institution, a string formed by combinations of 8 characters, is not sensitive, but related to the strings "key" or "access" would change to sensitive data. The following sections present methods used to address this challenge.

Regular Expressions

This method is based on the Theory of Computation where regular expressions are used to represent regular languages, in general terms, the alphabet is identified to form strings, which are used to create detection patterns. These patterns are called regular expressions (RE) and are used by search engines in word processing to validate, generate, extract or replace data. They are typically used for partial or exact detection of social security numbers, credit cards, personal and corporate records. With dictionaries on specific fields, they can speed up and improve the detection of sensitive data significantly.

In [14], RE are used to detect the appearance of critical patterns in the payloads of network packets, for which RE comparisons must be made in real time, and even when Deterministic Finite Automaton (DFA) perform the operation in a linear order time, traversing at most 2N states of the automaton when processing a string of length N, memory requirements can make their use prohibitive despite the improvements presented.

However, applied it in context-based intrusion detection systems have obtained satisfactory results.

In addition to the disadvantage that they comment in [14, 24], on the complexity in space, from our point of view other important limitations are: the complexity of expressing the requirements by means of an RE, they can only be used for regular languages, the application to strings of the language and the difficulty to represent context.

Classifiers

This section reviews some proposals for the evaluation of the sensitivity of information objects, seen as a problem of supervised classification. In [15, 18] the authors emphasize the application of a particular tool and approach, the methods of statistical processing of natural language and the use of machine learning and classification algorithms as decision trees, k -Nearest neighbors, Naive Bayes, Support Vector Machine, text classification algorithms, neural networks, n-grams, among others [25–32].

In general terms, among the limitations observed are: they only consider two classes of documents with a high and low level of confidentiality, or what would be two levels of sensitivity for us; they close the possibility of other kinds of documents; they require classification lists configured manually by the user, which implies that mistakes can be made. On the other hand, most only allow traits of numerical types, they use vectors (vector spaces) for the representation of objects, which excludes qualitative traits and the impossibility of incorporating criteria for the comparison of objects in terms of qualitative traits.

Statistical Analysis

In [19] they present an analysis of information object fingerprint methods and identify two main limitations. The first, that the detection of the leak can be avoided by rewriting the sensitive content and the second, because generally all the content of the document is processed, including non-sensitive parts, false alarms are produced. To remedy the above, they propose an extension of the n-gram matching method called k-jump in ordered-n-grams. As a description of the main idea of the method, it starts with the n-grams method, in which n strings (or portions) of a long sequence of text strings are taken, each selection of n-strings is used to calculate its hash function. In the jump-k method in n-grams it is allowed to skip or ignore up to k-elements of the n-grams. This possibility, when considering relationships between strings that are not adjacent, say the authors, which allows adding contextual information that is not achieved with the n-gram method.

Statistical methods usually consider the most frequently appeared content, while the sensitive content may be ignored if only occupy a small part in the training set.

Finally, in the k-jump proposal in n-ordered-grams, the advantage is offered that you can jump k in the n-chains, but now they are arranged in alphabetical form.

One aspect that we question is the use of a k value which there is no justification for its use, on the other hand, it does not work with incomplete information and assumptions are made on the training matrices.

From our point of view, considering only two classes, sensitive or non-sensitive, limits its application to problems in which different levels of sensitivity are required and even use degrees of sensitivity.

By eliminating articles, prepositions, common phrases, important information about the context in which the information object is generated is eliminated. But the most significant of the disadvantages is that in the representation of the documents the semantics of the terms are being overlooked, which we consider to be a deficiency.

4   Problems to Be Solved

In principle, the problem of determining the sensitivity of documents can be posed as a supervised classification problem, where the description of the information objects is given in terms of features that involve both the context and the content.

Allow quantitative, qualitative features or a mixture of both in the description of objects and use comparison criteria between objects on this basis.

The order in which the word combinations are presented must be considered in determining the sensitivity of documents.

On the other hand, although the determination of the sensitivity of a document has been planted in terms of classes, for example, secret, confidential and unclassified, a flexible way to deal with this problem is by assigning a degree of sensitivity in various levels (documents, paragraphs, sentences, words).

The need to use dynamic training matrices has been detected, that is, they can increase or decrease the number of elements in each class and even that the classes are not balanced and that comparison criteria are considered in which subdescriptions of objects can be compared.

It is important that in the method the procedure for the content analysis of the information object can be made independent of the application context and that it considers that the sensitivity of an information object is temporary, which means that the sensitivity of an object today, it may change at another moment or even cease to be.

With all these considerations, the methods for determining the sensitivity of information objects must be totally flexible and easily incorporated into the classification of documents.

5 Conclusions

In this study, which may not be exhaustive in the analysis of the methods and alternative solutions to the problem of determining the sensitivity of information objects, specifically documents, it has been shown that these solutions partially solve the problem and that there is still a long way to go to offer a tool for the automatic determination of the degree of sensitivity of any information object, particularly documents with unstructured information.

The search must continue from different approaches, the application or development of methods that consider all the factors present in the problem in an integral way, and that undoubtedly increase the complexity of the problem.

A problem to be solved is to develop a tool that is independent of the context, in such a way that said context is generated from a training process in which the context and content are bear in mind. The training would be carried out with sensitive and non-sensitive documents determined by the specialist in the application area. Even the possibility must be allowed that these classes are not disjunct.

The problem of automating the classification of the sensitivity of information objects is broader and more complex than it appears and a detailed study of each of the possible information objects, such as images, recordings and other forms of information object, each of which entails levels of complexity that merit studies analogous to those we have begun on the automation of the classification of sensitive texts.

References

1. Morales, S., Pérez, O., Ruiz, J.: Métodos para la determinación de la sensibilidad de documentos: un estado del arte. Serie Gris, Centro de Aplicaciones de Tecnologías de Avanzada, vol. 036, Habana, Cuba (2016)
2. Berardi, G., Esuli, A., Macdonald, C., Ounis, L., Sebastiani, F.: Semi-automated text classification for sensitivity identification. In: Proceedings of the 24th ACM International on Conference on Information and Knowledge Management, pp. 1711–1714. ACM (2015)
3. Alzhrani, K., Ruddy, E., Chow, C., Boulty, T.: Automated U.S diplomatic cables security classification: topic model pruning vs. classification based on clusters. In: Proceedings of the 2017 IEEE International Symposium on Technologies for Homeland Security (HST), pp. 1–6 (2017)
4. Salahdine, F., Kaabouch, N.: Social engineering attacks: a survey. Future Internet 11(4), 1–17 (2019)
5. Alneyadi, S., Sithirasenan, E., Muthukkumarasamy, V.: A survey on data leakage prevention systems. J. Netw. Comput. Appl. 62, 137–152 (2016)
6. Wynne, N., Reed, B.: Magic quadrant for enterprise data loss prevention. Gartner Group Research Note (2016)
7. Ahmad, N.: Do data almost always eventually leak?: Computer 54(2), 70–74 (2021)
8. Shabtai, A., Yuval, E., Lior, R.: A Survey of Data Leakage Detection and Prevention Solutions. Springer, Boston (2012). https://doi.org/10.1007/978-1-4614-2053-8

9. Jena, M.D., Singhar, S.S., Mohanta, B.K., Ramasubbareddy, S.: Ensuring data privacy using machine learning for responsible data science. In: Satapathy, S.C., Zhang, Y.-D., Bhateja, V., Majhi, R. (eds.) Intelligent Data Engineering and Analytics. AISC, vol. 1177, pp. 507–514. Springer, Singapore (2021). https://doi.org/10.1007/978-981-15-5679-1_49

10. Ávila, R., Khoury, R., Khoury, R., Petrillo, F.: Use of security logs for data leak detection: a systematic literature review. Secur. Commun. Netw. **2021**, 1–29 (2021)

11. Wadkar, H., Mishra, A., Dixit, A.: Prevention of information leakages in a web browser by monitoring system calls. In: Proceedings of the 2014 IEEE International Advance Computing Conference (IACC), pp. 199–204 (2014)

12. Liu, T., Pu, Y., Shi, J., Li, Q., Chen, X.: Towards misdirected email detection for preventing information leakage. In: Proceedings of the 2014 IEEE Symposium on Computers and Communication (ISCC), pp. 1–6 (2014)

13. Zilberman, P., Dolev, S., Katz, G., Elovici, Y., Shabtai, A.: Analyzing group communication for preventing data leakage via email. In: Proceedings of 2011 IEEE International Conference on Intelligence and Security Informatics, pp. 37–41 (2011)

14. Becchi, M., Crowley, P.: An improved algorithm to accelerate regular expression evaluation. In: Proceedings of the 2007 ACM/IEEE Symposium on Architecture for Networking and Communications Systems, pp. 145–154 (2007)

15. Sokolova, M., et al.: Personal health information leak prevention in heterogeneous texts. In: Proceedings of the Workshop on Adaptation of Language Resources and Technology to New Domains, pp. 58–69 (2009)

16. Chen, K., Liu, L.: Privacy preserving data classification with rotation perturbation. In: Fifth IEEE International Conference on Data Mining (ICDM 2005), pp. 1–4 (2005)

17. Aggarwal, C.C., Yu, P.S.: A general survey of privacy-preserving data mining models and algorithms. In: Aggarwal, C.C., Yu, P.S. (eds.) Privacy-Preserving Data Mining. ADBS, vol. 34, pp. 11–51. Springer, Boston (2008). https://doi.org/10.1007/978-0-387-70992-5_2

18. Brown, J.D., Charlebois, D.: Security classification using automated learning (SCALE): optimizing statistical natural language processing techniques to assign security labels to unstructured text. Defense Research and Development Canada, Ottawa (Ontario) (2010)

19. Shapira, Y., Shapira, B., Shabtai, A.: Content-based data leakage detection using extended fingerprinting. arXiv preprint arXiv:1302.2028 (2013)

20. Vijayalakshmi, V., Rohini, T., Sujatha, S., Ishali, A.: Survey on detecting leakage of sensitive data. In: World Conference on Futuristic Trends in Research and Innovation for Social Welfare (Startup Conclave), pp. 1–3. IEEE (2016)

21. Hart, M., Manadhata, P., Johnson, R.: Text classification for data loss prevention. In: Fischer-Hübner, S., Hopper, N. (eds.) PETS 2011. LNCS, vol. 6794, pp. 18–37. Springer, Heidelberg (2011). https://doi.org/10.1007/978-3-642-22263-4_2

22. Salton, G., Wong, A., Yang, C.S.: A vector space model for automatic indexing. Commun. ACM **18**, 613–620 (1975)

23. Carvalho, V.R., Balasubramanyan, R., Cohen, W.W.: Information leaks and suggestions: a case study using Mozilla thunderbird. In: CEAS 2009 Sixth Conference on Email and Anti-Spam (2009)

24. Nikitinsky, N., Sokolova, T., Engelstad Ehotskaya, E.: DLP technologies: challenges and future directions. In: The International Conference on Cyber-Crime Investigation and Cyber Security (ICCICS 2014), pp. 31–36 (2014)

25. Engelstad, P., Hammer, H., Yazidi, A., Bai, A.: Advanced classification lists (dirty word lists) for automatic security classification. In: Cyber-Enabled Distributed Computing and Knowledge Discovery, pp. 44–53. IEEE (2015)

26. Kowsari, K., Jafari, M., Heidarysafa, M., Mendu, S., Barnes, L., Brown, D.: Text classification algorithms: a survey. Information **10**(4), 150 (2019)

27. Zorarpacı, E., Özel, S.A.: Privacy preserving classification over differentially private data. Wiley Interdiscip. Rev.: Data Min. Knowl. Discov. **11**(3), e1399 (2021)
28. Guo, Y., Liu, J., Tang, W., Huang, C.: Exsense: Extract sensitive information from unstructured data. Comput. Secur. **102**, 102156 (2021)
29. Patil, D., Lokare, R., Patil, S.: Private data classification using deep learning. In: Proceedings of the 3rd International Conference on Advances in Science & Technology (ICAST) (2020)
30. Trieu, L.Q., Tran, T.N., Tran, M.K., Tran, M.T.: Document sensitivity classification for data leakage prevention with twitter-based document embedding and query expansion. In: 2017 13th International Conference on Computational Intelligence and Security (CIS), pp. 537–542. IEEE (2017)
31. Hassan, F., Sánchez, D., Soria-Comas, J., Domingo-Ferrer, J.: Automatic anonymization of textual documents: detecting sensitive information via word embeddings. In: 2019 18th IEEE International Conference on Trust, Security and Privacy in Computing and Communications/13th IEEE International Conference on Big Data Science and Engineering (TrustCom/BigDataSE), pp. 358–365. IEEE (2019)
32. Lu, Y., Huang, X., Li, D., Zhang, Y.: Collaborative graph-based mechanism for distributed big data leakage prevention. In: 2018 IEEE Global Communications Conference GLOBECOM, pp. 1–7. IEEE(2018)

Automatic Classification of Diabetic Foot Ulcers Using Computer Vision Techniques

José Daniel López-Cabrera$^{(\boxtimes)}$, Yusely Ruiz-Gonzalez , Roberto Díaz-Amador ,
and Alberto Taboada-Crispi

Universidad Central "Marta Abreu" de Las Villas, Santa Clara, Cuba
josedaniellc@uclv.cu

Abstract. Diabetic foot ulcers are one of the common complications that diabetic patients present. Poorly treated lesions can lead to the amputation of the limbs and even cause death. Therefore, the identification and follow-up of the lesions are of vital importance to apply a timely treatment. In this study, we performed the automatic classification of images of diabetic foot ulcers using computer vision techniques. We evaluated different approaches to traditional computer vision techniques and feature extraction from a convolution neural network. An SVM classifier using features extracted by the CNN Densenet201 obtained the best results. The results achieved here outperformed those reported in the literature for similar problems in terms of the $F1_{score}$ measure. That shows that the proposed alternative of combining a pre-trained CNN model as a feature extraction method and then using automatic classifiers is satisfactory in this task.

Keywords: Computer vision · Pattern recognition · Diabetic foot ulcers

1 Introduction

Diabetes is a chronic disease that currently affects more than 425 million people worldwide, and this number could increase considerably in the next 25 years [1]. The ailment is due to problems in the pancreas to synthesize the necessary insulin that the body needs, which causes a large number of complications for patients. One of the most severe complications is diabetic foot ulcer (DFU) [2]. Cellular dysfunction and biochemical imbalance characterize the DFU, which manifests with delayed healing. That can lead to infection and ischemia, followed by limb amputation or even death, in severe cases.

Efforts are currently underway to improve patient care and reduce the strain on healthcare systems. For this purpose, early detection of DFUs and regular follow-up is a vital task. One of the strategies for this purpose uses computer vision techniques. Recent research has focused on the development of detection algorithms that could be used as part of a mobile application to empower patients themselves or a caregiver in this regard [3]. These techniques have laid the groundwork for creating the first sets of DFU patient images for computer vision tasks. The crucial efforts have been in lesion identification and lesion segmentation, especially from the DFU Challenge 2020 [4, 5].

© Springer Nature Switzerland AG 2021
Y. Hernández Heredia et al. (Eds.): IWAIPR 2021, LNCS 13055, pp. 290–299, 2021.
https://doi.org/10.1007/978-3-030-89691-1_29

On the other hand, the automatic classification of these images has been less addressed, which is why the Diabetic Foot Ulcers Grand Challenge 2021 (DFUC202)[1] has been launched. That is to say, only a few works have been reported that classify DFU lesions. For example, in the work of [6], a new convolutional neural network (CNN) architecture called DFUnet is proposed to address the problem of binary classification of lesions into normal and abnormal. Other pre-trained CNNs such as LeNet, AlexNet, and GoogleNet were used in the same task. Furthermore, some variants of traditional computer vision techniques as features based on Local Binay Pattern (LBP), Histogram of Gradient (HOG), and the RGB, HSV, and LUV color spaces were also compared. On the other hand, the work of [7] was the first attempt to classify ischemia and infection, but in disjoint tasks. That is, two binary automatic classification tasks are evaluated. For this purpose, a new descriptor based on the color of the images was used after applying segmentation using SLIC Superpixel. Additionally, color-based features using RGB, CIELAB spaces, in addition to texture-based features such as LBP and HOG were used. Different CNN network architectures such as InceptionV3, ResnNet50, and InceptionResNetV2 were also evaluated. The best results were achieved for an ensemble of CNN. Recently in [8], for the first time, a classification task as a multiclass problem was performed. This problem is addressed only using the deep learning approach. The CNNs VGG16, ResNet101, InceptionV3, DenseNet121 and EfficientNet were evaluated. The best results were achieved for the last two aforementioned networks using data augmentation techniques. A micro-Average F1 of 0.64, an accuracy of 0.57, and a sensitivity of 0.58 were reported.

To our knowledge, this is the first study that uses the combination of traditional computer vision techniques and CNN to classify this type of image in a multiclass problem. On small image sets, traditional techniques have shown better results in image classification than using deep learning [9].

This paper aims to evaluate three feature extraction strategies for automatic classification on four classes of DFU images. For this purpose, the role played separately by the different strategies in the classification task was analyzed. It was shown that better classification rates are obtained from feature extraction based on a pre-trained CNN. We also showed that the variant involving the CNN obtained similar results in by class classification. These results suggest that the features extracted by DenseNet201 possess a high predictive value for this task. The results achieved outperformed those reported in the literature for similar problems.

2 Materials and Methods

2.1 Image Sets Used

The images used in this research are photographs collected from Lancashire Teaching Hospitals, United Kingdom, and belong to patients with DFU. Three cameras were used to capture the images of the feet, Kodak DX4530, Nikon D3300, and Nikon COOLPIX P100. Images were acquired with close-ups of the entire foot at a distance of about 30–40 cm with the orientation parallel to the plane of an ulcer. The use of flash as the main

---

[1] https://dfu-challenge.github.io/index.html.

light source was avoided and, instead, suitable room lights were used to obtain uniform colors in the image. A more detailed description of the image set appears in [8].

From the original image, the regions of interest (ROIs) that correspond to the lesions found are extracted. In the ROI extraction process itself, a natural data augmentation of the image set is performed. This process consisted of cropping the images to different sizes as shown in Fig. 1. Finally, all images were resized to $224 \times 224 \times 3$ pixels. It is important to note that those ROIs smaller than $224 \times 224 \times 3$, when resized, suffer the effect of low-pass filtering, and thus appear to be out of focus or blurred. This set of images belongs to DFUC2021. It is important to note also that, in this research, only a portion of the training set provided for DFUC2021 will be used, since so far this set is the only one that contains the class to which each image belongs. That is, the validation and test set have not yet been released. Table 1 shows the contents of the image set used in this work, which randomly splits the images per class into approximately 80% for training and 20% for testing.

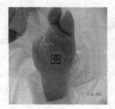

Fig. 1. The process of obtaining several replicas of the same lesion from the original image is called here natural data augmentation.

Table 1. Description of the image sets per-class used in training and testing, using the hold out validation strategy for an automatic classification task.

	Both	Infection	Ischemia	None
Training set	267	1036	98	792
Testing set	69	262	29	201

2.2 Image Set Curation

As reported by the owners of the set of images [8], the identifiers of the images were preserved, to perform the division of the set exclusively in training or testing. This ensures that there is no overlap between the sets. However, a thorough analysis carried out in this research revealed that there are images (due to the natural data augmentation) included in different sets.

An even more pernicious problem was also observed. Samples obtained from a same original foot appear labeled in different classes. Figure 2 illustrates some of the inconsistencies found so far. The name of the image and the class to which it belongs are depicted in the figure. Therefore, we discarded those conflicting images in this work.

To identify these errors, a color-based image retrieval search was performed, as will be explained in the section: "Color-based features". However, this method could not be fully automated to determine all similar images, which required visual analysis. This procedure allowed separating the samples obtained from a same original image, to use them in an automatic classification task without overlapping between the training and the test groups.

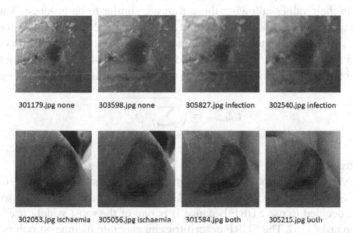

| 301179.jpg none | 303598.jpg none | 305827.jpg infection | 302540.jpg infection |

| 302053.jpg ischaemia | 305056.jpg ischaemia | 301584.jpg both | 305215.jpg both |

Fig. 2. Images obtained from a same original foot are wrongly identified in different classes in the DFUC2021 dataset.

2.3 Feature Extraction Strategies

In this study, we used three different strategies for feature extraction on images. The first two approaches are based on handcrafted features and the third one is based on a convolutional neural network. Figure 3 represents the pattern recognition process used in this research to obtain the classification of the images.

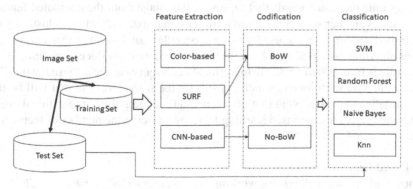

Fig. 3. General pattern recognition scheme.

Color-Based Features

Color is one of the distinguishing features of the images under study. In fact, in [5, 6], variants of conversion between color spaces have been used as features to perform classification. In this study, we evaluate a color-based feature extraction, which has not been studied in problems like this one. Firstly, we convert from the RGB color space to CIELAB. This new color space allows visual differences between colors to be quantified more easily. Thus, visually similar colors in the CIELAB color space will have smaller differences in their values, allowing those that are similar to be grouped. The average value per channel of the 8×8 nonoverlapping blocks in the $224 \times 224 \times 3$ image is then determined, which returns a tensor of dimensions $28 \times 28 \times 3$. This tensor is converted to a 784×3 matrix. Finally, it is normalized by row using the $L2_{norm}$, using the Eq. 1. The result obtained will be used to describe the color information of the image.

$$L2_{norm} = \sqrt{\sum\nolimits_{i=1}^{3} x_i^2} \tag{1}$$

Local Feature Detector

There are a variety of methods for local feature extraction such as FAST [10], BRISK [11], Harris-Stephens [12], KAZE [13], SURF [14] among others. However, as an initial study it was decided to use SURF because it is one of the most widely used in image classification tasks [15]. The SURF descriptor can generate its interest points on which it will subsequently extract features. However, experimenting with this strategy did not yield good results. Therefore, a dense sampling was performed to determine the points to be used in the calculation of the descriptor. To obtain a description at different scales of the image, square blocks of 32×32, 64×64, 96×96, and 128×128 pixels were used. The variant of 64 features per point of interest is used.

Bag of Words

The aforementioned descriptors, both color-based and SURF local feature detector, have high dimensionality. One of the techniques to address this problem that has been successful in increasing performance rates in computer vision tasks is Bag of Word (BoW) [16], which has its origins in text corpus analysis. In the case of computer vision, the idea is to determine the visual words that represent the image from the computed features. These features are then projected into an n-dimensional space, after that a clustering task is performed. In our case, we used a visual vocabulary of 1000. For this purpose, the k-means algorithm was used with $k = 1000$. This value was set after experimenting with various values from 500 to 1500. Histograms of occurrences of these "visual words" are then generated for each image, which constitutes the feature vectors that will be used in the classification stage. Note that, this technique reduces the computational cost of training classifiers for supervised learning tasks by reducing the number of features per image.

CNN-Based Features

The most widely used methods for working with images today are based on CNN [17]. These networks perform the feature extraction and classification stage by themselves.

However, they require millions of images to achieve satisfactory training, as well as computational resources such as specialized GPU and TPU cards. Note that these algorithms have to adjust millions of parameters in their training phase, which sometimes leads to the phenomenon of overfitting. They begin to worry the scientific community about the validity of their results [18].

In clinical settings, these quantities of images are generally not available. One technique to deal with this problem is transfer learning [19]. This technique consists of using pre-trained networks and modifying the classification stage to adjust it to the new problem to be solved, using the knowledge acquired by the network on a set of a large number of images. More recently, the potential of these pre-trained networks as feature extraction methods has been studied [9]. This new strategy consists of using the outputs of the CNN layers obtained for each image as a feature vector, which is used by other conventional classifiers. This variant is the one used in this research. For that, one of the best performing networks at present, called DenseNet201 [20], was used. This network contains 201 convolution layers, 98 routing layers, one avg pooling layer, 4 maxpooling, and one Softmax. In our case, the features are extracted from the layer called "avg_pool", which returns a vector of 1920 features. The features obtained by belonging to one of the final layers of the network contain information of a higher level of abstraction with high predictive value, which will be evaluated in the classification task.

2.4   Classification Algorithms and Performance Measures

In the final stage of this study, automatic classification of images is performed. For this purpose, four automatic classification algorithms were evaluated. These were SVM, Knn, Random Forest, and Naïve Bayes, which have shown very good performance in the scientific literature [21, 22].

The set of images used in this research, both for training and testing, is unbalanced. Therefore, to determine the effectiveness of the classifiers, it is necessary to use performance measures that take this problem into account and could perform a per-class analysis. To compare our results with those obtained in [7], we decided to estimate some of the same measures used in that study. These were $F1_{score}$ per class, as well as the average of the $F1_{scores}$, called $macroF1_{score}$. In addition, $macroAcc$ is used as a global metric, calculated as the average of true positive ratio (TPR) or Recall per class. Equations 2, 3, 4, 5 and 6 shows how to calculate these measures, with TP being the true positives, FP, the false positives, and FN, the false negatives, obtained from the confusion matrix, and C is the number of classes (4 in this study).

$$Precision = \frac{TP}{TP + FP} \tag{2}$$

$$Recall = \frac{TP}{TP + FN} \tag{3}$$

$$F1_{score} = \frac{2}{\frac{1}{Precision} + \frac{1}{Recall}} = \frac{2 * (Precision * Recall)}{Precision + Recall} \tag{4}$$

$$macroF1_{score} = \frac{1}{c} \sum_{i=1}^{c} F1_{score_i} \tag{5}$$

$$macroAcc = \frac{1}{c} \sum_{i=1}^{c} Recall_i \tag{6}$$

3 Results and Discussion

Tables 2, 3, and 4 show the performance indices achieved using the four classifiers for each of the feature extraction variants. The $F1_{score}$ value obtained is shown for each class, which allows us to evaluate the performance of the classifiers by class.

In the case of the color-based feature extraction strategy, the best values are reported for the SVM classifier (see Table 2). A similar performance was reported for the Knn classifier with values similar to the SVM. It can be seen that the most difficult classes to separate based on color were "both" and "none". This was because the "none" class shares many of the colors with the infection class, as well as, the "both" class with the "infection" class.

Table 2. Performance indices achieved using the color-based features.

	Per class $F1_{score}$				$macroF1_{score}$	$macroAcc$
	Both	Infection	Ischemia	None		
SVM	**0.370**	0.623	**0.679**	0.465	**0.534**	**0.519**
Random forest	0.250	**0.652**	0.421	**0.517**	0.460	0.424
Naïve Bayes	0.234	0.336	0.234	0.512	0.329	0.433
Knn	0.282	0.638	0.613	0.465	0.510	0.499

On the other hand, for the results using SURF local features, it can be seen that the best results are obtained for the Knn and SVM classifiers. In this case, the classes "ischemia" and "both" were difficult to separate (see Table 3). This table shows that for the Random Forest classifier, the $F1_{score}$ results for the "infection" class, as well as the $macroF1_{score}$, are undefined. This was because the classifier did not find any true positives (TP) for the class "ischemia". That is, all images for this class were misclassified.

Table 3. Performance indices achieved using the SURF local features.

	Per class $F1_{score}$				$macroF1_{score}$	$macroAcc$
	Both	Infection	Ischemia	None		
SVM	0.183	0.571	0.217	0.455	0.357	0.348
Random forest	0.000	**0.625**	–	0.353	–	0.281
Naïve Bayes	**0.265**	0.422	0.116	0.327	0.2825	0.372
Knn	0.190	0.543	**0.244**	**0.484**	**0.365**	**0.351**

In the case of the features extracted with CNN, the best results are reported for the SVM and Naïve Bayes classifiers (see Table 4). The Random Forest classifier again misclassified all images in the "ischemia" class, which undefined the $F1_{score}$ measure. From this variant, there is a balance in the results reported for each class. This was the approach that obtained the best results. From the point of view of global measures, the SVM classifier achieved the highest $macroF1_{score}$ and $macroAcc$ scores with values of 0.681 and 0.687.

Table 4. Performance indices achieved using CNN as features extractor.

	Per class $F1_{score}$				$macroF1_{score}$	$macroAcc$
	Both	Infection	Ischemia	None		
SVM	**0.693**	**0.698**	**0.702**	**0.630**	**0.681**	**0.687**
Random forest	0.517	0.695	–	0.538	–	0.435
Naïve Bayes	0.615	0.610	0.689	0.610	0.631	0.683
Knn	0.528	0.648	0.468	0.599	0.560	0.545

Taking as a reference the SVM classifier, which presented good performance indices for the three studied feature extraction strategies, Fig. 4 shows the value of the $F1_{score}$ measure per class for all the studied feature extraction variants as well as a global measure $macro\ F1score$. It also shows the value obtained in the work of Yap et al. [8]. Note also that the variant proposed in this research obtained a $macro\ F1_{score}$ 0.126 higher than the one proposed by Yap et al. (0.681 vs. 0.555).

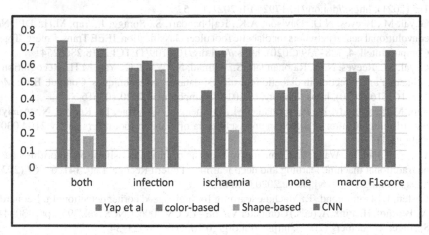

Fig. 4. Comparison of the three feature extraction strategies and the variant reported in the literature using $F1_{score}$.

4 Conclusions

In this study, three feature extraction alternatives for automatic DFU image classification were evaluated. It was observed that the best performing variant was found for the pre-trained CNN DenseNet201. On the other hand, the best performing classifier was SVM. The results achieved exceed those reported in the scientific literature. Despite the difficulty of classifying between the "infection" and "both" classes, our method showed balance in classification for all classes. These results suggest that our approach of using a pre-trained CNN as a feature extraction method and an SVM classifier is suitable to address this problem.

Acknowledgment. We gratefully acknowledge the support of DFU2021 Organizers who provided access to the data base resources.

References

1. Cho, N.H., et al.: IDF diabetes atlas: global estimates of diabetes prevalence for 2017 and projections for 2045. Diab. Res. Clin. Pract. **138**, 271–281 (2018). https://doi.org/10.1016/j.diabres.2018.02.023
2. Armstrong, D.G., Boulton, A.J.M., Bus, S.A.: Diabetic foot ulcers and their recurrence. N. Engl. J. Med. **376**, 2367–2375 (2017). https://doi.org/10.1056/NEJMra1615439
3. Goyal, M., Reeves, N.D., Rajbhandari, S., Yap, M.H.: Robust methods for real-time diabetic foot ulcer detection and localization on mobile devices. IEEE J. Biomed. Health Inform. **23**, 1730–1741 (2019). https://doi.org/10.1109/JBHI.2018.2868656
4. Yap, M.H., et al.: Deep learning in diabetic foot ulcers detection: a comprehensive evaluation. arXiv:2010.03341 [cs] (2020)
5. Cassidy, B., et al.: DFUC2020: analysis towards diabetic foot ulcer detection. Eur. Endocrinol. **1**, 5 (2021). https://doi.org/10.17925/EE.2021.1.1.5
6. Goyal, M., Reeves, N.D., Davison, A.K., Rajbhandari, S., Spragg, J., Yap, M.H.: DFUNet: convolutional neural networks for diabetic foot ulcer classification. IEEE Trans. Emerg. Topics Comput. Intell. **4**, 728–739 (2020). https://doi.org/10.1109/TETCI.2018.2866254
7. Goyal, M., Reeves, N.D., Rajbhandari, S., Ahmad, N., Wang, C., Yap, M.H.: Recognition of ischaemia and infection in diabetic foot ulcers: dataset and techniques. Comput. Biol. Med. **117**, 103616 (2020). https://doi.org/10.1016/j.compbiomed.2020.103616
8. Yap, M.H., Cassidy, B., Pappachan, J.M., O'Shea, C., Gillespie, D., Reeves, N.: Analysis towards classification of infection and ischaemia of diabetic foot ulcers. arXiv:2104.03068 [cs] (2021)
9. Wang, P., Fan, E., Wang, P.: Comparative analysis of image classification algorithms based on traditional machine learning and deep learning. Pattern Recogn. Lett. **141**, 61–67 (2021). https://doi.org/10.1016/j.patrec.2020.07.042
10. Rosten, E., Drummond, T.: Machine learning for high-speed corner detection. In: Leonardis, A., Bischof, H., Pinz, A. (eds.) Computer Vision – ECCV 2006. LNCS, vol. 3951, pp. 430–443. Springer, Heidelberg (2006). https://doi.org/10.1007/11744023_34
11. Leutenegger, S., Chli, M., Siegwart, R.Y.: BRISK: binary robust invariant scalable keypoints. In: 2011 International Conference on Computer Vision, pp. 2548–2555 (2011). https://doi.org/10.1109/ICCV.2011.6126542
12. Harris, C.G., Stephens, M.: A combined corner and edge detector. In: Proceedings of the 4th Alvey Vision Conference, pp. 147–152 (1988). https://doi.org/10.5244/C.2.23

13. Alcantarilla, P.F., Bartoli, A., Davison, A.J.: KAZE features. In: Fitzgibbon, A., Lazebnik, S., Perona, P., Sato, Y., Schmid, C. (eds.) Computer Vision – ECCV 2012. LNCS, vol. 7577, pp. 214–227. Springer, Heidelberg (2012). https://doi.org/10.1007/978-3-642-33783-3_16

14. Bay, H., Tuytelaars, T., Van Gool, L.: SURF: speeded up robust features. In: Leonardis, A., Bischof, H., Pinz, A. (eds.) Computer Vision – ECCV 2006. LNCS, vol. 3951, pp. 404–417. Springer, Heidelberg (2006). https://doi.org/10.1007/11744023_32

15. Arora, G., Dubey, A.K., Jaffery, Z.A., Rocha, A.: Bag of feature and support vector machine based early diagnosis of skin cancer. Neural Comput. Appl. (2020). https://doi.org/10.1007/s00521-020-05212-y

16. Fei-Fei, L., Fergus, R., Perona, P.: One-shot learning of object categories. IEEE Trans. Pattern Anal. Mach. Intell. **28**, 594–611 (2006). https://doi.org/10.1109/TPAMI.2006.79

17. López-Cabrera, J.D., Rodríguez, L.A.L., Pérez-Díaz, M.: Classification of breast cancer from digital mammography using deep learning. Intel. Artif. **23**, 56–66 (2020)

18. Geirhos, R., et al.: Shortcut learning in deep neural networks. Nat. Mach. Intell. **2**, 665–673 (2020). https://doi.org/10.1038/s42256-020-00257-z

19. Bengio, Y.: Deep learning of representations for unsupervised and transfer learning. In: Proceedings of ICML Workshop on Unsupervised and Transfer Learning, pp. 17–36 (2012)

20. Huang, G., Liu, Z., Pleiss, G., Van Der Maaten, L., Weinberger, K.: Convolutional networks with dense connectivity. IEEE Trans. Pattern Anal. Mach. Intell. 1–1 (2019). https://doi.org/10.1109/TPAMI.2019.2918284

21. López-Cabrera, J.D., Pereira-Toledo, A.: Análisis del comportamiento del algoritmo SVM para diferentes kernel en ambientes controlados. HOLOS **5**, 101–115 (2018)

22. Pereira-Toledo, A., López-Cabrera, J.D., Quintero-Domínguez, L.A.: Estudio experimental para la comparación del desempeño de Naïve Bayes con otros clasificadores bayesianos. Rev. Cuba. Cienc. Inform. **11**, 67–84 (2017)

Biometrics, Image, and Video Analysis

Image Segmentation Applied to Line Separation and Determination of GPN2 Protein Overexpression for Its Detection in Polyacrylamide Gels

Jorge Juárez[1] , María del Rayo Graciela Guevara-Villa[2] ,
Anabel Sánchez-Sánchez[1(✉)] , Raquel Díaz-Hernández[1] ,
and Leopoldo Altamirano-Robles[1]

[1] Instituto Nacional de Astrofísica, Óptica y Electrónica, Puebla 72840, México
{jjlucero,anabel,raqueld,robles}@inaoep.mx
[2] Universidad Politécnica de Puebla, San Mateo Cuanalá 72640, México
Maria.guevara495@uppuebla.edu.mx

Abstract. A new method was developed that allows analyzing the intensity profile of the histogram of an image of polyacrylamide gels within a binary mask of 1×400 pixels traversing the 600 pixels of a polyacrylamide gel image to detect the lanes that correspond to the different experiments present in the gel and, a mask of 1×50 pixels in the line desired to find the band related to specific proteins. The method also makes it possible to identify which lane has the highest and lowest overexpression of the studied protein. The proposed line detection method allows finding the position of the bands within a lane and, based on the loading buffer and interpolation methods the molecular weight of the protein of biological interest studied can be predicted. The article shows the results of the proposed method for the GPN2 protein.

Keywords: Protein image analysis · SDS-PAGE gels · Otsu segmentation

1 Introduction

The electrophoresis technique is used to separate proteins applying electrical charges to the samples causing their separations by moving due to the electrical force. They are distributed taking account their molecular weight and size. Each gel (see Fig. 1) has a two-dimensional arrangement of columns and rows, the first represent lanes (columns line or lanes) that belong to different experiments and, second (rows) represent the bands that correspond to different proteins present in each experiment [1, 2].

The gels are used as a detection method to find gene fragments [3, 4], specific proteins, or as a method of disease diagnosis [5–7].

The identification of genes are easier than proteins in an electrophoresis gel because they only present one band per lane while the proteins gel contains many bands in each lane, causing specialists to make some mistakes when looking for a specific protein

Y. Hernández Heredia et al. (Eds.): IWAIPR 2021, LNCS 13055, pp. 303–315, 2021.
https://doi.org/10.1007/978-3-030-89691-1_30

inside the gel, increasing the data analysis time and interpreting the gel subjectively or incorrectly due to different internal or external factors that include fatigue, sensitive vision or optical illusions [7–11].

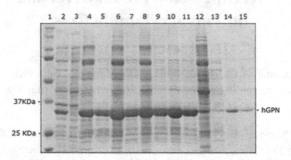

Fig. 1. Terminology used in SDS-PAGE gels. The vertical lanes (columns) represent different samples (experiments), numbered from 1 to 15, and the horizontal spots are the bands that represent different proteins per sample (such as hGPN located between 25 and 37 KDa).

The investigations carried out in the analysis of images of DNA or proteins gels have four processes in common: First, make corrections to eliminate background noise. Second, detect lines within the gel. Third, detect bands by looking for coincidences to quantify them. Fourth, group the bands of interest [2]. We will describe each step below.

For the elimination of background noise in protein gels, different processes have been applied, such as top-hat transforms, Gaussian low-pass filters, normalization, and filters in the image, changes in intensity, contourlet transforms, filters in each row of the image. To estimate the noise near to bands have been applied a second or median filters and analyze the histogram; adaptive median filters making corrections applying the geometrical constraint Rolling ball method; linear filters and nonlinear Gaussians combined with contourlet and wavelet transforms are used either. For DNA gels, Fourier analysis and fuzzy-c-means have been used to separate nucleotides, mixed with matrix convolution, cutting of regions of interest applying smoothing and averaging the intensity value of three consecutive pixels, contrast changes, and intensities methods. For 2D gels, different filters are used with greater emphasis on improving the quality of the device used to achieve images with the least possible noise [1, 2, 4, 7–9, 11–25].

For the detection of lanes and bands the following methodologies have been applied: Choosing a pair of high contrast pixels in relation to neighboring local pixels to use segmentation methods for edge detection with Bayesian approximations and use thresholding with segmentation of Otsu; manual isolation of regions with bands of interest, calculation of standard deviation taking a threshold value based on the intensity level of pixels that belong to each column of each experiment; normalization of intensity value of pixels comparing with a reference gel; use of Gaussian functions to determine the position of lanes; use of lane templates together with the average value of intensities; application of Sobel filters to calculate local maximums that allow detecting the space between lanes; measurement of changes in brightness; count the number of pixels in lanes and measure their distance by making variations in gray levels; calculation of density of spectrum and its use to analyze the average width of lanes to choose regions of the image; analysis of profile peaks of areas generated by bands and clustering by the K-means technique; delimitation of bands with ellipses avoiding intersection between them and, finally the choice of the bands manually is done, enclosing them in some region of interest [1, 2, 7–9, 11–26].

Current software developed to analyze images of DNA or proteins gels use filter bands and eliminate background noise (Scanalytics, GelcomparII, Gel-Pro Analyzer, TotalLab, PDQuest, Proteomweaver, Dcyder 2D, imageMAster, Melanie, BioNumerics, Redfin, Gel IQ, Z3, Delta2D Flicker) present the disadvantage of being semi-automatic, they require an operator to choose the columns or lanes manually to study and to select the bands of interest, in addition to the fact that the user needs to manipulate sensitivity to threshold changes and control the intensity, some are too complicated for the analyst and not all allow grouping of common elements [1, 13].

This paper is focused in the image analysis of polyacrylamide gel with over expression of GTPase GPN2 human protein. The GPN2 protein have a biomedical interest because this protein family over expression is related with invasives ductal and luminal breast cancer, some researchers are suggested to look over expression of GTPases like bio markers to detect this cancer type [27–30].

2 Methodology

The proposed methodology for this work is presented below:

2.1 Obtaining Gels

To obtain gels, 600 ml of the bacterium Escherichia coli (DL3) transformed with the hGPN2 gene expression vector were grown in a one-liter flask including 100 μM mL^{-1} of kanamycin until reaching the stationary phase. The induction of protein expression was carried out with Isopropyl ß-D-1-thiogalactopyranoside (IPTG) at 200 μM, and the culture medium was grown for 24 h at 10 °C. The samples were centrifuged at 4 °C with 13,000 revolutions per minute for 15 min to be resuspended in a buffer developed with 100 mM Tris-HCl, 100 mM KCl, 100 mM lysine, and 100 mM sodium glutamate with a pH of 8.2. The sample was sonicated and centrifuged at 13,000 rpm for 15 min at 4 °C. Subsequently, the sample was divided into the pellet and supernatant, the soluble part contains the protein of interest and polyacrylamide gel electrophoresis (SDS-PAGE) was performed and stained with coomassie blue. To purify the samples and detect the different concentrations of hGPN2, purification was carried out using IMAC chromatography (Immobilized Metal Affinity Chromatography) and washes were carried out with the same buffer following the methodology of [14].

2.2 Obtaining Images

The image of the gels was obtained on a Bio-Rad Gel Doc XR + System photo documenter based on high-resolution CCD, high sensitivity technology, and modular options including fluorescent and colorimetric detection. The system is controlled by the Image Lab Software program that optimizes the images and allows them to be saved in high resolution and different types.

2.3 Image Pre-processing

The images were resized to 600×400 pixels, if the analyzed sample is a total extract, dilation, color inversion, and erosion were applied. If the sample does not belong to total extract then the histogram equalization was performed before of the dilation, color inversion, and erosion were performed. (See Fig. 2).

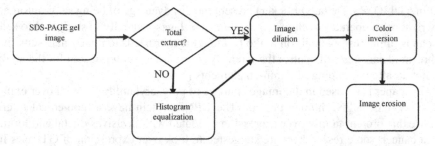

Fig. 2. Preprocessing applied to images of protein polyacrylamide gels.

2.4 Line Detection

For the detection of lines, a mask of 1×400 pixels was applied to cut the image, the histogram of the cut region was obtained applying the Otsu segmentation method from the arrangement of the data obtained in the histogram the last pixel was used to detect the intensity value in the white color, the intensity profile of the last values of the histogram of the entire gel image was finally plotted. (See Fig. 3).

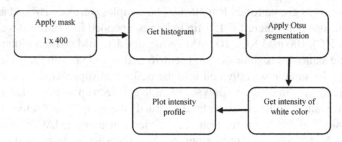

Fig. 3. The methodology used to detect the lines of the protein polyacrylamide gel.

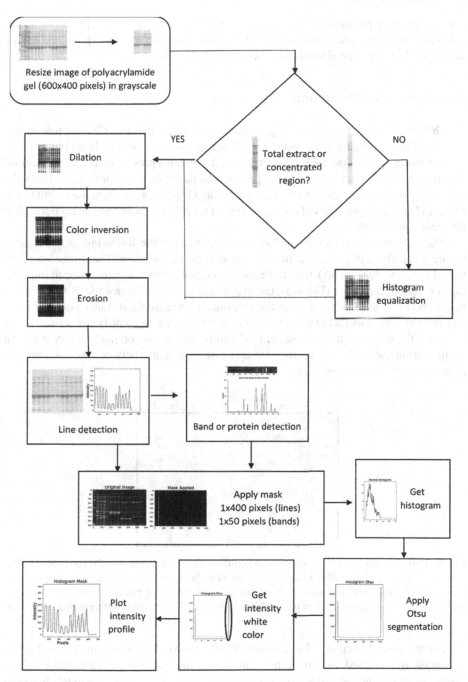

Fig. 4. Algorithm of the methodology used to detect lines and bands in a polyacrylamide gel.

2.5 Band Detection

For the detection of bands or proteins, a mask of 1×50 pixels was applied in a specific column or experiment and was developed the same methodology proposed to line detection. The complete algorithm is showed (see Fig. 4).

3 Results and Discussion

For this work, 10 polyacrylamide gels were obtained where the GPN2 protein was expressed recombinantly as shown in Fig. 5, the first line (column or lane) presents the loading buffer to know the molecular weight of the proteins present in the gel, the second contains the cell extract without the expression of the protein, the third lane shows the cell extract with the expression of the recombinant GPN2 protein, from the fourth to the fifteenth lane the expressions of the recombinant GPN2 protein are presented purified at different concentrations.

The images resized to 600×400 pixels underwent the following preprocessing before the analysis of band detection and protein over expression. The image was converted to grayscale (Fig. 6A), then the histogram equalization was performed to improve the contours of the image (Fig. 6B), the image was dilated to reduce the distance of the bands and make a first separation of the columns to increase the distance between them and to be able to detect a lower intensity in the white color to identify the separation of the lines, the colors were inverted (Fig. 6C) to be able to subsequently apply the Otsu segmentation and finally it was eroded to increase the distance between the columns and improve the detection (Fig. 6D).

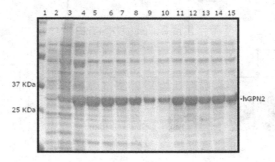

Fig. 5. Polyacrylamide gel of the expression at different concentrations of the recombinant GPN2 protein. Lane 1. Loading buffer. Lane 2. Cell extract without expression of the protein of interest. Lane 3. Cell extract with the expression of the recombinant GPN2 protein. Lane 4 non-purified sample. Lane 5 to 15. Expression of purified recombinant GPN2 protein at different concentrations.

For the lanes detection a difference with other researchers was implemented a 1×400 mask that crossed the image horizontally through each of the 600 pixels of the image, in each route the histogram was read at the time of applying the mask as shown in Fig. 7, where the graph corresponds to the gray distribution in the analyzed segment of the gel. Due to the fact that in this histogram information that allows identifying the data corresponding to the lines of the gel cannot be obtained, the detection was improved by applying the Otsu segmentation method [15] achieving the detection of the intensity of the black and white color present inside the mask (see Fig. 7). With the value of the intensity of the white color, the data of the intensity profile shown in Fig. 8 were obtained.

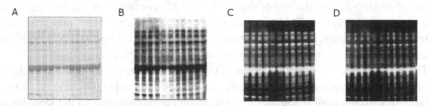

Fig. 6. Treatment was performed on the polyacrylamide gel before the detection of lines. A) Conversion to grayscale, B) Histogram equalization and dilation, C) Inversion of colors, D) Erosion of the image.

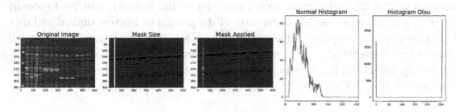

Fig. 7. Application of a 1 × 400 mask on the polyacrylamide gel to obtain the histogram of the analyzed region in gray level (normal histogram) and using the Otsu segmentation method (Histogram Otsu).

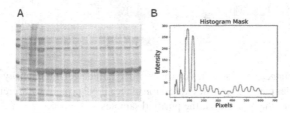

Fig. 8. A) Polyacrylamide gel analyzed. B) Intensity profile obtained from the gel.

When constructing the intensity profile, the separation between each of the columns corresponding to the different experiments could be seen, but those assigned to columns 5 to 15 (see Fig. 8) presented a low profile compared to the first four lanes. To solve this problem, the gel was divided into two regions, the first four lines have a high protein concentration (the first lane includes the loading buffer, lanes 2 and 3 contain the total protein extract with the presence and absence of GPN2, lane 4 contains an expression of unpurified GPN2); and the rest of the lanes (5 to 15) contain a low protein expression since they went through the IMAC purification process that eliminated proteins that are not required to maintain the analyzed protein of biological interest (GPN2) with some few contaminants compared to the sample that was not purified (lane 4).

The first four lanes were left as they were detected since the profile that allows them to be identified shows good expression and they are easily detected in the curve (see Figs. 8, 9A, and 9B). To improve the analysis of the region corresponding to the samples that were treated with IMAC purification, the image histogram was previously equalized and the methodology developed for line detection, explained above, was applied. Figure 9C and 9D show the result obtained where the detection of the lines was improved, achieving a better intensity profile, being able to perfectly visualize the separation of the lanes. Furthermore, the size of the peaks in the intensity profile makes it possible to identify which sample contains a higher expression of the protein of interest studied and those of smaller size are assigned to the samples with a lower expression of the protein. Figure 10 indicates which lane corresponds to a greater overexpression of the GPN2 protein (Fig. 10A and 10B) and which are assigned to the samples with a lower expression of the protein (Fig. 10C and 10D).

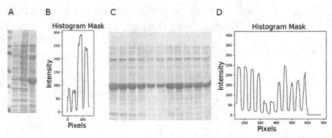

Fig. 9. A) Highly concentrated samples on the polyacrylamide gel. B) Intensity profile of the first four lanes. C) Samples purified with the expression of the GPN2 protein at different concentrations. D) Intensity profile of the gel lanes of the purified samples.

Having already established the methodology for the detection of bands, two regions of the polyacrylamide gel that correspond to the loading buffer and a sample of the purified GPN2 protein were taken, they were cut from the gel and the detection of lines was applied horizontally as show Fig. 11A and 11B.

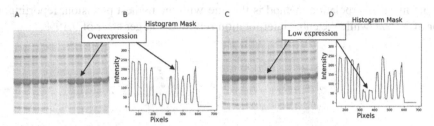

Fig. 10. Identification of the protein with the highest overexpression within the gel (A and B) and the one corresponding to the lowest expressions of the GPN2 protein (C and D).

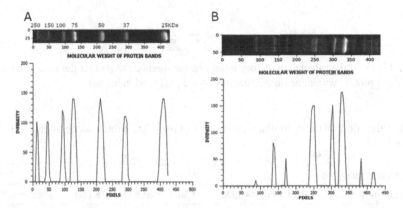

Fig. 11. A) Intensity profile of the loading buffer that indicates in the upper part the molecular weights of the proteins within the gel. B) Intensity profile of a sample containing the expression of recombinant GPN2.

The lane corresponding to the loading buffer shows the molecular weight of the proteins within the gel (upper values of Fig. 11A in kilodaltons). Its intensity profile was constructed (Fig. 11A) where each peak represents a band corresponding to the different molecular weights. With these data, a two-dimensional arrangement was generated with the values of the molecular weights in kilodaltons (KDa) and their corresponding values with the maximum value of the peaks of the intensity profile. Four interpolation methods were applied (cubic, Lagrange, linear and nearest) to evaluate which of them is the most appropriate to identify the molecular weight of the protein of biological interest (see Fig. 12). To identify the best interpolation method a sample of the expression of the protein of biological interest purified by IMAC was analyzed as shown in Fig. 11B and the methodology of detection of lines proposed was used. 8 peaks corresponding to the different proteins present in the gel were detected. GPN2 was detected at pixel number 330 (Fig. 11B and Fig. 12). Applying the interpolation methods, the prediction of the molecular weight corresponding to the GPN2 protein was calculated, obtaining the data shown in Table 1. The Lagrange interpolation was dropped out from the table due to its big error.

The absolute error was evaluated for each of the three interpolation methods when predicting the molecular weight for the protein of biological interest. The results showed that the linear interpolation method is the one with the highest precision, reporting an error of 3.36%, while the cubic interpolation reported a larger error of 9.19%.

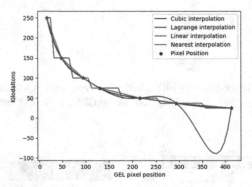

Fig. 12. Graph of the calculation of four interpolation methods to predict the molecular weight of the GPN2 protein within the image analysis of the polyacrylamide gel.

Table 1. Predictions of the molecular weight value of the GPN2 protein using three interpolation methods.

GPN2 protein analyzed			
Interpolation methods	Real weight (KDa)	Calculated weight (KDa)	Total error
Cubic	34.56	31.38	9.194960019
Lineal	34.56	33.4	3.35648148
Nearest	34.56	37.0	7.060185185

The best predicted value assigned to the GPN2 protein molecular weight is of 33.4 KDa having 34.56 KDa as the real weight.

A CPU times of the computational tests was not done because is not an objective of the research in the image analysis of polyacrylamide gel.

4   Conclusion

10 gels corresponding to samples with soluble proteins were prepared where the total cell extract containing the expression and absence of the GPN2 protein was obtained. The purification of the GPN2 protein was carried out at different concentrations and SDS-PAGE polyacrylamide gels were obtained. A new method was proposed that allows detecting the separation between the different experiments (columns) within a polyacrylamide gel using the intensity profile of a histogram only if the sample is highly concentrated, on the other hand, if the samples are not concentrated, a previous treatment is required consisting in the image dilation, color inversion, image erosion, equalizing of the image applying Otsu segmentation, get the intensity of white color and plot the intensity profile in a mask of 1×400 pixels.

The size of the curves related to the columns of images intensity profile also makes it possible to detect if the protein of biological interest is overexpressed, the larger value corresponds to overexpression and, the smaller contain less expressed protein.

The proposed methodology also allows locating the bands corresponding to the proteins expressed by each experiment either.

The loading buffer was used to correlate the molecular weight with the peaks of the intensity obtained with the methodology proposed to calculate the value in pixels used in four interpolation methods to predict the molecular weight of the GPN2 protein and it was found that linear interpolation produces the lowest error when predicting the molecular weight of the protein studied.

Is possible use the methodology proposed to find other kind of protein of biological importance, only is necessary to know their position or molecular weight and apply this method to find it.

References

1. Kaabouch, N., Schultz, R.R., Milavetz, B.: An analysis system for DNA gel electrophoresis images based on automatic thresholding and enhancement. In: IEEE International Electro/Information Technology, pp. 1–6 (2007)
2. Cai, F., Liu, S., Dijke, P.T., Verbeek, F.J.: Image analysis and pattern extraction of proteins classes from one-dimensional gels electrophoresis. Int. J. Biosci. Biochem. Bioinform. 7, 201–212 (2017)
3. Ferrari, M., Cremonesi, L., Carrera, P., Bonini, P.: Diagnosis of genetic disease by DNA technology. Pure Appl. Chem. 63, 1089–1096 (1991)
4. Intarapanich, A., Kaewkamnerd, S., Shaw, P.J., Ukosakit, K., Tragoonrung, S., Tongsima, S.: Automatic DNA diagnosis for 1D gel electrophoresis images using bio-image processing technique. BMC Genomics. 16, 1–11 (2015)
5. Wai-Hoe, L., Wing-Seng, L., Ismail, Z., Lay-Ham, G.: SDS-PAGE-based quantitative assay for screening of kidney stone disease. Biol. Proced. Online. 11, 145–160 (2009)
6. Jania, B., Andraszek, K.: Application of native agarose gel electrophoresis of serum proteins in veterinary diagnostic. J. Vet. Res. 60, 501–508 (2016)
7. Goez, M.M., Torres-Madroñcro, M.C., Röthlisberger, S., Delgado-Trejo, E.: Preprocessing of 2-dimensional gel electrophoresis images applied to proteomic analysis: a review. Genomic Proteomics Bioinform. 16, 63–72 (2018)

8. Ye, X., Suen, C.Y., Cheriet, M., Wang, E.: A recent development in image analysis of electrophoresis gels. In: Vision Interface 1999, Trois-Rivières, Canada (1999)
9. Jian-Derr, L., Chung-Hsien, H., Neng-Wei, W., Chen-Song, L.: Automatic DNA sequencing for electrophoresis gels using image processing algorithms. J. Biomed. Sci. Eng. **4**, 523–528 (2011)
10. Taher, R.S., Jamil, N., Nordin, S., Yusof, F.H., Bahari, U.M.: Poor DNA gel electrophoresis image enhancement: spatial vs. frequency domain filters. In: IEEE Conference on Systems, Process and Control, Malaysia (2013)
11. Koprowski, R., Wróbel, Z., Korzynska, A., Chwialkowska, K., Kwasniewski, M.: Automatic analysis of 2D polyacrylamide gels in the diagnosis of DNA polymorphisms. Biomed. Eng. **12**, 1–15 (2013)
12. Taher, R.S., Jamil, N., Nordin, S., Bahari, U.M.: A new false peak elimination method for poor DNA gel images analysis. In: International Conference on Intelligent Systems Design and Applications, Okinawa, Japan (2014)
13. Alnamoly, M.H., Alzohairy, A.M., Mahmoud, I., El-Henawy, I.M.: EGBIOIMAGE: a software tool for gel images analysis and hierarchical clustering. IEEE Access **8**, 10768–10781 (2019)
14. Juárez, J., Guevara-Villa, M.R.G., Sánchez-Sánchez, A., Díaz-Hernández, R., Altamirano-Robles, L.: Three-dimensional structure prediction and purification of human protein GPN2 to high concentrations by nickel affinity chromatography in presence of amino acids for improving impurities elimination. In: Arabnia, H.R. (ed.) Transactions on Computational Science and Computational Intelligence. Springer (2021, in press). ISSN: 2569-7072
15. Mohod, M., Hussain, Z., Ahmad, K.A., Ainihayati, A.R.: Gel electrophoresis image segmentation with otsu method based on particle swarm optimization. In: IEEE 7th International Colloquium on Signal Processing and its Applications, pp. 426–429 (2011)
16. Abadi, M.F.: Processing of DNA and protein electrophoresis gels by image processing. Sci. J. **36**, 3486–3494 (2015)
17. Abeykoon, A., Dhanapala, M., Yapa, R., Sooriyapathirana, S.: An automated system for analyzing agarose and polyacrylamide gel images. Ceylon J. Sci. **44**, 45–54 (2015)
18. Bajla, I., Holländer, I., Fluch, S., Burg, K., Kollár, M.: An alternative method for electrophoresis gel image analysis in the GelMaster software. Comput. Methods Programs Biomed. **77**, 209–231 (2005)
19. Brauner, J.M., et al.: Spot quantification in two dimensional gel electrophoresis image analysis: comparison of different approaches and presentation of a novel compound fitting algorithm. Bioinformatics **15**, 1–12 (2014). https://doi.org/10.1186/1471-2105-15-181
20. Efrat, A., Hoffmann, F., Kriegel, K., Schultz, C., Wenk, C.: Geometric algorithms for the analysis of 2D-electrophoresis gels. J. Comput. Biol. **9**, 1–20 (2001)
21. Fernández-Lozano, C., et al.: Texture analysis in gel electrophoresis images using an integrative kernel-based approach. Sci. Rep. **6**, 1–13 (2016)
22. Kaur, N., Sharma, P., Jaimni, S., Kehinde, B.A., Kaur, S.: Recent developments in purification techniques and industrial applications for whey valorization: a review. Chem. Eng. Commun. **207**, 1–16 (2019)
23. Labyed, N., Kaabouch, N., Schultz, R.R., Singh, B.B.: Automatic segmentation and band detection of protein images based on the standard deviation profile and its derivative. In: IEEE International Conference on Electro/Information Technology, pp. 577–582 (2007)
24. Magdeldin, S., et al.: Basic and recent advances of two dimensional- polyacrylamide gel electrophoresis. Clin. Proteomics **11**, 1–10 (2014)
25. Ramaswamy, G., Wu, B., MacEvilly, U.: Knowledge management of 1D SDS PAGE gel protein image information. J. Digit. Inf. Manag. **8**, 223–232 (2010)
26. Rezaei, M., Amiri, M., Mohajery, P.: A new algorithm for lane detection and tracking on pulsed field gel electrophoresis images. Chemometr. Intell. Lab. Syst. **157**, 1–18 (2016)

27. Humpries, B., Wang, Z., Yang, C.: Rho GTPases: big players in breast cancer initiation, metastasis and therapeutic responses. Cells **9**, 1–22 (2020)
28. Hanker, A.B., Der, C.J.: The roles of Ras family small GTPases in breast cancer. In: Bradshaw, R.A., Dennis, E.A. (eds.) Handbook of Cell Signaling, pp. 2763–2772. Academic Press (2010)
29. Lara-Chacón, B., et al.: Gpn3 is essential for cell proliferation of breast cancer cell independent of their malignancy degree. Technol. Cancer Res. Treat. **18**, 1–11 (2019).
30. Barroso-Sousa, R., Metzger-Filho, O.: Differences between invasive lobular and invasive carcinoma of the breast: results and therapeutic implications. Ther. Adv. Med. Oncol. **8**, 261–266 (2016)

Underwater Image Enhancement Using Adaptive Algorithms

Shaneer Luchman and Serestina Viriri[✉]

School of Mathematics, Statistics and Computer Science University
of KwaZulu-Natal, Durban, South Africa
viriris@ukzn.ac.za

Abstract. Images captured underwater suffer significantly from attenuation and degradation These characteristics entail that underwater images possess low contrast, weak natural light, and a low signal-to-noise ratio. Several image enhancement techniques have been developed to improve the visual appeal of an image, such as denoising, dehazing and contrast enhancement by histogram equalization. However, some of these methods have low adaptability and introduce discrepancies and distortions into the enhanced image. This paper proposes an adaptive dehazing method by dark channel prior (ADCP) with a combination of image enhancement methods. The proposed method can be used to improve images for real-world analysis such as feature extraction and detection in marine biology field. The proposed method shows that the enhanced images can be characterized by better exposure of the dark regions, improved global contrast, and improved image information content. The proposed method also mitigated certain limitations of the novel dehazing method.

Keywords: Underwater images · Attenuation and degradation · Dehazing · Image enhancement

1 Introduction

The oceans cover more than 70% of the Earth and are the source to some of the greatest biodiversity found on the planet [14]. Its sheer size and vastness mean that the ocean remains a mystery. Studies show only 20% of the ocean has been seen, explored, and mapped by humans [12]. Due to the lack of technologies and the deep sea's harsh natural conditions, exploration has been limited over the years. Feldman, an oceanographer at NASA, believed space exploration was far easier than exploring the deepest oceans [10]. His studies have shown the sea at low depths possessed three major challenges for explorers: Crushing amounts of pressure as researchers attempted to travel further below, extremely cold temperatures, and zero to minimal visibility. The constant advancements in technology have now provided researchers with autonomous underwater vehicles, such as the ROV Jason and AUV Sentry [17]. This means we can now discover

© Springer Nature Switzerland AG 2021
Y. Hernández Heredia et al. (Eds.): IWAIPR 2021, LNCS 13055, pp. 316–326, 2021.
https://doi.org/10.1007/978-3-030-89691-1_31

new energy resources, new food resources, find new species, and using the largely unexplored sea, we can uncover new information and data about the history of our planet [12].

Any form of successful research is highly dependent on the data extracted, meaning that only useful and correct data can produce useful and correct information. This supports the notion that transportation for deep-sea exploration is not the only problem that researchers and engineers have to solve. The unrelenting physical properties of the deep sea that Feldman mentions creates a major issue for the data we can extract from the ocean. Images and videos captured underwater have three major components for light: a direct component that comes from a specific source such as a strobe light or the sunlight [13]; a forward scattering component consisting of refracting or reflecting light from different objects and a backward scattering component caused by strobes lighting up objects and particles in the water in between the lens and the subject [6]. The backward scattering component formed through the suspended particles introduces noise [13] whilst the forward scattering component blurs the image [6]. The scattering components reduce image contrast, and as the sea depth increases, the direct light component severely attenuates [13]. This poses a significant problem for images that are captured deep underwater. These images suffer from degraded light, low contrast, diminishing colour, and suspended particles, which cause image distortion. These degraded images make it difficult for researchers to extract useful data and could cause them to deduce incorrect information. Hence, there has been a massive need to improve and enhance underwater images. This need for image enhancement has produced multiple methods to improve colour, contrast, and brightness of an image through image processing and computer vision.

Karrupusamy [9] conducted a review on underwater image enhancement techniques, some of which included Homomorphic Filtering, Contrast Stretching, Histogram Equalization, and Contrast Limited Adaptive Histogram Equalization (CLAHE). Vyas et al. [1] also reviewed several methods such as CLAHE, Dehazing by Dark Channel Prior (DCP), and the Polarization method. The polarization method pertained to taking multiple images of the same scene with different degrees of polarization and then fusing the images to form a new enhanced image. However, the sea's ever-changing environment and the movement of organisms posed a problem for researchers to successfully use this method. One of the most effective single image restoration methods for underwater images is dehazing by DCP [3]. The significant issues with DCP are that it is not robust and less effective for large bright patches in an image [3]. These issues lead to parts of the image with regions that look over-processed and unnatural. Another issue with DCP is that it causes halo artefacts to appear in whitened image areas, which introduces noise and causes colour distortions [3].

This paper proposes an adaptive dehazing method by dark channel prior (ADCP) and a combination of image enhancement methods, which will be used to improve an underwater image for real-world analysis. This includes improved feature extraction and faster object classification, which is used in machine learning. The ADCP algorithm will change the degree of how much it processes an image depending on the light intensity and entropy [15] of the image. The proposed method aims to adapt to the image to reduce possible distortions and halo artefacts from forming to produce a natural looking image.

2 Related Work

Luo et al. [7] proposed the idea of underwater image enhancement by performing Contrast Limited Adaptive Histogram Equalization (CLAHE) on the source image and further applying a homomorphic filter to produce an image with higher contrast. CLAHE is applied to the spatial domain of the image, and this entails computing several histograms of the image, each of a different area, and the pixels are distributed evenly in each area. The proposed method, while computationally efficient, showed a lack of major difference between the original image and result image, and the peak-signal-to-noise ratio (PSNR) values were not optimal as the other methods.

Yu et al. [21] proposed a method using dehazing by DCP with a double transmission map. First, they applied homomorphic filtering to the image to remove its colour deviations and improve image detail. They then used the dark channel map to estimate the 1st transmission map, this is commonly done in DCP. The method achieved a significant improvement in the restored image when compared to previous methods such as CLAHE, DCP, and Homomorphic filtering. The proposed method has complex processes, causing it to be computationally expensive.

Li and Guo [6] proposed a method that first dehazed an underwater image and then applied colour correction algorithms. They performed image dehazing by a medium transmission map. This transmission map is estimated by taking the difference of the maximum intensity of the red channel, with the maximum intensities of the blue and green channels. The proposed method performed well to mitigate the formation of noise and halo artefacts. However, the colour correction algorithms that were implemented introduced discrepancies in the image. Organic life forms in the underwater image changed colour, or their original colour was distorted, which may not produce desirable results for real-world marine analysis.

Xiang et al. [20] proposed an image enhancement methodology based on gamma correction and red channel weighted compensation. The red channel compensation is based on the "Gray World" theory. The theory enhances the images with retaining their natural colour. However, the improved image did not have a sufficient increase in image brightness in certain areas, and hence the method did not improve the details found in too dark images. Li et al. [4] proposed a dehazing method with minimal information loss and then performed contrast enhancement. This method produced two output images, a dehazed image with less attenuation, which had a better visual appeal; and a contrast enhanced image which is used for feature extraction and qualitative analysis. The proposed method worked well overall, but it did create incorrect colour estimations, which can adversely affect possible research and analysis.

3   Methods and Techniques

3.1   Contrast Limited Adaptive Histogram Equalization

CLAHE is a variation on adaptive histogram equalization (AHE). Histogram equalization is an effective method for improving the overall contrast of an image. It works by uniformly distributing the pixels of an image using a histogram [8]. AHE differs from normal histogram equalization as it segments an image into different areas and computes a histogram for each area [18]. It performs better than the normal method as it uses local contrasts for different areas rather than a single global contrast. However, Adaptive Histogram Equalization still has the disadvantage of over increasing the contrast in regions that are similar or constant, and this can introduce noise and irregularities [18]. Therefore, CLAHE is applied to the image as it introduces a ceiling to how much the contrast is amplified for each region [8]. We apply CLAHE by splitting the image into three separate channels (RGB). The CLAHE algorithm then partitions the channels into separate regions and applies histogram equalization to each region on each channel. We then recombine each channel to form the new image. This evens out the distribution of intensities for each channel and thus makes hidden features of the image more visible. The CLAHE equation is as follows [19] :

$$f = (f_{max} - f_{min}) * C(F) + f_{min};$$
(1)

where f is the computed pixel value per channel, f_{max} and f_{min} are the range of the pixel values, and $C(f)$ is the cumulative probability distribution.

3.2   Calculate Dehaze Factor

Entropy
Entropy in the context of digital images can be regarded as a measure of information content. It can be used to evaluate the quality of an image [10]. An image with high entropy means that the image has a high amount of information content and hence is good quality. Due to the high variation of image quality in underwater optics, entropy was considered when calculating the dehaze factor. The equation used for calculating entropy is as follows [16]:

$$E = - \sum_{i=0}^{2^S} p_i \log_2(p_i);$$
(2)

where S is the sum of the bits of the image, p_i is the probability of occurrence for colour i. We define $p_i = \frac{K_i}{M_1 * M_2}$ where $M_1 * M_2$ are the dimensions of the image and K_i is the frequency of occurrence for the colour i.

3.3   Dehazing by Adaptive Dark Channel Prior

In underwater optics, an image can be mathematically modelled as follows [3]:

$$I(x) = J(x)t(x) + A(1 - t(x)); \tag{3}$$

where I is the source image, and J is the generated haze-free image. $t(x)$ represents the transmission map, with A being the global atmospheric light, and x representing each pixel co-ordinate (x, y). We use the image's dark channel to calculate the $t(x)$ and A. This formula is manipulated to produce the enhanced image.

Dark Channel Prior

It has been observed that most underwater images have low contrast and diminishing light. These properties correlate that for every pixel, there exists at least one colour channel, where the intensity for that pixel is close to 0. This is used to produce the dark channel for the underwater image. The following equation is used to calculate the dark channel [3]:

$$J_{Dark}(x) = \min_{y \in \Omega(x)} (\min_{c \in [r,g,b]} J_c(Y)), \tag{4}$$

where J_c represents an intensity for each colour channel $c \in [r, g, b]$. $\Omega(x)$ represents a 15×15 kernel that is centered at x. The lowest pixel value among the three-colour channels and all the pixels in $\Omega(x)$ is chosen as the dark channel.

Global Atmospheric Light Estimation

Global atmospheric light is defined as the brightest regions of the image. It also tends to have no colour, meaning that it can look anything between white and grey [3], but it serves as an important parameter for the image restoration process. Natural attenuation caused at deeper depths significantly decreases the three colour channels' value in the local patch (x). This decrease implies that the dark channel can be a significant factor in estimating the atmospheric light. The following formula is used to estimate the atmospheric light by selecting the pixel with the highest intensity [3]:

$$A = I(argmax_x(I_{dark}(x)) \tag{5}$$

Transmission Map Estimation

Due to the natural conditions of the sea, light is scattered, and at lower scene depths, haze is significantly increased in the image. The transmission map estimation is important as the transmission map bears the most significance for the image recovery [2]. ADCP modifies the transmission map estimation by having it adapt to the type of image that is being processed. Using [3] the transmission map estimation for ADCP can be expressed as:

$$t(x) = 1 - f(\omega)(I_{Dark}(x)), \qquad (6)$$

where $f(\omega)$ is the function that controls to what extent the image is processed. In the standard methodology, ω is generally a constant set for all images; [3] suggested 0.9, whilst [1] chose 0.7. The high variation of underwater images and the use of this constant ω is the main reason why the standard DCP algorithm fails to be robust enough.

4 Results and Discussion

We sampled 100 images from the Underwater image enhancement benchmark (UIEB) dataset [5]. 60 images were selected at random and used to develop the adaptive algorithm, and 40 images were tested to review and analyze results. The resulting images from ADCP were compared to the standard dehazing algorithm, where ω is kept constant.

4.1 Analysis of Results

Figure 1 shows four underwater images taken from the sampled dataset used for implementing the algorithm. The original images are on the left, and the images processed by the proposed method are on the right. The enhanced images show significant improvements in color, contrast, and visibility. The proposed method increased the image's overall information content by revealing certain features that may not have been visible before. ADCP enhanced the colors in each image without distorting or changing them, keeping the image as natural looking as possible. ADCP did not introduce discrepancies in the image, nor did it produce halo artefacts and noise. This proved that ADCP mitigated common deficiencies found in the novel dehazing by dark channel prior algorithm.

4.2 Quantitative Analysis of Results

Two evaluation metrics were chosen for quantifying the results produced [11]: Mean Squared Error (MSE) and Peak Signal-to-Noise-Ratio (PSNR).

MSE is the absolute difference between the input image f(x,y) and the result image g(x,y). This technique aims to get a lower value as higher values mean the result image has been severely distorted [11].

PSNR is a common measure used for the evaluation of images, and it is effective for the measurement of white noise distortions [11]. It is the ratio between the value of the maximum signal in an image between the maximum noise factor that distorts the image. The source image f(x,y) and result image(x,y) are compared. The higher the PSNR value, the better the underwater image has been recovered to match the original image, which means the better the dehazing algorithm has performed.

(a) Image 1   (b) Image 1 after undergoing ADCP

(c) Image 2   (d) Image 2 after undergoing ADCP

(e) Image 3   (f) Image 3 after undergoing ADCP

(g) Image 4   (h) Image 4 after undergoing ADCP

Fig. 1. Images dehazing by Adaptive Dark Channel Prior (ADCP).

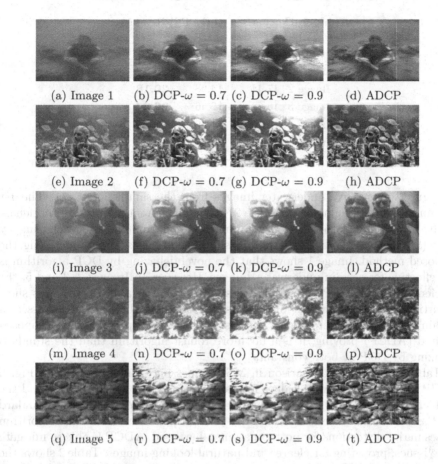

Fig. 2. Underwater images dehazing by Dark Channel Prior (DCP) and dehazing by Adaptive Dark Channel Prior (ADCP).

Table 1. Comparison of the MSE values

Image	DCP-0.7	DCP-0.9	ADCP
Image 1	1812.05	4985.52	**1142.69**
Image 2	3509.28	6189.09	**1871.45**
Image 3	4181.77	11062.36	**1844.62**
Image 4	4820.35	14106.49	**2557.07**
Image 5	17127.99	30499.06	**6164.28**

Table 2. Comparison of the PSNR values

Image	DCP-0.7	DCP-0.9	ADCP
Image 1	20.32	15.92	**22.32**
Image 2	17.44	14.98	**20.18**
Image 3	16.68	12.46	**20.24**
Image 4	16.07	11.40	**18.82**
Image 5	10.56	8.06	**15.00**

Figure 2 shows five underwater images from the sampled test set. The 1st column shows the original images, the 2nd column shows the images after dehazing by DCP ($\omega = 0.7$), the 3rd column shows the images after dehazing by DCP ($\omega = 0.9$), and the final column shows the images after undergoing the proposed method. Image 1 shows that the novel dehazing by DCP algorithm is still effective for certain underwater images. However, in Images 2, 3 and 5, the deficiencies in the DCP algorithm are shown. The 2nd and 3rd columns show distortions and halo artifacts forming, as well the image being over-processed in certain areas. These discrepancies and distortions are not present in the proposed method (ADCP) proving, it is a far more robust algorithm than the standard dehazing by DCP at both constants.

Table 1 shows the comparison in MSE values between the images in Fig. 2. ADCP produced the lowest values for each image, which meant that it had the least error between it and the original image, compared to the two standard DCP algorithms. In the images 5 and 7 in Fig. 2, the standard DCP algorithm causes major distortions for both constant values used. ADCP is able to mitigate these issues, providing far clearer and natural-looking images. Table 2 shows the comparison in PSNR values between the images in Fig. 2. ADCP produced the optimal results for all PSNR values.

Table 3 shows the PSNR values in [6] for three images that they tested. We compared the proposed method to theirs, and it can be seen that our PSNR values are greater, and therefore more optimal. Each enhanced image was reconstructed to be much closer to the original, and more natural-looking than the compared methods.

Table 3. Comparison of the proposed method using PSNR values

Image	PSNR (Li. et al. [6])	PSNR using ADCP
Single fish	12.05	**26.89**
Multiple fish	13.56	**18.22**
Coral	14.49	**18.11**

5   Conclusion

In this paper, a novel image dehazing technique for underwater images was explored and successfully implemented. A simple dehazing by dark channel prior based with adaptive capabilities was proposed with CLAHE, and image sharpening also being performed. ADCP has proven to far more robust than the novel dark channel prior algorithm. It is able to successfully enhance a wider variety of underwater images without introducing any distortions while also keeping the resulting image as natural looking as possible. ADCP has also proved that it can improve efficiency and effectiveness for feature classification and detection in the marine biology field. The standard DCP algorithm is less computationally expensive than ADCP. This is expected as the proposed method has to adapt to every picture to dehaze it. Due to the wide variation of deep underwater images, no single dehazing algorithm can produce optimal results for every picture. Future work should include a hybrid dehazing algorithm joined with machine learning. This could involve implementing several dehazing techniques to produce a set of enhanced images for each underwater picture. A machine learning algorithm can select the best-enhanced picture from that set.

References

1. Baajwa, D.S., Khan, S.A., Kaur, J.: Evaluating the research gaps of underwater image enhancement techniques. Int. J. Comput. Appl. **117**(20), 19–23 (2015)
2. He, K., Sun, J., Tang, X.: Single image haze removal using dark channel prior. IEEE Trans. Pattern Anal. Mach. Intell. **33**(12), 2341–2353 (2010)
3. Lee, S., Yun, S., Nam, J.H., Won, C.S., Jung, S.W.: A review on dark channel prior based image dehazing algorithms. EURASIP J. Image Video Process. **2016**(1), 4 (2016). https://doi.org/10.1186/s13640-016-0104-y
4. Li, C.Y., Guo, J.C., Cong, R.M., Pang, Y.W., Wang, B.: Underwater image enhancement by dehazing with minimum information loss and histogram distribution prior. IEEE Trans. Image Process. **25**(12), 5664–5677 (2016)
5. Li, C., et al.: An underwater image enhancement benchmark dataset and beyond. IEEE Trans. Image Process. **29**, 4376–4389 (2019)
6. Li, C., Guo, J.: Underwater image enhancement by dehazing and color correction. J. Electron. Imaging **24**(3), 033023 (2015)
7. Luo, M., Fang, Y., Ge, Y.: An effective underwater image enhancement method based on CLAHE-HF. J. Phys.: Conf. Ser. **1237**, 032009 (2019)
8. Mustafa, W.A., Kader, M.M.M.A.: A review of histogram equalization techniques in image enhancement application. J. Phys.: Conf. Ser. **1019**, 012026 (2018)
9. Karuppusamy, P.: Techniques for enhancement and denoising of underwater images: a review. J. Innov. Image Process. **1**(02), 81–90 (2019)
10. Petsko, E.: Why does so much of the ocean remain unexplored and unprotected? January 2019
11. Samajdar, T., Quraishi, M.I.: Analysis and evaluation of image quality metrics. In: Mandal, J., Satapathy, S., Kumar Sanyal, M., Sarkar, P., Mukhopadhyay, A. (eds.) Information Systems Design and Intelligent Applications, Advances in Intelligent Systems and Computing, vol. 340, pp. 369–378. Springer, New Delhi (2015). https://doi.org/10.1007/978-81-322-2247-7_3

12. National Geographic Society. Oceans, December 2020
13. Steiner, A.: Understanding the basics of underwater lighting, April 2019
14. Oceanpreneur Suzanne. 7 reasons why the ocean is so important, December 2020
15. Thum, Ch.: Measurement of the entropy of an image with application to image focusing. Optica Acta: Int. J. Opt. **31**(2), 203–211 (1984)
16. Torres, E., Garces, Y., Pereira, O., Rodriguez, R.: Behavior study of entropy in a digital image through an iterative algorithm of the mean shift filtering. Int. J. Soft Comput. Math. Control (IJSCMC) **4**(3), 21 (2015)
17. National Oceanic US Department of Commerce and Atmospheric Administration. Why the ocean is so important? July 2014
18. Wikipedia: Adaptive histogram equalization - Wikipedia. https://en.wikipedia.org/wiki/Adaptive_histogram_equalization. Accessed 22 June 2020
19. Wong, S.L., Yu, Y.P., Ho, N.A.J., Paramesran, R.: Comparative analysis of underwater image enhancement methods in different color spaces. In: 2014 International Symposium on Intelligent Signal Processing and Communication Systems (ISPACS), pp. 034–038. IEEE (2014)
20. Xiang, W., Yang, P., Wang, S., Bing, X., Liu, H.: Underwater image enhancement based on red channel weighted compensation and gamma correction model. Opto-Electron. Adv. **1**(10), 180024 (2018)
21. Yu, H., Li, X., Lou, Q., Lei, C., Liu, Z.: Underwater image enhancement based on DCP and depth transmission map. Multimedia Tools Appl. 1–18 (2020). https://doi.org/10.1007/s11042-020-08701-3

Improving the Robustness of DCT-Based Handwritten Document Image Watermarking Against JPEG-Compression

Ernesto Avila-Domenech[1]([⊠]) [iD] and Alberto Taboada-Crispi[2] [iD]

[1] Universidad de Granma, Carretera Central vía Holguín Km 1/2, Bayamo, Granma, Cuba
[2] Universidad Central Marta Abreu de Las Villas, Villa Clara, Cuba
ataboada@uclv.edu.cu

Abstract. Digital image watermarking is a powerful tool to secure digital images. An important step in these schemes is the quantification used to insert the watermark. In this paper, to improve the robustness of the watermark against JPEG-compression, different quantification variants are analyzed and optimized for a handwritten document image watermarking scheme. The results demonstrate that the embedded watermarks can be almost fully extracted from the JPEG-compressed images with high compression ratios.

Keywords: DCT · Handwritten · Image · QIM · Watermarking

1 Introduction

Digital watermarking is an important research branch of information hiding, which can be used to protect multimedia digital data, for example copyright protection, content verification and tamper detection.

Watermarking methods have been proposed for various image content and since the various types of content, each have their characteristics, a watermarking technique should be designed that takes account of their characteristics [11].

Digital watermarking schemes can be divided according to the working domain into spatial domain and frequency domain.

Spatial image watermarking techniques are commonly used in steganographic contexts because, hiding data into the least significant bits of an image can allow embedding a large quantity of data. Either it is useful in fragile schemes to determine the ownership integrity. However, the watermark will not be robust to common manipulations, e.g., JPEG-compression [6].

The frequency-domain schemes are generally considered more robust than the spatial domain schemes; these schemes consist of transforming an image from spatial domain to frequency domain. Some authors have made proposals based on Discrete Cosine Transform (DCT) [14,22], this is because it has good energy compaction property that is widely used in image compression.

© Springer Nature Switzerland AG 2021
Y. Hernández Heredia et al. (Eds.): IWAIPR 2021, LNCS 13055, pp. 327–336, 2021.
https://doi.org/10.1007/978-3-030-89691-1_32

On the other hand, handwritten documents hoarded in historical archives, libraries, and museums are an important source of knowledge and research for historians and the general public. Many of these manuscripts are being digitized to preserve their physical integrity and provide access to a greater number of people. In the digitization process, it is important to take into account security, as they can be modified and adjudicated to people illegally.

In this paper, to improve the robustness of the watermark against JPEG-compression, different quantification variants are analyzed and optimized for a handwritten document image watermarking scheme. Also, all the images of two datasets corresponding to handwritten documents have been marked and evaluated for imperceptibility and robustness.

The rest of the paper is organized as follows; Sect. 2 summarizes preliminaries. Section 3 describes the watermarking technique and its optimization. Our experimental results and discussion are given in Sect. 4, and Sect. 5 concludes the paper.

2   Preliminaries

2.1   Quantization Index Modulation (QIM)

QIM [7] is based on the set of $N-dimensional$ quantizers, one quantizer for each possible message m that needs to be transmitted. The message to be transmitted determines the quantizer to use. The selected quantizer is then used to embed the information. Refer to embedding information by first modulating an index or sequence of indices with the embedded information and then quantizing the host signal with the associated quantizer or sequence of quantizers.

QIM is "provably good" against arbitrary bounded and fully informed attacks, which arise in several copyright applications, and in particular, it achieves provably better distortion-robustness tradeoffs than currently popular spread-spectrum and low-bit(s) modulation methods [7].

A key aspect of the design of QIM systems involves the choice of practical quantizer ensembles for such systems, which we now explore.

We will define $Q_\Delta(x) = round(x/\Delta)\Delta$ where the function $round()$ denotes rounding value to the nearest integer, and Δ is the quantization step controlling the embedding strength of the watermark bit.

Variant 1: Dither Modulation (DM) is a special form of quantization index molulation which is applied an image watermarking system in order to assign one bit to each transformation coefficient. In [7], the watermarked signal is given by:

$$y_n = Q_\Delta(x_n, d_m) = Q_\Delta(x_n + d_m) - d_m \qquad m \in [0,1] \quad n = 1, 2, ..., L \qquad (1)$$

where d_0 and d_1 are used for embedding message bit "0" or "1", respectively. It is chosen d_0 pseudo-randomly with a uniform distribution over $[-\Delta/2, \Delta/2]$ and

$$d_1 = \begin{cases} d_0 + \frac{\Delta}{2} & d_0 < 0 \\ d_0 - \frac{\Delta}{2} & d_0 \geq 0 \end{cases} \qquad (2)$$

As suggested in [7], it takes $d_0 = \Delta/4$ and $d_1 = -\Delta/4$.

At the detector, the received signal y', possibly a corrupted version of y, is re-quantized with the family of quantizers used while embedding to determine the embedded message bit, i.e.

$$\hat{m} = \underbrace{arg\,min}_{m \in 0,1}|Q_\Delta(y', d_m) - y'| \tag{3}$$

Variant 2: One bit of the watermark can be embedded as [15,23,25,27]:

$$y = \begin{cases} Q_\Delta(x) + \Delta/2 & if \ \ Q_\Delta(x)/\Delta + m \equiv 0 \ (mod \ 2) \\ Q_\Delta(x) - \Delta/2 & otherwise \end{cases} \tag{4}$$

The watermark extraction process is given by:

$$\hat{m} = \begin{cases} 0 & if \ \lfloor y'/\Delta \rfloor \equiv 0 \ (mod \ 2) \\ 1 & otherwise \end{cases} \tag{5}$$

where $\lfloor \rfloor$ denote the floor function.

Although the authors present the formulas in different ways, [12] demonstrates their equivalence.

Variant 3: One bit of the watermark can be embedded as [12]:

$$y = \begin{cases} (\lfloor x/\Delta \rfloor + \frac{1}{2})\Delta & if \ \lfloor (x/\Delta) \rfloor + m \equiv 0 \ (mod \ 2) \\ (\lfloor x/\Delta \rfloor + \frac{3}{2})\Delta & otherwise \end{cases} \tag{6}$$

The watermark extraction process is given by:

$$\hat{m} = \begin{cases} 0 & if \ \lfloor y'/\Delta \rfloor \equiv 0 \ (mod \ 2) \\ 1 & otherwise \end{cases} \tag{7}$$

Variant 4: One bit of the watermark can be embedded as [10,26,28]:

$$y = \begin{cases} Q_\Delta(x) & if \ \ Q_\Delta(x)/\Delta \equiv m \ (mod \ 2) \\ Q_\Delta(x+1) & otherwise \end{cases} \tag{8}$$

The watermark extraction process is given by:

$$\hat{m} = \begin{cases} 0 & if \ \ Q_\Delta(y')/\Delta \equiv 0 \ (mod \ 2) \\ 1 & otherwise \end{cases} \tag{9}$$

Variant 5: One bit of the watermark can be embedded as [24]:

$$y = \begin{cases} Q_\Delta(x) - \Delta/4 & if\ m = 0 \\ Q_\Delta(x) + \Delta/4 & if\ m = 1 \end{cases} \tag{10}$$

The watermark extraction process is given by:

$$\hat{m} = \begin{cases} 0 & if\ y' - Q_\Delta(y') \le 0 \\ 1 & otherwise \end{cases} \tag{11}$$

Variant 6: In [13] the watermarked method is similar to variant 5, but to extract the watermark it is used:

$$\hat{m} = \underbrace{arg\,min}_{m \in 0,1} |Q_\Delta(y') + d_m - y'| \tag{12}$$

where $d_0 = -\Delta/4$ and $d_1 = \Delta/4$.

Variant 7: One bit of the watermark can be embedded as [21]:

$$y = \begin{cases} 2Q_\Delta(x) & if\ m = 0 \\ 2Q_\Delta(x-1) + \Delta & if\ m = 1 \end{cases} \tag{13}$$

The watermark extraction process is given by:

$$\hat{m} = \begin{cases} 0 & if\ round(y'/\Delta) \equiv 0\ (mod\ 2) \\ 1 & otherwise \end{cases} \tag{14}$$

3   Watermarking Techniques

3.1   Scheme Used

The robust watermarking method used is similar to the one proposed in [4,5] (see Fig. 1). Firstly, the binary watermark image is scrambled by Arnold transform [3]. Second, the cover image is transformed from RGB to YCbCr color space, and the Y component, corresponding to the luminance information, is divided into non-overlapping image blocks of 8×8 pixels. Next, some blocks equal to the number of bits to be inserted are selected from a given key, and each selected block is transform from spatial domain to frequency domain by DCT [1]. Then, the watermark bit is embedded into a coefficient using some quantification formula. Finally, the YCbCr to RGB color space is transformed to obtain RGB watermarked image.

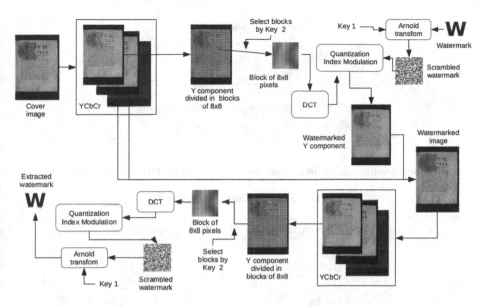

Fig. 1. Watermark embedding and extraction scheme. (Modified from [5]).

3.2   Quantification Formulas Optimization

Optimal AC coefficient and Δ values have been identified for each variant of the quantification formula using the Jaya algorithm [20], see Table 1. In this case, to achieve better approximation, a population opposite to the current population is generated and both are considered at the same time (Quasi-Oppositional-Based Jaya) [19], with an initial population of 15 elements and 30 iterations. The fitness function, which is used to evaluate the appropriateness of each candidate solution in each examined case, takes a form regarding the type of the used image quality index. In this context, and similar to [16], using Peak Signal-to-Noise Ratio (PSNR) as image quality index and the Bit Error Rate (BER), the fitness function F is defined as:

$$F = \alpha \max(PSRN - PSNR_{target},\ 0) + \beta \frac{1}{N} \sum_{i=1}^{N} (BER_i) \qquad (15)$$

where α and β are scaling factors equal to 0.02 and 10.0 respectively, $PSNR$ is the PSNR obtained, $PSNR_{target}$ is a desired PSNR value equal to 40 dB, N is the number of attacks encountered in the procedure, and BER_i is the BER of the ith compressions at different quality factor (QF={1, 3, 5, 10, 15, 20}) (Fig. 2).

Fig. 2. Image used in the optimization process. ("3.bmp" DIBCO2017 dataset [18]).

Table 1. Optimal values in each variant.

Variant	References	AC Coefficient (zig-zag)	Δ
1	[7]	8	273
2	[15, 23, 25, 27]	7	259
3	[12]	10	286
4	[10, 26, 28]	9	170
5	[24]	6	260
6	[13]	11	259
7	[21]	10	171

4   Experiments and Results

We used two image databases, consisting on handwritten RGB image documents, Saint Gall [8] and Parzival [9], and compressed them into JPEG images with various quality factors (QF).

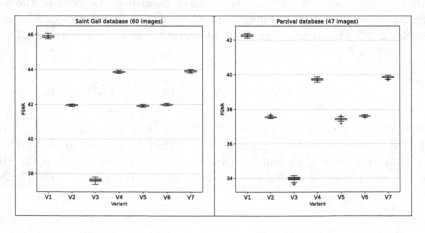

Fig. 3. Imperceptibility computed as PSNR (dB) for each variant by using the Saint Gall and the Parzival databases JPEG-compressed at QF = 100.

Imperceptibility means that the perceived quality of the host image should not be distorted by the presence of the watermark. As a measure of the quality of a watermarked image, the PSNR is typically used in decibels (dB). When evaluating the seven variants, the PSNR results greater than 37 dB in most cases were obtained; therefore, there is no perceptibility when the watermark is inserted. As seen in Fig. 3, the V1, V4 and V7 variants obtained better results. On the other hand, it is observed that the resulting V3 variant statistics are far below from the other variants, even obtaining results lower than 37 dB for Parzival dataset, indicating poor performance.

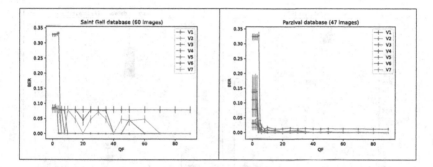

Fig. 4. Robustness computed as BER for each variant by using the Saint Gall and the Parzival databases JPEG-compressed at different quality factors.

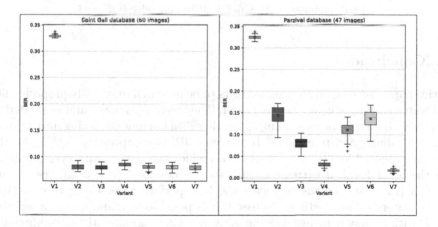

Fig. 5. Robustness computed as BER for each variant by using the Saint Gall and the Parzival databases JPEG-compressed at QF = 0.

To prove the robustness against JPEG compression, the watermarked images were compressed with different quality factors ($QF=\{0, 1, 2, 3, 4, 5, 6, 8, 10, 15, 20, 25, 30, 35, 40, 45, 50, 60, 70, 80, 90\}$). The Fig. 4 shows that the greatest difference in the results occurs when $QF \leq 5$. In real life instances, where compression with $QF \leq 5$ is not taken into account, using the V6 variant proposed in [13] would give the best results.

In the extreme case of JPEG compression with $QF = 0$ is observed for both datasets, the V7 variant used in [21] obtains better results (see Fig. 5).

Guetzli is a new JPEG encoder that aims to produce visually indistinguishable images at a lower bit-rate than other common JPEG encoders [2]. All the analyzed variants show good robustness parameters when using Guetzli, being the V1, V2, V5 and V6 variants where the best results are obtained (see Fig. 6).

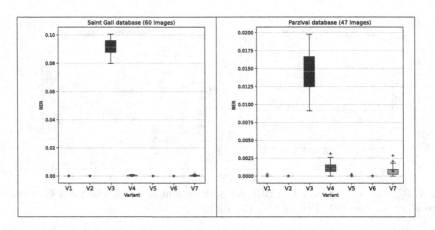

Fig. 6. Robustness to Guetzli JPEG encoder (QF = 84).

5   Conclusions

In this paper, seven quantization variants to be used in a previously proposed digital watermarking scheme were exposed. They were optimized and evaluated in two image datasets corresponding to handwritten documents taking into account imperceptibility and robustness. In extreme JPEG compression $(QF \leq 5)$, the variant proposed by [21] was the one with which the best results were obtained. On the other hand, if extreme compression is not used $(QF > 5)$, the variant used in [13] would be the one with the best performance. Using this variants in the watermarking method discussed, it is possible to maintain an acceptable BER without any perceptual changes, even using maximum JPEG compression (Guetzli included).

References

1. Ahmed, N., Natarajan, T., Rao, K.R.: Discrete cosine transform. IEEE Trans. Comput. **100**(1), 90–93 (1974)

2. Alakuijala, J., Obryk, R., Stoliarchuk, O., Szabadka, Z., Vandevenne, L., Wassenberg, J.: Guetzli: perceptually guided JPEG encoder. arXiv preprint arXiv:1703.04421 (2017)
3. Arnol'd, V.I., Avez, A.: Ergodic Problems of Classical Mechanics. The Mathematical Physics Monograph Series, Benjamin, W.A., New York (1968). http://cds.cern.ch/record/1987366
4. Avila-Domenech, E., Soria-Lorente, A.: Watermarking based on Krawtchouk moments for handwritten document images. In: Hernandez Heredia, Y., Milian Nunez, V., Ruiz Shulcloper, J. (eds.) Progress in Artificial Intelligence and Pattern Recognition, vol. 11047, pp. 122–129. Springer, Cham (2018). https://doi.org/10.1007/978-3-030-01132-1_14
5. Avila-Domenech, E., Soria-Lorente, A., Taboada-Crispi, A.: Dual watermarking for handwritten document image authentication and copyright protection for JPEG compression attacks. In: Nystrom, I., Hernandez Heredia, Y., Milian Nunez, V. (eds.) Progress in Pattern Recognition, Image Analysis, Computer Vision, and Applications, vol. 11896, pp. 656–666. Springer, Cham (2019). https://doi.org/10.1007/978-3-030-33904-3_62
6. Cardamone, N., d'Amore, F.: DWT and QR code based watermarking for document DRM. In: Yoo, C., Shi, Y.Q., Kim, H., Piva, A., Kim, G. (eds.) Digital Forensics and Watermarking, vol. 11378, pp. 137–150. Springer, Cham (2018). https://doi.org/10.1007/978-3-030-11389-6_11
7. Chen, B., Wornell, G.W.: Quantization index modulation: a class of provably good methods for digital watermarking and information embedding. IEEE Trans. Inf. Theor. 47(4), 1423–1443 (2001)
8. Fischer, A., Frinken, V., Fornés, A., Bunke, H.: Transcription alignment of Latin manuscripts using hidden Markov models. In: Proceedings of the 2011 Workshop on Historical Document Imaging and Processing, pp. 29–36. ACM (2011)
9. Fischer, A., et al.: Automatic transcription of handwritten medieval documents. In: 2009 15th International Conference on Virtual Systems and Multimedia, pp. 137–142. IEEE (2009)
10. Jin, C., Peng, J.: A robust wavelet-based blind digital watermarking algorithm. Inf. Technol. J. 5(2), 358–363 (2006)
11. Kang, J., Ji, S.K., Lee, H.K.: Spherical panorama image watermarking using viewpoint detection. In: Yoo, C., Shi, Y.Q., Kim, H., Piva, A., Kim, G. (eds.) Digital Forensics and Watermarking, vol. 11378, pp. 95–109. Springer, Cham (2018). https://doi.org/10.1007/978-3-030-11389-6_8
12. Li, X.: Optimization analysis of formulas for quantization-based image watermarking. Opto-Electron. Eng. 37(2), 96–102 (2010)
13. Liu, X., Han, G., Wu, J., Shao, Z., Coatrieux, G., Shu, H.: Fractional Krawtchouk transform with an application to image watermarking. IEEE Trans. Signal Process. 65(7), 1894–1908 (2017)
14. Muñoz-Ramirez, D.O., Ponomaryov, V., Reyes-Reyes, R., Kyrychenko, V., Pechenin, O., Totsky, A.: A robust watermarking scheme to JPEG compression for embedding a color watermark into digital images. In: 2018 IEEE 9th International Conference on Dependable Systems, Services and Technologies (DESSERT), pp. 619–624. IEEE (2018)
15. Niu, P.P., Wang, P., Liu, Y.N., Yang, H.Y., Wang, X.Y.: Invariant color image watermarking approach using quaternion radial harmonic Fourier moments. Multimedia Tools Appl. 75(13), 7655–7679 (2016)
16. Papakostas, G.A., Tsougenis, E., Koulouriotis, D.E.: Moment-based local image watermarking via genetic optimization. Appl. Math. Comput. 227, 222–236 (2014)

17. Pastor-Pellicer, J., Afzal, M.Z., Liwicki, M., Castro-Bleda, M.J.: Complete system for text line extraction using convolutional neural networks and watershed transform. In: 2016 12th IAPR Workshop on Document Analysis Systems (DAS), pp. 30–35. IEEE (2016)

18. Pratikakis, I., Zagoris, K., Barlas, G., Gatos, B.: ICDAR 2017 competition on document image binarization (DIBCO 2017). In: 2017 14th IAPR International Conference on Document Analysis and Recognition (ICDAR), vol. 01, pp. 1395–1403, November 2017. https://doi.org/10.1109/ICDAR.2017.228

19. Rao, R.V., Rai, D.P.: Optimisation of welding processes using quasi-oppositional-based Jaya algorithm. J. Exp. Theor. Artif. Intell. **29**(5), 1099–1117 (2017)

20. Rao, R.V.: Jaya: an advanced optimization algorithm and its engineering applications (2019)

21. Rosales-Roldan, L., Chao, J., Nakano-Miyatake, M., Perez-Meana, H.: Color image ownership protection based on spectral-domain watermarking using QR codes and QIM. Multimedia Tools Appl. **77**(13), 16031–16052 (2018)

22. Wang, J., Wan, W., Zhang, M., Zou, L., Sun, J.: A blind quantization watermarking scheme for screen content image. In: Sun, X., Pan, Z., Bertino, E. (eds.) Cloud Computing and Security, vol. 11066, pp. 61–71. Springer, Cham (2018). https://doi.org/10.1007/978-3-030-00015-8_6

23. Wang, X.Y., Liu, Y.N., Li, S., Yang, H.Y., Niu, P.P.: Robust image watermarking approach using polar harmonic transforms based geometric correction. Neurocomputing **174**, 627–642 (2016)

24. Wang, X., Shi, Q., Wang, S., Yang, H.: A blind robust digital watermarking using invariant exponent moments. AEU-Int. J. Electron. Commun. **70**(4), 416–426 (2016)

25. Xu-Dong, L.: Image watermarking method for resisting lightness-adjusting attack in DWT domain. Opto-Electron. Eng. **7** (2009)

26. Xuan, G., et al.: Identity verification system using data hiding and fingerprint recognition. In: 2005 IEEE 7th Workshop on Multimedia Signal Processing, pp. 1–4. IEEE (2005)

27. Yang, H.Y., Wang, P., Wang, X.Y., Niu, P.P., Miao, E.N., Zhang, Y.: Robust digital watermarking based on local invariant radial harmonic Fourier moments. Multimedia Tools Appl. **74**(23), 10559–10579 (2015)

28. Zhao, Y., Zheng, X., Li, N., Liu, G., Wang, Q.: A digital image watermark algorithm based on DC coefficients quantization. In: 2006 6th World Congress on Intelligent Control and Automation, vol. 2, pp. 9734–9738. IEEE (2006)

Automated System for the Detection of Lung Nodules

E. Martinez-Machado, M. Perez-Diaz$^{(\boxtimes)}$ (iD), and R. Orozco-Morales (iD)

Automatic Control Department, Universidad Central "Marta Abreu de Las Villas", Camajuani Road km 5 ½, 52830 Santa Clara, Cuba
mperez@uclv.edu.cu

Abstract. Lung cancer is the most frequent cause of cancer mortality in the world. The diagnostic procedure usually begins with a chest X-ray; however, it is difficult to interpret due to the set of anatomical structures overlapped. Computer-aided detection (CAD) systems are a diagnostic aid tool for radiologists. In the present work a CAD system is proposed for the detection of lung nodules on chest radiographs. Methods such as convolution, local normalization and homomorphic filters are used to pre-process images, using a multi-level threshold method supported by morphological operations for anatomical segmentation. This is followed by a candidate nodule detector using the local sliding-band convergence filter. The candidate nodules are segmented using an adaptive threshold based on distance. A set of characteristics for each candidate are calculated based on the segmentation. The system was tested by a free available database (DB) of 247 images, of which 154 are pulmonary nodules (100 malignant and 54 benign cases and 93 nodules). The results obtained indicate that the system is able of detecting 98.7% of the nodules of the DB with an average of 56.08 detections per image. Two false positive were obtained due to lung segmentation.

Keywords: CAD system · Lung nodules · Image processing

1 Introduction

Lung cancer is the second most common cancer that affects people and is the most frequent cause of cancer mortality in the world [1]. Statistics on survival in people depend on the disease stage at the time of diagnosis. This is why its early detection is of great importance, when it is still in the pulmonary nodule phase.

For diagnose a lung cancer, the first imaging tests is a chest x-ray. If the lesion is very small or of very low contrast, it is likely not to be detected (false negative). A pulmonary nodule is seen as a rounded opacity, discreetly well defined, and whose diameter is less than 3 cm [2], although they may also have irregular, spiculated or lobed edges [3].

With the development of technology, interest in developing algorithms for computer-assisted diagnosis (CAD), applied to the early detection of different types of cancer, has increased in radiography [4]. The purpose of these algorithms is to highlight suspicious opacities in the image, which may constitute a tumor, to get the radiologist's attention.

© Springer Nature Switzerland AG 2021
Y. Hernández Heredia et al. (Eds.): IWAIPR 2021, LNCS 13055, pp. 337–348, 2021.
https://doi.org/10.1007/978-3-030-89691-1_33

Most of the systems have the following stages: image pre-processing lung region seg-mentation, region's most likely to be nodules detection, extraction of suspicious regions characteristics and finally the lesion classification.

In the present work an automated system is developed that reduces image noise, segments the lung of the thoracic cavity, and then over the lung region, reveals and segments the anomalous regions (candidates for lung nodules). The approach used is based on image processing techniques.

2 Material and Methods

The database of the Japanese Society of Radiological Technology (JSRT) [5] was used. It is an annotated base, with 247 images, 154 of them are lung nodules (100 malignant cases, 54 benign cases and 93 non-nodules). The images are 2048 × 2048 pixels, for a pixel size of 0.175 mm and a depth of 12 bits per pixel.

Two tasks were performed during pre-processing, one aimed at obtaining better visibility in the image and another to facilitate segmentation of the lung region. In the first case, image smoothing was performed with the application of a convolution filter. During the convolution, elements of the image were averaged to their local neighbors, weighted by a smoothing kernel of 5 × 5 pixels [6]. For a two-dimensional (2D) input image $f(x, y)$ an output image $C(x, y)$ was generated.

$$C(x, y) = \sum_{i=-2}^{2} \sum_{j=-2}^{2} f(x - i, y - j)H(x, y) = H(x, y) * f(x, y) \qquad (1)$$

where $H(x, y)$ is the convolution kernel and * denotes convolution operation.

Then, through local normalization (LN) filtering, a global equalization of contrast was achieved. To normalize the contrast between different images and within each image, a local contrast improvement was made [7]). This operation is given by:

$$LN(x, y) = \frac{C(x, y) - \mu(x, y)}{\sigma(x, y)} \qquad (2)$$

where $LN(x, y)$ is the normalized image, $\mu(x, y)$ is an estimate of the local average, and $\sigma(x, y)$ is an estimate of the local standard deviation. The local average is calculated by:

$$\mu(x, y) = C(x, y) * h(x, y) \qquad (3)$$

where $h(x, y)$ is a Gaussian low pass filter, and the local standard deviation is calculated by:

$$\sigma(x, y) = \sqrt{C^2(x, y) * h(x, y) - \mu^2(x, y)} \qquad (4)$$

Finally, the edges were enhanced with a homomorphic filtering. A logarithmic map-ping in the space domain was performed to separate the lighting and reflectance com-ponents. To make the illumination of an image more uniform, the high frequency com-ponents (reflectance) are increased and the low frequency components (illumination) are decreased. High-pass filtering was used in this case to suppress low frequencies and amplify high frequencies. Let $LN(x, y)$ be the output image of the local normalization filter, it can be thought as:

$$LN(x, y) = i(x, y)r(x, y) \tag{5}$$

where $i(x, y)$ is the illumination and $r(x, y)$ is the reflectance.

During the second task the image intensity values were adjusted to highlight the lung region. Finally, the preprocessed images were resized from 2048×2048 pixels to 1024×1024 pixels, in order to reduce the computational load.

The equation was then transformed to the frequency domain to apply the high pass filter. However, it is very difficult to make a calculation after applying the Fourier transform to this equation, because it is no longer a product equation. Therefore, its logarithm was used.

$$\ln(LN(x, y)) = \ln(i(x, y)) + \ln(r(x, y)) \tag{6}$$

then, the Fourier transform was applied:

$$\mathcal{F}(\ln(LN(x, y))) = \mathcal{F}(\ln(i(x, y))) + \mathcal{F}(\ln(r(x, y))) \tag{7}$$

Next, the high pass filter was applied in the frequency domain.

$$\mathcal{F}(n(x, y)) = \mathcal{F}(h(x, y))\mathcal{F}(\ln(LN(x, y))) \tag{8}$$

where $h(x, y)$ is the kernel of the Gaussian high pass filter, so, to recover the filtered image in the space domain $n(x, y)$, the inverse Fourier transform is used.

Finally, the exponential function was used to eliminate the record used at the beginning to obtain the improved image.

$$ProcImage(x, y) = \exp(n(x, y)). \tag{9}$$

To adjust the intensity, new values were assigned to the image, to increase the contrast and highlight the region of interest (lungs) on the background. The *imadjust* function of Matlab was used with default settings. Because the input images may have different intensity values, the average image intensity was calculated, the range of the Intensity values to map is selected. For a mean less than or equal to 0.5, a range of 0.7 to 0.9 was taken, and for an average greater than 0.5, the range was 0.8 to 0.9. These values were obtained after a trial and error test.

During the segmentation of the lung region, the multilevel threshold method was used in two of the preprocessed images [8] to compute thresholds Th_1 and Th_2. Thresholded images are added, and morphological operations of opening and closing are applied. Then, because in some cases this method leaves parts of the lung region out, an auxiliary segmentation is performed, using another variant of the multi-level threshold method, in order to identify the outer edges of the lungs to correct the initial segmentation. Finally, an adjustment is made, because in this segmentation the retro-cardiac and sub-diaphragmatic regions, in which nodules may appear, also remain outside the lung field. This process is detailed below.

First this method is applied to both preprocessed images. Let Th_1 and Th_2 be the values of the output thresholds of this method.

$$bwBackg_1(x, y) = (ProcessedImage_1(x, y) \leq Th_1) \tag{10}$$

$$SegmentedImage_1(x, y) = 1 - bwBackg_1(x, y) \tag{11}$$

$$bwBackg_2(x, y) = (ProcessedImage_2(x, y) \leq Th_2) \tag{12}$$

$$SegmentedImage_2(x, y) = 1 - bwBackg_2(x, y) \tag{13}$$

The segmented images were added and the opening and closing morphological operations were applied. In this case, a disk-shaped structuring element with a diameter of 65 pixels in radius was used to obtain the initial segmentation. The aperture removed all pixels in regions that are smaller than the structuring element, the external protuberances were softened, the narrow sections were broken and the thin protuberances were eliminated. The morphological closing filled the holes and smaller concavities. Subsequently, the multilevel threshold method was reapplied for $ProcessedImage_1(x, y)$, thus obtaining auxiliary segmentation.

$$AuxiliarySegmentation(x, y) = (ProcessedImage_1(x, y) - Th_2) \tag{14}$$

Auxiliary segmentation is to define the edges of the lungs. This was done with adaptive morphology using the edge-linking algorithm [9]. This consisted of eliminating the segments of noisy edges, verifying the end points, applying adaptive dilation and thinning. First, the noisy edge segments were removed with a morphological closing operation, using a disk as a structuring element of 3 pixels of radius. Next, adaptive dilation was applied, using an elliptical structuring element. An angle $\alpha = 45°$ was rotated over the entire surface of the edges. With this, the edge segment was extended along the direction of the slope, by means of the shape of an ellipse.

After applying adaptive dilation at each end point, the edge segments were extended in the direction of the local slope. Because the elliptical structuring element was used, the edge segments grew to become thicker, so that, finally, morphological thinning was applied. Once the edges were defined, the image obtained from the initial segmentation was completed from the horizontal limits of the edges to the horizontal limits of the initial segmentation.

One of the deficiencies seen in this segmentation is that it does not include regions of low contrast lung field such as retro-cardiac and sub-diaphragmatic ones, in which nodules may also appear. To correct this aspect, an algorithm was designed that runs through the segmentation mask and detects the maximum and minimum limits of the internal region of the lungs, with which the missing areas of interest are completed.

The following Indices were used to measure the performance of the segmentation algorithm:

Accuracy index

$$A = (TP + TN)/(TP + FP + TN + FN) \tag{15}$$

Sensitivity index

$$S = TP/(TP + FN) \tag{16}$$

Overlay index

$$\Omega = TP/(TP + FP + FN) \tag{17}$$

where TP is the true positive (the area is correctly classified as a lung field), TN represents the true negative (the area is correctly classified as a background), FP is the false positive (the area is incorrectly classified as the lung field) and FN for false negatives (the area is incorrectly classified as background).

Next, a candidate nodule detection algorithm was executed to locate the regions of the image that can be potential lung nodules. For this, a local convergence filter (LCF) was used [10], with the difference that the convergence filter used in this case is a sliding band filter [11].

The LCF evaluates the degree of convergence of the gradient vectors within a local area (support region) towards a pixel of interest (central location of the area). The degree of convergence is related to the distribution of the directions of the gradient vectors and not to their magnitudes. This facilitates the definition of a global threshold, which is not affected by image illumination. The local convergence of a gradient vector in a given pixel can be defined as: the cosine of its orientation with respect to the line connecting that pixel and the central pixel of the area. Said convex shape detection is performed regardless of its contrast with the background. While the low contrast areas of the image may have a poorly defined gradient direction, and cause louder detections, this still allows a greater degree of invariance with respect to the image conditions. This is a valuable feature for the analysis of chest radiography images, due to the inherent low contrast they present.

The LCFs evaluate the convergence for each coordinate (x, y) in the image (excluding the border regions) [11]. In a discrete 2D space, the orientation of the image gradient within a convergence filter support region is defined as:

$$\alpha(x, y, \theta_i, m) = tan^{-1}\left(\frac{\delta I(x_0, y_0)/\delta x}{\delta I(x_0, y_0)/\delta y}\right) \tag{18}$$

with:

$$x_0 = x + m\sin(\theta_i) \tag{19}$$

$$y_0 = x + m\cos(\theta_i) \tag{20}$$

$I(x, y)$ is the image obtained from the lung segmentation, (θ_i, m) are polar coordinates within the support region, $\delta I/\delta x$ is the row-wise image gradient, and $\delta I/\delta y$ is the column-wise image gradient.

Gradients are calculated after a convolution with a 2D Gaussian filter to smooth the input noisy image. The polar coordinates of the support region are defined by m, which is measured in image pixels, and θ_i, which results from radial sampling, defined by:

$$\theta_i = \frac{2\pi}{N}(i - 1) \tag{21}$$

where N is the number of radial directions for which convergence is evaluated and i each direction.

The convergence for the coordinates (θ_i, m) within the support region can be defined using the cosine between the polar direction θ_i and the image gradient for the coordinates (x, y, θ_i, m):

$$CI(x, y, i, m) = \cos(\theta_i - \alpha(x, y, \theta_i, m)) \tag{22}$$

The overall convergence is obtained by adding all the individual convergences given by Eq. (22), within the specific support region of each filter.

Several types of LCF have been developed. Sliding band filter (SBF) was used in this work [11]. The SBF defines a support region formed by a band of fixed width, with a variable radius in each direction, to allow the convergence index to be maximized at each point. The formulation of SBF is given by:

$$SBF(x, y) = \frac{1}{N} \sum_{i=0}^{N-1} \max_{R_{min} \leq r \leq R_{max}} \left[\frac{1}{d} \sum_{m=r-\frac{d}{2}}^{r+\frac{d}{2}} CI(x, y, i, m) \right] \tag{23}$$

where d corresponds to the width of the band, which moves between R_{min} and R_{max}.

The corresponding shape radius for each radial line is given by:

$$r_{shape}(x, y, i) = \operatorname*{argmax}_{R_{min} \leq r \leq R_{max}} \left[\frac{1}{r} \sum_{m=r-\frac{d}{2}}^{r+\frac{d}{2}} CI(i, m) \right] \tag{24}$$

The programming of this filter was provided by the collaborative development platform: GitHub (https://codeload.github.com/EvaFlower/CVProject_celldetection/zip/master).

After candidate detection, an adaptive distance threshold (ADT) algorithm was applied to segment each candidate nodule [7]. The ADT works on the *ProcessedImage*(x, y) and begins with the next threshold operation.

$$s(x, y, T_0) = \begin{cases} 1 & ProcessedImage(x, y) > T(x, y, T_0) \\ 0 & otherwise \end{cases} \tag{25}$$

where $T(x, y, T_0)$ is the adaptive threshold function given by:

$$T(x, y, T_0) = \begin{cases} T_0 + \dfrac{T_\Delta \left(1 - e^{-\frac{d(x,y)}{r_{max}^2}} \right)}{1 - e^{-1}} & d(x, y) < r_{max}^2 \\ \infty & otherwise \end{cases} \tag{26}$$

This adaptive threshold is a function of the distance of a pixel given to the detection signal,

$$d(x, y) = (x - x_0)^2 - (y - y_0)^2 \tag{27}$$

where (x_0, y_0) is the detection reference point.

The maximum nodule radius, for segmentation purposes is specified by r_{max} in pixels. The range of thresholds from the reference point to r_{max} was specified by T_Δ. The adaptive threshold parameter is the offset T_0. For the results of the CAD system presented here, $r_{max} = 50$ pixels and $T_\Delta = 1.7$ were used. The idea behind the distance-based threshold (DBT) is to exploit the knowledge that the nodules tend to be approximately circular lesions. Increasing the threshold with distance tends to prevent segmentation from growing erroneously away from the reference point, along a bright structure, such as a rib.

Next, the binary image $s(x, y, T_0)$ is logically ANDed with the lung lobes mask, to prevent the segmentation from growing outside the defined lung boundaries. Then, a hole filling morphological operation, followed by a morphological opening, with a small circular structuring element with a one-pixel radius was applied. Finally, only the pixels connected to the reference point, which use the 4-connected neighbor criterion, were retained. This produced the denoted mask.

$$ARG(T_0) = \frac{1}{\left|\tilde{S}(T_0)\right|} \sum_{(k,l)\in\tilde{S}(T_0)} |g(x_0 + k, y_0 + l)|\cos\left(\theta_{x_0,y_0}(k, l)\right) \qquad (28)$$

where $\tilde{S}(T_0) = \left\{(k, l) : \tilde{S}(x_0 + k, y_0 + l, T_0) = 1\right\}$, $g(x_0 + k, y_0 + l)$ is the intensity gradient magnitude of the of *ProcessedImage* at pixel $(x_0 + k, y_0 + l)$, and $\theta_{x_0,y_0}(k, l)$ is the angle between the radial vector pointing from pixel $(x_0 + k, y_0 + l)$ to (x_0, y_0) and the intensity gradient vector at pixel $(x_0 + k, y_0 + l)$). T_0 was found, in the range $-2 \le T_0 \le 0$, which maximized ARG (T_0), and was used to generate the segmentation mask of the final nodule. The programming of this filter was provided by the GitHub collaborative development platform (https://github.com/roshniu/Lung-Nodule-Segmen tation-in-Chest-Radiographs--X).

3 Results and Discussion

The results of pre-processing procedure are showed in Fig. 1 and Fig. 2. In the last one is compares the visibility of lesions of different contrast in some regions of interest.

A   B

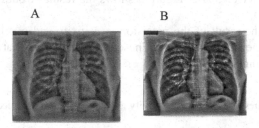

Fig. 1. A) Image obtained after applying the local normalization filter. B) Image obtained after applying homomorphic filtering.

Then, the segmentation of the lung region was performed. The results of the initial and final unsupervised segmentation performance were compared with the standard

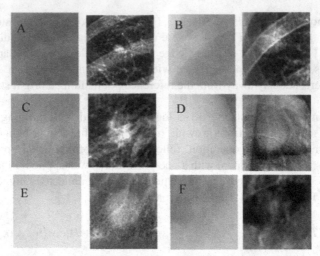

Fig. 2. Low contrast nodules with respect to the surrounding background, and which are highlighted with pre-processing. Case A (obvious), Cases B and C (relatively obvious), Cases D and E (subtle) and case F (very subtle).

Initial   Final

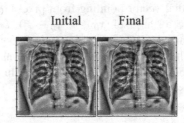

Fig. 3. Results of the initial and final segmentation for two chest X-rays in the JSRT database (the blue color indicates the segmentation by the proposed method, and the red color represents the reference contour offered by the database). (Color figure online)

references of the JSRT database. Figure 3 shows the result of both segmentations for one image of the BD.

Table 1 shows the result of the precision, sensitivity and overlap indexes for the initial and final segmentation proposed. These results indicated that both unsupervised segmentation algorithms were reliable.

Table 1. Average values of precision, sensitivity and superposition obtained for the detection of lung fields (%).

	Precision			Sensitivity			Overlap		
	Min	Med	Max	Min	Med	Max	Min	Med	Max
Initial segmentation	0,95	0,96	0,97	0,85	0,93	0,96	0,80	0,87	0,90
Final segmentation	0,90	0,92	0,94	0,88	0,94	0,97	0,65	0,74	0,81

As can be seen in general, the initial segmentation obtains better results than the final segmentation. This is because the segmentation reference provided by the DB does not include the regions of the low contrast lung field, for which the initial segmentation was modified. However, the final segmentation shows a small improvement in sensitivity, a very important parameter for later stages of the CAD system [14]. In addition, this segmentation includes most of the nodules found in regions of low contrast of the lung field, which are lost with the initial segmentation, so this segmentation is considered to be the most effective. Nevertheless, there were two nodules outside the segmentation, in the sub-diaphragmatic region, which were considered false negatives.

The information provided by the DB includes the center points of each nodule and information of its size. However, it does not provide information on how candidate nodules should be labeled in CAD systems for the detection of lung nodules. A variety of schemes can be found. For example, [12] declares a candidate for TP, if its center is 22 mm from the center of the lung nodule for candidates in the apical and peripheral regions, and 24 mm for a candidate in the hilum region. In [13], a candidate is labeled as TP, if there is an overlap between the truth circle and the bubble circle of the initial candidate's detection. Therefore, small nodules require that candidate detection be closer than for larger nodules. While this method is quite reasonable, it depends on the specific candidate detector used in the system, which makes a perfect reference comparison, impossible for CAD systems using other candidate detectors. In [7] authors adopted a 25mm fixed distance labeling rule. Although no scheme is perfect, it has been assumed in this paper that a fixed distance metric is consistent with the clinical objective. Any candidate with a reference point beyond 25 mm of a truth signal is labeled FP. Several candidates may be within 25 mm of a true signal, and multiple TPs must not be counted for the same nodule. Therefore, if the proposed CAD system generates any candidate that is within the 25 mm true signal, it is credited that the CAD detected that particular nodule. Additional detections within 25 mm of this same nodule are ignored.

For the detection of candidate nodules, the detector performance (SBF) was examined for different specificity values (number of detections per image). For a specificity of approximately 120 detections per image, a sensitivity of 100% was obtained (excluding the only two nodules that were lost in segmentation). Figure 4a) shows the fraction of the JSRT nodules with a detection within the specified distance on the horizontal axis. It is observed that all nodules had a detection within 14 mm, and more than 92.1% of the nodules had a detection within 7.5 mm. While this distance criterion is certainly relevant, it may be more illustrative to know that 97.4% of the nodules have a detection within their true signal radius. These results were obtained with a detection threshold of 4.4, with an internal and external contour energy value of 0.88 and 0.95 respectively, and a sigma value of 5 (Gaussian filter value was applied before detection).

By limiting the detection of adjacent nodules, that is, by increasing the distance that may exist between the candidates and increasing the sigma value to 20, a sensitivity of 100% is obtained (Fig. 4b). In this way, it is possible to maintain an optimal value of sensitivity, reducing the number of candidates per image, but this result has a tendency to increase the distance between the center of the detected nodule and the real center, with less precision. Unlike the previous case, all nodules had a detection within 19 mm, and only 77.48% of the nodules had a detection below 7.5 mm. In addition, 96.71% of the nodules had a detection within their true signal radius.

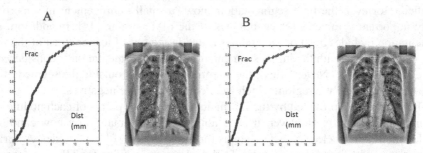

Fig. 4. A) Fraction of the JSRT nodules with an SBF detection within the specified distance on the horizontal axis (excluding the two nodules that are outside the segmentation). At this sensitivity, the SBF detector produces an average of 120 detections per image. B) Fraction of the JSRT nodules with an SBF detection within the specified distance on the horizontal axis (excluding the two nodules that are outside the segmentation). At this sensitivity, the SBF detector produces an average of 56 detections per image.

To put the performance of the detector (SBF) of candidate nodules into context, the operating point reported for candidate detectors in a system, previously published and using the same DB, is considered. According to [13] has a sensitivity of 96.4% with 134 detections per image (excluding 14 cases containing nodules in the retro-cardiac and sub-diaphragmatic regions). This sensitivity is based on the labeling method that seeks any overlap between the Laplacian of Gaussian (LoG) [11] detection circle and the true circle. Therefore, with a comparable specificity (that is, 120 detections per image) the detector (SBF) had a sensitivity of 97.4% in the present work.

Once all the radio-opacities in the image have been identified, each of these is segmented using the adaptive distance based threshold algorithm (ADT) (Fig. 5).

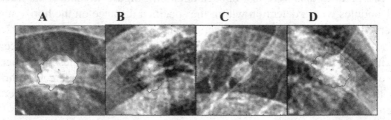

Fig. 5. Examples of segmented nodules using the ADT system for Case A (obvious), Case B (relatively obvious), Case C (subtle) and Case D (very subtle).

The main advantages of ADT segmentation lie in the way that the limits of segmentations do not extend too far from the reference point, without abruptly truncating segmentation. It also adapts better to irregularly shaped nodules and is less sensitive to having non-centralized reference points. The fundamental application of segmentation is aimed at the extraction of a set of characteristics that can be used for a future classification step, where all candidates can distinguish between nodules or non-nodules.

This system does not yet have a classification stage, for which a deep learning technique must be included, based on a convolutional neural network.

4 Conclusions

A CAD System was implemented that segments the lung region from known digital image processing tools, but which, combined in the way proposed in this work, detects the anomalies in the images. During the pre-processing stage, methods were successfully implemented to obtain better image visibility, such as a smoothing filter, a local normalization filter to equalize the contrast and homomorphic filtering to homogenize the lighting. The segmentation method that proved successful for lung segmentation was the multi-level threshold method supported by morphological operations of opening and closing the image. On the lung region, all regions in the image that could indicate the presence of cancer were successfully identified, using the local SBF. All the stages of image processing were integrated in a sequence comprising: preprocessing to enhance the anomalies, segment the lung region, detect all possible nodules and segment each of the candidates. The proposed CAD system presented a sensitivity of 98.7% with 56.08 detections per image with a maximum of 19 mm distance from the reference point. The two FPs that were obtained were due to segmentation.

References

1. American institute for cancer research Homepage. Worldwide cancer data. https://www.wcrf.org/dietandcancer/cancer-trends/worldwide-cancer-data. Accessed 18 Feb 2020
2. Dey, E., Hossain, M.: Chest X-ray analysis to detect mass tissue in lung. In: 2014 International Conference on Informatics, Electronics & Vision (ICIEV), Dhaka, Bangladesh. IEEE Xplore (2014). https://doi.org/10.1109/ICIEV.2014.6850788
3. Gabrielli, M., Muñoz, S., Passalacqua, S., Martinez, G., Plasencio, K., Troncoso, O., et al.: Nódulo pulmonar solitario: Desafío diagnóstico y terapéutico. Cuadernos de Cirugía 21(1), 65–74 (2018)
4. El-Regaily, S.A., Salem, M.A., Abdel-Aziz, M., Roushdy, M.I.: Survey of computer aided detection systems for lung cancer in computed tomography. Curr. Med. Imaging Rev. 14(1), 3–18 (2018)
5. Shiraishi, J., et al.: Development of a digital image database for chest radiographs with and without a lung nodule: receiver operating characteristic analysis of radiologists' detection of pulmonary nodules. Am. J. Roentgenol. 174(1), 71–74 (2000)
6. Solomon, C., Breckon, T.: Fundamentals of Digital Image Processing: A Practical Approach with Examples in Matlab, 12th edn. Wiley (2011)
7. Hardie, R.C., Rogers, S.K., Wilson, T., Rogers, A.: Performance analysis of a new computer aided detection system for identifying lung nodules on chest radiographs. Med. Image Anal. 12(3), 240–258 (2008)
8. Zhang, Y., Wu, L.: Optimal multi-level thresholding based on maximum Tsallis entropy via an artificial bee colony approach. Entropy 13(4), 841–859 (2011)

9. Shih, F.: Image Processing and Mathematical Morphology: Fundamentals and Applications. CRC press (2009)

10. Supanta, C., Kemper, G., Del Carpio, Ch.: An algorithm for feature extraction and detection of pulmonary nodules in digital radiographic images. In: 2018 IEEE International Conference on Automation/XXIII Congress of the Chilean Association of Automatic Control (ICA-ACCA), Chile. IEEE Xplore (2018). https://doi.org/10.1109/ICA-ACCA.2018.8609795

11. Esteves, T., Quelhas, P., Mendonça, A.M., Campilho, A.: Gradient convergence filters and a phase congruency approach for in vivo cell nuclei detection. Mach. Vis. Appl. **23**(4), 623–638 (2012)

12. Shiraishi, J., Li, Q., Suzuki, K., Engelmann, R., Doi, K.: Computer-aided diagnostic scheme for the detection of lung nodules on chest radiographs: localized search method based on anatomical classification. Med. Phys. **33**(7Part1), 2642–2653 (2006)

13. Schilham, A.M.R., van Ginneken, B., Loog, M.: A computer-aided diagnosis system for detection of lung nodules in chest radiographs with an evaluation on a public database. Med. Image Anal. **10**(2), 247–258 (2006)

14. Suarez-Aday, E., Perez-Diaz, M., Orozco-Morales, R.: Diseño de sistema automatizado para detección de anomalías en imágenes digitales de mama. J. Health Med. Sci. **5**(4), 229–243 (2019)

Video and Image Complexity in Human Action Recognition

Andrea Burgos-Madrigal$^{(\boxtimes)}$ and Leopoldo Altamirano-Robles

Computer Science, National Institute of Astrophysics, Optics and Electronics,
Puebla, Mexico
burgosmad@inaoep.mx
https://ccc.inaoep.mx/en/

Abstract. We analyze the relation of video complexity with the performance of Human Action Recognition (HAR) algorithms. The rationale behind this is that variations in image conditions (e.g. occlusion, camera movement, resolution, and illumination), and image content (e.g. edge density, and number of objects), both depicting scene complexity increase the difficulty to recognize activities for a computing model. The HAR algorithms used in this work are improved Dense Trajectories (iDT) [25], Motion-Augmented RGB Stream for Action Recognition (MARS) [5], and SlowFast [7] compared with the number of people and objects in the scene and to three statistical measures: entropy, number of regions and edge density. The results so far show a correlation between complexity and the classification performance. Mask-RCNN simulation for counting elements was carried in the supercomputer cluster of LSC-INAOE.

Keywords: Video complexity · Action recognition · Correlation

1 Introduction

Complexity is a term that has been largely studied and difficult to define. It may be related to the amount of information stored about a particular environment [1], required to reconstruct a message [8] or to specify a system [23]. Also, changes in light illumination, execution, style, size, appearance, or tilts of a camera variability's are possible indicators of scene and video complexity. Rosenholtz et al. [19] define complexity as 'the state in which excess items, or their representation or organization, lead to a degradation of performance at some task.' As a consequence, the concept of 'excess items that add information' appears related to that of complexity entering 'context' into the map. Two scenes with an equal number of objects could be rated very differently in complexity owing to differences in the nature of the objects, their affordances, their textures, and the nature and texture of the background [16]. In HAR, researchers conceptually categorize human activities into four different levels of complexity: gestures, actions, interactions, and group activities [2]. However, it is not always

Supported by CONACyT.

clear a-priori how challenging a HAR task actually is and what dimensions of an analysis pipeline are crucial for successful automated assessments [10]. This complexity term is not clearly defined being sometimes identified by using different parameters such as: average duration and deviation, duration of non repetitive patterns, predefined time of the activity, number of distinct location movements, number of people, and objects involved and so on [20].

In this work, we identify the complexity in videos and evaluate it with the performance of existent classification techniques. We depart from the idea that the classes with better performance should have less complexity.

2   Related Work

Studies in complexity of images or videos usually ask people to determine the levels of complexity manually to eventually compare the people perception with their metrics. Olivia et al. [17] represent the visual complexity in images by the perceptual dimensions where each one would be represented as a combination of low-level (e.g. contours, junctions) and medium-level features (e.g. symmetry) compared to people criteria. Nagle et al. [16], study complexity in images by comparing the correlation between human complexity criteria to scalar images features. The disadvantage of these studies is the dependence with people judge. Ali et al. [4] study the crowd movements by using trajectories and their topological entropy by their motion directions in order to analyze the complexity. The procedure is affected by the distance of the moving objects with the camera. Therefore, instead of comparing the entropy values of different locations, the goal in [3] is to regionally measure, and compare the entropy values of the same image and to determine how the values change over time generating a complexity map to show the crowd behavior. Also, authors [13] employ the appearance cues and motion cues to define the background complexity.

In this study, we take metrics that showed the best correlations to human perception in [16] and extend it to video. We also consider the number of objects or people present in the video by taking advantage of deep learning algorithms for object detection (Mask R-CNN [9]). As a first evaluation, we analyze the correlation of video complexity with precision in three classification algorithms.

3   Proposed Method

For the purpose of assessing the video complexity we used three image statistics: entropy, number of regions and edge density. Also, we get the total of people and objects in the scene. We compare the correlation between those metrics and the performance of classification algorithms.

3.1   Image Statistics

The entropy is a measure of the degree of randomness, in other words, it quantifies the uncertainty of a source of information [21]. For an image which is focused or detailed the entropy is usually large, contrary of an unfocused image (perhaps an image that captures movement). Then, we estimated segment counts using the Maximally Stable Extremal Regions (MSER) proposed by [14]. This algorithm defines regions by an intensity function building a tree of extremal components and finding the regions that stay nearly the same through a wide range of thresholds. MSER performs well on images containing homogeneous regions with distinctive boundaries and small regions but has problems with images that contain any motion blur. We get edge density using the Canny method [6] with a high and a low threshold of $[0.11, 0.27]$ to filter out edge pixels and a standard deviation of the filter $\sigma = 1$ such as [16].

3.2 Mask-RCNN

Mask R-CNN [9] extends Faster R-CNN detector [18] and is used to separate different objects in an image or video. Is conformed of two stages: a Region Proposal Network (RPN) that proposes candidate object bounding boxes (identical to Faster R-CNN), and in the second stage another neural network takes proposed regions to assign them to specific areas of a feature map level, scans these areas and generates object classes as also bounding boxes and masks.

3.3 Correlation Metric

As we did not ask yet people to rank or evaluate the complexity of the activities presented in the videos, we used the precision assuming that classes with low precision tend to be more complex than the ones with high precision. We estimate the ordinal association between the statistical metrics and the precision. We used Pearson's r correlation coefficient.

3.4 Classification Algorithms

iDT [25] is conformed of three concatenated descriptors Histograms of Oriented Gradients (HOG) to aggregate the gradient responses describing appearance and shape, Histogram of Optical Flow (HOF) to aggregate optical flow responses capturing local motion but being affected by camera motion, and Motion Boundary Histogram (MBH) that uses the gradients of optical flow to construct the descriptors in horizontal and vertical directions capturing the movement and being tolerant to camera movement. iDT is usually found as a complement for deep processes with the advantage of capturing motion information [24,26]. Then, MARS [5], which is focused on spatial information, avoids flow computation at test time by minimizing a feature-based loss compared to the flow stream and leverages both appearance and motion information effectively by training with a linear combination of the feature-based loss and the standard cross-entropy loss for HAR. Finally, SlowFast [7] that does not use optical flow. It is conformed by a Slow pathway, operating at low frame rate, to capture spatial semantics, and a Fast pathway, operating at high frame rate, to capture motion at fine temporal

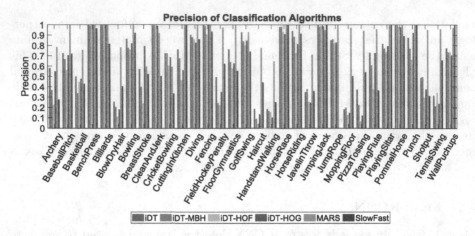

Fig. 1. Selected results as a sample of the precision differences between iDT, iDT-MBH, iDT-HOF, iDT-HOG, MARS, and SlowFast. As each algorithm captures different kind of information, the precision in every class have some variations depending on the action. (Color figure online)

resolution. In Fig. 1 we show the precision of some classes with this techniques to analyze in detail the different information captured by each one e.g. some actions are about interacting with specific objects being principally home-made videos with an inherent shaking of the camera making the spatial information the informative (such as in Archery, Baseball Pitch, or Breast Stroke observed in Fig. 1) and those algorithms that capture the spatial information shows better performance. There exist classes, where specific movement will be characteristic, that is, predominance in an axis such as Pull-ups with the aim of not getting confused with Push-ups. The analysis of their performance gave us a clue to correlate the features with the precision in order to diminish the dependence of human criteria during scene complexity analysis. Nevertheless, we do not have records of related work analyzing the video complexity in relation with classification performance.

4   Experiments and Results

4.1   Dataset

UCF101 [22] is composed of YouTube videos recorded by nonprofessionals with handy-cams containing camera motions, viewpoint variations, and resolution inconsistencies. With 101 action classes and at least 100 video clips for each class. The whole dataset contains 13320 video clips divided into Human-Object Interaction, Body-Motion Only, Human-Human Interaction, Playing Musical Instruments, and Sports.

Table 1. Image statistics and features taken as complexity measures correlated with several HAR algorithms (r for the correlation coefficient and p for p-value)

Method	Input	Whole image entropy	Regions	Edge density	People count	Objects count
2AFC paired comparisons [16]	Images	r = 0.43 p = −0.26	r = 0.45 p = 0.32	r = 0.42 p = −0.24	–	r = 0.49 p = 0.77
Frame edge length cue [13] vs iDT-HOF	Video	-	-	r = 0.2457 p = 0.0133	–	–
iDT	Video	r = 0.1341 p = 0.1811	r=0.2377 p=0.0167	r = 0.0958 p = 0.3404	r = 0.1484 p = 0.1373	r = −0.0090 p = 0.9284
iDT-MBH	Video	r = 0.1413 p = 0.1588	r=0.2624 p=0.0080	r = 0.1329 p = 0.1850	r = 0.1714 p = 0.0866	r = −0.0343 p = 0.7337
iDT-HOF	Video	r = 0.2053 p = 0.0395	r=0.3255 p=0.0008	r = 0.1962 p = 0.0493	r = 0.1523 p = 0.1284	r = 0.0236 p = 0.8151
iDT-HOG	Video	r = 0.1240 p = 0.2166	r=0.2255 p=0.0234	r = 0.1284 p = 0.2008	r = 0.1382 p = 0.1681	r = −0.0409 p = 0.6844
MARS+RGB	Video	r=0.1608 p=0.1083	r = 0.1208 p = 0.2288	r = 0.0224 p = 0.8241	r = 0.0552 p = 0.5833	r = 0.1503 p = 0.1335
SlowFast	Video	r = 0.0922 p = 0.3590	r = 0.0297 p = 0.7679	r = 0.0258 p = 0.7978	r = 0.00006 p = 0.9994	r = 0.0762 p = 0.4487

4.2 Complexity from Image Statistics

Complexity is quite related with noise and noise affects the precision during classification. We test the best statistics taken from the related work [16] and extended it to video action recognition by comparing with the precision obtained by applying iDT, MARS, and SlowFast. In addition, we compare our edge density with the frame edge length presented in [13]. In Table 1 we observe that the best statistic is regions by using the iDT-HOF with the Pearson correlation coefficient $r = 0.3255$ and that it is also the highest with the other iDT cases. This result suggested analyzing in detail the context so we extended the study to people and object count. However, the results were lower but with a high p-value which indicates there is not enough evidence yet for a correlation. Then, the whole image entropy is in second place with $r = 0.2053$ followed by the edge density with $r = 0.1962$. Noise such as movements, light or blur are elements that augment the complexity of videos. This is probably the reason why in Table 1 most measures presented very low p-values reflecting that the correlation coefficient is significantly different from zero. Nevertheless, we did not achieve an r as high as the evaluation of Nagle et al. [16] on images (which is compared to the human criteria and not to an automatic algorithm as classification performance). Besides, we achieved better results than the cue presented by Luo et al. [13] directly compared with iDT-HOF. Results for the Neural Networks MARS+RGB and SlowFast suggests that Neural Networks are not highly influenced by noise, in other words, Neural Networks manage to filter noise better and also, are not based on the context such as the number of regions, objects, or people.

4.3   Camera Movement Influence

We manually selected classes that does not suffer from camera movement (or only a little): ApplyEyeMakeup, ApplyLipstick, Billiards, BlowDryHair, CleanandJerk, HammerThrow, JumpingJack, PlayingCello, TableTennisShot, WallPushups, WritingOnBoard, and YoYo. In Table 2 the highest correlation achieved was $r = 0.7307$ with $p = 0.0094$ between entropy and the iDT-HOF probably because the small camera noise found affects both; the representatives of the characteristics used to obtain the classification performance and the amount of detail or information present and measured by the entropy. In fact, the correlation is high in all the cases of entropy for iDT without movement.On the other hand, we also manually selected classes that suffer from camera movement: BabyCrawling, Biking, FrisbeeCatch, Kayaking, LongJump, Lunges, MoppingFloor, ParallelBars, Skijet, and Swing. In these classes the use of a hand-camera is common what produce a lot of movement because the action requires to be followed. In this case (Table 2), the image feature that got the highest correlation with $r = 0.5376$ and $r = 0.5135$ is the regions feature. MSER is a method sensible to blur and HOF is also affected by the movement of the camera. Nonetheless MBH tries to mitigate the movement it is also affected because in these videos the movement is too abrupt. It is important to mention that for pure iDT the results of correlation are lower. This is quite related to the fact that the descriptors complement each other and the effect of different kind of noises are diminished.

4.4   Types of Activities

UCF-101 is divided into five types of activities and we analyze each one in Tables 4 and 3. Sports, which although they have a lot of movement they are usually captured with professional cameras, the context is really important so as the number of people in the scene, the objects, and the scenario. This is probably the reason why the statistic of regions measures achieved the highest correlations. The iDT-HOF with regions achieved $r = 0.4293$ and $p = 0.0018$ because both are affected by the motion blur. Surprisingly, the people and object count are not retrieving the highest correlation probably because the counting is made by Mask-RCNN which is a Neuronal Network making it more tolerant to noise. When we analyze the results using MARS and SlowFast we still do not find enough evidence for a high correlation between these two metrics. The highest was MARS which is centered on the spatial information but sports is a specific class that depends on temporal information too. The human-object interaction which typically has highly cluttered background and informative motions that occupy a small portion of the clips retrieves higher values with people count but unfortunately with a high p-value too $(p > 0.05)$. The highest correlation would

Table 2. Image statistics and features taken as complexity measures with several HAR recognition algorithms with or without camera movement.

Method	Whole image entropy	Regions	Edge density	People count	Objects count	Camera mov.
iDT	r=0.6845 p=0.0141	r = 0.3825 p = 0.2198	r = 0.5196 p = 0.0834	r = 0.3341 p = 0.2885	r = −0.0644 p = 0.8423	Without
iDT-MBH	r=0.7121 p=0.0094	r = 0.48 p = 0.1143	r = 0.6193 p = 0.0318	r = 0.3802 p = 0.2228	r = −0.0478 p = 0.8828	Without
iDT-HOF	r=0.7307 p=0.0069	r = 0.5075 p = 0921	r = 0.6552 p = 0.0207	r = 0.4115 p = 0.1838	r = 0.0274 p = 0.9326	Without
iDT-HOG	r = 0.603 p = 0.0379	r=0.6552 p=0.0207	r = 0.4621 p = 0.1304	r = 0.2550 p = 0.4237	r = −0.2407 p = 0.4510	Without
MARS	r = 0.3016 p = 0.3406	r = 0.4519 p = 0.1401	r=0.4922 p=0.1040	r = 0.3970 p = 0.2012	r = 0.4103 p = 0.1851	Without
SlowFast	r = −0.0050 p = 0.9875	r = −0.0601 p = 0.8528	r = −0.2159 p = 0.5001	r=−0.3353 p=0.2866	r = −0.00007 p = 0.9998	Without
iDT	r = 0.1562 p = 0.6664	r=0.3866 p=0.2697	r = 0.3520 p = 0.3184	r = 0.0964 p = 0.7911	r = −0.1033 p = 0.7764	With
iDT-MBH	r = 0.1249 p = 0.7309	r=0.5135 p=0.1289	r = 0.4920 p = 0.1486	r = 0.2085 p = 0.5631	r = −0.0504 p = 0.8900	With
iDT-HOF	r = 0.1356 p = 0.7087	r=0.5376 p=0.1089	r = 0.4876 p = 0.1527	r = 0.1817 p = 0.6154	r = −0.1295 p = 0.7214	With
iDT-HOG	r = 0.2218 p = 0.5379	r = 0.3403 p = 0.3358	r=0.4522 p=0.1894	r = 0.0344 p = 0.9249	r = −0.0696 p = 0.8485	With
MARS	r = 0.1673 p = 0.6440	r = −0.3113 p = 0.3812	r = −0.2290 p = 0.5244	r=−0.3913 p=0.2633	r = 0.0107 p = 0.9764	With
SlowFast	r = 0.2360 p = 0.51140	r = −0.0176 p = 0.9613	r=0.4773 p=0.1629	r = −0.0261 p = 0.9428	r = 0.2502 p = 0.4855	With

be between SlowFast and the edge density suggesting that both are sensitive to light changes. However, for body motion the highest correlation is reached when entropy $r = 0.4165$ but with a p-value. Then, we analyze the activity of playing musical instruments where the person usually occupies most of the frame creating a strong relationship with the statistics of regions and edge density with $r = 0.6742$ and $r = 0.7815$ using the algorithm of iDT-HOF. But, also between the objects count and the rest of the algorithms except for SlowFast which achieved $r = 0.5431$ with people count. Finally, the type of activity called human-human interaction is conformed by 5 classes which makes it difficult to find a relation, but it is worth mentioning that the entropy was the best statistic to measure the video complexity.

Table 3. Image statistics applied to each type of activity: sports(S), human-object interaction(H-OI), body-motion only (B-MO)

Method	Whole image entropy	Regions	Edge density	People count	Objects count	Type
iDT	$r = 0.2027$ $p = 0.1580$	**r=0.3094** **p=0.0287**	$r = -0.0522$ $p = 0.7187$	$r = 0.1701$ $p = 0.2376$	$r = -0.0781$ $p = 0.5899$	S
iDT-MBH	$r = 0.1865$ $p = 0.1946$	**r=0.3297** **p=0.0193**	$r = -0.0041$ $p = 0.9769$	$r = 0.2068$ $p = 0.1496$	$r = -0.0753$ $p = 0.6032$	S
iDT-HOF	$r = 0.2605$ $p = 0.0676$	**r=0.4293** **p=0.0018**	$r = 0.0767$ $p = 0.5963$	$r = 0.2000$ $p = 0.1637$	$r = -0.0378$ $p = 0.7943$	S
iDT-HOG	$r = 0.2245$ $p = 0.1169$	**r=0.3109** **p=0.0279**	$r = -0.0162$ $p = 0.9109$	$r = 0.1203$ $p = 0.4053$	$r = -0.1509$ $p = 0.2955$	S
MARS	$r = 0.1879$ $p = 0.1914$	$r = 0.1124$ $p = 0.4372$	$r = -0.0631$ $p = 0.6633$	$r = 0.1156$ $p = 0.424$	**r=0.2421** **p=0.0902**	S
SlowFast	$r = 0.1408$ $p = 0.3293$	$r = 0.1183$ $p = 0.4131$	$r = -0.0567$ $p = 0.6953$	$r = -0.0134$ $p = 0.9263$	**r=0.1731** **p=0.2292**	S
iDT	$r = -0.1710$ $p = 0.4837$	$r = 0.1707$ $p = 0.4846$	$r = 0.0945$ $p = 0.70029$	**r=0.2014** **p=0.4084**	$r = 0.1499$ $p = 0.5403$	H-OI
iDT-MBH	$r = -0.1214$ $p = 0.6203$	$r = 0.1855$ $p = 0.4470$	$r = -0.1634$ $p = 0.5038$	**r=0.2226** **p=0.3597**	$r = 0.0751$ $p = 0.7599$	H-OI
iDT-HOF	$r = -0.1414$ $p = 0.5634$	$r = 0.1946$ $p = 0.4244$	$r = 0.1530$ $p = 0.5315$	**r=0.2117** **p=0.3842**	$r = 0.1731$ $p = 0.4786$	H-OI
iDT-HOG	**r= −0.2078** **p=0.3932**	$r = 0.1743$ $p = 0.4753$	$r = 0.0455$ $p = 0.8529$	$r = 0.0806$ $p = 0.7428$	$r = 0.0954$ $p = 0.6976$	H-OI
MARS	$r = 0.1211$ $p = 0.6212$	$r = 0.1943$ $p = 0.4252$	$r = 0.1137$ $p = 0.6427$	$r = -0.1125$ $p = 0.6465$	**r= −0.2138** **p=0.3825**	H-OI
SlowFast	$r = -0.2003$ $p = 0.4108$	$r = -0.3758$ $p = 0.1127$	**r= −0.4282** **p=0.0673**	$r = -0.3220$ $p = 0.1792$	$r = -0.1393$ $p = 0.5690$	H-OI
iDT	**r=0.3976** **p=0.1272**	$r = 0.2107$ $p = 0.4332$	$r = 0.0341$ $p = 0.9000$	$r = -0.0483$ $p = 0.8589$	$r = -0.0048$ $p = 0.9859$	B-MO
iDT-MBH	**r=0.3789** **p=0.1477**	$r = 0.2640$ $p = 0.3231$	$r = 0.0360$ $p = 0.8946$	$r = -0.0986$ $p = 0.7164$	$r = 0.0072$ $p = 0.9790$	B-MO
iDT-HOF	**r=0.3234** **p=0.2217**	$r = 0.2365$ $p = 0.3776$	$r = 0.0619$ $p = 0.8197$	$r = -0.0107$ $p = 0.9687$	$r = 0.2266$ $p = 0.3986$	B-MO
iDT-HOG	**r=0.4165** **p=0.1084**	$r = 0.1796$ $p = 0.5054$	$r = 0.0225$ $p = 0.9339$	$r = 0.0290$ $p = 0.9152$	$r = 0.1975$ $p = 0.4635$	B-MO
MARS	$r = 0.2671$ $p = 0.3172$	$r = 0.2217$ $p = 0.4091$	**r=0.3424** **p=0.1941**	$r = 0.2030$ $p = 0.4506$	$r = -0.0247$ $p = 0.9275$	B-MO
SlowFast	$r = 0.0288$ $p = 0.9154$	$r = -0.2278$ $p = 0.3959$	$r = 0.0791$ $p = 0.7708$	**r= −0.3591** **p=0.1719**	$r = 0.02116$ $p = 0.9379$	B-MO

Table 4. Image statistics applied to playing musical instruments (PMI) and human-human interaction (H-HI)

iDT	$r = 0.0050$ $p = 0.9905$	$r = -0.0559$ $p = 0.8952$	$r = 0.3598$ $p = 0.3812$	$r = -0.4747$ $p = 0.2346$	**r= −0.7334** **p=0.0384**	PMI
iDT-MBH	$r = 0.1424$ $p = 0.7364$	$r = 0.2683$ $p = 0.5204$	**r=0.6742** **p=0.0666**	$r = -0.2373$ $p = 0.5715$	**r= −0.6676** **p=0.0704**	PMI
iDT-IIOF	$r = 0.3230$ $p = 0.4351$	**r=0.6742** **p=0.0666**	**r=0.7815** **p=0.0219**	$r = 0.0369$ $p = 0.9308$	$r = -0.3210$ $p = 0.4382$	PMI
iDT-HOG	$r = -0.2164$ $p = 0.6066$	$r = -0.1059$ $p = 0.8028$	$r = 0.1706$ $p = 0.6861$	$r = -0.4605$ $p = 0.2508$	**r= −0.7278** **p=0.0407**	PMI
MARS	$r = -0.0922$ $p = 0.8001$	$r = 0.0237$ $p = 0.9481$	$r = -0.3564$ $p = 0.3121$	$r = 0.3166$ $p = 0.3728$	**r= −0.3941** **p=0.2598**	PMI
SlowFast	$r = 0.4936$ $p = 0.1471$	$r = 0.3804$ $p = 0.2782$	$r = 0.4321$ $p = 0.2124$	**r=0.5431** **p=0.1047**	$r = 0.2386$ $p = 0.0.5067$	PMI
iDT	**r=0.6974** **p=0.1904**	$r = 0.1407$ $p = 0.8213$	$r = 0.3174$ $p = 0.6026$	$r = 0.2874$ $p = 0.6392$	$r = 0.1514$ $p = 0.8079$	H-HI
iDT-MBH	**r=0.7247** **p=0.1659**	$r = 0.1330$ $p = 0.8311$	$r = 0.3190$ $p = 0.6007$	$r = 0.2733$ $p = 0.6564$	$r = 0.1611$ $p = 0.7958$	H-HI
iDT-HOF	**r=0.7088** **p=0.1800**	$r = -0.0289$ $p = 0.9630$	$r = 0.1922$ $p = 0.7567$	$r = 0.1090$ $p = 0.8615$	$r = -0.0146$ $p = 0.9813$	H-HI
iDT-HOG	**r=0.6546** **p=0.2305**	$r = 0.0486$ $p = 0.9378$	$r = 0.2377$ $p = 0.7001$	$r = 0.2003$ $p = 0.7467$	$r = 0.0263$ $p = 0.9665$	H-HI
MARS	**r=0.6156** **p=0.2690**	$r = -0.0409$ $p = 0.9480$	$r = 0.2071$ $p = 0.7382$	$r = 0.0580$ $p = 0.9262$	$r = -0.1931$ $p = 0.7556$	H-HI
SlowFast	$r = 0.3493$ $p = 0.5645$	$r = 0.1185$ $p = 0.8494$	$r = 0.4204$ $p = 0.4810$	$r = 0.0469$ $p = 0.9403$	**r= −0.5142** **p=0.3754**	H-HI

5   Conclusions and Future Work

Although video complexity is a difficult issue to be objectively evaluated, humans can successfully interpret videos within a large range of complexity. We hypothesized that the video complexity can play an important role in the classification process, affecting its performance. In this work, we used the three classification algorithms in combination with five measures to assess the video complexity. We observed that the results are quite related to the type of activity which suggests looking for a fusion of the measures or for measures related to the temporal domain which is a weakness of 3DCNN solutions [12]. In fact, we humans use temporal reasoning to tolerate the spatial corruptions generated in acquisition and processing [11]. Understanding the elements that complicates a video, would help to decide the treatment needed to effectively classify and should diminishes the dependence on the dataset used to train. This would be one important step for classifying classes with only a few or none training example better known as few/zero shot learning [15]. Training deep architectures requires a large amount of annotated data, something that is not easily available for new action classes.

References

1. Adami, C.: What is complexity? BioEssays **24**(12), 1085–1094 (2002)
2. Aggarwal, J.K., Ryoo, M.S.: Human activity analysis: a review. ACM Comput. Surv. (CSUR) **43**(3), 1–43 (2011)

3. Akpulat, M., Ekinci, M.: Detecting interaction/complexity within crowd movements using braid entropy. Front. Inf. Technol. Electron. Eng. **20**(6), 849–861 (2019)
4. Ali, S.: Measuring flow complexity in videos. In: Proceedings of the IEEE International Conference on Computer Vision, pp. 1097–1104 (2013)
5. Crasto, N., Weinzaepfel, P., Alahari, K., Schmid, C.: Mars: motion-augmented RGB stream for action recognition. In: Proceedings of the IEEE/CVF Conference on Computer Vision and Pattern Recognition, pp. 7882–7891 (2019)
6. Ding, L., Goshtasby, A.: On the canny edge detector. Pattern Recogn. **34**(3), 721–725 (2001)
7. Feichtenhofer, C., Fan, H., Malik, J., He, K.: Slowfast networks for video recognition. In: Proceedings of the IEEE International Conference on Computer Vision, pp. 6202–6211 (2019)
8. Grünwald, P.D., Vitányi, P.M.: Kolmogorov complexity and information theory. With an interpretation in terms of questions and answers. J. Log. Lang. Inf. **12**(4), 497–529 (2003)
9. He, K., Gkioxari, G., Dollár, P., Girshick, R.: Mask R-CNN. In: Proceedings of the IEEE International Conference on Computer Vision, pp. 2961–2969 (2017)
10. Hiremath, S.K., Plötz, T.: Deriving effective human activity recognition systems through objective task complexity assessment. Proc. ACM Interact. Mob. Wearable Ubiquit. Technol. **4**(4), 1–24 (2020)
11. Lee, J.S., Ebrahimi, T.: Perceptual video compression: a survey. IEEE J. Sel. Top. Signal Process. **6**(6), 684–697 (2012)
12. Lin, Z.Y., Chen, J.L., Chen, L.G.: A 203 FPS VLSI architecture of improved dense trajectories for real-time human action recognition. In: 2018 IEEE International Conference on Acoustics, Speech and Signal Processing (ICASSP), pp. 1115–1119. IEEE (2018)
13. Luo, B., Li, H., Meng, F., Wu, Q., Ngan, K.N.: An unsupervised method to extract video object via complexity awareness and object local parts. IEEE Trans. Circ. Syst. Video Technol. **28**(7), 1580–1594 (2017)
14. Matas, J., Chum, O., Urban, M., Pajdla, T.: Robust wide-baseline stereo from maximally stable extremal regions. Image Vis. Comput. **22**(10), 761–767 (2004)
15. Mishra, A., Pandey, A., Murthy, H.A.: Zero-shot learning for action recognition using synthesized features. Neurocomputing **390**, 117–130 (2020)
16. Nagle, F., Lavie, N.: Predicting human complexity perception of real-world scenes. R. Soc. Open Sci. **7**(5), 191487 (2020)
17. Olivia, A., Mack, M.L., Shrestha, M., Peeper, A.: Identifying the perceptual dimensions of visual complexity of scenes. In: Proceedings of the Annual Meeting of the Cognitive Science Society, vol. 26 (2004)
18. Ren, S., He, K., Girshick, R., Sun, J.: Faster R-CNN: towards real-time object detection with region proposal networks. arXiv preprint arXiv:1506.01497 (2015)
19. Rosenholtz, R., Li, Y., Mansfield, J., Jin, Z.: Feature congestion: a measure of display clutter. In: Proceedings of the SIGCHI Conference on Human Factors in Computing Systems, pp. 761–770 (2005)
20. Sahaf, Y., Krishnan, N.C., Cook, D.J.: Defining the complexity of an activity. In: Activity Context Representation (2011)
21. Shannon, C.E.: A mathematical theory of communication. ACM SIGMOBILE Mob. Comput. Commun. Review **5**(1), 3–55 (2001)
22. Soomro, K., Zamir, A.R., Shah, M.: Ucf101: A dataset of 101 human actions classes from videos in the wild. arXiv preprint arXiv:1212.0402 (2012)

23. Standish, R.K.: Concept and definition of complexity. In: Intelligent Complex Adaptive Systems, pp. 105–124. IGI Global (2008)
24. Tokmakov, P., Hebert, M., Schmid, C.: Unsupervised learning of video representations via dense trajectory clustering. arXiv preprint arXiv:2006.15731 (2020)
25. Wang, H., Oneata, D., Verbeek, J., Schmid, C.: A robust and efficient video representation for action recognition. Int. J. Comput. Vis. **119**(3), 219–238 (2016)
26. Wang, L., Koniusz, P., Huynh, D.Q.: Hallucinating IDT descriptors and I3D optical flow features for action recognition with CNNs. In: Proceedings of the IEEE/CVF International Conference on Computer Vision, pp. 8698–8708 (2019)

A Wide 2D Median Filter for GPU Devices

Maikel Salas Zaldivar[✉]

Cuban Center for Neuroscience, Havana, Cuba
maikelsz8143@nauta.cu

Abstract. The median filter is a technique of nonlinear digital filter, often used to reduce some kinds of image noise. However, in its original form it is limited in part by its algorithmic complexity, which has led to faster algorithm versions. Still, these variants are not completely able to use the modern hardware such as its parallel computing capabilities and diverse compute architectures, leaving room for accelerations. It is therefore proposed a parallel execution modification of one of these variants to obtain faster processing speed with bigger filter sizes and execution in different processing environments.

Keywords: Denoise · Filter · GPU · Median · OpenCL

1 Introduction

The median filter is a non-linear filter that reduces the noise of an image or signal. It is one of the basic building blocks in many situations of image processing and is the foundation on which other advanced filters are based (Gonzales and Woods 2002). One of the advantages of this method is that it can preserve the edges, while eliminating noise. To eliminate noise, the algorithm processes element patterns of the input image or signal. For each pattern of elements in the neighborhood called support window, the algorithm finds the value of the median that is used as the filtered result for the central element of the window.

However, its usefulness is limited in some cases due to the processing time it requires. Its non-linearity or separability makes it very difficult to apply common optimization techniques. One common way to do it by brute force is to create an ordered list of the values of the pixels in the filter area (kernel). The median would then be the value located at the center of the list. In the general case, for every image pixel, it would have a complexity $O(n \log(r))$ where r is the radius of the filter. For a constant number of values, some methods decrease it to $O(r2)$. With small filter sizes, some variants reduce their complexity to $O(\log(r))$ (Devillard 1998).

© Springer Nature Switzerland AG 2021
Y. Hernández Heredia et al. (Eds.): IWAIPR 2021, LNCS 13055, pp. 360–369, 2021.
https://doi.org/10.1007/978-3-030-89691-1_35

A classic algorithm available and widely used has complexity O(r). The image is traversed by rows or columns, and a histogram is used to accumulate the pixels of the analysis window. Only a part is modified when moving from one pixel to another. As illustrated and pseudo-code in Fig. 1, only $2r + 1$ additions and $2r + 1$ subtractions are needed to update the histogram (Huang et al. 1979). This is the starting algorithm for our work.

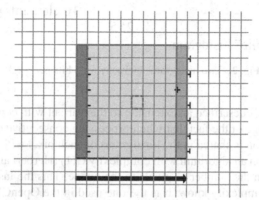

Input: Image X of size m ×n, r radii of the window
Output: Image Y, same size of X
Initialize histogram H of the filter window
for i = 1 ... m
for j = 1 ... n

   for k = −r ... r
    remove X(i+k , j−r−1) from H
    add X(i+k , j+r) to H
  end
  Y(i,j) = median(H)
 end
end

Fig. 1. Differential update of the filter values

To get the median, the histogram values are summed from one end and stopping when the sum reaches or exceeds $(2r + 1)2/2 + 1$. For 8-bit images, the histogram is made up of 256 elements and on average 128 comparisons and additions would be necessary; this would depend on the image. The worst case are images with many pixels of high values that force to travel almost the entire histogram. This would imply that, for filters of smaller radius, the time of histogram analysis may be longer than its creation, thus imposing a penalty on its use.

A way to reduce the search time is to use several histograms, from coarser (greater range of elements per position) to finner (lower range of elements per position). Each one contains the sum of a certain amount of the following positions in the hierarchy. The optimal size of each level is the square root of the lower level. For images of 8 bits per pixel, using three histograms, the bigger histogram has 256 positions, the next 16 and an the smallest would have 4 positions (Fig. 2). For example, with two levels of 16 and 256 positions, this hierarchy allows the worst case to go from 256 operations to only 32. With three levels, it would be further reduced to 24 operations.

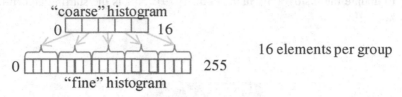

Fig. 2. Two histograms hierachy for 8 bits per pixel

In (Weiss 2006) is described an extension to this variant with complexity O(log(r)), which takes advantage of the fact that when processing consecutive columns (or rows), redundant information is shared in the histograms of each pixel with those of its neighbors. Finally, mention an algorithm with complexity O(1) (Herbert and Perreault 2007), that only depends on the number of pixels in the image. This the fastest and with lowest computationa complexity know. It is the one used in the OpenCV computer vision software library and is the reference implementation we test against. However, to do a parallel implementation of this one seems very difficult due to the complete dependence on the results of all the previous processed pixels, unless the image is processed by segments, something to investigate.

2   Methods and Materials

The median filter has been implemented several times for parallel accelerated execution in multicore CPUs (Intel 2012), GPUs (Perrot et al. 2013; Miyazaki and Koshimura 2018 and Salvador et al. 2018) and FPGAs (Tavse et al. 2012 and Lin et al. 2018). It has been made with different programming languages and technologies such as reconfigurable hardware, but none has been designed to work in more than one type of device or architecture. Also, those are usually limited implementations using small analysis windows (like 3 × 3 or 5 × 5), however, larger analysis windows of 11 × 11 pixels and more are necessary in some image and video processing (Hautiere and Tarel 2009 and Xiao and Gan 2012).

Modern computer systems have evolved towards incorporating processors with a greater number of execution units, since they cannot continue increasing clock speeds due to physical limitations. Some modern CPUs have more than two dozen cores while GPUs consist of thousands. Likewise, the shared execution capacity and data exchange between these processors has increased, blurring the separation line between them (Gaster et al. 2013). These changes are manifested from large computers to portable devices. Exploiting these heterogeneous computational architectures, requires development methodologies and tools different from those commonly used.

To create our variant of the median filter, OpenCL (Open Computing Language) (Khronos 2013) was used. It is a standard development framework, open and multiplatform, developed and maintained by Khronos Group. It is designed for develop general-purpose applications, capable of running on heterogeneous computing platforms, on devices such as CPUs, GPUs, FPGAs, DSPs, etc.; from mobile devices to supercomputers. While OpenCV has many OpenCL accelerated functions, the median filter larger than 5×5 only runs serially on CPU (Herbert and Perreault 2007).

Our implementation is relatively simple. Our first version (Salas 2017) was not optimized for any particular architecture but worked best on CPUs, having the GPUs a performance penalty. Then, we optimized for the particular architectures of GPUs. On GPUs, the image is processed simultaneously by columns, assigned to separated thread groups (work-groups). However, efficient memory access patterns must also be taken into account. On the GPUs the grouping of threads (work-items) in the work-groups was set to the width of the filter, that mean that each thread differentially process one pixel on the filter window last/next row. In addition, as we have many work-groups, we have many threads, increasing the hardware occupation and hiding the high memory latency. Also, the threads read consecutive memory positions, improving access to main and cache memory.

The two histograms are maintained by each work-group (GPU), and it is necessary to update both simultaneously. On the first pixel, the histograms are fully updated. Then, the differential update is performed. On GPU the two histograms are created in the local memory of each work-group, shared by its threads. Local memory on GPUs is located within the computing units and is the second fastest storage available (Munshi et al. 2012). Local and private memory are also of very limited size, and the amount used by each work-item should be as small as possible. Allocated local memory cannot pass a maximum amount. Therefore, the data type of the histograms is the smallest possible that can be used, in this case unsigned short, which represents 2 bytes (16 bits), then the two histograms consume only 544 bytes, allowing filtering windows of up to 256×256 pixels if local memory is limited to 16 KB. To update the histograms elements, atomic integer decrement and increment operations are used. This atomics make blocking updates to memory values and it is where most of the potentially serializations occurs.

While our first algorithm version could run on GPU, it posed a problem in its execution because the conditional operations and execution divergence of the work-items within a work-group. In GPUs this has a quite negative impact. GPUs are optimized to run many processing threads with the same operations on many same or continuous data elements, as straightforward as possible, and if possible, without comparisons or jumps (AMD 2012). Its memory system is built to make readings to aligned positions. As we assign one GPU work-group to each processed pixel column, this problem does not occur. There is only one main bifurcation on the work-group: the final median value for a pixel is obtained by only one work-item. This is done after a blocking local memory write sincronization, to assure all threads had updated its histogram value.

It must be taken into account how to process the edges of the image. To avoid going outside of the image when processing the pixels near the edges, controls methods can be applied when this condition is fulfilled: avoid processing the borders, take values form a different part of the imagen or keep the border values, modify the windows size, etc. The OpenCV median replicates the border values when the filter window goes off the image. For our method, we lock the analysis window to the border. Following, the complete code for our OpenCL GPU kernel function.

```
kernel void Median2D_GPU(__global uchar* srcImage, __global uchar* dstImage, int height)
{
        //one work-group (w-g) by each image column, global worksize = width * local work size
        const int x = get_group_id(0); //identifies the column to process
        const int lws = get_local_size(0);//local work size (w-g size). Same as Filter Width
        const int lid = get_local_id(0);//work item (w-i) id. One pixel on the filter width
        const int width = get_num_groups(0); //number of w-g on execution = image width
        const int radii = floor(lws / 2.0f); //filter radius
        const int medianStop = lws * lws / 2 + 1; //"cut" value of the median
        __local uint histogram_coarse[16]; //coarse histogram, local memory
        __local uint histogram_fine[256]; //fine histogram, local memory
        int u = min(max(xi + lid, 0), width - 1);
        for (int y = 0; y < height; y++)
        {//for every pixel along a column
                int endY = min(y + radii, height - 1);
                int iniPreY = max(y - radii - 1, 0);
                if (y == 0) { //on the first pixel, fully initialize the histograms
                        for (int i = 0; i < 16; i++)  histogram_coarse[i] = 0; //"#pragma unroll" can be used here...
                        for (int i = 0; i <= 255; i++) histogram_fine[i] = 0; //...and here
                        for (int v = -radii;  v <= radii; v++) {
                                uchar color = srcImage[u + clamp(y + v, 0, height) * width];
                                atomic_inc(&histogram_coarse[color / 16]);
                                atomic_inc(&histogram_fine[color]);
                        }//for
                }else{ //...then, only differentialy update the histograms
                        uchar color = srcImage[u + iniPreY * width];
                        atomic_dec(&histogram_coarse[color / 16]); //decrement the last row
                        atomic_dec(&histogram_fine[color]);
                        color = srcImage[u + clamp(endY, 0, height) * width];
                        atomic_inc(&histogram_coarse[color / 16]); //add the new row
                        atomic_inc(&histogram_fine[color]);
                }//else
                barrier(CLK_LOCAL_MEM_FENCE); //local thread synchronization
                if (lid == 0) {//only one thread do this final step. search median on the histograms, coarse first
                        uchar grayOut = 0;
                        uint sum = 0;
                        for (int m = 0; m < 16; m++) {
                                uint h = histogram_coarse[m];
                                sum += h; //accumulate values
                                if (sum >= medianStop) { //if equal or bigger than the "cut value"...
```

```
                        grayOut = m * 16;
                        sum -= h;
                        break; //...exit the coarse search loop...
                }//if
        }//for //...then search on the fine histogram, on the corresponding section
        for (int n = grayOut; n < grayOut + 16; n++) {
                sum += histogram_fine[n]; //accumulate values
                if (sum >= medianStop) { //if equal or bigger than the "cut value"...
                        grayOut = n; //...final result...
                        break; //...exit final search loop
                }//if
        }//for
        dstImage[x + y * width] = grayOut;//put final value on result image
    }//if
  }//for
}//kernel
```

3 Results

Verification of correct results is made by comparing to the reference median algorithm in the OpenCV computer vision and image processing library. This filter, although not parallel, also uses two histograms and SIMD instructions. It is an implementation of the median presented in (Hebert and Perreault 2007), of complexity O(1), since it only depends on the size of the image. The most commonly used cases for the filter size, 3 × 3 and 5 × 5 pixels, are made as two sorting networks (Knuth 1997) fixed in code.

The experiment were carried out by adding impulsive noise at the two extremes of the range of values (salt-and-pepper noise, black and white) to two standar 512 × 512 images. Then the images were filtered with a filter of size 3 × 3 in one and two iterations, and 7 × 7 and 11 × 11 in one iteration. This is to compare against the case that uses the sorting network and the one with the algorithm used in OpenCV.

Table 1 PSNR. OpenCV reference and our proposal

Image (degraded PSNR) >	Lenna (12.65 dB)		Baboon (12.43 dB)	
Filter size	OpenCV	Proposed	OpenCV	Proposed
3 × 3	29.82	29.82	19.90	19.90
3 × 3, 2 iter	32.29	32.28	20.11	20.11
7 × 7	28.71	28.70	18.12	18.12
11 × 11	26.62	26.62	17.62	17.61

Table 1 shows a quantitative evaluation of the results obtained in two cases, using the objective PSNR (Peak Signal-to-Noise Ratio). Our results are basically equal to the reference, with absolute differences usually less than one centh of dB (<0.01 dB), just inside of rounding errors to the tenth decimal place when the PSNR is calculated. As the values does not deviate from the reference, we can define the restoration quality of our algorithm as correct.

For the performance evaluation, three grayscale images of 1024 × 1024 pixels and 8 bits per pixel were used. An image is composed only of random noise that covers the entire range of values (0 … 255, noise image), one with only the minimum value (0, black image) and another with only the maximum value (255, white image). The noise image causes all the work-items (CPU) or work-groups (GPU) to have approximately the same probability of obtaining the result in a similar average time, and generates as many bifurcations as possible. The other two images test the cases in which a result is obtained immediately and more delayed, respectively. Thus we can test the three extreme cases.

The radius of the filter was increased in steps of 1 pixel up to size of 10. Then, in order to show the effects at a larger filter size, in increments of 5 pixels (11 in width). The results are the average of more than 100 continuous executions, discarding the first 10, which are taken as a warm-up.

The test hardware consists of 1 CPU and 2 GPUs, from different manufacturers and architectures. The CPU is the reference device, which executes the OpenCV reference median filter. The devices are: INTEL Core i5-4460 (desktop CPU), AMD Radeon RX 470 (desktop GPU), NVIDIA GeForce GTX1050Ti (laptop GPU). In our experiments, the data is already on device memory and mantained there, avoiding CPU to GPU data transfers. These data transfers between the host (CPU) and the device (GPU) can sometimes exceed the computation time, depending on its complexity, the volume of data and the speed of the data interface (Fig. 3).

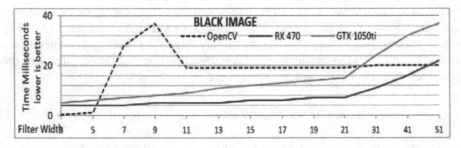

Fig. 3 GPU execution. "Black" image. Lower time is better

Processing the "black" or "white" images on the GPUs bring a total serialization inside the work-groups, due to all thread needing to update the very same positions in the histograms. One conclussion we can make from this, is that something like this can happen in images with very low contrast or many regions with very similar values. The case of the "white" image, it may takes longer as the last thread need to fully traverse both histograms (Fig. 4).

The "noise" image should be the most difficult test for all architectures because lots of bifurcations happens. Unlike the cases of the black/white images, where the work-goups maintain certain coherence but total thread serialization occurs, an image composed purely of noise generates extreme divergences on the execution. The work-groups stop processing a pixel and move to the next at different times, so loss of coherence of execution occurs with some negative impact on GPUs due to the characteristics of its

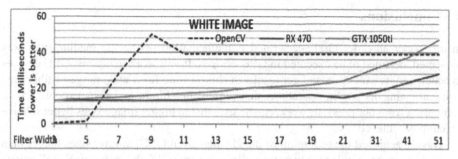

Fig. 4. GPU execution. "White" image. Lower time is better

architectures. But very high serialization like on the black/white test have higher impact on performance. If high loss of coherence have happened at thread level inside the work-groups, the impact have been a lot higher, as was in our previous work. The time differs little along the test as the average time for processing a pixel is similar (Fig. 5).

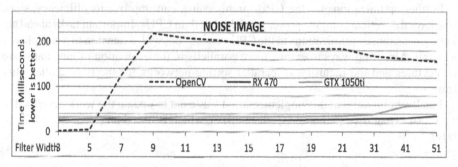

Fig. 5. GPU execution. "Noise" image. Lower time is better

In all cases, it can be seen the characteristic almost constant O(1) time of the OpenCV reference implementation is evident from a window size of 11 × 11. The instability of the sizes 7 × 7 to 11 × 11 can be given by characteristics of the implementation with respect to the architecture of the CPU, for example, how the cache is used. Also, because the cost of data initialization may be bigger than processing. The OpenCV reference implementation loss performance under random pixel values, as all the bifurcations are inside the unique execution thread. So the jump prediction and speculative execution mechanism of the CPU are almost useless due to the highly random nature of the data values. The time decreases and trend to stabilize with bigger filter sizes, as there are more shared data between pixels. Processing image with complex content and many details may have a behavior similar to this, as is more variation in the data. The more noise the image has, the more similar to this the processing will be.

The reference filter executes in a single thread/core and its performance depends fundamentally on the clock speed and the Instructions-Per-Cycle (IPC) of the processor where it is executed. Sizes 3 × 3 and 5 × 5 always get the fastest and same time, thanks to the use of sorting networks of fixed cost.

4 Conclusions

In this paper an order O(r) accelerated implementation of the 2D median filter was presented, destined to be executed in GPU devices. It will work in various GPU devices to accelerate its execution and get results in shorter time for a wide range of filter area sizes, allowing its use in operations that require big filters and fast response. Also, comparing from our previous work, can be seen that to bigger image sizes better relative speedup is achieved.

Having achieved the execution of the 2D median in GPU, at filter sizes bigger than others of this type found in the literature, allows in some GPGPU computing applications to eliminate the need for host-device-host transfers to apply the filter in the CPU, which imply additional times, unless the sum of the total time of the operation is lower. In general, the images processing time will be between the "noise" and the "black/white" results. In case of execution in GPU, the speeds is also given by the particularities of each architecture, its operation and characteristics of the algorithm. Modern models, with more general, powerful and efficient architectures are able to better execute complex flow code and scattered memory access.

Further optimizations for the GPUs architectures can improve its efficiency, since these have theoretical compute power much higher than CPUs. Important tasks ahead are to bring back those optimizations to the CPU version too, with extension to a complexity O(log(r)). Also, find ways to extract more parallelism, the evaluation of new hardware architectures and the inclusion of parallel sorting networks for the two smaller filter sizes.

Finally, point out that this implementation was used to update the work described in (Salas 2017) that uses (Salas and Collazo 2014), which is based on (Hautiere and Tarel 2009).

References

Gonzales, R., Woods, R.: Digital Image Processing. 2nd Edition, Prentice Hall, pp 123–124 (2002)

Devillard, N.: Fast median search: an ANSI C implementation (1998)

Huang, T., Yang, G., Tang, G.: A fast two-dimensional median filtering algorithm. IEEE Trans. Acoust. Speech Sig. Process. **27**(1), 13–18 (1979)

Weiss, B.: Fast median and bilateral filtering. In: ACM SIGGRAPH 2006, pp. 519–526 (2006)

Hebert, P., Perreault, S.: Median filtering in constant time. IEEE Trans. Image Process. **16**(9), 2389–2394 (2007)

INTEL Corp: Median Filter Sample. Intel SDK for OpenCL (2012)

Perrot, G., Domas, S., Couturier, R.: Fine-tuned high-speed implementation of a GPU-based median filter. J. Sig. Process. Syst. **75**(3), 185–190 (2013)

Miyazaki, T., Koshimura, Y.: A study on fast removal method of impulsive noise using parallel processing with GPU. In: Proceedings of the 6th IIAE International Conference on Industrial Applications Engineering (2018)

Salvador, G., et al.: Efficient GPU-based implementation of the median filter based on a multi-pixel-per-thread framework. In: IEEE Southwest Symposium on Image Analysis and Interpretation (2018)

Tavse, S., Jadhav, P., Ingle, M.: Optimized median filter implementation on FPGA including soft processor. Int. J. Emerg. Technol. Adv. Eng. **2**(8), 236–239 (2012)

Lin, S.H., Chen, P.Y., Lin, C.H.: Hardware design of an energy-efficient high-throughput median filter. IEEE Trans. Circ. Syst. II: Exp. Briefs **65**, 1728–1732 (2018)

Hautiere, N., Tarel, J.: Fast visibility restoration from a single color or gray level image. In: IEEE 12th International Conference on Computer Vision, pp 2201–2208 (2009)

Xiao, C., Gan, J.: Fast image dehazing using guided joint bilateral filter. Vis. Comput. **28**(6–8), 713–721 (2012)

Gaster, B., Kaeli, D., Mistry, P., Schaa, D.: Heterogeneous Computing with OpenCL. Elsevier Inc. (2013)

Khronos Group: The OpenCL Specification (2013)

Munshi A., et al.: The OpenCL Programming Guide. Addison Wesley (2012)

Knuth, D.E.: The Art of Computer Programming, Volume 3: Sorting and Searching, 3rd edn. Addison–Wesley, pp. 219–247 (1997).

Salas, M.: Propuesta de implementación del filtro de la mediana 2D para ejecución en dispositivos heterogéneos de cómputo paralelo. In: III Conferencia Científica RECPAT (2017)

Salas, M., Collazo, J.: Una propuesta paralela para la Recuperación Rápida de Visibilidad en Imágenes en Color y Escala de Gris en Dispositivos Gráficos, CEIS, CUJAE (2014)

Medical Image Watermarking
with Separable Moments

Yenner J. Díaz Núñez(✉)📷, Anier Soria Lorente📷, and Stefan Berres📷

Departamento de Tecnología, Universidad de Granma, Bayamo, Cuba
{ydiazn,asorial}@udg.co.cu

Abstract. In order to contribute to medical image watermarking methods, we evaluate the performance of several moment families and separable moments. We have modeled watermarking as a multi-objective optimization problem using particle swarm optimization with Conventional Weighted Aggregation. Additionally, we use dither modulation with a uniform quantizer to archive a better rate between imperceptibility and robustness. The proposed scheme was tested under common signal processing attacks. The results confirm the validity of the separable moments since they allowed to achieve in multiple cases a better performance than original moment families. The importance of studying moment families that have lacked of interest is also reinforced, given the relevant performance achieved by q-Krawtchouk moments in comparison to steady moment families in image watermarking.

Keywords: Medical image watermarking · Separable moments ·
Dither modulation · Particle swarm optimization

1 Introduction

With the development of radiology there is a growing need to exchange medical images between physicians and health institutions around the world; but this leads to important security and privacy problems, mainly during transmission over unsecured networks [4]. The watermarking has received a lot of attention in this regard, due to its proven potential to protect information. This technique can guarantee authenticity [14] and confidentiality [8], verify the integrity of the medical image, and even determine the location of modifications [1].

Watermarking methods must meet the requirements for fidelity and robustness; but doing so is challenging because uncontrolled improvement in one of these properties tends to worsen the other. Various strategies have been used to achieve the best tradeoff, one of them has been the use of orthogonal moments due their ability to capture the content information of images with minimum redundancy [10]. Nowadays, interest in moment-based watermarking methods and in separable moments (SMs) continues [3,12,13].

Supported by HPC UCLV.

Y. Hernández Heredia et al. (Eds.): IWAIPR 2021, LNCS 13055, pp. 370–379, 2021.
https://doi.org/10.1007/978-3-030-89691-1_36

In this work we evaluate the performance of a medical image watermarking method based on SMs. Tsougenis et al. [15] had already done a similar work; but we include moments derived from hypergeometric orthogonal polynomials (q-Krawtchouk, q-Hahn, q-Meixner and q-Charlier polynomial), which have been little reported in watermarking. Also, we use a different watermarking scheme which can addressed as an optimization problem. In short, we include 10 moment families and all their possible combinations for a total of 90 SMs. Our hypothesis is that given the large number of SMs evaluated, the inclusion of little-studied families and the modeling of the watermarking scheme as an optimization problem allows to identify those moments that provide better performance than steady moment families in watermarking.

2   Orthogonal Image Moments

Let C denote the cover image, let B_i be a block of $N \times N$ bytes of C, and let $\mathcal{B}_i$ be the corresponding block of $N \times N$ of the orthogonal moments of $(m+n)$-th order (forward moment transform), with $m, n = 0, \ldots, N-1$. The relationship between $\mathcal{B}_i$ and its inverse $B_i^w \equiv B_i$ (inverse moment transform) is given by

$$\mathcal{B}_i = \mathbb{A}(B_i)\mathbb{B}^T \quad \text{and} \quad B_i^w = \mathbb{A}^T(\mathcal{B}_i)\mathbb{B},$$

where

$$\mathbb{A} \equiv \mathbb{A}^{(k)} = \begin{pmatrix} \overline{P}_0^{(k)}(0) & \cdots & \overline{P}_{N-1}^{(k)}(0) \\ \vdots & \ddots & \vdots \\ \overline{P}_0^{(k)}(N-1) & \cdots & \overline{P}_{N-1}^{(k)}(N-1) \end{pmatrix},$$

and

$$\overline{P}_n^{(k)}(x) = \begin{cases} P_n^{(k)}(x)\sqrt{\dfrac{w^{(k)}(x)}{\|P_n^{(k)}\|_2^2}} & \text{for} \quad k = 1, \ldots, 9, \\[4mm] \sigma(n)\cos\left(\dfrac{\pi n(2x+1)}{2N}\right) & \text{for} \quad k = 10, \end{cases}$$

with

$$\sigma(n) = \begin{cases} \sqrt{1/N} & \text{if} \quad n = 0, \\ \sqrt{2/N} & \text{otherwise.} \end{cases}$$

Here, $P_n^{(k)}$ represents:

- The n-th-order discrete orthogonal polynomials, Krawtchouk ($k = 1$), Tchebichef ($k = 2$), Hahn ($k = 3$), Charlier ($k = 4$) and Meixner polynomials ($k = 5$), see [5].
- The n-th-order hypergeometric orthogonal polynomials, q-Krawtchouk ($k = 6$), q-Hahn ($k = 7$), q-Charlier ($k = 8$) and q-Meixner($k = 9$) polynomials ($k = 5$), see [6].

On the other hand, $w^{(k)}(x)$ and $\|P_n^{(k)}\|^2$ denote the weight function and the squared norm of $P_n^{(k)}$, respectively. Moreover, the matrix $\mathbb{B}$ is calculated in a similar way as $\mathbb{A}$. If we denote by $\mathcal{B}_i \equiv \mathcal{B}_i^{(k,j)}$, $\mathbb{A} \equiv \mathbb{A}^{(k)}$ and $\mathbb{B} \equiv \mathbb{B}^{(j)}$, then $\mathcal{B}_i^{(k,k)}$ with $1 \leq k \leq 9$ represents the orthogonal moments of Krawtchouk (K), Tchebichef (T), Hahn (H), Charlier (C), Meixner (M), q-Krawtchouk (qK), q-Hahn (qH), q-Charlier (qC) and q-Meixner (qM) respectively, and $\mathcal{B}_i^{10,10}$ represents the Discrete Cosine Transform (DCT). In addition, $\mathcal{B}_i^{k,j}$ with $k \neq j$ represents the combinations of the previous cases (SMs).

3   Proposed Method

We have modeled watermarking as a multi-objective optimization problem since we seek to guarantee the best trade off between imperceptibility and robustness, which are measured with Peak Signal-to-Noise Ratio (PSNR) and Bit Error Rate (BER), respectively [7]. Additionally, we use dither modulation [2] with a uniform quantizer to archive a better rate between these two competitive goals. The proposed method depends on two parameters that are intended to be optimized, (1) the step size Δ of the quantizer, and (2) the block coefficient index κ, where the payload is embedded.

3.1   Optimization Process

To address watermarking as multi-objective optimization problem, we use Particle Swarm Optimization (PSO) and Conventional Weighted Aggregation. Through a weighted combination, we aggregate the competing objective functions PSNR and BER in a single one by the function

$$f(x) = w_1 \cdot \text{PSNR}^*(x) + w_2 \left(\frac{1}{N} \sum_{i=0}^{N-1} \text{BER}_i(x) \right), \tag{1}$$

where w_1 and w_2 are non-negative weights such that $w_1 + w_2 = 1$, N is the number of attacks and

$$\text{PSNR}^* = \frac{|\text{PSNR} - \text{PSNR}_e|}{\text{VS}} \tag{2}$$

is a normalized PSNR in $[0, 1]$ scale, where VS is defined by

$$\text{VS} = \begin{cases} 10 \log_{10}(I_{\max}^2 \cdot X \cdot Y) - \text{PSNR}_e & \text{if} \quad \text{PSNR} > \text{PSNR}_e, \\ \text{PSNR}_e & \text{if} \quad \text{PSNR} \leq \text{PSNR}_e, \end{cases} \tag{3}$$

where X and Y are image dimensions and $I_{\max}$ is the maximum intensity. The input PSNR_e allows us to set beforehand a desired PSNR value, allowing us to conduct a fair evaluation. During the fitness evaluation, PSNR^* approaches zero when PSNR approaches PSNR_e, therefore solution candidates with PSNR scores close to $PSNR_e$ are considered better than those that deviate further from the desired value.

Clearly, now we address a single-objective optimization where the goal is the minimization of

$$\min_{\triangle,\kappa} f(x), \tag{4}$$

Figure 1 shows the flow diagram on how a new position of the i-th particle $x_i(\triangle_i, \kappa_i)$ is evaluated.

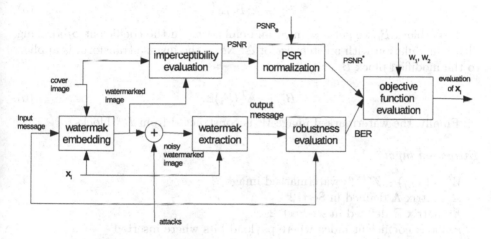

Fig. 1. Flow diagram for the evaluation of the new position of a particle.

3.2 Watermarking Scheme

In this work we use a blind watermarking scheme in the transform domain using SMs. We divide the cover image into 8×8 pixels of non-overlapping blocks and then we embed a single message bit m_i per block into the transform domain using dither modulation with a uniform quantizer. Each m_i is embedded in the same coefficient κ and with the same strength $\triangle$.

Details of the embedding and extraction processes are explained below.

Embedding input

- $C = (c_{i,j}) \in \mathbb{Z}^{m \times n}$: cover image
- $M = \{m_i \in 0, 1 : 1 \leq i \leq |M|\}$: message as bit sequence
- $\mathbb{A}$: matrix $\mathbb{A}$ defined in Sect. 2
- $\mathbb{B}$: matrix $\mathbb{B}$ defined in Sect. 2
- κ: block coefficient index where payload bits are inserted
- $\triangle$: quantizer step size

Embedding output $W = (w_{i,j}) \in \mathbb{Z}^{m \times n}$: watermarked image

As mentioned earlier, we embed only one message bit per block; therefore, firstly we check that the whole message M can be embedded asserting that there are enough blocks. Then we divide a copy of the cover image C into 8×8 pixels of non-overlapping blocks B, and for each message bit m_i, we apply a forwards moment transform to block B_i, obtaining the block $\mathcal{B}_i$ in the transform domain as follows:

$$\mathcal{B}_i \leftarrow \mathbb{A}(B_i)\mathbb{B}^T. \tag{5}$$

From block $\mathcal{B}_i$ we get a scan S_i and embed m_i in the coefficient $S_i[\kappa]$ using dither modulation with an step size of $\triangle$. Next, the inverse transform is applied to the modified block $\mathcal{B}_i$ as follows:

$$B_i^w \leftarrow \mathbb{A}^T(\mathcal{B}_i)\mathbb{B}. \tag{6}$$

Finally, the watermarked image W is constructed from B^w blocks.

Extraction input

- $W = (w_{i,j}) \in \mathbb{Z}^{m \times n}$: watermarked image
- $\mathbb{A}$: matrix $\mathbb{A}$ defined in Sect. 2
- $\mathbb{B}$: matrix $\mathbb{B}$ defined in see Sect. 2
- κ: block coefficient index where payload bits where inserted
- $\triangle$: quantizer step size

Extraction output $\hat{M} = \{\hat{m}_i \in 0, 1 : 1 \leq i \leq |\hat{M}|\}$: extracted message

Firstly, $\hat{M}$ is initialized with an empty sequence, next the watermarked image W is divided into 8×8 pixels of non-overlapping blocks B, then we apply a forwards moment transform to each block Bi, obtaining the block $\mathcal{B}_i$ in transform domain as follows:

$$\mathcal{B}_i \leftarrow \mathbb{A}(B_i)\mathbb{B}^T. \tag{7}$$

From each block $\mathcal{B}_i$ we get a scan S_i, after that we extract a bit message $\hat{m}_i$ from coefficient $S_i[\kappa]$ using dither modulation with a step size of $\triangle$, finally $\hat{m}_i$ is appended to $\hat{M}$. For simplicity, it is assumed that in each block one bit has been inserted.

4   Experimental Study

To evaluate the performance of SMs, experiments were conducted with grayscale 8 bit 512×512 medical brain images from *The Cancer Imaging Archive* (see Fig. 2). The following attacks where applied: Salt & Pepper noise (1%, 5%), Gaussian noise (10%, 15%, 20%), Median filter (2×2, 4×4, 8×8) and JPEG attack ($Q = 10\%$, $Q = 20\%$, $Q = 40\%$). In addition, one bit was hidden in each image block for a 4096-bit payload.

Table 1 show the meta-parameter of the binary PSO used in the experiments and the parameters of the proposed method. Particularly, for $PSNR_e$ we chose a reference value reported in similar work [11], while weight w_1 allowed us to assign the same importance to PSNR and BER in the multi-objective optimization process carried out.

For the systematic experiments a software was developed in the python programming language that uses several programming libraries such as pyswarms [9] for PSO. In total, 100 moments were evaluated, derived from DCT, Krawtchouk (K), Tchebichef (T), Hahn (H), Charlier (C), Meixner (M), q-Krawtchouk (qK), q-Hahn (qH), q-Charlier (qC) and q-Meixner (qM). Hereafter, for example, to refer to Tchebichef-based moments, we use the acronym TMs, while for example, to refer to SMs derived from DCT and Meixner (M) in that order, we use the term DCTMMs.

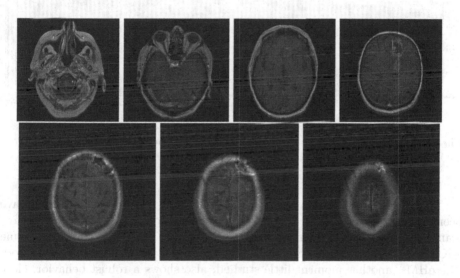

Fig. 2. Images included in the experiments.

The optimization process together with the use of $PSNR^*$ in the objective function allowed to achieve PSNR values in the vicinity of the expected value $PSNR_e$ and therefore to create the necessary conditions for a fair evaluation of robustness. In short, the mean PSNR was 44.01 (SD = 0.02).

Table 1. PSO meta-parameters and proposed method parameters.

Inertia	Cognitive	Social	Particles	Iteration	Neighbors	κ	$\triangle$	$PSNR_e$	$I_{\max}$	w_1
0.9	0.5	0.5	20	80	20	$[1, 63]$	$[1, 255]$	44	255	0.5

4.1   Robustness Evaluation

Figure 3 shows the BER mean values of all attacks and images. The first thing to highlight is the capacity of SMs to outperform original moment families. DCTMs, qKMs and TMs, in that order, are the most robust original moments; but there are several SMs that outperform them. Note that of moments with higher ability to detect the watermark, the first eleven are SMs, all of them formed from DCT, q-Krawtchouk or Tchebichef. Moreover, despite HMs show a relative moderate performance, the BER mean suggest than HTMs, THMs and HDCTMs are an even better choice than DCTMs.

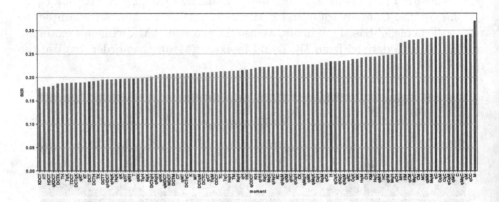

Fig. 3. BER mean scores for all images under combined attack. Classical moment families are highlighted.

The performance of qKMs is especially relevant, considering that they have been under-reported in watermarking research. The qKMs show a better performance than the steady moment families TMs, KMs and HMs. Moreover, some q-Krawtchouk-derived SMs even improve the robustness of the proposed method. The qHMs, another moment little studied, also shows a robust behavior, close to KMs; however, Krawtchouk-derived SMs provide better performance; in fact, the KDCTM is the only one that provides a BER less than 0.18. On the other hand, clearly the CMs, qCMs, qMMs and MMs are less effective detecting the watermark.

The DCTMs and TMs are the most resistant methods to the JPEG attack with $Q = 40\%$, but they are outperformed by qKMs and qHMs in the JPEG attack with $Q = 20\%$, and DCTMs become least effective in the JPEG attack with $Q = 10\%$. The TqKMs stands out under JPEG attack with $Q = 20\%$, not only because it provides the lowest BER score, but also because it achieves a 17% improvement over the second most robust moment. The HMs, qHMs and KMs provide the highest robustness under JPEG attack with $Q = 10\%$ among original moment families and those with a modest behavior to the JPEG ($Q = 40\%$), like MMs with the worst performance, show now a better relative performance.

It seems that qHMs and qKMs, in that order, are the better choices based on mean BER for JPEG attacks, beyond that some separable moments are able to overcome them; furthermore, qHMs is the one who shows the most stable performance for all compression levels.

There are several SMs that provide a close but less BER mean than DCTMs, the original moment family is more resistant to Gaussian noise. The TMs show a behavior similar to DCTMs, in fact TMs is little more resistant under Gaussian noise (0.1%). The KMs and qKMs also show a robust behavior while qMMs, qCMs, CMs, and MMs are notably less robust than the other original moment families.

The KMs and qKMs are the most remarkable original families under the 2×2 median filtering attack. There are several SMs with a satisfactory performance, some of them with a better performance than KMs. On the other hand, the most notable SMs are derived from combinations of Krawtchouk and q-Krawtchouk polynomials. The mean result is similar under 4×4 medial filtering, but in this case qKMs shows the lowest BER mean value including the SMs.

The DCTMs show a performance significantly higher than the rest of original moment families under 8×8 median filter, with the exception of the TMs which show a close score. The ability of SMs to improve the robustness of the proposed method is evidenced by HTMs, as they provide better performance than DCTMs, despite that HMs do not show a satisfactory performance for this level. The KDCTMs seem to be the best choice under median filtering according to BER mean among three noise levels, while DCTMs, TMS and qKMs moments stand out among the original moment families. The KDCTMs also show the relevance of SMs, as they show the lowest BER mean values under 8×8 median filtering among all moments studied; however, the KMs no longer show satisfactory behavior at this level.

In the case of Salt & Pepper noise, the most interesting thing is the fact that MMs, qCMs, CMs and qMMs achieve a much superior performance than DCTMs, qKMs and TMs, contrary to what happens for the rest of attacks. The SMs built from the combination of these first families also show a robust behavior under this attack type.

Table 2 show original moment families (OMFs) and SMs with the best performance per attack type and the best of all.

Table 2. Moment families with best performance.

	Gaussian	Salt & Pepper	Median filter	JPEG
SMs	DCTTMs DCTqMMs	MqCMs qCMMs	KDCTMs qKDCTMs	TqKMs qHHMs
OMFs	DCTMs TMs	MMs qCMs	DCTMs TMs	qHMs qKMs
Best	DCTMMs	MqCMs	KDCTMs	TqKMs

4.2   Discusion

Clearly, separable moments allow a better balance between robustness and imperceptibility under a combined attack and also under a particular attack. The relevance of separable moments varies according to the attack type; for Gaussian noise there are multiple separable moments that outperform original moment families with the lowest BER mean value while under JPEG attack only two SMs show a more robust behavior. But beyond these variations, the results under combined attack indicate that there are several SMs that outperform the original moment families. Furthermore, all the best performing moments are SMs, as can be seen in Table 2. Interestingly, the combination of well performing original moment families with a much more modest performance under a given attack, can result in a SMs that outperforms the better component moment family; even some of these SMs are among moments with the more robust behavior.

DCTMs is undoubtedly the most remarkable original moment family: in addition to being the best performer under combined attacks, most of the best located SMs are conformed from DCTMs and only achieves discrete performance when combined with the worst performing: qCMs, CMs, qMMs, and MMs. Note, that SMs derived form these last moment families are also among with worst robustness; however, they show a robust behavior under Salt & Pepper noise when another moment families fail in extract watermark.

The other element to highlight is the performance showed by moment families little studied in watermarking.The qKMs are only outperformed under combined attack by DCTMs, which are widely used in watermarking application during many years. In fact, qKMs are among two moment families that are more robust under JPEG attack beside qHMs, another moment family little studied. This remark is supported by qCMs and qMMs performance under Salt & Pepper noise, as they were more robust than steady moment families.

Conclusions

The results confirm the relevance of the SMs for watermarking, since they allow to achieve in multiple cases a better balance between imperceptibility and robustness. Even some SMs derived from moment families with modest performance under a given attack are able to outperform their component moment families. The SMs derived from DCT, Tchebichef and q-Krawtchouk, deserve special attention, as they provided the best performance among all moments studied. The importance of studying new moment families is also reinforced, given the relevant performance achieved by the qKMs under combined attack and by qCMs and qMMs under Salt & Pepper noise. Although significant, the outputs are preliminary; further studies are required with larger databases, different embedding methods and with higher capacity watermarking schemes.

References

1. Al-Haj, A., et al.: Secured telemedicine using region-based watermarking with tamper localization. J. Digit. Imag. **27**(6), 737–750 (2014). https://doi.org/10.1007/s10278-014-9709-9
2. Chen, B., Wornell, G.W.: Quantization index modulation: a class of provably good methods for digital watermarking and information embedding. IEEE Trans. Inf. Theory **47**(4), 1423–1443 (2001). https://doi.org/10.1109/18.923725
3. Daoui, A., Yamni, M., Karmouni, H., Sayyouri, M., Qjidaa, H.: Biomedical signals reconstruction and zero-watermarking using separable fractional order Charlier-Krawtchouk transformation and sine cosine algorithm. Sig. Process. **180**, 107854 (2021). https://doi.org/10.1016/j.sigpro.2020.107854
4. Dugonjić, I., Travar, M., Bajić, G.: Safety aspects in shared medical it environment. JITA-J. Inf. Technol. Appl. **16**(2) (2018). https://doi.org/10.7251/JIT1802086D
5. Ismail, M., Ismail, M.E., van Assche, W.: Classical and Quantum Orthogonal Polynomials in One Variable, vol. 13. Cambridge University Press (2005). https://doi.org/10.1017/CBO9781107325982
6. Koekoek, R., Lesky, P.A., Swarttouw, R.F.: Hypergeometric Orthogonal Polynomials and Their q-Analogues. Springer, Heidelberg (2010). https://doi.org/10.1007/978-3-642-05014-5
7. Singh, A.K., Kumar, B., Singh, G., Mohan, A. (eds.): Medical Image Watermarking. MSA, Springer, Cham (2017). https://doi.org/10.1007/978-3-319-57699-2
8. Kundu, M.K., Das, S.: Lossless ROI medical image watermarking technique with enhanced security and high payload embedding. In: 2010 20th International Conference on Pattern Recognition, pp. 1457–1460. IEEE (2010). https://doi.org/10.1109/ICPR.2010.360
9. Miranda, L.J.: PySwarms: a research toolkit for particle swarm optimization in Python. J. Open Source Softw. **3**(21), 433 (2018). https://doi.org/10.21105/joss.00433
10. Papakostas, G.: Moments and moment invariants: theory and applications. Sci. Gate **1**, 3–32 (2014). https://doi.org/10.15579/gcsr.vol1
11. Papakostas, G.A., Tsougenis, E., Koulouriotis, D.E.: Moment-based local image watermarking via genetic optimization. Appl. Math. Comput. **227**, 222–236 (2014)
12. Senapati, R.K., Srivastava, S., Mankar, P.: RST invariant blind image watermarking schemes based on discrete Tchebichef transform and singular value decomposition. Arab. J. Sci. Eng. 1–23 (2020). https://doi.org/10.1007/s13369-020-04387-9
13. Setyono, A., et al.: Tchebichef image watermarking based on PN-sequence. In: 2019 International Seminar on Application for Technology of Information and Communication (iSemantic), pp. 1–5. IEEE (2019). https://doi.org/10.1109/ISEMANTIC.2019.8884270
14. Sharma, A., Singh, A.K., Ghrera, S.P.: Robust and secure multiple watermarking for medical images. Wirel. Pers. Commun. **92**(4), 1611–1624 (2017). https://doi.org/10.7251/JIT1802086D
15. Tsougenis, E., Papakostas, G., Koulouriotis, D.: Image watermarking via separable moments. Multimed. Tools Appl. **74**, 3985–4012 (2015). https://doi.org/10.1007/s11042-013-1808-y

Signals Analysis and Processing

Intra-day Population Fluxes from Mobile Phone Data in Havana, Cuba

Milton García-Borroto[1]([✉]), Orlando Martínez-Durive[2], Eduardo Sánchez[1],
Humberto Díaz[1], and Alejandro Lage-Castellanos[2]

[1] Universidad Tecnológica de La Habana CUJAE, 114 #1 Marianao,
La Habana, Cuba
{mgarciab,esancheza,hdiazp}@ceis.cujae.edu.cu
[2] Universidad de La Habana, La Habana, Cuba
{omartinez,lage}@fisica.uh.cu

Abstract. For the first time in Cuba, we use Location Update records from the mobile phone network to generate origin-destination matrices in Havana. We used 15-days telecom anonymized data from 2020 to approximate trips identified as sequences of cellphone towers. We projected these trips over transport areas and municipalities, and showed the plausibility of the fluxes by comparing it with known behaviour of the city and data from census and work-home survey.

Keywords: Big data · Population mobility · Mobile phone data

1 Introduction

Cuba's transport situation resembles that of Latin America and Europe in the 1960s with very low vehicle ownership [3]. Many boroughs in Havana are compact, having most services available within walking distance. One thing that is unique to Cuba is the travel behaviors and the land use planning strategies to streamline travels [3]. In this situation, aggravated by increased penalties associated with the USA blockade, understanding mobility flows is crucial, because it would allow optimal use of the limited economical resources.

Understanding the dynamics of traffic demand over space and time is very important for most applications in the transportation domain [2]. Since transport planners have no direct access to the location of every person at all times, they need an estimation of the time-dependent relation between travel origin and destination [7]. This estimation is frequently expressed as an origin-destination matrix (O-D matrix). In an O-D matrix, the cell $c_{i,j}$ contains the estimated number of travels between locations i and j.

O-D matrices can be calculated in many different ways; traditional methods were based on surveys, travel diaries, or vehicle re-identification systems[7]. In recent years, there has been an increasing interest in the development of technologies that can succeed in collecting, processing, and analyzing mobility data with efficient and privacy-preserving procedures [8]. In particular, the widespread

© Springer Nature Switzerland AG 2021
Y. Hernández Heredia et al. (Eds.): IWAIPR 2021, LNCS 13055, pp. 383–392, 2021.
https://doi.org/10.1007/978-3-030-89691-1_37

and high penetration rates of mobile networks enable mobile phone operators to collect an enormous quantity of up-to-date geolocation data from Call Detail Records (CDR), at a very low cost [1,10].

O-D matrices calculation based on mobile phone records has received a lot of attention, mostly in developed countries, which have large cell covering with large investing in infrastructures [1,4,8,9]. On the other hand, few results appear in developing countries, mostly because of infrastructure limitations and limited access to funds [5,6,11].

The case of Cuba is particular, since mobile techonology has become common only recently. However, the number of lines is now above 6 millions in a population of 12 millions, which guarantees a large representative sample. Up to this research, mobile phone data has not been used as a tool for understanding intra-day flows in Cuba.

In this article we study intra-day population fluxes, obtained from Location Area Update data from the Cuban telecommunication company ETECSA. After collecting the data, cleaning it, and processing it with BigData techniques, we obtained a variety of O-D matrices characterizing the intra-day mobility at the level of transport zones in the city. Results, validated using two different existing sources, prove to be accurate and a valid alternative for such studies.

2 Mobile Phone Data and Human Mobility

We were granted access to 15 days of telecom data between February and March 2020, just before the COVID broke out in Cuba. Data comes from the 2G and 3G infrastructures of ETECSA, the single telecom company in Cuba, and is duly anonymized and regulated by a confidentiality agreement. Furthermore, raw data, even anonymized, is not taken from the telecom servers but analyzed *in situ* and only aggregated data can be extracted for scientific purposes and publications.

The data consists of Location Update Registries (LUR) which are network-driven events (see Table 1). Location Areas are labels classifying groups of antennas. Instances of LUR records are generated in any of the following situations: the phone is turned on or off, the phone receives calls or SMS through 2G and 3G protocols, the phone moves from antennas in one Location Area, to those in a different Location Area, and when neither of the previous has occurred in a lapse of 2h or 4h, depending on the location of the cellphone (city or countryside areas).

Table 1. Sample of Location Area Update registries as provided by ETECSA. IMSI field is a hash code, and has no trivial relation to the real line/mobile or user identifier. CELL field is a label for small groups of towers, always within the same location area.

ID	IMSI	CELL	DATETIME
234768	67981	dfk-78	2020-03-05 15:00:10
234769	61911	dhk-80	2020-03-05 15:00:11
234770	57981	lab-51	2020-03-05 15:00:11

The data we are using consists of the available LUR registries of some days between 19 February 2020 and 23 March 2020, distributed as one Monday, five Tuesdays, three Wednesdays, four Thursdays, and two Fridays. The GPS positioning of the CELLS is also provided by ETECSA, allowing for an estimation of the user position, that we can later map to Transport zones, or municipalities. The days provided coincide with the arrival of the SARS-CoV2 to Cuba, but precede the adoption of measures to restrict population mobility. Therefore we retain them as a valid snapshot of normal mobility in the city.

3   Trip Identification

The nature of LUR is particularly suitable to detect movement, since displacement will produce tower handovers, and, whenever towers are from different Location Areas, there shall be a register generated for the new LA that handles the phone.

We define a trip as a sequence of towers (and times) that span more than 2 km in total length with time intervals between consecutive towers that are no larger than 2 h. If a user is moving on a long trip and makes a stop of more than 2 h in the middle, that trip is split into two different trips.

For each of the 12 typical workday (Tuesday to Thursday) given, we compute all trips resulting in a total of 7 million trips. Each of these trips has an initial and a final tower and time. Each tower is mapped to a Transport Area. Counting the number of trips that occur between two given TAs, we build the matrix $T_{i,j}$, which is the origin-destination matrix of all trips in a typical workday.

Furthermore, we can restrict our matrix to account for trips in the morning or the afternoon or starting within any particular range in time. For instance, we could analyze all trips that start between 5 am and 10 am, which most home-work trips should take place. With this restriction, we have 161 thousand trips identified and we call this morning matrix $M_{i,j}$. On the other hand, if we restrict ourselves to trips starting in the 2 pm- 6 pm interval, we find also 161 thousand trips and we call the resulting matrix $A_{i,j}$.

Both matrices are not the same but do have some visible correlation and some properties one would expect if they are capturing the home-work fluxes.

First, let's focus on the total amount of people departing from transport area i, $m_i = \sum_j M_{i,j}$ and $a_i = \sum_j A_{i,j}$, and the total amount of people arriving at i, $\tilde{m}_i = \sum_j M_{j,i}$ and $\tilde{a}_i = \sum_j A_{j,i}$. In Fig. 1 we visually compare the correlations between these quantities. The lower plots show the correlation with the amount of people leaving and entering a given TA, both in the morning and in the afternoon, and they are less correlated than the plots on top. The best correlation is obtained between the number of people that leave one transport area in the morning and those who arrive at that transport area in the afternoon, and vise-versa. This shows that trips do alter the amount of population within each TA during the day, but restore it to the initial values at the end of the day. This is expected if those trips are capturing the intra-day house-work pendularity.

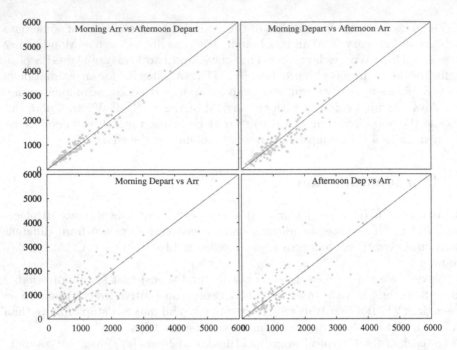

Fig. 1. Correlations between the total numbers of outgoing and incoming people at every transport area. The best correlation is obtained for the fluxes that restore the system: morning outgoing vs afternoon incoming, and vice-versa.

3.1 Frequent Night and Day Locations as Proxies for Home and Work

We defined a night location as any tower signal appearing in the interval $\mathcal{T}_n = [1am : 6am]$ and a day location as those appearing in the complementary interval $\mathcal{T}_d = [7am : 2pm]$. To define a single "house" and "work" locations, we follow these steps.

1. For each of the 15 days given, and for each user, we selected all the night and day locations
2. Each location is transformed to a corresponding Transport Area (TA);
3. We count for each user, how many days each TA appears in either category (night and day);
4. A TA appearing in more than 8 days is considered a valid candidate to represent the "house" or "work" locations";
5. Among all possible candidates for home and work, we select the pair that is more spatially distant, and consider this to be the house - work definition for the user.

In other words, we are selecting the repetitive behavior, and within it selecting the most distant options as the transport areas for house and work.

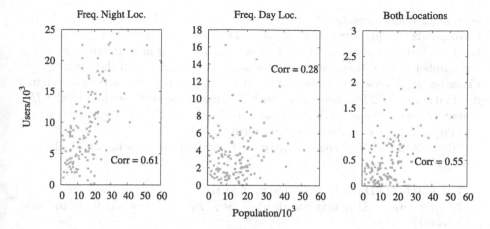

Fig. 2. Correlations between the total number of users with a known night (left), day (center), and both (right panel) locations for every transport area, compared to the census population living within each of these areas.

When applying this procedure to all 15 days at hand, we are capable of identifying 1.1 million users with a known house TA, and 171 thousand users with both house and work TAs identified. In Fig. 2, we showed how does the known population living within each transport area correlates with the identified number of users with a frequent night location (roughly 0.61). In the middle panel, we show that the number of users that have a frequent day location does not correlate as well with the census population, which is consistent with the idea that jobs are not evenly distributed within the city. However, the number of users that we can identify with both frequent day and night locations still correlates well (when aggregated over the night location) with the population of each area, as expected if we pretend to have an unbiased sampling of the home-work mobility in the city. Still, this correlation is far from perfect (~ 0.55), and there are some reasons why this could be:

- 4G technology, which is absent from our data, was still expanding at the moment of the study, meaning that some neighborhoods had it, some didn't. This puts a bias against the identification of users in the areas with 4G.
- people living in the city downtown are more often close to their jobs than people in the periphery, which puts a bias towards identifying the workplaces of the former since our method is more sensitive to people mobility.

In what follows, we will use the set of 171'000 users that have a known night and day location to compute the matrix $H_{i,j}$ with the number of users that dwell at i and work at j.

3.2   Trips and Trips to Work

Among the trips identified in the previous section, there is a part corresponding to regular home-work (or home-school also) trips, and a part related to more occasional displacements. We can extract the part T^w of the matrix T that corresponds to trips between home and work. For every single user, if it is among the 171 thousand that have a known home and work transport areas, we count the number of trips between these locations that we identify in the working days (Tuesday to Thursday) of the given data. We can produce a typical origin - destination matrix for these trips. Such T^w matrix should be close to the $H_{i,j}$ matrix of known home/work locations, and should also be similar to the average mobility (all trips considered) in the morning M.

Figure 3 shows the correlation between these four matrices for a typical working day:

- T, the total O-D matrix for all identified trips
- M, the total O-D matrix for all identified trips in the 6 am–9 am morning interval.
- T^w, the O-D matrix for trips occurring between home and work.
- H, the home-work matrix for the users with identifiable night and day frequent locations

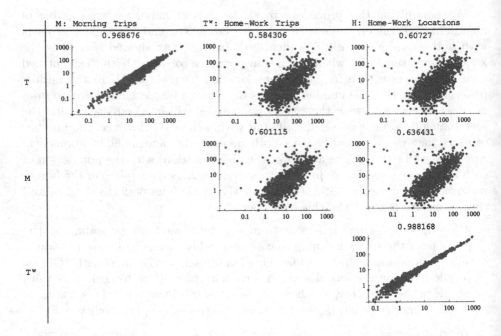

Fig. 3. Correlation between all four matrices T, M, T^w and H.

4   Understanding the Fluxes

As seen in the bottom two figures in Fig. 1, there is not good correlation between the number of people leaving one TA and the amount arriving at it. This means that fluxes are asymmetrical. In Fig. 4 we plot the morning unbalance $m_i - \tilde{m}_i$ vs the afternoon unbalance $a_i - \tilde{a}_i$. The negative correlation is consistent with the known fact that some areas are morning sources and afternoon sinks of population.

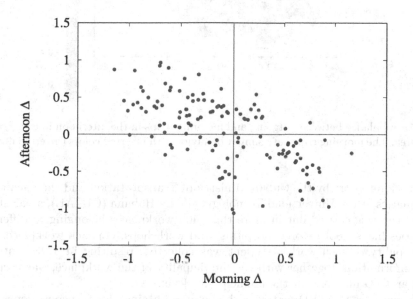

Fig. 4. Unbalance between in-going and outgoing trips at every transport area. The anticorrelation states that the sign of the unbalances changes between morning and afternoon as expected.

In Fig. 5, we color-coded this unbalance over the transport areas in Havana. Zones with positively unbalanced fluxes correspond to known sinks of mobility, like Old Havana and Central Habana, in the west side of the bay, while zones with negatively unbalanced fluxes are located mostly in the periphery, as is the case of Alamar urbanization in East Havana.

4.1   Validation with Job Survey

It is hard to show, beyond the plausibility of the obtained results, that it is a fair description of mobility flows in the city. There is no ground truth on this matter, and the best we can do is compare to demographic data (as we did with the census) or to surveys.

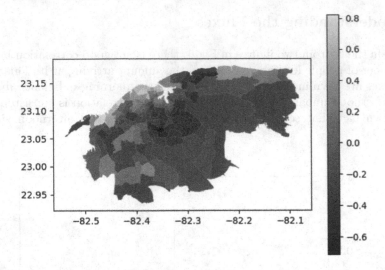

Fig. 5. Unbalance between outgoing and incoming trips in the afternoon in each transport area. The morning trips have similar behavior with inverted colors (inverted fluxes)

In a joint effort by the Cuban Ministry of Transportation and the Faculty of Informatics at the Universidad Tecnológica de La Habana (CUJAE), a painstaking survey was carried out in more than 400 workplaces belonging to different activities like schools, stores, hospitals, and workshops. On each workplace, the municipality of each worker/student was collected, resulting in 37480 entries. This information, together with the municipality of the workplace, was used to build an O-D matrix S at the municipality level.

To compare this O-D matrix with the ones obtained for transport zones, we need to scale down the latter, since Havana has 15 municipalities but 134 transport zones. Fortunately, though, transport zones do not intersect more than one municipality, making trivial the process of collapsing the 134×134 matrices into 15×15 ones, by adding columns (and rows) that belong to the same municipality.

We scaled down to the municipal level all four matrices T, M, T^w and H of the previous section and computed the correlations between them and the survey matrix S. Two cases are shown in Fig. 6, with correlations 0.885 for the matrix T^w of the average trips between home and work, and the correlation 0.813 for the matrix M of all trips identified in the 6 am to 9 am interval. Matrices T and H have similar behaviors, with correlations 0.799 and 0.882 respectively.

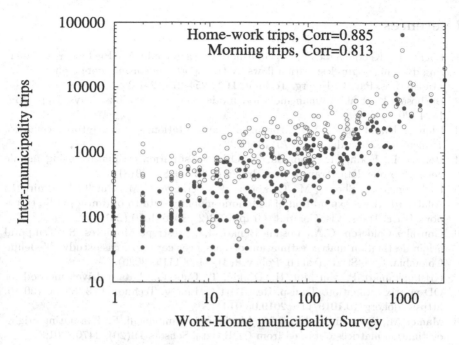

Fig. 6. Correlations between Home-Work municipality survey and the scaled down version of mobility matrices from cellphone data.

5   Conclusions

We have shown, for the first time in Cuba, that Location Update records from the Cuban telecom ETECSA can be used to extract models of intra-day population mobility patterns.

We worked in an ad-hoc manner, using our insight into the dynamics of the city transport system to define parameters to identify trips and relevant locations. With the trips identified we produced O-D matrices and compared them to census data and data coming from a survey of more than 400 workplaces.

The correlation between population estimates or mobility estimates coming from cellphone data and that from census or surveys is generally high (above 0.6). We showed that morning trips capture the same (0.9 correlated) inter-municipal dynamics as a detailed survey of home-work mobility.

Overall this study suggests that transport planning as well as many other sociological and geographical approaches to the dynamics in Havana can be readily based on Big Data techniques from mobile phone data, as is becoming more and more customary around the world.

References

1. Bachir, D., Khodabandelou, G., Gauthier, V., El Yacoubi, M., Puchinger, J.: Inferring dynamic origin-destination flows by transport mode using mobile phone data. Transp. Res. Part C: Emerg. Technol. **101**, 254–275 (2019)
2. Barbosa, H., et al.: Human mobility: models and applications. Phys. Rep. **734**, 1–74 (2018)
3. Blanco, H., Moudon, A.V.: Havana's transportation system: future scenarios. Transp. Res. Procedia **25**, 4679–4691 (2017)
4. Bonnel, P., Fekih, M., Smoreda, Z.: Origin-destination estimation using mobile network probe data. Transp. Res. Procedia **32**, 69–81 (2018)
5. Di Lorenzo, G., Sbodio, M., Calabrese, F., Berlingerio, M., Pinelli, F., Nair, R.: Allaboard: visual exploration of cellphone mobility data to optimise public transport. IEEE Trans. Vis. Comput. Graph. **22**(2), 1036–1050 (2015)
6. Gonzalez-Calderon, C.A., Posada-Henao, J.J., Restrepo-Morantes, S.: Temporal origin-destination matrix estimation of passenger car trips. case study: Medellin, Colombia. Case Stud. Transp. Policy **8**(3), 1109–1115 (2020)
7. Krishnakumari, P., van Lint, H., Djukic, T., Cats, O.: A data driven method for OD matrix estimation. Transp. Res. Part C: Emerg. Technol. **113**, 38–56 (2020). https://doi.org/10.1016/j.trc.2019.05.014
8. Mamei, M., Bicocchi, N., Lippi, M., Mariani, S., Zambonelli, F.: Evaluating origin-destination matrices obtained from CDR data. Sensors **19**(20), 4470 (2019)
9. Tolouei, R., Psarras, S., Prince, R.: Origin-destination trip matrix development: Conventional methods versus mobile phone data. Transportation research procedia **26**, 39–52 (2017)
10. White, J., Wells, I.: Extracting origin destination information from mobile phone data. In: Proceedings of the Eleventh International Conference on Road Transport Information and Control. IET (2002)
11. Zagatti, G.A., et al.: A trip to work: estimation of origin and destination of commuting patterns in the main metropolitan regions of Haiti using CDR. Dev. Eng. **3**, 133–165 (2018)

Semantic Segmentation of Radio-Astronomical Images

Carmelo Pino[1(✉)], Renato Sortino[1,2], Eva Sciacca[1], Simone Riggi[1],
and Concetto Spampinato[2]

[1] INAF, Catania, Italy
{carmelo.pino,eva.sciacca,simone.riggi}@inaf.it,
renato.sortino@phd.unict.it
[2] PeRCeiVe Lab, University of Catania, Catania, Italy
concetto.spampinato@unict.it

Abstract. In the context of next-generation radio-astronomical visual surveys, automated object detection and segmentation are necessary tasks to support astrophysics research from observations. Indeed, identifying manually astronomical sources (e.g., galaxies) from the daunting amount of acquired images is largely unfeasible, greatly limiting the huge potential of big data in the field. As a consequence, the astrophysics research has directed its attention, with increasing interest given the recent success in AI, to learning-based computer vision methods. Several automated visual source extractors have been proposed, but they mainly pose the source identification as an object detection. While this may reduce the time needed for visual inspection, it presents an evident shortcoming in case of objects consisting of multiple, spatial distant, parts (e.g., the same galaxy appearing as a set of isolated objects). This specific limitation can be overcome through semantic segmentation. Consequently, in this paper we evaluate the performance of multiple semantic segmentation models for pixelwise dense prediction in astrophysical images with the objective to identify and segment *galaxies*, *sidelobe*, and *compact sources*. Performance analysis is carried out on a dataset consisting of over 9,000 images and shows how state-of-the-art segmentation models yield accurate results, thus providing a baseline for future works. We also employ the output segmentation maps for object detection and results are better than those obtained with Mask-RCNN based detectors that are largely used in the field.

Keywords: Tiramisu · Object detection · Galaxy visual inspection

1   Introduction

The recent technological advancement has led to an exponential growth in data availability, which in turn, has brought out the pressing need for computational

C. Pino and R. Sortino—Equal contribution.

© Springer Nature Switzerland AG 2021
Y. Hernández Heredia et al. (Eds.): IWAIPR 2021, LNCS 13055, pp. 393–403, 2021.
https://doi.org/10.1007/978-3-030-89691-1_38

tools and innovative knowledge extraction methods to make sense of the collected data. Astronomy and astrophysics, among the others, are fields that in the last decades have produced an impressive amount of data coming from sky observation and surveys. This trend is bound not to change, but even more data is expected to be collected. For example, the Evolutionary Map of the Universe (EMU) [16] planned with the ASKAP system [3] will survey 70% of the sky, leading to an unprecedented quantity of data.

Typically, astronomy and astrophysics visual data may be of different modalities (e.g., radio-interferometric images, infrared images, etc.), and the main required task for supporting surveys is *source finding*, i.e. identifying and extracting astronomical sources like compact or point-like source, galaxies and sidelobes. However, beside cumbersome, this task is far from being trivial (both for humans and for computational methods) because of strong artifacts due to physical limitations of the acquisition process, especially in cases of extended sources or diffuse emissions. This requires an extensive manual pre- and post-processing phase that, however, is error-prone and time-consuming, other than almost infeasible on a volume of data such as the one predicted with systems like ASKAP.

Thus, there is an unmet need for automated and reliable computational methods for source detection. Indeed, several automated astronomical source detectors have been proposed, such as CAESAR [18], to address this need, yet these are based on classic computer vision methods requiring ad-hoc and complicated calibration and tuning steps. Standard learning-based techniques, e.g., shallow neural networks [18], have been adopted to overcome the limitations of computer vision methods. Despite the initial encouraging results, these methods tend to fail with extended and faint objects. At the moment, few source finders [19,20] are providing dedicated algorithms for extended sources but their performance is still inferior to what is achieved for compact sources.

With the resurgence of artificial intelligence, due to deep learning architectures, object detection methods based on convolutional neural networks have been proposed for galaxy classification [23,25], supernova remnant detection [2] and celestial object detection [4,6,8,11,26]. Nevertheless, even these deep learning–based object detectors are not able to detect accurately specific astronomical sources, especially galaxies that usually appear as composed by several fragments (see Fig. 1), thus limiting the effectiveness of the existing solutions. Motivated by the failures of the existing object detectors, in this paper we face the source identification problem from a different perspective, i.e., pixel-wise dense prediction for segmenting anatomical sources (Fig. 1 shows the advantage of semantic segmentation models over object detectors in case of galaxy detection). More in detail, we pose the source localization problem as a semantic segmentation task and propose a first, to our knowledge, benchmark analysis of state of the art approaches on astronomical images. Beside evaluating the performance in terms of segmentation accuracy, providing a first baseline for future works, we also leverage the segmentation masks to perform source detection obtaining better performance than Mask-R CNN [7], which is the most employed detector in prior works. These obtained results thus highlight that employing semantic segmentation models is a interesting research direction in the astronomical image analysis field, as they allow scientists not only to detect automatically objects/sources but also to study morphological information about these sky objects.

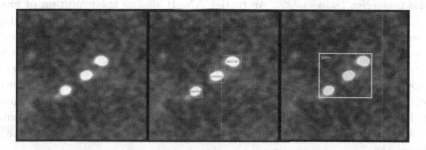

Fig. 1. Typical example of object detector failure. Usually astronomical images, especially small crops, contain one galaxy consisting of multiple non-connected parts [Left]. In this example, MaskR-CNN detects three single objects as sources [Center], while instead there is only one galaxy. A semantic segmentation method, as the one tested in this paper, identifies correctly the three objects as part of only one galaxy [Right].

2   Related Work

Automatic source detection in astronomical images has been developed mainly along two directions: either using classic computer vision techniques or deep learning methods. There exist several works on source finding based on classic computer vision techniques, such as [5], that applies Latent Dirichlet allocation to image pixels in order to segment them as source or background and [18], which performs source segmentation using the k-means algorithm based on pixels spatial and intensity proximity measure. Such works are mainly limited by the impossibility of generalizing well on unseen data. For this reason, recent works have been increasingly focused on deep learning models for automated source detection.

ConvoSource [14] uses a minimal configuration of a CNN, composed by three convolutional layers, one dropout layer and a dense layer to generate a binary map containing sources. Such an approach lacks the ability to distinguish among classes as it performs only binary classification. DeepSource [24] uses a CNN architecture composed by 5 layers with ReLU activation, residual connection and batch normalization, to first increase the signal-to-noise ratio of the input image and then apply a post-processing technique to identify the predicted source. In this case, the CNN is not used to directly perform object detection, but only to enhance image quality. The described methods use basic implementations of CNNs and do not allow for learning high-level features, which could be a problem in the case of more complex sources or fainted objects. An improvement on this architecture is made with the employment of state-of-the-art object detection methods that make use of RPN (region proposal network) backbones, to yield more accurate results. CLARAN [25] performs domain adaptation on the Faster R-CNN architecture [17], replacing the RoI Pooling layer with differentiable affine transformations and fine-tuning the model from weights pre-trained on the ImageNet Dataset [22]. Astro R-CNN [1] applies the evolution of Faster R-CNN model, Mask R-CNN [7], to perform object detection on a simulated dataset. Mask Galaxy [4] uses Mask R-CNN as well to adapt it to the astronomical domain by performing transfer learning from weights learned on COCO dataset [13] using only one class. Thus, the state of art contains several works employing object detection in astronomical images, but, to the best of our knowledge, no study yet exists that applies semantic segmentation to the source finding task. Hence, the main contribution of this work is to explore the application of such approach to the source finding task as to provide a proper baseline for future works.

3   Semantic Segmentation

This section briefly describes the semantic segmentation models applied to astronomical images. Existing semantic segmentation methods typically use an encoder-decoder architecture based on U-Net [21]. The base U-Net model in the years has been improved through combining segmentation maps created at different scales [12], or devising new loss functions [28] or through deep supervision [27] or through residual and squeeze excitation modules [15]. One significant change in the U-Net architecture was introduced in Tiramisu [10] that employs a sequence of DenseNet [9] blocks, rather than standard convolutional blocks. The *Tiramisu* network consists of a downsampling path for feature extraction and an upsampling path for output generation, with skip connections. Its architecture is shown in Fig. 2.

The input to the model consists of an image resized to 132×132 (in our case) and pre-processed by applying z-scale transform to adjust the contrast. Each image is passed to a convolutional layer to expand the feature dimensions. The resulting feature maps obtained from the first block, traverse a downsampling path consisting of five sequences of dense blocks, and transition-down layers. The transition-down layers are implemented to employ max-pooling in order to reduce feature map size. After the transition-down step, the encoded representation of the input image is obtained. The following upsampling path is symmetric to the downsampling one. Finally, a convolutional layer outputs a 2-channel segmentation map, respectively encoding the log-likelihoods of object and non-object pixels.

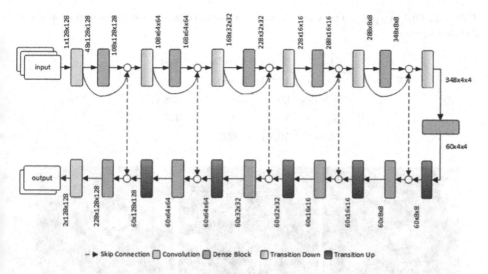

Fig. 2. The proposed Tiramisu segmentation architecture, consisting of a downsampling path and an upsampling path, interconnected by the bottleneck layer.

4 Experiments

4.1 Dataset

Performance analysis is carried on dataset containing 9,192 grayscale image cutouts extracted from different radio-astronomical survey maps taken with the Australian Telescope Compact Array (ATCA), the Australian Square Kilometre Array Pathfinder (ASKAP) and the Very Large Array (VLA). Each image has size 132×132 and may contain multiple objects of the following three classes (examples of them are in Fig. 3):

- **Source** (*19,000 samples*): Compact or point-like radio sources, with unknown astrophysical classification, having rounded and single-component morphology.
- **Sidelobe** (*1,280 samples*): A class of imaging artefacts, introduced by the map making process, often mimicking real radio sources and mostly appearing as elongated or ring-like regions around bright compact sources.
- **Galaxy** (*3,202 samples*): Extended multi-component radio galaxies, often comprising two or more disjoint regions (or islands), typically aligned along the radio structure axis and symmetrical around a center or core region.

The images are stored in FITS file format, although, for being fed to the model, they are converted into PNG format. Before conversion, each crop is normalized using a Z-Scale value of 0.3, in order to enhance the contrast. Each image in the dataset comes with a color-coded segmentation mask (see Fig. 4), which serves as ground truth during training. The whole dataset contains 23,481 different objects that are split for training, validation and test as shown in Table 1.

Table 1. Object splits. The whole dataset consists of 9,192 images containing about 23,000 objects.

Class	Train	Validation	Test
Source	13,300	3,800	1,900
Sidelobe	896	256	128
Galaxy	2,241	640	320
Total	16,437	4,696	2,348

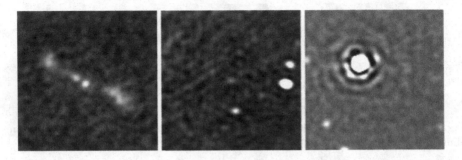

Fig. 3. Examples of (left) galaxies, (center) sources and (right) sidelobes.

4.2   Architecture and Training Details

We test multiple segmentation models on our dataset, namely, a standard encoder-decoder model, Tiramisu and U-Net. The latter has been tested in two variations: baseline and with deep supervision. The baseline version is the one reported in [21], which includes skip connections. Deep supervision consists in computing the distance between the deeper stages of the decoder and the down-sampled ground truth mask and add these distances to the final loss, so to guide the decoder to give a meaningful output even in the deeper layers. Input size is set to 132 × 132, training is carried out for 100 epochs using negative log likelihood as a loss function. Initial learning rate is set to 0.0001, weight decay to 0.0001 with RMSProp as optimizer. Given a strong imbalance among classes, the loss is weighed by a different factor for each class, which results in a different update in the gradients during backpropagation, according to the class of the ground truth. For each class, the factor is computed as

$$w_j = S/(C * S_j) \tag{1}$$

where w_j is the weight for the j-th class, S stands for the total number of samples in the dataset, C is the number of classes and S_j is the number of samples for the j-th class.

This way, the classes with a smaller number of samples will have a higher loss, which pushes the model to better learn such underrepresented classes, counterbalancing the bias. Code is written in Pytorch and experiments executed on a NVIDIA GPU RTX 3090 (24 GB memory).

4.3   Results

For performance evaluation, commonly employed metrics for semantic segmentation and object detection are used. Accuracy, precision, recall and F1 score are computed according to their definition, by using true positives, true negatives, false positives and false negatives. More in detail:

$$Accuracy = \frac{TP + TN}{TP + FP + TN + FN}$$

$$Precision = \frac{TP}{TP + FP}$$

$$Recall = \frac{TP}{TP + FN}$$

$$F_1 = \frac{2 * Precision * Recall}{Precision + Recall} = \frac{2 * TP}{2 * TP + FP + FN}$$

For semantic segmentation and object detection, TP, TN, FP, FN are computed in different ways:

- **Semantic Segmentation**: For each class i, with $i = 1 \cdots$ N (number of classes) a binary mask is generated, where values are ones if they correspond to pixels predicted class i, zeros otherwise. True positives and true negatives correspond to correctly predicted pixels (respectively for the correct class or for the background). False positives correspond to pixels not belonging to class i, predicted as class i. False negatives correspond to pixels with zero prediction where the ground truth is class i.
- **Object Detection**: To allow comparison with object detection models, the binary segmentation mask is converted into a sparse matrix where each connected component (i.e. an object) is identified separately from the others. Then, each object O_i is compared with the corresponding ground truth GT_i using the Intersection over Union (IoU) metric and defining a threshold α.

$$IoU = \frac{O_i \bigcap GT_i}{O_i \bigcup GT_i}$$

True positives are objects of class i with IoU $> \alpha$. False positives occur when the predicted object is not in the correct position with respect to its ground truth (i.e. IoU $< \alpha$). False negatives mean no prediction for the ground truth object GT_i. In this case, there are no true negatives, so the accuracy is not computed.

Table 2 reports semantic segmentation accuracy indicating how the Tiramisu models is the best performing one. All models yield good performance, especially for source and galaxy classification. Sidelobe segmentation performance is in generally lower because of both the limited representativeness in the dataset and their morphological structure. Indeed, sidelobes show a huge appearance variability as they are generated by distortions. This explains the lower number

Table 2. Comparison between Tiramisu and U-Net variations. *DS* stands for deep supervision.

Model	Class	Accuracy	Recall	Precision	F_1
Encoder-Decoder	Sidelobe	0.45	0.38	0.26	0.33
	Source	0.65	0.65	0.72	0.68
	Galaxy	0.74	0.70	0.84	0.76
U-Net	Sidelobe	0.57	0.5	0.33	0.41
	Source	0.74	0.70	0.79	0.76
	Galaxy	0.83	0.76	0.86	0.81
↳+DS	Sidelobe	0.56	0.52	0.35	0.42
	Source	0.76	0.74	0.79	0.76
	Galaxy	0.87	0.88	**0.93**	0.90
Tiramisu	Sidelobe	**0.85**	**0.85**	**0.50**	**0.63**
	Source	**0.90**	**0.90**	0.82	**0.86**
	Galaxy	**0.97**	**0.97**	0.90	**0.93**

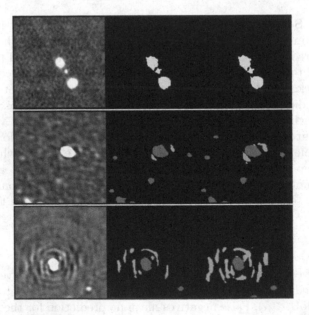

Fig. 4. Output segmentation maps. (right) input image, (middle) ground truth mask, (right) prediction mask. Yellow pixels belong to galaxies, blue ones to sidelobes and red ones to sources. First two rows show success cases, while the last row some failures on sidelobe segmentation.

of sidelobe samples in our dataset w.r.t. the other two classes: annotators often mislabel or miss often them. Among all the U-Net variants, the one employing deep supervision outperforms the others, while it underperforms the Tiramisu

Table 3. Object detection results of Tiramisu and MaskR-CNN.

Model	Class	F_1	Precision	Recall
Tiramisu	Sidelobe	**0.52**	0.46	**0.59**
	Source	**0.83**	**0.81**	0.84
	Galaxy	**0.90**	**0.91**	0.90
MaskR-CNN	Sidelobe	0.30	**0.47**	0.23
	Source	0.74	0.66	**0.86**
	Galaxy	0.77	0.66	**0.93**

model. Examples of good and wrong segmentations are given in Fig. 4. The failures (last row of Fig. 4) mainly pertain identification of sidelobes due to the reasons highlighted earlier.

Table 3 shows the object detection results, computed using a IoU threshold value of 0.5 and compared to those obtained by MaskR-CNN. Here we observe how Tiramisu model outperforms (in terms of F_1 measure, MaskR-CNN one, especially on the precision metrics for galaxy class, thus substantiating our original claim on a major effectiveness of semantic segmentation models over object detectors for that class. Similar to semantic segmentation task, lowest performance is achieved on sidelobes.

5   Conclusion

Both detection and segmentation of astronomical objects in radio images are of key importance for extracting useful information to support astrophysics research. In this work we provide a different perspective to the current object detection approach employed for source identification, i.e., performing semantic segmentation followed by a downstream localization method. To this end, we carried out a benchmark analysis of state-of-the-art semantic segmentation methods to define a baseline for future works. Beside this, we show that using semantic segmentation leads to better detection performance than MaskR-CNN, especially for galaxies. As in terms of segmentation performance, Tiramisu yields an average F_1 score of about 0.93 for galaxies, 0.86 for sources and 0.63 for sidelobes. The reduced performance on sidelobs mainly lies in the low quality of the annotations in the employed dataset. Indeed, the massive presence of sidelobes in astronomical images and their huge variability in appearance make rather complex to annotate all instances. This opens two possible research directions: (a) enhancing the quality of annotated datasets beside increasing the number of classes and instances per class; (b) investigating unsupervised and semi-supervised methods to reduce the annotation burden while keeping the same level of accuracy.

Acknowledgements. The research leading to these results has received funding from the European Commissions Horizon 2020 RIA programme under the grant agreement No. 863448 (NEANIAS) and from the INAF PRIN TEC programme (CIRASA).

References

1. Burke, C.J., et al.: Deblending and classifying astronomical sources with mask R-CNN deep learning. Monthly Not. R. Astron. Soc. **490**(3), 3952–3965 (2019)
2. Cunningham, F., et al.: Ensembl 2019. Nucleic Acids Res. **47**(D1), D745–D751 (2019)
3. DeBoer, D.R., et al.: Australian SKA pathfinder: a high-dynamic range wide-field of view survey telescope. Proc. IEEE **97**(8), 1507–1521 (2009)
4. Farias, H., et al.: Mask galaxy: morphological segmentation of galaxies. Astron. Comput. **33**, 100420 (2020)
5. Friedlander, A.E.A.: Latent Dirichlet allocation for image segmentation and source finding in radio astronomy images. In: ACM International Conference Proceeding Series (2012)
6. González, R.E., Muñoz, R.P., Hernández, C.A.: Galaxy detection and identification using deep learning and data augmentation. Astron. Comput. **25**, 103–109 (2018)
7. He, K., et al.: Mask R-CNN. In: ICCV (2017)
8. Hou, Y.C., et al.: Identification and extraction of solar radio spikes based on deep learning. Solar Phys. **295**(10), 1–11 (2020)
9. Huang, G., et al.: Densely connected convolutional networks. In: CVPR (2017). https://doi.org/10.1109/CVPR.2017.243
10. Jégou, S., et al.: The one hundred layers tiramisu: fully convolutional densenets for semantic segmentation. In: CVPRW (2017)
11. Jia, P., et al.: Detection and classification of astronomical targets with deep neural networks in wide field small aperture telescopes. arXiv 159(5) (2020)
12. Kayalibay, B., et al.: CNN-based segmentation of medical imaging data. arXiv preprint arXiv:1701.03056 (2017)
13. Lin, T.Y., et al.: Microsoft COCO: common objects in context. In: Fleet, D., Pajdla, T., Schiele, B., Tuytelaars, T. (eds.) ECCV 2014. LNCS, vol. 8693, pp. 740–755. Springer, Cham (2014). https://doi.org/10.1007/978-3-319-10602-1_48
14. Lukic, V., Gasperin, F.D., Brüggen, M.: ConvoSource: radio-astronomical source-finding with convolutional neural networks (2019)
15. Murabito, F., et al.: Deep recurrent-convolutional model for automated segmentation of craniomaxillofacial CT scans. In: 2020 25th International Conference on Pattern Recognition (ICPR) (2021)
16. Norris, R.P., et al.: EMU: evolutionary map of the universe. Publ. Astron. Soc. Aust. **28**(3), 215–248 (2011)
17. Ren, S., et al.: Faster R-CNN: towards real-time object detection with region proposal networks. IEEE Trans. Pattern Anal. Mach. Intell. **39**, 1137–1149 (2015)
18. Riggi, S., et al.: Caesar source finder: recent developments and testing. Publ. Astron. Soc. Aust. **36** (2019)
19. Riggi, S., et al.: Automated detection of extended sources in radio maps: progress from the SCORPIO survey. Monthly Not. R. Astron. Soc. **460**(2), 1486–1499 (2016)
20. Robotham, A., et al.: ProFound: source extraction and application to modern survey data. Monthly Not. R. Astron. Soc. **476**(3), 3137–3159 (2018)
21. Ronneberger, O., et al.: U-Net: convolutional networks for biomedical image segmentation. In: Navab, N., Hornegger, J., Wells, W., Frangi, A. (eds.) MICCAI 2015. LNCS, vol. 9351, pp. 234–241. Springer, Cham (2015). https://doi.org/10.1007/978-3-319-24574-4_28

22. Russakovsky, O., et al.: ImageNet large scale visual recognition challenge. Int. J. Comput. Vis. (IJCV) **115**(3), 211–252 (2015)
23. Shimwell, T., et al.: The LOFAR two-metre sky survey-II. First data release. Astron. Astrophys. **622**, A1 (2019)
24. Vafaei-Sadr, A., et al.: DeepSource: point source detection using deep learning. Monthly Not. R. Astron. Soc. **484**(2), 2793–2806 (2019)
25. Wu, C., et al.: Radio galaxy Zoo:CLARAN - a deep learning classifier for radio morphologies. Monthly Not. R. Astron. Soc. **482**(1), 1211–1230 (2018)
26. Xie, Z., Ji, C., Wang, H.: Single and multiwavelength detection of coronal dimming and coronal wave using faster R-CNN. Adv. Astron. **2019** (2019)
27. Zhou, Z., et al.: Unet++: a nested U-Net architecture for medical image segmentation. In: Stoyanov, D., et al. (eds.) DLMIA 2018, ML-CDS 2018. LNCS, vol. 11045, pp. 3–11. Springer, Cham (2018). https://doi.org/10.1007/978-3-030-00889-5_1
28. Zhu, Q., et al.: Deeply-supervised CNN for prostate segmentation. In: 2017 International Joint Conference on Neural Networks (IJCNN). IEEE (2017)

Content-Based Image Retrieval for Surface Defects of Hot Rolled Steel Strip Using Wavelet-Based LBP

Fatma Zohra Boudani[1,2(✉)], Nafaa Nacereddine[1], and Nacera Laiche[2]

[1] Research Center in Industrial Technologies CRTI, P.O. Box 64, 16014 Cheraga, Algiers, Algeria
fboudani@usthb.dz, n.nacereddine@crti.dz
[2] Faculty of Electronic and Computing, USTHB, BP 32 El-Alia, 16111 Bab Ezzouar, Algiers, Algeria
nlaiche@usthb.dz

Abstract. Quality control by artificial vision with applications in industrial manufacturing is a challenging task due to the significant variability of surface defects. In this work, we propose to use content based image retrieval CBIR to manage the large data produced by surface inspection systems. The performance of the CBIR system was evaluated using textural features extracted from NEU database that collects six kinds of surface defects of the hot-rolled steel strip. Different similarity measurements were used to retrieve the most similar images to the query image. The effectiveness of Wavelet based local binary patterns WLBP features was shown in the experimental results for the retrieval of surface defects. WLBP features using Chi square distance achieved the highest retrieval values compared to LBP, GLCM, and EHD features.

Keywords: Surface defects · CBIR · Hot-rolled steel strip · Textural features · Feature extraction · Wavelet · LBP · Chi square

1 Introduction

In recent years, products of many industries such as aerospace, marine, automobile, iron and steel industry, electronics, and so on have made huge contributions to the development of the global economy. The competitiveness of manufacturing industry has been accompanied by a large number of surface defects in the final products which is very costly and would lead to enormous economic and reputation losses. Hence, there have been an increasing surface quality control demands for the industrial manufacturing [1–5]. Automatic surface inspection systems produce thousands of defect images on a daily basis. These huge image data are composed of various surface defects with large inter class similarities and intra-class diversities [4]. Therefore, it is very exhausting and time-consuming to analyze all these images on a daily basis. Content based image retrieval (CBIR) systems are suitable tools to handle this problem, since their performance is accurate for large databases with the advantage of bringing human expertise in the

© Springer Nature Switzerland AG 2021
Y. Hernández Heredia et al. (Eds.): IWAIPR 2021, LNCS 13055, pp. 404–413, 2021.
https://doi.org/10.1007/978-3-030-89691-1_39

decisions making step [6, 7]. The process of CBIR is based on analyzing the visual features of images database such as colors, shapes and texture [6, 8]. In this context, quality control experts use images of serious defects as queries and train the CBIR system employing features extraction techniques and similarity measurements to retrieve images that look similar to the queries [7, 9]. This will give the experts an overview of the defects occurred in the production lines which will allow them to refine the performance in the future. The industrial surface inspection is mainly a texture analysis problem [2, 4]. Scholars have conducted significant research to inspect local textural irregularities on different types of surfaces such as Steel, stone, textile, wood, and ceramic tiles [1–5]. Publications of the last 3 decades classified texture feature description approaches into four categories, including statistical approaches, filtering based methods, model-based methods, and methods based on machine learning [1–5]. The local binary patterns LBP are a widely used statistical method for describing local texture features of an image by comparing the gray values of every pixel with its neighbors [10]. Many LBP variants have been developed to extract features of various surface defects from images of steel strips [11–14]. In this paper, we present a wavelet based LBP Method WLBP to extract features from hot-rolled steel strip database for an effective retrieval and detection of surface defects.

2 Content Based Image Retrieval

Content based image retrieval CBIR has become an active research field in computer vision. Research interest in this field has increased due to the deployment of large image databases in various professional fields. Accessing requested images from these large and varied image databases is fundamental for the users. Content-based means that the search will analyze the visual features of the image such as colors, shapes, and texture [6]. CBIR systems are created to retrieve images that are visually similar to a query image using two steps [6, 8]:

- Feature Extraction: The first step in the process is extracting features from the image database, allowing the database indexing.
- Matching and comparison: The second step involves matching and comparing these features to yield a result that is similar to the query.

Texture is the most important describing features of industrial surface inspection images [1–5]. It is essentially characterized by the spatial distribution of gray levels in a neighborhood. Textured image contains important information about the structural arrangement of the surface, and the relationship of the surface to the surrounding environment [8].

3 Local Binary Pattern

The local binary pattern LBP is a widely used method for describing local texture features of an image by comparing the gray values of every pixel with its neighbors. LBP was first introduced by Ojala et al. [10]. The original LBP descriptor is defined in a 3×3

window. It uses the gray value of the center pixel (g_c) as a threshold for its 8 neighbors ($g_0, ..., g_7$). If the gray value of a neighbor pixel is higher or equal to the threshold than 1 is assigned to this pixel, otherwise it gets 0. The eight binary values will be concatenated in a clockwise direction to form a binary number. Then, the LBP code of the center pixel $g_c(x_c, y_c)$ is obtained by converting the binary number into a decimal number using Eq. 1. An example of LBP operator is shown on Fig. 1. The local texture features of the whole image can be described by computing the 256 bins histogram of the LBP codes.

$$LBP(x_c, y_c) = \sum_{n=0}^{7} 2^n sgn(g_n - g_c) \qquad (1)$$

where, $sgn(g_n - g_c)$ is the sign function defined as

$$sgn(g_n - g_c) = \begin{cases} 1, g_n \geq g_c \\ 0, g_n < g_c \end{cases} \qquad (2)$$

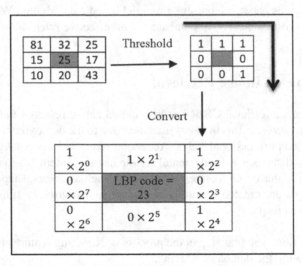

Fig. 1. Example of LBP operator.

4   Image Retrieval Using Wavelet Based Local Binary Patterns

Wavelet transforms have been commonly used in different applications, such as image denoising [15], clustering [16], and features extraction [17–19]. The result of the wavelet transform is a multilevel decomposition of the image into approximation and details coefficients [20]. In this paper, we extract textural features using local binary patterns of the wavelet sub bands. This feature extraction method is the first step of the CBIR process, it consists of the following tasks:

(1)   Multilevel decomposition of the images via Haar based Discrete Wavelet Transform DWT [20].

(2) Computation of LBP codes of the wavelet coefficients (approximation and details).
(3) Concatenation of LBP feature vectors of all DWT coefficients to form a single feature vector for each image.

The second step of the process is to compute the similarity between the feature vector of the query image and feature database of the selected descriptor. The similarity measures are then stored and sorted in increasing order and the most similar images are displayed as a retrieval result. The diagram of the proposed image retrieval process is presented in the following Fig. 2:

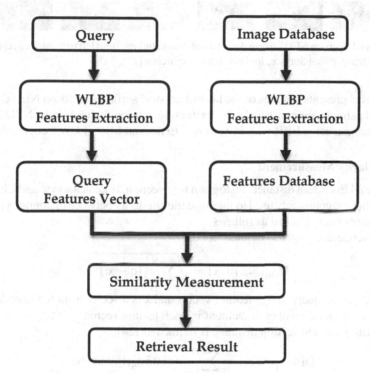

Fig. 2. Diagram of the proposed image retrieval system.

5 Experimental Results

In this section, the performance of WLBP features for content based image retrieval is compared with other feature extraction methods, namely Gray level Co-occurrence matrix (GLCM) [21], Edge Histogram Descriptor (EHD) [22], and the original LBP [10]. We select NEU Surface Defect Database that includes 1,800 Gy scale images for experiments [11]. It is an open source dataset comprising six kinds of typical surface defects of the hot-rolled steel strip with 300 images for each defect, i.e., Crazing (Cr), Inclusion (IN), Patches (PA), Pitted Surface (PS), Rolled-in Scale (RS), and Scratches

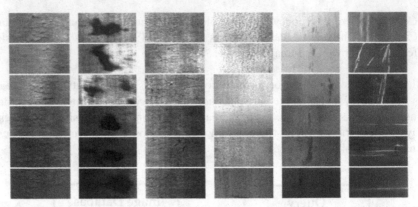

Fig. 3. Steel defects on NEU surface defect database including, from left to right, Rolled-In Scale, Patches, Crazing, Pitted Surface, Inclusion, and Scratches [11].

(Sc). Figure 3 presents samples of the hot-rolled steel surface defects on NEU database. Features databases are constructed by extracting images features from NEU Surface Defect Database using LBP, GLCM features, EHD, and LBP of DWT coefficients.

5.1 Similarity Measurement

We have used Euclidean distance, histogram intersection, Bhattacharyya, and Chi square distance, that are commonly used to measure the similarity between histograms [23, 24]. These distances are obtained as follows.

The Euclidean distance is defined as [25]:

$$D_{Euclidean}(q, x) = \sqrt{\sum_{i=1}^{N} (q - x_i)^2} \tag{3}$$

where, q is the query image feature vector and x is a vector from features database. N represents the total number of element in each feature vector.

The histogram intersection distance is defined as [24]:

$$D(hist_q, hist_x) = \sum_{i=1}^{N} \min(hist_q(i), hist_x(i)) \tag{4}$$

where, $hist_q$ is the histogram-based feature vector of the query image, and $hist_x$ is a vector from the histogram-based features database.

The Bhattacharrya distance between two histograms is defined as [25]:

$$D_{Bhattacharyya}(hist_q, hist_x) = \sqrt{1 - \sum_{i=1}^{N} \frac{\sqrt{hist_q(i).hist_x(i)}}{\sqrt{\sum hist_q(i). \sum hist_q(i)}}} \tag{5}$$

The Chi square distance between two histograms is defined as [24]:

$$D_{chisquare}(hist_q, hist_x) = \frac{1}{2} \sum_{i=1}^{N} \frac{(hist_q(i) - hist_x(i))^2}{(hist_q(i) + hist_x(i))} \tag{6}$$

The distances are then stored and sorted in increasing order based on similarity distance and most similar images are displayed as a retrieval result.

5.2 Performance Evaluation Metrics

We have evaluated the retrieval system using the Mean Average Precision (MAP) which is one of the most used metrics in literature to measure the retrieval performances [26]. It is computed as the mean of average precision values for each query. The mathematical representations of the Precision, the Average Precision, and the Mean Average Precision are given below:

- Precision (P) is equivalent to the ratio of retrieved relevant images to the total number of retrieved images N:

$$P(k) = \frac{1}{N} \sum_{k=1}^{N} relevant(k) \tag{7}$$

where, relevant (k) is a function that returns 1 if the image at position k is relevant, and returns 0 otherwise.

- The Average Precision (AP) is calculated for a single query by averaging the precision values at each relevant image:

$$AP = \frac{\sum_{k=1}^{N} P(k) \cdot relevant(k)}{\text{number of relevant images}} \tag{8}$$

- The MAP for a set of queries Q is given by:

$$MAP = \frac{\sum_{q=1}^{Q} AP(q)}{Q} \tag{9}$$

5.3 Retrieval Results

Experimental results of the proposed system are presented in Table 1. For each descriptor, all images were chosen one by one as a query image and top 10 images were retrieved based on Euclidean distance, Histogram intersection, Chi square, and Bhattacharyya distance. For the WLBP, we have tested up to three levels of the DWT decomposition using Haar wavelet.

According to Table 1, best results in terms of similarity measures were obtained using Chi square, and Bhattacharyya distance. It has been shown that LBP features achieve a good MAP value of 90.26%; it outperforms both EHD and GLCM features with a MAP difference of about 20%. Further experiments on WLBP demonstrate the superiority of this descriptor over the previously tested descriptors. Two decomposition levels of the WLBP using Chi square distance yields the highest value of MAP with an improvement of 3% compared to the results of LBP features. However, a decrease in performance has been detected when using more than two decomposition levels.

Table 1. Comparison of MAP@10 of the selected descriptors using different similarity measures

Distance metrics	GLCM	EHD	LBP	WLBP 1 level	WLBP 2 levels	WLBP 3 levels
Euclidean distance	0.3721	0.6467	0.8933	0.9104	0.9103	0.9116
Histogram intersection	0.4438	0.6869	0.8211	0.8314	0.8083	0.8283
Bhattacharyya	**0.6834**	0.7032	**0.9026**	**0.9236**	0.9298	0.8871
Chi square	0.5200	**0.7081**	0.8959	0.9216	**0.9329**	**0.9170**

More experiments have been done to assess the performance of the descriptors on each defects class. Table 2 illustrates the MAP values of the top 10 images retrieved based on the Chi Square distance. The CBIR systems using LBP, 1 level WLBP, and 2 levels WLBP features succeed to retrieve all images from the defects class "Rolled in scale" with a MAP value equals to 100%. Two levels WLBP yields the highest MAP values for the classes of Crazing and Patches. The best results for the class of Pitted surface have been achieved by LBP features. However, EHD outperforms the other descriptors in retrieving images of "inclusion", it achieves a MAP value equals to 94.66% which is higher by more than 7% compared to the closest results obtained by 2 levels WLBP. In addition, even though the total MAP using GLCM features is the worst with a value of 52%, these features achieve the best MAP score for the class of Scratches. The MAP value of GLCM features is 7% higher compared to the closest result obtained by 3 levels WLBP.

Table 2. Comparison of retrieval results based on map@10 for different defect classes using chi square.

Defect classes	MAP@10 Using Chi Square distance					
	GLCM	EHD	LBP	WLBP 1 level	WLBP 2 levels	WLBP 3 levels
Crazing	0.4664	0.8498	0.9680	0.9940	**0.9996**	0.9979
Inclusion	0.3697	**0.9466**	0.8521	0.8677	0.8690	0.8583
Patches	0.4707	0.4985	0.8494	0.9346	**0.9829**	0.9485
Pitted surface	0.3272	0.4219	**0.9453**	0.9413	0.9239	0.8712
Rolled in scale	0.5891	0.8709	**1.0000**	**1.0000**	**1.0000**	0.9988
Scratches	**0.8969**	0.6607	0.7607	0.7917	0.8222	0.8274
Whole database	0.5200	**0.7081**	0.8959	0.9216	**0.9329**	0.9170

Retrieval results of a query from the class of patches defects using LBP and 2 levels WLBP are shown in Figs. 4 and 5 respectively. Similarity measures using Chi square distance are displayed below each image. The CBIR system using LBP features is not effective for the selected query according to Fig. 4, since it retrieved only 4 relevant images including the query. This retrieval result presents confusion with the class of Crazing defects. The wavelet based LBP performs better with 10 relevant images out of 10 retrieved as shown in Fig. 5.

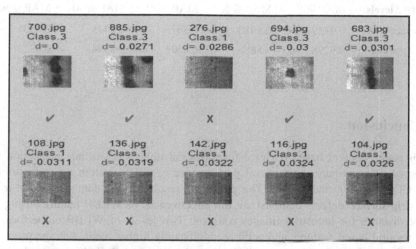

Fig. 4. Image retrieval results for a query (top-left image) of the defect class (Patches) using LBP features.

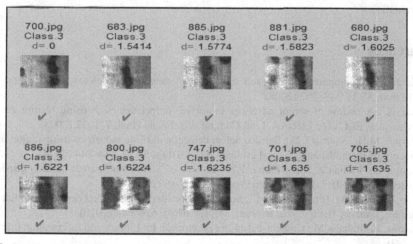

Fig. 5. Image retrieval results for a query (top-left image) of the defect class (Patches) using WLBP features.

To further evaluate the retrieval performance, top 10, 20, 30, 40 and 50 images of the CBIR system using 2 levels WLBP features are retrieved. MAP value is calculated for all the retrieved images of the NEU database based on Chi square, and Bhattacharyya distance. As summarized in Table 3, the best results were obtained using the Chi square distance. In addition, 2 levels WLBP features retain their effectiveness for the entire scope with a MAP value that's greater than 83%.

Table 3. Performance of the wlbp features at five top ranks (10, 20, 30, 40, 50)

WLBP 2 levels	MAP @10	MAP @20	MAP @30	MAP @40	MAP @50
Chi square	0.9329	0.8930	0.8673	0.8475	0.8306
Bhattacharyya	0.9298	0.8880	0.8603	0.8394	0.8223

6 Conclusion

In this paper, content based retrieval for industrial images of surface inspection was addressed. We compare the retrieval performance of CBIR system using features of LBP, GLCM, EHD, and WLBP. The promising results on the database of hot-rolled steel strip surface defects demonstrate the effectiveness of WLBP features using Chi square distance for industrial images retrieval. Two levels of WLBP outperform the other textural based features and achieve significantly higher mean average precision, especially for the defects classes of Crazing, Patches, and Rolled in scale. In future work, we plan to further boost the retrieval performance by combining descriptors and using features selection techniques. Also, more industrial databases will be considered for evaluation.

References

1. Kumar, A.: Computer-vision-based fabric defect detection: a survey IEEE Trans. Ind. Electron. **55**(1), 348–363 (2008)
2. Xie, X.: A review of recent advances in surface defect detection using texture analysis techniques. ELCVIA: Electron. Lett. Comput. Vis. Image Anal. **7**, 1–22 (2008)
3. Karimi, M.H., Asemani, D.: Surface defect detection in tiling industries using digital image processing methods: analysis and evaluation ISA Trans. **53**(3), 834–844 (2014)
4. Neogi, N., Mohanta, D.K., Dutta, P.K.: Review of vision-based steel surface inspection systems EURASIP J. Image Video Process. (1), 1–19 (2014)
5. Luo, Q., Fang, X., Liu, L., Yang, C., Sun, Y.: Automated visual defect detection for flat steel surface: a survey IEEE Trans. Instrum. Measur. **69**(3), 626–644 (2020)
6. Eakins, J., Graham, M.: Content-based image retrieval. In: Library and Information Briefings (1999)
7. Iivarinen, J., Rautkorpi, R., Pakkanen, J., Rauhamaa, J.: Content-based retrieval of surface defect images with PicSOM Int. J. Fuzzy Syst. **6**, 3–160 (2004)
8. Juneja, K., Verma, A., Goel, S., Goel, S.: A survey on recent image indexing and retrieval techniques for low-level feature extraction in CBIR systems. In: 2015 IEEE International Conference on Computational Intelligence & Communication Technology, pp. 67–72 (2015)

9. Nacereddine, N., Ziou, D., Hamami, L.: Fusion-based shape descriptor for weld defect radiographic image retrieval Int. J. Adv. Manuf. Technol. **68**(9–12) 2815–2832 (2013)
10. Ojala, T., Pietikäinen, M., Harwood, D.: A comparative study of texture measures with classification based on featured distributions Pattern Recogn. **29**(1), 51–59 (1996)
11. Song, K., Yan, Y.: A noise robust method based on completed local binary patterns for hot-rolled steel strip surface defects Appl. Surf. Sci. **285** 858–864 (2013)
12. Luo, Q., Sun, Y., Li, P., Simpson, O., Tian, L., He, Y.: Generalized completed local binary patterns for time-efficient steel surface defect classification IEEE Trans. Instrum. Measur. **68**(3), 667–679 (2018)
13. Luo, Q.: Surface defect classification for hot-rolled steel strips by selectively dominant local binary patterns IEEE Access **7** 23488–23499 (2019)
14. Liu, Y., Xu, K., Xu, J.: An improved MB-LBP defect recognition approach for the surface of steel plates Appl. Sci. **9**(20), 4222 (2019)
15. Boudani, F.Z., Nacereddine, N.: Diffusion in the wavelet domain for denoising radiographic images of welding defects. In: 2019 International Conference on Advanced Electrical Engineering (ICAEE), pp. 1–5. IEEE. Algeria (2019).
16. Chetih, N., Messali, Z., Serir, A., Ramou, N.: Robust fuzzy c-means clustering algorithm using non-parametric Bayesian estimation in wavelet transform domain for noisy MR brain image segmentation IET Image Process. **12**(5), 652–660 (2018)
17. Moh'd Shamaileh, A., Rassem, T.H., Chuin, L.S., Al Sayaydeh, O.N.: A new feature-based wavelet completed local ternary pattern (Feat-WCLTP) for texture image classification. IEEE Access **8**, 28276–28288 (2020)
18. Chaudhari, C.V.: Steel surface defect detection using glcm, gabor wavelet, hog, and random forest classifier Turkish J. Comput. Math. Educ. (TURCOMAT) **12**(12), 263–273 (2021)
19. Deepa, B., Sumithra, M. G., Kumar, R. M., Suriya, M : Weiner filter based hough transform and wavelet feature extraction with neural network for classifying brain tumor. In: 6th International Conference on Inventive Computation Technologies (ICICT), pp. 637–641. IEEE, India (2021)
20. Shensa, M.J.: The discrete wavelet transform: wedding the a Trous and Mallat algorithms IEEE Trans. Sig. Process. **40**(10), 2464–2482 (1992)
21. Mohanaiah, P., Sathyanarayana, P., GuruKumar, L.: Image texture feature extraction using GLCM approach Int. J. Sci. Res. Publ. **3**(5), 1–5 (2013)
22. Won, C.S., Park, D.K., Park, S.J.: Efficient use of MPEG-7 edge histogram descriptor ETRI J. **24**(1) 23–30 (2002)
23. Cha, S.H., Srihari, S.N.: On measuring the distance between histograms Pattern Recogn. **35**(6), 1355–1370 (2002)
24. Marín-Reyes, P.A., Lorenzo-Navarro, J., Castrillón-Santana, M.: Comparative study of histogram distance measures for re-identification. arXiv preprint arXiv:1611.08134 (2016)
25. Rahman, M.M., Bhattacharya, P., Desai, B.C.: Similarity searching in image retrieval with statistical distance measures and supervised learning. In: Singh, S., Singh, M., Apte, C., Perner, P. (eds.) ICAPR 2005 LNCS 3686 Springer, pp. 315–324 Heidelberg (2005)
26. Deselaers, T., Keysers, D., Ney, H.: Features for image retrieval: an experimental comparison Inf. Retrieval **11**(2), 77–107 (2008)

Decision Rules for Radar Detection in the Moments Space with Arbitrary Correlation Degree and Constant False Alarm Rate

Camilo Guillén[(✉)] [iD] and Nelson Chávez[iD]

Technological University of Havana "José Antonio Echeverría", CUJAE, La Habana, Cuba
{camilo.gs,nelson}@tele.cujae.edu.cu

Abstract. At the end of the last century, radar detection in the moments space was proposed. The main motivations for its use are to increase the discriminative ability of the signal parameters and to decrease the uncertainty about their distribution. For achieving detection, it is necessary to determine the decision rules that establish the operations performed by the detector. This work details the obtaining of the optimal decision rule following the Neyman-Pearson criterion and the rule that allows to maintain a constant false alarm rate (CFAR), both for moments with arbitrary correlation degree. The probability densities of the decision statistics are also proposed, which will allow to evaluate the performance of radar detection through statistical moments.

Keywords: Radar detection · Statistical moments · Anomaly detection · CFAR detection · Mahalanobis distance

1 Introduction

The detection in the moments space is one of the techniques that seeks to improve the quality of radar detection [1–3]. Its essence relies on transferring the decision making to a space formed by a certain number of statistical moments (mean, average power, etc.), computed from the echo-signal parameters (amplitude, frequency, etc.). Among its main advantages are the reduction of the uncertainty about the distribution of the parameters [4] and the increase of the discriminative ability [3, 5].

In order to implement this technique, the DRACEC method (a Spanish acronym for Radar Detection through the Analysis and Classification of Cellular Emission) was developed [1]. The initial proposal of DRACEC assumes statistical independence between the moments to obtain the optimal decision rule in a simple way, applying the Neyman-Pearson criterion [6]. In addition, DRACEC devised an adaptation stage to dynamically estimate the interference characteristics. However, in practice there is some error due to the assumption of independence between the moments, since this is a particular case where the correlation is null [7, 8], which is a very difficult condition to achieve strictly. On the other hand, the former adaptive algorithm did not propose a decision statistic that

© Springer Nature Switzerland AG 2021
Y. Hernández Heredia et al. (Eds.): IWAIPR 2021, LNCS 13055, pp. 414–423, 2021.
https://doi.org/10.1007/978-3-030-89691-1_40

satisfies the constant false alarm rate (CFAR) property [9], which is an essential element in dealing with interference variations.

The SM-CFAR (Statistical Moments-CFAR) detector [5] was recently conceived to solve both of the above problems. It achieves CFAR detection using moments with arbitrary correlation degree, through a combination of the principles of classical sliding window detectors [9] with a decision statistic based on the square of the Mahalanobis distance [10]. However, no previous work has addressed the details of obtaining the optimal and the CFAR decision rules for the moments space. Therefore, the goal of the following sections will be to obtain the optimal decision statistic for the case of moments with arbitrary correlation degree and then identify a statistic that preserves the CFAR property. Also, the probability densities for both decision statistics are proposed for the first time.

2 The Moments Space for Radar Detection

In the following, the only considered parameter will be the amplitude of the video-signal, for a monostatic pulse radar that scans a two-dimensional superficial searching window (range and azimuth) [11]. The index $u = 1, ..., U$ identifies the U resolution cells that compose the window, whose dimensions will depend on the range resolution and the antenna's half-power beam width.

The amplitude of the video-signal is a continuous random process. By properly sampling this process [5, 11], it is possible to associate to each resolution cell a set of samples Ψ_u, which will be a discrete random process, often referred to as cellular emission. If any anomaly occurs in the searching window, the corresponding cellular emission Ψ_u will carry out information about the produced changes. As the "natural" behavior of Ψ_u is affected, the variation will be reflected in the moments that describe its joint probability density of statistic order G [7]. By selecting S moments and sorting them according to the indices $(1), (2), ... (S)$, it is possible to calculate N values for each one and associate to each resolution cell the set

$$\Phi_u = \{\mu\}_{n=1,...,N} = \left\{\varepsilon_{(1)}, \varepsilon_{(2)}, ..., \varepsilon_{(S)}\right\}_{n=1,...,N}, \tag{1}$$

formed by N vectors (or patterns) denoted by μ, whose components (or features) $\varepsilon_{(1)}, \varepsilon_{(2)}, ..., \varepsilon_{(S)}$ are the moments. Thus, the statistical behavior of any cellular emission is characterized by Φ_u in an S-dimensional space: the moments space.

The expression for computing N values of the (s)-th moment from N random samples of size M is given by

$$\left\{\varepsilon_{(s)}\right\}_{n=1,...,N} = \frac{1}{M}\sum_{m=1}^{M}X_{m,n} = \frac{1}{M}\sum_{m=1}^{M}\left[\prod_{g=1}^{G}x_g^{l_g}\right]_{m,n}, \tag{2}$$

where $X = \prod_{g=1}^{G} x_g^{l_g}$ is a sample element composed by the samples of the video-signal $x_1, ..., x_G$ multiplied and raised to the corresponding l_g. The sum $L = \sum_{g=1}^{G} l_g$ is the moment order for the statistic order G [7, 8].

The goal of the detector in moments space is to use the information contained in Φ_u to assign each resolution cell to the classes background or anomaly. The background is associated with processes that take place "normally" in the searching window, e.g., the clutter. Likewise, phenomena outside the "normality" will be treated as anomalies, which constitute the targets to be detected.

3   Optimum Decision Rule for Moments with Arbitrary Correlation Degree

Detection in the moments space is a typical test between the two hypotheses: (i) μ belongs to the background class or (ii) μ belongs to the anomaly class. Using the Neyman-Pearson criterion, the decision rule is designed to maximize the detection probability (P_D) under the constraint of a fixed false alarm probability (P_{FA}) [6]. For the moments space, the criterion can be stated as follows: to maximize P_D by taking $P_{FA} = \alpha$, decide that μ belongs to the anomaly class if

$$\Lambda(\mu) = \frac{f_\mu(\mu|A)}{f_\mu(\mu|B)} > \Lambda_0, \tag{3}$$

where the threshold Λ_0 must guarantee

$$P_{FA} = \underset{\{\mu:\Lambda(\mu)>\Lambda_0\}}{\int \cdots \int} f_\mu(\mu|B)d\mu = \alpha. \tag{4}$$

The function $\Lambda(\mu)$ is known as the likelihood ratio [6, 9], while $f_\mu(\mu|A)$ and $f_\mu(\mu|B)$ are the joint probability density functions (PDF) of the patterns for the anomaly and the background, respectively. The integration region $\{\mu : \Lambda(\mu) > \Lambda_0\}$ is the one where the S-dimensional patterns satisfy the condition $\Lambda(\mu) > \Lambda_0$.

When the S Gaussian moments of μ have an arbitrary correlation degree, their joint PDF will be multivariate normal and is given by [4, 7, 12]

$$f_\mu(\mu|C) = \frac{\exp\left\{-\frac{1}{2}(\mu - \overline{\mu}_C)\Sigma_C^{-1}(\mu - \overline{\mu}_C)^T\right\}}{(2\pi)^{S/2}|\Sigma_C|^{1/2}}, \tag{5}$$

where $C = A, B$ for the anomaly or the background respectively, $\overline{\mu}_C$ is the mean vector and Σ_C^{-1} is the inverse of the covariance matrix; $|\Sigma_C|$ denotes the determinant and T the transpose. Taking (5) into account, the likelihood ratio would be

$$\Lambda(\mu) = \frac{|\Sigma_B|^{1/2}}{|\Sigma_A|^{1/2}} \exp\left\{\frac{1}{2}(\mu - \overline{\mu}_B)\Sigma_B^{-1}(\mu - \overline{\mu}_B)^T - \frac{1}{2}(\mu - \overline{\mu}_A)\Sigma_A^{-1}(\mu - \overline{\mu}_A)^T\right\}. \tag{6}$$

The exponent of the above equation constitutes a monotonically increasing function of $\Lambda(\mu)$, thus is taken as a sufficient decision statistic [3, 9], which allows the application of a rule that is easier to compute [6, 9]. Denoting the sufficient statistic as Z, the decision rule can be written directly as

$$
\begin{aligned}
Z = (\mu - \overline{\mu}_B)\Sigma_B^{-1}(\mu - \overline{\mu}_B)^T - (\mu - \overline{\mu}_A)\Sigma_A^{-1}(\mu - \overline{\mu}_A)^T \geq Z_0 \Rightarrow \mu \in A \\
Z = (\mu - \overline{\mu}_B)\Sigma_B^{-1}(\mu - \overline{\mu}_B)^T - (\mu - \overline{\mu}_A)\Sigma_A^{-1}(\mu - \overline{\mu}_A)^T < Z_0 \Rightarrow \mu \in B.
\end{aligned}
\tag{7}
$$

Since $Z > Z_0$ implies $\Lambda(\mu) > \Lambda_0$, the threshold Λ_0 of $\Lambda(\mu)$ will corresponds to the threshold Z_0 of Z. This threshold is chosen to guarantee the design P_{FA} according to

$$
P_{FA} = \int_{Z_0}^{\infty} f_Z(Z|B)\,dZ,
\tag{8}
$$

where $f_Z(Z|B)$ is the PDF of Z for the background class.

3.1 Mahalanobis Distance and Its Relation to Optimal Detection

From Eq. (7) it can be identified that both terms of Z constitute two squares of the Mahalanobis distances (SMD), each one defined as [10]

$$
D_C(\mu) = (\mu - \overline{\mu}_C)\Sigma_C^{-1}(\mu - \overline{\mu}_C)^T.
\tag{9}
$$

$D_C(\mu)$ provides a measure of the separation between the pattern μ and the cluster associated with the joint PDF of the class C, described by the covariance matrix Σ_C and mean vector $\overline{\mu}_C$. All patterns that satisfy a constant $D_C(\mu)$, describe an ellipsoid (ellipse for the two-dimensional case) centered on the mean vector and with semi-axes proportional to the variance in their directions.

Taking Eq. (9) into account, the rule in (7) could be rewritten as follows

$$
\begin{aligned}
Z = D_B(\mu) - D_A(\mu) \geq Z_0 \Rightarrow \mu \in A \\
Z = D_B(\mu) - D_A(\mu) < Z_0 \Rightarrow \mu \in B,
\end{aligned}
\tag{10}
$$

where becomes clear that the optimal detector is a comparator between two SMDs, a relationship illustrated in Fig. 1. The SMD $D_B(\mu_1)$ of the pattern μ_1 with respect to the background cluster has a value less than $Z_0 + D_A(\mu_1)$, therefore, it is classified as background. The opposite is true for μ_2, since $D_B(\mu_2)$ is greater than $Z_0 + D_A(\mu_2)$ and consequently it will be classified as anomaly.

3.2 Probability Density Function of the Sufficient Decision Statistic

To establish the threshold that guarantees the probability of false alarm, it is necessary to evaluate the integral in (8). In this sense, it is very useful to have the analytical expression of the PDF of Z for both classes. Based on Eq. (10), when the patterns belong to the background the values of $D_B(\mu)$ will be small compared to those of $D_A(\mu)$ and Z will take its smallest (negative) values. The opposite happens when the patterns belong to the anomaly, so Z will reach its largest (positive) values. Therefore, the distribution of Z

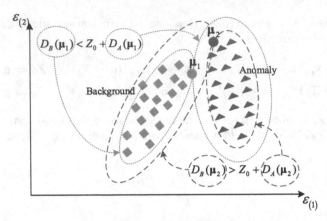

Fig. 1. Optimum detection and its relation to the SMD.

will follow the distribution of its extreme values: that of the minima for the background and that of the maxima for the anomaly.

Based on this reasoning, we resort to the Extreme Value Theory [13], whose purpose is to study extreme events and is widely used in disciplines such as communications [14] or radar [15–17]. The Fisher-Tippett-Gnedenko theorem [13, 18] states that the distribution of the extreme values of a random variable can only converge to one of the following three types: Gumbel, Frechet and Weibull. In turn, these can be grouped into a single distribution with three parameters, known as the generalized extreme value distribution (GEV), whose PDF is given by [18]

$$
f_Z(Z|C) = \begin{cases} \frac{1}{\beta_C}\left(1 + \kappa_C \frac{Z-\zeta_C}{\beta_C}\right)^{-1-\frac{1}{\kappa_C}} \exp\left[-\left(1 + \kappa_C \frac{Z-\zeta_C}{\beta_C}\right)^{-\frac{1}{\kappa_C}}\right] & \kappa_C \neq 0 \,;\, 1 + \kappa_C \frac{Z-\zeta_C}{\beta_C} > 0 \\ \frac{1}{\beta_C} \exp\left[-\exp\left(-\frac{Z-\zeta_C}{\beta_C}\right) - \frac{Z-\zeta_C}{\beta_C}\right] & \kappa_C = 0 \end{cases},
$$

$$(11)$$

where $\kappa_C, \beta_C, \zeta_C$ are the shape, scale and location parameters, respectively. The subscript C indicates again the corresponding class.

Figure 2 shows an example of the estimated PDFs of Z for both classes and their fits to (11). In this case, the samples of the video-signal for the background corresponds to the internal noise of the radar receiver, so they are ruled by the Rayleigh model [9]. On the other hand, the anomaly is a non-fluctuating target, thus the samples follow the Rice model [9]. The components of μ are the first and second order moments. The parameters of the PDFs of Z are computed using the Maximum Likelihood Estimation method [19] and the threshold that guarantees a P_{FA} of 10^{-3} is calculated using a step-descendent algorithm [20].

Table 1 shows two common coefficients [4] for measuring the goodness of the previous fits. They are the Mean Square Error (MSE) and the Normalized Mean Square Error (NMSE). Values close to 0 for the MSE and close to 1 for the NMSE indicate an ideal fit, so the proposal of the GEV distribution seems adequate. The complete validity of this models for practical purposes require exhaustive analysis of hypothesis testing and goodness-of-fit that will be the center of future works.

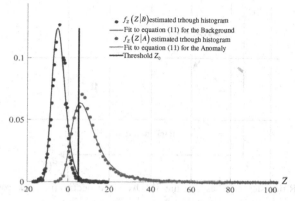

Fig. 2. Probability densities functions of Z for both classes.

Table 1. Coefficients of goodness-of-fit to the GEV distribution for both classes.

	MSE	NMSE
$f_Z(Z|B)$	$1.181 \cdot 10^{-5}$	0.957
$f_Z(Z|A)$	$2.523 \cdot 10^{-6}$	0.986

4 CFAR Decision Rule in the Moments Space

From Eq. (10) it can be seen that optimal detection in moments space is reduced to a comparison between two SMDs. However, in real situations the characteristics of the anomaly ($\overline{\mu}_A$ and Σ_A) are unknown a priori, thus some alternative to (10) is needed as a decision statistic. The immediate variant is illustrated in Fig. 3 and only comprises the SMD with respect to the background cluster, in order to define the ellipsoid

$$D = D_B(\mu) = (\mu - \overline{\mu}_B)\Sigma_B^{-1}(\mu - \overline{\mu}_B)^T = D_0, \tag{12}$$

which will allow the association of any pattern in the inside (μ_1) to the background, while the patterns in the outside are declared as anomaly (μ_2). The decision rule for this situation would be

$$D = D_B(\mu) \geq D_0 \Rightarrow \mu \in A$$
$$D = D_B(\mu) < D_0 \Rightarrow \mu \in B, \tag{13}$$

where the differences with (7) or (10) must be noted.

The two key elements to determine the previous ellipsoid lie in (i) the choice of the patterns that contribute to estimate $\overline{\mu}_B$ and Σ_B, and (ii) the computation of the threshold D_0 that establishes its size as a function of the P_{FA}. The solution to the first issue is possible by a reasoning similar to that used by traditional CFAR detectors: the cells contiguous to the cell under test are taken as reference channels to describe the background. The paper [5] discusses the details of the mechanism devised for this purpose, so that hereafter it is assumed that $\overline{\mu}_B$ and Σ_B are correctly estimated.

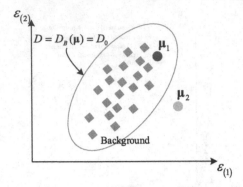

Fig. 3. CFAR decision rule based in the SMD with respect to the background cluster.

To solve the issue concerning the computation of the D_0 that defines the size of the ellipsoid according to the P_{FA}, we have that the relationship between both elements is

$$P_{FA} = \int_{D_0}^{\infty} f_D(D|B)dD = \int_{D_0}^{\infty} \frac{D^{S/2-1}\exp(-D/2)}{2^{S/2}\Gamma(S/2)}dD, \tag{14}$$

where $f_D(D|B)$ is the PDF of D for the background patterns, S is the number of moments and $\Gamma(\cdot)$ is the gamma function. It should be noted that $f_D(D|B)$ is a Chi-square distribution, with S degrees of freedom, as corresponds to the SMD of any S-dimensional pattern belonging to a cluster (the background cluster in this case) [6].

Since the P_{FA} of (14) is independent of the background characteristics $\overline{\mu}_B$ and Σ_B, the decision statistic D satisfies the CFAR property [9, 21]. Evaluating D for each pattern and applying the rule (13) in order to know if they are outside the ellipsoid $D = D_0$ that guarantees (14), will exhibit a CFAR behavior. As Fig. 4 shows for three background types, changes in their characteristics are manifested in the mean vectors and covariance

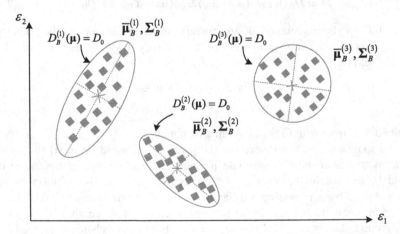

Fig. 4. Maintenance of the CFAR condition in the face of background changes.

matrices defining the clusters shapes. However, all ellipsoids correspond to the same D_0 computed to satisfy (14), which only dependency is on the patterns dimension ($S = 2$ for the figure) and therefore the P_{FA} is kept constant for each case.

The PDF for the anomaly $f_D(D|A)$ can be obtained as in Sect. 3.2. The SMD for patterns not belonging to a cluster take its highest values, so the distribution of D follows that of its maximum values and will be of GEV, similarly to (11). Figure 5 shows an example of the densities of D for both classes, their fits to the Chi-square and to (11), as well as the threshold that guarantees a P_{FA} of 10^{-3}. The components of the patterns and the models for the samples of the video-signal are the same used for Fig. 2. Finally, Table 2 shows the goodness-of-fit coefficients, whose values suggest the utility of the proposal.

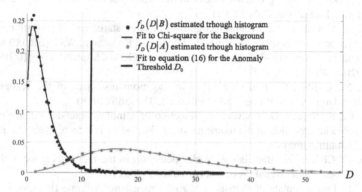

Fig. 5. Probability densities of D for both classes.

Table 2. Coefficients of goodness-of-fit to the Chi-square and the GEV distributions.

	MSE	NMSE
$f_D(D|B)$	$8.976 \cdot 10^{-6}$	0.974
$f_D(D|A)$	$3.282 \cdot 10^{-4}$	0.955

5 Conclusions

The importance of the optimal decision rule following the Neyman-Pearson criterion and generalized to take into account moments with arbitrary correlation degree, lies in considering correlation levels very difficult to control in real situations. The rule initially proposed by DRACEC is a particular case of the generalized one, so that the latter remains valid for applications where the moments are independent.

From the mathematical expression of the sufficient decision statistic, a fundamental analytical issue is highlighted: the optimal detector in moments space consists of a comparator between two SMDs. This allows us to identify the SMD with respect to the background class as a decision statistic in the moments space that guarantees the CFAR property.

The proposals of probability densities for the decision statistics in the moments space is an unprecedented topic. Although the objectives of this work do not include obtaining theoretical receiver operating curves (ROC), the proposal will allow this analysis to be carried out in future work. It is recommended to conduct hypothesis testing and goodness-of-fit studies that contribute to the validation of the suggested models.

References

1. Chávez, N.: Detección y alcance de radar: la alerta temprana de blancos en fondos enmascarantes y una solución al problema. Doctor in Sciences dissertation, Instituto Técnico Militar "José Martí", La Habana, Cuba (2002)
2. Chávez, N., González, A.L.: Radar recognition through statistical classification of cellular emission in the moment space. In: Ruiz-Shulcloper, J., Kropatsch, W.G. (eds.) CIARP 2008. LNCS, vol. 5197, pp. 325–331. Springer, Heidelberg (2008). https://doi.org/10.1007/978-3-540-85920-8_40
3. Chávez, N., Guillén, C.: Radar detection in the moments space of the scattered signal parameters. Digit. Signal Process. **83**(December), 359–366 (2018)
4. Guillén, C., Rodríguez, G., Chávez, N.: Selection of sampling interval and size of random sample for radar detection in the moments space. Periodica Polytech. Electr. Eng. Comput. Sci. (2021, online-first)
5. Guillén, C., Chávez, N., Bacallao, J.: Radar detection in the moments space with constant false alarm rate. Digit. Signal Process. **114**, 103080 (2021)
6. Kay, S.M.: Fundamentals of Statistical Signal Processing, Volume II: Detection Theory. Prentice Hall, Upper Saddle River (1998)
7. Papoulis, A.: Probability, Random Variables and Stochastic Processes, 3rd edn. McGraw-Hill, New York (1991)
8. Peebles, P.Z.: Probability, Random Variables and Random Signals Principles, 2nd edn. MacGraw-Hill, New York (1987)
9. Richards, M.A.: Fundamentals of Radar Signal Processing, 2nd edn. McGraw-Hill Education, New York (2014)
10. Webb, A.R., Copsey, K.D.: Statistical Pattern Recognition, 3rd edn. Wiley, Malvern (2011)
11. Guillén, C., Casas, G., Frómeta, D., Chávez, N.: Simple communication interface for a radar detector in the moments space. Int. J. Eng. Technol. Innov. **9**(4), 314–326 (2019)
12. Guillén, C., Chávez, N.: Densidad de probabilidad conjunta normal multivariada para momentos correlacionados. In: XVIII Convención Científica de Ingeniería y Arquitectura. La Habana, Cuba (2016)
13. Falk, M.: Multivariate Extreme Value Theory and D-Norms. Springer, Cham (2019)
14. Nourshamsi, N., West, J.C., Bunting, C.F.: Investigation of electromagnetic complex cavities by applying the generalized extreme value distribution. In: IEEE Symposium on Electromagnetic Compatibility, Signal Integrity and Power Integrity, Long Beach, CA (2018)
15. Bai, J., Li, Y.: Modeling high-resolution SAR images with generalized extreme value distribution. In: IEEE Advanced Information Management, Communicates, Electronic and Automation Control Conference. Xian, China (2016)
16. Ding, H., Huang, Y., Liu, N., Xue, Y., Wang, G.: Modeling of sea spike events with generalized extreme value distribution. In: European Radar Conference, Paris, France (2015)
17. Vrba, J.: Adaptive novelty detection with generalized extreme value distribution. In: International Conference on Applied Electronics, Pilsen, Czech Republic (2018)

18. Ahsanullah, M.: Extreme Value Distributions. Atlantis Press, Paris (2016)
19. MathWorks: Matlab Help. version R2017a (2017)
20. Guillén, C., Chávez, N.: Two-dimensional determination of the decision boundary for a radar detection method in the moment space. J. Aerosp. Technol. Manag. **11**, e2219 (2019)
21. Richards, M.A., Scheer, J.A., Holm, W.A.: Principles of Modern Radar, Vol. I: Basic Principles. SciTech Publishing, Raleigh (2010)

Interpretable Diagnosis of ADHD Based on Wavelet Features and Logistic Regression

Julián D. Pastrana-Cortes[1](✉) [iD], Maria Camila Maya-Piedrahita[1] [iD],
Paula Marcela Herrera-Gómez[2] [iD], David Cárdenas-Peña[1] [iD],
and Alvaro A. Orozco-Gutierrez[1] [iD]

[1] Automatics Research Group, Universidad Tecnológica de Pereira, Pereria,
Risaralda 660003, Colombia
{j.pastrana,camila.maya,dcardenasp,aaog}@utp.edu.co
[2] Research Group Psiquiatría, neurociencias y comunidad, Universidad Tecnológica de Pereira,
Pereria, Risaralda 660003, Colombia
p.herrera@utp.edu.co
http://www.utp.edu.co

Abstract. Despite arising in childhood, attention deficit hyperactivity disorder (ADHD) can persist into adulthood, compromising the individual's social skills. ADHD diagnosis is a real challenge due to its dependence on the clinical observation of the patient, the information provided by parents and teachers, and the clinicians' expertise. Therefore, there is great interest in studying objective biomarkers extracted from electroencephalographic (EEG) signals supporting accurate diagnoses. However, the non-stationarity and non-linearity characteristics of the EEG hinders the development of such tools. This paper presents a methodology for supporting the ADHD diagnosis by extracting features from the Discrete Wavelet transform of EEG signals. Due to the failed inhibitory control symptom, we consider EEG signals recorded under the Reward Stop Signal Task paradigm. Then, the logistic regressor learns the linear boundary discriminating between ADHD and healthy control subjects. As a benefit, the weighting vector supporting the classification also provides a straightforward interpretation of features in spatial locations and decomposition levels. The cross-validated classification results prove that the approach reaches an F1 score of 96% on a dataset of 34 children. Besides, the interpretability results support the hypothesis that the motivational effect leads the poor impulse control in ADHD.

Keywords: Attention deficit hyperactivity disorder (ADHD) ·
Electroencephalograpy (EEG) · Discrete Wavelet Transform (DWT) ·
Interpretability

1 Introduction

Attention deficit hyperactivity disorder (ADHD) is the most common chronic disease in childhood, with a high probability of persistence throughout the lifespan. ADHD can lead to learning difficulties, low self-esteem, substance abuse, and delinquent activities

© Springer Nature Switzerland AG 2021
Y. Hernández Heredia et al. (Eds.): IWAIPR 2021, LNCS 13055, pp. 424–433, 2021.
https://doi.org/10.1007/978-3-030-89691-1_41

in adolescents [1]. Currently, clinicians diagnose ADHD according to the clinical symptoms described in the Diagnostic and Statistical Manual of Mental Disorders (DSM-5), gathered from children, parents, and teachers. However, the overlap of attentional and behavioral symptoms with other disorders yields high rates of overdiagnosis [2]. Therefore, clinicians require objective tools to support specific and sensitive diagnosis from biomarkers and complement the regular clinical evaluation. Most of the objective diagnostic strategies of neural disorder rely on electroencephalographic (EEG) recordings due to the low cost and non-invasivity. EEG allows the understanding of neuropathologies through physiological brain responses. For instance, the FDA-approved Theta-Beta power Ratio (TBR) contrasts slow Theta waves (4–7 Hz) and fast Beta waves (13–30 Hz) under resting-state, under the assumption that slow waves emerge with more power in ADHD than in controls [3]. Also, other studies found a significant decrease in alpha band energy in the ADHD group compared to controls, especially in those electrodes located over the left frontal region, along with changes in the theta band that may differentiate ADHD patients in terms of gender [4]. Therefore, changes in the energy level of brain waves allow identifying biomarkers related to the disorder.

Although several studies decompose the signals using the Fourier transform, the EEG non-stationarity hampers the quality and confidence of the resulting analysis [5]. Despite the short-time Fourier transform potentially solves such an issue, fitting the processing window may lead to poor resolutions [6]. The Discrete Wavelet Transform (DWT) overcomes that limitation by decomposing the signal into several scales with different time and frequency resolutions. Besides, DWT adapts to the spectral content of the examined recordings, thus better decoding the time-frequency patterns and better explaining the electrophysiological changes [7].

Hence, this work proposes a methodology for supporting the ADHD diagnosis using statistical features extracted from the DWT decomposition of EEG signals. Contrary to previous works relying on the Oddball and resting state paradigms, EEG data in this contribution was recorded on subjects while performing a Reward Stop Signal Task (RSST), which takes into account the executive inhibition modulation through motivation, as behavioral and electrophysiological landmarks associated with the disorder [8,9]. The feature extraction stage computes the average coefficient, standard deviation, average peak location, standard deviation of the peak location, and maximum absolute coefficient per channel and scale. Lastly, a logistic regressor predicts the conditional probability of the ADHD diagnosis given the extracted features and provides the prediction. Thanks to the tuned feature-wise weights of the logistic regressor, the whole framework become endowed with spatial and spectral interpretability [10].

The paper agenda is as follows: Sect. 2 describes the mathematical framework, including the DWT-based signal decomposition, extraction of statistical features, and interpretable classification using logistic regression. Section 3 presents the experimental setup, introducing the considered EEG dataset, the signal processing details, and parameter tuning. Section 3.2 focuses on the attained supported diagnosis results. Finally, Sect. 4 discusses the main findings and proposes a future work.

2   Materials and Methods

2.1   Dataset and Preprocessing

For evaluating the proposed methodology, we considered an EEG dataset obtained recorded during the execution of the *Reward Stop-Signal Task* (RSST). The RSST paradigm commands the participant to press a key when confronted with a frequent stimulus, labeled as *Go*, unless an infrequent stimulus appears after the *Stop* signal. The dataset holds 34 children diagnosed as either Healthy Control (HC) or ADHD and aging between 7 and 12 years old. The combined mean age for both girls and boys participating from the study was 9.1 ± 1.5 years. Sex ratio (boys:girls) was $2.4 : 1$. Each child executed four blocks of four minutes length, receiving a reward when succeeding in inhibiting the motor response after being presented with the Stop signal. The paradigm included a *Smiley* sticker reward, followed by a *Low* amount of candies and a *High* amount of candies. Only trials in which children pressed a key despite the Stop stimulus (failed inhibitions) constitutes the database to identify the pathological error monitoring associated with neuropsychiatric conditions [11]. Table 1 summarizes the number of children per diagnosis, along with the average number of failed inhibitions on each reward.

Table 1. Number of children and average number of failed inhibitions in the dataset.

Diagnosis	N	*Smiley*	*Low*	*High*
Control	17	10.0 ± 07	9.05 ± 05	8.01 ± 05
ADHD	17	14.6 ± 06	14.0 ± 04	13.3 ± 05

Regarding the time series details, EEG signals were recorded 250 Hz and 32 channels distributed over the scalp, registering activity over the medial frontal [12], left frontal [13], ventromedial orbitofrontal, and prefrontal cortices known to evoke event-related negative (ERN) waves [14], as shown in Fig. 1. Each trial is trimmed 200 ms before and 800 ms after the *Go* stimulus, producing time series $F \in \mathbb{R}^{D \times T}$ lasting $T = 250$ time instants over $D = 32$ channels.

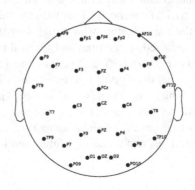

Fig. 1. 10–20 EEG montage of RSST dataset.

For the preprocessing stage, muscular activity artifacts and eye movements rejection was conducted through a semi-automatized procedure via custom MATLAB scripts [15]. Firstly, Independent Components Analysis (ICA) based on the Infomax algorithm extracts sources from each multidimensional trial. Then, the clinician visually identifies and rejects noisy components. Lastly, spherical spline interpolation reconstructs the rejected channels if they exist.

2.2 DWT-Based Feature Extraction

A DWT system considers two types of real valued functions to decompose a single-channel signal, namely, a scaling function and wavelet function. The first one is an energy function with non-zero frequency component and unit norm, denoted by $\varphi(t) \in L^2$. The successive translation and scaling of such a function creates an orthogonal set spanning a subspace of L^2 as $Span_j\{\varphi_{j,k}(t) = \{2^{j/2}\varphi(2^j t - k)\}$, being $j \in \mathbb{Z}$ and $k \in \mathbb{Z}$ the scale and translation indexes. Similarly, both time transformations in the wavelet function $\psi(t) \in L^2$, that holds a zero frequency component, spans the subspace $Span_j\{\psi_{j,k}(t) = \{2^{j/2}\psi(2^j t - k)\}$.

Thus, a single channel in an EEG trial $f_c(t) \in L^2$ can be written as a linear combination of the basis functions spanning $Span_j\{\varphi_{j,k}(t)\}$ and $Span_j\{\psi_{j,k}(t)\}$:

$$f_c(t) = \sum_{k=-\infty}^{\infty} a_{j_0,k}\varphi_{j_0,k}(t) + \sum_{j=j_0}^{\infty}\sum_{k=-\infty}^{\infty} d_{j,k}\psi_{j,k}(t) \tag{1}$$

where j_0 is the level of detail of $f(t)$, a_{jk} the approximation coefficient, and d_{jk} the detail coefficient. Note that the first summation approximates $x(t)$ at the scale j_0, while the double summation holds the detail to rebuild $x(t)$. Since, $\varphi_{j-1,k}(t) = \sum_{\tau} h_0(\tau)\varphi_{j,k}(t-\tau)$ and $\psi_{j-1,k}(t) = \sum_{\tau} h_1(\tau)\varphi_{j,k}(t-\tau)$, the representation coefficients at any level of decomposition or detail are calculated from the coefficients of the immediately upper level of decomposition:

$$a_{j-1,k} = \sum_m h_0(m - 2k)a_{jk} \tag{2}$$

$$d_{j-1,k} = \sum_m h_1(m - 2k)a_{jk} \tag{3}$$

with h_0 and h_1 as low pass and high pass filters, respectively.

Applying the DWT decomposition channel-wise in an EEG trial results in a set of coefficients representing the signal in the wavelet domain: $F_i \rightarrow \{a_{i,j,k}, d_{i,j,k} : j \in [-J, 0], k \in [1, \lceil T \cdot M_n \cdot 2^j + 1 \rceil]\}$, being J the number of considered decomposition levels, $i \in [1, M_n]$, and M_n the number of trials in the subject n.

Since M_n varies from child to child, we extract a set of statistical features to build a fixed length representing vector with physiological interpretability. Firstly, DWT decomposes each trial channel into J levels for detail coefficients and one for approximation. At each level, including the approximation, we compute the following five statistical features from each set of coefficients $c_{i,j,k} \in \{a_{i,j,k}, d_{i,j,k}\}$, as a subdivision of the conventional features of EEG [16]:

1. **Average coefficient**

$$\mu_{i,j} = \frac{1}{T \cdot M_n \cdot 2^j + 1} \sum_{k=0}^{T \cdot M_n \cdot 2^j} c_{i,j,k} \tag{4}$$

2. **Coefficient deviation**

$$\sigma_{i,j} = \sqrt{\frac{1}{T \cdot M_n \cdot 2^j + 1} \sum_{k=0}^{T \cdot M_n \cdot 2^j} (c_{i,j,k} - \mu_{i,j})^2} \tag{5}$$

3. **Average peak location** computed from the set of local maxima:

$$\mathcal{K}_{i,j} = \{k : c_{i,j,k} > c_{i,j,k+1} \wedge c_{i,j,k} \geq c_{i,j,k-1} \wedge c_{i,j,k} > 0\}$$

Then, the average peak location becomes:

$$\bar{k}_{i,j} = \frac{1}{|\mathcal{K}_{i,j}|} \sum_{k \in \mathcal{K}_{i,j}} k \tag{6}$$

4. **Standard deviation of the peak location**

$$\varsigma_{i,j} = \sqrt{\frac{1}{|\mathcal{K}_{i,j}|} \sum_{k \in \mathcal{K}_{i,j}} (k - \bar{k}_{i,j})^2} \tag{7}$$

5. **Maximum absolute coefficient**

$$max_{i,j} = \max_k |c_{i,j,k}| \tag{8}$$

As a result, the feature matrix $X = \{\mu_{i,j}^n, \sigma_{i,j}^n, \bar{k}_{i,j}^n, \varsigma_{i,j}^n, max_{i,j}^n\}_{n,i,j} \in \mathbb{R}^{N \times P}$ holds the descriptors extracted for each subject n, channel i and decomposition level j, being N the number of subjects and $P = 5D(J+1)$ the total number of features. Hence, the band-pass filtering of DWT makes features independent among scales and EEG rhythms.

2.3 Interpretable Classification Through Logistic Regression

This work considers a logistic regression classifier due to its simplicity and efficiency. Also, $L1$ regularization allows controls of the sparseness of the solution. The weights obtained in the logistic regression classifier measure feature relevance and how these can be altered with a minimum cost, easing the interpretability [10]. Let the matrix X, where the row $x_n \in \mathbb{R}^P$ represents the n-th child with label $y_n \in \{0, 1\}$ (HC and ADHD, respectively). The logistic regressor predicts the posterior probability for the target class $y = 1$ given the feature vector x and a weighting vector $w \in \mathbb{R}^P$ as:

$$p(y = 1 \mid x) = \sigma\left(w^\top x\right) = \frac{1}{1 + \exp\left(-w^\top x\right)} \tag{9}$$

with $\sigma(\cdot)$ as the sigmoid function. To tune the weighting vector, the cross-entropy loss is minimized constrained by the L_1 norm of w.

$$\min_{\mathbf{w}} - \sum_{n=1}^{N} y_n \log p\left(1 \mid \mathbf{x}_n\right) + \left(1 - y_n\right) \log\left(1 - p\left(1 \mid \mathbf{x}_n\right)\right)$$

$$\text{subject to } \|\mathbf{w}\|_1 \leq C \tag{10}$$

being $C \in \mathbb{R}^+$ the inverse regularization parameter. The resulting weights rank extracted features and select the fewest of them maximizing the HC/ADHD separability. Consequently, the selected wavelet-based features can be straightforward interpreted as the spatial locations and decomposition levels enhancing the ADHD discrimination.

3   Results

3.1   Parameter Tuning

The proposed methodology uses a Daubechies 4 mother wavelet for the DWT (see Fig. 2) as it has been widely used to highlight or detect relevant features in electrophysiological signals [17]. To identify the optimal signal decomposition level discriminating ADHD and HC subjects, the DWT decomposes the signals using $J \in \{1, \ldots, 5\}$ levels. The described statistical moments and peak descriptors fit the logistic regressor in a five-fold cross-validated grid search within $C \in \{10^{-4}, \ldots, 10^2\}$. Table 2 presents the average F1-score achieved over the test set for the optimal C at each reward and decomposition level. Note that $J = 3$ exhibits the highest scores and lowest standard deviations, being used hereafter as the tuned decomposition level.

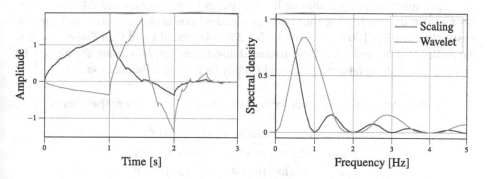

Fig. 2. Daubechies 4 set in time (left) and spectral density magnitude (right)

Table 2. F1 classification scores for each decomposition level and reward. Average and standard deviation over five test folds are presented.

Rewards	Decomposition levels				
	1	2	3	4	5
Smiley	88 ± 10	86 ± 12	**94 ± 07**	91 ± 11	85 ± 08
Low	91 ± 11	91 ± 11	**96 ± 08**	96 ± 08	93 ± 09
High	86 ± 08	85 ± 08	**88 ± 07**	85 ± 08	88 ± 10

Figure 3 illustrates the tuning curve for the inverse regularization parameter C using the optimal $J = 3$ at each reward. Note that the F1-score considerably increases from $C = 0.1$ for the Low and High rewards. For Smiley, the SVM needs to be less regularized ($C > 0.1$) to highlight the motivational effect. Therefore, a box constraint between 0.1 and 1 enhances the classifier performance and highlights the discriminative capacity of the wavelet-based features.

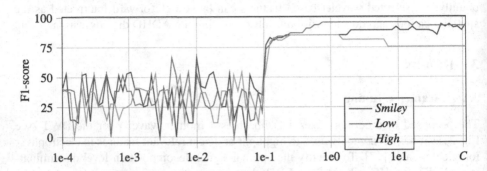

Fig. 3. Box constraint tuning curve. Five test folds are averaged for each reward.

3.2 Performance Analysis

Table 3 presents the F1 score, precision, recall, and area under the ROC attained at each reward level. The average and standard deviation are computed from five test folds using the optimal parameters for the methodology. Regarding *Smiley*, its metrics reach similar values, resulting in a suitable trade-off between false positives and false negatives. On the contrary, the *High* reward benefits the recall compromising the overdiagnosis. Lastly, *Low* reaches 100% precision with a 2% lower recall score than *Smiley*. Despite the *Smiley* reward evokes the most balanced discrimination, *Low* attain the highest F1 score by diminishing false positives and slightly increasing false positives.

Table 3. Performance measures for the three reward types the optimal parameters.

Reward	F1	Precision	Recall	AUC
Smiley	94±07	95±10	95±10	98±03
Low	**96±08**	**100±0**	93±13	**100±0**
High	88±07	86±12	93±13	93±06

Figure 4 distributes the logistic regressor weights over the head scalp according to their decomposition level and kind of statistical descriptor for the *Low* reward. Red and blue regions indicate leading contributions to the discrimination, either by a positive or negative weight, respectively. In turn, green areas denote close-to-zero weights and a lack of effect on the classifier prediction. Note that peak-related descriptors (third and fourth columns) result in the least relevant, implying that locating the maximum wavelet coefficient is less discriminant than the coefficient values themselves. On the contrary, features associated with the wavelet coefficient magnitude such as mean, standard deviation, and maximum absolute value hold the most discriminative information.

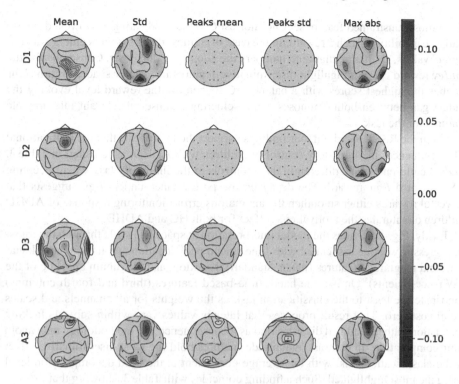

Fig. 4. Spatial interpretation of the weights obtained from the logistic regressor for each feature and decomposition level at the *Low* reward. (Color figure online)

4   Discussion and Concluding Remarks

This paper proposes a methodology for the supported diagnosis of ADHD from EEG recordings, wavelet-based features, and a logistic regressor. Following the RSST paradigm, the proposed approach describes each subject from its failed inhibition trials using magnitude and location features. Such features feed a logistic regressor that facilitates the interpretability of the classification results needed for diagnostic tasks. To identify the optimal decomposition for each of the three rewards, we inspected up to five levels. Each tested number of decomposition levels included all detail coefficients and the last ones for approximation. Performance metrics in Table 2 show that the best number of decomposition levels is $J = 3$. Considering that the frequencies captured at the third decomposition level range from 15.6 Hz to 31.2 Hz, the methodology highlights the role of the Beta brain rhythm as an ADHD biomarker, agreeing with the clinical literature [18]. Besides, including higher decomposition levels introduces noisy features, so hampering the classification performance.

In the parameter tuning, we searched the optimal box constraint C for each reward. From Fig. 3, it is worth noting that the F1 score considerably increases when $C > 0.1$ for the three reward levels, implying a low regularization requirement for the classification problem. Nonetheless, the *High* reward, which underperforms *Smiley* and *Low*, results in the most constrained feature set (the shortest C value), indicating the lowest discrimination capability of such a reward. In the case of Smiley, the best scores emerge at very high C values, so that regularizing hampers the supported diagnosis. Consequently, the *Smiley* reward can not highlight discriminative features in scale or space. In turn, *Low* reaches the highest scores with a balanced C, becoming the reward level evoking the widest gap between both diagnoses while selecting a subset of relevant interpretable features for the task.

From the RSST paradigm, our findings support the hypothesis that the motivational effect influences the inhibitory control of children with ADHD, as reflected in Table 3. ADHD children engage differently than controls in the inhibitory task when receiving a *Smiley* or a *Low* reward. The decay on the performance under *High* suggests that powerful rewards either smoothen the anomalous error monitoring response of ADHD children or saturates the motivational effect for both HC and ADHD.

Lastly, Fig. 4 provides the model interpretation at space and scale through the logistic regressor weights associated with time (mean peak location and its standard deviation) and magnitude features (mean, standard deviation, and maximum absolute of the DWT coefficients). On the one hand, time-based features (third and fourth columns) contribute the least to the classification task as the weights for all channels and scales are almost zero. That result proposes that latency values vary within subjects lacking correlation with the studied disorder, and as a consequence, the methodology may avoid their computation. In contrast, magnitude features hold the most discriminative effect in the classification task, with the average coefficient at the third decomposition level being the most highlighted. Such a finding coincides with Table 3, showing that extracting the Beta rhythm in a decomposition level improved the supported diagnosis.

For future work, we devise the following research directions: Firstly, we will extend the methodology to other feature sets, e.g. connectivity measures, to gain knowledge about the disorder. Secondly, we will analyze other cognitive tasks targeting clinical ADHD symptoms on the space, time, and frequency domains, aiming at optimizing the paradigm, EEG recording montage, and feature set for supported diagnosis of ADHD. Thirdly, we will introduce a subject-wise interpretable machine learning strategy, such as the Shapley additive explanations, so that the model not only suggests a diagnosis but also describes the EEG features and values leading it.

Acknowledgment. This work was supported by the research project number 111080763051 and the project number 6-20-10 funded by MinCiencias.

References

1. Khoshnoud, S., Nazari, M.A., Shamsi, M.: Functional brain dynamic analysis of ADHD and control children using nonlinear dynamical features of EEG signals. J. Integr. Neurosci. **17**(1), 17–30 (2018)
2. American Psychiatric Association, et al.: Diagnostic and statistical manual of mental disorders (DSM-5®). American Psychiatric Publishing (2013)
3. Arns, M., Conners, C.K., Kraemer, H.C.: A decade of EEG theta/beta ratio research in ADHD: a meta-analysis. J. Atten. Disord. **17**(5), 374–383 (2013)

4. Swartwood, J.N., Swartwood, M.O., Lubar, J.F., Timmermann, D.L.: EEG differences in ADHD-combined type during baseline and cognitive tasks. Pediatr. Neurol. **28**(3), 199–204 (2003)
5. Saad, J.F., Kohn, M.R., Clarke, S., Lagopoulos, J., Hermens, D.F.: Is the theta/beta EEG marker for ADHD inherently flawed? J. Atten. Disord. **22**(9), 815–826 (2018)
6. Gabriel, R., Spindola, M.M., Mesquita, A., Neto, A.Z.: Identification of ADHD cognitive pattern disturbances using EEG and wavelets analysis. In: 2017 IEEE 17th International Conference on Bioinformatics and Bioengineering (BIBE), pp. 157–162. IEEE (2017)
7. Joy, R.C., George, S.T., Rajan, A.A., Subathra, M.: Detection of attention deficit hyperactivity disorder from EEG signal using discrete wavelet transform. In: 2019 5th International Conference on Computing, Communication, Control and Automation (ICCUBEA), pp. 1–5. IEEE (2019)
8. Maya-Piedrahita, M., Cárdenas-Peña, D., Orozco-Gutierrez, A.: Diagnosis of attention deficit and hyperactivity disorder (ADHD) using hidden Markov models. In: 2020 28th European Signal Processing Conference (EUSIPCO), pp. 1205–1209. IEEE (2021)
9. Herrera, P.M., et al.: Expectation of reward differentially modulates executive inhibition. BMC Psychol. **7**(1), 1–10 (2019)
10. Murdoch, W.J., Singh, C., Kumbier, K., Abbasi-Asl, R., Yu, B.: Definitions, methods, and applications in interpretable machine learning. Proc. Natl. Acad. Sci. **116**(44), 22071–22080 (2019)
11. Groen, Y., Wijers, A.A., Mulder, L.J., Waggeveld, B., Minderaa, R.B., Althaus, M.: Error and feedback processing in children with ADHD and children with autistic spectrum disorder: an EEG event-related potential study. Clin. Neurophysiol. **119**(11), 2476–2493 (2008)
12. Ridderinkhof, K.R., Ullsperger, M., Crone, E.A., Nieuwenhuis, S.: The role of the medial frontal cortex in cognitive control. Science **306**(5695), 443–447 (2004)
13. van Meel, C.S., Heslenfeld, D.J., Oosterlaan, J., Sergeant, J.A.: Adaptive control deficits in attention-deficit/hyperactivity disorder (ADHD): the role of error processing. Psychiatry Res. **151**(3), 211–220 (2007)
14. Garavan, H., Ross, T., Murphy, K., Roche, R., Stein, E.: Dissociable executive functions in the dynamic control of behavior: inhibition, error detection, and correction. NeuroImage **17**(4), 1820–1829 (2002)
15. Croce, P., Zappasodi, F., Marzetti, L., Merla, A., Pizzella, V., Chiarelli, A.M.: Deep convolutional neural networks for feature-less automatic classification of independent components in multi-channel electrophysiological brain recordings. IEEE Trans. Biomed. Eng. **66**(8), 2372–2380 (2019)
16. Haloi, R., Hazarika, J., Chanda, D.: Selection of appropriate statistical features of EEG signals for detection of Parkinson's disease. In: 2020 International Conference on Computational Performance Evaluation, ComPE 2020, pp. 761–764 (2020)
17. Chrapka, P., de Bruin, H., Hasey, G., Reilly, J.: Wavelet-based muscle artefact noise reduction for short latency rTMS evoked potentials. IEEE Trans. Neural Syst. Rehabil. Eng. **27**(7), 1449–1457 (2019)
18. McAuliffe, D., et al.: Increased mirror overflow movements in ADHD are associated with altered EEG alpha/beta band desynchronization. Eur. J. Neurosci. **51**(8), 1815–1826 (2020)

Evaluation of GOI Detectors in EGG Signals Assuming Different Models for the Pulse Length Variability

Carlos A. Ferrer Riesgo[1,2] ⓘ, Reinier Rodríguez-Guillén[1] ⓘ, and Elmar Nöth[2(✉)] ⓘ

[1] Informatics Research Center, Central University "Marta Abreu" de Las Villas, Santa Clara, Cuba
cferrer@uclv.edu.cu, reinierrg@uclv.cu
[2] Pattern Recognition Lab, Friedrich Alexander University Erlangen-Nuremberg, Erlangen, Germany
elmar.noeth@fau.de

Abstract. In this paper, three Glottal Opening Instants Detectors are simultaneously evaluated with three glottal measures and two concepts of pulse boundaries. Performance has to be evaluated in the absence of reference locations. The evaluation is made over a subset of 120 pathological voice samples. Results show that, among detectors, the crossing over the 3/7 of the pulses' amplitude span performs better. Considering ratios of pulse phases' duration, results support the modeling of the effect of jitter in the glottal pulse as a constant warping between glottal closure instants.

Keywords: EGG · GCI · GOI · Jitter

1 Introduction

1.1 The Glottal Pulse

The glottal flow pulse waveform $g(t)$ is one of the two main elements of the source-filter theory of speech production [1]. The audible acoustic pressure waveform $s(t)$ is usually modeled as the convolution in time of $g(t)$ with the vocal tract's impulse response $h(t)$ and the radiation at the lips $r(t)$. Since the latter is generally considered as a derivative operation, it is frequent to model $s(t)$ as the convolution of $g'(t)$, conceived as the source, with $h(t)$, identified as the filter [2–4].

Synthetic voices are mostly obtained by generating a $g(t)$ departing from an analytical expression, with other alternatives, e.g. physical models of the oscillating tissues still lacking generalization. The $g(t)$ is schematically divided into open and closed phases [5], with durations O_p and C_p, respectively, as shown in Fig. 1 (top panel). During C_p there can't be a net flow (i.e. $g(t) = 0$) since the glottis remains closed. In the corresponding derivative $g'(t)$, depicted in the bottom panel of Fig. 1, the relevant features are being non-zero during O_p, and the prominent sudden change in the transition from O_p to C_p. This sudden change is known as glottal closure instant (GCI), and in some mathematical

© Springer Nature Switzerland AG 2021
Y. Hernández Heredia et al. (Eds.): IWAIPR 2021, LNCS 13055, pp. 434–443, 2021.
https://doi.org/10.1007/978-3-030-89691-1_42

expressions for $g(t)$ it involves a discontinuity in $g'(t)$ [6]. Conversely, the point where C_p transitions into its posterior O_p is defined as the glottal opening instant (GOI).

In normal phonation $g(t)$ is quasi-periodic, hence the time elapsed between same instants (e.g. GOI or GCI) corresponding to two adjacent pulses is expected to be roughly constant and equal to the period of the signal, T0. Both ways of measuring T0 have been depicted in Fig. 1, one denoted T_{O-O} which comprises an O_p and its posterior C_p (thus bounded by GOI positions), and the other denoted T_{C-C}, which contains a C_p and its posterior O_p (conversely bounded by GCIs).

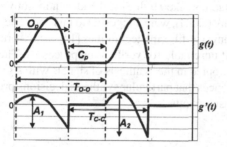

Fig. 1. Schematic graph of $g(t)$ and its phases (top), and its derivative $g'(t)$ (bottom) for a jittered signal. Vertical dashed lines at GOIs, dash-dot lines at GCIs.

It is frequent to obtain several indexes like Open Quotient (OQ), Speed Quotient (SQ), etc., as ratios between the durations of the different pulse phases (opening, closing, closed, pulse length) which have proven to relate to the spectral roll off towards the high frequencies [7]. In non-pathologic, quasi-periodic voice, these indexes are constant across pulses.

In pathological voices it is frequent to find that T0 varies more than 1% from its value measured in a given pulse to its neighbor's [8–11]. When this T0 variability (jitter) is present, the equivalence of using either GOIs or GCIs as pulse boundaries cannot be taken for granted [12, 13]. This fact is conceptually explored in [13], where three controversial points were raised:

The Jitter-Induced Warping of Glottal Pulses: With several models described in [13], the most relevant ones were a "Constant Warping" (CW) and a "Piecewise Warping" (PW). In the CW all the included phases are warped proportionally to the variation in T0, while in the main PW alternative all the variation is made to one of the phases (C_p in that case). OQ, SQ, and other indexes can be constant across pulses on a model and variable on the other.

The Pulse's Starting Point Problem: The choice of any given point (either GOI or GCI) can be seen as arbitrary, but can yield very different results when measuring jitter, especially for signals synthesized using the CW model [13].

The Jitter-Induced Shimmer: If the open phase duration (O_p) varies across pulses, $g'(t)$ will show peak-to-peak amplitude (PPA) variability (shimmer) irrespective of the $g(t)$ pulses being of constant amplitudes (see A_1 and A_2 in Fig. 1). This effect is present in the CW model, but not in the PW variant, producing a significant amount of $s(t)$ shimmer [13]. The fact that the choice of the synthesis model produces such different outcomes regarding shimmer cannot be neglected.

The three mentioned conflicting views regarding the possible effects of jitter on the glottal pulse waveform were described in [13], and the possible magnitude of their effects demonstrated in terms of the automated measurement of signal parameters (jitter, shimmer, noise). It was then recommended that the different views were evaluated in terms of their fit to real life data of the duration of pulses and phases, and direct measures of vocal fold dynamics, like High Speed Videoendoscopy, Videokymography, or even Electroglottography (EGG), were suggested to this end. The actual $g(t)$ is generally estimated by means of inverse-filtering techniques [14], which are prone to fail in pathological voice, making it unreliable for verification processes. The most close-to-reality model should then be adopted in the synthesis of signals with significant jitter, given the magnitude of the differences that particular synthesis decisions produced in the resulting jitter and shimmer measurements.

1.2 Objectives

In this research, while trying to shed some light on the previous controversies, we decide to use EGG signals due to their availability and the relatively higher sampling frequencies allowing for higher precision in the location of the pulse's GCI and GOI. Typical High Speed Videoendoscopy frame frequency is still 4 kHz, while EGG is in the range of tens of KHz. For a female voice with F0 = 400 Hz, there would be only 10 samples on a glottal pulse, making sampling errors a lot higher than the variability to be measured.

We evaluate three GOI detectors, according to three measures (OQ, CQ and T0), on the assumption of both possible pulse boundaries (T_{O-O} or T_{C-C}), in the absence of reference annotated markings of pulse boundaries. To this end, a minimum variability model is assumed.

2   Materials and Methods

2.1   The Closure and Opening Instants Detection on EGG Signals

The basic principle behind EGG is the change in electrical conductivity as measured across the vocal cords as they get in contact during the closed phase of the glottal cycle and separate and later get closer during the open phase. Depending on the actual physical magnitude measured, either impedance or its inverse, the admittance, the resulting variability signal keeps the original EGG acronym [15] or is referred to as Lx [16] (for electrolaryngography), respectively. The EGG waveform directly relates to $g(t)$ (higher values of flow correspond to higher values of impedance) while Lx relates inversely.

In the EGG signals, as in $g(t)$, the GCIs correspond to the points where the derivative reaches its larger peak [17]. Since the EGG signals used here are actually Lx, the peak in the derivative corresponding to the GCI in a pulse is the positive maximum (see Fig. 2). Opposite to the behavior in $g(t)$, in both types of EGG signals the flattest part occurs

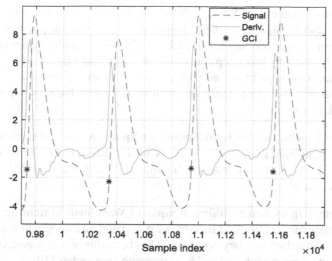

Fig. 2. Smoothed EGG /Lx signal (dashed) and its derivative (solid) as extracted from a segment of signal ID#110 (vertical axis in arbitrary units). GCIs are shown as asterisks.

prior to the GCI (corresponding to the O_p phase) while the inner part of the C_p phase (after GCI) presents large rising and falling excursions, as shown in Fig. 2.

Contrary to the case of GCIs, the detection of the GOIs is reportedly a difficult problem [17, 18], with errors being typically twice as large as the reported for GCIs [19]. For this reason, we decided to include an evaluation of several GOI Detectors as part of this work.

2.2 GOI Detectors Evaluated

The three GOI detectors considered are described in the following sections. Since all of them require the previous extraction of the GCIs from the EGG waveform, a GCI detector was first implemented. Since the EGG signals used here are actually Lx, the peak in the derivative corresponding to the GCI in a pulse is the positive maximum (see Fig. 2). Opposite to the behavior in $g(t)$, in both types of EGG signals the flattest part occurs prior to the GCI (corresponding to the O_p phase) while the inner part of the C_p phase (after GCI) presents large rising and falling excursions, as shown in Fig. 2.

A peak picking method for GCI detection, as reported elsewhere [17], proved to work in our set of signals if applied to a smoothed version of EGG. The peaks were obtained using the *FindPeaks* function of Matlab on the derivative of the smoothed EGG, tweaking three parameters for the function: '*MinPeakDistance*' to 1/3 of an estimate of T0 (obtained as the inverse of the first harmonic in an FFT analysis of the whole EGG), '*MinPeakProminence*' to $(m_x - m_n)/6$ (being m_x the global maximum of the EGG and m_n the global minimum), and 'MinPeakHeight' to $m_x/12$. The mentioned smoothing was performed in a two-step filtering process, first a median filter to remove possible noise outliers, followed by a moving average consisting of a Hanning window. Both filters operate over windows of 41 samples (0.8 ms) which for the moving average represents a low-pass cutoff frequency of ~850 Hz.

Derivative-Based Detection: Some authors link the GOI to the extreme value of the derivative of opposite sign to the GCI. However, this significant point is not as well defined as the one corresponding to the GCI. The falling excursion where the GOI is to be located is significantly less steep than the rising excursion where the GCI is detected. For this reason, it is frequent to find multiple local minima in the falling section (see 1st and 3rd occurrences in Fig. 2) and the position in time of the largest peak can vary within the falling section.

Crossing by a Fraction of the Total Amplitude Span: A reported alternative is not to relate GOI to significant points of the EGG or its derivative, but to locate it in a place where the EGG waveform descends to a fraction of its full excursion (3/7 showed the best results in [17, 20]).

Inflection Detection by Least Minimum Squares Waveform Matching: Both previous approaches can be criticized in terms of its dependence on single point measurements. In acoustic pulse boundary detection, it has been shown that waveform matching techniques outperform peak based and zero-crossing approaches [10].

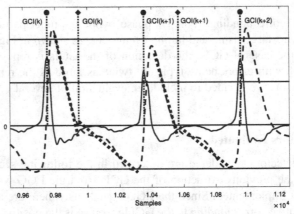

Fig. 3. Illustration of the functioning of the Waveform Matching method for the detection of the inflection point. GCIs shown in filled circles, and GOIs in filled diamonds. Best-fit lines are shown thick-dotted.

Here, we introduce an optimization method fitting two sections of the EGG waveform. The sections modeled are the falling excursion within the C_p, and the flatter part occurring prior to the next GCI. Each section is modeled as a straight line, obtained from a best fit to the EGG waveform. Using an auxiliary margin value of $m = 0.05(GCI_{(k+1)} - GCI_{(k)})$, the lines are defined in the intervals $[t_{peak} + m, t_{mid}]$ and $[t_{mid}, GCI_{(k+1)} - m]$, respectively, being t_{peak} the instant of the maximum of EGG between $GCI_{(k)}$ and $GCI_{(k+1)}$. The $GOI_{(k)}$ is the value of t_{mid}, evaluated in the interval $[t_{peak} + 3m, GCI_{(k+1)} - 3m]$, for which the total squared error of fit (considering both lines) is minimized. GOI is then expected to be located on the point of inflection between both fit lines.

A sample representation of the resulting best fit lines and the consequential GOIs detected by this Waveform-Matching procedure are shown in Fig. 3:

2.3 Datasets

The dataset of signals used in this study is extracted from the Saarbrücken Voice Database (SVD) [21], which contains simultaneous recordings of speech and Lx signals from thousands of healthy and pathological subjects, and is freely downloadable from its website. The subjects are recorded pronouncing five vowels (a, e, i, o, u) at three pitches (low, normal and high) and a sentence in German, with fs = 50 kHz. Although the signals are actually Lx, they will still be referred to by the more general term of EGG, unless otherwise noted.

From this huge amount of data, which has even been used for deep learning algorithms [22], we chose to work with EGG recordings from the vowel /a/ in normal tone. Visual inspection was then performed by the first author on all the pathologic cases, searching for segments with evident pulse to pulse variability on one hand (as to find some correspondence through correlational analysis) and a well-defined pulse pattern in the other (so that an automatic marking procedure could work reliably). After this inspection, 114 signals were selected, from which 120 EGG segments were extracted.

The total amount of glottal pulses detected was 5763, varying across segments from a minimum of 8 to a maximum of 302, for a mean of 48. The segments excluded from each signal were either too regular to provide useful variability or too irregular to perform the desired measurements.

2.4 Evaluation Procedure: Assumptions and Measures Considered

A main drawback of the dataset used is the lack of annotations of the actual GCIs and GOIs. References have been obtained in previous works [17, 19] by inspection of High Speed Videoendoscopy, which as we have pointed out is too inaccurate when compared to the variability to be evaluated here (easily below 5%). In the absence of this reference, we will use the resulting variability of a measure as a performance criterion. For each of the 120 segments we obtain a vector of values (a value per glottal pulse in the segment) of a given measure M. We can conceive the variance $\sigma^2_{Outcome}$ of each of these vectors as a sum of contributing factors:

$$\sigma^2_{Outcome} = \sigma^2_{GOI-Det} + \sigma^2_{Measure} + \sigma^2_{Noise} \qquad (1)$$

Here, $\sigma^2_{Measure}$ is the variability that the presence of jitter in the pulse duration introduces in the particular measure. For instance, if the measure chosen is the OQ, and the segment behaves as in a Constant Warping model, then OQ (defined as $O_p/T0$) would be constant. In the ideal case, with the GOI detector committing no errors ($\sigma^2_{GOI-Det} = 0$), and in the absence of other sources of error (represented by σ^2_{Noise}) $\sigma^2_{Outcome}$ would then be zero. We then assume that the smaller the value of $\sigma^2_{Outcome}$, the better the fit of the measure to be constant in the particular model, and, simultaneously, the better the performance of the GOI detector.

The measures chosen are five: OQ in two variants (for T0 = T_{O-O} and T0 = T_{C-C}), CQ (defined as $C_p/T0$) in the same two variants, and the pulse length as measured between GOIs: T_{O-O}. With these 5 measures conclusions can be drawn regarding both the type of warping of the pulse, and its boundaries.

As a proxy for $\sigma_{Outcome}$, for a given measure M, we actually calculate the most typical formula for variability in voice research, frequently used for *jitter* [23] due to the normalization effect of the denominator:

$$jitter_{(GOI-Det,Measure,Segment)} = \sum_{n=1}^{N-1} \frac{2|M(n+1) - M(n)|}{M(n+1) + M(n)} \tag{2}$$

where M is the vector of N values of the measure for each of the pulses in the segment. These *jitter* values are calculated for each GOI detector, measure, and segment, resulting in a $(3 \times 5 \times 120)$ matrix of values.

3   Results and Discussion

An illustration of the behavior of the three GOI detectors is shown in Fig. 4. The inconsistency of the minimum of the derivative is evident from the different behavior on pulses 1 & 3 (marking GOI on extremely high values in Lx) vs. the pulses 2 & 4, at a little lower values. The durations of the C_p are also excessively small.

A Kruskall-Wallis test for the difference of the medians was performed considering the 15 vectors (3 GOI Detector times 5 measures) of 120 elements (segments). The results of the multiple comparisons are shown in Fig. 5, where each random variable (vector) is named according a X-YY-ZZ code. X stands for the GOI detector (M-Matching, F-Fraction, D-Derivative), YY for the measure (OQ, CQ, or PL: Pulse-Length as T_{O-O}), and ZZ for assumed boundary (OO for T_{O-O} or CC for T_{C-C}).

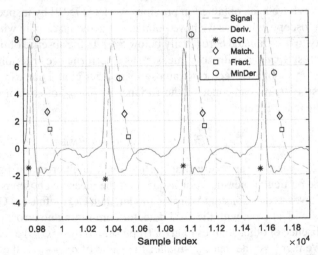

Fig. 4. GOIs detected by the tree methods on the same pulses from Fig. 2. Circles: the (minimum of) Derivative, Squares: the Fraction (3/7) of the amplitude span between GCIs, Diamonds Waveform Matching method.

It can be seen that the OQ measure obtained from GOIs detected by the 3/7 method and considering the pulse bounded by GCI (F-OQ-CC) is an almost absolute winner. The only other method slightly overlapping the confidence interval is F-CQ-CC. A first conclusion from these two best performers points towards the likelihood of the CC boundary. A second one points towards a constant warping (CW) [13] model for the influence of jitter in the pulse phases. For the contending piece-wise warping to be considered, only one of the opposite measures (either OQ or CQ) for the same boundary can have a low variability.

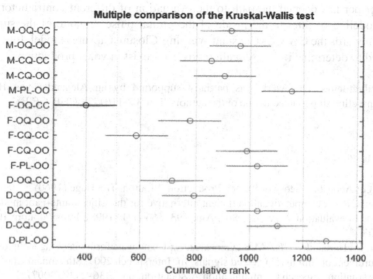

Fig. 5. Multiple comparison test of the variability of the different measures selected, for the different GOI detectors and the two possible boundaries considered.

Additionally, we show in Table 1 the number of segments for which each measure had the lowest (best) variability measured according to Eq. (2).

The outstanding performance of F-OQ-CC is reinforced by noticing that it is the best fit in more than half the segments (62 out of 120).

Table 1. Count of #1 ranks by each Detector, on each Measure's variability.

GOI Detector	OQ (C-C)	OQ (O-O)	CQ (C-C)	CQ (O-O)	PL(O-O)
Matching	1	3	5	9	3
Fraction (3/7)	62	9	6	2	3
Derivative	12	3	2	0	0

4 Conclusions

The reported good performance of the GOI detector based on a 3/7 thresholding is ratified by the results obtained. The low variability of the OQ also tends to confirm the assumption it being constant across pulses. However, the tendency of OQ to remain constant is strong only when considering the pulse as bounded by GCIs and not by GOIs, being the latter the standard model used for synthesis. As a whole, results support the modeling of the effect of jitter in the glottal pulse as a constant warping between glottal closure instants.

This paper has opened the path to the evaluation of different contradictory views on the modeling of jitter to the inside of the glottal pulse. In spite of the supporting evidence towards the CW-CC (Constant Warping-Closure Closure) model, further work is required to determine if different alternatives co-exist in voice production.

Acknowledgements. This work was partially supported by an Alexander von Humboldt Foundation Fellowship granted to one of the authors (Ref 3.2-1164728-CUB-GF-E).

References

1. Fant, G.: Acoustic Theory of Speech Production. Mouton, The Hage (1960)
2. Veldhuis, R.: A computationally efficient alternative for the Liljencrants-Fant model and its perceptual evaluation. J. Acoust. Soc. Am. **103**, 566–571 (1998). https://doi.org/10.1121/1.421103
3. Ferrer, C., Hernández-Díaz, M.E., González, E.: Using waveform matching techniques in the measurement of shimmer in voiced signals. In: Interspeech 2007: 8th Annual Conference of the International Speech Communication Association, pp. 2436–2439 (2007)
4. Hanquinet, J., Grenez, F., Schoentgen, J.: Synthesis of disordered voices. In: Faundez-Zanuy, M., Janer, L., Esposito, A., Satue-Villar, A., Roure, J., Espinosa-Duro, V. (eds.) NOLISP 2005. LNCS (LNAI), vol. 3817, pp. 231–241. Springer, Heidelberg (2006). https://doi.org/10.1007/11613107_20
5. Drugman, T., Alku, P., Alwan, A., Yegnanarayana, B.: Glottal source processing: from analysis to applications. Comput. Speech Lang. **28**, 1117–1138 (2014). https://doi.org/10.1016/j.csl.2014.03.003
6. Rosenberg, A.E.: Effect of glottal pulse shape on the quality of natural vowels. J. Acoust. Soc. Am. **49**, 583–590 (1971). https://doi.org/10.1121/1.1973515
7. Kreiman, J., et al.: Variability in the relationships among voice quality, harmonic amplitudes, open quotient, and glottal area waveform shape in sustained phonation. J. Acoust. Soc. Am. **132**, 2625–2632 (2012). https://doi.org/10.1121/1.4747007
8. Lieberman, P.: Some acoustic measures of the fundamental periodicity of normal and pathologic larynges. J. Acoust. Soc. Am. **35**, 344–353 (1963). https://doi.org/10.1121/1.1918465
9. Titze, I.R.: Workshop on Acoustic Voice Analysis: Summary Statement. NCVS. 36 (1994). https://doi.org/10.1016/S0892-1997(97)80022-7.
10. Boersma, P.: Should jitter be measured by peak picking or by waveform matching? Folia Phoniatr. Logop. **61**, 305–308 (2009). https://doi.org/10.1159/000245159
11. Horii, Y.: Some statistical characteristics of voice fundamental frequency. J. Speech Hear. Res. **18**, 192–201 (1975)

12. Roark, R.M.: Frequency and voice: perspectives in the time domain. J. Voice. **20**, 325–354 (2006). https://doi.org/10.1016/j.jvoice.2005.12.009
13. Ferrer, C.A., Torres, D., González, E., Calvo, J.R., Castillo, E.: Effect of different jitter-induced glottal pulse shape changes in periodicity perturbation measures. In: Proceedings of the Annual Conference of the International Speech Communication Association, INTERSPEECH (2015)
14. Degottex, G., Kane, J., Drugman, T., Raitio, T., Scherer, S.: COVAREP – A Collaborative Voice Analysis Repository for Speech technologies. In: IEEE International Conference on Acoustics, Speech and Signal Processing, pp. 960–964 (2014)
15. Childers, D., Larar, J.N.: Electroglottography for laryngeal function assessment and speech analysis. IEEE Trans. Biomed. Eng. **BME-31**(12), 807–817 (1984). https://doi.org/10.1109/TBME.1984.325242
16. Abberton, E., Fourcin, A.: Electrolaryngography. In: Ball, M.J., Code, C. (eds.) Instrumental Clinical Phonetics, pp. 119–148. Whurr Publishers Ltd., London (1997)
17. Henrich, N., d'Alessandro, C., Doval, B., Castellengo, M.: On the use of the derivative of electroglottographic signals for characterization of nonpathological phonation. J. Acoust. Soc. Am. **115**, 1321–1332 (2004). https://doi.org/10.1121/1.1646401
18. Baken, R.J.: Electroglottography. J. Voice. **6**, 98–110 (1992). https://doi.org/10.1097/000 02508-199209000-00009
19. Krishnamurthy, A., Childers, D.: Two-channel speech analysis. IEEE Trans. Acoust. Speech Signal Process. **34**(4), 730–743 (1986). https://doi.org/10.1109/TASSP.1986.1164909
20. Howard, D.M.: Variation of electrolaryngographically derived closed quotient for trained and untrained adult female singers. J. Voice. **9**, 163–172 (1995)
21. Pützer, M., Barry, W.J.: Saarbruecken Voice Database. http://stimmdb.coli.uni-saarland.de/. Accessed 16 Mar 2018
22. Harar, P., Alonso-Hernandez, J.B., Mekyska, J., Galaz, Z., Burget, R., Smekal, Z.: Voice pathology detection using deep learning: a preliminary study. In: International Conference and Workshop on Bioinspired Intelligence, IWOBI 2017. pp. 1–4. IEEE Xplore, Madeira (2017)
23. Ferrer, C., Torres, D., Hernández-Díaz, M.E.: Using dynamic time warping of T0 contours in the evaluation of cycle-to-cycle Pitch Detection Algorithms. Pattern Recognit. Lett. **31**, 517–522 (2010). https://doi.org/10.1016/j.patrec.2009.07.021

Author Index

Printed in the United States
by Baker & Taylor Publisher Services